Tort Law

CONCEPTS AND APPLICATIONS

Second Edition

Hillary J. Michaud, ESQ., CPA

Paralegal Program Coordinator and Professor of Law
Stevenson University

PEARSON

Boston   Columbus   Indianapolis   New York   San Francisco   Upper Saddle River
Amsterdam   Cape Town   Dubai   London   Madrid   Milan   Munich   Paris   Montreal   Toronto
Delhi   Mexico City   São Paulo   Sydney   Hong Kong   Seoul   Singapore   Taipei   Tokyo

Editorial Director: Vernon R. Anthony
Senior Acquisitions Editor: Gary Bauer
Editor, Digital Projects: Nichole Caldwell
Editorial Assistant: Tanika Henderson
Director of Marketing: David Gesell
Marketing Manager: Stacey Martinez
Senior Marketing Coordinator: Alicia Wozniak
Senior Marketing Assistant: Les Roberts
Senior Project Manager: Rex Davidson
Production Manager: Holly Shufeldt

Creative Director: Andrea Nix
Art Director: Jane Conte
Cover Designer: Suzanne Behnke
Cover Image: Shutterstock
Media Project Manager: Karen Bretz
Full-Service Project Management and Composition: PreMediaGlobal
Printer/Binder: LSC Communications
Cover Printer: LSC Communications

Photo Credits: David Graham/Pearson Education: pp. 1, 30, 31, 46, 47, 74, 75, 98, 99, 124, 125, 151, 178, 179, 195, 226, 227, 244, 245, 276, 277, 290, 291, 309, 326, 365
Pearson Education: p. 150
Image Source/Alamy: p. 197
© Orange Line Media/Shutterstock: p. 310
Stephen Coburn/Shutterstock: p. 327

Library of Congress Cataloging-in-Publication Data

Michaud, Hillary J.
    Tort law : concepts and applications / Hillary J. Michaud, ESQ., CPA, paralegal program
        coordinator and professor of law, Stevenson University. — Second Edition.
        pages cm
    Includes bibliographical references and index.
    ISBN-13: 978-0-13-297373-1
    ISBN-10: 0-13-297373-1
    1. Torts—United States.   2. Legal assistants—United States—Handbooks, manuals, etc.   I. Title.
    KF1250.Z9M53 2014
    346.7303—dc23

2012044320

ISBN 10: 0-13-297373-1
ISBN 13: 978-0-13-297373-1

Dedication

For Kate and Davis

CONTENTS

PREFACE

FROM THE AUTHOR

In developing and writing this text, I focused on dual needs: the need to present a comprehensive and detailed review of the vast body of substantive U.S. tort law, and the need to integrate practical applications in tort law to meet the American Bar Association's legal specialty course requirement to develop practical paralegal employment skills throughout a law course. This book is that marriage, for me, designed and written specially to meet the goals of a course that goes beyond theory, to explore the realm of practical application, useful to paralegal, prelaw, business, and other undergraduate majors, especially those with a career focus. My classroom teaching experience, my experience as a lawyer practicing in the area of tort law and products liability litigation, among other areas, and my knowledge and experience as the director of an ABA-approved paralegal studies bachelor's degree program have all prepared me to write this book.

What a pleasure it has been the past couple of years for me to teach my torts classes using my own textbook! What an opportunity it has been, as well, to evaluate the effectiveness of the content and organization of the book as I use it in classes. In this second edition, I have revised the book based on my own evaluation of how it is working in class, as well as recommendations and comments given to me by peers who have reviewed the text, as well as used it in their own classes.

Tort law governs wrongful conduct in the civil law system. It is a complex and dynamic area of law, sometimes as perplexing as it is interesting, in which a deluge of multimillion-dollar jury awards has made "tort reform" a household phrase. To study tort law is to study an important system, constructed largely by our judiciary, to compensate persons for personal injuries and property damage they suffer at the hands of others who have acted in certain unjust ways.

CHAPTER ORGANIZATION AND FEATURES

The book is organized to cover and merge both substantive tort law and its practical application. It is designed to be comprehensive, and instructors may find it contains more information than they can cover in a three-credit torts class. In that situation, instructors can pick and choose chapters or parts they want to include in their courses and refer students to the other chapters or parts for independent study and/or reference.

The text incorporates a variety of features designed to accommodate alternative learning styles and to ensure that students learn not only the concepts but how to apply them in the workplace.

CHAPTER FEATURES

Each chapter contains the following features:

- **A chapter introduction** that includes the chapter objectives and questions to be addressed in the chapter
- **Margin definitions** for easy student reference

- **Cases on Point** to be read, briefed, and discussed in class
- **Tables** highlighting important material, such as the essential elements of certain torts
- **Boxed features** containing highlighted material, ancillary topical material for classroom discussion, international considerations, and the like
- **Legal ethics** notes and applications integrated into each chapter
- **Chapter summary** summarizing the major topics covered in the chapter

END-OF-CHAPTER EXERCISES AND ASSIGNMENTS

At the end of each chapter are materials to assess a student's grasp of basic terminology and concepts, and a wealth of exercises and applications to develop critical thinking and workplace skills. Exercises are organized into two sections:

Concept Review and Reinforcement

- **Questions for Review** allow students to check their mastery of basic concepts presented in the chapter.

Developing Your Paralegal Skills

- **Critical Thinking Exercises** allow students and the class to apply the substantive law covered in the chapter by using knowledge gained in the problem-solving exercises.
- **Assignments and Practical Applications** develop skills such as legal research, legal writing, analyzing and synthesizing complex information, data gathering, negotiating, case briefing, and legal document drafting.
- **Technology Resources and Internet Exercises** familiarize students with performing research using Internet resources.
- **Ethical Applications** allow students to research and apply the rules of legal ethics to situations that could be encountered by tort law practitioners.
- **Video Case Study** provides students with a window into the real-world practice of tort law. Each chapter includes a video case study that presents a legal situation related to the chapter's content. Each video case study is accessible to students as well as the instructor and can be assigned as homework or can be shown in class to stimulate class discussion.

CHANGES IN THE SECOND EDITION

Cases and Statutes Added

Sixty new Cases on Point and Statutes on Point have been added to the text in the second edition. These summarize the actual law on different aspects of torts in various jurisdictions in the United States.

Intentional Torts

The topic of intentional torts has been split into two chapters because of the extensive content covered. There is now a chapter focusing on intentional torts against persons and a separate chapter on intentional torts against property and commercial interests. The topics of misrepresentation, tortious interference, and the *prima facie* tort doctrine, previously in separate chapters in a later part of the first edition, have been moved to the new intentional torts chapter and are included as intentional torts against commercial interests. Having split the material into two chapters, more content was added, including many more Cases on Point illustrating the different intentional torts.

Negligence

This topic has been split into two chapters because of the extensive content covered in the second edition. To fill what now is two chapters, additional material has been added on the topic of negligence, including new Cases on Point. There is now a chapter focusing on the first two of the four essential elements of the tort of negligence, namely duty of care and breach of the duty of care. A new second chapter covers the last two of the four essential elements, namely causation and damages. It also covers other negligence-related topics such as mass torts, the role of insurance, and workers' compensation.

Reorganization of Topics

In response to peer evaluations, some reorganization of the text materials has been made in the second edition. The topics of joint tortfeasors and vicarious liability have been moved to near the front of the text in the second edition, before specific torts are studied. Mass torts, the role of insurance in tort law, and workers' compensation have been moved to be included in the second of the two negligence chapters. The topics of survival, wrongful death, and wrongful birth and life, related to negligence, were moved forward in the text to be included in the negligence material in the second edition. The defense of immunity, its own chapter in the first edition, has been combined with other material and has been moved to the chapter on defenses to negligence. Practice applications appear in the first, introductory chapter (how to research tort law as well as read and brief cases) and then more extensively in the new, final chapter of the second edition.

New Practice Applications Material

New practice applications material has been added. An overview of a tort case has been added to the second edition. In addition, instruction on how to draft tort-related documents, such as legal correspondence, legal memoranda, pleadings and discovery requests/responses, and settlements agreements, has been expanded in the second edition, with samples of these documents included in the chapter materials. Material on how to conduct interviews, factual investigations, and negotiations has been expanded and some sample documents, such as interview questionnaires and intake forms, have been added in the second edition.

RESOURCES FOR INSTRUCTORS

Instructor's Manual for Tort Law: Concepts and Applications, by Hillary J. Michaud

The Instructor's Manual includes content outlines for classroom discussion, teaching suggestions, and answers to end-of-chapter questions from the text.

Comprehensive Test Bank and Test Generator, by Hillary J. Michaud

The Test Bank is arranged by chapter, containing a variety of question formats such as multiple choice, short answer, essay, and key term matching. Many of these questions have been "vetted" through use in the author's torts classes over the last several years.

PowerPoint Lecture Presentations, by Hillary J. Michaud

PowerPoint presentations, prepared for each chapter, outline and summarize the major points covered, and correspond to the organization of the text and the chapter's learning objectives.

Tort Law Video Case Studies

All video case studies are available for instructor and student access at www.pearsonhighered.com/careers.

ACKNOWLEDGMENTS

When my son asked me what kind of book I was writing, I replied, "I am writing a tort law textbook." My son was just 12 years old at the time, so I had to follow that statement with a basic explanation that tort law protects people from other people's wrong behavior. After my explanation, I (jokingly, of course) mentioned that he was my inspiration for writing this text, and that I would dedicate this book to him, "for all his wrongful conduct." As he laughed and told me I should do that, I knew that the dedication belonged to Davis, for his good humor. And to his sister, Kate, who displays very little wrongful conduct—but whose teenage years have just begun. I want to thank my family for supporting me throughout this and my other writing projects, for much of my time is spent in front of a computer, drafting and revising manuscripts. I also want to thank my hundreds of torts students over the years, who, as unwitting guinea pigs, showed me what works, and what does not, in a tort law course. What they taught me has been translated into this book.

I wish to acknowledge and thank Tom Goldman for his work on the video case studies and for inspiring me to keep on writing. I also wish to thank Alice Barr, my Pearson Prentice-Hall representative, who first got me started writing law textbooks. In addition, I wish to thank Gary Bauer, my executive editor, for making these books happen. Also, I want to thank Linda Cupp for her help with manuscript review, revision, and development.

I also wish to thank the educators whose review of my first edition provided valuable insights, many of which have now been incorporated into this second edition. They have made the text more complete and helped me craft a better teaching tool. Reviewers include Barbara A. Dralnick, Pima Community College; Patty Greer, Berkely College; Dena Sukol, Community College of Philadelphia; and Tasha Wardy, Pulasky Technical College.

I hope that you enjoy using this text. As an educator, I welcome feedback on any aspect of the textbook and its accompanying supplements. Feel free to contact me at hmichaud@stevenson.edu.

Now, let's begin. . . . A tort is not a dessert.

ABOUT THE AUTHOR

Hillary Michaud is a full-time law professor and director of an ABA-approved baccalaureate paralegal studies program at Stevenson University in Maryland. She is an active member of the Maryland State Bar Association and the State Bar of Georgia, and she maintains a part-time law practice as an administrative hearing officer. The author started her career as a certified public accountant for an international accounting firm before attending law school at the University of North Carolina at Chapel Hill School of Law, where she graduated with honors. As a lawyer, she has practiced as in-house legal counsel to The Coca-Cola Company, as well as for law firms and for Baltimore City.

At Stevenson University, the author directs a law clinic, performing *pro bono* legal services in tax and family law. In addition, she is a member of the Maryland State Bar Association's Special Committee on Paralegals, the American Association for Paralegal Education, and is a contributor to AAfPE's *The Paralegal Educator*.

Tort Law: Concepts and Applications was her first textbook published by Pearson Prentice Hall. She is also the author of *Paralegal Studies,* published in 2012.

chapter **1**

INTRODUCTION TO TORT LAW

This chapter provides a basic understanding of the substance and nature of tort law and places it within the context of the U.S. legal system. The chapter reviews the definition of tort law and how tort law is distinguished from other areas of law. It examines the sources of tort law, how tort law is researched, and how to read, analyze, and brief tort cases. It also reviews the classification of torts. Essential elements of torts are defined. How legal ethics applies to tort law is reviewed. A discussion of tort reform is included. The chapter ends with a discussion of careers in tort law, including paralegal opportunities. We begin our study with a look at the definition of tort.

Definition of Tort

To study tort law, the first question to be answered is, "What is a tort?" Most basically, a **tort** is a civil wrong, other than a breach of contract. In fact, the French word for "wrong" is *tort*. Tort **liability** arises when a person commits a wrongful act for which she is held legally responsible. That person is called a **tortfeasor**.

Through tort law, a person who suffers an injury as a result of the wrongful, or tortious, conduct of another can receive compensation for that injury. Where tort liability is established, a court will provide a **remedy**, often in the form of money **damages**. Therefore, tort law has two major concerns: wrongful conduct and compensation.

The purpose of tort law is to provide compensation or other legal remedy to those who are injured and/or whose property is damaged by the wrongful conduct of another. In essence, it is to provide one or more remedies for the invasion of protected interests. A **protected interest** is a right that a person has, under the law, to be protected from certain kinds of conduct. Tort law covers a variety of protected interests, as do other areas of law, such as contract law. Examples of protected interests under tort law include one's interest in her own personal safety from physical harm, in her own freedom of movement, in maintaining her privacy, and in protecting her personal property from destruction or damage. Each of these interests, and many more, is protected under tort law. As we study each tort, we will identify the interest that each protects.

LEARNING OBJECTIVES

1.1 Define a tort.

1.2 Explain how tort law differs from other areas of law, such as contract law or criminal law.

1.3 Identify and discuss the sources of tort law.

1.4 Understand how to research tort law and brief tort cases.

1.5 Explain how different torts are classified.

1.6 Identify and describe the "essential elements" of various torts.

1.7 Understand how legal ethics applies to tort law.

1.8 Explain tort reform and the arguments for and against it.

Tort
A civil wrong, other than a breach of contract.
Liability
Legal responsibility.
Tortfeasor
The person who commits a tort.
Remedy
The relief given to a party to enforce a right or to compensate for the violation of a right.
Damages
A remedy awarded at law, in the form of money.
Protected interest
A right that a person has, under the law, to be protected from certain kinds of conduct.

How is tort law similar to other areas of law? What distinguishes tort law from other areas of law? How does tort law relate to other areas, such as criminal law? Certain other areas of law need to be discussed to be able to put tort law into perspective within the U.S. legal system.

Tort Law Distinguished from Other Areas of Law

Contract
A legally enforceable agreement between parties.

Tort law is distinguishable from contract law. A ***contract*** is a legally enforceable agreement between parties. It arises out of a voluntary, mutual agreement or exchange of promises between two or more parties. One party may sue the other for breach of contract if the other party fails to fulfill his obligations under the contract. Distinguish that notion, of voluntary agreement to make and abide by promises, with torts. Contracts involve voluntarily undertaken obligations, consented to by the parties. Torts differ in that they involve forced obligations, meaning ones placed on persons without regard to their agreement to them. More specifically, torts involve conduct that is wrongful. What constitutes wrongful conduct normally is defined by case law, and is based on society's view of what duties and obligations one person owes to another. For instance, it is a tort, namely, the tort of battery, to hit another person without justification. So while tort law involves the general notion of wrongful conduct, contract law involves the concept of legally enforceable promises. Breaking one's promises under a contract, while constituting wrongful conduct in lay terms, is called "breach of contract" in the legal system, and it is remedied under contract law principles. Both tort law and contract law are part of the civil law system. What, then, is civil law?

Civil law
The system of law dealing with the definition and enforcement of all private or public rights.

Criminal law
The system of law dealing with wrongful actions perpetrated against society, for which society demands redress.

Lawsuit
A civil legal action brought by a party against another.

Plaintiff
The party bringing suit in a civil case.

Defendant
The party being sued in a civil case or the party being prosecuted in a criminal prosecution.

Burden of proof
A party's duty to prove a disputed assertion in a lawsuit or prosecution.

Preponderance of the evidence
The standard of proof typically applied in a civil case, by which the party must demonstrate that it is more likely than not that the allegations are true.

Civil law is the system of law dealing with the definition and enforcement of all private or public rights. It can be distinguished from ***criminal law***, which is the system of law defining and governing actions that constitute crimes, as defined by statutes. Criminal law deals with wrongful actions perpetrated against society, although these actions most certainly may affect an individual's rights, and for which society demands redress.

For a detailed comparison of these two systems of law, see Table 1-1. Civil law is concerned with rights and duties between private persons, or between private persons and the government, concerning noncriminal matters. The parties to a civil action, called a ***lawsuit***, are the ***plaintiff***, who brings the action, and the ***defendant***, who is being sued. The ***burden of proof*** in a civil case, meaning a party's duty to prove a disputed assertion, is typically a ***preponderance of the evidence***, meaning that the allegations are "more likely than not" true. Remedies may be awarded where liability is found. Remedies awarded are meant to compensate the injured party for the injuries sustained with the goal of making the injured party "whole" again.

Criminal law concerns wrongs committed against society as a whole, prosecuted by the government. The parties to a criminal action are the government

TABLE 1-1 Distinguishing Civil and Criminal Law

Area of Distinction	Civil Law System	Criminal Law System
Who brings the action?	A private person* who suffers harm (called a plaintiff)	The government, either state or federal
What is the wrongful act being addressed?	Injury or harm to a person* or to his property	A criminal statute prohibiting certain conduct has been violated
Who is concerned?	Rights and duties between private persons* and other persons* and/or their government	Society, because crimes are offenses against society as a whole
What is the legal action called?	Lawsuit	Prosecution
What is the standard of proof?	Preponderance of the evidence (typically)**	Beyond a reasonable doubt
What is the issue?	Liability	Guilt
What is the result?	Remedy, at law or in equity, usually in the form of money damages	Punishment, through penalties, in the form of fines, imprisonment, probation, or even death

*Person(s), in the legal sense, includes not only humans but also businesses and other entities.

**In some civil cases the standard of proof is "clear and convincing evidence." This standard of proof is higher than "preponderance of the evidence" but lower than "beyond a reasonable doubt." It is typically applied in cases where the loss of an important legal interest—such as potential termination of parental rights—is involved. "Clear and convincing evidence" means the party must demonstrate that it is *substantially* more likely than not that the allegations are true; in other words, the evidence establishes the truth of a disputed fact by a high probability.

(normally the state, but sometimes the federal government) and the criminal defendant. The burden of proof in a criminal case, called a **prosecution**, is **beyond a reasonable doubt**, meaning the prosecution must prove its case leaving no reasonable doubt as to the guilt of the defendant in the minds of the jurors. **Penalties** may be imposed on a wrongdoer found guilty of the commission of a crime, including fines, imprisonment, and even death. The constitutional protections found in the Bill of Rights, such as the right to counsel and the right to a speedy public trial before an impartial jury, apply to criminal defendants, not defendants in civil cases. Remember that the purpose of criminal law is to protect society and punish convicted perpetrators; its purpose is not to compensate injured victims.

Most crimes are also torts. While crimes are defined by statute, usually state statute but sometimes federal, most of them define conduct of a heinous enough nature to also meet the definition and elements of one or more torts. Crimes can often be torts because many crimes involve the violation of private rights as well as public interests. For example, the conduct that constitutes the *crime* of kidnapping is likely to constitute the *tort* of false imprisonment. There are some exceptions, however, where conduct considered criminal is not also considered tortious. For instance, victimless crimes, such as illegal drug use and prostitution, are not normally torts. Therefore, most but not all crimes are also torts.

Conversely, some but not all torts are also crimes. Many of the intentional torts, especially those against people, such as battery, assault, and false imprisonment, define conduct that is also criminal under a jurisdiction's criminal statutes. However, some torts do not rise to the level of constituting criminal conduct as well. For example, causing a car accident because you are driving

Prosecution
The legal action brought against a defendant alleging the commission of a crime.

Beyond a reasonable doubt
The standard of proof applied in a criminal case by which the prosecution must prove the case sufficiently so that there is no reasonable doubt in the mind of any juror that the defendant committed the crime.

Penalty
What is imposed on a defendant found guilty in a criminal prosecution.

CASE on Point

Orenthal James (O. J.) Simpson

A single action can constitute both a crime and a tort. Consider the case of O. J. Simpson.

On June 12, 1994, Nicole Brown Simpson, ex-wife of O. J. Simpson, the former professional football player and Heisman trophy winner, and her friend Ronald Goldman, were found stabbed to death outside Brown's home in Brentwood, California. After an infamous, televised, slow-speed chase of O. J. Simpson in his white Ford Bronco driving down Interstate 405 in the Los Angeles area, Simpson was arrested and criminally prosecuted for the murders of both Brown and Goldman. The criminal trial, conducted in 1995, included 134 days of televised testimony. In his closing argument, Johnny Cochran, one of Simpson's defense lawyers, famously quipped, "If it doesn't fit, you must acquit," in reference to a glove, covered in the victims' blood and produced as evidence during the trial, which appeared to be too small for the defendant to wear. After only three hours of deliberation concluding a trial lasting from January 25 until October 3, 1995, Simpson was acquitted of both murders by a jury of his peers.

Unsatisfied with the outcome of the criminal trial, the families of the victims brought a tort action against O. J. Simpson for the wrongful deaths of Brown and Goldman. In 1997, a civil jury found Simpson liable for the wrongful deaths of both victims, and rendered a judgment against O. J. Simpson in the amount of $33.5 million. To date, that judgment remains largely unpaid.

Why the different results? The reason for the difference in results reached in the two cases, beyond a difference in jurors, is the difference in burden of proof. As discussed, the burden of proof in a criminal case is very high, and the defense need only establish a reasonable doubt for the verdict to be not guilty. However, the burden of proof in a civil case is much lower, with the plaintiff needing only to establish his claim by a preponderance of the evidence—meaning it is more likely than not that the plaintiff's allegations are true.

unreasonably, applying makeup while negotiating traffic, may constitute the tort of negligence, but it is not criminal conduct.

Because many crimes are also torts, why don't many crime victims sue the perpetrators in tort for the harms they suffered? As the O. J. Simpson case suggests, these tort claims can be won, even when the criminal prosecution fails. The answer to the question is, simply, money. More victims of crimes do not bring tort actions against the perpetrators because of the lack of ability of most perpetrators to pay a judgment rendered against them. These tort cases can be won; it is just that, often, no judgment is collectable. It is only when the defendant has "deep pockets," meaning the ability to pay an adverse judgment, that it makes practical sense to bring such a tort suit. Examples of defendants with deep pockets, who are thus practical candidates to be sued for their tortious conduct, include employers and other business entities, insurance companies insuring the perpetrators, and wealthy individuals.

Now, knowing what a tort is, and how tort law is distinguished from other areas of law, we will examine where tort law comes from, and why.

Sources of Tort Law

There are four main sources of American law: constitutional law, statutory law, common law, and administrative law. In the absence of statutes controlling in an area, courts can make laws. Courts can also interpret laws derived from other sources, such as from the federal or state constitutions or from statutes enacted by the various legislatures in the United States. Court-made law, established by judges in their court opinions, is called case law or common law.

Tort law is derived, mainly, from common law. *Common law,* also called *case law*, is judge-made law, created by the courts and found in court opinions. Most torts are made in the absence of *statutes* or other controlling authority. Legislatures can enact tort statutes, and there are some statutorily enacted torts, including some we will examine in this text. However, most torts, including those we will study, are derived from the common law.

Now, knowing what tort law is and where it comes from, we will examine how to research tort law.

Common law
Judge-made law created by the courts and found in court opinions; also called case law.

Statute
A law enacted by a legislature.

Researching Tort Law

Legal research is a critical part of the job, both for attorneys and for paralegals. It is important to know how to research the law to (1) know what it is and (2) determine how it affects your client. Most law and paralegal students take one to two courses devoted specifically to the conduct of legal research and writing.

Legal research may be conducted manually, using printed material (law books), or with the use of technology, specifically, computerized legal research (using proprietary software or the Internet). Because the most reliable and widely used computerized legal research database services, available through Westlaw and Lexis, are very expensive, not all employers use them, or allow unrestricted use of these databases by their employees. Therefore, all lawyers and paralegals need to know how to conduct both manual and computerized legal research, though computerized legal research is conducted frequently today, and increasingly so.

As already discussed, the main source of American tort law is case law. Most tort law comes from court decisions. Therefore, it is important for a tort lawyer or paralegal to know how to research case law.

To research case law, the researcher must first define the issue or issues to be researched. In other words, the researcher must preplan what she is looking for in conducting the research—what question(s) she seeks to answer by performing this legal research. Knowing what her goal is, the researcher may begin searching for *cases on point*, meaning previous cases involving similar facts and legal issues. What the researcher is ultimately looking for in researching tort case law is binding authority on the case. *Binding authority*, also called *mandatory authority*, is legal authority that a court must follow in deciding the issue, such as a prior case that is precedent in the jurisdiction. Note that for a case to be binding authority on an issue, it must be both on point and from a higher court within the jurisdiction. When researching tort case law, then, the best binding case law authority is decisions made by the highest court in the

Case on point
A previous court decision involving similar facts and legal issues.

Binding authority
Legal authority that a court must follow in deciding the issue at hand; also called mandatory authority.

Key Point

Requirements to be Binding Authority
For a case to be binding authority on a legal issue, it must be (a) on point, and (b) from a higher court within the jurisdiction.

SIDEBAR

PLAN YOUR RESEARCH

Before beginning tort law research, a researcher should plan by defining the issues to be researched and knowing what questions she wants to be able to answer using her research results.

Key Point

Secondary Sources of Law

Secondary sources of law—resources that summarize or interpret the law—include materials such as case digests, legal encyclopedias, *Restatements of Torts* (*Second* and *Third*), *American Law Reports,* and law reviews.

Secondary sources of law
Resources that summarize or interpret the law but are not law themselves.

Primary sources of law
Resources that establish the law on an issue, such as a court decision, constitution, statute, or administrative regulation.

Key Point

Primary Sources of Law

Primary sources of law—establish the law on an issue—include such sources of law as court decisions, constitutions, statutes, and administrative regulations.

Key Point

Researching Tort Law

In researching tort law, a researcher is searching primarily for state case law.

Case name
Identifies the parties to a court case; also called a case title.

Case citation
A case's locator reference, which includes the volume number of the reporter where the case is published, the name of the reporter, the page number on which the case begins, identification of the court rendering the decision, and the year of the decision.

jurisdiction, as those cases have greatest precedential value (other than U.S. Supreme Court cases, and not many of those involve tort law). How, then, does a researcher find these cases?

A researcher often begins her research by searching secondary sources of law. **Secondary sources of law** are resources that summarize or interpret the law; they are not law themselves. They are research tools, used to get the researcher headed in the right direction in finding the relevant law. Secondary sources of law that a researcher might use in researching tort cases include case digests, legal encyclopedias, treatises, *Restatements of Torts* (*Second* and *Third*), *American Law Reports,* and law reviews. By reviewing secondary sources of law, the researcher can gain an understanding of the issue and its context within tort law and obtain citations to primary sources of law.

Primary sources of law establish the law on an issue and include such sources of law as court decisions, constitutions, statutes, and administrative regulations. Ultimately, it is the primary sources of law the researcher is searching for in conducting legal research. In tort law research, the relevant primary source of law is case law, as most tort law is derived from court cases. In addition, most tort law is a matter of state, rather than federal, law. Therefore, in researching tort law, a researcher is searching primarily for state cases.

Most state *trial* court decisions are not published but are merely filed in the clerk of court's office, where they are available for public inspection; today, however, with the advent of computerized databases, more and more unpublished opinions can be found in these databases—such as Westlaw and Lexis—using electronic resources. *Appellate* cases are routinely published in state reporters. Each state has its own official reporter (sometimes more than one), as designated by the state's legislature, and/or unofficial reporters, which are often published by West's National Reporter System. Reporters are published in numbered, multivolume sets, chronologically by date of decision. In addition, state court opinions are also published in regional reporters, published by West's National Reporter System. These regional reporters group states by geographic region in publishing regional court decisions, which can be useful for researchers who need to know case law in their own and in neighboring states.

A case, once identified, can be located using the case's name and citation. A **case name**, also called a **case title**, identifies the parties to the action. A **case citation** is a case's locator reference and typically includes the following information: the volume number of the reporter in which the case is published, the name of the reporter, the page number on which the case begins in that volume of that reporter, identification of the court rendering the decision, and the year of the decision.

It may be that the researcher cannot find binding authority on an issue in the relevant jurisdiction. In that case, the researcher may turn to sources of persuasive authority to gain insight in answering the legal issue. ***Persuasive authority*** is legal authority that is not binding on a court but may be used as guidance by a court in making its decision. Examples of persuasive authority in tort law research include previous court opinions from other jurisdictions or from lower courts in the jurisdiction, legal encyclopedias, or law reviews and similar scholarly legal periodicals.

When using a case, it is important to check to make sure the case is still good law and has not been reversed or modified by an appellate court. A prudent attorney or paralegal always checks to make sure a case he wishes to cite is still good law by performing a search of its subsequent history, meaning what happened to it in later court proceedings, such as appeals, if any occurred. Citation services, such as Shepard's Citations and KeyCite, are useful print and computerized resources for verifying that a case is still good law. Online citators are more up to date than printed ones, and many attorneys and paralegals find technology particularly useful when it comes to checking citations, including case citations.

As mentioned earlier, legal researchers have the choice of using printed materials found in a law library or computerized legal research services to perform their research. Which legal research method is better? Both methods have advantages and disadvantages.

Obviously, when conducting legal research using printed materials, the researcher must visit a law library where the necessary resources can be found. Many lawyers and paralegals today use computers to perform legal research, rendering a trip to the law library unnecessary. Another advantage to conducting computerized research is that the materials, including case law, are updated more frequently and more quickly, making research results more timely and up to date. A major disadvantage of the use of computerized legal resource technology, whether through a proprietary software license or via the Internet, is its cost. The cost of subscriptions to the two main legal research service databases, Westlaw and Lexis, is notable. As a result, as already mentioned, not all employers subscribe to these services, or allow unrestricted use of these services by their employees. Accordingly, all legal researchers must know how to research using both computer technology and printed materials.

Many primary sources of law can be found on the Internet, including state and federal statutes and regulations and written court cases. Secondary sources, such as legal encyclopedias, are less readily available online. Because tort law

Persuasive authority
Legal authority that is not binding on a court but that may be used as guidance in making its decision.

Key Point
Case Citations
Case citations follow the case name and include the reporter volume number, reporter name, page number on which the case begins, identification of the court rendering the decision, and the year of the decision. For example, "*Palsgraf v. Long Island R.R. Co.,* 162 N.E. 99 (N.Y. 1928)" is the case name and citation for the famous *Palsgraf* tort case examined in Chapter 6.

SIDEBAR

SITE CHECKING

Manual citation checking is performed using Shepard's Citations, a print source. Online citation checking is performed using KeyCite (from Westlaw) or Shepard's (from Lexis).

CONSIDER THE SOURCE

When you are performing computerized legal research, know that the site you are using contains dependable information before you use primary sources of law from it!

researchers typically look for court opinions, a primary source of law, computerized legal research is a good way to find them, financial resources permitting.

Although most computer users are accustomed to performing Google searches and finding what they need online, legal research requires something more than a generalized search using a search engine of that type. The reason is that, in searching for law, particularly primary sources of law, it is imperative that the computerized database used contain *reliable* and *accurate* information. For example, a tort case available online should be the verbatim case published in print form or released to the clerk of court for public filing. The researcher should be able to trust the reliability of the data on the site before using primary sources of law from it. That is why Westlaw and Lexis are the main sites used to perform computerized legal research, as they are well-established and well-known providers of computerized legal research services, with by far the most accurate and comprehensive databases available. Subscribers to Westlaw and Lexis, who pay a substantial fee for use of the services, have access to extensive collections of legal and business databases maintained by the sites, through which legal researchers can access specific documents, such as cases, and check citations. Government sites are also reliable in obtaining statutory materials from their jurisdiction, but statutes do not play a large role in tort law practice.

Once an attorney or paralegal finds a case she needs through legal research, she must read and analyze the case in order to understand the law for which it stands. The next section discusses how to read, analyze, and brief tort cases.

How to Read and Brief Tort Cases

Case briefing
The process of reading, analyzing, and summarizing court cases; also called briefing a case.

As discussed earlier, most tort law is derived from case law, meaning opinions rendered by judges in court. To understand tort law, then, one must understand how to read and analyze cases. This process is called *case briefing* or *briefing a case*. To brief a case is, in essence, to read, analyze, and summarize it.

Cases vary in size and complexity, from one or two pages to hundreds of pages of complex legal rulings and supporting reasoning. Like any other form of writing, some case authors write more clearly, and better, than others. Accordingly, some cases are easier to read and understand than others. To understand any case you read, however, it is likely you will have to reread at least portions of it, perhaps several times, to understand fully the court's ruling and its reasoning. No matter the complexity of the case or how well or poorly it is written, understanding the components of a case will help the reader understand the case. Here are the usual components of a case.

First, a case has a name or title. This indicates the names of the parties to the litigation, separated by a "v." which means "versus." Normally, the plaintiff's name appears first, followed by the defendant's name. On appeal, however, the order may change. For instance, when the defendant is the appellant, the appellate court may list the appellant's name first. The facts of the case will clarify who the parties are if the order of the appearance of their names in the title leaves this unclear.

A case citation is found near the case title, usually just above or below it. The case citation indicates the volume number, reporter, and page number where the case is reported, identification of the court rendering the decision, and the date of the decision. It sometimes includes the date of the arguments when the case is an appellate one. In addition, a docket number assigned by the clerk of court follows the case title. Although the docket number is not part of the official case citation, it is a useful tool in researching the case for previous or subsequent cases and/or related legal briefs.

A case syllabus typically follows the docket number. The case syllabus is normally a paragraph containing a condensed statement of the facts of the case, the issues facing the court, and the court's ruling. For official reporters, the courts may prepare the syllabi, but for unofficial reporters, they are usually prepared by the reporter's publisher. Keep in mind that when briefing cases, the court's opinion itself reflects the law, not the publisher's summary of what it thinks the opinion is saying, found either in syllabi or in headnotes, discussed next.

Unofficial reporters, which are very widely used because they are very helpful to researchers, often contain headnotes. Headnotes are paragraph breakdowns of the case in summary form. Like syllabi from unofficial reporters, headnotes are written by publishers, not the courts, and they are not part of the court's opinion. Thus, they are not the law set forth in the case, no matter how well the publisher summarizes the law in them.

The names of counsel representing the parties, if they are represented by counsel, normally appear after the syllabi (and headnotes, if there are any). The name of the judge or justice authoring the opinion, or a notation that the decision was authored *per curium*, meaning by the entire court, immediately precedes the opinion.

Although the term "opinion" is commonly used to refer to an entire court decision, the precise meaning of the term is more restricted. In fact, an ***opinion*** is the formal—usually lengthy—analysis, decision, and reasoning of the court in ruling on a case. The opinion normally includes a statement of the facts of the case, a summary of the legal issues raised, the remedies sought by the parties, errors of law in the lower court if the case is on appeal, and the application of the law to the facts of the case. Courts normally cite other laws, such as statutes, administrative regulations, or case precedents, or relate public or social policies or other nonlaw considerations, in support of their rulings in their reasoning. An appellate opinion is called a ***unanimous opinion*** when all the judges agree to it, or a ***majority opinion*** when only a majority of the judges agree to it.

The opinion of the court is normally followed by the court's conclusion. If the decision of the court was set forth earlier, in the opinion itself, then it is normally reiterated, clearly and concisely, in the court's conclusion. If the

Key Point

Components of a Case

- Case name/title and case citation
- Date decided (and perhaps the date of appellate arguments)
- Docket number
- Syllabus and (sometimes) headnotes
- Names of counsel representing the parties, and the judge or justice writing the opinion
- Opinion (or body) of the case
- Conclusion
- Concurring and/or dissenting opinions (may follow)

Opinion
The formal, usually lengthy, analysis, decision, and reasoning of the court in ruling on a case.

Unanimous opinion
A court opinion in which all the judges agree.
Majority opinion
A court opinion in which a majority of the judges agree.

case is an appellate one, the conclusion also states whether the lower court's decision is being affirmed, reversed, or remanded for further proceedings. A sample court case is given in Schedule 1-1.

Schedule 1-1 Sample Court Case

[Reporter citation]
457 F.Suppl.2d 590, 34 Media L. Rep. 2574

[Court hearing the case]
United States District Court,
D. Maryland.

[Case title—names the parties to the case, docket number, and date of decision]
Tonya BARNHART
v.
PAISANO PUBLICATIONS, LLC.
Civil No. JFM-06-318.
Oct. 17, 2006.

[Case syllabus—a brief summary of the case, prepared by the courts for official reporters and by the publishers for unofficial reporters; *this summary was prepared by the text author as an example*]
Plaintiff brought suit against defendant publisher for the tort of invasion of privacy. Defendant publisher moved for summary judgment.

The District Court held that plaintiff's conduct in baring her chest at a public event could not reasonably constitute a private act, the photograph taken at the event did not constitute false light, and publication of plaintiff's photograph did not constitute appropriation of plaintiff's likeness.

Defendant's motion for summary judgment was granted and judgment entered against plaintiff.

[Headnotes—paragraph summaries regarding different aspects of the case, prepared by the publisher; *using online legal research technology (such as Westlaw or Lexis) or a law library containing the F. Supp. Reporter, locate and review the numerous headnotes prepared by the publisher, West, for this case*]

[Counsel for the parties]
David Ellin, Melissa A. Proctor, Law Office of David Ellin PC, Baltimore, MD, for Tonya Barnhart.

Michael D. Sullivan, Thomas Curley, Levine Sullivan and Koch LLP, Washington, DC, for Paisano Publications, LLC.

MEMORANDUM

[Judge authoring the opinion]
MOTZ, District Judge.

[Opinion of the court]
This action arises from the publication of a photograph of the Plaintiff, Tonya Barnhart, in the March 2005 issue of Easyriders, a magazine published by Defendant Paisano Publications. Ms. Barnhart appears partially nude in the photograph. As a result of its publication, she asserts several claims for invasion of privacy against the Defendant. Paisano Publications has filed a motion for summary judgment. For the following reasons, the motion will be granted.

I.

The undisputed facts are as follows. Tonya Barnhart is a 29-year-old woman employed as a retail clerk; she is not a celebrity, and she has never been paid to perform or to make any other public appearance. On August 28, 2004, Ms. Barnhart attended the Toop's Troops Second Annual Pig Roast.[1] The Pig Roast was a fund-raising event attended by motorcycle enthusiasts, and included music, food, games, and vendors selling motorcycling paraphernalia. At least 200 people were present. The party was "bring your own" alcohol, and continued all day and into the early hours of the next morning. At some point during the day women began removing their shirts in return for being given beads. Ms. Barnhart, swept up by the Mardi Gras type atmosphere, was hoisted onto the shoulders of two men and voluntarily lifted up her shirt. At that moment, Bill Cromwell, a photographer who often submitted his pictures to Easyriders magazine for publication, snapped a photograph of Ms. Barnhart in her exposed state. He later submitted that picture to Easyriders, and it was published in the magazine's March 2005 edition.

II.

A.   Motions for summary judgment should be granted when the record establishes that there is no genuine issue of material fact, and the moving party is entitled to judgment as a matter of law. Fed.R.Civ.P. 56(c); Celotex Corp. v. Catrett, 477 U.S. 317, 322, 106 S.Ct. 2548, 91 L.Ed.2d 265 (1986). The substantive law of the cause of action determines which facts are material. Anderson v. Liberty Lobby, Inc., 477 U.S. 242, 248, 106 S.Ct. 2505, 91 L.Ed.2d 202 (1986). The existence of other factual disputes between the litigants does not defeat an otherwise proper motion for summary judgment if none of the material facts are in dispute. Id. A dispute about a material fact is genuine and summary judgment is inappropriate if the evidence is such that a reasonable jury could return a verdict for the nonmoving party. Id. at 248, 106 S.Ct. 2505. In analyzing whether a genuine issue of material fact exists, the evidence and reasonable inferences from that evidence must be viewed in the light most favorable to the non-moving party. Id. at 255, 106 S.Ct. 2505.

B.   This is a diversity action, and Maryland's choice of law provisions apply. "In tort actions, Maryland applies the doctrine of lex loci delicti, which provides that *593 the substantive law of the state where the wrong occurs governs." Rockstroh v. A.H. Robins Co., 602 F.Supp. 1259, 1262 (D.Md.1985). In this case, the event at which plaintiff was photographed was held in Maryland, and plaintiff and defendant both assume that Maryland law applies. The fact that Easyrider magazine is distributed nationally does not provide a basis for overturning this assumption, and I will apply Maryland law.

The Restatement of Torts defines four different types of the tort of invasion of privacy: 1) unreasonable intrusion upon the seclusion of another, 2) unreasonable publicity given to another's private life, 3) publicity that unreasonably places another in a false light before the public, and 4) appropriation of another's name or likeness. Under Maryland law a plaintiff may assert a claim for any of these types of invasion of privacy, see Lawrence v. A.S. Abell Co., 299 Md. 697, 475 A.2d 448, 450-51 (2001), and Maryland cases look to the definitions and comments contained in the Restatement in applying invasion of privacy law. See Hollander v. Lubow, 277 Md. 47, 351 A.2d 421, 424-26 (1976); see also Bagwell v. Peninsula Regional Medical Center, 106 Md.App. 470, 665 A.2d 297, 318-19 (1995).

---

[1] The record is unclear as to whether the name of the organization is "Toop's Troops" or "Tube's Troops." "Toop's Troops" is the name used in the Declaration of a member of the organization. (Dec. of Ralph Stambaugh 1).

III.

An intrusion upon seclusion claim requires that the matter into which there was an intrusion is entitled to be private and is kept private by the plaintiff. Hollander, 351 A.2d at 424 (citing W. Prosser, The Law of Torts, 808 (4th ed.1971)); Restatement Second of Torts § 652B (1977). Likewise, an unreasonable publicity claim requires that the matter that is publicized is private in nature. In that regard the Maryland Court of Appeals has ruled that "anything visible in a public place can be recorded and given circulation by means of a photograph, to the same extent as by a written description, since this amounts to nothing more than giving publicity to what is already public and what anyone would be free to see." Hollander at 426 (quoting W. Prosser, The Law of Torts, 810 (4th ed. 1971)). The court went on to say that "facts disclosed to the public must be private facts, and not public ones. Certainly no one can complain when publicity is given to information about him which he himself leaves open to the public eye." Id. at 427 (quoting Prosser, Privacy, 48 Cal. L.Rev. 383 (1960)).

Here, plaintiff's lifting up of her shirt cannot reasonably be said to have constituted a private act. She exposed herself at an outdoor fund-raising event open to any member of the public who purchased a ticket. According to plaintiff's own estimate, about 200 people were present at the event. Although she alleges that at the moment she removed her shirt she was in the company of only about 10 people, all of whom she knew and trusted, the fact remains that she exposed herself in a public place where anyone could have seen her.

Furman v. Sheppard, 130 Md.App. 67, 744 A.2d 583 (2000), is very much on point. There, the defendant had trespassed onto the property of a private club and filmed plaintiffs on their yacht without their consent. The court held that plaintiff's intrusion claim had been properly dismissed because they were seen participating in activities that could have been observed by non-trespassing members of the public as well. Id. at 587. Likewise, in Solomon v. National Enquirer, 1996 WL 635384 (D.Md.1996), the court held that a photograph taken of a woman as she stood inside her house by the window could not give rise to an invasion of privacy because any passerby on the street could have viewed her through the window. Furman *594 and Solomon both mandate the entry of summary judgment for defendant on plaintiff's seclusion and unreasonable publicity claims.[2]

IV.

To establish a successful claim for false light invasion of privacy, a plaintiff must prove 1) that the defendant gave "publicity to a matter concerning another that places the other before the public in a false light," 2) that "the false light in which the other person was placed would be highly offensive to a reasonable person," and 3) that "the actor had knowledge of or acted in reckless disregard as to the falsity of the publicized matter and the false light in which the other would be placed." Bagwell v. Peninsula Regional Medical Center, 106 Md.App. 470, 513-14, 665 A.2d 297 (Md.App.1995). A defendant is entitled to judgment as a matter of law if the facts disseminated regarding the plaintiff are true. Id.

[2]Plaintiff relies heavily upon Capdeboscq v. Francis, 2004 WL 463316, 2004 U.S. Dist. LEXIS 3790 (E.D.La.2004), in which the court denied a motion for summary judgment filed by defendants where plaintiff had been photographed lifting their tee shirts and exposing their breasts. Capdeboscq, of course, was decided under Louisiana, not Maryland, law. Moreover, in denying defendants' motion, the court noted that plaintiffs alleged that they had been photographed only after having been asked to do so several times and after being told that they would not appear on any "Girls Gone Wild" video. In fact, their photographs ultimately appeared on the cover of a video/dvd titled "Girls Gone Wild Doggie Style." Even under those circumstances, the court found that it was "a close call" as to whether defendants' summary judgment motion should be denied.

In Furman v. Sheppard, supra, the Maryland Court of Special Appeals found that because the videotape there at issue recorded the plaintiff's activities accurately, it was not actionable under a false light theory. 130 Md.App. 67, 744 A.2d 583, 587-88 (2000). Similarly, in AIDS Counseling and Testing Centers v. Group W Television, 903 F.2d 1000 (4th Cir.1990), the Fourth Circuit held that summary judgment had properly been entered for defendant on a false light claim because any inaccuracies in a television station's reporting were minor and did not cause the story to produce a different effect on the audience than would have been produced had the truth been reported. Id. at 1004.

Here, however, plaintiff's claim is not that the published photograph somehow distorts her true appearance, but that the photograph's publication gives the impression that she is the type of person who consents to having a topless photograph of herself published in Easyriders magazine. There does not appear to be a Maryland case directly on point, in which plaintiffs claimed not that the information contained in the picture or article itself was false, but that the publication gave the false impression that the plaintiff consented to the dissemination of the information. Cases in other jurisdictions, however, have addressed the issue.

Braun v. Flynt, 726 F.2d 245, 247 (5th Cir.1984), involved an accurate picture of the plaintiff published in a hard core men's magazine called Chic. The picture depicted the plaintiff performing her routine as an entertainer at an amusement park, in which a pig dove into a pool and swam to the plaintiff, who was waiting with a bottle of milk for him. The picture was accompanied by a caption written in a tongue in cheek manner.[3] The court upheld the *595 jury's finding of liability, finding the fact that the plaintiff's picture had been placed without her consent in a "magazine devoted exclusively to sexual exploitation and disparagement of women" was sufficient for the jury to find that she had been placed in a false light. Id. at 255.

The same result was reached in Douglass v. Hustler Magazine, 769 F.2d 1128 (7th Cir.1985). There, Robyn Douglass, a model and actress, consented to being portrayed in the nude in Playboy magazine. Id. at 1131. Her picture, however, was published in Hustler magazine instead. Id. The court delineated the differences between Hustler and Playboy as shown by the record and found that the evidence was such that a reasonable jury could find that it was degrading for a woman to be portrayed as the type of person who would consent to be published in Hustler even if she had consented to be published in Playboy. Id. at 1137. In addition, the court found that the accompanying text in Hustler could have been understood to insinuate that Ms. Douglass was a lesbian, which she is not. Id. at 1135. Thus, although the court reversed a jury verdict in plaintiff's favor on other grounds, it concluded that plaintiff had a viable false light claim.

In Braun and Douglass the plaintiffs presented voluminous evidence demonstrating in detail the degrading and lewd content of Chic and Hustler. Plaintiff has presented no such evidence here. Unquestionably, the record discloses that a few of the pictures in Easyriders are a bit racy, including bikini-clad women and two women (one of whom is plaintiff) lifting up their shirts. However, the only direct evidence concerning the nature of Easyriders is contained in the deposition of Kimberly James Peterson, the editor of the "In The Wind" section of the magazine in which plaintiff's picture was published. According to Peterson,

---

[3] The caption read: "SWINE DIVE—A pig that swims? Why not? This plucky porker performs every day at Aquarena Springs Amusement Park in bustling San Marcos, Texas. Aquarena staff members say the pig was incredibly easy to train. They told him to learn quick, or grow up to be a juicy ham sandwich." Id. at 248 n. 2.

the purpose of that portion of the magazine is to illustrate the "exhilaration" of the motorcycling lifestyle. (Dep. of Kimberly James Peterson 12). Likewise, the caption accompanying plaintiff's photograph says only "Pegging the fun meter." This caption is not itself offensive, and did not imply, as did some of the text in the Hustler magazine involved in Douglass, that plaintiff is a lesbian.

Most importantly, there is nothing in the record to suggest that Easyriders is more sexually explicit than Playboy, and in Douglass the very premise of the court's holding was that plaintiff's consent to have her photograph appear in Playboy did not give rise to a false light claim. It was only because the court found that a consent to be photographed for Playboy was qualitatively different from a consent to be photographed for Hustler that the court held that plaintiff's false light claim was viable.

V.

The final claim asserted by plaintiff is for appropriation of her likeness. The Restatement of Torts provides that "[o]ne who appropriates to his own use or benefit the name or likeness of another is subject to liability to the other for invasion of his privacy." Restatement (Second) of Torts § 652C (1977). The tort is intended to protect against a person using the identity of another to advertise his business or for other commercial purposes. Thus, an appropriation claim does not arise from incidental uses of a person's identity or likeness. Id. As set forth in the Restatement the value of a person's image is not appropriated when it is published for purposes other than taking advantage of his reputation, prestige, or other value associated with *596 him, for purposes of publicity. No one has the right to object merely because his name or his appearance is brought before the public, since neither is in any way a private matter and both are open to public observation. It is only when the publicity is given for the purpose of appropriating to the defendant's benefit the commercial or other values associated with the name or likeness that the right of privacy is invaded. The fact that the defendant is engaged in the business of publication, for example of a newspaper, out of which he makes or seeks to make a profit, is not enough to make the incidental publication a commercial use of the name or likeness. Thus a newspaper, although it is not a philanthropic institution, does not become liable under the rule stated in this Section to every person whose name or likeness it publishes. Id.

Applying the rules of the Restatement, in Lawrence v. The A.S. Abell Company, supra, the Maryland Court of Appeals held that because the plaintiffs' picture was taken while they were in a public place at a newsworthy event, an action for appropriation could not lie. 475 A.2d at 453. Furthermore, the court stated that even if the use of the plaintiffs' photograph in an advertising campaign was not merely "incidental," a person's likeness must also have some commercial or other value before an action for appropriation can succeed. Id. Because the plaintiffs in Lawrence were neither famous nor professional models, they could not show that the newspaper had taken advantage of any special value associated with their pictures. Id.

Lawrence is controlling here. The record does not establish that plaintiff is famous or a professional model or that there is any special value associated with her likeness. Moreover, as in Lawrence, plaintiff's photograph was taken at a public, outdoor event. Accordingly, her appropriation claim fails as a matter of law.[4]

---

[4]In her opposition papers, plaintiff argues that she did not consent to the publication of her photograph. That is immaterial. The issue of whether a plaintiff consented is relevant only in determining whether a defendant has a defense to the plaintiff's invasion of privacy claim. See Bagwell v. Peninsula Regional Medical Center, 106 Md.App. 470, 665 A.2d 297, 319 (Md.1995). Here, for the reasons I have stated, plaintiff cannot meet the threshold requirements for any invasion of privacy claim.

A separate order effecting the rulings made in this memorandum is being entered herewith.

[Conclusion and order of the court]

ORDER

For the reasons stated in the accompanying memorandum, it is, this 17th day of October 2006.

ORDERED

1. Defendant's motion for summary judgment is granted; and
2. Judgment is entered in favor of defendant against plaintiff.

When an appellate judge agrees with the court's decision, but for different reasons, or disagrees with the court's decision altogether, that judge (or judges) may write a ***concurring opinion*** (in which she agrees with the decision but for different reasons) or a ***dissenting opinion*** (in which she disagrees with the ruling of the court). Concurring and dissenting opinions, when they exist, follow the majority opinion of the court.

In reading a case, only certain statements within it are legally binding. The legally binding principle(s) established by the case is called the court's holding(s). Other statements made by the court that do not directly address the specific facts and issues of the case, but are the judge's "editorializing" about the case or merely explain or provide additional information and are not essential to the case, are called *dicta*. **Dicta**, such nonlaw statements made by judges in their opinion, have no precedential value and are not binding in later court decisions. Only the court's holding is considered precedent in subsequent cases, and a case reader must be able to distinguish between the court's holding and *dicta*.

A ***case brief*** is a mechanism for summarizing, in written form, the case, as read and analyzed by the brief's author. If in conducting legal research you find a case on point that you want to use in your research findings, perhaps to include in a legal memorandum or a legal brief (different from a case brief, and written for the court) you are writing, you can summarize your understanding of the case in a case brief. This summary will provide you with the case name/title and citation, the important facts of the case and perhaps its procedural history, the legal issue(s) addressed by the court in the case, the court's holding(s) that state the rule of law established by the case and answer the issue(s), and the court's reasoning for its holding(s).

The form of a case brief can vary, depending on the author and/or the requestor of the brief (for instance, a paralegal's supervising attorney may request that the paralegal brief a case in a certain format). However, case briefs generally contain the following parts, numbered and labeled: (1) case name/title and citation, (2) a summary of the material facts of the case (may include the case's procedural history), (3) a statement of the issue(s) presented by the case, (4) the court's holding(s), and (5) a summary of the court's reasoning for its decision (may include law relied on by the court in reaching its decision). A sample case brief is given in Schedule 1-2.

Concurring opinion
An opinion written by a judge or judges who agree with the court's majority opinion, but for different reasons.

Dissenting opinion
An opinion written by a judge or judges who disagree with the court's majority opinion.

Dicta
Nonlaw statements made by judges in an opinion.

Case brief
A mechanism for summarizing, in written form, a court case.

Key Point

Contents of a Case Brief

1. Case name/title and citation
2. Summary of the key facts (may include the case's procedural history)
3. Issue(s)
4. Holding(s)
5. Summary of the court's reasoning (may include law relied on by the court in reaching its decision)

Schedule 1-2 Sample Case Brief
Using the Case from Schedule 1-1

I. *Barnhart v. Paisano Publ'ns, LLC*, 457 F.Suppl.2d 590 (D. Md. 2006).

II. The plaintiff, an adult woman who is not a celebrity, attended an outdoor fundraising event for motorcycle enthusiasts. The event was open to the general public. At the event, there was music, food, games, motorcycle vendors, and drinking alcohol was allowed. Women began removing their shirts in exchange for being given beads, Mardi Gras style. The plaintiff, upon being lifted onto the shoulders of two men, voluntarily lifted her shirt and exposed her breasts. A photographer at the event took a photograph of the plaintiff's exposure and submitted it, for publication, to Easyriders magazine, published by the defendant. The magazine published the photograph. The plaintiff sued the defendant for invasion of privacy as a result of this publication.

Procedure: On defendant's motion for summary judgment. Motion granted.

III. a. Has the plaintiff stated a claim for the invasion of privacy tort of intrusion on seclusion?

   b. Has the plaintiff stated a claim for the invasion of privacy tort of false light?

   c. Has the plaintiff stated a claim for the invasion of privacy tort of appropriation?

IV. a. No, the plaintiff has not stated a claim for the invasion of privacy tort of intrusion on seclusion.

   b. No, the plaintiff has not stated a claim for the invasion of privacy tort of false light.

   c. No, the plaintiff has not stated a claim for the invasion of privacy tort of appropriation.

V. The plaintiff chose to lift up her shirt at an outdoor fund-raising event which was open to the public and where about 200 people were present, according to the plaintiff's own estimate. Her actions in exposing her breasts in public could not reasonably have constituted a private act giving rise to a claim of intrusion upon seclusion. Rather, it was a public act. For an intrusion on seclusion claim to exist, that matter into which there was an intrusion must be a private one, not a public one.

There was no actionable claim of false light because the photograph's publication did not give the false impression that the plaintiff consented to the dissemination of the information contained in the photograph. Further, the photograph did not distort the plaintiff's appearance in any way, its caption was not offensive ("Pegging the fun meter"), and there was no evidence that the magazine published degrading and lewd content.

In regards to her appropriation claim, there was no appropriation of the plaintiff's likeness where there was mere incidental use, and not commercial use, of the likeness. Further, the plaintiff was not famous or a professional model, and there was no other special value associated with her likeness. Without commercial or other value to one's name or likeness, an appropriation claim does not lie under Maryland law.

SIDEBAR

THE BLUEBOOK: A UNIFORM SYSTEM OF CITATION

The Bluebook (as it is called) is widely regarded as the authority for proper legal citation form. It is accurately marketed as the leading legal citation guide used in the United States, and it is widely used by lawyers, judges, legal scholars, law students, and other legal professionals such as paralegals. *The Bluebook* is published by the Harvard Law Review Association. It is typically a required text in law schools and paralegal education programs.

The first part of a case brief is the case name/title and citation. Abbreviations may be used. The names of multiple plaintiffs or defendants may be omitted. *The Bluebook* style of legal citation is used by most lawyers and judges in uniformly citing legal authority, including case citations.

The second part of a case brief is a summary of the key facts of the case. Key facts are those that are material, meaning important, to understanding the decision rendered by the court. For instance, that the plaintiff is a female might not be important in a breach of contract case, but it is likely material to a Title VII gender discrimination case. Extraneous facts should be omitted, and material facts should be presented succinctly—this is a case "brief." In reading a case to find the important facts, remember that facts often appear at the beginning of the case, but they can appear anywhere in the case.

In this second section of a case brief, the brief writer may wish to include a short procedural history of the case, in one or two sentences, indicating how the case got to the present court. This is especially true if the procedure is relevant to the court's decision in the case. If the procedural history of the case is not relevant to the court's decision or useful to the brief writer, it may be omitted from the case brief.

The third part of a case brief is the issue or issues presented by the case. An issue should be phrased concisely and should set forth the essential question to be decided by the court. There are normally multiple issues in any one case. Each issue should be stated separately, normally in the form of a question that can be answered "yes" or "no," in sufficient detail that its answer will reflect the court's holding in the case. The following is an example of how to phrase an issue: "Did the plaintiff's unreasonable conduct contribute to the injury she suffered?"

SIDEBAR

OTHER CITATION SYSTEMS

The Bluebook is the most widely used legal citation system, but it is not the only one. The *ALWD Citation Manual* is compiled by the Association of Legal Writing Directors as an alternative professional system of citation for legal materials. It has been adopted by some law schools, paralegal programs, law reviews, moot-court competitions, and courts. Some states utilize their own legal style manuals as well.

The fourth part of a case brief is the court's holding or holdings. A court's holding is the decision it renders on an issue in the case. The holding constitutes the law of the case. There may be one, or multiple, holdings in a case, correlating to the number of issues presented. The holding or holdings should state succinctly the rule(s) of law established in the case. Usually, a holding is phrased "yes, ..." or "no, ..." and answers the question set forth in the issue. Based on the previous example, the holding might be, "Yes, the plaintiff's unreasonable conduct contributed to the injury she suffered." In the holding, some brief writers state who won the case, if that would be useful to them. Remember, however, that the court's decision regarding who won the case is a different concept than the holding, which is the rule of law established by the case, and which may become precedent.

The final part of a case brief is a summary of the court's reasoning. The court's reasoning may include specific facts about the case, law being relied on or interpreted by the court, public or social policy, and any other factors that affect the court's holding. The summary of the court's reasoning is often the longest part of a case brief. In this part, the brief writer summarizes the reasons why the court made the ruling that it did. Further developing the above example, the court's reasoning might be, "By speeding excessively while driving her car, the plaintiff contributed to the injury she suffered in the car collision caused by the defendant's negligence."

SIDEBAR

THE IRAC METHOD

Another common format for briefing cases is the IRAC method. IRAC means I-issue, R-rule, A-application, C-conclusion.

"Issue" means the legal issue(s) presented in the case.

"Rule" means the law to be applied to the facts of the case.

"Application" means application of the law to the facts of the case.

"Conclusion" means the decision of the court after applying the law to the facts of the case.

To use IRAC, do the following for *each* legal issue presented in the case:

1. State a legal issue presented. For example, "The issue is whether Bob committed the tort of battery when he kissed Pam without her consent."

2. State the law involved. Articulate the rule of law to be applied by the court to the facts of the case in order to make its determination. For example, case law in the jurisdiction defines the essential elements of the intentional tort of battery as (a) an act, (b) harmful or offensive contact with the plaintiff's person, (c) intent, and (d) causation.

3. Apply the law to the facts of the case. Here is where the case briefer analyzes the facts of the case in conjunction with the law that applies. In this example, the act of committing the unconsented-to kiss is evaluated based on the essential elements defined in part 2.

4. Make a conclusion about each issue using logical analysis that relates the rule of law to the facts of the case. For example, the conclusion may be that Bob committed the tort of battery when he kissed Pam without her consent.

Just like with the summary of the key facts, this part of the brief should be a summary, preferably in the brief writer's own words, and not simply a recitation of the court's reasoning—again, it should be "brief."

Remember, in briefing cases, different people may brief in different formats. Nonetheless, those who are reading, analyzing, and summarizing cases, for whatever use (to discuss in a law school class, to use in a court document, or to note in a research memorandum for a supervisor), are synthesizing the same information and, ultimately, also determining the rule of law established by the case, and the reasons for it.

Now that we have reviewed how to research tort law and brief tort cases, we will review how torts are classified. These classifications provide a framework for studying and understanding each of the individual torts.

Classification of Torts

Torts are classified into three main categories: intentional torts, negligence, and strict liability torts. Some torts do not fit neatly into these main categories, such as defamation and invasion of privacy. However, most torts fall within one or more of these categories. We will study torts within the framework of these categories.

Intentional torts are those torts in which the tortfeasor either desired to bring about the consequences of his actions or failure to act, or knew with substantial certainty that the consequences would follow from his actions or failure to act. "Intent" is an essential element of all the intentional torts. The other tort classifications do not require intent.

Negligence is the failure to use reasonable care, resulting in harm to a person or his or her property. Negligence is the most common tort action, by far. Most personal injury cases are negligence cases, though personal injuries can result from intentional torts, such as battery, and strict liability torts, such as products liability.

Strict liability is tort liability imposed without regard to fault. It is also called absolute liability. Under strict liability theory, a tortfeasor can be held responsible for injuries she causes to others, without regard to blameworthiness.

Each of the torts, no matter what classification, is defined by its essential elements. Before we study each tort's essential elements, we must first understand the concept of essential elements.

Intentional torts
Those torts in which the tortfeasor either desired to bring about the result or knew with substantial certainty that the result would follow from the person's actions or failure to act.

Negligence
The failure to use reasonable care, resulting in harm to a person or to his or her property.

Strict liability
Liability imposed without regard to fault, for which a tortfeasor is held responsible without regard to blameworthiness; also called absolute liability.

Essential Elements of Torts

Every tort can be broken down into its ***essential elements***. Essential elements are the component parts of each ***cause of action***, meaning each legal theory in a lawsuit. Each essential element must be supported by the facts of the case in order to state and prove a cause of action for that tort. If an essential element of a tort is missing, then that tort has not been committed or has not been proven. That is why each element is considered *essential*.

Throughout this book, you will study the essential elements of each tort. Remember that these elements are normally defined by judges in cases, as the main source of tort law is common law.

Essential elements
The building blocks, or component parts, of a cause of action, which must be established by the person bringing the action.
Cause of action
A legal theory in a lawsuit.

PRIMA FACIE CASE

When a plaintiff has established each of the essential elements of a claim, he is said to have made a *prima facie* case. *Prima facie* is a Latin term meaning "on its face." In other words, the plaintiff has made a claim on its face.

However, establishing a *prima facie* case does not necessarily mean that the plaintiff wins. The defendant may defeat one or more of the essential elements of the plaintiff's claim. Or the defendant may assert an affirmative defense, which in essence permits or justifies his conduct. Once the plaintiff has established a *prima facie* case, though, the burden of proof shifts to the defendant to show some legal reason why the plaintiff should not win on the claim.

Attorneys and paralegals must abide by the legal ethics rules in performing legal services. Next, we will examine how legal ethics applies to tort law.

Legal Ethics and Tort Law

Legal ethics and professional responsibility apply to tort law, just as they do to all areas of the law. Attorneys, who are licensed by the state(s) in which they practice law, are regulated by the ethical codes and rules adopted by those states.

Violations of ethical rules by attorneys can result in sanctions against them, including disbarment, suspension of their licenses, and reprimand in the form of a private or public warning or scolding by the disciplinary body, as well as malpractice liability and termination of employment, among other negative consequences.

Paralegals and other members of the legal services delivery team must also abide by the rules of legal ethics and professional responsibility when they practice their professions. Although state codes and rules of ethics apply directly to attorneys, they also apply, albeit indirectly, to the rest of the legal services delivery team. For instance, if a paralegal violates the confidentiality rules by disclosing confidential information about a case to someone outside the legal services delivery team, the attorney supervising the paralegal may be disciplined for that ethical violation even though it was committed by another (the paralegal) under the attorney's supervision. Certainly, that would have adverse employment consequences for the paralegal! In addition, a paralegal could be sued for professional negligence, known as malpractice, just as an attorney can be.

Many legal ethics rules come into play when someone is engaged in the practice of tort law. For instance, only licensed attorneys may engage in the practice of law. It is both an ethical violation and a crime, in most states, for anyone else to do so. Therefore, a nonattorney should never give legal advice, such as by recommending to a client a course of action in tort litigation.

Numerous other legal ethics rules also apply in the tort law arena. Here is a broad overview of many of these requirements.

The ethical rules regarding confidentiality require that client confidences be maintained. They require that conflicts of interest be avoided and that attorneys exercise utmost loyalty in representing their clients. Although advertising and solicitation of clients is allowed, limitations are placed on both by the ethics rules of every state. Many personal injury lawyers engage in very public advertising, such as in television commercials and on roadway billboards. Ethical restrictions on lawyer advertising and solicitation must be followed when building and maintaining a personal injury law practice. Although legal fees are normally set using the hourly method, it is common to have contingency fees in personal injury tort cases. **Contingency fees** are legal fees based on a percentage of the plaintiff's recovery. Ethical rules require that fees be reasonable, and courts may scrutinize excessive fees. Also, ethics rules, and tort law on malpractice, require that attorneys act competently in their representation of clients, represent their clients zealously, communicate effectively with their clients, and pursue client matters without unreasonable delay.

Contingency fee
A legal fee based on a percentage of the plaintiff's recovery.

SIDEBAR

LEGAL FEES AND ETHICS

Legal fees are normally structured as either fixed fees, hourly fees, or contingency fees.

Fixed fees are flat fees charged for the performance of a task, for example, $500 for incorporating a business or $400 for drafting a simple will. Fixed fees are not commonly used in tort matters.

Hourly fees are based on actual time spent on a matter. The most common fee arrangement with clients is an hourly fee arrangement. In order to bill hourly fees, lawyers and paralegals must keep track of their time, and maintain complete and accurate timekeeping records. Hourly fee arrangements are common in tort practice.

Contingency fees are allowed only in certain types of cases, pursuant to legal ethics rules. Contingency fees are most often used in personal injury cases. The reason for them is that many potential plaintiffs who are injured by another's wrongful conduct may not be able to afford a lawyer on an hourly fee basis. Without being able to afford a lawyer, many would be denied access to the justice system. Contingency fees are a way to provide access to the courts for those who would not otherwise be able to afford access.

With contingency fees, plaintiffs pay a portion of their recovery as the legal fee, such as 20 or 30 percent. What if the plaintiff loses at trial? In that case, the lawyer does not get paid, because a percentage of nothing is nothing. If you think that 30 percent of a plaintiff's recovery is too high a fee, remember that the lawyer is assuming the risk that she could work on a matter for many months or years but recover nothing (and hence be paid nothing). The contingency fee amount must reflect this assumption of the risk of not being paid, or of being paid very little. The use of contingency fees is considered necessary by our legal system and society in order to provide more people with access to justice.

Note that with contingency fees, even if the client recovers nothing so the lawyer receives no fee, the client may still be responsible for litigation costs and expenses, in accordance with the client's fee arrangement with his or her lawyer.

These many ethics rules affect tort law, and the practice of lawyers, paralegals, and other members of the legal services delivery team who practice in the area of tort law. These topics will be discussed more thoroughly throughout this book. Competence in understanding and applying ethical rules is essential to the practice of tort law.

In recent times, there has been a movement in our society to reform tort law. This movement has arisen as a result of the ever-increasing cost of insurance and the large damages awards being rendered by some courts, normally via juries, in personal injury cases. Some of these judgments seem disproportionate to the harm, and the media gets involved in raising public awareness from the media's viewpoint. Next, we will consider tort reform, and the arguments for and against it.

Tort Reform

The Sixth and Seventh Amendments to the U.S. Constitution give citizens a right to jury trial in most legal disputes. As a result, most tort cases that go to trial are decided by juries unless both parties waive their right to jury trial (but note that most cases, whether tort or otherwise, are settled or otherwise resolved before trial, such as through dismissal). Interestingly, most developed countries other than the United States do not allow juries to hear tort cases.

Tort cases often involve personal injuries. In their pursuit of justice, some juries, especially lately, render huge judgments in favor of injured plaintiffs. The "McDonald's coffee case" discussed in the Case on Point is a well-known example because of the significant media attention paid to it.

Tort reform
Changing the rules and applications of tort law to reverse the upward trend in compensation being awarded by juries today, particularly in personal injury cases.

Advocates of **tort reform** argue that such large jury awards, exponentially disproportionate to the injury sustained, are raising insurance and health care costs for the rest of Americans. Who, for instance, actually pays when an insurance company has a multimillion-dollar judgment rendered against it or the person it insures? Tort reformists argue that these costs are passed on to the citizens who pay premiums to insure themselves through these companies, raising the cost of insurance for all.

Advocates for tort reform include insurance companies, who desire to pay smaller damage awards on behalf of their insureds. The medical profession has also been successful so far in advocating for tort reform in such a way as to effectively lobby for judgment caps in some states. For example, in Texas there is an overall $750,000 cap on noneconomic damages that can be awarded in health care lawsuits and a $250,000 cap on noneconomic damages that can be awarded against doctors in medical malpractice lawsuits. Advocates favoring tort reform have proposed, among other possibilities, capping damage awards and limiting the number of claims that can be brought, hoping to curb the filing of frivolous lawsuits and the awarding of excessive damage judgments. Some damage caps have been enacted in a variety of jurisdictions. For another example, in 1975 the state of California passed the Medical Injury Compensation Reform Act. This statute caps noneconomic damages, such as pain and suffering, emotional distress, loss of enjoyment of life, and disfigurement at $250,000 per occurrence.

CASE on Point

Liebeck v. McDonald's Rests., P.T.S., Inc., 1995 WL 360309[1]

In this case, a 79-year-old woman went through a drive-thru at a McDonald's restaurant in Albuquerque, New Mexico. She was riding in the front-passenger seat of her car, which was being driven by her grandson. The grandson parked the car so that Liebeck could add cream and sugar to her coffee. Liebeck placed the cup of coffee between her knees and pulled the lid tab toward her. In the process, she spilled the entire cup of coffee in her lap. Liebeck was wearing cotton sweatpants at the time, and the coffee was absorbed and held against her skin as Liebeck sat in the spill for about ninety seconds. Liebeck suffered third-degree burns over 6 percent of her body during the coffee scalding, spent eight days in the hospital, and received numerous skin grafts.

At the end of her tort trial, the jury awarded Liebeck $2.86 million for her injuries. The trial judge reduced the award to $640,000. The parties later settled out of court for an undisclosed amount (less than the trial judge's reduced award) before judgment was rendered on McDonald's appeal.

As presented in the media, this case demonstrates well the point of tort reformists about excessive jury awards.[2] Interestingly, not much media attention was paid to the fact that McDonald's had faced a large number of claims because of its scalding coffee—this was hardly the first.

Not everyone agrees that tort reform is necessary, or advantageous. Consumer advocate groups are a good example of opponents of tort reform. Remember that the purpose of tort law is to provide compensation for those who are wrongly injured by others. Is it fair to cap that compensation at some arbitrary amount? What if, for instance, it is your loved one who is severely harmed by the negligence of a surgeon performing an operation on your beloved? What if your loved one suffers irreparable brain damage as a result of the surgeon's unreasonable conduct in performing the operation? If a damage cap of, say, $250,000 per occurrence was in place, as tort reformists would support, how would your loved one be made whole, which is the goal of compensatory damages? Common sense in the jury deliberation room goes a long way in making jury awards in these extreme cases more reasonable. Further, those opposed to tort reform argue that if damage awards are capped, is that not a disincentive for medical practitioners, drivers, and other major categories of personal injury tortfeasors to use care in their actions? For example, it is counterintuitive to expect improved patient care by medical professionals when damage awards for medical malpractice are capped.

Tort reform has been a national trend at the state level. The extent of tort reform and their specific reforms vary from state to state. For example, some states have enacted caps on noneconomic damage awards, many states limit the joint and several liability of joint tortfeasors, a handful of states limit punitive damage awards, some states limit joint and several liability when there are multiple tortfeasors who cause an injury, and several states restrict the amount an attorney can charge on a contingency fee basis in medical malpractice cases.

The federal government also considers tort reform issues in legislating. For example, it considered prohibiting punitive damages in asbestos cases (the Asbestos Compensation Fairness Act of 2003) and limiting damage awards in medical malpractice cases (the Common Sense Medical Malpractice Reform Act of 2003), though neither of these bills was passed into law. The Volunteer Protection Act of 1997 is a good example of current federal tort reform. The Volunteer Protection Act protects people who volunteer for nonprofit organizations or government entities from tort liability for damages caused by their negligent conduct.[3]

This debate will continue as the cost of insurance continues to rise (although the cost of litigation and jury verdicts is only one component contributing to the increase in premiums) and excessive damage awards continue to be rendered by juries.

Next we will consider what careers are available to attorneys and paralegals who are interested in tort law practice.

Careers in Tort Law

Many types of careers are available in the field of tort law, for both lawyers and paralegals. As a distinct practice area, tort law deals with personal injury and property damage. It is invoked when persons are injured, or their property is harmed, because of the conduct of another.

Tort practice is litigation-intensive. Therefore, tort practitioners are typically litigators and trial attorneys. Because it is its own specialty area, tort cases are often handled by specialists in the field. As litigators, successful tort practitioners possess good litigation skills, including conducting legal research, drafting pleadings, motions, and other court documents, and making persuasive arguments in court documents and at trial. In addition, because most tort cases are settled before trial, good tort litigators must have strong negotiating skills to achieve early settlement of disputes.

Interestingly, in the area of personal injury law more than any other area of law, contingency fee structure is common. The use of contingency fees in this area expands access to lawyers and the legal system to injured persons who might otherwise be unable to afford to seek redress under the law for harms they suffer because of the wrongful conduct of another.

Plaintiff's attorney
A lawyer who represents an injured person in a tort lawsuit.

Tort lawyers may represent injured plaintiffs. Although this is a generalization, often plaintiffs in tort actions are represented by solo practitioners or by small firms that specialize in tort litigation. These attorneys are called ***plaintiff's attorneys*** or plaintiff's firms. Tort lawyers may represent defendants who are sued for legal liability by injured plaintiffs. Defendants in these cases may be people but are often business entities, such as corporations that manufacture, distribute, or sell products. When the defendants are companies or insurance companies, they are often represented by larger firms or by the company's in-house lawyers. Tort lawyers may represent insurance companies that have entered into special contracts, called insurance policies, to protect people and entities against certain risks of loss. Typically, tort lawyers represent either plaintiffs *or* defendants and insurance companies (but not always, as some practitioners will represent either side in tort litigation).

PLAINTIFF'S ATTORNEY

An attorney who represents an injured person in a tort lawsuit is often referred to as a plaintiff's attorney.

Within the field of tort law, a lawyer may handle a variety of types of cases. Most common are negligence cases. Negligence cases are often referred to as *personal injury cases* or PI cases. They involve injuries caused to a person because of another's failure to exercise reasonable care. These cases range from "slip-and-fall" cases, such as a customer slipping on a wet floor in a defendant's store and being injured, to mass torts, such as train derailments that result in numerous injuries and even death. The most common type of PI case, however, arises out of negligently caused car accidents. Accordingly, insurance defense litigation is a big part of PI litigation, as laws in every state require drivers to carry automobile insurance or otherwise prove financial ability to pay in the event of a loss.

Malpractice, or professional negligence, is another specialty in the field of tort law. Malpractice litigation has grown in recent years, as persons are more willing to sue professionals, such as doctors, lawyers, and accountants, for injuries sustained because of their professional misconduct. Malpractice litigation, because of its complex subject matter, often requires the use of expert witnesses, so practitioners in this area must be capable of working with experts and their testimony. Insurance is typically involved when malpractice claims are made, and, like other types of tort litigation, these claims are often settled prior to trial.

The number of medical malpractice lawsuits, like other forms of malpractice lawsuits, has increased exponentially over the last few decades. This growth has given rise to a debate that medical malpractice litigation is raising the cost of medical care and insurance for all, even forcing some doctors and specialists, such as obstetricians, out of their fields. While the debate continues, one must recognize the balancing of competing interests involved, namely, the interest an injured person has in receiving compensation for the harm she suffers versus the interest society has that the injured person bear the risk of harm or loss in order to make the cost of care reasonable for all. At some point, the risk of harm or loss should shift from the injured person to the professional who negligently caused the injury, and malpractice attorneys represent the interests of those persons.

Tort law practitioners may also represent parties in intentional tort lawsuits, such as cases involving assault, battery, intentional infliction of emotional distress, invasion of privacy, or defamation. These cases are much less common than negligence cases. Further, insurance may not be involved in these situations, because insurance coverage is typically disclaimed expressly, in the policy, for intentional misconduct committed by the insured. Without the presence of insurance, it is usually not very lucrative for plaintiffs who bring intentional tort claims, and the decision of whether to bring such claims

Personal injury cases
A name for negligence cases resulting in personal injury to a plaintiff, often known by the abbreviation PI.

against intentional tortfeasors will depend, at least in part, on the particular defendant's ability to pay an adverse judgment that might ultimately be rendered against him.

Strict liability cases are also handled by tort law practitioners. The most common type of litigation in this area is products liability. Normally, products liability cases are brought under the strict liability theory because that theory makes it easier for plaintiffs to establish the essential elements of their claims and prove their cases. Products liability shifts the risk of loss caused by defective products from the injured person to the one who places the defective product into the stream of commerce. The rationale for this treatment is that products liability is a cost of doing business for manufacturers, distributors, and sellers of products. Products liability cases are typically defended by either big law firms representing the companies that made, distributed, or sold the products or the companies' in-house counsel. Products liability is examined, in detail, in Chapter 11.

Careers in tort law, then, typically involve litigation practice. Many lawyers specialize in tort litigation. Although ethics rules and state criminal statutes permit lawyers, and only lawyers, to represent clients in court, there is a role for paralegals in tort law. This role is discussed next.

The Role of Paralegals in Tort Law

Like most areas of law, tort law offers many employment opportunities for paralegals. Statistically, most paralegals work in litigation, and most work for law firms. Because tort law is litigation-intensive, it is common today to see paralegals involved in tort law practice. Further, because much of tort litigation is handled by law firms, many law firms employ paralegals to specialize in tort law practice. That said, many companies large enough to have in-house corporate legal departments also employ paralegals. Among areas of law in which in-house paralegals may practice is tort law.

Whether employed by a law firm or an in-house legal department, the role of paralegals in the field of tort law is, by and large, to support litigation attorneys in representing parties to tort litigation. As mentioned above, tort law practice is litigation-intensive, typically involving a lawsuit brought by one who has suffered personal injury or property damage because of the wrongful conduct of another. As in other areas of litigation, paralegals may assist attorneys in most aspects of litigation, with the exception of giving legal advice and representing clients in court, both of which are prohibited by legal ethics rules.

For example, paralegals may set up and maintain client files, conduct factual investigations in evaluating claims, gather and review documents through discovery, interview clients and witnesses, obtain and review medical and employment records to determine the plaintiff's injuries and lost wages, draft documents for filing with the court, arrange for service of process and prepare subpoenas, track discovery and litigation deadlines, perform legal research in establishing or defending claims, and assist in the preparation of a case for hearing or trial such as by making a trial notebook, preparing exhibits, organizing evidence, and assisting with witness preparation.

Key Point

Tasks Performed by Personal Injury Paralegals

Tasks performed by personal injury paralegals include

- Interviewing clients and witnesses
- Setting up and maintaining client files
- Conducting factual investigations of accidents or other occurrences
- Gathering and reviewing records
- Drafting legal documents such as pleadings and settlement agreements
- Assisting in drafting motions and legal briefs
- Preparing discovery requests and responses
- Summarizing records and depositions
- Tracking discovery and litigation deadlines
- Performing legal research
- Scheduling and preparing witnesses for deposition and trial
- Arranging for service of process
- Preparing subpoenas for trial
- Organizing exhibits and preparing trial notebooks

Skills that are often useful for paralegals who work in the field of tort litigation include the ability to speak and write clearly and well, to be a good listener and an effective interviewer, to be able to analyze and synthesize complex information, to be well organized and effective in managing time, to work well with others, to act in a professional manner, to maintain client confidences, to be responsible and willing to take on responsibility, and to use technology well and effectively.

In conclusion, as a legal specialty, tort law offers many career options for paralegals with an interest in providing litigation support, both for law firms and in in-house corporate legal departments.

CHAPTER **SUMMARY**

- A tort is a civil wrong, other than a breach of contract. It is distinguished from a criminal wrong, which is prosecuted in the criminal law system. A tortfeasor can be held liable, for damages or other remedies, for tortious conduct that causes injury or harm to another.

- The purpose of tort law is to protect certain interests of persons, including interests in their physical safety and toward their property. The main source of tort law is common law.

- Legal research, a critical part of the job for attorneys and paralegals, may be conducted using print material or using computer technology, and attorneys and paralegals need to know how to research both ways.

- To research case law, the main source of tort law, the researcher must first plan the research project. Next, she conducts the research, using either print materials or computer technology, and using secondary and primary sources of law, primarily state cases. In researching state case law, she locates cases using their names and citations, which citations include the volume number of the reporter in which the case is published, the name of the reporter, the page number on which the case begins in that volume of that reporter, identification of the court rendering the decision, and the year of the decision. Using a citation service, either in print or online, tort law researchers must make sure the cases they used are still good law, and that they have not been reversed or modified by an appellate court.

- Once an attorney or paralegal finds the case he needs through legal research, he next must read, analyze, and summarize the case using a process called case briefing. Briefing a case involves reading (and rereading) a case, analyzing what the case says, then summarizing it in the following format: case name and citation, a summary of the key facts, the issue(s) of the case, the holding(s) of the court, and a summary of the court's reasoning.

- Torts can be classified into three major categories: intentional torts, negligence, and strict liability torts. Each tort can be broken down into its essential elements, which define the tort.

- Legal ethics and professional responsibility have a clear role in the area of tort law. Legal ethics codes and rules apply directly to attorneys. They apply indirectly to other members of the legal services delivery team, including paralegals. Ethical issues, like the reasonableness of contingency fees and attorney advertising and solicitation, play a particular role in the field of tort law.

- Tort reform is the notion of changing the rules and applications of tort law to reverse the upward trend in compensation being awarded by juries today, particularly in personal injury cases.

- Many types of careers are available in the field of tort law, for both lawyers and paralegals, especially in litigation practice, as plaintiff's attorneys, defense attorneys, or attorneys for insurers, or as paralegals working for any of them. As litigators, successful tort practitioners practice such litigation skills as conducting legal research, drafting pleadings, motions, and other court documents, negotiating, and making persuasive arguments in court documents and at trial. Negligence cases are often referred to as personal injury, or PI, cases, and they involve injuries caused to a person because of another's failure to exercise reasonable care. These are the most common types of cases in tort law practice.

- Legal ethics rules and state criminal statutes permit lawyers, and only lawyers, to represent clients in court, but there is a role for the paralegal in tort law, namely, to provide support to the litigation attorney by performing tasks such as setting up and maintaining client files, conducting factual investigations, reviewing and gathering documents, interviewing clients and witnesses, obtaining and reviewing medical and employment records, drafting documents, tracking litigation deadlines, performing legal research, and assisting in the preparation of a case for hearing or trial. Skills often useful for paralegals who work in the field of tort litigation include the ability to speak and write clearly and well, to be a good listener and an effective interviewer, to be able to analyze and synthesize complex information, to be well organized and effective in managing time, to work well with others, to act in a professional manner, to maintain client confidences, to be responsible and willing to take on responsibility, and to use technology well and effectively.

CONCEPT REVIEW AND REINFORCEMENT

QUESTIONS FOR **REVIEW**

1. What is a tort?
2. What is the purpose of tort law?
3. How is tort law different from other areas of law?
4. What are the major differences between the civil law system and the criminal law system?
5. What is the main source of tort law?
6. How is tort law researched?
7. Because tort law is mainly case law, how do you research cases?
8. How do you read and analyze cases?
9. What are the steps in briefing a case?
10. What are the three major classifications of torts?
11. What are the essential elements of a tort?
12. What role do legal ethics play in tort law?
13. What is tort reform?
14. What careers are available in tort law?
15. What career opportunities are specifically available to paralegals?
16. What is the paralegal's role in the field of tort law?

DEVELOPING YOUR PARALEGAL SKILLS

CRITICAL THINKING **EXERCISES**

1. Lenny Lucas is in love. Unfortunately for Lenny, his love is unrequited. The object of Lenny's affection, Virginia Riley, loves another—her husband, Martin Riley. Lenny and Virginia work together at Millford Bank & Trust Co. One day, Lenny finds himself alone in the break room with Virginia. Lenny's passion for Virginia is unleashed, and he professes his love for her, takes her by the hand, and gently kisses it. Virginia is appalled by Lenny's actions.

   Has Lenny engaged in wrongful conduct from an ethical (as opposed to legal) standpoint? Has he engaged in tortious conduct? Has he committed a crime? In considering this case, know that the tort of battery is defined as an intentional, harmful, or offensive contact with another person.

2. Refer to the *O. J. Simpson* Case on Point. How could O. J. Simpson be found not guilty of the murders of his ex-wife and her friend, yet be held liable for their wrongful deaths?

3. The standard of proof in a criminal case is "beyond a reasonable doubt." The standard of proof in a civil case typically is "preponderance of the evidence." Which standard is higher, meaning that it requires a greater amount of proof? Does this make sense? Why or why not?

4. Does being found "not guilty" in a criminal prosecution mean the defendant is innocent? Why or why not? How does your answer affect tort law, under which the conduct alleged might constitute both a crime and a tort?

5. Why is a victimless crime, such as illegal drug use, not also a tort?

ASSIGNMENTS AND PRACTICAL **APPLICATIONS**

1. Go to your school's law library (or, if your school has none, use the Internet website for "FindLaw") and research the tort and crime in your jurisdiction (your state) for the wrongful act of punching one's archenemy. Is this act a crime in your state? What is the crime called? Is this act a tort in your state? What is the tort called? Hint: Remember that crimes usually are defined by statute, and torts by case law, so look in your state's code for the crime and your state's court opinions for the tort.

2. The murder and wrongful death trials involving O. J. Simpson were not the last of his legal entanglements. More recently, O. J. Simpson was arrested, charged with, and, in 2008, convicted of criminal actions relating to entering another's hotel room in Las Vegas and taking property not belonging to him. To locate and read the criminal complaint in this case, using the Internet, go to http://hosted.ap.org/specials/interactives/_documents/simpson_complaint.pdf. Simpson is currently serving a multiyear prison sentence for these criminal actions.

3. Go to your school's or a local law library and find and review the secondary sources of law that may be useful to tort law researchers, including legal encyclopedias (*American Jurisprudence* and *Corpus Juris Secundum* are the two main legal encyclopedias), case digests for your state, the *Restatement (Second)* and *(Third) of Torts*, tort law treatises, and the *American Law Reports*.

4. Review current events in tort law by examining newspapers and news magazines. Look for pending tort cases, as well as conduct that could be tortious and actionable. See how tort law relates to everyday life. Share your results with the class.

5. Research the legal ethics rules in your jurisdiction regarding the reasonableness of fees and the allowed use of contingency fee arrangements. What restrictions does your jurisdiction place on fees and contingency fee arrangements? How do these restrictions affect attorneys' ability or desire to accept representation of clients in tort matters? Discuss your research results with the class.

6. Research the local newspapers in your area to see what employment opportunities are available. See the classified advertisements section for paralegal and attorney positions. In particular, if your area has a legal newspaper or journal, review its classified ads for employment opportunities. (Often, the online classified advertisements for these publications contain substantially more advertisements than the hard copy versions do.) Can you find any advertisements for tort lawyers or paralegals? If so, what are the positions? Where are they (for law firms, companies, insurance companies)? Share your research results with the class.

TECHNOLOGY RESOURCES AND INTERNET **EXERCISES**

Go on the Internet and see what computerized legal research resources are available by typing in searches such as for "legal research," using a search engine such as Google, AOL Search, or Yahoo! In your search, find the following: Cornell Law School's informative site at *www.law.cornell.edu*, the popular free legal site FindLaw at *www.findlaw.com*, and the two leading computerized legal research databases, Westlaw (*http://web2.westlaw.com*) and Lexis (*www.lexis.com*). See also the Duke Law website (*www.law.duke.edu/lib/researchguides/formbks*) for useful information on form books and how to locate legal forms online, such as through Westlaw, Lexis, and FindLaw.

See *www.pacificwestlaw.com/physicians/micra.htm* for more information about the California Medical Injury Compensation Reform Act.

For an interesting review of the debate surrounding tort reform, see the Wikipedia website on tort reform (*www.en.wikipedia.org/wiki/Tort_reform*).

Go to the website for the American Tort Reform Association (*www.atra.org*) and search for specific tort reforms in your state by selecting "state and federal reforms."

See the U.S. Department of Justice's Bureau of Justice Statistics website (*http://bjs.ojp.usdoj.gov/*) for information tracking the amount and types of litigation occurring in the United States.

Model jury instructions, also called pattern jury instructions, are forms of jury instructions approved by a state bar association or similar group regarding matters arising in a typical case. A good way for students to learn the essential elements of the different torts and how those elements are defined is to review the jury instructions used in their

state. These can often and easily be found on the Internet. Locate jury instructions used in your state for the various torts as they are discussed in upcoming chapters.

Go to the Cornell Law School website (*www.law.cornell.edu/ethics/md/code*). Perform a search for the legal ethics code in Maryland. Using either this resource or your own state's legal ethics rules, answer the questions in the following Ethical Applications section.

ETHICAL **APPLICATIONS**

Maria Jones is a paralegal working for the personal injury law firm, Carmichael & Wright, P.C. Around 4:00 p.m. one Friday afternoon, Maria is in a hurry to finish a project for her supervising attorney, George Harris. She has been researching the current state of the law on contributory negligence in Maryland. She believes she heard that contributory negligence continues to be a defense to negligence in Maryland, but she cannot seem to quickly pinpoint recent case law on point. Wanting to beat rush-hour traffic, she "embellishes" the results of her research, and reports to her supervisor that she has confirmed (though she has not) the

law on this issue, and that contributory negligence is a valid defense to negligence in the state of Maryland at this time. She is *correct*. George thinks this sounds reasonable, and he does not review or follow up on Maria's work.

Under your state's legal ethics rules, has Maria Jones violated an ethical duty? Can she be sanctioned by her state bar's disciplinary board? Has George Harris violated an ethical rule or duty? Can he be sanctioned by the state bar that licenses him? Can either, or both, be held liable for malpractice because of their actions or inactions?

VIDEO **CASE STUDY**

Difference Between a Civil Criminal Case

Synopsis: Interview with trial court Judge Kenny, who discusses the difference between a civil case and a criminal case.

Questions

1. What is the difference between a criminal prosecution and a civil lawsuit?
2. How does this difference apply to tort cases?
3. If certain conduct can both be a violation of criminal law and result in civil liability in tort, what is the difference in the burden of proof between a criminal case and a tort case? Why is there a difference?

chapter 2
TORT LIABILITY

This chapter provides a basic understanding of tort liability and the people who can be held liable for committing torts. The chapter examines the impact of "foreseeability" on tort law. It reviews the definition of "tortfeasor." The chapter explores the concepts of joint tortfeasors and joint and several liability. Vicarious liability of a person for the tortious conduct of another is examined. We begin our study with a look at the impact of foreseeability on tort law.

The Concept of Foreseeability in Tort Law

Foreseeability in tort law means the predictability of an event or occurrence. The concept of foreseeability is relevant in many areas of tort law. Because of this concept, a wrongdoer who causes injury or harm to another might not be liable for the harm she causes if the harm was not foreseeable or if the person harmed (the plaintiff) was not foreseeable. For example, in negligence, a duty of care may not be owed to an "unforeseeable" plaintiff. As another negligence example, a wrongdoer might not be found liable for harm he unreasonably caused when the nature of the harm was not foreseeable. Foreseeability is studied in this chapter because it impacts when a person can be held liable for her tortious conduct—so it impacts tort liability.

Foreseeability is determined by considering the occurrence before, rather than after, the fact. Foreseeability involves the quality of being able to reasonably anticipate that harm will result from the occurrence. This means that you judge whether the outcome was foreseeable *before it happens*, rather than in hindsight.

Throughout this text, we will study foreseeability as it applies to various torts. We will practice applying the concept of foreseeability to specific torts. When doing so, remember that "unforeseeability" may negate or limit a tortfeasor's liability, depending on the circumstances.

Foreseeability impacts whether or not tort liability is imposed. That liability is imposed on a person who commits a tort. The concept of tortfeasor is discussed next.

LEARNING OBJECTIVES

2.1 Explain the concept of "foreseeability" in tort law.

2.2 Define a tortfeasor.

2.3 Understand and explain the concept of joint tortfeasors.

2.4 Explain the concept of joint and several liability.

2.5 Define vicarious liability and explain how it applies to tort law.

Foreseeability

In tort law, the predictability of an event or occurrence.

Tortfeasors

Tort liability
Arises when a person commits a wrongful act.

Tortfeasor
A person who commits a tort.

As discussed in Chapter 1, **tort liability** arises when a person commits a wrongful act. A person who commits a tort is called a **tortfeasor**. Any person who suffers an injury to his person or property as a result of a tortfeasor's conduct can receive compensation for that injury in the form of a court award of damages. Therefore, a tortfeasor incurs tort liability.

What if there is more than one person who causes harm to another? In other words, what if multiple tortfeasors act together in committing a tort? They are joint tortfeasors. The issue of multiple tortfeasors is examined next.

Joint Tortfeasors

Joint tortfeasors
Persons who act with other persons in causing a tortious wrong, who can be sued together by the injured party.

Joint tortfeasors are two or more tortfeasors who contribute to causing another's injury and who can be joined as defendants in the injured party's tort claim. To be a joint tortfeasor, the person must have participated in the wrongful conduct or encouraged and facilitated it. For example, suppose that three individuals, acting together, negligently install a chandelier in a ballroom. During a ball, the chandelier falls to the ground, shattering crystals in every direction and injuring the plaintiff. All three individuals acted negligently in causing this one harm; thus all three are joint tortfeasors.

How does being a joint tortfeasor affect legal liability? If more than one person contributes to causing the harm, to what extent is each person liable for the harm? Joint liability is liability shared by two or more persons. Joint liability is based on the notion that all joint and concurrent tortfeasors are independently at fault for their wrongful act(s). Joint and several liability allows a plaintiff who is injured by joint tortfeasors to sue one, some, or all of the joint tortfeasors. Joint and several liability is discussed next.

Joint and Several Liability

Joint and several liability
A legal doctrine under which a plaintiff, in a tort or other action, may sue all of the responsible parties, jointly, or any one or more of them, severally, at his option.

Joint and several liability means that a plaintiff, in a tort or other action, may sue all of the responsible parties, jointly, or any one or more of them, severally, at his option. Therefore, in a tort action involving joint tortfeasors, a plaintiff may sue any one joint tortfeasor for all of the damages suffered, may sue more than one joint tortfeasor for all of the damages suffered, or may sue all of them. The plaintiff can choose which, and how many, of the joint tortfeasors to sue, and may sue any one or more of them for the entire harm. Note that in some jurisdictions this common law application of joint and several liability has been modified by statute to limit the liability of joint tortfeasors for damages proportionate to their respective degrees of fault as a tort reform measure.

In the earlier hypothetical involving the negligently installed crystal chandelier, the plaintiff could choose to sue all three of the joint tortfeasors, or one or two of them. Whether she sues one, two, or three of them, she can sue for the entire harm. In other words, she could sue just one of the joint tortfeasors, yet sue him for the entire amount of the damages she seeks to recover.

How does the plaintiff decide which joint tortfeasor(s) to sue? Obviously, a plaintiff is most likely to sue the joint tortfeasor(s) with the deepest pockets, meaning the greatest ability to pay the judgment if the plaintiff wins her case.

The purpose behind the doctrine of joint and several liability is to relieve the plaintiff of the burden of having to sue each joint tortfeasor for his proportionate share of the harm. Instead, the plaintiff is allowed to choose whom to sue, shifting the burden to the joint tortfeasors to pursue contribution of proportionate shares of the judgment from each other, as discussed below.

The plaintiff may only recover one time for the entire harm, however. So if the plaintiff sues less than all of the joint tortfeasors and recovers, that recovery is the end of the line for the plaintiff. She is not entitled to multiple recoveries just because there are multiple tortfeasors. If, however, the plaintiff sues one joint tortfeasor and is unable to collect the entire judgment, she can then sue any of the other joint tortfeasors until the whole judgment is collected.

What happens if the plaintiff sues only one of the joint tortfeasors? What rights does that joint tortfeasor have, who is forced to pay the entire judgment even though he is only partially responsible for the harm the plaintiff suffered? In such a case, any joint tortfeasor who pays more than his proportionate share of the entire harm may seek contribution from the other joint tortfeasors in jurisdictions that allow contribution.

Contribution is the right of a joint tortfeasor who has paid a judgment to be proportionately reimbursed by the other joint tortfeasors for their share of the harm. In other words, each joint tortfeasor should contribute proportionately to the judgment. Not all states allow contribution, and when and how they allow it differs among jurisdictions. For example, when contribution is allowed may depend on whether the tortious conduct was negligent or intentional. For another example, how contribution is allowed varies, with some states permitting contribution in equal shares and others authorizing contribution proportionate to fault. Keep in mind, however, that whether contribution occurs is of no consequence to the plaintiff. The plaintiff is entitled to satisfaction of the judgment from any individual tortfeasor(s), severally. Contribution is an issue for, and among, the joint tortfeasors.

Indemnity is a method of forcing a person who has not paid the judgment to reimburse the person who paid it for the full amount of the judgment paid. Indemnity is also called ***subrogation***. It is a way for a party who is secondarily liable for a judgment, who has paid it, to obtain reimbursement from the party who is primarily liable for it. Whereas contribution shifts a portion of the loss to other joint tortfeasors, indemnity shifts the entire loss to another. Indemnity can arise either by contractual agreement, such as through an insurance policy, or by operation of law, such as when an employer seeks to be reimbursed by an employee for the wrongful acts of the employee for which the employer was held responsible under the doctrine of *respondeat superior,* a vicarious liability principle discussed below.

If a joint tortfeasor has paid the entire judgment, the plaintiff is deemed to have received satisfaction and is not entitled to sue the other joint tortfeasors, because she can only recover once for her injury. ***Satisfaction*** is full payment of a judgment by a liable party. If full satisfaction is received from one joint

Contribution
The right of a joint tortfeasor who has paid a judgment to be proportionately reimbursed by the other joint tortfeasors for their share of the harm.

Indemnity
A method of forcing a person who has not paid the judgment to reimburse the person who paid it for the full amount of the judgment paid; also called subrogation.

Satisfaction
Full payment of a judgment by a liable party.

Release
A document that formally relinquishes a plaintiff's legal claim.

tortfeasor, the other joint tortfeasors may no longer be sued by the plaintiff, who is not allowed multiple recoveries. If the plaintiff has received satisfaction on a judgment, she may be asked to execute a release. A *release* is a legal document in which a plaintiff gives up and relinquishes her claim—which is reasonable, because she has already been compensated for it. Releases, although they may be executed gratuitously (for free), normally are executed upon the receipt of consideration, such as the payment of a settlement or judgment in full. If the plaintiff releases all joint tortfeasors, then her claims against all of them are extinguished. If, however, she releases one or only some of the joint tortfeasors, does the release act to relinquish the claim the plaintiff has against the rest of the joint tortfeasors? In most states, it does, unless a special statute exists to change that result.

In jurisdictions that recognize that the release of one joint tortfeasor operates to release all of them, the joint tortfeasor who pays, rather than executing a release, may obtain a covenant not to sue from the plaintiff. A *covenant not to sue* is a legally enforceable promise by the plaintiff not to sue the person in whose favor the covenant is made—the joint tortfeasor who paid. A covenant not to sue does not affect the plaintiff's ability to sue the remaining joint tortfeasors.

Covenant not to sue
A legally enforceable promise by the plaintiff not to sue the person in whose favor the covenant is made.

We have just examined liability of multiple tortfeasors. Now we will shift gears and examine the concept of when one person can be held liable for the tortious conduct of another. This is the notion of vicarious liability.

Vicarious Liability

Vicarious liability
Legal responsibility of one person for the wrongful conduct of another.

Vicarious liability is legal responsibility imposed on a person for the wrongful conduct of another. That wrongful conduct can be tortious conduct, so vicarious liability applies to tort law. Vicarious liability, in effect, is a shifting of legal responsibility from the one who caused the harm to another, who gets to pay for it.

To understand vicarious liability, it helps to distinguish independent liability from derivative, or indirect, liability. The person who engages in the wrongful conduct can, normally, be held responsible for it. There are exceptions, for instance, if the person is a young child, who may not be held responsible for his actions because of his inability to understand their consequences. When the actor is held responsible, it is called independent liability. At the same time, another person may be vicariously liable for the harm as well. Thus, vicarious liability is indirect, or derivative, liability, derived from the wrongful act of another. Nonetheless, vicarious liability is full legal liability.

When does vicarious liability arise? Vicarious liability arises out of certain relationships. In tort law, a particular kind of vicarious liability, that of the employer for the wrongful acts of its employees, is of particular importance. That liability derives from the doctrine of *respondeat superior*. Other vicarious liability situations involving tort law include joint enterprise liability, automobile consent statutes, the family purpose doctrine, and parental liability. These topics are examined next.

THE DOCTRINE OF *RESPONDEAT SUPERIOR*

The doctrine of *respondeat superior* illustrates the most common form of vicarious liability. *Respondeat superior* is Latin for "Let the master respond." Under the **doctrine of *respondeat superior***, an employer can be held vicariously liable for the wrongful conduct, including the tortious conduct, of its employees committed within the course and scope of their employment.

The doctrine of *respondeat superior* applies only to the employment relationship. Remember, there must be an employment relationship—an employer and an employee. If a worker is an independent contractor, rather than an employee of the employer, then the doctrine is not applicable. An ***independent contractor*** is one who works for another but whose working conditions and methods are not controlled by the hiring party. How is the determination made of whether a person is an employee or an independent contractor? There is no clear, universal definition of "employer" under U.S. law, but courts and regulatory agencies have generally defined an ***employer*** as one who hires another to perform work on his behalf, and who has the right to control the details of how the work is performed.

The courts determine whether an employment relationship exists by considering several factors enumerated by the U.S. Supreme Court, with the overall determination ultimately a matter of the degree of control the employer exercises over the worker. An ***employee*** is a worker who is subject to an employer's control over the details of the work. Generally speaking, an employer is not liable for the tortious conduct of independent contractors in the performance of the contract because the employer does not have sufficient control over the details of the performance to warrant such liability. Read and brief the *Darden* U.S. Supreme Court case at the end of the chapter for the application of these factors in an employment relationship determination.

Remember that even if an employment relationship exists, the employer is only vicariously liable for the tortious conduct of the employee that occurs within the course and scope of her employment. What is the course and scope of employment? Generally speaking, an employee's conduct is within the ***course and scope of employment*** if the employee is performing employment duties. In other words, while the employee is acting in the interests, or on behalf, of the employer, her conduct is within the course and scope of employment. Otherwise, it is not, perhaps even if it is engaged in on the employer's premises or while on an employer-sponsored business trip.

Doctrine of *respondeat superior*
A legal doctrine under which an employer can be held vicariously liable for the wrongful conduct, including the tortious conduct, of its employees committed within the course and scope of their employment.

Independent contractor
One who works for another but whose working conditions and methods are not controlled by the hiring party.

Employer
One who hires another to perform work on his behalf, and who has the right to control the details of how the work is performed.

Employee
A worker who is subject to an employer's control over the details of the work.

Course and scope of employment
Conduct of an employee performed in the interests, or on behalf, of the employer.

COURT FACTORS IN DETERMINING EMPLOYEE VERSUS INDEPENDENT CONTRACTOR STATUS

In determining whether a worker is an employee or an independent contractor, the court is, in effect, determining whether an employment relationship exists. These are the factors that courts consider in making this determination, as set forth by the U.S. Supreme Court in *Nationwide Mut. Ins. Co. v. Darden,* as follows:

- The skill required to perform the work
- The source of the tools and instrumentalities of the work
- The location where the work is performed
- The duration of the relationship of the parties
- The hiring party's right to assign additional projects
- The worker's discretion over when and how long to work
- The method of payment of the worker
- The worker's role in hiring and paying assistants
- Whether the work is part of the hiring party's regular business
- Whether the worker is in business
- Whether employment benefits are provided to the worker
- The tax treatment of the worker

The answer to the question of whether an employee's conduct is within the course and scope of his employment is not always clear. Think of the issue as a spectrum, on which one side of the spectrum is conduct within the course and scope of employment and the other side is conduct outside the course and scope of employment. Where a particular case falls on the spectrum depends on the facts and circumstances of the case, and courts will evaluate those facts and circumstances to determine whose interests, overall, were being served when the incident occurred—the employer's business interests or the employee's personal interests, as illustrated in the examples below.

The mere fact that the employee is in the general employment of the employer does not necessarily mean that an act performed by the employee is within the course and scope of employment. Consider this example. Joe is a chef at Masters Steak House and while he is in Florida on vacation, he injures

COURSE AND SCOPE OF EMPLOYMENT DETERMINATION

To fall within the course and scope of employment means that the employee must be performing employment duties or otherwise be acting in the interests, or on behalf, of the employer. In making this determination, ask yourself whether the employee was acting to further the employer's business or was acting to further her own personal interests.

someone by driving negligently. Would Masters Steak House be vicariously liable for Joe's negligent conduct? No, because the conduct was not committed within the course and scope of his employment despite the fact that Joe is an employee of Masters Steak House. Joe is on vacation, a purely personal interest of his own. Joe's vacation is serving no business purpose for his employer. The conduct is outside the course and scope of Joe's employment.

What if Joe, while making a cake at work one day, carelessly puts insect poison in the batter thinking it is flour? The Masters Steak House patrons who eat slices of the cake become very ill and need medical care. Is Masters Steak House liable for the patrons' injuries? Yes, under the doctrine of *respondeat superior*, because Joe, its employee, was acting within the course and scope of his employment, as its chef, when he made the cake with the poisonous ingredient. Of course, Joe could be held liable as well; Joe has independent liability. However, the patrons are more likely to sue Masters Steak House because it has a greater ability to pay a large judgment; it has deeper pockets.

What if Joe, in preparing his menu for that evening, shops for fresh produce and fish at the local market? If Joe drives negligently in the market parking lot, injuring a pedestrian, is Masters Steak House liable for that injury? This is a more difficult question than the previous examples. It may depend on whether shopping for ingredients is part of chef Joe's job responsibilities. If shopping for fresh ingredients is part of Joe's job responsibilities, then the accident likely occurred within the course and scope of his employment, for which Masters Steak House may be held vicariously liable under the doctrine of *respondeat superior*. However, what if shopping for ingredients is not part of Joe's employment duties, as other employees are assigned to shop for ingredients and provide them to the chef? Although shopping is not part of Joe's job duties, because Joe is acting in the interests, and on behalf, of his employer in performing this task, a court may still consider the conduct to be within the course and scope of Joe's employment.

But what if Joe, while driving to the market to buy fresh ingredients, first stops at a drug store to purchase a tube of toothpaste for his son? Joe negligently runs over a pedestrian in the drug store parking lot. Is Joe's conduct within the course and scope of his employment? In this case, Joe is not acting within the course and scope of his employment. Rather, he is on a *frolic and detour*.

Frolic and detour occurs when an employee makes a physical departure from the service of the employer. If the employee is on a **frolic and detour**, he has deviated from or abandoned the employer's business interests and is acting in furtherance of his own personal interests. A frolic occurs when the employee's departure from the employer's business is major, meaning the employee is acting on his own and for his own benefit. A detour occurs when the employee's departure from the employer's business is minor. In the case of a frolic, the employer is relieved of vicarious liability for the acts of the employee because they are considered outside the course and scope of the employment. If the employee is merely on a detour, however, the employer may still remain vicariously liable for the employee's wrongful acts. Courts consider factors such as the amount of time taken for the departure, the place where the departure occurred, the foreseeability and normalcy of the employee's departure, and the purpose for

Frolic and detour
When an employee deviates from or abandons the employer's business interests and acts in furtherance of her own personal interests.

the departure in making determinations about frolics and detours and an employer's vicarious liability under the doctrine of *respondeat superior*.

Remember that even under the doctrine of *respondeat superior*, the employee remains liable for his own tortious conduct. This is his independent liability. It is just that, under the doctrine of *respondeat superior*, the employer is also liable. The victim may recover only once, however. The victim cannot recover twice, both from the tortfeasor and from his employer. Because the employer is likely to have deeper pockets, meaning greater ability to pay a judgment, the employer is more likely to be the one the plaintiff chooses to sue, though he can choose to sue them both, or just the employee.

Another type of vicarious liability with a role in tort law is examined next. It is joint enterprise liability.

JOINT ENTERPRISE LIABILITY

Joint enterprise liability
A legal doctrine under which persons who are working together for some common business purpose may be held vicariously liable for the acts of the others in the joint enterprise.

Another situation in which vicarious liability is authorized occurs when persons are engaged in a joint enterprise, working together for some common business purpose. A joint enterprise is much like a partnership, but for a more limited purpose and/or formed for a short duration. In a joint enterprise, as in a partnership, each person involved has the express or implied authority to act on behalf of the others in fulfilling the common purpose of that joint enterprise. Therefore, each of the persons involved in the joint enterprise may be held vicariously liable for the acts of the others. This is the doctrine of *joint enterprise liability*.

Joint enterprise liability applies in tort law when one party to the joint enterprise engages in tortious misconduct. Because of the vicarious liability theory, other parties to the joint enterprise may be held vicariously liable for those wrongful acts.

Consider the following example. Brooks, Cal, José, and Hank decide to operate a summer camp for underprivileged teenagers. At this camp, these men teach baseball skills they learned while playing in the major leagues. A small group of campers are ill-behaved, and they talk and joke while José is demonstrating proper throwing technique. Irritated by the disrespectful interruptions of these few children, José lobs a ball at them, hitting one child in the nose and breaking it. Certainly, José could be independently liable for the tort of battery.

SIDEBAR

JOINT ENTERPRISE REQUIREMENTS

For persons to be engaged in a joint enterprise, there must be

1. An express or implied agreement between or among them to participate in the common enterprise

2. A common purpose, normally of a financial or business nature

3. A common monetary interest

4. A mutual right to control and direct the joint enterprise

CASE on Point

Reimer v. City of Crookston, 421 F.3d 673 (8th Cir. 2005)

In this case, a boiler repairman suffered serious burn injuries while inspecting a boiler at a swimming pool facility. He was injured when he accidentally struck and dislodged a corroded component on the boiler, causing the boiler to release hot steam and scalding water on him (his medical expenses exceeded $700,000).

The Eighth Circuit Court of Appeals found that the swimming pool facility was operated by the city and the school district as a joint enterprise. Therefore, the city and the school district bore joint responsibility for the damages awarded to the injured boiler repairman.

But what about Brooks, Cal, and Hank? None of them threw the ball. Could any or all of them be held liable for the child's injuries? Yes, under the vicarious liability theory of joint enterprise liability, because their baseball camp endeavor was a joint enterprise.

Vicarious liability may also be imposed under automobile consent statutes. These statutes are examined next.

AUTOMOBILE CONSENT STATUTES

Automobile consent statutes are legislative acts that make the owners of automobiles vicariously liable for the negligence of any person to whom they entrust their automobiles. Accordingly, these statutes, where they have been enacted, render the owners liable for any harm caused by the negligence of drivers to whom they entrust their automobiles. The purpose of these statutes is to place the financial responsibility for harm caused by automobile accidents on the persons responsible for insuring the automobiles.

The automobile owner must entrust the automobile to the other driver, meaning he must consent to the other's use of his car. For instance, a car owner is not vicariously liable for injuries caused by a car thief who is driving his car.

Automobile consent statutes
Legislative acts that make the owners of automobiles vicariously liable for the negligence of any person to whom they entrust their automobiles.

STATUTE on Point

Mich. Comp. Laws Ann. § 257.401 (2009)

Pursuant to Michigan's automobile consent statute, the owner of a motor vehicle is liable for injuries caused by the negligent operation of the motor vehicle, whether the negligence consists of a violation of a Michigan statute or the ordinary care standard required by the common law of negligence. However, the owner of a motor vehicle is liable only if the motor vehicle is being driven with the owner's express or implied consent or knowledge. It is presumed that the motor vehicle is being driven with the knowledge and consent of the owner if it is driven at the time of the injury by his or her spouse, father, mother, brother, sister, son, daughter, or other immediate member of the family.

DISTINGUISHING AUTOMOBILE CONSENT STATUTES AND AUTOMOBILE GUEST STATUTES

In studying negligence in Chapter 6, we will discuss automobile guest statutes. These statutes protect drivers from lawsuits by nonpaying passengers so long as the driver's conduct was not grossly negligent or reckless. Do not confuse automobile guest statutes and automobile consent statutes—they are different.

OMNIBUS CLAUSES IN AUTOMOBILE INSURANCE POLICIES

Omnibus clause
A clause in many standard automobile insurance policies that provides that liability insurance for the designated automobile applies to the named insured in the policy, any member of the named insured's household, and any person using the automobile with the named insured's permission.

Today, many drivers purchase standard automobile insurance, which normally includes an omnibus clause. An *omnibus clause* provides that liability insurance for the owner's automobile applies to the named insured in the policy, any member of the named insured's household, and any person using the automobile with the named insured's permission, so long as the use was within the scope of the owner's permission—which would be exceeded if the owner gave permission to a third party to use the car for a day, and the third party kept and drove the car all week.

These clauses make automobile consent statutes unnecessary because they protect third parties who are injured by accidents caused by anyone who is driving the insured automobile with the owner's consent. Of course, not every driver has automobile liability insurance even where it is required by law, and not every automobile insurance policy contains an omnibus clause, rendering automobile consent statutes of continued usefulness.

The person to whom the owner entrusts the car need not be a family member, though consent of the owner may be presumed if the driver is an immediate family member—see the Michigan Statute on Point—it can be a friend or neighbor, even a stranger in an emergency. But statutory construction issues regarding what constitutes an owner's "consent" have caused courts to have to interpret the meaning of that term, and define the words and acts that demonstrate consent by an owner to another using his automobile.

As you have learned, automobile consent statutes impose vicarious liability on automobile owners under certain circumstances. Another type of vicarious liability involving automobiles is examined next, namely, the family purpose doctrine.

THE FAMILY PURPOSE DOCTRINE

Family purpose doctrine
A doctrine that allows a plaintiff to sue the owner of an automobile for the negligent acts of members of the owner's family when an immediate family member is driving the automobile for family purposes; also called the family car doctrine.

The *family purpose doctrine*, also called the *family car doctrine,* is another application of vicarious liability that is recognized in some, but not all, states. Where it is recognized, the family purpose doctrine allows a plaintiff to sue the owner of an automobile for the negligent acts of members of the owner's family when a family member drives the automobile for family purposes. In other

SIDEBAR

RECOVERY UNDER THE FAMILY PURPOSE DOCTRINE

Jurisdictions that recognize the family purpose doctrine do not agree on all of its elements, but generally, for a plaintiff to recover from an automobile owner who is not the driver under the family purpose doctrine, the plaintiff must be able to show that

1. The defendant owned or controlled the use of the automobile involved in the accident
2. The automobile owner made the automobile available to family members for family use, rather than for business use
3. The driver was an immediate family member of the owner
4. The driver was using the automobile for a family purpose at the time of the accident
5. The driver had the express or implied permission of the owner to use the automobile at the time of the accident

words, it makes automobile owners vicariously liable for certain driving accidents caused by members of their families.

Family purposes under this doctrine include uses such as driving the automobile to run errands (to shop for household groceries, for example) or to take a family member to school, work, or an appointment. However, family purposes are construed even more broadly by the courts—using the automobile merely for convenience, pleasure, or enjoyment will constitute a family purpose under this doctrine.

Courts restrict the family purpose doctrine's application to members of the automobile owner's immediate family. The doctrine is often applied to hold parents liable for the actions of a child driver if that young driver causes injury to someone while driving his parents' automobile. Vicarious liability is extended even if the parent is not in the automobile at the time of the accident.

Further, most courts that recognize this doctrine restrict its application to automobiles. For an exception, where a court extended the doctrine to cover a family motorboat, read and brief a case on that point that is included in the exercises at the end of the chapter.

As with the application of automobile consent statutes, what constitutes "consent" of the owner for another to drive his vehicle is not always clear. Courts grapple with this issue, defining words and acts that constitute express or implied consent.

If a parent can be held vicariously liable for certain driving accidents caused by her children in a jurisdiction that recognizes the family purpose doctrine, are parents vicariously liable for all torts committed by their children? That question is answered next.

PARENTAL LIABILITY

The traditional rule is that parents are not vicariously liable for the tortious conduct of their minor children simply because they are their parents. However, most jurisdictions will impose liability under special circumstances, such as if the parent entrusts the child with an instrumentality that, because of the child's lack of age and maturity, may become a source of danger to others (such as a car or rifle); if the child, in committing the tort, is employed by the parent and the parent authorizes the commission of the tort; if the parent knows of the child's wrongdoing and consents to or sanctions it; or if the parent fails to exercise reasonable supervision and control over the child despite the fact that he knew or, in exercising due care, should have known that harm to a third party was a likely consequence. These special circumstances basically make parents liable for their own negligent acts in raising and supervising their children.

Some states have enacted statutes that impose vicarious liability on parents for the torts of their minor children in certain situations, but only up to a limited dollar amount, such as a few thousand dollars. For example, by statute in many states, parents are liable for intentional, willful, malicious, or reckless property damage caused by their child, perhaps up to a dollar limit. Some states hold parents liable for personal injury, theft, shoplifting, and vandalism resulting from intentional, willful, malicious, or reckless acts of their children, which again may be limited to a certain dollar amount. Less common, some state statutes extend parental liability for merely negligent acts of their children, especially when children are operating a motor vehicle. Review examples of such parent liability statutes in the following Statutes on Point.

Consider this example. Thomas, a 10-year-old boy, instigates a fight and knocks another child off his bike. May the injured child sue Thomas's parents for the battery that Thomas committed? Not successfully, under the common law, because parents are not normally liable for the tortious acts of their minor children. However, if a parent liability statute has been enacted in the jurisdiction, the parents may be liable for Thomas's tortious act, up to the dollar limits set forth in that statute.

When engaged in the practice of tort law, as with other areas of law, it is critical to understand the codes and rules of legal ethics regulating lawyer conduct. In addition, it is important to understand how legal ethics rules apply to nonlawyers who work as part of the legal services delivery team, including paralegals. Next, we introduce the concept of legal ethics as applied to tort law.

STATUTES on Point

Parental Liability Statutes

In Colorado, a person may recover actual damages in an amount not to exceed $3,500 from the parents of a minor under the age of 18 years, living with the parents, for both malicious and willful destruction of property and causing bodily injury.[1]

Compare the Colorado statute to one enacted in Florida. In Florida, a person may recover damages from the parents of a minor under the age of 18 years, living with the parents, who maliciously or willfully destroys or steals property. That recovery is limited to actual damages and taxable court costs.[2]

CHAPTER **SUMMARY**

- The concept of foreseeability has special meaning in tort law. Although people are normally liable for wrongful conduct that results in injury to another, if the injury or the victim is not foreseeable, then legal liability in tort may be cut off.

- A tortfeasor is a person who commits a tort. A joint tortfeasor is a person who acts with other persons in causing a tortious wrong. To be a joint tortfeasor, the person must participate in the wrongful conduct or encourage and facilitate it.

- Joint and several liability means that a plaintiff, in a tort or other action, may sue all of the responsible parties, jointly, or any one or more of them, severally, at his option. The plaintiff can choose which, and how many, of the joint tortfeasors to sue for the entire harm.

- A joint tortfeasor who pays more than his proportionate share of the entire harm may seek contribution from the other joint tortfeasors in jurisdictions that allow contribution. Contribution is the right of a joint tortfeasor who has paid a judgment to be proportionately reimbursed by the other joint tortfeasors for their share of the harm.

- Indemnity, also called subrogation, is a method of forcing a person who has not paid the judgment to reimburse the person who has paid the judgment, for the full amount paid. Indemnity can arise either by contractual agreement or by operation of law.

- If a joint tortfeasor has paid the entire judgment, the plaintiff is deemed to have received satisfaction, and is not entitled to sue the other joint tortfeasors. Satisfaction is full payment of a judgment by a liable party. If the plaintiff has received satisfaction on a judgment, she may be asked to execute a release, meaning the formal giving up or relinquishing of her legal claim.

- In jurisdictions that recognize that the release of one joint tortfeasor operates to release them all, rather than execute a release, the paying joint tortfeasor may obtain a covenant not to sue from the plaintiff. A covenant not to sue is a legally enforceable promise by the plaintiff not to sue the person in whose favor the covenant is made, but it does not affect the plaintiff's ability to sue the remaining joint tortfeasors.

- Vicarious liability is legal responsibility of one person for the wrongful conduct of another. Vicarious liability applies to tort law because the wrongful conduct of another may be tortious conduct. In its tort law application, vicarious liability is imposed under the doctrine of *respondeat superior*, joint enterprise liability, automobile consent statutes, the family purpose doctrine, and, to a limited extent, parental liability.

- Under the doctrine of *respondeat superior*, an employer can be held liable for the wrongful conduct, including the torts, of its employees committed within the course and scope of their employment. This doctrine applies only to the employment relationship, and courts consider several factors in making the determination as to whether an employment relationship exists.

- Vicarious liability is authorized when persons are engaged in a joint enterprise, working together for some common business purpose. Automobile consent statutes make the owners of automobiles vicariously liable for the negligence of any person to whom they entrust their automobiles. The family purpose doctrine, recognized in some states, allows a plaintiff to sue the owner of an automobile when it is driven, with the owner's consent, by an immediate family member for a family-related purpose. Normally, parents are not liable for the tortious conduct of their minor children, unless a statute has been enacted in the jurisdiction to impose such liability, typically for up to a limited dollar amount.

CONCEPT REVIEW AND REINFORCEMENT

QUESTIONS FOR **REVIEW**

1. What does foreseeability mean in tort law?
2. Who is a tortfeasor?
3. Who are joint tortfeasors?
4. What is joint and several liability?
5. What is vicarious liability?
6. How does vicarious liability apply to tort law?
7. What is the doctrine of *respondeat superior,* and to whom does it apply?
8. What is joint enterprise liability?
9. What are automobile consent statutes, and how do they affect tort liability?
10. What is the family purpose doctrine, and how does it relate to automobile accident liability?
11. Are parents vicariously liable for the torts committed by their children?

DEVELOPING YOUR PARALEGAL SKILLS

CRITICAL THINKING **EXERCISES**

1. In this chapter, we examined joint and several liability, vicarious liability, automobile consent statutes, the family purpose doctrine, and liability of parents for the tortious acts of their children. States differ in their laws, including in some of these areas. Research the law in your jurisdiction on these topics. What similarities and differences do you find compared to the rules of law of most jurisdictions, as set forth in this chapter? Discuss your research results in class.

2. Clark Lake Camp is a sleep-over summer camp that is owned and operated by Camps-R-Us, Inc. The company hires several camp counselors to supervise and stay with the children. Marsha, Greg, Jan, Peter, Cindy, Bobby, Mike, Carol, and Alice are hired as camp counselors for the season. During one camp session, while Marsha, Greg, Jan, and Peter are assigned the duty of supervising the campers during a lake swim, those counselors decide to drive to town to buy soda and chips for a snack (for everyone). While they are away and the swimmers are left unsupervised, one of the campers drowns in the lake.

   a. *Under what theory might Marsha, Greg, Jan, and Peter be sued together? Who would they be sued by (in other words, who would bring the action)?*

   b. *Under the theory of joint and several liability, must they all be sued together, or may the family of the victim, in bringing a tort action for the injury sustained (death) by the camper, sue one or less than all of the counselors?*

   c. *In reality, would the family of the victim choose to sue the counselors, or would they be more likely to sue someone else? If so, who? Under what doctrine?*

   d. *If Marsha is 17 years old, Greg is 18 years old, Jan is 15 years old, and Peter is 16 years old, would the parents of the counselors who are minors be liable for the tortious conduct of their children? Why or why not?*

3. Percy and Ronald decide to go in together to get a permit to operate a hot dog, sausage, and drink stand outside the entrance to Oriole Park at Camden Yards in Baltimore, along with other vendors who sell game food and drinks before home games. Percy and Ronald take turns operating the stand. One day, when it is his turn to operate the stand, Ronald forgets to refrigerate the raw meat and leaves it out all day. That proves to be a problem for the sausage, for when Ronald later cooks and sells it, several customers who eat the spoiled meat become sick and are hospitalized.

   a. *Could Ronald be held liable for the injuries sustained by these customers? Why or why not?*

   b. *Could Percy be held liable for the injuries sustained by these customers? If so, under what theory?*

4. Tom purchased a classic Corvette. His neighbor, Steve, asked to borrow the car from Tom, to drive his young son around the neighborhood (the son is a huge car enthusiast, as many young boys are), and generous Tom happily agreed. While he was driving around the neighborhood, Steve took his eyes off the road in order to change the radio station, just as a child chased a ball into the street. If Steve had been watching the road, he would have been able to avoid hitting the child. Unfortunately, he was not, and the child was hit and injured.

   a. *Can Steve be held liable for the child's injuries? Why or why not?*

   b. *Can Tom be held liable for the child's injuries? Pursuant to what law?*

   c. *What if Steve is Tom's son (and neighbor), making the car enthusiast Tom's grandson. Under what doctrine might Tom be held liable for the injuries caused by Steve?*

ASSIGNMENTS AND PRACTICAL **APPLICATIONS**

1. In the chapter, we learned that joint liability is based on the notion that all joint and concurrent tortfeasors are independently liable for their wrongful act(s). Read and brief the following case on this point: *Anne Arundel Med. Ctr., Inc. v. Condon,* 649 A.2d 1189 (Md. Ct. Spec. App. 1994).

2. Joint tortfeasors are jointly and severally liable for the entire damage sustained, but the plaintiff may only obtain one satisfaction of the claim. On this point, read and brief *Morgan v. Cohen,* 523 A.2d 1003 (Md. 1987).

3. The U.S. Supreme Court identified twelve significant factors to be used in determining whether a worker is an employee or an independent contractor. Read and brief *Nationwide Mut. Ins. Co. v. Darden,* 503 U.S. 318 (1992) for these factors.

4. Course and scope of employment can be an interesting determination. Read and brief *Goodyear Tire and Rubber Co. v. Mayes,* 236 S.W.3d 754 (Tex. 2007), in which it was held that an employee was not acting within the course and scope of his employment when he negligently caused an accident by falling asleep while driving on a late-night personal errand, even though he was driving the employer's truck (containing the employer's tires, for delivery the next day) when he caused the accident.

5. For a case involving the question of whether a worker was an employee or an independent contractor, whether conduct occurred within the course and scope of employment, and whether joint enterprise liability applied under the facts, read and brief *Bell v. VPSI, Inc.,* 205 S.W.3d 706 (Tex. App. 2006).

6. Go to a law library and find form books containing forms for drafting a release. Review the different forms of releases in several different form books. Think about under what circumstances the different types of releases would apply (normally, the forms are labeled or their use is described). Using one or more of the forms you find that you think is appropriate, draft a release to relinquish the claims against two joint tortfeasors (Adam Presley and Christopher Hartley), where Adam has paid $100,000 in full settlement of the claims in a negligence action asserted by the plaintiff (Susan Brady), docket number cv-419265 in the Circuit Court of Baltimore City, Maryland. Share your draft agreement in class.

7. For a case involving Michigan's automobile consent statute (set forth in the chapter), read and brief *Kaiser v. Allen,* 746 N.W.2d 92 (Mich. 2008).

8. Does your state have an automobile consent statute? Perform legal research to see if it does. If your state does not have an automobile consent statute, do any of your neighboring states have one? For the one you find, discuss with your class what liability is imposed by the statue and on whom is it imposed.

9. Research whether your jurisdiction recognizes the family purpose doctrine, and if so, what elements it requires. Discuss your research results in class.

10. Does the family purpose doctrine apply to a family motorboat as it would an automobile? Read and brief *Stewart v. Stephens,* 166 S.E.2d 890 (Ga. 1969). See the following Technology Resources and Internet Exercises regarding the family purpose doctrine in Georgia and application of the family purpose doctrine to motorboats, by statute, in North Carolina.

11. Research whether your jurisdiction has a statute authorizing the vicarious liability of parents for the torts of their minor children. If so, what are the dollar limits of that liability, if any? Discuss your research results in class.

TECHNOLOGY RESOURCES AND INTERNET **EXERCISES**

Using the Internet, research your state's law on contribution by joint tortfeasors. Does your state allow contribution? If so, when is contribution allowed? Is a distinction made between negligent and intentional conduct? How are shares determined? Are they equal, or proportionate to fault? Share your research results in class.

Various government agencies define "employees" and "employers" differently. Consider how the Internal Revenue Service of the U.S. government defines the terms after reviewing its website, *www.irs.gov/businesses/small /article/0,,id=99921,00.html.*

For an article on the concept of frolic and detour, which takes an employee's conduct outside the course and scope of employment, see *www.legalzoom.com/legal-articles /frolic-and-detour.html.*

According to the Georgia Injury Lawyer Blog, the family purpose doctrine is alive and well in Georgia. Review comments in this regard at *www.georgiainjurylawyerblog.com/2007/06/.*

By statute in North Carolina, the family purpose doctrine is extended to include the operation of motorboats and vessels. See *http://law.justia.com/northcarolina/codes /chapter_75a/gs_75a-10.1.html.*

Go to the Cornell Law School website (*www.law.cornell .edu/ethics/md/code*). Perform a search for the legal ethics code in Maryland. Using either this resource or your own state's legal ethics rules, answer the questions in the following Ethical Applications section.

ETHICAL **APPLICATIONS**

In this chapter, the concept of people acting jointly was considered in the context of tort law. What about when lawyers from different firms work jointly on a case? Consider the following. Rupert Hill is a real estate lawyer with a solo practice. One of his clients is Top Notch Properties, Inc. Top Notch Properties was recently sued. The party bringing the lawsuit claims to own certain real property that Top Notch Properties claims to own and is currently marketing for sale. Rupert, having little experience as a litigator, contacts Melanie Duncan, a competent civil trial lawyer in the area, and asks her to help him with the case. They agree on a mechanism for sharing the fee, and the client agrees (in writing).

Have the lawyers breached any legal ethics requirements by agreeing to work jointly on this matter? Are Rupert and Melanie allowed to share the fee?

What if Rupert does not wish to work on the litigation matter at all. Instead, he refers the case to Melanie, for her competent handling. Rupert asks Melanie for a referral fee for referring his client's matter to her. Melanie agrees, and pays Rupert $3,000 as a referral fee.

Have Rupert and Melanie breached any legal ethics requirements by agreeing to, and paying, a referral fee? Why or why not?

VIDEO **CASE STUDY**

Truck Driver's Deposition: Agent on a Detour and Liability of the Principal

Synopsis: At the deposition of the truck driver for Ace Trucking Company, testimony is elicited regarding the events leading up to the collision involving the school bus.

Questions

1. Can Ace Trucking Company, the employer of the truck driver, be held liable for the wrongful acts of its employee committed within the course and scope of his employment? Why or why not?

2. What is a frolic and detour? In this case, when did the frolic and detour begin and when did it end? Is that relevant to the tort liability of the employer? Is that relevant to the tort liability of the employee?

3. What is the effect of the frolic and detour on the employer's vicarious liability for the employee's wrongful acts?

4. What is the effect of the frolic and detour on the employee's independent liability for his tortious act?

chapter 3

INTENTIONAL TORTS AGAINST PERSONS

This chapter introduces the first major classification of torts, intentional torts. The topics of intent and the doctrine of transferred intent are discussed. The chapter also thoroughly examines each of the intentional torts against persons.

Remember from Chapter 1 that there are three main classifications of torts: intentional, negligence, and strict liability. Some torts fall neatly within one category, whereas others fall within more than one category or outside the categories altogether. The intentional torts that we will cover in this chapter include battery, assault, false imprisonment, false arrest, intentional infliction of emotional distress, malicious prosecution, and abuse of process. These torts are intentional torts against persons. In Chapter 4, we will discuss intentional torts against property, the related nuisance doctrine, and intentional torts against commercial interests.

Every intentional tort has, as one of its essential elements, the element of "intent." We begin our examination of intentional torts by answering the question, "What is 'intent'?"

LEARNING OBJECTIVES

3.1 Explain the concept of "intent" as it relates to tort law.

3.2 Discuss the doctrine of transferred intent.

3.3 Identify and list the various intentional torts against persons.

The Intent Requirement

Intent, in tort law, means the desire to bring about the consequences of an act or knowledge with substantial certainty that the consequences will result from the act. The *Restatement (Second) of Torts* helps to define "intent." It says that intent in tort law exists when a person desires to bring about or cause the consequences of his act or when a person believes that the consequences are substantially certain to result from his act.[1] Intent is a required, or essential, element of each of the intentional torts. Unlike other torts, these torts can only be committed purposefully.

In Chapter 1, we discussed the distinction between the civil and criminal law systems. We said that many crimes are also torts. Most of the torts that also constitute crimes are intentional torts. Remember the *O. J. Simpson* Case on Point from Chapter 1, where it

Intent
The desire to bring about the consequences of the act or knowledge with substantial certainty that the consequences will flow from the act.

WHAT IS THE *RESTATEMENT (SECOND) OF TORTS?*

The *Restatement (Second) of Torts* is one of the many Restatements written and published by the American Law Institute. Restatements are written by legal scholars, judges, and practicing lawyers to set forth and explain the law, especially law from common law sources. The *Restatement of Torts,* published for the first time in 1965, is now in its second edition, hence the name *Restatement (Second).* A *Restatement (Third) of Torts: Products Liability* was published in 1998 to supersede Section 402A of the *Restatement (Second) of Torts* on the topic of products liability. Restatements are considered secondary sources of law. Thus, the *Restatement of Torts* does not constitute law, but it serves as a good guide for judges and practitioners working in the tort law field, and it may be cited as persuasive (though not binding) authority.

was demonstrated that a single act can constitute both a crime (murder) and a tort (wrongful death). Intentional torts are the torts most likely to meet the *mens rea* requirement for a crime, for they all have an "intent" element to their commission.

There is an important distinction between "intent" in criminal law and "intent" in tort (civil) law. Intent in criminal law means a concrete mental state defined by the criminal statute for a particular crime. For example, Nebraska's second-degree murder statute requires a person to cause the death of another person "intentionally, but without premeditation." Intent in tort law is different. It means intent to perform the conduct that brings about the consequences of the tortious act or injury. In tort law, intent does not mean intent to cause harm or injury. It merely means intent to perform the conduct; what injury or harm is the consequence of that conduct impacts the damages a plaintiff can recover in her tort action.

There is some overlap in terminology between the criminal and civil law systems with regard to intentional torts. For instance, the tort of battery in one jurisdiction may coincide with the crime of battery in that jurisdiction, or the jurisdiction may name the crime "assault and battery," or something else. In tort law, the tort of assault and the tort of battery are separate and distinct, each

TWO ELEMENTS OF CRIMINAL LIABILITY: *ACTUS REUS* AND *MENS REA*

There are two elements that must be present for a crime to be committed. The first is the *actus reus,* which means the "guilty act." It is not enough to think about committing a crime. A perpetrator must actually commit the act before a criminal wrong has occurred. The other element of criminal liability is *mens rea.* For a crime to be committed, the perpetrator must act with a wrongful mental state. *Mens rea* is the requirement of "evil intent."

with its own set of essential elements. However, criminal statutes may use either, or both, of these terms in defining the crime of unlawful physical contact with another person.

This overlap in terminology can be confusing for students. Always remember that the civil and criminal law systems are separate and distinct. Although the same conduct can be both tortious and criminal, whether it is one or both depends on whether the facts and circumstances meet the elements of the tort, as defined by the courts in case law, and/or meet the statutory definition of the crime, as enacted by the legislature.

In some cases involving unintended plaintiffs and unintended torts, intent may be transferred, in effect broadening the scope of the tortfeasor's liability. The doctrine of transferred intent is discussed next.

The Doctrine of Transferred Intent

The *doctrine of transferred intent* applies when a tortfeasor intended to commit a tort against one person, but instead committed that tort against another person (the "unintended plaintiff"), or when a tortfeasor intended to commit one tort against a person, but in fact committed another tort (the "unintended tort") against that person. Under the doctrine of transferred intent, the intent to commit a tort against one person may be transferred to another person (the unintended plaintiff), or the intent to commit one tort may be transferred when the tortfeasor commits a different tort against the intended person (the unintended tort).

Consider this hypothetical situation. Bob dislikes his classmate Harry, the class "brain." One day, Harry is seated in class, waiting for the instructor to arrive and chatting with his friend Marsha, who is seated next to him. Bob, having a bad day anyway, thinks he sees Harry smirk at him when Bob arrives for class. In fact, Harry, who also dislikes Bob, did smirk at him. This enrages Bob, who throws his Constitutional Law book at Harry. Fortunately for Harry, Bob has bad aim and misses him. Unfortunately for Marsha, she is knocked in the head by this 500-page book and injured. Has Bob committed an intentional tort against *Marsha*?

As you will see when we examine each of the intentional torts, the act of purposefully making a harmful or offensive contact with another person constitutes the tort of battery. How is this definition affected by the fact that Bob intended to hit Harry, but mistakenly hit Marsha? Did Bob have the intent required to commit battery as to Marsha?

The answer is "yes." Marsha is an "unintended plaintiff." Under the doctrine of transferred intent, Bob's intent to harm Harry is transferred to Marsha, so she could recover from Bob for the tort of battery.

What about the following situation? What if Bob, when he threw the book, missed both Harry and Marsha? In fact, the book hit no one; it simply fell, uneventfully, to the floor. Bob, in fact, was trying to hit Harry with the book. He intended to commit the tort of battery against Harry. When Harry saw the heavy, hard-cover book being hurled toward him, he felt afraid. His fear did not pass until it was clear that the book had missed him.

The tort of assault is the purposeful act of causing an apprehension of a harmful or offensive contact to another person. In this situation, Bob intended to commit the tort of battery against Harry because he intended to hit Harry with the book. Instead, because of his poor aim, Bob merely caused Harry to feel apprehension of a harmful contact. Did Bob, then, have the requisite intent required to meet that essential element of the tort of assault?

The answer to this modified scenario is, again, "yes." Bob's intent to commit battery is transferred to the tort of assault, meeting that essential element. This is an example of the "unintended tort." Therefore, Harry could recover from Bob for the tort of assault even though Bob intended to commit the tort of battery.

Importantly, the doctrine of transferred intent applies to five intentional torts: battery, assault, false imprisonment, trespass to land, and trespass to chattels. Remember that it does not apply to all torts, or to all the intentional torts. So, if you have a situation involving an intentional tort other than these enumerated ones—say, for example, the tort of intentional infliction of emotional distress—the doctrine of transferred intent does not apply. In that case, the defendant would have to intend to commit that specific tort against that particular plaintiff in order to meet the intent element.

Now that we understand the element of intent and the doctrine of transferred intent, we will examine specific intentional torts. Intentional torts can be committed against persons or their property and commercial interests. We begin our study of intentional torts with intentional torts against persons.

Intentional Torts Against Persons

Intentional torts against persons, also called intentional torts against the person, are those torts in which the defendant acts purposefully, resulting in injury to another. The injury normally can be physical and/or emotional.

Each of these torts has its own essential elements. These essential elements must be established by the plaintiff in order to state a claim for which relief can be granted in litigation. When the plaintiff establishes these elements, it is said that he has established a *prima facie* case. If the plaintiff establishes a *prima facie* case, then the burden of proof shifts to the defendant to defend herself from the claim by defeating one or more of the essential elements or raising one or more affirmative defenses. We will discuss the concept of defenses to intentional torts in Chapter 5.

SIDEBAR

ESSENTIAL ELEMENTS AND THE *PRIMA FACIE* CASE

Each essential element of a claim, including a tort claim, must be stated in the complaint and established by the plaintiff in order for the plaintiff to make a *prima facie* case. Failure of the plaintiff to establish a *prima facie* case will result in the court's dismissal of the action on the grounds of failure to state a claim for which relief can be granted.

THE INTENTIONAL TORT OF "STALKING"

By statute in some jurisdictions, an intentional tort against the person called "stalking" has been enacted. For example, in California, a person is liable for the tort of stalking if the plaintiff can prove the following:

- The defendant engaged in a pattern of conduct the *intent* of which was to follow, alarm, or harass the plaintiff;

- As a result of the pattern of conduct the plaintiff reasonably feared for his or her safety or the safety of an immediate family member; and

- The defendant made a credible threat with the *intent* to place the plaintiff in reasonable fear for his or her safety or the safety of an immediate family member and at least once the plaintiff clearly demanded that the defendant cease and the defendant did not *or* the defendant violated a restraining order.

There are several intentional torts against the person. The main intentional torts against the person are battery, assault, false imprisonment, false arrest, intentional infliction of emotional distress, malicious prosecution, and abuse of process. We will now examine each of these torts in detail.

BATTERY

Battery is a purposeful and unwanted harmful or offensive contact with another person. In Chapter 1, you learned that each tort protects an individual interest or right. The interest protected by the tort of battery is the right of a person to be free from unwanted, intentional physical contact with another person, made without permission. The essential elements of the tort of battery are (1) an act, (2) harmful or offensive contact with the plaintiff's person, (3) intent, and (4) causation.

Now we will examine each of these essential elements. An "act" is a voluntary movement of the defendant's body. For example, if Joyce throws a punch at Jerry, that is a voluntary movement of Joyce's body. But what if Joyce punches Jerry in the eye while suffering an epileptic seizure? Did Joyce commit the tort of battery against Jerry? No, because there was no voluntary act on Joyce's part.

Harmful or offensive contact with the plaintiff's person is contact that brings about physical damage, impairment, pain, or illness (harmful contact), or that offends the personal dignity of an ordinary person who is not unduly sensitive (offensive contact). The contact can be very slight, such as an unwanted kiss. Or it can be severe, such as a blow to the head with a baseball bat. Of course, the severity of the contact and the injury sustained affect the amount of damages awarded, but any degree of harmfulness or offensiveness is sufficient to meet this element.

A "reasonable person" test is used to determine whether contact is harmful or offensive. Would a hypothetical reasonable person, not unduly sensitive, consider the contact to be harmful or offensive? This is an objective standard. It does not normally consider what that particular plaintiff felt; what matters in

Battery
Purposeful and unwanted harmful or offensive contact with another person.

Key Point
The Essential Elements of Battery
1. An act
2. Harmful or offensive contact with the plaintiff's person
3. Intent
4. Causation

CASE on Point

Britton v. City of Crawford, 803 N.W.2d 508 (Neb. 2011)

In this case, the personal representative of a deceased police shooting victim brought a tort action against the city that employed the officers involved. The shooting victim was a 16-year-old burglary suspect. Two officers were involved in the shooting, one a police officer and the other a conservation officer with the Nebraska Game and Parks Commission; together they were investigating the burglaries. The deceased was shot by both officers when, upon their finding the burglary suspect in hiding, the suspect sprang up, pointed his gun at the officers, and refused to drop the gun when commanded to do so.

The Nebraska Supreme Court said that the state of Nebraska defined the intentional tort of battery as "an actual infliction of an unconsented injury upon or unconsented contact with another." The court ultimately determined that this shooting incident constituted the tort of battery under Nebraska law. It noted that, regarding the element of intent, the focus is whether the actor intended the acts alleged in the claim.

this determination is what a reasonable person would have experienced. That said, a reasonable person expects a certain amount of contact with others as a part of daily living. Would a tap on the shoulder to get someone's attention, if not invited, constitute harmful or offensive contact? In making this determination, a court would apply the facts to the "reasonable person" test. Applying that test to these facts, the court would determine whether a reasonable person would be harmed or offended by a tap on the shoulder to get her attention.

However, there is an exception to the application of this "reasonable person," objective test. If the defendant knows that the plaintiff is unduly sensitive and acts in a purposeful way to exploit or violate those sensitivities, a subjective standard is used. In such a case, the question is whether this *particular plaintiff* considered the contact to be harmful or offensive rather than what a hypothetical reasonable person would have experienced. So, if the defendant knows that the plaintiff is a germaphobe but touches her on the shoulder anyway in an attempt to get her attention, the test is not whether a reasonable person would have been harmed or offended by the contact, but whether this particularly sensitive plaintiff was harmed or offended by it.

What is the "plaintiff's person"? The "plaintiff's person" is broadly defined. It includes one's body, anything attached to one's body, or anything so closely associated with one's body so as to be identified with it. For example, a purse hanging from your shoulder, a book in your hand, or a horse you are riding are all part of your "person" under this broad definition. Battery, then, means causing a harmful or offensive contact to anything so closely associated with the plaintiff's body as to be identified with it, including but not limited to contact with the plaintiff's physical body.

The contact can be direct, such as one person touching another person. Contact can also be indirect, if the defendant uses objects other than his body to make the contact. To demonstrate, although it is harmful or offensive contact for a defendant to hit you, it is also harmful or offensive contact for a defendant to throw a rock at you. Other examples of indirect contact include shooting a bullet into a victim, poisoning someone's food, or pulling a chair out from under someone about to sit on it (see the *Garratt v. Dailey* case in the end-of-chapter materials). Remember that contact can be made by use of a weapon or other object or device; it is not limited to one person directly touching another person.

It is not necessary for the plaintiff to be aware of the contact at the time it is made. The contact can occur while the plaintiff is asleep or unconscious, so long as the other essential elements of this tort are met. In other words, contact with the plaintiff's person can be harmful or offensive even if it is learned of after it occurs. Consider this example. A man puts Rohypnol, a "date rape" drug, in his date's drink. When the woman is rendered unconscious by the drug, the man rapes her. The woman learns she was raped after the drug wears off and she awakens. Not only is the woman a victim of the crime of rape, she is also a victim of the tort of battery despite the fact that she was not aware of the both harmful and offensive contact until after it occurred.

As this is an intentional tort, the element of intent must be established. Intent, for purposes of this tort, means that the defendant must act consciously and knowingly, with the purpose of causing contact with the plaintiff. Note that "intent" here does not mean ill will or malice. No evil motive is required. Consider this hypothetical situation. Melvin is in a hurry to get to an important meeting. To secure a spot on a crowded subway car and avoid having to wait for the next train, Melvin pushes Larry to the side. Now, Melvin is a nice guy, and he never intended to cause Larry harm. Unfortunately, the push knocks Larry off balance, causing him to fall against the closing subway car doors, injuring him. Has the "intent" element for battery been met? The answer is "yes." Melvin knew with substantial certainty that the results would follow from the act: that by pushing Larry, he might fall. That Melvin did not intend to harm Larry is irrelevant to the determination of whether the tort of battery was committed, although it could affect the amount of damages awarded. The test of intent is whether the defendant desired to bring about the consequences of the act or knew with substantial certainty that the consequences would result from it.

The last essential element of the tort of battery is causation. The defendant must be the cause of the intentional harmful or offensive contact. So, if Jane pushes Ted, Jane is the cause of the harmful contact. There are two tests for determining causation, the "but for" test and the "substantial factor" test. The "but for" test is used when there is one causal event, such as in this scenario. But for Jane's action, Ted would not have been harmed. The "substantial factor" test is used when there is more than one causal event contributing to the harm, such as if Jane and Maggie push Ted. In this case, Jane is a substantial factor contributing to the harm suffered by Ted. So is Maggie. The causation element is met as to both possible defendants.

Now assume that Jane pushes Ted, who falls into Melanie, hurting Melanie. Did Jane commit battery as to Ted? Sure. She was the "but for" cause of Ted's injuries. But what about Melanie? Was not Ted the one who actually injured Melanie? Not really. Jane started the chain of events leading to Melanie's injury. She did, in fact, cause the injury because, had Jane not pushed Ted, Melanie would not have suffered injury in this way at this time. This type of causation, determined using the "but for" or "substantial factor" test, is called "actual cause." The issue raised by this scenario is that Melanie's injuries were less of a foreseeable consequence of Jane's act than were injuries to Ted. This issue introduces another part of causation, the legal doctrine of proximate cause.

In tort law, not only must the defendant's act be the actual cause of the plaintiff's harm, there also must be a sufficient connection between the defendant's act and the plaintiff's harm to justify imposing liability on the defendant. This is called "legal cause," or more commonly, "proximate cause." Proximate cause is a legal doctrine that requires there to be a sufficient causal connection between the act and the injury to justify imposing legal liability. It is based on the notion of foreseeability, introduced in Chapter 2. Normally, a tortfeasor, including one who commits the tort of battery, is liable for the foreseeable consequences of his actions, but not for the unforeseeable ones. When Jane pushed Ted, it was a foreseeable consequence that Ted might fall and be harmed. When Jane pushed Ted, who fell into Melanie and hurt Melanie, the harm Melanie suffered was less foreseeable, though maybe still a foreseeable consequence of Jane's act. What if Jane pushed Ted, who fell into Melanie, who lost her balance and stepped on George's dog, who was on a leash at George's feet? Did Jane in fact cause the dog's injury? Yes, in that the dog would not have suffered injury at this time in this way had not Jane set in motion the chain of events leading to Melanie stepping on him. However, was injury to George's dog the foreseeable consequence of Jane's act (pushing Ted)? Maybe not. In that case, Jane's liability may be cut off, or extinguished, because the trier of fact (the jury in a jury trial or the judge in a bench trial) may determine that she was not the proximate cause of the dog's injuries. This is true even though Jane was the actual cause of the harm the dog suffered. The reason, under the law, for this cutoff test of proximate cause is that at some point along the chain of events set in motion by a tortfeasor such as Jane, she should no longer be held legally responsible for the results. Foreseeability is the test. The two parts to causation are much more thoroughly examined later in the text under the topic of negligence, where proximate cause is more often an issue.

Notice that "injury" or "harm" is not an essential element of this, or many, of the intentional torts, though the nature and seriousness of the injury or harm suffered by the plaintiff affects the amount of damages a court will award. Later, when we study some of the other categories of torts (negligence and strict liability), you will see that "damages" is an essential element of certain torts—just not many of the intentional torts.

SIDEBAR

APPLICATION OF THE DOCTRINE OF TRANSFERRED INTENT

Remember that under the doctrine of transferred intent, which applies to the tort of battery, Jane's intent toward Ted is transferred to Melanie, as Melanie is the "unintended plaintiff."

These concepts are applied in the exercises and problems at the end of the chapter. To practice applying the elements of battery and the other intentional torts to hypothetical situations and real cases, make sure to review those materials.

ASSAULT

The next major intentional tort we will discuss is the tort of assault. **Assault** is a purposeful act that causes an apprehension of a harmful or offensive contact. It is very similar to the tort of battery. However, instead of having harmful or offensive contact, you have the *threat* of such contact. If the threat results in contact, then a battery has been committed, too. In other words, both torts may be committed if all the essential elements of both are present. The injury sustained by the plaintiff in the tort of assault involves mental harm or anguish rather than physical harm from contact. The interest protected by this tort is the right of an individual to be free from the apprehension of a harmful or offensive contact. The essential elements of this tort are (1) an act, (2) the reasonable apprehension of an immediate harmful or offensive contact with the plaintiff's person, (3) intent, and (4) causation.

Many of the elements of this tort are identical to the elements of the tort of battery. To start, an "act" is a voluntary movement of the defendant's body. This

Assault
A purposeful act that causes an apprehension of a harmful or offensive contact.

Key Point

The Essential Elements of Assault

1. An act
2. The reasonable apprehension of an immediate harmful or offensive contact with the plaintiff's person
3. Intent
4. Causation

CASE on Point

Hilgefort v. Stewart, 2011 WL 290509 (Ohio Ct. App. 2011)[2]

This case, heard by the Court of Appeals of Ohio, was brought by a bartender named Hilgefort who was working at the Moose Lodge in Sidney, Ohio. The lodge posts rules for proper attire, including a requirement that hats be worn "straight," with the bill forward. A patron, Stewart, wore his hat "backwards" despite being asked to turn it around by another bartender, then by Hilgefort. When Hilgefort informed Stewart that he would have to leave the lodge if he did not turn his hat around, Stewart rose from his chair, directly faced Hilgefort within about 6 inches of his face, and told Hilgefort that if he wanted the hat reversed, he would have to "turn it around for him." Hilgefort refused to turn Stewart's hat around, at which point Steward picked up Hilgefort and slammed him to the floor "with great force and violence," injuring him, including dislocating his elbow. Hilgefort sued Stewart for the torts of assault and battery.

Regarding the assault claim, the court defined the tort of assault as "the willful threat or attempt to harm or touch another offensively, which threat or attempt reasonably places the other in fear of such contact." It noted that a key element of the tort of assault is whether the defendant "knew with substantial certainty that his or her act would bring harmful or offensive contact." Testimony at trial revealed that Stewart was much larger in height and weight, and much stronger, than Hilgefort. The court found all the elements of the tort of assault (as well as the tort of battery) present in this case, noting that Stewart "willfully threatened or attempted to harm or touch Hilgefort offensively and that Hilgefort was placed in fear of such harm or contact."

is similar to that element in the tort of battery. One is not liable for assault for an action one did not voluntarily take. Note, however, that words alone may not be sufficient to constitute a tortious assault. Many courts require some type of action beyond mere words, such as a verbal threat accompanied by a threatening gesture—for example, making a fist or brandishing a weapon.

In addition, the essential element of intent is virtually the same for this tort as it is for the tort of battery. The defendant must have acted with intent, meaning consciously and knowingly, with the purpose of causing apprehension in the plaintiff by way of the threat. There is no requirement of ill will or evil motive. In meeting the intent requirement, remember that the doctrine of transferred intent applies to this tort. Also, as for battery, causation is an essential element. The defendant must cause the threat the plaintiff experiences for there to be a tortious assault.

Where the tort elements differ is in the element of "reasonable apprehension of an immediate harmful or offensive contact with the plaintiff's person." Although this element has several similarities to the tort of battery, it also presents some twists. In terms of similarities, the concept of reasonableness is the same. The test for determining whether there was a reasonable apprehension of harmful or offensive contact is the same "reasonable person" test used in the battery tort. It is an objective test, asking, "Would a reasonable person, not unduly sensitive, be apprehensive that an immediate harmful or offensive contact may occur?" Once again, however, an exception may be made, and a subjective standard used, when the defendant knows that the plaintiff is unduly sensitive but nonetheless proceeds to exploit this sensitivity and cause apprehension.

The meaning of the "plaintiff's person" part of this essential element is the same as it is with the tort of battery. The "plaintiff's person" extends beyond the body of the plaintiff, to anything attached to the body or otherwise so closely associated with it as to be identified with it, such as the book in the plaintiff's hand or the horse on which the plaintiff is riding.

A new concept within this essential element is the notion of "apprehension." What is "apprehension"? Apprehension is an understanding, awareness, anticipation, belief, or knowledge of something. It does not have to rise to the level of fear or anxiety, but it can. For instance, the threat of an unwelcome kiss may cause apprehension in a reasonable person, depending on the circumstances. Keep in mind, however, that for this tort to be committed, the plaintiff must be aware of the threat. For example, if the plaintiff slept through the threat, or was facing the other direction at the time and was not aware of it, there is no tort of assault.

The apprehension must be one of immediate, or imminent, harmful or offensive contact. A threat of future contact is not covered by this tort. In other words, the defendant must have the apparent present ability to carry out the act threatened. For instance, if a law professor promises, in earnest, to slap any student who does not get an "A" on the first torts exam next week, and really means to do it, there is no tort of assault committed today. The threat, while entirely real, is not immediate. What about if Joe, over the telephone, threatens to beat up James? There is no threat of imminent contact unless Joe and James are in each other's presence. On this point, remember that the defendant's act must cause a reasonable expectation that imminent contact will occur.

Notice that injury or harm is not an essential element of this tort. It is enough for the plaintiff to establish a *prima facie* case of assault by demonstrating the tort's essential elements; the plaintiff need not show she was harmed or injured to recover, though the extent of her injury or harm may affect the amount of damages she recovers.

For practice applying these elements to more hypothetical situations and real cases, be sure to do the assignments and exercises at the end of this chapter.

FALSE IMPRISONMENT

Another intentional tort against the person is false imprisonment. *False imprisonment* is the intentional confinement of another within fixed boundaries set by the defendant. It protects the right of individuals to be free from intentional restraints on their freedom of movement. The essential elements of the tort of false imprisonment are (1) an act that completely confines the plaintiff within fixed boundaries set by the defendant, (2) intent to cause confinement (of the plaintiff or a third party), (3) causation, and (4) consciousness of the confinement or physical harm to the plaintiff (required only in some jurisdictions).

In analyzing these elements, first, there must be an act that completely confines the plaintiff within fixed boundaries set by the defendant. There are several ways to confine a plaintiff by restricting the plaintiff's freedom of movement. First, a defendant can restrain a plaintiff's movement by physical barrier. For instance, the defendant can lock the plaintiff in a windowless room that does not permit reasonable escape. Second, a defendant can restrain a plaintiff's movement by physical force, such as by holding the plaintiff firmly by the arms and not letting her walk away. Third, a defendant can restrain a plaintiff's movement by threat of present physical force. If a defendant holds a gun to the plaintiff's head and tells the plaintiff, "Don't move or I'll shoot," the defendant does not feel free to move away. So this action not only constitutes the tort of assault but also meets the confinement element of the tort of false imprisonment. Note that for both confinement by physical force and confinement by threat of physical force, these notions extend beyond physical force or threat of physical force to the plaintiff. They extend to include physical force, or the threat of it, against the plaintiff's immediate family or her property. So a physical threat against a plaintiff's spouse, made in the presence of both the plaintiff and the spouse, confines not only the spouse but also the plaintiff, who does not feel free to leave his or her beloved in peril. Fourth, a defendant can restrain a plaintiff's movement by asserting legal authority to confine. Consider a Los Angeles city police officer, on vacation in Dallas, making an arrest of a suspected shoplifter. Assuming the officer has no legal authority to make such an arrest outside his jurisdiction, making his acts not privileged, the wrongful arrest of the plaintiff constitutes confinement. Finally, a defendant can restrain a plaintiff's movement by refusing to release a plaintiff. For example, assume that the plaintiff had been validly imprisoned but has served his complete sentence. If the jailor

False imprisonment
Intentional confinement of another within fixed boundaries set by the defendant.

Key Point

The Essential Elements of False Imprisonment

1. An act that completely confines the plaintiff within fixed boundaries set by the defendant
2. Intent to cause confinement (of the plaintiff or a third party)
3. Causation
4. Consciousness of the confinement or physical harm to the plaintiff (in some jurisdictions)

Key Point

Five Methods of Confinement

1. Confinement by physical barrier
2. Confinement by physical force (against the plaintiff, his immediate family, or his property)
3. Confinement by threat of present physical force (against the plaintiff, his immediate family, or his property)
4. Confinement by assertion of legal authority
5. Confinement by refusal to release

fails to release the plaintiff, who has the legal right to be released, that failure to release constitutes confinement. All of these forms of confinement meet this essential element.

The length of the confinement does not matter in establishing this essential element. Being held hostage for two days is, obviously, confinement. A very short period of confinement, such as being physically restrained for thirty seconds, is still confinement, because it is a violation of a person's right to freedom of movement. Though a short period of confinement is still confinement, the duration and nature of the confinement may affect the amount of damages awarded.

What if the plaintiff has the means to escape the confinement? If the plaintiff has a reasonable means of escape, then there is no confinement. So if the plaintiff, an athletic 20-year-old man, is locked in a first-floor room that has many large windows opening onto a grassy yard, there may not be confinement if the man can reasonably climb out a window safely. What if the plaintiff is locked in a store by the defendant? There is a back door out of the store, but it is barricaded by stacks of boxes of inventory in a storeroom, and the plaintiff does not know the door exists and cannot even see it because of the boxes stacked in front of it. Is the plaintiff confined? Yes, because he is not reasonably aware of the means to escape. Although a person who has a reasonable means of escape is not confined for purposes of this intentional tort, a person is not required to risk danger to escape, such as by jumping out of a five-story window. Nor is a person required to embarrass herself by attempting escape, such as if she is naked and would have to escape without wearing clothing.

What "intent" is necessary for this tort? The intent element of this tort of false imprisonment is met when the defendant acts with the purpose to confine or knowledge with substantial certainty that confinement will result from the defendant's actions. Just as with battery and assault torts, no ill will or evil motive is required. What if Eric inadvertently locks Marta in a room, not realizing she had entered it? Eric has not committed the tort of false imprisonment because the "intent" element is not met; he did not act with the purpose of confining Marta, or know with substantial certainly that confinement would result from his actions. In establishing the element of intent, remember that the doctrine of transferred intent applies to the tort of false imprisonment.

Finally, the defendant must cause the confinement. Causation is an essential element of this tort. If the defendant entices the plaintiff into a house, and then a mudslide barricades the doors and windows of the house, the defendant did not cause, actually or legally, the confinement.

In some jurisdictions, the plaintiff must be aware of the confinement for this tort to be committed. In such jurisdictions, if the plaintiff sleeps through the period of confinement and has no knowledge of it, there is no tort of false imprisonment. These jurisdictions may make an exception, however, if the plaintiff suffered actual harm during the confinement, such as by getting sick during it, even though he was not aware of the confinement during the time it was occurring. Other jurisdictions do not require that the plaintiff be aware of the confinement; in those states, it is enough that the plaintiff was confined.

CASE on Point

Bellanger v. Webre, 65 So.3d 201 (La. Ct. App. 2011)

On May 23, 2007, Typhoon Dodge, an infant, was killed by a gunshot wound sustained during a shootout initiated when the child's father, Albert Dewayne Dodge, who was an aggravated battery suspect, unexpectedly fired a hidden weapon at point-blank range at a sheriff's deputy. At the time the deputy was attempting to arrest Dodge inside his trailer. Dodge also died, from gunshot wounds sustained.

The child's mother, Bellanger, brought a claim against the sheriff's office for false imprisonment based on her detention by police officers following the gun battle in her trailer. The police officers detained Bellanger because she attempted to conceal Dodge's presence there in order to prevent his arrest. In fact, she was handcuffed and placed in custody when she was arrested for obstruction of justice for lying to sheriff's deputies about Dodge's presence in the trailer (though she was not ultimately prosecuted for that crime).

The Court of Appeal of Louisiana said that "the tort of false arrest or false imprisonment occurs when one arrests and restrains another against his will and without statutory authority." It noted two essential elements to the tort: (1) detention of the person; and (2) unlawfulness of the detention. In this case, the court determined that Bellanger was detained, but that her detention was lawful. Therefore, the tort of false arrest, a type of false imprisonment, was not committed. Note that this case illustrates that false arrest is one type of false imprisonment.

Also see the Case on Point, appearing in the next section, entitled *Mathis v. Coats,* for another case involving false arrest, distinguishing false arrest and false imprisonment and setting for the essential elements of a claim for false imprisonment.

As with the other intentional torts we have studied so far, the plaintiff need not establish that she was actually injured or harmed by the act in order to establish a *prima facie* case, though the extent of her harm will affect the amount of her damage award. The confinement is considered damage enough to recover under this tort.

Defenses will be covered later in this book, but an important privilege relating to this tort warrants discussion now. Many states recognize a type of merchant protection called "shopkeepers' privilege," which allows merchants (shopkeepers, such as your local department store) or their agents to reasonably and temporarily detain a suspected shoplifter for the sole purpose of questioning him about whether shoplifting occurred. The shopkeeper must be reasonable both in suspecting that the person has committed the crime of shoplifting and in the scope and duration of the investigation. The detainment must be temporary, and it must be for the sole purpose of investigating the possible shoplifting. Reasonable force may be used by the shopkeeper or his agent to carry out the investigation, as well. See the end-of-chapter assignments to research whether your jurisdiction recognizes a form of shopkeepers' privilege via a merchants' protection statute.

WHAT IS A PRIVILEGE?

A "privilege" is a special legal right allowing a person to act in a way that would, under normal circumstances, subject him to legal liability.

FALSE ARREST

False arrest
The unprivileged arrest of an individual.

The next intentional tort we will discuss is false arrest. False arrest is a type of false imprisonment. It restricts an individual's freedom of movement. *False arrest* is an arrest that is not privileged. It has the same essential elements as the tort of false imprisonment, as is demonstrated by the Cases on Point.

Both law enforcement officers and private citizens have a privilege to arrest another, depending on the facts and circumstances surrounding the arrest. Obviously, law enforcement officers have a broader privilege in this area than do private citizens; in fact, making arrests of suspected criminals is a major duty of law enforcement officers.

The tort issue is that an arrest made without that privilege is an unlawful restraint of another's freedom. The person making the unprivileged arrest can be subject to liability for this intentional tort because of this wrongful conduct. That person, if working within the course and scope of his employment, may subject his employer to vicarious liability for the

CASE on Point

Bonkowski v. Arlan's Dep't Store, 162 N.W.2d 347 (Mich. Ct. App. 1968)

In this case, Mrs. Bonkowski was walking to her car with her husband when she was stopped in the parking lot of the defendant's store by a member of the store's private security team, an off-duty policy officer. She was asked to accompany the security officer back toward the store, which she did. The security officer stated that someone had seen her put three pieces of costume jewelry into her purse without paying for them. Mrs. Bonkowski denied that she had taken anything unlawfully; still, the security officer asked to see the contents of her purse. Mrs. Bonkowski, standing on a cement step in front of the store, emptied the contents of her purse into her husband's hands. Among the contents were sales slips for the items she had purchased. Satisfied, the security officer returned to the store.

Mrs. Bonkowski sued the store and the security officer for, among other things, false arrest. The court found the existence of a privilege permitting a merchant, including the merchant's agent, who reasonably believes someone has taken goods unlawfully, to detain that person for the purpose of conducting a reasonable investigation of the facts. This court was willing to extend the privilege to not only the physical location of the store itself but also the parking lot outside the store.

STATUTE on Point

Ariz. Rev. Stat. § 13-3884 (2012)

A private person may make an arrest when

a. The person to be arrested has in his presence committed a misdemeanor amounting to a breach of the peace, or committed a felony.

b. A felony has been in fact committed and he has reasonable grounds to believe that the person to be arrested committed it.

employee's wrongdoing under the doctrine of *respondeat superior*, discussed earlier, in Chapter 2.

Generally, when a law enforcement officer has a warrant, based on probable cause, which basically means a reasonable suspicion, to arrest an individual, the arrest is privileged so long as the warrant is fair on its face. "Fair on its face" means that it does not appear to be obviously defective. The privilege is lost if the warrant is not fair on its face, such as if it fails to state the crime charged. The privilege also may be lost if the law enforcement officer arrests the wrong individual, if the mistake as to identify is unreasonable under the circumstances. A law enforcement officer may, under certain circumstances, make an arrest without a warrant if probable cause exists but the circumstances do not permit the officer to obtain a warrant, such as in an emergency situation—perhaps the officer has witnessed a bank robbery and takes immediate action to apprehend the perpetrator. If a law enforcement officer makes a warrantless arrest and probable cause is lacking, he may be exposed to tort liability for false arrest.

Private citizens also have a privilege to arrest, though it is less broad than that of law enforcement officers, who make arrests as part of their employment duties. The circumstances under which private citizens may make arrests differ from jurisdiction to jurisdiction. For one example, see the Arizona Statute on Point. However, keep in mind that an arrest made by a private citizen that fails to meet the jurisdictional requirements for a proper citizen's arrest may constitute an intentional tort. That citizen may be held liable for false arrest.

CASE on Point

Bellanger v. Webre, 65 So.3d 201 (La. Ct. App. 2011)

In this case already discussed (in the section on the tort of false imprisonment), the court treated the tort of false arrest as the tort of false imprisonment, stating "the tort of false arrest or false imprisonment occurs when one arrests and restrains another against his will and without statutory authority."

CASE on Point

Mathis v. Coats, 24 So.3d 1284 (Fla. Dist. Ct. App. 2010)

A motorist, Ms. Mathis, was observed by a sheriff's deputy veering from her lane and striking the center median, nearly side-swiping another vehicle, then striking the center median again. A backup deputy stopped Ms. Mathis, saw that she exhibited signs of intoxication, and administered a series of field sobriety tests that Ms. Mathis could not satisfactorily complete. Then Ms. Mathis was arrested for driving under the influence (DUI). She was handcuffed, transported involuntarily via police cruiser to Central Breath Testing, and subjected to another set of field sobriety tests, a breath test, a urine test, and a drug evaluation. Ms. Mathis was given a DUI citation and taken to jail, where she stayed until noon the next day. All the test results came in (days later) negative. Subsequently, Ms. Mathis sued the sheriff for false arrest.

The District Court of Appeal of Florida ruled that Ms. Mathis's claim of false arrest "must fail" because "probable cause existed to arrest [her] at the scene of the traffic stop" so there was no unlawful arrest. The court went on to say that "[f]alse arrest and false imprisonment are closely related, but false imprisonment is a broader common law tort; false arrest is only one of several methods of committing false imprisonment." Then the court went on to state that false imprisonment means "forcibly, by threat, or secretly confining, abducting, imprisoning, or restraining another person without lawful authority and against her or his will."

The court noted that a person improperly detained pursuant to a lawful arrest may have the right to bring an action for false imprisonment, as was the case here, when Ms. Mathis was lawfully arrested but that probable cause "evaporated at some point after she was transported to CBT and jailed." So while Ms. Mathis did not have a valid claim of false arrest, she might have a claim for false imprisonment for the detention that occurred later. The essential elements of a cause of action for false imprisonment, as noted by this court, were (1) the unlawful detention and deprivation of liberty of a person; (2) against that person's will; (3) without legal authority or "color of authority"; and (4) which is unreasonable and unwarranted under the circumstances.

Intentional infliction of emotional distress
The purposeful causing of severe mental anguish by an act of extreme or outrageous conduct.

Key Point

The Essential Elements of Intentional Infliction of Emotional Distress

1. An act of extreme or outrageous conduct
2. Intent to cause severe emotional distress
3. The plaintiff suffers severe emotional distress
4. Causation

INTENTIONAL INFLICTION OF EMOTIONAL DISTRESS

Another intentional tort against the person is intentional infliction of emotional distress. *Intentional infliction of emotional distress* is the purposeful causing of severe mental anguish by an act of extreme or outrageous conduct. This tort is also called the tort of "outrage." Emotions such as fear, anxiety, horror, humiliation, grief, worry, and other such strong, negative emotions constitute severe emotional distress, or mental anguish, the harm targeted by this tort. The interest this tort protects is the right of individuals to be free from emotional distress and psychological harm that is intentionally, or perhaps recklessly (as discussed later), caused by another. The essential elements of the tort of intentional infliction of emotional distress are (1) an act of extreme or outrageous conduct, (2) intent to cause severe emotional distress, (3) the plaintiff suffers severe emotional distress, and (4) causation.

The first essential element of the tort of intentional infliction of emotional distress is the requirement that the defendant act in an extreme and outrageous manner. The defendant's conduct must be so extreme that an ordinary person would regard it as appalling, atrocious, and completely and totally intolerable. Court opinions demonstrate that this is a difficult element to establish. To meet this high standard, the conduct of the defendant must shock the conscience of society. See the exercises at the end of the chapter for some cases to read and brief on this point. This high standard is why the tort is also called the tort of outrage. The courts, in defining the conduct this way, are limiting frivolous lawsuits. As members of society, we experience emotional distress. That is just part of life. This tort does not cover everyday distress that all people face. Rather, it covers conduct that is so outrageous that most people never experience it. An example of conduct that would be outrageous enough to constitute this tort is putting a loaded gun to the head of an elderly person—and likely this would constitute the tort of assault, too. Similarly, threatening to push a pregnant woman into traffic is outrageous enough. What about threatening to kick someone's new Porsche convertible? That would not be outrageous enough conduct to meet the requirements of this tort, even though it is likely to cause the Porsche owner considerable distress.

In judging whether conduct is extreme and outrageous, consideration is given to plaintiffs' particular vulnerabilities, such as young or old age, or physical or mental illness. However, a perfectly healthy, young adult can be a victim of this tort. If the tortfeasor intentionally drives through a parking lot and tries to run down a 25-year-old professional athlete, the conduct would meet the "extreme and outrageous" test, even as to this strong and healthy plaintiff. It is just that when the plaintiff has vulnerabilities, such as a physical illness or old age, it is easier to establish that the defendant's conduct was extreme and outrageous.

In terms of the intent requirement, the defendant must act with the specific intent to inflict severe emotional distress on the plaintiff or act with such utter recklessness that emotional distress is a foreseeable consequence. For this tort, in many jurisdictions, intent includes reckless conduct so long as it is also outrageous. Holding a gun to someone's head and threatening to shoot him demonstrates an act with the specific intent to cause severe emotional distress. Consider, however, the following example. Dorothy, a police dispatcher, dispatches a police officer to the home of Emily Baker, to inform Emily that her husband, John Baker, has been killed in a car accident. In fact, Emily's husband is alive and well, busy at work. Another person named "John Baker" was killed in the automobile accident, but that person is no relation to Emily. If Dorothy had checked her information for accuracy, she would have learned that the unfortunate accident victim was named John Martin Baker, and Emily's husband is named John Edward Baker. Emily, upon hearing the news that her husband was killed in a car accident, faints. Has Dorothy purposefully inflicted emotional distress on Emily? No. However, her actions were reckless in that she failed to verify the identity of the accident victim before delivering this tragic news to the wrong recipient. Reckless conduct is conduct that is extremely careless, even indifferent to the consequences it causes, but beyond mere failure to exercise reasonable care. Degrees of failure in exercising reasonable care are discussed more fully in Chapters 6 through 9 on the tort of negligence. In many jurisdictions, recklessness is sufficient to meet the "intent" requirement for this tort. Remember, too, that the doctrine of transferred intent does not apply to the tort of intentional infliction of emotional distress—it is not one of those five enumerated torts.

For this tort to be committed, the plaintiff must actually suffer severe emotional distress. It is not enough for the defendant to intend to cause severe emotional distress; the defendant's conduct must result in the consequence of severe emotional distress being suffered by the plaintiff. Severe emotional distress means significant, substantial mental anguish. Minor inconvenience, annoyance, indignity, insult, or other insubstantial degree of emotional distress is not sufficient. The severity of these emotions is measured by their intensity and duration. To determine the severity of the emotional distress, the "reasonable person" test normally is used: Would a reasonable person, of ordinary sensibilities, meaning not unduly sensitive, have suffered severe emotional distress as a result of the defendant's conduct?

What if the plaintiff is unduly sensitive and the defendant knows about the plaintiff's vulnerability? For instance, consider the horticulturist plaintiff with a history of mental illness and who is overly attached to his Princess Diana rosebush. In fun, the defendant tells the plaintiff that the bush is infested with beetles and is half-eaten. The plaintiff breaks down emotionally and is propelled into severe depression. In that case, a subjective standard is used to determine the severity of the emotional distress. Although a reasonable person would not suffer emotional distress from this news, because the defendant knew about the plaintiff's particular vulnerability and acted anyway, the court would use a subjective standard in determining the severity of this plaintiff's emotional distress.

When a plaintiff actually suffers severe emotional distress, must that distress manifest itself in physical injury or harm for this tort to be committed? Most jurisdictions do not require that the plaintiff suffer any physical injury or harm as a result of the defendant's conduct to establish this tort, though the existence of such physical injury or harm would affect any damage award. However, a few jurisdictions require that some physical injury or harm exist, in addition to the emotional distress, to establish a *prima facie* case of intentional infliction of emotional distress. That injury or harm can be actual injury or harm to the plaintiff that accompanies the act causing the distress; it can also be some physical manifestation of the emotional distress itself, such as sleeplessness, nausea, or fainting. The reason for this restriction, where it exists, is to deter false claims.

Finally, the defendant must be the cause of the emotional distress that the plaintiff suffers. The defendant is not liable for emotional distress suffered by another resulting from something other than his conduct. Consider this example. Susan, six months pregnant, is not well liked in her neighborhood, causing much trouble within her homeowners' association. One day, several of the neighborhood wives are drinking tea on a porch. Seeing Susan approaching on a walk, Brea confronts Susan about recent homeowners' issues, and a verbal spat ensues. Brea, whose anger has become explosive, threatens to knee Susan in the stomach. The other ladies laugh at this ridiculous interchange between Brea and Susan. Susan is not only emotionally hurt but also humiliated by the ladies' laughter.

CASE on Point

Griffin v. State of New Jersey, 2011 WL 6782438 (N.J. Super. Ct. App. Div. 2011)[3]

In this case, some coworkers lodged complaints of harassment against the plaintiff, Ms. Griffin. As a result, Ms. Griffin was told by her supervisor that she was being suspended from work, was directed to leave the building, and then a New Jersey State trooper escorted her to her office to clear her desk and leave the building. Ms. Griffin sued the State of New Jersey for intentional infliction of emotional distress as a result of this incident.

The court stated that in order to establish a tort claim for intentional infliction of emotional distress, a plaintiff must prove that (1) the defendant intended to inflict emotional distress or knew or should have known that emotional distress was the likely result of the conduct; (2) the conduct was extreme or outrageous; (3) the actions of the defendant were the cause of the plaintiff's distress; and (4) the emotional distress suffered by the plaintiff was severe. Focusing on the second element, the court here said that being escorted from her place of employment by a State trooper was merely embarrassing; it was not the equivalent of atrocious conduct nor "beyond all possible bounds of decency." The court reasoned that Ms. Griffin was not handcuffed or in any way restrained. Her escort simply guaranteed her removal from the building in an orderly manner.

Have these *other ladies* committed the tort of outrage against Susan? No, because there is no causation. Brea was the cause of Susan's humiliation. Note that Brea, via her threat, likely committed the tort of assault against Susan, as well.

As several of the previous examples indicate, it is possible for the tort of intentional infliction of emotional distress to be committed simultaneously with other intentional torts. For another example, threatening a child by holding a knife to her side is both an assault *and* the tort of outrage. This tort may also be committed on its own. For example, if a magazine publishes an advertisement that a well-known minister engaged in an incestuous relationship with his mother, the tort of outrage may be committed (see the exercises at the end of the chapter for a case on these facts, although the verdict in favor of the minister was overturned by the U.S. Supreme Court on free-speech grounds).

Some jurisdictions recognize a separate tort for the *negligent,* rather than intentional, infliction of emotional distress. Although we examine negligence in detail later in this book, it is important to mention this tort now because of its relationship to the intentional tort. The tort of **negligent infliction of emotional distress** is the causing of emotional distress by an act of unreasonable conduct. In these cases, the requisite "intent" for the intentional tort is not met, which includes recklessness in some jurisdictions, as we discussed. The defendant's conduct is merely "unreasonable" with this tort. Unreasonableness of the defendant's conduct is the essence of the tort of negligence, as you will learn when we examine the tort of negligence. The most common application of the tort of

Negligent infliction of emotional distress
Causing emotional distress by an act of unreasonable conduct.

negligent infliction of emotional distress is cases involving persons who witness the injury or death of loved ones caused by another's negligence.

Consider the following situation. Mary is walking down the sidewalk, next to the street. Charlie is driving down the street, talking on his cell phone and exceeding the speed limit, meaning that his driving is unreasonable. Charlie takes his eyes off the road momentarily, and his car veers onto the sidewalk. It is approaching Mary! Thankfully, Mary sees the car approaching her on the sidewalk, and she jumps to safety. Mary is physically uninjured, though she suffered substantial anxiety and fear, albeit briefly, over the incident. As you will see when we discuss the tort of negligence, unless Mary suffers actual damage or harm, the tort of negligence has not been committed. Assume that Mary suffered no actual harm. She would not be able to recover for negligence. However, could she recover from Charlie for intentional infliction of emotional distress? No, she could not, because the "intent" element could not be established. But what about for negligent infliction of emotional distress? To recover for negligent infliction of emotional distress, most courts require that the mental anguish be accompanied by some physical harm or injury, such as if the fear causes a heart attack. The courts reason that the emotional distress is too trivial if it does not arise out of or cause some physical injury or harm. What if the physical injury or harm occurs later in time? For instance, what if Mary was

CASE on Point

Griffin v. State of New Jersey, 2011 WL 6782438 (N.J. Super. Ct. App. Div. 2011)

In the Case on Point from the previous page, Ms. Griffin pursued a negligent infliction of emotional distress claim, along with her intentional infliction of emotional distress claim (discussed earlier), related to the police escort from her place of employment she experienced as a result of her suspension from employment due to harassment complaints made by coworkers. The court said that in order to establish a claim for negligent infliction of emotional distress, a plaintiff must prove that (1) the defendant owed the plaintiff a duty of reasonable care; (2) the duty was breached; (3) the plaintiff suffered severe emotional distress; and (4) the breach of the duty was the proximate cause of the injury.

This court ruled that using the State Police to escort Ms. Griffin out of the building was not a breach of any duty it may have owed to her. The court reasoned that this police escort was necessary to prevent contact between Ms. Griffin and her coworkers. Such contact might have been perceived as harassing or potentially intimidating. So the court recognized the obligations owed by the employer/defendant to others in the workplace. Accordingly, with no breach of a duty of reasonable care, there was no valid claim for negligent infliction of emotional distress in this case.

Further, with regard to the third and fourth essential elements, the court ruled that the employer/defendant had no reason to foresee that its actions would lead an employee in Ms. Griffin's position to experience fright or shock sufficient to cause substantial injury.

CASE on Point

Trisuzzi v. Tabatchnik, 666 A.2d 543 (N.J. Super. Ct. App. Div. 1995)

In this case, a dog-bite victim's wife brought an action against dog owners for negligent infliction of emotional distress after witnessing her husband being attacked by the dog owners' German Shepherd. The court said that to state a cause of action for negligent infliction of emotional distress, a plaintiff must prove (1) the death or serious physical injury of another caused by the defendant's negligence, (2) a marital or intimate familial relationship between the plaintiff and the injured person, (3) observation of the death or injury at the scene, and (4) severe emotional distress. After reviewing the case, the appellate court found that neither the physical injuries that the wife observed her husband sustain (bites to his hands and groin area that did not disable him) nor her resulting emotional distress (a fear of dogs, causing her nightmares) was serious enough to give rise to liability.

twelve weeks pregnant at the time of the incident? Because of the stress she experienced as a result of the incident, Mary suffered a miscarriage three days later. Some courts permit recovery in these cases. Other courts permit recovery if this harm is accompanied by some other physical impact on the plaintiff at the time of the event, such as falling when she jumped out of the car's way—the impact at the time does not have to produce the physical harm suffered later; is it enough that the emotional distress caused the harm later. Still other courts will deny recovery if the physical harm or injury and the emotional distress did not occur simultaneously. Remember that jurisdictions that recognize the tort of negligent infliction of emotional distress are not uniform in their treatment of cases when physical harm does not immediately accompany the cause of the emotional distress.

Keep in mind that, under traditional negligence theory (which we will study later), plaintiffs can recover damages for emotional distress that accompany physical injury or harm. These damages are called "pain and suffering." These concepts must be distinguished. The tort of negligent infliction of emotional distress is a separate and distinct tort, distinguishable from damages for pain and suffering.

MALICIOUS PROSECUTION

Another intentional tort against the person is malicious prosecution. *Malicious prosecution* is the initiation of a criminal prosecution or a civil lawsuit against another party with malice and without probable cause. This tort protects the right of individuals to be free from the initiation of unjustified or unwarranted legal action against them. It is one of two torts, the other being abuse of process, designed to curb misuse of our legal system. Consider a lawsuit brought to harass or intimidate another person. This is considered tortious because it is a misuse of our judicial system and a waste of resources. The essential elements of the tort of malicious prosecution are (1) the initiation or continuance of a criminal or civil proceeding against the plaintiff, (2) without

Malicious prosecution
Initiation of a criminal prosecution or a civil lawsuit against another party with malice and without probable cause.

Key Point

The Essential Elements of Malicious Prosecution

1. The initiation or continuance of a criminal or civil proceeding against the plaintiff
2. Without probable cause
3. With malice
4. The proceeding terminates in favor of the plaintiff

probable cause, (3) with malice, and (4) the proceeding terminates in favor of the plaintiff.

Some states separate this tort into two distinct torts. These states reserve the tort of *malicious prosecution* for wrongfully brought and maintained criminal prosecutions. They define a similar, but separate, tort called "wrongful" or "unjustified" civil proceedings for civil lawsuits wrongfully brought or maintained. The essential elements are virtually the same. For purposes of this discussion, we will combine both civil and criminal actions in the definition of malicious prosecution.

Regarding the first essential element, the defendant must initiate, procure the initiation of, or continue a legal proceeding against the plaintiff. The tortfeasor becomes the defendant in the malicious prosecution case brought by the plaintiff; remember that the plaintiff in the tort suit is the defendant in the wrongfully brought or continued legal action. For example, by reporting a false claim to the police that the plaintiff assaulted her, the defendant in the tort suit initiates a legal prosecution against the plaintiff.

Additionally, the legal action, whether civil or criminal, must be initiated without probable cause. Probable cause in a criminal matter means reasonable suspicion, in other words a suspicion based on the circumstances that is strong enough to permit a reasonable person to believe a criminal charge against a person is true. In a civil matter, for this tort, probable cause means that good grounds exist to warrant bringing a civil action against the plaintiff. If probable cause exists in the underlying action, there is no tort of malicious prosecution. For example, a false claim of rape made by a stripper against certain—say, Duke University—lacrosse players, which is completely and intentionally made up by the claimant, lacks probable cause, and constitutes procurement of the initiation of legal proceedings against the players.

CASE on Point

Farrell v. Hitchin' Post Trailer Ranch, 2011 WL 6057930 (Ariz. Ct. App. 2011)[4]

This was a malicious prosecution case arising out of a landlord/tenant dispute. Farrell purchased a mobile home that was permanently embedded on property owned by the defendant, Hitchin' Post Trailer Ranch. Farrell experienced problems with his electrical and water service and withheld rent owed to the defendant as a result. The defendant filed a forcible entry and detainer action against Farrell resulting in Farrell's eviction (so the defendant won the eviction action).

The Court of Appeals of Arizona stated that to prevail on a malicious prosecution claim, a plaintiff must prove that the defendant instituted a civil action that was motivated by malice, begun without probable cause, and terminated in favor of the plaintiff.

Note that Arizona is one of the states that covers both criminal and civil actions in its malicious prosecution tort. In this case, because Farrell, the plaintiff in the action, had not prevailed in the underlying civil action (the eviction action), judgment was rendered in favor of the defendant on this malicious prosecution claim.

CASE on Point

The Duke University Lacrosse Players' Scandal

The 2006 Duke University lacrosse players' scandal demonstrates a malicious prosecution suit that was not brought, but surely would have been a winner. In April and May 2006, three white members of the Duke University lacrosse team were indicted for rape after being accused by Crystal Mangum, an African American woman who had been performing exotic dancing for the team at a party at the house of two of the team's captains. The charges were brought by Durham County District Attorney Mike Nifong, who was seeking reelection at the time, and who later was forced to resign and then was disbarred by the North Carolina State Bar Association for his unethical conduct related to the bringing of these charges. On April 11, 2007, North Carolina's Attorney General dropped all charges against the three lacrosse players, declaring them innocent and victims of a tragic rush to accuse. Although the three wrongfully accused players never sued their accuser for malicious prosecution, the essential elements of the tort were present. They did sue the city of Durham and District Attorney Nifong, among others with deeper pockets than the accuser, on other theories relating to the violation of their civil rights. Interestingly, the accuser was convicted of child abuse and vandalism in 2010, then indicted in 2011 for first-degree murder for stabbing her boyfriend to death—using a kitchen knife.

Further, the legal action must be brought or maintained with malice. "With malice" means that the defendant had an improper motive in initiating, procuring the initiation of, or continuing the legal action. The proper motive for bringing a legal action is to pursue justice. Any other motive, such as to harass, intimidate, or blackmail another, is improper.

Finally, the proceedings must terminate in favor of the plaintiff. This means the plaintiff must win the underlying case, whether civil or criminal. Most states require that the plaintiff win "on the merits" rather than on a technicality. To win on the merits means that the evidence supports the verdict or judgment for the plaintiff. To win on a technicality means that the plaintiff wins for a reason other than the weight of the evidence, such as a procedural violation or the running of the statute of limitations. Remember that winning a criminal case does not necessarily mean that there was no probable cause to bring the action; probable cause merely requires that there be a reasonable suspicion that the defendant committed the crime. You can have probable cause to bring an action without having sufficient evidence to prove the claim or win a guilty verdict.

Another intentional tort that, along with the tort of malicious prosecution, helps prevent the abuse of our legal system is the tort of abuse of process.

ABUSE OF PROCESS

The intentional tort of **abuse of process** is the use of civil or criminal proceedings for an improper purpose or for an ulterior motive. The interest protected by this tort is the right of individuals to be free from misuse of the legal process to achieve improper objectives. The essential elements of the tort of abuse of

Abuse of process
The use of civil or criminal proceedings for an improper purpose or for an ulterior motive.

CASE on Point

Reardon v. CTRE, LLC, 2011 WL 6270529 (Conn. Super. Ct. 2011)[5]

The Superior Court of Connecticut stated that "[a]n action for abuse of process lies against any person using a legal process against another in an improper manner or to accomplish a purpose for which it was not designed." It noted the *Restatement (Second) of Torts'* comment that the most significant part of an action for abuse of process is the use of a legal process "against another *primarily* to accomplish a purpose for which it is not designed." The term "primarily" is meant to exclude from liability the situation when the process is used for the purpose for which it is intended but there is an incidental motive of spite or an ulterior purpose that benefits the defendant.

This case involved a real estate transaction in Mystic, Connecticut. Reardon, the defendant in the case, was alleged to have interfered with a contractual relationship between two other parties to derail the sale of certain real property. Reardon argued that his motive was to enjoin the property sale that he believed was fraudulent. The court in this case ruled that a determination must be made by a trier of fact to determine what Reardon's intent was by looking at the evidence and determining his credibility in order to make a ruling on the abuse of process claim.

Key Point

The Essential Elements of Abuse of Process

1. The use of civil or criminal proceedings
2. For an improper purpose or for an ulterior motive

process are (1) the use of civil or criminal proceedings, and (2) for an improper purpose or for an ulterior motive.

It is important to distinguish abuse of process from malicious prosecution. With the tort of malicious prosecution, a legal action is wrongfully initiated. However, with the tort of abuse of process, the legal action is properly brought, but for improper reasons.

Note that this tort does not require that there be lack of probable cause, one of the essential elements of the tort of malicious prosecution. Probable cause may exist. In fact, with abuse of process, the civil or criminal proceeding is, in fact, properly brought.

Nor does this tort require that the underlying action terminate in favor of the plaintiff. The outcome of the underlying matter is irrelevant to the abuse of process determination.

The conduct giving rise to this tort is use of the legal system for some reason other than the pursuit of justice. Improper motives are any motives other than the pursuit of justice, such as harassment, embarrassment, or intimidation of another person. What about when a person tries to coerce another by threatening to pursue a valid legal claim? For instance, what if Pamela threatens to report her ex-boyfriend Steven's tax evasion unless Steven agrees to allow Pamela to keep the house they shared? In that situation, the person making the threat has an ulterior motive—she is attempting to force another to yield to her will via threat of legal action, albeit valid legal action. Extortion is not the proper purpose of our legal system, and this constitutes the tort of abuse of process.

Together, the torts of abuse of process and malicious prosecution are intended to reduce the misuse of our legal system.

CHAPTER **SUMMARY**

- Intentional torts have a common essential element: the element of intent. "Intent" means the desire to bring about the consequences of the act or knowledge with substantial certainty that the consequences will result from the act. Without this element of intent, no intentional tort is committed.

- The doctrine of transferred intent is used to establish the intent element when there is an "unintended plaintiff" or an "unintended tort." This doctrine only applies to five of the intentional torts, namely, battery, assault, false imprisonment, trespass to land, and trespass to chattels.

- Intentional torts against the person are torts in which the defendant acts purposefully to injure the plaintiff. The main intentional torts against the person are battery, assault, false imprisonment, false arrest, intentional infliction of emotional distress, malicious prosecution, and abuse of process.

- Battery is a purposeful and unwanted harmful or offensive contact with another person.

- Assault is a purposeful act that causes an apprehension of a harmful or offensive contact.

- False imprisonment is the intentional confinement of another within fixed boundaries set by the defendant.

- False arrest is an arrest that is not privileged.

- Intentional infliction of emotional distress is the purposeful causing of severe mental anguish by an act of extreme or outrageous conduct; it is also called the tort of outrage.

- Malicious prosecution is the initiation of a criminal prosecution or a civil lawsuit against another party with malice and without probable cause.

- Abuse of process is the use of civil or criminal proceedings for an improper purpose or for an ulterior motive.

CONCEPT REVIEW AND REINFORCEMENT

QUESTIONS FOR **REVIEW**

1. What is an intentional tort?
2. What is intent?
3. What is the doctrine of transferred intent? When and how does it apply?
4. What are the main intentional torts against the person?
5. What is the tort of battery?
6. What is the tort of assault?
7. What is the tort of false imprisonment?
8. What is the tort of false arrest?
9. What is the tort of intentional infliction of emotional distress?
10. What is the tort of negligent infliction of emotional distress?
11. What is the tort of malicious prosecution?
12. What is the tort of abuse of process?

DEVELOPING YOUR PARALEGAL SKILLS

CRITICAL THINKING **EXERCISES**

1. In this chapter, we studied the essential elements of the intentional torts of battery, assault, false imprisonment, false arrest, intentional infliction of emotional distress, malicious prosecution, and abuse of process. Each state may "customize" these elements in its case law. Research the law in your state

with reference to the essential elements of each of these intentional torts to see in what way(s), if any, they differ from most states' elements for those torts. An excellent starting point for your research is a case law digest for your state. For example, in Maryland, the resource *Maryland Digest 2d* by West includes cases from Maryland establishing essential elements for each of these torts. Review these essential elements in class.

Here is a list of cases stating Maryland law on the various intentional torts covered in this chapter, as an example of jurisdiction-specific legal research:

Battery: First Financial Ins. Co. v. GLM, Inc., 88 F.Supp.2d 425 (D. Md. 2000).

Assault: Lee v. Pfeifer, 916 F.Supp. 501 (D. Md. 1996).

False imprisonment and false arrest: Gray v. Maryland, 228 F.Supp.2d 628 (D. Md. 2002). This case states that under Maryland law, the essential elements of these two torts are the same.

Intentional infliction of emotional distress: Young v. Hartford Acc. and Indem. Co., 492 A.2d 1270 (Md. 1985). Note that this case recognizes "reckless" as meeting the intent requirement under Maryland law.

Malicious prosecution: In Maryland, both criminal and civil actions fall under this malicious prosecution tort, but civil actions have additional essential elements to their malicious prosecution claim. For the essential elements when the action is based on a criminal case: *Krashes v. White,* 341 A.2d 798 (Md. 1975). For the essential elements when the action is based on a civil case: *Dostert v. Crowley,* 394 F.2d 178 (4th Cir. 1968).

Abuse of process: Campbell v. Lyon, 26 F. App'x 183 (4th Cir. 2001).

2. Mattie is late for class and is running through the hallway. In her haste, she trips and falls to the ground, knocking into Sylvia along the way. Sylvia suffers a concussion during this mishap.

   Has Mattie committed the tort of battery against Sylvia? Why or why not?

3. Joe intentionally terrifies Mary by holding a gun to her head, threatening to shoot her, then shifting the gun slightly to the left and discharging it. Mary is not hit by the bullet, thank goodness. However, Mary's mother, Fran, is in the room and suffers severe emotional distress, thinking that her daughter has just been shot in the head.

   Has Joe committed an intentional tort against Mary? If so, which one(s)? Has Joe committed an intentional tort against Fran? If so, which one(s)?

4. Howie is a germaphobe. He is sincerely and seriously afraid of catching germs from others. In fact,

it is common knowledge among his acquaintances that Howie will not shake hands when greeting others; rather, he bumps fists with them to lessen the physical contact and his exposure to germs. Phillip, a friend, knows this about Howie. Phillip invites Howie to a party. When Howie arrives, Phillip, in good fun, embraces Howie in a bear hug. Howie is aghast. He sulks in a corner throughout the party, then sleeps fitfully the next two nights, worried that he is about to catch a cold, or worse, the flu, from Phillip's embrace.

Has Phillip committed the tort of battery against Howie? Why or why not?

5. Tom, intending to mug Shawnna, points a gun at her head and says, "Give me your wallet or else!" Fortunately, a nearby noise frightens Tom, who is afraid of being caught by the police, and he runs away.

   Has Tom committed the tort of assault against Shawnna? Why or why not?

6. Christopher, trying to elude the police after committing a robbery, enters the home of Trudy Shore and her daughter, Isabelle. Both women are at home at the time, watching television in the den. Christopher, armed with a sharp-looking knife, enters the den. He tells Trudy, "You are free to go." Trudy does not leave. Then Christopher yells at her, "Get out of here now!"

   Has Christopher committed the tort of false imprisonment against Isabelle? Why or why not? What about against Trudy? Why or why not?

7. Lily enters her bedroom and falls asleep on the bed. While she is sleeping, Enid locks the door to the room. Before Lily wakens, Enid unlocks the door. Lily has a nice nap, wakes up refreshed, and goes on her way.

   Has Enid committed the tort of false imprisonment against Lily? Why or why not?

8. Gerald purchased a used army uniform from a thrift store. From time to time, he likes to dress up in the uniform and venture around town. One day, he goes to the home of a family whom he knows has a son, Brian, serving in the U.S. Army, and who is stationed in Iraq (during wartime). Gerald has no further knowledge about Brian other than that he is in the Army and serving in Iraq. Gerald rings the doorbell. Marianne, the soldier's mother, answers the door. Gerald says, "I'm very sorry, ma'am. Your son was killed in action yesterday. Please accept the condolences of the United States Army, and we thank you for your family's sacrifice to our great nation." Marianne goes into shock. In fact, Brian is safely sound asleep in his tent on the outskirts of Baghdad.

Has Gerald committed the tort of intentional infliction of emotional distress against Marianne? Why or why not?

9. William and Hilery are going through a messy divorce. Their only son, Chase, is grown and on his own, so child custody is not an issue in the divorce litigation. However, the couple has substantial marital property between them, and the fight over who gets what and how much is explosive. Fed up, Hilery makes William an offer he cannot refuse. Hilery tells William that if he will give her the house, free and clear, and three-quarters of the money in their investment and bank accounts, all in settlement of the divorce litigation, she will forego reporting to the Internal Revenue Service William's failure to report substantial amounts of income on his income taxes last year (last year, Hilery filed her own taxes, using a proper filing status—married filing separately—and correctly reporting her income). William really did commit tax fraud.

Has Hilery committed the tort of malicious prosecution or abuse of process against William? If so, which one, and why? If not, why not?

ASSIGNMENTS AND PRACTICAL **APPLICATIONS**

1. Assign to students various intentional torts against persons and ask the students to make up their own hypothetical situations for these torts, for sharing and discussing with the class. Students should consider all the essential elements of each tort when preparing their hypothetical situations.

2. Research the law in your state. Using your law library or Internet resources, determine whether your state recognizes a form of shopkeepers' privilege. If so, what does it cover? What are its limitations? Who does it protect? Review your research results in class.

3. Read, analyze, and brief the following cases involving "intent." The first involves a man who develops lung cancer after exposure to second-hand smoke. He sues a cigarette manufacturer for the tort of battery: *Shaw v. Brown & Williamson Tobacco Corp.*, 973 F. Supp. 539 (D. Md. 1997). Now, read and brief the case of *Garratt v. Dailey*, 279 P.2d 1091 (Wash. 1955). Compare and contrast the different courts' "intent" requirements for the tort of battery. For another case on "intent," this one involving an incident occurring on the field during a professional football game, read and brief *Hackbart v. Cincinnati Bengals, Inc.*, 601 F.2d 516 (10th Cir. 1979).

4. Read and brief the following battery case involving a heckling baseball spectator who was injured by a ball thrown by a Baltimore Orioles pitcher (while playing at Fenway Park against the Boston Red Sox): *Manning v. Grimsley*, 643 F.2d 20 (1st Cir. 1981).

5. What is "outrageous" enough conduct to constitute the tort of outrage? The courts find this a high standard to reach, making the tort rarely viable and used sparingly. Read and brief the cases of *Figueiredo-Torres v. Nickel*, 584 A.2d 69 (Md. 1991) (involving a psychologist treating a couple for marital problems while engaging in a sexual relationship with the wife at the same time) and *Borchers v. Hrychuk*, 727 A.2d 388 (Md.App. 1999) (involving a pastor counseling a woman on her marital problems while engaging in a sexual relationship with her). What about the situation in which a famous minister is depicted in a magazine ad as engaging in an incestuous relationship with his mother? Read and brief *Hustler Magazine v. Falwell*, 485 U.S. 46 (1988).

6. Some jurisdictions recognize the tort of negligent infliction of emotional distress. Read and brief the case of *Dillon v. Legg*, 441 P.2d 912 (Cal. 1968), involving a mother who witnessed her child being run over by an automobile and killed.

7. What constitutes "confinement" for the tort of false imprisonment? Read and brief the case of *Teichmiller v. Rogers Memorial Hospital, Inc.*, 597 N.W.2d 773 (Wis. Ct. App. 1999).

8. Some states require that the plaintiff know he is being confined in order for the tort of false imprisonment to be committed. Research whether your state has a "consciousness" requirement for false imprisonment.

9. Using the *Restatement (Second) of Torts*, research the definitions of the intentional torts of battery and assault. How are these definitions similar? How do they differ?

TECHNOLOGY RESOURCES AND INTERNET **EXERCISES**

As discussed in the chapter, in 2006, three Caucasian members of the Duke University lacrosse team were accused of rape by an African American woman who had been performing for the team at a party at the house of two of the team's captains. On April 11, 2007, North Carolina's Attorney General dropped all charges against the three, declaring them "innocent" and victims of a "tragic rush to accuse." The charges had been brought by Durham County District Attorney Mike Nifong, who was seeking reelection at the time, and who later was forced to resign and then was disbarred by the North Carolina State Bar Association for his unethical actions involving this prosecution. See *http://en.wikipedia.org/wiki/2006_Duke_University_lacrosse_case* for this interesting case of malicious prosecution.

Although contingency fees are most often used in personal injury cases, lawyers and paralegals normally bill their time based on hourly rates. In order to do this, they must keep accurate records of their time, and how much time is spent doing what tasks and for which client. In the age of technology, these records are normally kept electronically, updated at least once a day by the legal professional. Perform an Internet search for timekeeping software. Look at what the different software programs offer in terms of applications. Pay particular attention to whether the software is designed for certain professions, such as lawyers or accountants. You can "demo" the popular Timeslips legal timekeeping software via their website. See if you can input a week's worth of hypothetical timekeeping using that demo software.

ETHICAL **APPLICATIONS**

Wayne Pilar is your client. You are defending him in a tort action. In what appears to be an episode of domestic violence, Wayne's girlfriend, Clarise, was beaten up pretty badly, requiring a two-day hospital stay and ten stitches. Wayne spent a few days in the county jail as a result. Almost eight months after the incident, Clarise sued Wayne for the intentional torts of battery, assault, and false imprisonment. You have been representing Wayne in this matter for almost a year. You believe the case may go to trial within the next six months. The closer the dispute gets to litigation, the more irate Wayne appears to be over the situation. One day, in your office, Wayne declares, "I'm going to take care of this problem. I'm going to make it go away. I'm going to make Clarise go away. I have a plan on how to do it and not get caught. I know you, as my attorney, can't mention my plans to anyone because of attorney–client confidentiality, but I wanted to get this off my chest and you're a good listener. Heck, I pay you to listen to me."

Using your state's legal ethics rules, or those of the state of Maryland from the exercises in Chapter 1, answer the following questions.

Is Wayne right? Do the legal ethics rules on confidentiality require that an attorney not disclose this information? Hint: The "plan" Wayne proposes sounds like both the commission of at least one crime and at least one intentional tort—and Wayne seems to be experienced in committing intentional torts against Clarise. In the alternative, do the ethics rules require an attorney to disclose confidential information to prevent a client from committing a future crime such as this one? If so, to whom should the lawyer disclose this information? Clarise and/or the police? Could an attorney be held liable for not reporting the threat?

VIDEO **CASE STUDY**

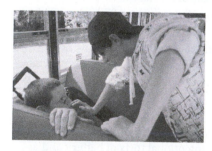

Altercation on the School Bus: Legal Duties and Liabilities

Synopsis: During a ride home from school, a student on a school bus is attacked by another student. The school bus driver gets involved, separating the students, and is injured while restraining the instigating student.

Questions

1. Has the instigating student (who is a minor) committed any intentional tort(s)?
2. Has the school bus driver committed any intentional tort(s)?
3. What are the essential elements of the torts of assault and battery, and do they apply in this case?
4. What are the essential elements of the tort of false imprisonment, and do they apply in this case?

chapter 4

INTENTIONAL TORTS AGAINST PROPERTY AND INTENTIONAL TORTS AGAINST COMMERCIAL INTERESTS

This chapter examines other types of intentional torts. First, it reviews intentional torts against property, such as trespass to land, the common law nuisance doctrine, conversion, and trespass to chattels. Then it discusses several intentional torts against commercial interests: misrepresentation, tortious interference, and the *prima facie* tort doctrine. Whereas the intentional torts discussed in Chapter 3 dealt with harms against persons, these intentional torts deal with wrongs against property and wrongs against businesses and similar commercial interests. We begin with a discussion of intentional torts against property.

Intentional Torts Against Property

Intentional torts against property are those torts in which the defendant acts purposefully to interfere with another person's rights in property. These torts can be perpetrated against real property or personal property. Keep in mind that the purpose of tort law is to protect certain interests. Among the protected interests is the right to freely enjoy one's own personal and real property.

By way of review, *real property* is land and anything permanently affixed to it, such as a house, barn, imbedded fence, or fruit tree

Intentional torts against property
Those torts in which the defendant acts purposefully to interfere with another person's rights in property.

Real property
Land and anything permanently affixed thereto.

Personal property
All property that is not real property; also called chattels.

growing on the land. *Personal property* is the residual; it is all property that is not real property, such as a computer, a shoe, or a picked flower. Another name for personal property is *chattels*.

The main intentional torts against property are trespass to land, conversion, and trespass to chattels. While not on its own a separate tort, we will discuss the common law doctrine of nuisance and how it relates to the torts against property, particularly trespass to land.

TRESPASS TO LAND

Trespass to land
Intentional and unlawful entry onto or interference with the land of another, without permission.

Trespass to land is the intentional and unlawful entry onto or interference with the land of another, without permission. The interest protected by this tort is the right to exclusive possession of land in its present physical condition. The essential elements of the tort of trespass to land are (1) an act, (2) intrusion onto land, (3) in possession of another, (4) intent to intrude on the land of another, and (5) causation. We will now discuss each of these elements, in turn.

The element of "an act" means a voluntary movement of the body that leads to the intrusion on the land. The "voluntary movement" concept is similar to that required for the intentional torts of battery and assault. To walk across another's land is such a voluntary movement, but to be pushed onto another's land during a car collision is not.

Intrusion onto the land includes going on the land of another. However, it also encompasses using an extension of the body, such as a thrown object, to enter the land of another. Further, remaining on the land without consent, even if one was initially invited onto the land, is also intrusion. Causing something to remain on the land, even if initially permitted—such as leaving a car parked on someone else's land for an extended period of time—can be intrusion. Finally, entering a prohibited portion of the land, even if entering another portion is permitted, constitutes intrusion onto the land. Trespass to land can occur, then, when a person, without permission, enters the land of another, causes something to enter the land, remains on the land, permits something to remain on the land, or enters a prohibited portion of the land.

The land must be in the possession of another. This means that the land must be actually occupied by an owner or tenant, or that another person (not the defendant) has the right to immediate occupancy. Remember that not merely owners of land have the legal right to possession. Tenants, for example, may have the lawful right to possess the land under a lease agreement.

The intent required to commit this tort is the intent to intrude on the land of another. Similar to other intentional torts, it is not the intent to cause harm or damage. There is no evil motive requirement to this intent element. Remember also that the doctrine of transferred intent, discussed in Chapter 3, applies to this tort.

Finally, the defendant must cause the intrusion onto the land of another in order to be liable for this tort. Here are some examples of the application of these elements to hypothetical situations.

The obvious way to commit the tort of trespass to land is to physically enter the land of another without permission. However, trespass to land can be committed when someone causes an object to enter the land of another. For instance, throwing your trash on another person's land constitutes trespass to

Key Point

The Essential Elements of Trespass to Land

1. An act
2. Intrusion onto land
3. In possession of another
4. Intent to intrude on the land of another
5. Causation

Key Point

Intrusion onto Land
Intrusion onto land can occur when, without permission, a person

- Enters the land of another
- Causes something to enter the land of another
- Remains on the land of another
- Permits something to remain on the land of another
- Enters a prohibited portion of the land of another

land. Trespass to land can occur when one is lawfully on another's land but then remains on the land after the permission ends. For instance, Jan is invited to Henry's house for dinner. Well after dinner, Jan simply will not leave. Finally, Henry tells Jan, "Please be on your way." Jan refuses to leave. Jan, who was initially invited onto Henry's land, becomes a trespasser to land when the consent expires and she refuses to leave Henry's real property.

In further example, because land includes a portion of the airspace above the ground, only the landowner has the right to use that airspace. Consequently, it is trespass to land to build a roof overhang that extends over the property line into your neighbor's airspace. In the same vein, a property owner is entitled to the use of space below the ground. It would therefore be trespass to land to dig a tunnel that extends into another person's underground space.

What if a person mistakenly walks across the land of another? Is such an innocent mistake still the tort of trespass to land? Courts have ruled that yes, it is, even if the mistake was reasonable. The "good faith" aspect of the conduct may reduce the damage award, but the essential elements of the tort of trespass to land are met.

Notice that a plaintiff does not have to establish that the land was harmed or damaged in any way for this tort to be committed. Damage is not an essential element of this tort, so harm to the land is not necessary. It is enough for the plaintiff to prove intrusion on the land of another in order to establish liability, although if the land is not actually harmed, the damage award may be nominal. On the other hand, if a trespasser harms the land, he can be held liable for that damage.

CASE on Point

Reeves v. Meridian S. Ry., LLC, 61 So.3d 964 (Miss. Ct. App. 2011) on the Tort of Trespass to Land

In this case Reeves alleged, among other things, that Meridian Southern Railway (Meridian) trespassed on its land when it placed railcars on a spur (a small segment of railway track that branches off from the main line) without the owner's permission. Originally, the spur was owned by Clarke County and Meridian was given an oral license to use it to store railcars. Without Reeves's knowledge, Clarke County sold the land to Rega (defendant Reeves is a shareholder of Rega). Not knowing of the sale, Meridian continued to use the spur to store its railcars.

Regarding the trespass to land claim, the court said that a trespass to land is committed when a person intentionally invades the land of another without a license or other right. It went on to say that trespass can be committed by, among other acts, placing an object on the other person's land. A trespass is committed even if the trespasser has a good faith belief that he has the right to enter the land.

Applying this law to the facts of the case, the court held that Meridian placed railcars on Rega's spur without Rega's consent. While Meridian argued that it had a good faith belief that it had the right to use the spur, the court held that this was not a defense to a trespass to land claim. Accordingly, Meridian was found to have trespassed on Rega's land by leaving its railcars on Rega's spur.

Chapter 5 examines defenses to intentional torts. In that chapter you will see that a trespasser can be removed by a landowner through the use of reasonable force. Chapter 5 also reviews remedies for successful intentional tort claims. Although damages are the typical remedy in intentional tort cases, an equitable remedy, namely, an injunction, can be an appropriate remedy in trespass to land cases involving continuing trespass if the plaintiff desires to stop the trespass rather than recover money.

Is it trespass to land if light, sound, or odor from one person's property filters over to another's? No. Courts routinely hold that such things do not constitute trespass to land. However, they may constitute a nuisance. The common law doctrine of nuisance liability is discussed next.

THE COMMON LAW TORT DOCTRINE OF NUISANCE LIABILITY

Nuisance

A common law doctrine under which persons can be held liable for using their property in a manner that unreasonably interferes with other persons' use and enjoyment of their property.

Nuisance is a common law tort doctrine under which persons can be held liable for using their property in a manner that unreasonably interferes with other persons' use and enjoyment of their own property. Although we are discussing the nuisance doctrine as part of intentional torts against land, note that nuisance may also result from conduct that is merely negligent, meaning unreasonable, such as when there is no intent to interfere with the plaintiff's use and enjoyment of his land, but rather there is failure of another party to take reasonable precautions to prevent such interference. An example of an intentional nuisance is the dumping of pollutants into a public waterway. An example of a negligent nuisance is carelessly allowing a public building to deteriorate to the point that it becomes unsafe. The materials at the end of this chapter include two cases illustrating the difference between intentionally and negligently caused nuisance liability.

A nuisance cause of action can be brought when the defendant's conduct results in unreasonable interference with other persons' use and enjoyment of land. Nuisance situations commonly involve the leaking of substances, such as liquids, odors, or fumes, from one person's property onto her neighbor's property. There are two types of nuisance actions, private nuisance and public nuisance.

Private nuisance

Unreasonable interference with another's interest in the private use and enjoyment of his or her land.

Private nuisance is the unreasonable interference in another's interest in the private use and enjoyment of land. It is essentially a wrong committed against an owner or lawful possessor of land. Private nuisance is distinguished from trespass, however, because it does not require any type of physical entry onto the plaintiff's land, though private nuisance may accompany such a trespass to land. The interference can occur in a variety of ways. For example, it can be interference with the physical condition of the premises, such as by conducting blasting activities on adjacent land. It can be interference with a health condition, such as maintaining unsanitary conditions on adjacent property. It can be an inconvenience, such as odor emissions or noise emanating from adjoining property. It can be interference with comfort, such as by operating a drug trafficking establishment on adjoining property. All of these interferences constitute private, rather than public, nuisances, because the land interest interfered with is that of a private person or entity.

On the other hand, ***public nuisance*** is unreasonable interference with a right that is common to the general public. Examples of public nuisance include obstructing public lands, polluting a public waterway, and maintaining unsafe public buildings. Causes of action for public nuisance are normally reserved to government, while private nuisance actions may be instituted by private persons. Historically, for a public nuisance to justify relief in tort, the conduct must also have constituted a crime. See the following Case on Point for an example. Over time, however, public nuisance law has evolved, in large part because of the concern for environmental protection, to define public nuisance broadly, in terms of an interference with a right that is common to the general public. Whether the conduct violates a criminal statute is only one factor in determining whether there is an unreasonable interference. Other factors can include whether the conduct involves a substantial interference with public health, public safety, public peace, public comfort, or public convenience. Today in the United States, many legislatures have enacted criminal statutes covering public nuisances as well, such as statutes making it a crime to pollute the environment or to operate a building where illegal drugs are traded. Conduct that constitutes a private nuisance may also constitute a public nuisance, such as when it interferes with someone's private use and enjoyment of his land and also constitutes a crime, such as operating a house of prostitution on adjoining land.

Public nuisance
Unreasonable interference with a right that is common to the general public.

CASE on Point

Pope v. Edward M. Rude Carrier Corp., 75 S.E.2d 584 (W. Va. 1953)

This case involved injury caused by an explosion that occurred when dynamite was transported by a contract carrier over a public highway. The injured plaintiff sued the carrier using the theory of public nuisance, among other theories. The plaintiff argued that the transportation of dynamite on a public highway by a licensed contract carrier constituted a public nuisance. However, the court disagreed.

In defining the term "nuisance," the court said that it applied to "that class of wrongs which arises from the unreasonable, unwarrantable, or unlawful use by a person of his own property and produces such material annoyance, inconvenience, discomfort, or hurt that the law will presume a consequent damage." Further, the court noted that "[p]ublic nuisances always arise out of unlawful acts, and that which is lawful, or is authorized by a valid statute, or which the public convenience imperatively demands, cannot be a public nuisance."

In applying those rules to the facts of the case, the court noted that this transport was by a licensed contract carrier under "an act of Congress and pursuant to regulations of the Interstate Commerce Commission, and under the laws of this State." Further, the court reasoned the carrier had the right to receive and transport, by motor vehicle on the public highways, the dynamite that it was transporting at the time of the explosion. Because the manufacture and shipment of dynamite and its transportation by common carrier "are lawful and essential business enterprises" and that "[h]igh explosives, such as dynamite, are valuable, important and necessary articles of commerce and industry," the court found there was no public nuisance.

Key Point

Factors That Courts Consider in Making Nuisance Determinations

- The location and type of neighborhood in which the property is located
- The nature of the acts resulting in the interference
- The frequency of the interference
- Whether the interference is continuing and ongoing
- The burden on the plaintiff and/or defendant to minimize or avoid the interference
- The defendant's motive
- The nature and severity of the resulting damage or annoyance

Conversion

Intentional exercise of dominion and control over another's personal property which seriously interferes with the owner or possessor's right to possession.

Key Point

The Essential Elements of Conversion

1. Personal property/chattel
2. That the plaintiff is in possession of the chattel or is entitled to immediate possession
3. Intent to exercise dominion or control over the chattel
4. Serious interference with the plaintiff's possession
5. Causation

With both private and public nuisance, the interference must be *unreasonable*. Courts consider several factors in determining whether an interference is unreasonable. The factors include the location and type of neighborhood in which the property is located, the nature of the acts resulting in the interference, the frequency of the interference, whether the interference is continuing and ongoing, the burden on the plaintiff and/or defendant to minimize or avoid the interference, the defendant's motive, and the nature and severity of the resulting damage or annoyance.

In distinguishing between the common law doctrine of nuisance and trespass to land, remember that the tort of trespass to land protects one's interest in the exclusive right to possession of land. Nuisance, in contrast, protects against unreasonable interference with a person's interest in the reasonable use and enjoyment of his or her own land. The same conduct may result in both trespass to land and nuisance, though the interests invaded are different.

The other intentional torts against property involve personal, not real, property. The most serious of these torts against personal property is conversion.

CONVERSION

Conversion is the intentional exercise of dominion and control over another's personal property which seriously interferes with the owner's or possessor's right to possession. The interest protected by this tort is the right to be free from serious intentional interferences with one's personal property. Conversion is a substantial interference with the plaintiff's use or possession of his personal property. You will see, when trespass to chattels is discussed, that these two torts are very similar. The difference between them is the degree of seriousness of the interference. The essential elements of the tort of conversion are (1) personal property, (2) that the plaintiff is in possession of the personal property or is entitled to immediate possession, (3) intent to exercise dominion or control over the personal property, (4) serious interference with the plaintiff's possession, and (5) causation.

Conversion is a tort involving personal property, also called chattels. Note that it is not a real property tort. In reviewing the essential elements, also notice that damage to the property is not necessary for this tort to be committed. Here are the tort's requirements.

The plaintiff must be in possession of the chattel or be entitled to immediate possession. The plaintiff may be the owner of the chattel. However, the tort is not limited to being committed against personal property owners. Someone who is not the owner but is legally entitled to possession, such as a lessee under a car lease, may be the plaintiff in a conversion action. The defendant must intend to exercise dominion or control over the property. Intent to harm the property is not necessary. Dominion and control means exerting complete power and authority over the object. The defendant's actions must constitute *serious interference* with the plaintiff's possession. With the tort of conversion, the defendant's interference is of such a serious nature and degree that the plaintiff is fully deprived of the ownership and possession rights in that property, and the defendant converts the property to his own use. In determining the seriousness of the interference, sometimes called a taking, courts look at several factors. These factors include

- The extent and duration of the taking (the more substantial the interference, and the longer its duration, the more likely the tort is conversion rather than trespass to chattels, which is discussed below)
- Whether the defendant intended to assert a right in the property that was inconsistent with the plaintiff's rights in ownership or possession (a factor favoring the more serious tort of conversion)
- Whether the defendant acted in bad faith (lending the determination toward conversion, whereas good faith acts by the defendant favor a trespass to chattels determination, as discussed below)
- Whether the interference resulted in damage or harm to the property (a factor weighing in favor of conversion)
- Whether the plaintiff suffered expense or inconvenience as a result of the defendant's interference with the property (another factor weighing in favor of conversion, especially the greater the expense or inconvenience)

Again, the more serious the interference, the more likely it is that the tort of conversion has been committed. The less serious the interference, the more likely it is that the tort of trespass to chattels, discussed in the next section, has been committed. Consider this example. Joan watched Lucy park her bicycle at the school's bike rack. After Lucy walked away, Joan removed the bike from the rack. Then Joan put the bike in the back of her truck and drove it to a bike shop. There, she sold the bike to the shop for $45. Joan committed the tort of conversion, not trespass to chattels. By taking the bike and selling it to a third party, she exerted dominion and control over Lucy's chattel and significantly interfered with Lucy's ownership rights in the property. This is a clear case of "substantial interference."

CASE on Point

Reeves v. Meridian S. Ry., LLC, 61 So.3d 964 (Miss. Ct. App. 2011) on the Tort of Conversion

In this case, already discussed in the section on trespass to land, Reeves also alleged that Meridian committed the tort of conversion by converting a railroad spur by using the spur to store railcars on. Regarding the conversion claim, the court said there is a conversion when there is an intent to exercise dominion and control over goods that is inconsistent with the true owner's right. It defined the tort of conversion as an intentional exercise of dominion and control over personal property that so seriously interferes with the right of another to control that property that the tortfeasor may justly be required to pay the other the full value of the property.

Applying that definition to these facts, the court held that there was no conversion. It determined that the spur was a fixture—so it was part of realty, meaning real property (because it was something permanently affixed to the land). Since the spur was real property, not personal property, it could not be converted.

What if Joan had a bike that was almost identical to Lucy's? When Joan took the bike to the bike shop and sold it, she honestly believed the bike was hers, though it really was Lucy's. Did Joan convert Lucy's bike? Probably not. Still, Joan had no legal right to take Lucy's bike. Therefore, Joan's conduct may still be a tortious interference, even if it is not conversion. Is it a valid defense that Joan, honestly and in good faith, believed the bike was her own? No. In these cases, mistake is not a defense, nor is acting in good faith. However, both are factors considered by the court in determining the seriousness of the defendant's interference. Thus, they affect whether the court determines the tort committed to be conversion or trespass to chattels. In this scenario, because of the presence of these factors that tend to lessen the seriousness of the taking or interference, it is more likely that the tort of trespass to chattels was committed. Trespass to chattels is examined next.

TRESPASS TO CHATTELS

Trespass to chattels
Intentional dispossession or intermeddling by the defendant with the plaintiff's right to use or possession of personal property.

Trespass to chattels is the intentional dispossession or intermeddling by the defendant with the plaintiff's right to use or possession of personal property. It is similar to the tort of conversion, discussed above. However, it involves a less serious interference with property than does the tort of conversion.

The interest protected by this tort is the right to be free from intentional interference with one's personal property that results in dispossession or intermeddling. The essential elements of the tort of trespass to chattels are (1) personal property, (2) that the plaintiff is in possession of the chattel or is entitled to immediate possession, (3) intent to dispossess or to intermeddle with the chattel, (4) dispossession or intermeddling, (5) causation, and (6) damages (most, not all, courts require). Note the similarities, and differences, in the essential elements for the tort of trespass to chattels and the tort of conversion.

This tort, like conversion, is a tort involving personal property. For the commission of this tort, the defendant must intentionally dispossess or intermeddle with the plaintiff's property, interfering with the plaintiff's right to use or possession. What distinguishes this tort from conversion is the degree of the defendant's interference. For the tort of conversion, the defendant must exercise complete dominion and control over the plaintiff's property. For trespass to chattels, something less is required—namely, dispossession or intermeddling. Dispossession means taking physical control and possession over the property without the rightful possessor's consent, stopping short of exercising dominion over it. Intermeddling is the defendant's wrongful contact and interference with the property, but again, something less than a complete exercise of dominion and control over it.

Consider this example. Joan sees Lilly's bike parked at the school's bike rack. While Lilly is away, and without her permission, Joan takes Lilly's bike for a quiet ride around campus. About a half-hour later, after riding over some glass that causes a flat tire, Joan returns the bike to the rack. Two hours later, Lilly returns for her bike and walks it home. Does Joan's act constitute the tort of trespass to chattels? The unauthorized use of the bike may be sufficient interference to constitute this tort. The use of the bike for a "joy ride" (and causing a flat tire)

Key Point

The Essential Elements of Trespass to Chattels

1. Personal property/chattel
2. That the plaintiff is in possession of the chattel or is entitled to immediate possession
3. Intent to dispossess or to intermeddle with the chattel
4. Dispossession or intermeddling
5. Causation
6. Damages (most, but not all, courts require)

CASE on Point

Jamgotchian v. Slender, 170 Cal. App. 4th 1384, 89 Cal. Rptr. 3d 122 (Cal. Ct. App. 2009)

In this case, the owner of a racehorse brought an action for trespass to chattels against a racing steward (the person in charge of a horse race and track) and the horse's trainer. The owner alleged that the steward refused to allow the owner to remove his horse, named JKG, from the racetrack grounds. Then the steward and the trainer raced the owner's horse against the owner's express instructions. JKG injured her front foot running the race, causing her to be lame.

Regarding the tort of trespass to chattels, the court said that this tort allows recovery for interferences with possession of personal property not sufficiently important to be classed as conversion, calling the tort the "little brother of conversion." For the tort to be committed, the defendant's interference must cause some injury to the chattel or to the plaintiff's rights in it. California law permits liability for trespass to chattels where there is an intentional interference with the possession of personal property that proximately causes injury. In such cases, the owner of the property may recover only the actual damages suffered by reason of the impairment of the property or its loss of use. Quoting the *Restatement (Second) of Torts*, the court said that a trespass to chattels may be committed either by intentionally dispossessing another of the chattel or by intentionally using or intermeddling with the chattel in the possession of another; dispossession can be committed by intentionally barring the possessor's access to the chattel.

Applying the facts of the case to the law, the court found that a triable issue of fact existed as to whether the steward's conduct in preventing the owner from removing his horse from the racetrack grounds was a substantial factor in causing the owner's harm (a horse is considered personal property of its owner). The court reasoned that if the horse had been removed from the grounds, a feat the owner tried diligently to accomplish but the steward effectively blocked through use of security, the horse would not have been raced and injured.

is probably not a serious enough interference or taking to constitute the tort of conversion, however.

Note that under the essential elements, the defendant need not intend to harm the property; the intent required for this tort is the intent to dispossess or intermeddle. However, note that most, but not all, courts hold that damages are an essential element of this tort. This is unlike the tort of conversion, for which there is no damage requirement. Although the defendant need not intend to damage the property, many courts hold that for the plaintiff to recover for this tort, the defendant's interference must result in some damage to or loss of the property. Remember from Chapter 3 that the doctrine of transferred intent applies to this intentional tort, but not to the tort of conversion.

Now that we have reviewed the intentional torts against property, we will discuss the last major group of intentional torts. These are the intentional torts against commercial interests. We will begin with an examination of the tort of misrepresentation.

Misrepresentation

Misrepresentation, also called *fraudulent misrepresentation*, *fraud*, or the *tort of fraud or deceit*, is the intentional making of a material false statement, or the failure to disclose when a duty to disclose exists, which causes the plaintiff a pecuniary (financial) loss. The interest protected by this tort is the right to be free from pecuniary loss caused by another's false statement(s) or omission(s). The essential elements of the tort of misrepresentation are the intentional making of a material false statement of a fact, or nondisclosure when there is a duty to disclose, on which the plaintiff justifiably relies, causing her damages.

The essence of this tort is making a false statement of material fact. The statement can be made expressly, in words, such as by stating, "The car has 13,542 miles on it," when the car has in fact been driven more than 20,000 miles. The statement need not be express, however. It may be implied as a result of a person's actions, such as by turning back the odometer on a used car. It may also be implied by nonverbal communication, as by a gesture such as an affirmative nod of the head that the used car offered for sale was never involved in an accident, when it had been in three. See the *Salzman* Case on Point, later in this chapter, which illustrates misrepresentation through actions rather than words.

The statement must be one of fact, not merely an opinion. A **statement of fact** is a statement that can be objectively verified (proven), such as, "That automobile is a 2007 model." A **statement of opinion** is a vague statement, or value judgment, that is not objectively verifiable, such as, "That car is the best used car on the lot." Facts contain objective terms, while opinions contain more subjective ones.

For misrepresentation to be committed, more than seller's talk, called sales puffery, must be involved. **Sales puffery** is that "sales talk" engaged in by a salesperson, often exaggerating the good qualities of the item offered for sale, in order to induce the sale. These types of statements are not considered actionable misstatements. This is so because prospective buyers cannot justifiably rely on them in making buying decisions, as they are known exaggerations. Note, however, that a statement of opinion may constitute misrepresentation if the opinion giver possesses superior knowledge of the subject matter, such as when an accountant gives an opinion regarding a company's financial statements.

The statement must be material, meaning "significant" in the decision-making process, for misrepresentation to occur. In other words, it must be basic to the transaction. The concepts of materiality and justifiable reliance, which will be examined shortly, are related.

To be a misrepresentation, the statement must be false. A false statement is one that is not true, obviously. Not so obviously, it can also be a misleading, ambiguous, or incomplete statement and be actionable misrepresentation. If the statement of fact is true, however, there is no fraud.

Sometimes, failure to disclose—in other words, concealment—can constitute misrepresentation. This is so even though no "statement" has been made. Failure to disclose occurs when a person owes a duty to disclose some fact to another, and does not disclose it. For instance, a seller of a house, when asked

---

Misrepresentation
The intentional making of a material false statement, or the failure to disclose when a duty to disclose exists, which causes the plaintiff a pecuniary loss; also called fraudulent misrepresentation, fraud, or the tort of fraud or deceit.

Statement of fact
A statement that can be objectively verified (proven), as distinguished from a statement of opinion.

Statement of opinion
A vague statement or value judgment that is not objectively verifiable, as distinguished from a statement of fact.

Sales puffery
The sales talk engaged in by salespersons in order to induce a sale.

Key Point

The Essential Elements of Misrepresentation

1. A false statement of material fact, or nondisclosure when a duty to disclose exists
2. Made with the intent to induce the plaintiff's reliance
3. Justifiable reliance by the plaintiff
4. Causation
5. Damages

by a prospective buyer whether the house is structurally sound, might wish to say nothing if, in fact, there is a major crack in the house's foundation. However, such fraudulent concealment may constitute misrepresentation if the rest of the essential elements of the tort are met. That said, a duty to disclose does not automatically arise in all situations. Only if there is a duty to disclose may silence constitute misrepresentation. When, then, is there a duty to disclose?

A duty to disclose normally arises in fiduciary relationships, such as those between business partners, spouses, doctors and patients, and lawyers and clients. It also arises when one party to a transaction specifically asks the other party to the transaction a question regarding a material fact related to the transaction. For example, a prospective car buyer may ask a used car salesperson, "Has this vehicle ever been involved in an accident?" The salesperson may not have owed a duty to disclose this information absent some other law requiring disclosure, but once she has been asked this question of material fact by a prospective purchaser, a duty to disclose arises. The salesperson should answer the question truthfully to avoid committing the tort of fraud. Also, if there is a latent defect in the property that is known to the seller, a duty to disclose exists. Consider the example above regarding the major crack in the foundation of the house offered for sale. That defect, if a latent one—meaning it is not obvious to a prospective buyer—and if known to the seller, gives rise to a duty of the seller to disclose it. If a duty to disclose exists, the person owing the duty must make a truthful statement regarding the matter; otherwise he has committed misrepresentation so long as the other essential elements of the tort are present.

Because misrepresentation is an intentional tort, the defendant must intend to induce the plaintiff's reliance. This means that the defendant must want the plaintiff to believe the statement or rely on the omission, and to act, or refrain from acting, based on that belief.

Although misrepresentation is an intentional tort, some jurisdictions also recognize a tort of negligent misrepresentation. The tort of negligent misrepresentation, where it is recognized, involves unreasonably made false statements; the "intent" element is lacking. These cases involve defendants who make false statements or omissions carelessly, for example, by not taking reasonable precautions to confirm the accuracy of their statements before making them to the plaintiff.

SIDEBAR

NEGLIGENT MISREPRESENTATION

Some jurisdictions recognize a tort of negligent misrepresentation. Its essential elements are that the defendant, in the course of his business, profession, or employment, makes a false statement, believing it is true but without reasonable grounds for his belief, on which the plaintiff justifiably relies and which causes her injury. Note that if the false statement leads to physical harm, such as injury to the plaintiff's person, a traditional negligence action may be brought. However, if only pecuniary loss results (such as when a painting's value is not as high as promised by the seller), then many states permit the plaintiff to sue for negligent misrepresentation.

For there to be fraud, the plaintiff must rely on the defendant's false statement or omission. Reliance by the plaintiff means that the plaintiff must take action, or refrain from acting, because of the false statement or omission. Consider this example. A home inspector, after being engaged by a prospective purchaser to perform an inspection of a home, tells the prospective purchaser he sees no major problems with the home's electrical system. The prospective purchaser is likely to rely on that statement in considering whether to purchase the house.

What if the home inspector was engaged by the seller, not the prospective purchaser? After the seller's inspection, the prospective purchaser hires her own inspector and has her own inspection performed. The prospective purchaser relies on the results of her inspection in making a purchase decision. If the seller's inspector makes a false statement, it may not be actionable fraud if the prospective purchaser does not rely on it—if, instead, she relies on the statement made by her own inspector.

For a plaintiff to rely on the statement, the statement must be material—meaning significant—to her decision making. For example, a false statement that a car was manufactured in Florida when it was in fact manufactured in Georgia probably is not material to the prospective purchaser, though whether it was made in the United States or a foreign country may be material to her purchase decision.

For there to be misrepresentation, reliance by the plaintiff must be justifiable. This means that the plaintiff's reliance must be reasonable given the facts

CASE on Point

Salzman v. Maldaver, 24 N.W.2d 161 (Mich. 1946)

The parties to this case were both dealers in aluminum. The plaintiffs were buyers obtaining aluminum to resell to manufacturers of aluminum products. The defendants operated a salvage company and had purchased certain scrap aluminum from the Ford Motor Company. The parties entered into a contract whereby the plaintiffs agreed to purchase a surplus lot of aluminum sheets from the defendants for a certain price per pound.

The buyers brought this action against the sellers for the tort of deceit and fraud. The buyers alleged that the sellers knew the aluminum sheets were corroded and damaged and deceived the buyers by bundling the sheets with an undamaged sheet on top, to cover corroded and damaged sheets beneath. Thus, they alleged that the sellers misrepresented the quality and condition of the aluminum being sold.

The Supreme Court of Michigan agreed. It said, "[T]he defendants knew the aluminum sheets stored in the warehouse were damaged and corroded and that, for the purpose of deceiving and defrauding plaintiffs, they had placed a good, or undamaged, sheet on the top of each bundle of corroded and damaged sheets." The court found that the plaintiffs had properly stated a cause of action for deceit and fraud.

Note that, in this case, the defendants committed misrepresentation through actions, not words, by hiding the corroded and damaged aluminum inside bundles.

and circumstances. Consider this example. A salesperson tells a prospective customer, "You should buy as many of our everlasting batteries as possible, because the sun is going to burn out before the end of this year." The customer, who happens to be prone to paranoia, relies on the statement and buys the salesperson's entire inventory of everlasting batteries. The plaintiff's reliance on the salesperson's ridiculous statement is not justifiable, hence there is no misrepresentation.

Recall the discussion of sales puffery. Sales puffery does not constitute misrepresentation because customers do not take these statements seriously; no consumer can justifiably rely on seller's talk in making a purchase decision, as such statements are known and expected exaggerations.

For there to be misrepresentation, the plaintiff's justifiable reliance on the material statement of fact or omission must cause her damages, the final two essential elements of this tort. The causation element means that there must be a causal link or connection between the false statement and the injury suffered. Further, actual damages must be suffered as a result of the plaintiff's reliance on the false statement or omission. Courts normally allow recovery for injury to persons or property caused by the misrepresentation, including the possibility of punitive damages because this is an intentional tort (remedies for intentional torts are discussed more fully in the next chapter).

Misrepresentation is one tort against commercial interests. Tortious interference is another. We examine tortious interference next.

Tortious Interference

Tortious interference is harm that is intentionally caused to a plaintiff's contractual or other business relationships. The tort of tortious interference was first established in the old English case entitled *Keeble v. Hickeringill* (see the Case on Point).

There are different types of tortious interference. One type specifically involves contractual relationships and is called tortious interference with a contractual relationship. The contractual relationship may or may not be a business relationship. Another type of tortious interference involves business relationships or activities that do not involve a contract; that tort is called tortious interference with a business relationship. Still another type of tortious interference is tortious interference with employment. We examine the first of these, tortious interference with a contractual relationship, next.

TORTIOUS INTERFERENCE WITH A CONTRACTUAL RELATIONSHIP

Tortious interference with a contractual relationship occurs when a tortfeasor induces a party to breach its contract with the plaintiff, or otherwise disrupts the party's performance under the contract, causing the plaintiff harm.

The essential elements of tortious interference with a contractual relationship require intentional interference with an existing contract that causes damage to the plaintiff. Note that the defendant must know about the existence of the contract between the parties in order to commit this tort.

Tortious interference
Harm caused intentionally to a plaintiff's contractual or other business relationships.

Tortious interference with a contractual relationship
When a tortfeasor induces a party to breach its contract with the plaintiff, or otherwise disrupts the party's performance under the contract, causing the plaintiff harm.

Key Point

The Essential Elements of Tortious Interference with a Contractual Relationship

1. A valid, enforceable contract between two or more parties
2. The defendant knows of the existence of the contract
3. Interference with that contract by the defendant
4. Intent to interfere with the contractual relationship
5. Damages
6. Causation

CASE on Point

Keeble v. Hickeringill, 103 Eng. Rep. 1127 (1707)

The plaintiff had built a pond as part of establishing a duck hunting business. The defendant was a business competitor of the plaintiff. The defendant, inspired purely by malice, fired shotguns to frighten ducks away from the plaintiff's pond in order to prevent the plaintiff (and his customers) from being able to hunt them. Although the ducks were wild, the court found that "where a violent or malicious act is done to a man's occupation, profession, or way of getting a livelihood, there an action lies in all cases." The court noted that the defendant would have the right to draw ducks away, to a pond of his own. It raised as a comparison a case in which a schoolmaster opened a new school that drew students away from an existing school, and no cause of action was found to exist. However, as in this case, if the motivation is mere malice, the otherwise proper act becomes tortious.

The first element requires that there be a valid, enforceable contract in existence. The contract can be between two or more parties, but the defendant is not a party to it. The contract cannot violate public policy or otherwise be unenforceable.

The second element is the requirement that the defendant know about the existence of the contract. It is not tortious interference with a contractual relationship if the defendant does not know about the existence of the contract, though it could be the second type of tortious interference tort, discussed in the next section.

The defendant must interfere with that contractual relationship, according to the third element. She can do this by inducing a party to breach the contract. She can also do this by making it very difficult, or even impossible, for a party to perform his obligations under the contract.

The defendant must intend to interfere with the contractual relationship. The fourth element of this tort is the "intent" element. It is not tortious interference with a contractual relationship if the defendant accidentally interferes with another's contract. Nor is it this tort if the defendant negligently, meaning unreasonably, interferes with another's contract. The interference must be intentional: The defendant must act either knowing her conduct will result in the desired interference, or with substantial certainty that the desired interference will result.

Finally, the last two elements of this tort require that the defendant's interference actually cause the plaintiff damages. Actual damages must be established by the plaintiff, but they can be nominal. Punitive damages may be awarded if the facts and circumstances warrant, as this is an intentional tort.

Consider this example. Lyle entered into a contract with Mercedes to paint her home this week, in time for an open house planned for next week, when Mercedes lists her home for sale. Kristin wants Lyle to do some painting at her home before the weekend, when Kristin will be hosting a holiday party. Kristin knows about the contract between Lyle and Mercedes. Kristin offers Lyle $500 more than Mercedes is paying to get Lyle to paint her house this week, instead

CASE on Point

Lumley v. Gye, 118 Eng. Rep. 749 (Q.B. 1853)

This early English case involved tortious interference with a contractual relationship between the plaintiff, who was the manager of the Queens Theatre, where operas were performed, and a singer named Johanna Wagner. Wagner was to perform in the Queens Theatre for a designated time, and she agreed not to perform elsewhere during the term of the contract. The defendant, who ran Covent Garden, a competing venue, knew of the contract and its commitments, promised to pay Wagner more, and "enticed and procured Wagner to refuse to perform."

The court phrased the issue as, "Whether an action will lie by the proprietor of a theatre against a person who maliciously procures an entire abandonment of a contract to perform exclusively at that theatre for a certain time; whereby damage was sustained?" "[I]t seems to me that it will," the court held, reasoning that "an action will lie by a master against a person who procures that a servant should unlawfully leave his service."

of Mercedes's house. Lyle accepts Kristin's offer and paints her house, instead of Mercedes's house, this week.

In terms of contract law, Lyle may well have breached his contract with Mercedes to paint her house this week, depending on the terms of their agreement, especially the termination provision. In addition to the breach of contract action between Mercedes and Lyle, Kristin tortiously interfered with Lyle and Mercedes's contractual relationship. Kristin knew about the contract, intentionally induced Lyle to breach it, and thereby caused damage to Mercedes, who either would not have her house painted in time for the open house or would have to find another painter, and quickly!

Note that a breach of contract action may be brought by the nonbreaching party to the contract. That is a separate and distinct legal action from the tort action the nonbreaching party to the contract can bring against the party interfering with that contract by inducing its breach or nonperformance.

Sometimes a person interferes with the business or activity of another, but there is no underlying contract between two or more parties involving that business or activity. Such a situation is not tortious interference with a contractual relationship because there is no contract with which the defendant interferes. Rather, it may be tortious interference with a business relationship, which is examined next.

TORTIOUS INTERFERENCE WITH A BUSINESS RELATIONSHIP

Tortious interference with a business relationship occurs when a tortfeasor interferes with a business or activity of another, causing harm. Unlike tortious interference with a contractual relationship, an underlying contract between the plaintiff and a third party is not present.

Tortious interference with a business relationship
When a tortfeasor interferes with a business or activity of another, causing harm.

Key Point

The Essential Elements of Tortious Interference with a Business Relationship

1. A reasonable expectation by the plaintiff of economic advantage through a business or activity
2. Interference with that business or activity by the defendant
3. Intent to interfere with the plaintiff's business or activity
4. Damages
5. Causation

For this tort, and in many other areas of law, the law distinguishes free competition from predatory behavior and other forms of unfair competition. Because predatory behavior and unfair competition unlawfully harm the marketplace and marketplace competitors, this tort is among the laws that encourage fair competition. Accordingly, interference with a business relationship that is unfair and anticompetitive may be tortious.

The essential elements of tortious interference with a business relationship are almost identical to those of the tort of tortious interference with a contractual relationship. Where they differ is the requirements that there be a valid, enforceable contract about which the defendant knows. Those elements are replaced with the element that there be a reasonable expectation of economic advantage through a business or activity. When this tort is committed, the defendant has unreasonably interfered with the plaintiff's reasonable expectation of economic benefit expected to be derived from a business or activity.

Consider the following examples. The defendant opens a snowball (a frozen treat) stand on his property, which is located directly next to the plaintiff's property. The plaintiff already operates a snowball stand on his property. The defendant's conduct, though likely to hurt the plaintiff's business, is conduct that constitutes fair, competitive marketplace behavior, offering greater supply and driving snowball prices down, for the benefit of snowball consumers.

However, what if the defendant desires to take over the land on which the plaintiff operates his snowball stand? To achieve this objective, the defendant threatens the plaintiff's prospective customers, driving them away. The defendant's behavior constitutes tortious interference with a business relationship, namely, the relationship the plaintiff has with his customers and prospective customers. Determining whether there are damages, and if so, the extent of them, is the issue, for these damages can be speculative. Because the plaintiff had no contractual right to the benefit, such as a contractual right to a sale of a snowball, at the time of the defendant's interference, establishing that the defendant actually caused harm to the plaintiff, and the extent of that harm, can be problematic.

CASE on Point

Tuttle v. Buck, 119 N.W. 946 (Minn. 1909)

In this early case of tortious interference with a business relationship, a wealthy and influential banker established a barber shop in order to lure customers from the plaintiff's barber shop. He did this not for any legitimate purpose of his own, but for the sole purpose of maliciously injuring the plaintiff. He accomplished his objective. As a result of the defendant's actions, after more than ten years in prosperous business, the plaintiff's barber shop was forced to close.

The Supreme Court of Minnesota said, "When a man starts an opposition place of business, not for the sake of profit to himself, but regardless of loss to himself, and for the sole purpose of driving his competitor out of business, and with the intention of himself retiring upon the accomplishment of his malevolent purpose, he is guilty of a wanton wrong and an actionable tort."

Another type of tortious interference involves employment relationships. Tortious interference with employment is examined next.

TORTIOUS INTERFERENCE WITH EMPLOYMENT

Tortious interference with employment is the taking of adverse employment action by an employer, in violation of the law. This tort is also known as wrongful discharge when employment termination is involved. However, the interference could involve adverse employment actions not related to termination, such as interfering in order to prevent another's promotion or to sabotage someone's being hired.

If an employee and an employer have a contractual relationship, the terms of the contract govern termination and other aspects of employment. However, most employment relationships are "at will." This means that the employer and/or the employee can terminate the relationship at any time, for any reason, other than for an illegal reason, such as discrimination or retaliation.

If an employee suffers an adverse employment action, such as demotion or termination, in violation of the law, such as when discrimination or retaliation is involved, then she may have a claim of tortious interference with employment against her employer.

This tort differs from the other tortious interference torts, however. In the other tortious interference torts, a third party is interfering, either with a contractual relationship or with another's business or activity. Distinguishingly, with tortious interference with employment, there is no third party interfering with the employment relationship; rather, the employer itself is acting wrongfully in taking an adverse employment action. However, there may be a third party interference (see the Case on Point for an example).

> **Tortious interference with employment**
> The taking of adverse employment action by an employer, in violation of the law.

CASE on Point

McNett v Worthington, 2011 WL 4790759 (Ohio Ct. App. 2011)

In this case, McNett, a terminated employee, brought an action for defamation and interference with an employment relationship against a former coworker, Worthington. McNett alleged that Worthington made false statements about him to coworkers and management of their employer, leading to his termination from employment.

The court said that the essential elements of a claim of tortious interference with an employment relationship are (1) the existence of an employment relationship between the plaintiff and the employer, (2) the defendant was aware of the relationship, (3) the defendant intentionally interfered with the relationship, and (4) the plaintiff was injured as a proximate result of the defendant's acts.

Applying the facts of the case to these elements, the court found that Worthington's statements made to management personnel were privileged because he had a right to report his concerns. Further, the court found that McNett failed to prove that Worthington's statements were the proximate cause of his employment termination.

The *Prima Facie* Tort Doctrine

The **prima facie tort doctrine** is a catch-all tort doctrine covering certain intentional misconduct that does not fit the essential elements of the other recognized intentional torts. It is not recognized in most jurisdictions. However, a few jurisdictions, and in particular, New York, which carefully developed the doctrine in its case law, have adopted it, also via case law, to provide a tort remedy when an intentional lawful act is committed with the intent to injure another. Where it has been adopted, the application of this tort has generally been limited to protecting economic interests.

The tort was first recognized by the Supreme Court in the case of *Aikens v. Wisconsin*, 195 U.S. 194 (1904). In that case, Justice Oliver Wendell Holmes, Jr., conceptualized the *prima facie* tort doctrine when he opined, "*Prima facie*, the intentional infliction of temporal damages is a cause of action which as a matter of substantive law, whatever may be the form of the pleading, requires a justification if the defendant is to escape."

The essential elements of the *prima facie* tort require the intentional infliction of harm, which causes special damages.

In applying these essential elements, many courts require that the defendant act maliciously, rather than merely intentionally, adding a "bad faith" requirement beyond what is normally required of intentional torts—that is, the defendant must intend the harm, not merely intend to commit the act. Early New York case law on this doctrine restricted its application to cases in which malice was the sole motivation for the act, but today, jurisdictions that recognize this tort take the approach of the *Restatement (Second) of Torts*. In doing so, they balance the defendant's bad motivation in performing the act that caused the injury against the defendant's claimed justification for the act in determining whether the act's societal value outweighed the defendant's wrongful motive in attempting to injure the plaintiff. See the following Case on Point for an illustration of this application.

Besides bad motivation by the defendant, special damages must be proved by the plaintiff in establishing a *prima facie* tort claim in many jurisdictions that recognize this tort. Special damages, defined fully in the next chapter, are based on measurable dollar amounts of actual loss, such as medical expenses paid. So, although the jurisdictions that recognize this tort doctrine mean to provide a

SIDEBAR

THE *PRIMA FACIE* TORT DOCTRINE IS NOT RECOGNIZED IN ALL JURISDICTIONS

Most jurisdictions consider that the problems involved in defining both this tort and its defenses outweigh its benefits. Rather, these jurisdictions prefer to expand the boundaries of their existing torts, when possible, to "catch" more types of wrongful conduct. The *Restatement (Second) of Torts*, section 870 and its comments, sets forth the considerations that should be balanced by a court in determining whether to declare a new cause of action for the *prima facie* tort doctrine or to extend the boundaries of an existing tort action.

remedy for certain intentional acts that do not fit within the other intentional tort theories, they do not mean for it to apply to all wrongful conduct that is not "caught" by the other torts. Rather, this conduct must be committed maliciously, and special damages must be suffered. If these items, as well as the other essential elements (infliction of harm and causation) are not present, then even this catch-all tort will not "catch" the misconduct.

A defendant may defend a *prima facie* tort action by demonstrating that his act was justified. Justification is a valid defense to this tort doctrine. The Missouri Court of Appeals, in *Porter v. Crawford & Co.*, stated that if a defendant can prove sufficient justification for his act, he will not be liable under the *prima facie* tort doctrine. In that case, the court said the defendant "may,

CASE on Point

Porter v. Crawford & Co., 611 S.W.2d 265 (Mo. Ct. App. 1980)

According to the facts of this case, the plaintiff was injured in an automobile collision involving a motorist insured by the one of the defendants. Another defendant, acting as the agent and adjuster for the insurance company defendant, settled the plaintiff's insurance claim and drafted a check to the plaintiff in settlement of the claim. After the settlement check was deposited, the plaintiff proceeded to write checks of his own against these funds in his account. Unknown to him, the agent had stopped payment on the draft, and the plaintiff's checks were dishonored for insufficient funds, for which his bank assessed him fees. The plaintiff sued to recover for the injury he sustained as a result of the bank service charges, and also for the embarrassment, humiliation, and damage to reputation he suffered when his checks bounced. The theory the plaintiff advanced was the *prima facie* tort doctrine.

The issue before the Missouri Court of Appeals in this case was whether the law of Missouri permitted recovery in tort for a lawful act performed maliciously and with intent to cause harm to a plaintiff. It answered this issue in the affirmative. In doing so, the court set forth the elements of the *prima facie* tort doctrine, as follows: "1. Intentional lawful act by the defendant. 2. Intent to cause injury to the plaintiff. 3. Injury to the plaintiff. 4. An absence of any justification or an insufficient justification for the defendant's act."

Holding that the *prima facie* tort doctrine applied in Missouri, the court reasoned that "modern scholarship considers that there exists a reside of tort liability which has not been explicated in specific forms of tort action and which is available for the courts to develop as common law tort actions as the needs of society require such development." The court noted emerging products liability recovery theories and the recovery of damages for the intentional infliction of emotional distress as illustrations of its point. Another important reason to adopt the *prima facie* tort doctrine given by the court was that the *Restatement (Second) of Torts*, in section 870, "stated a guide for the development of new forms of intentional torts, expressed a rationale for imposing such liability, and provided guidelines for the imposition of such liability." That Missouri, in the past, had not been reluctant to adopt new forms of action in tort based on *Restatement* principles, and the fact that several other states had developed this doctrine in their jurisdictions, influenced the court's decision to adopt the *prima facie* tort doctrine in that state.

of course, plead and prove any facts establishing a justification for the act of stopping payment on the draft," and in doing so, may defeat the plaintiff's claim.

Once a plaintiff establishes a *prima facie* case of an intentional tort, then the burden of proof shifts to the defendant to defend himself from the plaintiff's claim. The next chapter will address the defenses one can assert to defend against an intentional tort claim. It will also examine the remedies available when intentional tort liability is found.

CHAPTER **SUMMARY**

- Intentional torts against property are torts in which the defendant acts purposefully to interfere with another person's rights in property. The main intentional torts against property are trespass to land, conversion, and trespass to chattels.

- Trespass to land is the intentional and unlawful entry onto or interference with the land of another, without permission.

- Under the common law doctrine of nuisance liability, a person may be held liable for using his property in a manner that unreasonably interferes with another person's use and enjoyment of her property. Nuisance can occur separate from, or in conjunction with, the tort of trespass to land and can be private or public.

- Conversion is the intentional exercise of dominion and control over another's personal property which seriously interferes with the owner or possessor's right to possession. It is a more serious interference than trespass to chattels.

- Trespass to chattels is the intentional dispossession or intermeddling by the defendant with the plaintiff's right to use or possession of personal property. It is a less serious interference than conversion.

- Misrepresentation, also called fraudulent misrepresentation, fraud, or the tort of fraud or deceit, is the intentional making of a false statement, or the failure to disclose when a duty to disclose exists, which causes the plaintiff a pecuniary loss.

- Tortious interference is harm that is intentionally caused to a plaintiff's contractual or other business relationships. There are two main types of tortious interferences, one specifically involving contractual relationships, called tortious interference with a contractual relationship (which may or may not be a business relationship), and one involving business relationships or activities that do not involve a contract, called tortious interference with a business relationship. There can also be tortious interference with employment.

- Tortious interference with a contractual relationship occurs when a tortfeasor induces a party to breach its contract with the plaintiff, or otherwise disrupts the party's performance under the contract, causing the plaintiff harm.

- Tortious interference with a business relationship occurs where a tortfeasor interferes with a business or activity of another, causing harm. An underlying contract between the plaintiff and a third party is not present. With this tort, the defendant unreasonably interferes with the plaintiff's reasonable expectation of economic benefit expected to be derived from the business or activity.

- Another type of tortious interference is tortious interference with employment. If an employee suffers adverse employment action in violation of the law, she may have a claim of tortious interference with employment against the employer.

- The *prima facie* tort doctrine is a catch-all tort doctrine covering certain intentional misconduct that does not fit the essential elements of the other recognized intentional torts, but it is recognized in only a few jurisdictions. Where it is recognized, it provides a tort remedy when an intentional lawful act is committed with the intent to injure another. A defendant can successfully defend a *prima facie* tort claim by proving he had sufficient justification for committing the act.

CONCEPT REVIEW AND REINFORCEMENT

QUESTIONS FOR **REVIEW**

1. What are the main intentional torts against property?
2. What is trespass to land?
3. What is the common law nuisance doctrine?
4. What is conversion?
5. What is trespass to chattels?
6. What is misrepresentation, and what are its essential elements?
7. What is tortious interference?
8. What are the different types of tortious interference?
9. What is the *prima facie* tort doctrine?

DEVELOPING YOUR PARALEGAL SKILLS

CRITICAL THINKING **EXERCISES**

1. In this chapter, we studied the essential elements of the intentional torts against property including trespass to land, conversion, and trespass to chattels. Each state may "customize" these elements in its case law. Research the law in your state with reference to the essential elements of each of these intentional torts to see in what way(s), if any, they differ from most states' elements for those torts. An excellent starting point for your research is a case law digest for your state. For example, in Maryland, the resource *Maryland Digest 2d* by West includes cases from Maryland establishing essential elements for each of these torts. Review these essential elements in class.

   Here is a list of cases stating Maryland law on the various intentional torts against property covered in this chapter, as an example of jurisdiction-specific legal research:

   Trespass to land: Adams v. NVR Homes, Inc., 193 F.R.D. 243 (D. Md. 2000)

   Conversion: Allied Inv. Corp. v. Jasen, 731 A.2d 957 (Md. 1999)

   Trespass to chattels: Diamond v. T. Rowe Price Assoc., Inc., 852 F.Supp. 372 (D. Md. 1994)

2. It is Halloween. Jake and his friends, in a festive prank, "egg" Mr. Steven's house. They do a great job, lobbing two dozen eggs—splat—toward Mr. Steven's garage door, and only missing twice. The boys consider this skillful throwing, as they had to stand in the road, outside Mr. Steven's fenced yard, to throw the eggs.
   Have Jake and his friends committed trespass to Mr. Steven's land? Why or why not?

3. a. Bob is in the neighborhood park, walking his darling yellow lab, Milo. Sarah, a dog lover, approaches. Without asking permission, she reaches out and pats Milo on the head.
   Has Sarah committed an intentional tort against property by patting Milo without Bob's permission? Why or why not? If so, which one?

   b. Sarah, while reaching to pet Milo, accidentally spills her cup of hot coffee on the poor dog. A patch of his skin is scalded.
   Has Sarah committed an intentional tort against property now? If so, which one, and why?

   c. Larry is in the same park, playing with his beautiful black lab, Otis. Otis is running around without a leash. Sarah is watching them play, admiring Otis's beauty and his fine disposition. A woman approaches Larry to ask him directions. While Larry is preoccupied helping this woman, Sarah lures Otis to her. Seizing the moment, Sarah takes Otis by the collar and runs away with him. Sarah keeps Otis, and renames him Oreo.
   Has Sarah committed an intentional tort against property now? If so, which one and why?

4. On a trip to Los Angeles, California, Jacob Matthews is walking through the airport when he glimpses a famous movie star nearby. Excited by this, Jacob gets out his camera and approaches the celebrity, asking him, "May I take your picture?" The celebrity denies Jacob's request. Jacob, just feet from the object of his photographic desire, takes several pictures anyway. Enraged by Jacob's intrusive actions, the celebrity lunges at Jacob, grabs his camera, and shoves

both, forcefully, to the ground. Jacob is injured and his camera is destroyed by the celebrity's actions. Because the celebrity has "deep pockets," Jacob considers it worthwhile to sue the celebrity for the intentional torts of battery and conversion.

a. *Jacob retains you to represent him in this matter. Draft the complaint necessary to initiate this lawsuit.*

b. *If the celebrity had been a noncelebrity, "regular Joe" type instead, would you recommend that Jacob pursue this tort suit? Why or why not? Would you agree to represent Jacob in the suit? Why or why not?*

5. In this chapter, we studied the torts of misrepresentation, tortious interference, and the *prima facie* tort doctrine. What are the essential elements of the torts of misrepresentation and tortious interference in your state? Is the *prima facie* tort doctrine recognized in your jurisdiction? If so, what are its elements? Does it have a malice requirement? An excellent starting point for your research is a case law digest for your state. For example, in Maryland, the resource *Maryland Digest 2d* by West includes cases from Maryland dealing with these applications. Discuss your research results in class.

6. Patrick has been hired as a telemarketer for a nonprofit organization. He calls S. Bob, a cancer survivor, to solicit a contribution. Patrick tells S. Bob that the organization performs important medical research to find a cure for cancer and therefore deserves S. Bob's financial support. In fact, the organization rescues unwanted pets. During their telephone conversation, Patrick learns that S. Bob is an avid scuba diver. Patrick tells S. Bob that he, too, is an avid scuba diver. Patrick has never been scuba diving; in fact, he cannot swim. S. Bob donates $100 to the organization. Then S. Bob gets his wife, Sandy, on the telephone to speak with Patrick. Sandy, who like her husband is also an avid scuba diver, hears from Patrick

everything he told S. Bob. Sandy donates $5,000 to the organization. Later, S. Bob and Sandy learn that the organization does not research cancer cures and that Patrick does not scuba dive.

a. *As a class, discuss whether S. Bob could win a misrepresentation suit against Patrick. Should S. Bob win? Why or why not?*

b. *As a class, discuss whether Sandy could win a misrepresentation suit against Patrick? Should Sandy win? Why or why not?*

7. Doctor Stevens tells his patient, Ernest Brown, that continuing his employment as a coal miner at the Pennsylvania Mining Company's Scranton coal mine could further damage the health of his lungs. As a result of this statement, Ernest quits his job, and the coal mine has to replace him and train a new worker.

Has the doctor committed any kind of tortious interference? If so, what kind? Might a defense apply? If so, which one?

8. The Landers hired Rogers Construction Co. to renovate their home and construct an addition. When Rogers Construction Co. completed the work, the Landers were unhappy with its quality and requested that the contractor perform certain repairs. The contractor refused. The Landers wanted to hurt Rogers Construction Co.'s business, so they posted a sign on their property stating, "Rogers Construction Co. renovated our house—contact us before they renovate yours!"

If Rogers Construction Co. wants to sue the Landers for (a) damages and (b) an injunction requiring them to remove the offending sign, what legal theory might the company use? Have the Landers committed an intentional tort against Rogers Construction Co.? Do the Landers have the right to post this sign (remember that the Constitution guarantees the right to free speech)? This fact pattern is based loosely on the case of Morrison v. Woolley, 45 A.D.3d 953 (N.Y. App. Div. 2007).

ASSIGNMENTS AND PRACTICAL **APPLICATIONS**

1. Assign to students various intentional torts against property and ask the students to make up their own hypothetical situations for these torts, for sharing and discussing with the class. Students should consider all the essential elements of each tort when preparing their hypothetical situations.

2. For an intentional nuisance case, read and brief *Morgan v. High Penn Oil Co.*, 77 S.E.2d 682 (N.C. 1953); for a negligent nuisance case, read and brief *Schindler v. Standard Oil Co.*, 232 S.W. 735 (Mo. App. 1921). To distinguish the tort of trespass from

nuisance, read and brief *Nissan Motor Corp. in U.S.A. v. Maryland Shipbuilding and Drydock Co.*, 544 F.Supp. 1104, *aff'd*, 742 F.2d 1449 (D. Md. 1982).

3. When they are asked for recommendations or references, many employers today provide only the dates of employment and the former employee's title. To provide more information, such as the quality of the employee's performance or the reason for termination, could render the employer liable in tort. Normally, employers fear defamation actions when the

statements they make are untrue and hurt the reputation of the applicant. However, misrepresentation could be committed if a recommendation letter provides only half-truths to the prospective employer. Read and brief *Randi W. v. Muroc Joint Unified School District*, 929 P.2d 582 (Cal. 1997) on this issue.

4. When is a plaintiff's reliance on a defendant's statement justifiable for the tort of misrepresentation? Negligence is the yardstick by which Maryland courts measure justifiable reliance on representations. On this point, read and brief *Moseman v. Van Leer*, 263 F.3d 129 (4th Cir. 2001).

5. Regarding the tort of misrepresentation, what sorts of situations give rise to a duty to disclose? Perform legal research for examples, from your jurisdiction, of when a duty to disclose arises under the tort theory of misrepresentation. Discuss your research results with the class.

6. Regarding the tort of misrepresentation, under Maryland law, a duty to disclose arises when one party is in a fiduciary or confidential relationship with another, or when one party makes a partial and fragmentary statement of fact. Read and brief *Hill v. Brush Engineered Materials, Inc.*, 383 F.Supp.2d 814 (D. Md. 2005) on this point.

7. Does your state recognize the tort of negligent misrepresentation? Perform legal research to answer that question. If it does, what are the essential elements of

that tort in your jurisdiction? Discuss your research results in class.

8. What about interference with contracts to marry? Contracts to marry have received special treatment under the law. Almost all courts hold that it is not a tort to induce a party to breach a contract to marry. They reason that such contracts are highly personal agreements, and third parties should be free to advise the parties to them to change their minds. Read and brief *Brown v. Glickstein*, 107 N.E.2d 267 (Ill. App. Ct. 1952) regarding interference with contracts to marry.

9. The essential elements of tortious interference with a contractual relationship under District of Columbia law can be found in *Murray v. Wells Fargo Home Mortgage*, 953 A.2d 308 (D.C. 2008). Read and brief this case.

10. The essential elements of tortious interference with a business relationship under Maryland law can be found in *Contech Stormwater Solutions, Inc. v. Baysaver Techs., Inc.*, 534 F.Supp.2d 616 (D. Md. 2008). Read and brief this case.

11. For a recent *prima facie* tort case in New York, defining the tort and its essential elements and recognizing its limits, read and brief *Denaro v. Rosalia*, 59 A.D.3d 584 (N.Y. App. Div. 2009).

TECHNOLOGY RESOURCES AND INTERNET **EXERCISES**

Fraud, silent fraud, and innocent misrepresentation are explained on ExpertLaw.com. See *www.expertlaw.com /library/business/fraud.html*.

Go to the Wikipedia Internet site to see its discussion of the famous early English case of *Lumley v. Gye*, cited in the chapter, regarding tortious interference with a contractual relationship (*http://en.wikipedia.org/wiki /Lumley_v._Gye*).

Using the Internet site nolo.com, review that site's definitions of the tortious interference torts.

Locate a current misrepresentation or tortious interference case using the Internet. Share your research results with the class.

Using the Internet, find out whether your state recognizes the *prima facie* tort doctrine. What states, besides New York, recognize it?

ETHICAL **APPLICATIONS**

Brian Turner, an attorney with a tort law practice, wishes to expand his law practice through effective advertising. He hires an advertising firm to prepare print and radio ads in which Brian says, "If you have a telephone, you have a lawyer who can win your case for you." As a result of these ads, Brian's business is growing because many clients want to have a lawyer who is confident that he can win their cases.

Although Brian had good business intentions in making and using these ads, and U.S. laws and economic policy certainly favor free competition, is there any problem with this advertising given that Brian is a lawyer and his business is a law practice? What legal ethics rules in your jurisdiction regulate advertising by lawyers? How is it regulated?

VIDEO **CASE STUDY**

A Salesman's Courtroom Testimony: Fact or Misrepresentation?

Synopsis: A salesman for Acme Brake Company is providing courtroom testimony about his sale of unlabeled "seconds" brake pads to the truck mechanic for Ace Trucking Company.

Questions

1. Who would most likely call the salesman as a witness, and why?
2. What constitutes actionable fraudulent misrepresentation?
3. Has the salesman in this scenario committed fraud?

chapter 5

INTENTIONAL TORTS: DEFENSES AND REMEDIES

This chapter discusses what happens after a plaintiff has established a *prima facie* case of one or more intentional torts. At that point, the burden of proof shifts to the defendant to defend himself from the plaintiff's asserted claim. If the defendant is unable to defend himself fully from the claim, the court will award a remedy to the plaintiff. To begin, we examine the concept of legal defenses and then we review the major defenses to intentional torts including consent, self-defense, defense of others, defense of property, reentry onto land, recapture of chattels, necessity, discipline, justification, and statutes of limitations.

LEARNING OBJECTIVES

5.1 Define defenses.

5.2 Identify and discuss the major defenses to intentional torts.

5.3 Define remedies.

5.4 Identify and discuss the specific remedies available for intentional tort claims.

Definition of Defense

A *defense* is a legal reason why a claim should be denied or reduced. It is asserted by a person who is defending himself against a legal claim by stating why the plaintiff should not recover what is sought in the lawsuit. By asserting a defense, a defendant, or a plaintiff if counterclaims are filed, is providing reasons why he should be exonerated from all liability, or why his liability should be reduced or limited.

A defendant may defend himself in one of two ways. First, the defendant may assert that the plaintiff failed to establish, through evidence, the existence of one or more of the essential elements of his claim. In the case of tort actions, the defendant can assert that the plaintiff failed to establish at least one, if not more, of the essential elements of the tort alleged. This means that the plaintiff failed to establish a *prima facie* case for that tort. If so, the plaintiff's action fails. What if the plaintiff is successful in establishing a *prima facie* case for a tort?

If the plaintiff has established a *prima facie* case for one or more torts, then the burden of proof shifts to the defendant to establish that the plaintiff is not entitled to recovery. He does this by establishing an affirmative defense. An *affirmative defense* is a defense to a claim that goes beyond the complaint made by the plaintiff and sets out new facts and arguments for why the defendant should win the case or his liability

Defense
A legal reason why a claim should be denied or reduced.

Affirmative defense
A defense to a claim that goes beyond the complaint made by the plaintiff and sets out new facts and arguments for why the defendant should win the case or his liability be reduced.

Privilege

A defense that justifies otherwise tortious conduct and is derived from the right of a person to act contrary to the right of another person without being subject to liability for his actions.

Immunity

A defense related to the status of a party that protects the party from liability for his tortious conduct.

Consent

A plaintiff's voluntary willingness to let the defendant's conduct occur and to accept its consequences.

be reduced. The burden of proof of an affirmative defense is on the party asserting one (or more). Affirmative defenses apply to all legal actions asserted by plaintiffs (or by defendants via counterclaims). These include intentional tort actions. What affirmative defenses may be asserted in intentional tort cases?

Many tort defenses are either privileges or immunities. A **privilege** is a defense that, in effect, justifies otherwise tortious conduct; it is derived from the right of a person to act contrary to the right of another person without being subject to liability for his actions. Examples of privileges are consent, self-defense, defense of others, defense of property, reentry onto land, recapture of chattels, necessity, discipline, and justification. These defenses are discussed in this chapter because many of them apply specifically to intentional torts. **Immunity** is a defense related to the status of the party that protects the party from liability for his tortious conduct. Examples of immunity include sovereign immunity, charitable immunity, diplomatic immunity, and family immunity. Immunities are discussed more fully in the negligence chapters because they apply to tortious conduct generally, not specifically to intentional torts, and negligence is the most common tort action. Other tort defenses, such as statutes of limitations, are neither privileges nor immunities. The statute of limitations defense is discussed in this chapter.

Major Defenses to Intentional Torts

The major defenses to intentional tort actions are consent, self-defense, defense of others, defense of property, reentry onto land, recapture of chattels, necessity, discipline, justification, and statutes of limitations. As with all defenses, they are asserted by someone defending himself from claims—in our case, intentional tort claims. The first major intentional tort defense we examine is consent.

CONSENT

Consent is a plaintiff's voluntary willingness to let the defendant's conduct occur and to accept its consequences. The rational for this defense is that a defendant should not be liable for conduct to which the plaintiff agreed. To succeed with this defense, the defendant must establish several things. First, he must be able to establish that the consent was given *voluntarily* and *knowingly*.

For consent to be voluntary, it must actually be agreed to by the plaintiff. So, if the defendant coerces or tricks the plaintiff into agreement, there is no legal consent. Also, the plaintiff's consent must be knowingly given. For consent to be knowingly given, the plaintiff must actually be aware of and understand the nature and consequences of the defendant's conduct and the harm that might result. Consider the tort of battery and the consent a doctor receives from a patient to allow the doctor to perform a medical procedure. Most of the time, certain emergencies excepted, a patient must give informed consent to a medical procedure before it is performed. To give such consent, the patient or his legal representative or guardian must be informed of the risks and other important information involving the procedure. It could be the tort of battery for a physician to perform a procedure without first informing the patient of the

CASE on Point

Peterson v. Sorlien, 299 N.W.2d 123 (Minn. 1980)

This case was an action for false imprisonment, as well as intentional infliction of emotional distress, that arose when a 21-year-old woman's parents, along with some others named as defendants, sought to deprogram the woman, Susan Peterson, from her involvement with a youth cult ministry called The Way. In an effort to have Peterson deprogrammed, her parents brought her to a home where several young people and a professional deprogrammer were present for the purpose of trying to break Peterson's involvement in the youth cult ministry. Peterson stayed in this situation for sixteen days. During that time she took many excursions to public places like to parks, roller-skating rinks, shopping centers, and swimming facilities. But after that time, she returned to the cult's headquarters, was directed to legal counsel, and brought this legal action against her parents and their agents who had sought to extricate Peterson from the cult.

As to the defense of consent, the court said that for consent to be a defense to a claim of false imprisonment, the evidence must show that the plaintiff consented, voluntarily, to the confinement. "Damages may not be assessed for any period of detention to which one freely consents," said the court.

The court found that Peterson only regained her "volitional capacity to consent" after engaging in the first three days of the deprogramming process. But the court went on to say that her parents and their agents sought to extricate Peterson from what they reasonably believed to be religious or a pseudo-religious cult and that their actions did not constitute meaningful deprivations of personal liberty sufficient to support liability for false imprisonment.

risks and other material factors involved, and obtaining the patient's consent to be touched. To protect themselves from legal liability, medical practitioners normally require this patient consent to be in writing.

How does one give consent? A person can manifest a willingness to accept the consequences of the defendant's conduct by words, such as by saying, "It is okay for you to come on my land to fish in my pond." A cautious defendant might ask for that consent in writing. Words are not required, however, for there to be consent. Actions may also be sufficient to constitute consent. A person can consent through conduct demonstrating a willingness to accept the consequences of the defendant's conduct, such as by nodding one's head in agreement. As another example, by leaning in toward a date, who appears to be trying to kiss the plaintiff goodnight, the plaintiff may consent to a goodnight kiss.

What if the plaintiff, at the end of the date, reaches out her hand to shake hands goodnight? The defendant, in the mood for romance, fully embraces the plaintiff and proceeds to try to kiss her passionately; the plaintiff, not interested in romance with the defendant, pushes him away. Although the plaintiff consented to a handshake, she did not consent to an embrace or a kiss. Lawsuits for unwanted hugs and kisses such as these may seem frivolous, but an unwelcome and unconsented-to kiss may meet the essential elements of the tort of battery, as discussed in Chapter 3, depending on the circumstances. Keep in mind that the conduct performed must be substantially the same as the conduct consented to. See the Case on Point involving this issue, among other consent issues.

CASE on Point

Barbara A. v. John G., 145 Cal. App. 3d 369 (1983)

This case included a claim of battery by a female client of an attorney. The client alleged that she suffered an ectopic pregnancy after she engaged in sexual intercourse with her attorney after the attorney told her that "I can't possibly get anyone pregnant." One of the client's legal theories was that the act of impregnation exceeded the scope of her consent to intercourse and that her consent to intercourse was fraudulently induced.

The court determined that the client properly stated a cause of action for battery. The court defined battery as "an *unconsented* invasion of [a person's] interest in freedom from intentional, unlawful, and harmful or offensive contact with her person." Regarding the issue of consent, the court said that consent to an act that is otherwise a battery "vitiates the wrong." However, the court found that the client's consent in this case was not valid because the act of impregnation exceeded the scope of her consent to intercourse and because her consent to intercourse was fraudulently induced.

Not everyone has legal capacity to consent. Minors, for example, mental incompetents, and perhaps even intoxicated persons may not be able to give legal consent. Keep in mind that the legal guardian(s) of a minor child, usually the parents, have the legal right to give consent for their wards.

Certain kinds of actions may never be consented to, for example, killing a person. One cannot consent to another person inflicting deadly harm on him. The law will not permit such consent. In less egregious circumstances, however, if consent is knowingly and voluntarily given, it is a valid defense to an intentional tort.

Certain other defenses to intentional torts are considered self-help privileges. These self-help privileges are self-defense, defense of others, defense of property, reentry onto land, recapture of chattels, necessity, and discipline. First, we examine the privilege of self-defense.

SELF-DEFENSE

Self-defense
The right of a person to use reasonable force to prevent an immediate harmful or offensive contact by another against himself.

Self-defense is the right of a person to use reasonable force to prevent an immediate harmful or offensive contact against him by another. This type of defense is called a self-help privilege. As noted earlier, a privilege is the right of a person to act contrary to the right of another person without being subject to tort liability for his actions.

The privilege of self-defense permits a person to use reasonable force to prevent an immediate harmful or offensive contact against him by another. There must be *current* force being used against the plaintiff, or the *immediate* threat of it. This threat can be real (an actual, true threat) or apparent (the defendant reasonably believes that she is being threatened) for this privilege to apply. See the Critical Thinking Exercises at the end of the chapter for a detailed example of an apparent threat. The person defending himself normally cannot

SIDEBAR

RESTATEMENT (SECOND) OF TORTS AND SELF-DEFENSE

Regarding the privilege of self-defense, the *Restatement (Second) of Torts* says that a person may use reasonable force to defend herself against an unprivileged harmful or offensive contact or other harm to her person that she reasonably believes another person is about to intentionally inflict on her.[1]

What about the use of deadly force in self-defense? The *Restatement (Second) of Torts* says that, in self-defense, a person may use deadly force, that is, force intended or likely to cause death or serious bodily harm, if and when she reasonably believes that another person is about to intentionally inflict on her physical contact or other harm to her person that would put her in peril of death or serious bodily harm.[2] The *Restatement* limits this use of deadly force to situations where the threatened harm by another can be safely prevented only by the immediate use of deadly force in self-defense.[3]

be the initial aggressor, meaning the one instigating the threat or force. However, the law allows a person to reasonably defend himself from the threat or use of force by another. How much force can be used? Can deadly force be used in self-defense?

How much force a defendant can use is the amount that is *reasonable under the circumstances*. The force used must be proportionate to, not greater than, the force faced or threatened. This can include deadly force if one is facing the use or threat of force likely to cause death or serious bodily harm. How much force a person can use in defending himself, then, is whatever force is reasonably necessary to prevent the threatened harmful or offensive contact. For example, Jack sees John approach him, brandishing a sinister-looking knife. Jack believes he is about to be attacked by John, and using an old football move from his youth, lunges at John's legs to tackle him and attempt to wrestle the knife from John. Did Jack commit battery against John by tackling him? Remember, John was not touching Jack. John did, however, at least appear to be threatening Jack with immediate harmful contact. In this case, Jack's tackling of John would fall under the privilege of self-defense. Jack used reasonable force against an apparent, immediate threat, to protect

SIDEBAR

WHO IS THE AGGRESSOR?

Normally the aggressor who initially instigated the threat or force cannot assert the privilege of self-defense because he created the threat or force from which he then needed to defend himself. However, there is an exception when the aggressor may be able to lawfully engage in self-defense. He may defend himself when, although he was the aggressor, he stopped using force, while the other party continued to use force; this makes it necessary for the aggressor to then defend himself. Depending on the circumstances, this may be permitted self-defense.

CASE on Point

Roberts v. American Employers Ins. Co., Boston, Mass., 221 So.2d 550 (La. Ct. App. 1969)

In this case, Roberts sued a police officer, among others, for injuries sustained from a gunshot wound. Roberts went to a bar one evening, but the bar was holding a private party and would not serve him. Roberts refused to leave, ate some snacks that the party invitees had brought, and created a disturbance. The bartender called the police. Before the police arrived at the scene, Roberts went across the street to a pool hall. Police officer Randolph investigated the complaint at the bar and tracked down Roberts. After questioning Roberts, the officer placed him under arrest for violation of a city ordinance against disturbing the peace. Walking out to the police car, Roberts stopped twice, cursed, and said he refused to go to jail. When they neared the car, Roberts grabbed for the officer, at which time the officer fired one shot from the hip. The shot hit Roberts in the lower-left jaw, though he survived.

In defending tort claims for assault and battery, the police officer asserted the privilege of self-defense. Regarding this privilege, the court said that the privilege of self-defense in tort actions is now well recognized. When a person reasonably believes he is threatened with bodily harm, he may use whatever force appears to be reasonably necessary to protect against the threatened injury. The court said that each case depends on its own facts, including the relative size, age, and strength of the parties, their reputations for violence, who was the aggressor, the degree of physical harm reasonably feared, and the presence or absence of a weapon. Roberts was a single, 24-year-old African American male weighing about 150 pounds and with a known and long criminal record, including acts of violence; also he had been drinking that night. The officer weighed about 165 pounds and was substantially older than Roberts. Roberts' actions in cursing and saying he would not go to jail, then grabbing for the officer, led the officer to belief that Roberts was going to resist arrest by physical force.

The court determined that Roberts was the aggressor; he was in the officer's custody under lawful arrest, which he attempted to resist by physical force. The court held that the officer reasonably believed he was in danger of substantial physical harm and that the force he used to defend himself was not unreasonably excessive. Therefore, the court ruled that the officer's privilege of self-defense barred Roberts' recovery for the torts of assault and battery.

himself from harmful contact. Jack would not be liable for the tort of battery against John, even if John is injured by the tackle, because of the privilege of self-defense.

Always remember, when considering the privilege of self-defense, that the defendant's response must be equal to, or less than, the threat. Excessive force is not allowed and in fact could be tortious. Consider this example. Marla is sick and tired of Beatrice flirting with Marla's boyfriend, Steve. Catching Beatrice winking at Steve, Marla approaches Beatrice and raises her hand in what looks like will be a slap across Beatrice's face. Quick to the draw, Beatrice brandishes a pistol and shoots Marla. Marla was, in fact, about to slap

Beatrice across the face. Were Beatrice's actions, in shooting Marla, privileged self-defense? Certainly not. Beatrice used excessive force, meaning force greater than the threat to which she was responding. Beatrice can be held liable for her tortious conduct.

What about others? Does the privilege of self-defense extend to defending not only oneself but also other people?

DEFENSE OF OTHERS

There is a separate self-help privilege that permits people to reasonably defend others. **Defense of others** is the right of a person to use reasonable force to prevent an immediate harmful or offensive contact by another against someone other than himself. Though under early common law this privilege was limited to protecting members of one's immediate family, it has been extended. Today, it does not matter whether the other person is a family member, a friend, or a stranger. People have the legal right to reasonably defend other people—any people—from real or threatened harm.

Just as under the privilege of self-defense, reasonable force includes deadly force if it is used in response to a force or threat of force likely to cause death or serious bodily harm. Just like self-defense, the threat must be immediate.

What if the defendant makes a mistake? What if he is mistaken in believing that he, or another, is threatened? Or what if he is mistaken as to the amount of force needed to protect himself or the other person, and uses excessive force as a result? The privileges of self-defense and defense of others, while otherwise the same, differ on this point.

Defense of others
The right of a person to use reasonable force to prevent an immediate harmful or offensive contact by another against someone other than himself.

CASE on Point

Gortarez v. Smitty's Super Valu, Inc., 680 P.2d 807 (Ariz. 1984) on Defense of Others

In this case Gortarez, a 16-year-old boy, and his 18-year-old cousin, Hernandez, were detained in a store parking lot after a store clerk mistakenly accused them of shoplifting. They were detained by Gibson, the store's security officer and an off-duty police officer, among other store employees. During the parking lot confrontation, Gortarez observed Gibson grab Hernandez, push him against the car, and search him. Seeing this, Gortarez ran around his car and pushed Gibson away from Hernandez. Then Gibson put Gortarez in a choke hold. At this point, Gibson identified himself as the store's security guard.

The court discussed, among other things, the right of Gortarez to come to the defense of his cousin, Hernandez. The court said there is a privilege to come to the defense of another where that action is called for or sanctioned by recognized social usage or commonly accepted standards of decent conduct. The privilege permits use of "all force reasonably necessary for such defense." So the court noted that even though Hernandez was the person first physically seized by Gibson, Gortarez was entitled to defend Hernandez—as well as himself (the privilege of self-defense)—to the same extent as if Gortarez had been physically seized.

Regarding the privilege of self-defense, most jurisdictions hold that the defense is not lost so long as the defender's mistake was reasonable. It does not matter if the mistake was about whether there was a real or apparent threat or whether the mistake was about the amount of force that was reasonable. Most states protect the defendant in these cases. However, if a defendant makes a mistake regarding his need to defend another, or the amount of force that is reasonable in defense of another, most jurisdictions will find that the privilege is lost; this subjects the defendant to liability in tort for even reasonable mistakes, though a minority of jurisdictions hold that a reasonable mistake in defending others will not defeat the privilege.

So far we have discussed defending people. Is there a self-help privilege to defend one's property? In other words, does the privilege of self-defense or defense of others extend to cover defense of property? The answer is yes, to a degree.

DEFENSE OF PROPERTY

Defense of property is the right of a person to use reasonable, but never deadly, force to prevent immediate interference with his property or to end interference that is already occurring. Like the self-help privileges of self-defense and defense of others, a person may use reasonable force in attempting to remove intruders from his home or to otherwise defend his property; however, force that is likely to cause death or serious bodily injury can never be justified to protect property. The reasoning behind this limitation is the courts' view that human life is more valuable than property. Keep in mind that this defense applies to both real and personal property, so persons may defend their houses and their personal property.

The following Case on Point is a well-known and interesting case illustrating the limitations on the defense of property. It answers the question, "Can a person use force, and if so, potentially deadly force, to protect property?"

When evaluating a defendant's conduct, be sure to distinguish defense of property from self-defense and defense of others. For instance, one has the right to attempt to remove intruders from one's home; that constitutes the privilege of defense of property. Deadly force may never be used in that case. However, what if the intruder is armed, and the defendant is home with his family? In that case, the defendant has the right to use reasonable force to defend himself and his family, including deadly force, if such force is reasonable. When the intruder presents a real or apparent threat to the defendant and/or his family, reasonable force, including deadly force if confronted by the threat of deadly force by the intruder, is privileged.

What is the impact of mistake on this privilege? If the defendant is mistaken, reasonably or unreasonably, as to his right to posses the property he defended and protected, the privilege is lost. However, if the defendant is mistaken only as to the amount of force needed to protect the property (assuming deadly force was not used), the privilege is not lost so long as the mistake is reasonable.

Besides protecting one's property via the privilege of defense of property, a possessor of real property may be able to reclaim possession of her property if

Defense of property
The right of a person to use reasonable, but never deadly, force to prevent immediate interference with his property or to end interference already occurring.

CASE on Point

Katko v. Briney, 183 N.W.2d 657 (Iowa 1971)

In 1957 the defendant, Bertha Briney, inherited her parents' farmland, including an 80-acre tract on which her grandparents had lived. No one occupied the farmhouse after her grandparents, although Mrs. Briney's husband, Edward, attempted to care for the land.

Over a period of about ten years, a series of trespassings and house break-ins occurred on the unoccupied farm, which resulted in some damage to the property and "loss of some household items." Over the years, the Brineys boarded up the windows and doors of the house to try to keep out intruders. They also posted "No Trespassing" signs on the land, including one that was located 35 feet from the house.

On June 11, 1967, the Brineys set a "shotgun trap" in the north bedroom of the house by securing a 20-gauge shotgun to an iron bed with the barrel pointed at the door. Rigged with wire from the doorknob to the gun's trigger, it was set to fire at an intruder's legs if the door was opened. The Brineys nailed tin over the bedroom window so the spring gun could not be seen from the outside. No warning of its presence was posted.

On July 16, 1967, the plaintiff, Marvin Katko, and his companion, Marvin McDonough, broke into the house to steal old bottles and dated fruit jars that "they considered antiques." These two had trespassed on the premises before, taking old bottles and jars for their collection of antiques. That day, they entered the house by removing a board from a porch window. While McDonough searched the kitchen, Katko approached the north bedroom and opened the door. As he opened the door, Katko was shot in the right leg, blowing much of it away. He spent forty days in the hospital recovering from the shotgun injury.

Katko pled guilty to a criminal charge of larceny and was fined $50 plus costs. He was paroled for good behavior during a sixty-day jail sentence. Despite his crime, Katko brought suit against the defendants for compensation for the injuries he sustained by being shot.

The primary issue of the case was whether an owner may protect personal property in an unoccupied, boarded-up farmhouse against trespassers and thieves using a spring gun capable of inflicting death or serious injury. The defendants argued that the law permitted use of a spring gun in a dwelling or warehouse to prevent "the unlawful entry of a burglar or thief." This argument failed.

The Iowa Supreme Court held that the use of force calculated to cause death or serious bodily harm was unreasonable as a means to repel trespassers or thieves in order to protect property. The court reasoned that the law places a higher value on human safety than on rights in property. It said that there was no privilege to use deadly force to defend property without an accompanying threat of deadly force against a person to justify self-defense.

Quoting the *Restatement of Torts* the court said, "A possessor of land cannot do indirectly and by a mechanical device that which, were he present, he could not do immediately and in person." The court also noted that in addition to civil liability, many jurisdictions, by statute, hold landowners criminally responsible for homicide or serious injury caused by spring guns.

she is wrongfully dispossessed of it. We begin our review of this type of defense by addressing the retaking of real property, and follow that discussion with one about the retaking of personal property. What can be done when a defendant is wrongly dispossessed of his land by another? Can a defendant forcibly retake possession of the land? The answer is "sometimes." Reentry onto land as a defense is examined next.

REENTRY ONTO LAND

Reentry onto land
The limited right to use reasonable, nondeadly force to reenter and reclaim real property when the plaintiff has wrongfully dispossessed the defendant.

Reentry onto land is the *limited* right to use reasonable, nondeadly force to reenter and reclaim real property when the plaintiff has wrongfully dispossessed the defendant (so the defendant is asserting this defense to justify retaking possession of the land). Note that the plaintiff is the one crying foul, because the defendant, who is rightful possessor of the land, is using force to take it back.

Most states have enacted statutes governing repossession of land, requiring use of legal proceedings. This is most often seen in landlord/tenant cases involving tenant evictions. Rightful possessors of the land must comply with statutory requirements to be able to forcibly remove the plaintiffs who have wrongfully

CASE on Point

Miceli v. Foley, 575 A.2d 1249 (Md. Ct. Spec. App. 1990)

This case involved a landowner, Miceli, bringing a lawsuit against his neighbors. Part of the lawsuit involved a claim of adverse possession by the neighbors. Adverse possession is a process pursuant to which title to real property can be acquired without compensation where a person takes possession of the property in a manner that conflicts with the owner's rights. If the person who takes possession of the land owned by another possesses it in an actual, open, notorious, exclusive, and hostile manner, under claim of title or ownership (so claiming to be the property owner), continuously for a requisite period (twenty years in Maryland, where this case was heard), the possessor of the land can acquire title to it.

To try to defeat the adverse possession claim, Miceli argued that the neighbors' possession of the land was interrupted and not continuous, as is required for adverse possession—he argued reentry onto the land. The court noted that the running of the statutory period for adverse possession may be interrupted by the owner's reentry on the land. The reentry must be made with a clearly demonstrated intention to repossess the land; reentry onto land must be made openly and under claim of right. The court also said that entry sufficient to interrupt an adverse possession claim can be made by the owner's agent; it need not be made by the owner personally. In this case, Miceli commissioned a land survey of the property and his surveyor and crew surveyed the land for two years during the twenty-year statutory period. The court ruled that reentry onto the land for the purpose of conducting a survey, without a claim of right to the land, does not interrupt the running of the statute sufficient to oust an adverse possessor. So Miceli's reentry onto land was not sufficient to defeat the neighbors' claim of adverse possession.

THE MODEL PENAL CODE

The Model Penal Code is a model act drafted by the American Law Institute in 1962 and updated from time to time. Its purpose is to provide guidance to states in standardizing penal law from jurisdiction to jurisdiction. Although the Model Penal Code is not, itself, law, it is a model, written by penal law experts, that can be, and is, considered by state lawmakers in defining their states' penal codes. Most states have adopted at least part of it, and many states have adopted almost all of it.

dispossessed them, to avoid running afoul of the law themselves. Self-help by the landlord in tenant evictions is likely to result in tort liability for the landlord. In most cases, the landlord must pursue his remedies in court. In some states, the criminal system is faster and more efficient than the civil system in getting a nonpaying tenant out of possession—by charging the tenant with a misdemeanor and forcing him to vacate the realty after ten days or so or his property will be removed by the sheriff.

The Model Penal Code, adopted in many states, permits the use of nondeadly force to reenter land (or recapture personal property, discussed next) if a person believes that he, or the person for whom he is acting, was unlawfully dispossessed of the property, and the nondeadly force was used either right after the act of dispossession or the person believed the dispossessor had no legal basis for possessing the property.[4]

However, reentry onto land, as distinguished from recapture of personal property, is *not* permitted unless the defendant also believes that it would constitute an "exceptional hardship" to delay reentry until he can obtain a court order.

What if it is not land that the defendant is trying to take back, but rather is personal property? Does the defendant have the right to take back chattels rightfully belonging to her? We discuss recapture of chattels next.

RECAPTURE OF CHATTELS

Recapture of chattels is the *limited* right to use reasonable force to regain possession and control over one's personal property, or chattels. It allows a rightful owner to recover personal property. It is important to distinguish recapture of chattels from the privilege of defense of property. Under the privilege of defense of property, the rightful owner has possession of the property and another person is interfering with that possession. In recapture of chattels, another person (the plaintiff) has wrongfully dispossessed the rightful owner or possessor (the defendant), who wants to recapture it, meaning take it back.

The privilege to recapture chattels must be asserted *immediately*, meaning close in time to when the wrongful dispossession occurs. So a purse owner may chase down a purse snatcher and snatch back her purse, but if she sees the thief, two weeks later, carrying her stolen purse through the mall, she can no longer snatch it back without herself committing a tort, as too much time has passed since she was dispossessed of the purse by the thief. In that case, the owner

Recapture of chattels
The limited right to use reasonable force to regain possession and control over one's personal property.

would have to resort to the justice system, rather than self-help, to recover her purse. She should contact the police.

Recapture of chattels can only be asserted if the property was wrongfully taken from the rightful owner or possessor. If the purse owner gives her purse to another, then wishes to take it back and does, the recapture of chattels privilege does not apply because she was not wrongfully dispossessed of the property.

In addition, the force used must be reasonable, and it can never be deadly force. This is so because only property, not human life, is involved. Before using any force, however, the dispossessed person must first request that the property be returned, unless making this request would be either futile or unsafe.

What if the dispossessor obtains possession rightfully, via permission from the owner, but then refuses to give back the property? Can the privilege of recapture of chattels be used in that instance? For example, suppose Helen obtains permission from Charlie to take Charlie's dog for a walk in the park. After the park walk, Helen decides to keep the dog. Can Charlie take back his dog, using immediate, reasonable force? The answer is no. Because Charlie initially gave Helen possession of the dog, Charlie was never wrongfully dispossessed of the property (his dog). To recover the dog, Charlie would need to, and should, pursue a legal action. This self-help privilege of recapture of chattels is not available to him, and his use of force in this instance would be tortious.

What if the property owner makes a mistake about his right to possess the chattel? What if, for instance, Charlie sees Helen walking his dog in the park. Assume Charlie never gave permission for this. Charlie, immediately and using reasonable force, takes back the dog. Shortly after reclaiming his dog, Charlie realizes this dog is not—but sure looks like—his! How does Charlie's honest, reasonable mistake affect the use of this defense? The privilege is lost when a mistake as to right to possession is made, even if it is reasonable. If a defendant uses force to repossess a chattel, he should be sure to have the legal right to possession first, to avoid liability in tort.

CASE on Point

Gortarez v. Smitty's Super Valu, Inc., 680 P.2d 807 (Ariz. 1984) on Recapture of Chattels

This case, discussed earlier in the section on defense of others and involving an erroneous accusation of shoplifting, also addresses the common law privilege to recapture a chattel. Here the court said that there is a limited privilege for an owner whose property has been wrongfully taken, while in fresh pursuit, to use reasonable force to recapture a chattel. The property owner must be correct as to the facts that he believes grant him the privilege, and faces liability for damages that may result from any mistake, even a reasonable mistake. The force privileged must be reasonable under the circumstances and it must not be calculated to inflict serious bodily harm. The court also said that ordinarily the use of any force is not justified until there has been a demand made by the property owner for the return of the property.

Could a person ever have the legal right to use the property of another without permission? The answer is yes, in limited situations. In such a case, the privilege of necessity may protect such actions by a defendant.

NECESSITY

Necessity is the privilege to make reasonable use of another's property in order to prevent immediate harm or damage to persons or property. The issue with necessity is whether the defendant may harm the property interests of another if it is necessary to prevent *greater* harm to himself, others, or property. This defense involves a balancing of interests between the plaintiff's exclusive rights in his own property and the right of another to avoid even greater harm. In effect, it is a choice between a lesser and a greater harm.

Understandably, the normal rule is that an owner of property, whether real or personal property, is the one with the exclusive right to use that property, and the one with the legal authority to grant that right to others. However, the necessity defense constitutes an excuse for the defendant to use the real or personal property of another, without permission, if the use is undertaken to prevent even greater harm to himself or other persons in the form of personal injury or property damage.

If the defendant's use of the plaintiff's property is undertaken to protect a substantial number of people, then the privilege is one of public necessity. For instance, if a small lake in your town is threatening to flood and you enter another's land, without permission, to help construct a make-shift dam on that property to protect the adjoining neighborhoods from flood waters, that is a public necessity.

Necessity
The privilege to make reasonable use of another's property in order to prevent immediate harm or damage to persons or real or personal property.

SIDEBAR

BALANCING OF INTERESTS

The balancing of interests is pervasive in U.S. law. It can be found in many court decisions, including U.S. Supreme Court opinions, in which courts try to balance the competing interests of the litigants. Because the Supreme Court hears many cases involving the U.S. Constitution, many opinions are written in which the Supreme Court balances the competing interests of a private litigant and a governmental entity, such as Fourth Amendment search and seizure cases, in which the interest of the individual in his freedoms guaranteed by the Constitution conflicts with the government's interest in pursuing criminal justice on behalf of society.

Among the many examples in which balancing of interests can be seen in the tort arena are invasion of privacy cases, in which the privacy interests of an individual may conflict with a public right, such as a celebrity being photographed while engaging in a private activity. Also consider the case of nuisance, in which a court must balance the interests of neighboring property occupiers when one's use interferes with the other's quiet use and enjoyment of his property and the court must determine whether the interference is unreasonable. In making these determinations, the courts must decide which party has the more compelling interest warranting legal protection.

CASE on Point

Trisuzzi v. Tabatchnik, 666 A.2d 543 (N.J. Super. Ct. App. Div. 1995)

In this case already discussed in Chapter 3, the defense of private necessity succeeded. This was a case involving a dog attack. A German Shepherd attacked Mr. Trisuzzi while he, his wife, and grown daughter were taking an evening walk. The defendants (the dog's owners) claimed that Mr. Trisuzzi came upon their property to fight with the dog, when Mr. Trisuzzi used martial arts kicks and other moves against the dog, as well as beat the dog with a tree branch.

The court said that Mr. Trisuzzi could have been lawfully on the defendants' property in order to protect himself or his family from his perceived threat from the dog. It said that Mr. Trisuzzi had a right by "implied invitation" to be on the defendants' property if he was there to protect himself or his family members from serious physical harm. The court defined the privilege of necessity as follows: "One is privileged to enter or remain on land in the possession of another if it is or reasonably appears to be necessary to prevent serious harm to" the person or to a third person.

When the defendant's use of the plaintiff's property is undertaken to protect the defendant himself, or another person, then the privilege is one of private necessity. For instance, if you use a stranger's car, without permission, to rush a family member to the hospital in an emergency, that is a private necessity.

The distinction between public and private necessity is important in determining whether the defendant is responsible for any damage he causes to the other person's property while using it without permission. If it is a private necessity, the defendant may use the other person's property, without permission, to prevent a greater harm to himself or another person or property. However, she is legally responsible for any damages or harm she may cause to the property. In contrast, under the common law, a defendant is not legally responsible to provide compensation for harm caused by public necessity. However, many states have enacted statutes to modify this common law result, imposing on the defendant the responsibility to compensate the property owner in certain situations, usually when the harm is committed by public employees, such as police officers and fire fighters.

When it comes to necessity, remember that it is a defense allowing a person to commit one type of harm, namely, use of another's property without permission, in order to avoid a more serious harm. Compensation to the person with the right to possession of the property may be required.

What about a parent's or a teacher's right to discipline a child? Is there a defense to intentional torts, such as battery, for engaging in discipline? The answer is yes, in certain circumstances.

DISCIPLINE

Discipline
The privilege to use reasonable force or confinement to control, train, or educate a child.

Discipline is the privilege to use reasonable force or confinement to control, train, or educate a child. The *Restatement (Second) of Torts* says that a child's parent may use reasonable force or impose reasonable confinement on a child if she reasonably

CASE on Point

Illinois v. Green, 957 N.E.2d 1233 (Ill. App. Ct. 2011)

In this criminal case, a mother was prosecuted for domestic battery against her minor son. The court discussed a parent's right to corporally punish his or her child. It said the Constitutional right to privacy encompasses the right to care for, control, and discipline one's own children and noted that the discipline allowed is "reasonable corporal punishment." Balancing different rights, the court noted that while parents have a right to privacy in the manner in which they raise their children, this right to privacy must be balanced against the state's interest in preventing and deterring the mistreatment of children. A parent who inflicts corporal punishment that exceeds the boundaries of *reasonable* may be subject to prosecution for cruelty to children.

The court recited the common law rule that parents may take reasonable steps to discipline their children when necessary, and like self-defense, discipline is a legal justification for an otherwise criminal act. The court noted several factors to be considered in determining whether discipline is reasonable: the degree of injury inflicted on the child, the likelihood of future punishment that might be more injurious, the psychological effects of the discipline on the child, and whether the parent was calmly attempting to discipline the child or was lashing out in anger.

In this case, the court determined that the mother exercised unreasonable discipline and was guilty of the crime of domestic battery for several reasons. First, the mother struck her son with multiple hard blows on his torso and legs over a several-minute period, with a snow brush about 2.5 feet long. She stood over her son, striking downward while he lay in a faceup position. During the incident, the son had his arms up trying to defend himself and he was crying. The mother continued to strike her son despite his pleas. Only after a witness called the police did the mother drive away with her son. As she drove away, the son put his hands out of the vehicle, looked at the witness, and flexed his finders in a way interpreted to mean he was asking for help.

believes it is necessary for the reasonable control, education, or training of the child.[5] Someone other than a parent who by law was given or who has voluntarily assumed the role of controlling, educating, and training the child may use the same reasonable force or confinement so long as the parent has not restricted that privilege.[6]

The force used to discipline a child must be reasonable, and it can never be excessive. Reasonableness depends on factors such as the child's age, size, behaviors, mental abilities, and the like. Local and state statutes regulate this conduct more particularly, especially in the criminal arena relating to child abuse.

Justification is yet another defense to intentional torts. It is applied in the interest of fairness, when the other intentional tort defenses do not fit. Justification is discussed next.

JUSTIFICATION

Justification is a reasonable belief by the court that the defendant's actions were justified and it would be unfair to hold the person liable for his actions. Where it is recognized, it operates as a complete defense to the plaintiff's tort claim. Consider the following Case on Point.

Justification
A reasonable belief by the court that the defendant's actions were justified and it would be unfair to hold the person liable for his actions.

CASE on Point

Sindle v. New York City Transit Auth., 307 N.E.2d 245 (N.Y. 1973)

At about noon on June 20, 1967, the 14-year-old plaintiff boarded a school bus owned by the defendant, New York City Transit Authority, and driven by its employee, the defendant Mooney. It was the last day of the term, and the seventy or so students on the bus were in a boisterous, exuberant mood. In their excitement, some students on the bus committed vandalism by breaking lights, windows, ceiling panels, and advertising poster frames on the bus. There was no evidence that the plaintiff committed any vandalism.

The bus made several of its appointed stops. On at least one occasion, the driver admonished the students about excessive noise and damage to the bus. When he reached the Annadale station stop, the driver discharged several more passengers, went to the rear of the bus, inspected the damage, and notified the remaining passengers that he was taking them to the St. George police station.

The driver closed the doors of the bus and proceeded to drive, bypassing several normal stops. As the bus slowed to turn on to Woodrow Road, several students jumped from a side window at the rear of the bus, apparently without injuring themselves. Several more students followed, again without apparent harm, when the bus turned onto Arden Avenue. At the corner of Arden Avenue and Arthur Kill Road, departing from its normal route, the bus turned right in the general direction of the St. George police station. The plaintiff, intending to jump from the bus, positioned himself in a window on the right-rear side. As the bus turned right, the right rear wheels hit the curb and the plaintiff either jumped or fell to the street. The right rear wheels of the bus then rolled over the midsection of his body, seriously injuring the plaintiff.

The plaintiff sued the defendants for negligence and false imprisonment, but waived the negligence cause of action at the start of the trial. At the close of the plaintiff's case, the court denied the defendants' motion to amend their answers to plead the defense of justification and excluded all evidence relating to the justification defense.

The New York Court of Appeals ruled that it was an abuse of discretion for the trial court to deny the defendants' motion to amend and to exclude the evidence supporting the justification defense. The court reasoned that it was the defendants' burden to prove justification, noting that a plaintiff in a false imprisonment action should be prepared to meet the justification defense. Further, the court outlined some of the considerations relevant to the issue of justification. It said that "restraint or detention, reasonable under the circumstances and in time and manner, imposed for the purpose of preventing another from inflicting personal injuries or interfering with or damaging real or personal property" in one's lawful possession or custody is not unlawful. Applying these considerations to the facts of the case, the court said "a school bus driver, entrusted with the care of his student-passengers and the custody of public property, has the duty to take reasonable measures for the safety and protection of both." In determining the reasonableness of his actions, the court said to consider all of the circumstances, including "the need to protect the persons and property in his charge, the duty to aid the investigation and apprehension of those inflicting damage, the manner and place of the occurrence, and the feasibility and practicality of other alternative courses of action."

The court concluded that if the jury determines that the plaintiff was falsely imprisoned but that he acted unreasonably "by placing himself in a perilous position in the window of the bus preparatory to an attempt to alight," his recovery would be barred by the justification defense.

CASE on Point

Tuttle v. Buck, 119 N.W. 946 (Minn. 1909)

Recall this case from Chapter 4, in which a wealthy man forced the local barber out of business by opening a competing barber shop for the sole purpose of driving the local barber out of business. In *dicta* in that case, the Supreme Court of Minnesota said, "To divert to one's self the customers of a business rival by the offer of goods at lower prices is in general a legitimate mode of serving one's own interest, and justifiable as fair competition." Although the defendant's conduct in that case was not considered justifiable, the court noted that fair competition is legitimate, lawful conduct.

The defense of justification is often used as a defense to tortious interference claims. For example, if the defendant had a contract to sell gloves to a wholesaler, knowing the wholesaler had a contract to resell the goods to a retailer, the defendant could stop shipment of the goods if the wholesaler breaches his contract with her despite the fact that the retailer might be injured as a result. Justification would be a valid defense to a tortious interference with a contractual relationship claim in that situation. Accordingly, it is a defense to the tortious interference torts if the interference was justified. The interference may be justified if it is undertaken to protect the defendant's own interests (in the glove example, above) or the legitimate interests of another. It may also be justified when it constitutes bona-fide competitive behavior. Although unfair competition is disfavored under U.S. law, bona-fide competitive behavior is not only accepted, but encouraged. The interference must be beyond the limits of bona-fide business competition to constitute a tort. Consider the following examples. Effective advertising, which lures customers to one's business, is acceptable competitive behavior. Lowering prices and offering rebates are acceptable competitive practices even though they are designed to increase one's business at the expense of another's. Deceptive advertising, on the other hand, which wrongly lures customers to another's business, is unfair competition and unlawful. So is the use of monopoly power to force customers to pay higher prices. There is a distinction between bona-fide business competition and business competition that is tortious. See the above Case on Point for an example.

The defense of justification is also often used to defend against claims brought under the *prima facie* tort doctrine. A defendant may defend a *prima facie* tort action by demonstrating that his act was justified. The Missouri Court of Appeals, in *Porter v. Crawford & Co.*, a Case on Point from Chapter 4, stated that if a defendant can prove sufficient justification for his act, he will not be liable under the *prima facie* tort doctrine. In that case, the court said the defendant "may, of course, plead and prove any facts establishing a justification for the act of stopping payment on the draft," and in doing so, may defeat the plaintiff's claim.

Another defense to intentional torts is statutes of limitations. Statutes of limitations are examined next.

CASE on Point

Doe v. Johnson, 817 F.Supp. 1382 (W.D. Mich. 1993)

In this case, a female plaintiff and her infant child brought legal action, including a battery claim, against her male sex partner because of his transmission to her of the human immunodeficiency virus (HIV). In defending this claim, the defendant argued that the statute of limitations in Michigan required the plaintiffs to bring their action for battery within two years, which they failed to do. The court responded that Michigan courts follow the discovery rule to determine when a cause of action accrues to start the running of a statute of limitations. Under the discovery rule, a claim does not accrue until the plaintiff discovers or through the exercise of reasonable diligence should have discovered that the plaintiff was injured and what a likely cause of the injury was. The court ruled that the plaintiffs did not know or have reason to know that Johnson had infected them with HIV until June 1991 (despite the fact that the sexual encounter between the adult female plaintiff and the defendant occurred on June 22 or 23, 1990). Since the plaintiffs brought the action on October 30, 1992, they brought it within the two-year period required by the Michigan statute of limitations for the tort of battery.

STATUTES OF LIMITATIONS

Statutes of limitations
Statutes enacted by legislatures that set time limits during which plaintiffs may bring certain types of legal actions including tort actions.

Every tort action has a time limit within which the action must be brought. It if is not brought within that time limit, it can never be brought. These deadlines are set forth in ***statutes of limitations***. The limitations periods are set forth in the statutes, enacted by legislatures, and differ from tort to tort and from jurisdiction to jurisdiction. The statute of limitations operates as a defense if it is asserted by the defendant in arguing that a plaintiff's claim was brought too late.

The purpose of statutes of limitations is to encourage plaintiffs to bring their causes of action in a diligent manner, when evidence is still available and witnesses' memories are clearer. It is considered unfair, under the law, to expect a defendant to be able to defend himself too long after the incident or occurrence, when the plaintiff could have brought the action sooner.

If the defendant is able to defend herself successfully, either by establishing that the plaintiff failed to establish a *prima facie* tort claim by failing to provide sufficient evidence of one or more of the essential elements of a tort, or by establishing an affirmative defense as discussed above, then the defendant will win the lawsuit by having a verdict entered in her favor. If

STATUTE on Point

Ga. Code Ann. § 9-3-32 (2009)

In Georgia, actions for conversion or destruction of personal property must be brought within four years after the cause of action accrues. This is an example of a statute of limitations.

the defendant fails to so defend an intentional tort claim made by a plaintiff, then the plaintiff will win the lawsuit by having a verdict entered in his favor. In that case, the court will award some sort of remedy to the plaintiff. What, then, are remedies? Remedies are discussed next.

Definition of Remedies

Remedies are the way legal rights are enforced or the violations of rights are prevented, redressed, or compensated. They are awarded by a court to successful parties in litigation.

There are two types of remedies, remedies at law and remedies in equity. *Remedies at law* are monetary awards, called *damages*. Damages are the usual form of remedy in most cases, including tort cases. For instance, if Wally committed the tort of battery against Sarah, causing her physical injury and emotional harm, Sarah, if she won her tort claim, could recover damages, meaning money, for the physical injury and emotional harm she suffered.

Sometimes, however, damages are not adequate to compensate the victim of a wrong. For instance, suppose Lance trespasses across Georganna's real property every day when he walks to work. Lance does not cause physical harm to the property. If Georganna sues Lance for the tort of trespass to land, Georganna will not want to recover damages from Lance. He has not actually harmed her land. Rather, Georganna will want to stop Lance from continuing to walk across her land. In that case, Georganna will seek a remedy other than damages. She will seek a remedy in equity.

Remedies in equity, also called *equitable remedies*, are all remedies other than remedies at law. Hence, they are all remedies other than money damages. They include remedies such as injunctions, specific performance, reformation, and rescission. Equitable remedies are awarded in the court's discretion, when remedies at law are not adequate. In Georganna's case, she would want the equitable remedy of an injunction. An *injunction* is a court order requiring a person to do or refrain from doing a certain act. Georganna would want to enjoin, meaning stop, Lance from trespassing across her property. What remedies, then, are typically awarded in intentional tort cases?

Remedies for Intentional Torts

The usual remedy for a successful intentional tort claim is damages. As mentioned above, damages are compensation in the form of money. Several types of damages may be awarded, and they can be awarded together—they are not independent. As summarized in Table 5-1, the following types of damage awards may be made in intentional tort claims: compensatory, nominal, punitive, and pain and suffering.

Compensatory damages are damages awarded to compensate, meaning reimburse, the plaintiff for actual harm suffered. They are intended to make the plaintiff whole. This type of damages is the most common type awarded in tort actions. Included in compensatory damages are, among other things, amounts recoverable to pay medical bills, to compensate for lost wages, and to recover the value of damage to property.

Remedies
The way legal rights are enforced or the violations of rights are prevented, redressed, or compensated.

Remedies at law
Recovery in a civil lawsuit in the form of money damages.

Damages
The remedy at law.

Remedies in equity
Forms of recovery in a civil lawsuit other than money damages, which are awarded by a court, in its discretion; also called equitable remedies.

Injunction
A court order requiring a person to do or refrain from doing a certain act.

Compensatory damages
Damages awarded to compensate, or reimburse, the plaintiff for the actual harm suffered and awarded to make the plaintiff whole again.

TABLE 5-1 Damages

Type	Use
Compensatory	To compensate the victim for the actual injury suffered
Nominal	When wrongdoing has occurred but there is little or no actual harm or damage suffered by the plaintiff
Punitive	To punish the tortfeasor for committing the wrongful conduct and to deter future similar misconduct
Pain and suffering	To recover for actual pain, fear, anxiety, humiliation, depression, loss of companionship, and similar emotional harms suffered

General damages
Those compensatory damages that are normally and reasonably expected from the defendant's actions; also called direct damages.

Special damages
Those compensatory damages that are incurred beyond and in addition to the general damages suffered and expected from the defendant's conduct, which are specific, or peculiar, to the plaintiff and which must be specifically pled; also called consequential damages.

Nominal damages
Damages awarded when wrongdoing has occurred, but little or no injury or harm is suffered by the plaintiff.

Punitive damages
Damages awarded to the plaintiff to punish the defendant and to deter future wrongdoing; also called exemplary damages.

Compensatory damages may be general or special. *General damages* are those compensatory damages that are normally and reasonably expected to result from the defendant's actions. These are the kinds of damages that normally flow from the kind of wrong committed by the defendant. They are also called *direct damages* because they arise directly out of the plaintiff's injury. General damages are presumed to flow from the type of wrong committed. For example, medical bills are normally expected to be incurred by a plaintiff who suffers injury because of a tortious battery, and they are considered general damages. *Special damages* are those compensatory damages that are incurred beyond and in addition to the general damages suffered and expected from the defendant's conduct. They do not flow directly from the injurious act, but rather result indirectly from the act. They are specific, or peculiar, to the particular plaintiff, and are sometimes called particular damages. For instance, an element of compensatory damages is lost wages for a plaintiff who is out of work recovering from his injury. The amount of lost wages depends on the particular plaintiff—how injured he is, how long he is out of work, and how much compensation he earns at work. Going beyond general damages, these damages must be specially pled by the plaintiff (in the complaint) when the lawsuit is brought in order to be recovered. Special damages are also called *consequential damages*.

Nominal damages are awarded when wrongdoing has occurred, but little or no injury or harm is suffered by the plaintiff. They are small in amount, often $1. Their point is to establish that the defendant's conduct was wrongful. Most lawsuits for nominal damages are brought as a matter of principle; given the significant expense of litigation, these suits are not often cost effective.

Punitive damages, also called *exemplary damages*, are damages awarded to the plaintiff to punish the defendant and to deter future wrongdoing. When they are awarded, they are in addition to compensatory damages. Punitive damages can be calculated based on the defendant's conduct and/or the defendant's income. Although recovering punitive damages is not standard, they may be recovered in intentional tort cases because the tortfeasor acted with intent and caused harm to the person or property. The more egregious the defendant's conduct in an intentional tort case, the more likely punitive damages may be awarded. Punitive damages are also common in products liability cases—these cases are studied later in the text. Tort reform, aimed at curbing excessive personal injury awards, is in part triggered by large punitive damages awards, such as in the McDonald's coffee case discussed in Chapter 1. In that products liability case, in addition to compensatory damages of $200,000, the jury awarded punitive damages of $2.7 million, which was calculated to be one to two days' worth of McDonald's coffee revenues.[7] So, although this award was a huge amount given the circumstances, it was relatively small considering the magnitude of McDonald's revenues. This case demonstrates the calculation of punitive damages based on the defendant's income.

In addition to compensation for medical bills, lost wages, damage to property, and the like, plaintiffs are also entitled to recover damages for pain and suffering incurred as a result of the defendant's wrongful conduct. ***Pain and suffering damages*** include recovery for harms such as actual pain, fear, anxiety, humiliation, depression, loss of companionship, and the like. Although they are not as easy to measure as lost wages or medical bills, they are nonetheless recoverable. It is up to the court, often a jury, to determine the amount.

What about when damages are not adequate to make the plaintiff whole? Sometimes, damages are not sufficient to right the wrong committed against the plaintiff. Recall the situation involving Lance trespassing on Georganna's land. In such cases, equitable remedies may be awarded by the court, in its discretion. Of the many types of equitable remedies already mentioned, including reformation, rescission, and specific performance (more normally associated with contract law cases), injunctions are the likely equitable remedy awarded in cases involving intentional torts. Remember that injunctions are court orders requiring a defendant to do or refrain from doing something. In Lance's case, the appropriate remedy to do justice would be an injunction ordering him not to trespass on Georganna's land. Also remember the tortious interference torts discussed in Chapter 4. When the interference is threatened or continuing, rather than accomplished, damages may be an inadequate remedy. In such a case, an injunction to compel the defendant to stop the interference may be warranted.

A plaintiff has a duty to mitigate, or lessen, her damages whenever it is reasonable to do so. This is the ***mitigation of damages doctrine***, also called the ***doctrine of avoidable consequences***. The mitigation of damages doctrine applies in tort law as well as in other areas of law, such as contract law. It also applies to all types of torts, including intentional torts, negligence, and strict liability. Failure to mitigate damages may reduce or limit the plaintiff's recovery in a tort case, including an intentional tort case. For instance, if the plaintiff is physically injured from a battery committed against her by the defendant, she is obligated under the mitigation of damages doctrine to seek reasonable medical care for her injuries. If the plaintiff refuses reasonable medical care and is harmed further by lack of proper medical treatment, the defendant is not legally responsible for the additional harm the plaintiff suffers. Rather, the defendant is liable only for the original harm he caused the plaintiff. So even though the defendant caused the plaintiff's injuries, he is not liable for any further harm caused by the plaintiff's failure to obtain reasonable medical treatment. The plaintiff has a duty to mitigate her damages, to protect herself, and to minimize the extent of harm she suffers, and is responsible for the consequences from not doing so.

Whether at law or in equity, a plaintiff who is harmed by the purposeful wrongful conduct of another may be entitled to legal relief in the form of some remedy or remedies. This is the case when intentional torts are committed.

Pain and suffering damages
Damages awarded to recover for actual pain, fear, anxiety, humiliation, depression, loss of companionship, and similar emotional harms suffered.

Mitigation of damages doctrine
The legal requirement that a person who has suffered injury because of another's misconduct must take reasonable steps to mitigate, or lessen, the damages she suffers or her recovery may be denied or reduced by the amount of harm she could have avoided; also called the doctrine of avoidable consequences.

CHAPTER **SUMMARY**

- A defense is legal reason why a claim should be denied or reduced. A defense is asserted by a party who is defending himself against a legal claim.

- The major defenses to intentional tort actions are consent, self-defense, defense of others, defense of property, reentry onto land, recapture of chattels, necessity, discipline, justification, and statutes of limitations.

- Consent is a plaintiff's knowing and voluntary willingness to let the defendant's conduct occur and to accept its consequences.

- Self-defense is the right of a person to use reasonable force to prevent immediate harmful or offensive contact by another against himself.

- Defense of others is the right of a person to use reasonable force to prevent immediate harmful or offensive contact by another against someone other than himself.

- Defense of property is the right of a person to use reasonable, but never deadly, force to prevent immediate interference with his property or to end interference already occurring.

- Reentry onto land is the limited right to use reasonable force to reenter and reclaim real property when the plaintiff has wrongfully dispossessed the defendant.

- Recapture of chattels is the right to use reasonable force to regain possession and control over one's personal property.

- Necessity is the privilege to make reasonable use of another's property in order to prevent immediate harm or damage to persons or to real or personal property.

- Discipline is the privilege to use reasonable force or confinement to control, train, or educate a child.

- Justification is a reasonable belief by the court that the defendant's actions were justified and it would be unfair to hold the person liable for his actions.

- Statutes of limitations are time limits established by legislatures during which plaintiffs must bring their causes of action. Any tort action brought after the running (expiration) of the relevant statute of limitations is untimely, and the defendant can successfully assert the running of the statute of limitations as a defense to the tort claim.

- Remedies are the way legal rights are enforced or the violations of rights are prevented, redressed, or compensated. They are awarded by a court to successful parties in litigation, including intentional tort litigation.

- There are two types of remedies, remedies at law and remedies in equity. Remedies at law are, essentially, money damages. Remedies in equity are all remedies other than remedies at law, thus, other than damages. They include remedies such as injunctions and specific performance. Equitable remedies are awarded in the court's discretion.

- The usual remedy for a successful intentional tort claim is damages. The following types of damage awards may be made: compensatory, nominal, punitive, and pain and suffering.

- Compensatory damages are damages awarded to compensate, or reimburse, the plaintiff for the actual harm suffered, to make the plaintiff whole again. This type of damages is the most common type awarded in tort actions. Compensatory damages may be general or special. General damages are those compensatory damages that are normally and reasonably expected from the defendant's actions. They are also called direct damages because they arise directly out of the injury to the plaintiff. Special damages are those compensatory damages that are incurred beyond and in addition to the general damages suffered and expected from the defendant's conduct. They are specific, or peculiar, to the particular plaintiff. Special damages are also called consequential damages and must be specifically pled to be recoverable.

- Nominal damages are awarded when wrongdoing has occurred but little or no injury or harm is suffered by the plaintiff. They are small in amount, but they do establish that the defendant's conduct was wrongful.

- Punitive damages, also called exemplary damages, are damages awarded to the plaintiff to punish the defendant and to deter future wrongdoing. When they are awarded, they are in addition to compensatory damages. They may be calculated based on the defendant's conduct and/or the defendant's income. They may be recovered in intentional tort cases because the tortfeasor acted with intent and caused harm to the person or property.

- Plaintiffs are also entitled to recover damages for pain and suffering incurred by them as a result of the defendant's wrongful conduct. Pain and suffering damages include recovery for harms such as actual pain, fear, anxiety, humiliation, depression, loss of companionship, and the like.

- Sometimes money damages are not sufficient to right the wrong committed against the plaintiff. In such cases, equitable remedies may be awarded by the court, in its discretion. An example of an equitable remedy is an injunction, which is a court order requiring a defendant to do or refrain from doing something, such as an order requiring the defendant to stop trespassing on another's land.

- A plaintiff has the duty to mitigate, or lessen, her damages whenever it is reasonable to do so. Failure to mitigate damages may reduce or limit the plaintiff's recovery in a tort case, including an intentional tort case.

CONCEPT REVIEW AND REINFORCEMENT

QUESTIONS FOR **REVIEW**

1. What is a defense?
2. What are the major defenses to intentional torts?
3. What are remedies?
4. How is a remedy at law distinguished from a remedy in equity?
5. What different remedies are available for intentional tort claims?
6. How are the different types of damages distinguished?

DEVELOPING YOUR PARALEGAL SKILLS

CRITICAL THINKING **EXERCISES**

1. In this chapter, we studied the defenses to intentional torts including consent, self-defense, defense of others, defense of property, reentry onto land, recapture of chattels, necessity, discipline, justification, and statutes of limitations. As you know, each state may "customize" these defenses in its case law (or, for statutes of limitations, enact them in their relevant statutes). Research the law in your state on each of these defenses to intentional torts to see in what way(s), if any, they differ from most states' laws. An excellent starting point for your research is a case law digest for your state. For example, in Maryland, the resource *Maryland Digest 2d* by West includes cases from Maryland establishing each of these common law defenses. You should search for your state's statutes of limitations in your state code. Share your research results in class.

2. Michael is scheduled to undergo a surgical procedure on Wednesday. On Tuesday, he visits his surgeon's office for some preliminary lab work and to complete paperwork in anticipation of his upcoming surgery. The surgeon meets with Michael to explain what will

happen during the next day's surgery. He provides Michael with a detailed explanation of the benefits and risks of that particular surgery. Afterward, the physician's assistant gives Michael several papers to read and sign. One of the papers is entitled "Patient's Informed Consent." The several paragraphs on that page summarize the discussion Michael just had with the surgeon, explaining the benefits and risks of this surgery. Michael signs that paper, along with all the others. The next day, during surgery, Michael suffers an adverse reaction to the anesthesia and is injured. He sues the doctor for the tort of battery (not malpractice, which we will examine later).

Will the doctor be able to successfully defend himself by asserting that Michael consented to the contact that constituted the surgery performed? Why or why not?

3. Bryce is walking to her car, parked in a dark and deserted parking lot. Tony, needing directions to the local hospital to visit his ailing mother, approaches Bryce quickly from behind. He intends to ask her for directions. Bryce, feeling threatened by the presence of someone coming up behind her, reaches into her purse and takes out a can of pepper spray. She waits a few seconds to allow Tony to get a bit closer. Then, suddenly, Bryce spins around, aims, and sprays Tony in the face with her pepper spray.

Were Bryce's actions privileged self-defense, or did she just commit the tort of battery against Tony? Why or why not? Remember, Tony was only approaching her to ask for directions to the hospital to visit his sick mother.

4. Daniel is picking a fight with Gerald. Gerald, a peaceable man, is trying his best to ignore Daniel, though without much success. Taylor, observing the situation from across the street, comes to Gerald's defense. When it appears that Daniel is about to push Gerald in the chest, Taylor punches Daniel in the stomach, causing Daniel to double over in pain.

Were Taylor's actions within the privilege of defense of others, or has Taylor committed the tort of battery against Daniel? Why or why not?

5. a. Frank is asleep in his bed one night. A noise causes him to wake. Frank hears shuffling sounds and movement coming from inside the house. Terrified that there is an intruder, Frank approaches the hallway to investigate the source of the noise. Entering the hallway, Frank is confronted by an intruder. Each is surprised at the sight of the other. Catching the intruder temporarily off guard, Frank grabs the intruder by the shirt and shoves him sideways, down the cellar steps, then slams shut the cellar door and locks it. He hurries to call 911 and alert the police.

Has Frank committed a tort against the intruder by grabbing him and shoving him down the cellar stairs? Why or why not?

b. Now assume that when Frank is awakened by the noise, he quietly retrieves a pistol from his nightstand. When he is confronted by the intruder in his hallway, Frank shouts, "Don't move or I'll shot." The intruder turns to run, and Frank keeps his word—shooting the intruder in the back.

Is Frank's conduct within the privilege of defense of property? Why or why not?

c. Now assume that, when Frank and the intruder run into each other in the hallway, Frank sees the intruder standing there, armed with a shotgun. Before the intruder can raise his weapon, Frank raises his pistol and fires, shooting the intruder. The next day, the intruder dies of his injuries while being treated at the hospital.

Should Frank be liable in tort for the injury (death) he caused to the intruder? Why or why not?

6. a. Ruby leaves her backpack on a table in the library while she goes to make a copy of an assignment. Upon returning to the table, she discovers her backpack is missing. Quickly scanning the area for a sign of her property, Ruby sees Dahlila leaving the library wearing Ruby's backpack. Ruby scurries after Dahlila and catches up to her in the common area outside the library. Placing herself in Dahlila's path, Ruby says, "That's my backpack. Please give it back to me now." Dahlila refuses. Ruby grabs the pack and pulls, getting it off Dahlila. Mission accomplished, Ruby promptly leaves the scene with her backpack.

Did Ruby have the legal right to take her backpack from Dahlila? Why or why not?

b. Now assume that, after retaking her backpack, Ruby returns to her dorm room and opens the book compartment. Looking inside the backpack, she realizes that this is not her bag, and not her stuff. It all belongs to Dahlila.

What is the impact of mistake on the relevant self-help privilege?

7. Melody is hiking through the woods one hot, summer afternoon. A monstrous thunderstorm blows in. Lightning is so fierce that Melody must seek shelter, if she can find it. She does find it—in the plaintiff's barn. Melody trespasses onto the land of the plaintiff, breaks into her barn, and waits out the storm.

Did Melody have the legal right to do what she did? Why or why not?

8. Doug, Jill's 9-year old son, is behaving horribly. In the middle of his sister's birthday party, Doug pitches a tantrum, kicking his mother and calling her disrespectful names. Not wanting to raise a juvenile delinquent, Jill forcibly ushers Doug to the dining room, where she gives him a spank on the behind with her bare hand, and puts him in a twenty-minute "time out." Jill threatens to spank Doug if he moves out of time out before he is allowed.

Has Jill committed the torts of battery, assault, and/or the tort of false imprisonment against Doug by spanking him, forcibly removing him to another room, and threatening to spank him if he moves from the room before his "time out" is completed? Why or why not?

ASSIGNMENTS AND PRACTICAL **APPLICATIONS**

1. Assign students one or more of the defenses to intentional torts and ask the students to role-play their defenses, using their own hypothetical situations, for the class.

2. Read and brief the *Katko v. Briney* and *Sindle v. New York City Transit Auth.* cases discussed in this chapter.

3. Research whether your state will uphold the privilege of defense of others when the defendant makes a reasonable mistake in believing the other person was threatened, or in the amount of force needed to counter the threat. Remember that most states say even a reasonable mistake will defeat this privilege. Discuss your research results with the class.

4. Research whether your state has adopted Model Penal Code section 3.06(1)(b) permitting reentry onto land and recapture of chattels under the circumstances discussed in this chapter. If there are differences, discuss these in class.

5. On informed consent of patients and the disclosure of HIV status of a surgeon, read and brief *Faya v. Almaraz*, 620 A.2d 327 (Md. 1993).

6. Read and brief the following cases involving self-defense and the reasonable use of force: *Roberts v. Am. Employers Ins. Co.*, 221 So.2d 550 (La. Ct. App. 1969) (on self-defense and the reasonable belief that one is under attack); now compare that case to *Taran v. State*, 186 A.D.2d 794 (N.Y. App. Div. 1992) (the force used must be equal to the threat).

7. Read and brief other intentional tort defense cases: *Ploof v. Putnam*, 71 A. 188 (Vt. 1908) (on the defense of private necessity and the protection of human life); *Vincent v. Lake Erie Transp. Co.*, 124 N.W. 221 (Minn. 1910) (necessity and the right of a plaintiff to receive compensation); *Hackbart v. Cincinnati Bengals, Inc.*, 601 F.2d 516 (10th Cir. 1979) (whether a player in a professional football game consents to harmful or offensive contact by another during the game); *Mohr v. Williams*, 104 N.W. 12 (Minn. 1905) (battery and the issue of patient consent); *Kirby v. Foster*, 22 A. 1111 (R.I. 1891) (when a property owner may use force to recapture a chattel); *Gillett v. Gillett*, 335 P.2d 736 (Cal. Dist. Ct. App. 1959) (the reasonable scope of discipline of a child by a caregiver).

TECHNOLOGY RESOURCES AND INTERNET **EXERCISES**

Informed consent is a critical issue in medical malpractice cases. To protect themselves from malpractice claims, medical professionals routinely ask patients to sign informed consent forms. Using the Internet, research the law in your state on informed consent pertaining to medical malpractice. What is required of a medical professional to obtain the informed consent of a patient?

Using the Internet resource FindLaw, research your state's law on tenant eviction procedures used by landlords. In many jurisdictions, this legal process is called "unlawful detainer." See *http://realestate.findlaw.com/tenant /tenant-eviction*.

Using enotes.com's Encyclopedia of Everyday Law, read about child discipline and abuse, including a brief summary of the child abuse statute in your (as well as each) state. See *www.enotes.com/everyday-law-encyclopedia /child-abuse-child-safety-discipline#state-laws*.

ETHICAL **APPLICATIONS**

Justin is a paralegal working for a personal injury law firm. Justin is working on a matter with George Walker, Esq. George is in court this week. On Monday, one of their clients, Phillip Jetts, telephones and asks to speak with George. Not hearing from George, who is busy at trial, Phillip calls back every day that week. By Thursday, Justin starts taking Phillip's calls, to try to answer the client's questions in George's absence. Phillip asks Justin his advice on whether he can defend a battery tort action filed against him by asserting the privilege of self-defense. Phillip explains all the relevant facts to Justin. Having studied tort law in college, Justin is quite sure Phillip has a good chance of establishing this defense and succeeding at trial. Justin believes George would support his conclusion. In fact,

Justin has been working in the field of personal injury law for twice as long as George has.

Is it permissible for Justin to render an opinion to Phillip on whether self-defense could be used to defend against this tort claim? Why or why not?

VIDEO **CASE STUDY**

Meet the Courthouse Team

Synopsis: This is an interview with trial court Judge Kenney, who introduces members of the courthouse team and describes their roles.

Note: This video introduces students to the "players" involved in courtroom proceedings. These people are present when tort cases go to trial.

chapter **6**

NEGLIGENCE: AN INTRODUCTION, AND THE ELEMENTS OF DUTY OF CARE AND BREACH

The next two chapters provide a comprehensive examination of the tort of negligence and its essential elements. This chapter introduces the tort of negligence. Then it examines the first two of four essential elements of this tort, namely, duty of care and breach of the duty of care. We start our discussion with an introduction to the tort of negligence.

Definition of Negligence

Negligence is the largest of the three main classifications of torts, the others being intentional torts and strict liability. The tort of negligence covers a wide variety of unreasonable conduct, including both unreasonable acts and unreasonable failures to act, that causes harm or injury to others or their property. *Negligence* is defined as harm caused by failure to use reasonable care. There is no *intent* requirement for this tort, as there is for the intentional torts; this means that with negligence, the tortfeasor neither wishes to bring about the consequences of the act nor believes the consequences will result. Rather, the tortfeasor's unreasonable conduct merely creates a risk of the consequences occurring. The risk he creates is the basis for negligence liability.

Now that we understand the basic concept of negligence, we will consider each of its essential elements, in turn. Like the intentional torts we covered earlier in the text, the tort of negligence is defined by its essential elements.

LEARNING OBJECTIVES

6.1 Define and explain the concept of negligence.

6.2 List and discuss the essential elements of the tort of negligence.

6.3 Explain the element of duty of care.

6.4 Explain the element of breach of the duty of care.

Negligence
Harm to persons and/or property caused by failure to exercise reasonable care.

Essential Elements of the Tort of Negligence

Key Point

The Essential Elements of Negligence

1. Duty of care
2. Breach of the duty of care
3. Causation (including cause in fact and proximate cause)
4. Damages

There are four essential elements of the tort of negligence. They are duty of care, breach of the duty of care, causation, and damages.

When the plaintiff has established these four elements, she has established a *prima facie* case of negligence. Then the burden of proof shifts to the defendant to defend himself by showing that his conduct was reasonable or by providing some other valid legal defense. Defenses to negligence are the subject of Chapter 9.

Duty of care is the first essential element of the tort of negligence; accordingly, we will discuss it first. Without there being a duty of care owed to the plaintiff by the defendant, there is no negligence.

Duty of Care

Duty of care
An obligation to conform to a standard of conduct prescribed by law.

Duty of care is an obligation to conform to a standard of conduct prescribed by law. It is a duty imposed by law from which an obligation arises to act with due care, meaning reasonably. Normally it is the court's responsibility to determine as a matter of law the question of whether a duty of care exists; later the jury in a jury trial can determine whether the duty of care was breached, and if so, if that breach caused the plaintiff harm. In determining whether there is a duty of care owed, several questions must be considered. When does a duty of care arise?

SIDEBAR

DISTINGUISHING NEGLIGENCE FROM INSURANCE LAW

Negligence is distinguishable from insurance law. Negligence is a tort, for which a successful plaintiff may recover a remedy, normally damages. A fundamental notion of negligence is that the defendant's conduct must be unreasonable. Contrast this with insurance law. Insurance law deals with contracts. For instance, automobile insurance a driver purchases is a contract, covering certain types of losses, up to certain dollar amounts, and paid for by insurance premiums. When an accident occurs, payment to those involved in the accident is based on the terms of the insurance contract, called a policy. Payment is made only in accordance with the terms of the policy.

Automobile insurance contracts cover not only accidents caused by unreasonable conduct (when negligence is present) but also accidents occurring in the absence of negligence. For example, a car losing traction while being driven in a rain storm, veering from its lane and colliding with another car, causes compensable loss under the insurance policy even in the absence of unreasonable driving by the person causing the accident.

Injured parties are automatically compensated for losses covered under the terms of the relevant insurance policy, which is just a special type of contract. All that is needed to recover is a covered person, a covered injury, and causation. Negligence involves much more than just causing injury—negligence requires the injury be caused by wrongful, unreasonable conduct.

CASE on Point

Bryant v. Better Bus. Bureau of Greater Md., Inc., 923 F.Supp. 720 (D. Md. 1996)

The essential elements of the tort of negligence in Maryland are set forth in this case. They are identified by the District Court of Maryland as duty of care, breach of the duty of care, causation, and damages. The court said that to establish a claim of negligence, a plaintiff must prove the existence of "a duty owed by a defendant to him (or to a class of which he is a part), a breach of that duty, a legally cognizable causal relationship between the breach of duty and the harm suffered, and damages."

In this case a hearing-impaired employee brought an action against her employer and its president alleging, among other things, negligent selection, supervision, or retention of an employee. The court said that in order to prove such a cause of action, the plaintiff must prove that her injury was caused by the tortious conduct of a coworker; that the employer knew or should have known by the exercise of reasonable care that the coworker was capable of inflicting harm of some type; that the employer failed to use proper care in selecting, supervising, or retaining that employee; and that the employer's breach of its duty was the proximate cause of the plaintiff's harm. Here the court found the employee failed to establish this negligence cause of action.

When it arises, what is the extent, or scope, of this duty? Who owes a duty of care? To whom is a duty of care owed?

A duty of care arises when someone's conduct creates a foreseeable risk of harm to someone else's person or property. What is the extent, or scope, of this duty? The duty is to take reasonable precautions to prevent the harm. What is reasonable depends on the facts and circumstances. The more foreseeable the harm, and the greater the potential harm, the more precautions must be taken to be "reasonable." The duty of care, then, is triggered by the foreseeability of the harm.

Note that a duty of care is not a duty to *prevent* harm. It is not a guarantee against harm. Rather, it is a duty to use reasonable care to prevent harm. For example, consider this hypothetical scenario. John is driving in the rain, at night. To whom does John owe a duty of care? John owes a duty of care to those toward whom his conduct creates a foreseeable risk of harm, such as other cars and their drivers and passengers who are on the road near John. What is the duty of care that John owes these persons? The duty of care is to use reasonable care to prevent injury to them or harm to their property. How does John accomplish this? He accomplishes this by driving more slowly, by turning on his headlights and windshield wipers, and by increasing the distance between his car and the car in front of him, as a reasonable person would do in driving in the rain at night. The duty of care does not require John to stay at home rather than drive in the rain at night. It is not a duty to prevent, or guarantee against, harm. Remember that the duty is to take reasonable precautions to prevent harm, not to guarantee against harm.

A duty of care is owed by a person if it is reasonably foreseeable that his conduct creates a foreseeable risk of harm to another's person or property. This test defines the normal case, or general rule, of who owes a duty of care, and to whom it is owed.

Sometimes, however, the person harmed by the defendant's conduct is unforeseeable. Consider the case of the unforeseeable plaintiff.

THE UNFORESEEABLE PLAINTIFF

When is a duty of care owed to an unforeseeable plaintiff? In determining who is owed a duty of care, if the plaintiff is foreseeable—meaning a person can reasonably foresee that his actions create a foreseeable risk of harm to another person or her property—then a duty of care is owed to her. But what about a plaintiff who is unforeseeable yet is nonetheless injured by the actor's conduct? Can a duty of care be owed to an unforeseeable plaintiff? Consider this example. Julia is driving her car at night in the rain, driving too fast and tailgating the car in front of her. Julia hits the car in front of her, causing part of its bumper to dislodge and fly through the air. Penelope, who is standing at a bus stop waiting for her bus, is struck by the dislodged piece of bumper and is injured. To whom did Julia owe a duty of care? Clearly, she owed one to the driver and passengers of the car she was tailgating; they are foreseeable plaintiffs because it is reasonably foreseeable that Julia's conduct created a foreseeable risk of harm to them and their property. However, what about the bystander who was hurt in the incident? The bystander is an example of an unforeseeable plaintiff. When is a duty of care owed to an unforeseeable plaintiff? According to the *Palsgraf* case, one of the most famous tort cases of all time, which is described in the Case on Point, in both the majority and the dissenting opinions, the answer to the question of whether a duty of care is owed to an unforeseeable plaintiff is "sometimes."

The majority opinion in the *Palsgraf* case, written by Judge Benjamin N. Cardozo, defines the **zone of danger test**, ruling that a duty of care is owed to an unforeseeable plaintiff, such as a bystander, if the plaintiff was within the foreseeable zone, or orbit, of danger. This test of whether an unforeseeable plaintiff is owed a duty of care is still followed in some jurisdictions today. Other jurisdictions follow the world at large test, which is set forth in the *Palsgraf* dissent. As the *Palsgraf* case illustrates, the issues of whether a duty of care is owed to an unforeseeable plaintiff and whether there is proximate cause, a part of the causation element of negligence discussed further in Chapter 7, are intertwined.

Consider this example. Brad is walking down the street. Carl is on the roof of a building along the street, where he is standing on a scaffold doing construction work. The scaffold was negligently constructed by employees of World Construction Products, Inc. The scaffold collapses and Carl falls to the ground, injured. During his fall, Carl dislodges construction materials piled near the roof's edge. These materials fall to the street, causing drivers to veer around the debris. One of the drivers inadvertently hits some debris, causing it to fly through the air, where Brad is struck by it and injured. Did World Construction Products, Inc., owe a duty of care to Carl? Yes, because its employees' conduct, in constructing the scaffold negligently, created a foreseeable risk of harm to him. Carl is a foreseeable plaintiff. But what about Brad?

CASE on Point

Palsgraf v. Long Island R.R. Co., 162 N.E. 99 (N.Y. 1928)

Chief Judge Benjamin Cardozo, a leading figure in the development of U.S. common law and later a Supreme Court justice, wrote the majority opinion in this famous case.

The plaintiff, Mrs. Helen Palsgraf, was standing on a Long Island Railroad platform waiting for her train. Another train stopped at the station, and two men ran to catch it as it started to pull away. One of the men jumped, without incident, onto the moving train. The other man, who was carrying a package, jumped on board a train car but seemed unsteady and about to fall. A guard on the train car reached forward to help the passenger in while another guard on the platform pushed the passenger from behind. The package, about 15 inches long and covered in newspaper, was dislodged from the passenger's hands and fell onto the train rails. The package contained fireworks that exploded when they hit the rails. The explosion "threw down some scales on the other end of the platform," striking the plaintiff and injuring her. As a result, the plaintiff brought a negligence action against the railroad company.

The Court of Appeals of New York said that the "conduct of the defendant's guard, if wrong in its relation to the holder of the package, was not a wrong in relation to the plaintiff," who was standing far away. "Relative to her, it was not negligence at all," said the court regarding the plaintiff, who was "removed" from the peril. The court reasoned that there must be a "duty to the individual complaining" that is breached rather than a person being a "vicarious beneficiary of a breach of duty to another." The court said that in this case, if there was a wrong at all, it was a wrong "to a property interest" of the passenger whose package was dislodged from his hands. The court was unwilling to extend to the plaintiff a right "to bodily security" based on a wrong "to a property interest" committed against another. In defining the zone, or orbit, of danger test, the court said: "[T]he orbit of the danger as disclosed to the eye of reasonable vigilance would be the orbit of the duty."

The court continued, "What the plaintiff must show is 'a wrong' to herself... and not merely a wrong to someone else," nor conduct "wrongful" generally but not "a wrong" to anyone. Further, the "risk reasonably to be perceived defines the duty to be obeyed, and risk imports relation; it is risk to another or to others within the range of apprehension." The court concluded that there was nothing to suggest that the package wrapped in newspaper would cause "wreckage through the station." Mrs. Palsgraf was found by the court to be an unforeseeable plaintiff outside the orbit of danger, and she was denied recovery for negligence.

The dissent in the *Palsgraf* case, written by Judge William S. Andrews, defined a broader test, the ***world at large test***. Today, in jurisdictions that follow the world at large test rather than the zone of danger test, the duty owed to an unforeseeable plaintiff is even more broadly defined, to include anyone injured as a result of a person's unreasonable conduct that places someone, not necessarily the plaintiff, in the foreseeable zone of danger.

Judge Andrews's dissenting opinion can be summarized as follows: A duty of care is imposed "on each one of us to protect society from unnecessary danger, not to protect A, B, or C alone." Everyone "owes to the world at large the duty of refraining from those acts that may unreasonably threaten the safety of others." Not only is one harmed to whom harm "might reasonably be expected to result," but also he who is in fact injured even if he is outside "the danger zone."

World at large test
A duty of care is owed to an unforeseeable plaintiff if, as a result of the defendant's unreasonable conduct, someone (not necessarily the plaintiff) was within the foreseeable zone of danger.

Key Point

Two Tests for Duty of Care and the Unforeseeable Plaintiff

Zone of Danger—A duty of care is owed to an unforeseeable plaintiff if the plaintiff was within the zone of danger of the foreseeable risk of harm created by the defendant's conduct.

World at Large—A duty of care is owed to an unforeseeable plaintiff if anyone in the world at large was within the zone of danger of the foreseeable risk of harm created by the defendant's conduct.

Brad is an unforeseeable plaintiff, a bystander injured by another's unreasonable conduct. Depending on the jurisdiction, either the zone of danger or the world at large test would be used to determine whether the company owed Brad a duty of care. Under the world at large test, the answer would be yes, because the company employees created a foreseeable risk of harm to someone (Carl). Under the zone of danger test, however, the issue is less clear. In a jury trial, it would be up to the jury to determine whether Brad himself, rather than some other person, was within the zone of danger resulting from the defendant's conduct. Note that this hypothetical situation raises a causation question as well—that of proximate cause. Did the defendant (World Construction Products, Inc.) cause Brad's injury? Duty of care and proximate cause are closely related, and both rely on principles of foreseeability. Causation is discussed in the next chapter.

An unreasonable act, such as constructing a scaffold improperly, can constitute negligence. What about an unreasonable failure to act?

Misfeasance
Misconduct by affirmative act.
Nonfeasance
Misconduct by failure to act.

Key Point

Distinguish Misfeasance and Nonfeasance

Misfeasance is an unreasonable action.
Nonfeasance is an unreasonable failure to act.

Key Point

Duty of Care Rule in a Nonfeasance Case

No duty of care is owed in a nonfeasance case unless (1) the injury to the plaintiff is foreseeable, (2) the defendant had the opportunity to prevent the injury, and (3) the plaintiff and the defendant are in a special relationship.

MISFEASANCE AND NONFEASANCE

A person can be negligent through his actions or through his failure to act. In a *misfeasance* case, a person commits an unreasonable act by engaging in affirmative conduct, such as driving too fast during a rainstorm. Sometimes negligence arises from a person's failure to act when a reasonable person would. These inactions are acts of omission and are known as cases of *nonfeasance*. For example, suppose someone sees another person in danger, being swept away by a riptide while swimming in the ocean. Would the observer who does nothing have breached a duty of care to the imperiled swimmer? The answer is no: No duty of care is owed in this instance. So what is the duty of care rule in nonfeasance cases?

In nonfeasance cases, the general rule is that no duty of care is owed unless the following three elements are present: (1) The injury to the plaintiff is foreseeable, (2) the defendant had the opportunity to prevent the injury, and (3) the parties (plaintiff and defendant) are in a special relationship. The first and second elements are self-explanatory. Regarding the third element, special relationships between the plaintiff and defendant in which such a duty of care is owed include parent and child, spouse and spouse, employer and employee, innkeeper and guest, landlord and tenant, common carrier and passenger, student and teacher, day care provider and child, and the person who created the danger and the potential victim of it. It is for the court to determine whether a relationship between the parties constitutes a special relationship that would give rise to a duty of care in a nonfeasance case. There is no set list of qualifying relatives, for example. So although one owes no duty of care to a stranger to attempt to rescue him from a riptide, that same person would owe a duty of care toward his spouse or child, and would be required, by law, to undertake a reasonable rescue effort in such a case.

There are several important special doctrines and statutes dealing with negligence, including the doctrine of *res ipsa loquitur*, the doctrine of negligence *per se*, the danger invites rescue doctrine, Good Samaritan statutes, and dram shop statutes. Each of these will be discussed, in context, within the framework of the relevant essential elements of negligence.

CASE on Point

City Check Cashing, Inc. v. Manufacturers Hanover Trust Co., 764 A.2d 411 (N.J. 2001)

In this case, a check-cashing service brought an action against a drawee bank (the bank that pays the check) to recover for negligence and for the untimely dishonor of a purportedly certified check that was for a large amount ($290,000) and was obviously altered. The court considered, among other things, whether the bank owed a duty of care to the plaintiff, who was not its customer, to support a claim of negligence.

 The court recognized this as a nonfeasance case, where the bank failed to act by not responding to the plaintiff's inquiry about the validity of the check within a two-hour time period imposed by the plaintiff. The court went on to say that in negligence actions based on nonfeasance, there must be "some definite relation between the parties of such a character that social policy justifies the imposition of a duty to act." Without a special relationship, it said, courts will typically bar negligence claims brought by non-customers against banks. Here, the court found that the plaintiff was a non-customer who made an unsolicited call to the customer service line of the drawee bank to verify whether a check in its possession was good; this was not sufficient to establish a special relationship between the parties to create a duty of care in a nonfeasance case.

THE GOOD SAMARITAN RULE AND GRATUITOUS UNDERTAKINGS

We have seen that no duty of care is owed in nonfeasance cases absent the presence of a special relationship. Unless some special statute or other rule imposes a duty when common law negligence does not, no action to come to the aid of others is required by law. In other words, absent some other law requiring it, there is no legal duty to be a "Good Samaritan" under the common law of negligence; this is the **Good Samaritan rule**.

 What if no duty of care is owed by one person to another, such as when a person observes a stranger imperiled in a riptide, *yet the observer attempts a rescue anyway*? The observer, who did not owe a duty of care, has voluntarily assumed one. This is known as a **gratuitous undertaking**. Once the actor has voluntarily assumed a duty of care, she must act reasonably to avoid negligence liability. If the Good Samaritan causes injury in the attempted rescue, she can be held liable, in negligence, for that injury under the common law of negligence.

 However, many states have sought to modify this common law result by enacting **Good Samaritan statutes** to relieve from liability for ordinary negligence certain Good Samaritans who come to the emergency aid of others. These statutes protect covered Good Samaritans from civil liability for ordinary negligence in their rescue efforts, and a few go even further and impose an affirmative duty to render aid in certain situations. Note that this statutory protection covers ordinary negligence only. Good Samaritans whose conduct is grossly negligent, or willful, wanton, and reckless, are not shielded from liability under Good Samaritan statutes.

Good Samaritan rule
Absent a special relationship, in nonfeasance cases, no duty of care is imposed on a person to come to the aid of another in an emergency.

Gratuitous undertaking
Voluntarily assuming a duty of care when none is imposed by law.

Good Samaritan statutes
Statutes enacted in many states to limit the ordinary negligence liability of Good Samaritans who come to the emergency aid of others.

Key Point

The Good Samaritan Rule

The Good Samaritan rule states that, in nonfeasance cases, absent a special relationship, no duty of care is imposed on a person to come to the aid of another in an emergency.

SIDEBAR

SPECIAL NEGLIGENCE STATUTES

Good Samaritan Statutes

Special negligence statutes called Good Samaritan statutes have been enacted in many states to encourage people to provide emergency aid to others. A few, but not most, of these statutes impose an affirmative duty on persons to assist those needing aid in an emergency if they can do so without endangering themselves or others. For example, the Good Samaritan statute in Minnesota imposes a duty on a person to provide reasonable assistance to another at the scene of an emergency where the person knows that the other is exposed to or has suffered grave physical harm.[1] Such assistance is required, however, only where the person can assist without endangering or imperiling herself or others.[2]

Most of these Good Samaritan statutes limit the civil liability to which Good Samaritans are exposed by rendering emergency action when they owe no legal duty to act. Normally, such Good Samaritans cannot be held liable for negligence in their actions. They can only be held liable for gross negligence or willful, wanton, and reckless conduct, both of which are forms of extreme, or super, negligence, when their conduct is wholly unreasonable.

Dram Shop Statutes

Other special negligence statutes, called dram shop statutes, affirmatively impose legal liability on owners of bars and taverns, and others who serve alcoholic beverages to the public, for injuries resulting from accidents caused by intoxicated persons when the sellers or servers contribute to the intoxication. Some of these statutes expand liability to include social hosts, such as persons hosting parties at their own homes. Unlike Good Samaritan statutes, which limit negligence liability for Good Samaritans' actions, dram shop statutes impose liability on those who serve alcohol to others who then cause harm to third parties.

DANGER INVITES RESCUE DOCTRINE

Related to the concept of Good Samaritans is the doctrine of danger invites rescue. Under the **danger invites rescue doctrine**, liability is extended to protect rescuers who are injured while coming to the emergency aid of others. The tortfeasor who created the dangerous situation is liable not only for the harm suffered by the person he imperiled, but also for the harm suffered by the person who came to the victim's rescue.

STATUTE on Point

Illinois Dram Shop Act

Illinois Dram Shop Act, part of that state's Liquor Control Act, states that a commercial vendor may be held liable for any injuries or damages caused by an intoxicated person if (a) the vendor sold alcohol to the person causing the injury, (b) the alcohol sold by the vendor caused or materially contributed to the person's intoxication, and (c) the intoxication was the proximate cause of the plaintiff's injuries. This dram shop act imposes liability on persons who sell or furnish the alcohol to the intoxicated person, and on persons who own, rent, or lease the property where the alcohol is sold or provided.

SIDEBAR

DANGER INVITES RESCUE DOCTRINE

A doctrine related to the Good Samaritan rule that covers people coming to the aid of others is the danger invites rescue doctrine. Pursuant to this doctrine, if a person commits an unreasonable act that endangers another, and a rescuer sustains injury while coming to the aid of the imperiled person, the tortfeasor can be held liable not only for the injury sustained by the person he put in peril, but also for any injury sustained by the person who came to the rescue, because danger invites rescue!

What about landowners and possessors of land? Do they owe a duty of care to those injured on their premises?

PREMISES LIABILITY: THE DUTY OWED BY LANDHOLDERS

When does a landholder, meaning an owner or occupier (such as a tenant) of land, owe a duty of care to persons coming on the land? This is the question of premises liability. Landholders often owe a duty of care, depending on the facts and circumstances. Whether a duty of care is owed or not, and the extent of the duty, depend on the status of the person coming on the land—whether that person is a trespasser, a licensee, or an invitee. When the owner of land has lawfully relinquished the right of possession to the occupier, then the occupier of the land, such as a tenant, rather than the owner, owes the duty.

A **trespasser** is a person who intrudes on the land of another without permission or privilege. Recall the discussion of the intentional tort of trespass to land in Chapter 4.

Key Point

Visitor Status

An entrant on land may be a trespasser, a licensee, or an invitee.

Trespasser

A person who intrudes on the land of another without permission or privilege.

CASE on Point

O'Connor v. Syracuse Univ., 66 A.D.3d 1187 (N.Y. App. Div. 2009)

In this case, the plaintiff (O'Connor) witnessed a university hockey game and saw a member of the defeated team, while wearing full hockey gear and surrounded by teammates, punch a spectator. The spectator, named McNeil, was a stranger to the plaintiff. The plaintiff jumped to McNeil's aid and ended up being pulled across a barrier, along with McNeil, where they were attacked by members of the defeated hockey team. McNeil was pulled from the pile of players by a fire safety officer and was not seriously hurt. However, O'Connor, his rescuer, was seriously injured, suffering a broken ankle and shin in the fracas.

The plaintiff invoked the danger invites rescue doctrine, saying that in coming to McNeil's aid (O'Connor grabbed him around the waist to try to keep the hockey players from pulling him over the barrier, but both ended up being pulled across the barrier and into the ensuing fight), he was motivated by a reasonable belief of imminent peril warranting application of the danger invites rescue doctrine. The court found that the danger invites rescue doctrine applied, and that it was sufficient that the plaintiff held a reasonable belief of imminent peril of serious injury to another.

Licensee
A person who enters the land of another, with permission, for his own purposes or benefit.

Invitee
A person who enters the land of another, with permission, for the benefit of the land owner or occupier or the mutual benefit of both parties, or for the purposes for which the owner or occupier holds his property open to the public.

A *licensee* is a person who enters the land of another, with permission, for his own purposes or benefit. A social guest, such as a dinner party guest, is an example.

An *invitee* is a person who enters the land of another, with permission, for the benefit of the landholder or for their mutual benefit, or for the purposes for which the owner or occupier holds his property open to the public. A customer in a retail store and a client in a business office are two examples.

TRESPASSER RULE

A trespasser is one who enters another's land unlawfully, without the consent of the landholder or the privilege to be there. The general rule is that a landholder owes no duty of care to a trespasser. However, there are important exceptions to this general rule. If the trespasser is a discovered trespasser, meaning that he is known to the owner or occupier, is a constant trespasser on limited portions of the land, meaning the owner or occupier knows the trespasser enters a part of his land frequently, or is a child trespasser anywhere on the land, then a duty of care is owed to the trespasser.

What is the nature and extent of this duty of care? A trespasser is owed the lowest duty of care of the three statuses of entrants on the land. The landholder must use reasonable care to avoid injuring the trespasser. Reasonable care to avoid injury to the trespasser includes a duty to warn a trespasser about potential dangerous conditions or activities existing or occurring on the land—for instance, by posting a warning sign that a guard dog patrols the property. The landholder may be expected to take reasonable precautions to avoid injury from dangerous conditions or activities on the land that he knows about, such as by fencing in an abandoned well. However, the landholder is not expected to

CASE on Point

Sholer v. ERC Mgmt. Group, LLC, 256 P.3d 38 (Okla. 2011)

In this case, Cassidy Sholer sustained severe injuries, rendering her a quadriplegic, when she dove head first into the shallow end of swimming pool and hit her head on the bottom of the pool. The swimming pool was at an apartment complex owned and operated by the defendant and Sholer was visiting a friend at the apartment complex. Sholer said that she and her friend went to swim in the pool at about 11:30 p.m., and she admitted that she had been drinking alcohol that night. A few feet from where Sholer dove into the pool was a marker clearly indicating the water was 3 feet deep.

The court said that the threshold question in a negligence case is whether the defendant owed a duty of care to the plaintiff. In cases of landlord liability, to answer this threshold question a court must identify the status of the person as that of a trespasser, a licensee, or an invitee. The court went on to say that if the person is a trespasser, the landlord's only duty is to avoid willful or wanton injury. But a landlord owes a licensee a greater duty, the duty to exercise reasonable care in disclosing dangerous defects known to the landlord but unlikely to be discovered by the licensee; that obligation extends to hidden dangers, traps, snares, and similar conditions. A landlord owes an invitee the additional duty of exercising reasonable care to keep the premises in a reasonably safe condition for the invitee. The court stated that although the invitee is entitled to the greatest protection of the three categories, the landlord need not guard the invitee against dangers so apparent and readily observable that the conditions should be discovered.

inspect the land to protect trespassers from dangerous conditions or activities that are hidden or of which the landholder is not otherwise aware.

TRESPASS AND THE ATTRACTIVE NUISANCE DOCTRINE

Under the ***attractive nuisance doctrine***, the duty of care is expanded to protect trespassing children who are of a young age and cannot fully appreciate the dangers present, who may be attracted to property because of some artificial condition on the land or some dangerous activity conducted there. A landholder owes a duty of care to trespassing children to take reasonable precautions to protect them from reasonably foreseeable harm for artificial conditions and dangerous activities on the land.

In deterring the presence of trespassers, remember from the study of defenses to intentional tort in Chapter 5 that a landholder may not commit intentional torts against a known trespasser, except in self-defense, defense of others, or if some other privilege allows the use of reasonable force. A trespasser can be removed using reasonable force under the self-help privilege.

If a trespasser may be owed a duty of care in some situations, what about a licensee?

Attractive nuisance doctrine
A legal doctrine that states that a duty of care is owed to trespassing children of young age who cannot fully appreciate certain dangers and who may be attracted to artificial conditions or dangerous activities on the premises.

SIDEBAR

ATTRACTIVE NUISANCE DOCTRINE

Courts developed the attractive nuisance doctrine to protect children from dangerous artificial conditions and activities on others' land that, because of their young age and lack of maturity, they would find attractive and enticing. To establish a duty of care under the attractive nuisance doctrine, the plaintiff must demonstrate several things: that the defendant had reason to know there was a dangerous condition or activity on the land, such as a railroad yard, a swimming pool, an abandoned building, a barn, timber cutting, and the like, and that children are likely to trespass there; that the defendant had reason to know that the dangerous condition or activity posed an unreasonable risk of injury to children; that young children, because of their lack of maturity and experience, would not appreciate the extent of the danger presented; that the financial burden of making the condition or activity safer is slight compared to the extent of the danger posed to children; and that the defendant failed to take reasonable precautions to prevent trespassing children from being injured.

The purpose of this doctrine is to protect young children who cannot appreciate the dangers to which they are enticed. There is no precise age cutoff. Most cases allowing recovery under the attractive nuisance doctrine involve children under the age of 12, however. A few courts have fixed an arbitrary age of 14, while other courts allow recovery by teenagers when the circumstances are such that the teenagers would not be expected to appreciate the danger involved. The age of the child is relevant in determining what dangers he is expected to be mature and experienced enough to be able to fully appreciate.

The condition on the land must be an artificial—meaning man-made—one, such as a swimming pool or building, rather than a natural condition, such as a natural pond. However, courts are not consistent in distinguishing an artificial condition from a natural one. Further, as the case in the exercises at the end of the chapter demonstrates, a swimming pool is not always considered to be a proper subject of the attractive nuisance doctrine. The doctrine extends to activities conducted on the land to which children might be attracted, such as mining activities or timber cutting, as well as artificial conditions on it.

LICENSEE RULE

A licensee is a person who enters the land of another, with permission, but for her own benefit rather than for the benefit of the landholder. For example, if Julie gets permission to enter Martin's land to fish in his pond, Julie is a licensee. Does Martin owe Julie a duty of care while she is on his land? The answer is yes.

What is the nature and extent of this duty of care? The landholder owes a duty of care to the licensee at least as great as would be owed to a trespasser. This means that the landholder must warn the licensee of any dangerous natural or artificial conditions or activities on the land of which he has actual knowledge. It does not mean the landholder must inspect the property to investigate for dangerous conditions that are hidden, meaning those dangers of which he is not aware. Further, an occupier of land must carry on activities on the premises using reasonable care to avoid injuring his licensees.

If a duty of care is owed to licensees, is one owed to invitees? If so, is the extent of that duty the same?

INVITEE RULE

An invitee is a person who enters the land of another, with permission, for the benefit of the landholder, for the mutual benefit of them both, or for the purposes for which the property is held open to the public, such as a customer in a store or restaurant, or a client to a business. The landholder owes the greatest duty of care to this person. The extent of this duty of care is the highest duty of care of the three statuses of entrants onto land. It requires taking full reasonable care measures to reasonably prevent foreseeable harm to invitees, including not

CASE on Point

Folley v. United Bldg. & Loan Ass'n of Hackensack, 186 A. 591 (N.J. 1936)

In this case, the plaintiff Folley entered into a lease with the landlord, to commence on February 15. On February 12, three days before the lease was to begin, the plaintiff, without the landlord's permission or knowledge, went onto the premises. When there, the heel of one of her shoes sank into the linoleum on the landing of the cellar stairway and she lost her footing and fell. The plaintiff brought an action against the landlord for negligence in breaching its duty of care owed to her.

The court considered whether the landlord owed the plaintiff a duty of care. The court noted that the plaintiff was not a tenant because her lease term had not yet commenced and she paid no rent yet. The plaintiff argued that she was an invitee. However, the court found that the plaintiff's premature taking of possession of the property was to further her own interests, and did not advance the interests of the landlord; there was "no mutuality of interest" of the plaintiff and the landlord. Accordingly, the court determined the plaintiff's status was that of a licensee. As a licensee, said the court, the plaintiff could not recover from the landlord for injuries caused by of the defective condition of the property.

SIDEBAR

OUTSIDE THE PREMISES

What are the duties of a landholder for injuries sustained by persons outside the land? Note that in these cases there is no entry onto the land by the injured party. A landholder normally owes no duty of care to prevent injury to persons outside the land who might be injured by natural conditions that exist on the land; regarding artificial conditions and activities on the land, the landholder owes a duty of reasonable care to prevent injury to persons outside the land who might be injured by those conditions or activities.

only warning about dangerous conditions or activities on the land, but also taking reasonable actions to make the premises safe. This includes inspecting the premises for possible dangerous artificial and natural conditions and dangerous activities on the land that are hidden, and then taking reasonable precautions to make them safe for invitees.

COMMON AREAS

Landlords often retain control over the common areas of their properties, such as lobbies, walkways, hallways, stairways, elevators, laundry rooms, and the like, though they otherwise do not remain in possession of their property. When

CASE on Point

Tolbert v. Jamison, 794 N.W.2d 877 (Neb. 2011)

A negligence action was brought against landlords, who owned a Section 8 federally subsidized two-story single-family home, by relatives of a tenant (a mother) and the tenant's daughter who lived in that home. Both the tenant and the daughter were killed in a house fire that was intentionally set by a third party; another occupant of the house escaped to safety through a window. Representatives of the fire victims brought the negligence action alleging that the landlords failed to provide appropriate ingress and egress, working fire alarms, and fire extinguishers or other extinguishing equipment.

The court stated that as a general rule, in the absence of a statute, covenant, fraud, or concealment, a landlord who gives a tenant full control and possession of the leased property will not be liable for personal injuries sustained by the tenant or other persons lawfully on the leased property. In order to hold the landlord liable for injuries suffered as a result of the condition of the leased premises, it must appear that the landlord had a right to present possession or present control or dominion over the premises. In the absence of an express agreement otherwise, the landlord does not warrant the fitness or safety of the premises and the tenant takes the premises as she finds it.

The court recognized that the landlord may be required to use reasonable care in the maintenance of the common areas over which the landlord retains control and has not demised to the tenants. But there was no such common area in this single-family dwelling.

CASE on Point

Jones v. Basha, Inc., 2011 WL 3903241 (Fla. Dist. Ct. App. 2011)[3]

In this case, a convenience store customer, who was the victim of an attempted carjacking outside the store, brought a premises liability action against the landlord of the premises where the store was operated. The landlord leased the premises to a tenant, and the tenant operated the convenience store.

The court noted that it is generally the court's responsibility to determine, as a matter of law, the threshold question of whether a duty of care exists. In cases of premises liability of landlords, the court must determine whether the landlord exercised some control over the premises and public access to it to trigger a duty of care. If the landlord surrenders possession and control over the premises to a tenant, the landlord is not liable for injury to a third party that occurs on the premises. The court determined that this landlord did not exercise control over the premises so it owed no duty of care to this customer of its tenant.

landlords retain control over these common areas, they assume the duty to reasonably inspect and maintain these areas to prevent others from foreseeable harm, extending not only to tenants, but also to their guests. Also, although the general rule is that tenants assume liability for injuries caused by conditions or activities on their land as occupiers of the land, some state statutes require landlords to maintain the premises, including the tenants' space, in a safe condition, and can impose criminal penalties for serious violations.

We have finished our examination of the first element of negligence, duty of care. After the plaintiff establishes that the defendant owed her a duty of care, the next element for the plaintiff to demonstrate in setting forth a claim for negligence is that the defendant breached this duty of care. Breach of the duty of care is examined next.

Breach of the Duty of Care and the Reasonable Person Standard

Breach of the duty of care, the second essential element of the tort of negligence, incorporates the concept of "reasonableness." The defendant's conduct must be reasonable. In other words, his action, or failure to act, must be reasonable under the circumstances. What standard of care is used to determine whether a defendant's conduct is reasonable under the circumstances? The standard is the "reasonable person" standard.

The **reasonable person standard** is that standard of behavior expected of a hypothetical reasonable person. A court will ask *how a reasonable person would have acted in the same or similar circumstances.*

The rationale for the reasonable person standard is that, as part of a greater society, individuals must be expected to tolerate certain conduct

Breach of the duty of care
Failure to use reasonable care under the circumstances, judged by the reasonable person standard.

Reasonable person standard
The standard of behavior expected of a hypothetical reasonable person under the same or similar circumstances.

SIDEBAR

REASONABLE PERSON STANDARD

Regarding the reasonable person standard, the *Restatement (Second) of Torts* says that a person must recognize that her conduct creates or involves a risk of invading another person's legal interests if a reasonable man would recognize this while exercising the attention, memory, intelligence, judgment, and the like that a reasonable man would have.[4] In addition, a reasonable man must use or exercise any superior attention, memory, intelligence, and judgment as he may possess relative to other people.[5]

Notice that the *Restatement* uses a reasonable "man" standard. In recent years, this standard has been made gender-neutral and is now more commonly known as a reasonable *person* standard. Reasonable care was commonly called "due care" in the past, so you may see older cases referencing that as well.

but are not expected to tolerate other conduct. What conduct an individual should be expected to tolerate is defined by this tort as conduct that is reasonable, meaning conduct that, under similar circumstances, others would be able to tolerate. Therefore, a defined standard of conduct is used to determine what conduct is tolerable and what is not. That defined standard of conduct is the reasonable person standard. How, then, is the reasonable person standard applied?

As mentioned earlier, a reasonable person is a hypothetical one placed in the same or similar circumstances as the defendant. A reasonable person is not a perfect person; she does not guarantee against harm and she does not undertake every possible precaution to prevent harm. Nor is a reasonable person careless, taking insufficient precautions against possible harm to others or their property. Rather, a reasonable person is a person who takes reasonable precautions to avoid reasonably foreseeable risks of harm to others and their property. She is an ordinary, prudent person, not perfect but not careless either. Because a reasonable person is not perfect, she can injure others; she just does not injure others by being careless.

Consider how the following types of persons would drive during a severe rainstorm: a perfect person, a reasonable person, and a careless person. The perfect person would not drive during a severe rainstorm; she would stay home until the storm passes, thereby avoiding causing harm to another by driving during unfavorable conditions. A reasonable person would still drive but would drive carefully, including taking such reasonable precautionary measures as reducing speed (to perhaps well below the statutory speed limit), increasing the distance to other cars, and using headlights and windshield wipers. A careless person would drive too fast, tailgate, and so on, falling short of taking reasonable precautions to prevent others and their property from foreseeable harm. A perfect person will cause no injury in this scenario. The reasonable person may cause injury, but not because of carelessness. The careless person is even more likely to cause injury, and can be held liable, in negligence, for failure to take reasonable precautions to avoid causing harm to others or their property.

The reasonable person standard is considered an objective standard of care. It is considered to be objective because it normally considers how hypothetical reasonable people would act, not how a particular person would act, under the same or similar circumstances. However, sometimes the reasonable person standard is made subjective, by considering particular characteristics of the person involved. For example, a court will consider special physical characteristics of a person in evaluating the reasonableness of his actions, such as holding a blind person to the reasonableness standard of other blind people under the same or similar circumstances. It will also hold individuals who possess superior knowledge or skill, including professionals such as doctors, lawyers, and accountants, to a higher standard of care because of their special knowledge, education, and training.

What constitutes reasonable care depends on the circumstances. The greater the danger, the greater are the precautions needed to meet this standard. Courts look at several factors in determining whether a person's actions were reasonable. These are some of those factors:

- Courts consider whether the incident was reasonably foreseeable. The more foreseeable the incident causing harm, the more precautions a reasonable person would take to avoid it. In this determination, courts evaluate the manner in which the act was performed, whether it was performed carelessly or carefully, and the precautions taken.
- Courts evaluate whether the act was commonplace and usual, or unusual or even outrageous. The more unusual or outrageous the act, the more precautions a reasonable person would take to avoid causing injury by performing it.
- Courts consider whether the nature and extent of the injury or damage that resulted from the incident was reasonably foreseeable. The more foreseeable the type of harm caused or the more serious the harm, the more precautions a reasonable person would take to avoid causing that harm.
- The burden or inconvenience involved in taking the precautions necessary to avoid the incident is also considered by courts in evaluating the reasonableness of a defendant's actions. The less the defendant's burden or inconvenience involved in taking the precautions necessary to avoid the incident, the more reasonable it is that a defendant should take on this burden or inconvenience to avoid causing the harm.
- Courts consider the importance or social utility of what the defendant was trying to do before the incident occurred. The more beneficial or useful the defendant's activity, the more likely it is that a reasonable person would take on the risks associated with the activity in order to perform it. For instance, saving a child from drowning in a swimming pool has greater social utility than driving to a restaurant for dinner. Fewer precautions may be permitted by the person rendering emergency aid to a drowning child.

So far, we have discussed the general rule on when a duty of care is breached. Some court doctrines help to establish that there has been a breach of the duty of care. One of these is the doctrine of *res ipsa loquitur*.

OBJECTIVE VERSUS SUBJECTIVE STANDARD

A standard is a yardstick by which something is measured. Overall, the reasonable person standard is an objective standard. It uses a basis of comparison to measure whether a particular person's conduct is reasonable. The comparison is made using other, hypothetical, people, to determine what they would do in the same or similar circumstances. For instance, in judging whether a person was exercising reasonable care by driving at the speed limit during a downpour, the court will measure this conduct against how a reasonable hypothetical person would drive during such a downpour—which may be well below the speed limit.

A subjective standard is one that takes into account particular characteristics of a person. The reasonable person standard, while mainly an objective standard, sometimes takes on subjective characteristics by taking into account particular physical or mental characteristics of the person. Generally, physical characteristics, such as handicaps, are taken into account, and mental characteristics, such as intelligence, are not taken into account when defining the standard of care.

If a person has special skills or abilities, such as special training and education in a profession, then that person is held to a reasonable person standard that takes into account these special abilities. So, the conduct of a surgeon performing surgery would be compared to that of other surgeons with similar training, education, and experience, not other people who are not surgeons. This standard, sometimes called the professional community standard of care, is based on the custom and practices among those working in that professional activity and includes not only doctors, lawyers, and accountants, but also professionals such as plumbers, contractors, financial advisors, beauticians, electricians, therapists, and the like.

A person's physical limitations are taken into account in comparing his actions with those of a hypothetical reasonable person. Therefore, a physically handicapped person is compared to others with the same physical handicap. For instance, a blind person's conduct would be compared to that of a hypothetical blind person.

Unlike with physical characteristics, however, a person's mental characteristics, such as intelligence or mental or emotional illness, are not normally taken into account. Courts consider mental characteristics to be much harder to determine and define than physical ones, and instead defer to the objective reasonable person standard in evaluating these cases.

That said, courts do make exceptions when the mental characteristic at issue is easily defined. Such is the case when dealing with children. Children do not possess the same level of maturity and experience as do adults, and courts recognize this. Courts therefore consider the mental characteristics of children in defining the relevant standard of care, because childhood is easy to define. Children are normally held to the standard of care of hypothetical children of similar age and intelligence, unless the child is engaged in an adult activity, such as operating an automobile. Children engaged in an adult activity are evaluated using the objective, reasonable person—meaning adult—standard.

CASE on Point

RES IPSA LOQUITUR DOCTRINE

Res ipsa loquitur doctrine
A legal doctrine that infers negligence simply because an event occurred, if it is the type of event that would not normally occur in the absence of negligence; *res ipsa loquitur* means "the event speaks for itself."

Key Point

The *Res Ipsa Loquitur* Doctrine
The *res ipsa loquitur* doctrine permits negligence—specifically, the essential element of breach of the duty of care—to be inferred simply because an event occurred, if the event is one that would not normally occur in the absence of negligence.

Res ipsa loquitur means that "the event speaks for itself." The **res ipsa loquitur doctrine** permits negligence to be inferred simply because an event occurred, if it is the type of event that would not normally occur in the absence of negligence. This doctrine helps plaintiffs prove the essential element of breach of the duty of care for certain types of accidents. Typical applications of this doctrine are found in catastrophic accidents such as railroad derailments, airplane crashes, elevator crashes, and the like, where the plaintiff has limited ability to determine what the defendant did wrong, but just that the event occurred demonstrates "common sense" negligence. For example, that a train derailed, that an airplane fell from the sky, that an elevator plummeted to the ground, or that a surgical instrument was left inside a patient's body demonstrate such common sense negligence, and situations in which this doctrine may be applicable to infer breach of a duty of care.

The doctrine of *res ipsa loquitur* applies only when certain requirements are met: (1) The event would not ordinarily occur without the presence of

CASE on Point

CASES on Point

Simmons v. Neuman, 50 A.D.3d 666 (N.Y. App. Div. 2008); *Pope v. Edward M. Rude Carrier Corp., 75 S.E.2d 584* (W. Va. 1953)

In *Simmons v. Neuman*, the plaintiff sued to recover damages for medical malpractice after she allegedly suffered burns to her right thigh during surgery on her right shoulder. She relied on the doctrine of *res ipsa loquitur* to establish breach of the duty of care by the defendants. The court said that in order to rely on the doctrine of *res ipsa loquitur,* a plaintiff must demonstrate that (1) the injury is of a kind that does not occur in the absence of someone's negligence, (2) the injury is caused by an agency or instrumentality within the exclusive control of the defendants, and (3) the injury is not due to any voluntary action on the part of the injured plaintiff. The New York Supreme Court, Appellate Division, upheld the trial court's denial of the plaintiff's motion for summary judgment on the issue of negligence liability, finding that the doctrine of *res ipsa loquitur* "allows, but does not require, the fact finder to infer that the defendant was negligent" and that "*res ipsa loquitur* evidence does not ordinarily or automatically entitle the plaintiff to summary judgment."

Compare this case to *Pope v. Edward M. Rude Carrier Corp.* In this case, which we discussed in Chapter 4 with reference to the nuisance doctrine, the plaintiff was injured when an explosion occurred when a licensed contract carrier was transporting dynamite on a public highway. In discussing the doctrine of *res ipsa loquitur,* the court said that "when a person who is without fault is injured by an instrumentality at the time within the exclusive control of another person and the injury is such as in the ordinary course of events does not occur if the person who has control uses due care, the injury is charged to the failure of such other person to exercise due care." Further, "[i]t does not dispense with the requirement that negligence must be proved by him who alleges it but relates only to the method of proving such negligence. . . . [T]he facts and circumstances accompanying an injury may be such as to raise a presumption, or at least permit an inference, of negligence on the part of the defendant."

The Supreme Court of Appeals of West Virginia found that the doctrine of *res ipsa loquitur* applied in this case. It held that "whenever the thing that explodes is shown to have been under the control and management of the defendant, and the explosion is such a one as, in the ordinary course of events, would not happen if due care is exercised, the fact of injury itself will be deemed to afford sufficient evidence to support a recovery, unless the defendant gives an explanation of the occurrence tending to show that the injury was not due to his want of care."

negligent conduct; (2) the event was caused by some instrumentality exclusively under the defendant's control; and (3) the act was not caused, even in part, by the plaintiff's actions or failure to act. In such cases, the defendant is presumed to have breached his duty of care and acted negligently just because the event occurred. To establish a *prima facie* case of negligence, then, the plaintiff merely has to establish that the accident occurred and caused him injury, and that such an accident does not normally occur in the absence of negligence. At this point, the burden of proof shifts to the defendant to show that the instrumentality that caused the plaintiff's injury was not under his exclusive control, that the plaintiff contributed to his own injuries, or that his conduct was not negligent.

Res ipsa loquitur is not the only legal doctrine that makes it easier for plaintiffs to establish a breach of the duty of care. Another court doctrine that helps establish a breach of the duty of care is negligence *per se*.

NEGLIGENCE *PER SE*

Negligence per se Negligence *per se* is an act or failure to act in violation of a statutory require-
An act or omission in violation of ment. It literally means "negligence by itself." Pursuant to the negligence *per se*
a statute; it literally means "negli- doctrine, a court can infer a breach of the duty of care if the plaintiff can estab-
gence by itself." lish that the defendant's act or omission was in violation of a statute. For this doctrine to apply, the plaintiff must demonstrate several things: (1) The defendant violated a statute; (2) the violation of the statute was not excused; (3) the statute was intended to avoid this kind of harm; (4) the defendant's violation of the statute caused (using the "but for" or "substantial factor" test) the plaintiff's injuries; and (5) the plaintiff was in the class of persons protected by the statute. In effect, under this doctrine, the reasonableness of a defendant's conduct is determined not by the reasonable person standard, but by the requirements of the relevant statute.

Different jurisdictions treat negligence *per se* in different ways. In some states, if the requirements of negligence *per se* are met, the violation of a statute is considered to be unreasonableness *per se,* and the defendant may not offer any evidence of reasonableness in rebuttal. Other states treat negligence *per se* as merely a presumption, or inference, of negligence, and allow the defendant to rebut the presumption by offering evidence of reasonableness.

If the requirements of negligence *per se* are not met, then violation of a statute by the defendant is not conclusive evidence of breach of the duty of care. Rather, violation of a statute is mere evidence of breach of a duty of care and is not an inference or presumption of it. Consider this example. State law requires that all drivers carry proof of insurance with them when they drive. Nancy is driving, in a careful manner but without proof of insurance, which she inadvertently left in her other purse. Nancy causes a car accident while backing out of a parking space because she did not see a driver who was already backing out of the space behind her. Is this negligence *per se*? Nancy was in violation of the

CASE on Point

Sodders v. Fry, 32 A.3d 882 (Pa. Commw. Ct. 2011)

This court affirmed the granting of a new trial so that the jury could be instructed on the doctrine of negligence *per se.* In this case, the plaintiff, Sodders, was a motorist who was injured when he was struck by a police car driven by Officer Fry. Just before the accident, three police cars were approaching Sodders, with the police cars travelling about 35 miles per hour in a 25-miles-per-hour zone. Even though they were responding to a disturbance call, none of the police officers in the cars were using their lights or sirens at the time. The first two police cars passed Sodders, but then Sodders' vehicle was struck by Officer Fry's police car.

In reviewing the case, the court said that negligence *per se* applies when a person violates an applicable statute, regulation, or ordinance designed to prevent a public harm. The court went on to note that proof that an applicable statute exists and that the defendant violated the statute establish only the first two elements of negligence—namely duty of care and breach. The court noted that even after establishing negligence *per se,* to recover a plaintiff must also prove that the negligence was the proximate or legal cause of the injury. Because Officer Fry was not using his lights or siren and was speeding, violations of statutes designed to prevent public harm, the jury should have been instructed on the doctrine of negligence *per se.*

state statute requiring that she carry evidence of insurance with her while driving. However, Nancy not having such evidence with her did not, in fact, cause the accident. Therefore, violation of this statute by Nancy would not constitute negligence *per se,* so it would not be conclusive evidence of breach of the duty of care.

Similarly, *compliance* with a statute is not conclusive evidence of the reasonableness of conduct. It is merely evidence of it. For example, if the speed limit is 45 miles per hour and Carla is driving 44 miles per hour, her driving may seem reasonable, at least in terms of her speed. However, driving at this legal rate of speed is not conclusive evidence of reasonableness because weather conditions could warrant her to drive more slowly. If, for instance, Carla is driving in a severe snow storm, a speed of 44 miles per hour in a 45-miles-per-hour zone may well constitute unreasonable conduct even though she is complying with the speed limit statute.

So far, we have discussed ordinary negligence. Ordinary negligence is the most common form of negligence, in which a defendant fails to take reasonable precautions to avoid or prevent foreseeable risk of harm to others or their property. What about where the defendant's conduct is more than merely unreasonable, yet short of intentional, for the intentional torts? What if the defendant's conduct is wholly and utterly unreasonable? This conduct may constitute a form of super, or extreme, negligence, such as gross negligence.

GROSS NEGLIGENCE

Gross negligence
A form of extreme negligence in which a tortfeasor fails to use even a small amount of care to avoid causing foreseeable harm to others or their property.

Sometimes a defendant's conduct is so wholly unreasonable that it is deemed to be more than ordinary negligence. Shooting a gun in a crowd is an example. A defendant may be extremely negligent in a couple of ways. *Gross negligence* is the failure to use even a small amount of care to avoid foreseeable harm to others or their property. Street racing is another example of such extreme, or super, negligence; it demonstrates failure to use even a small amount of care to avoid harming others or their property.

WILLFUL, WANTON, AND RECKLESS CONDUCT

Willful, wanton, and reckless conduct
A form of extreme negligence in which a person's act or omission is likely to cause harm to others or their property.

Willful, wanton, and reckless conduct is another form of extreme negligence. It is an act or omission that is likely to cause harm to others or their property. For example, driving an automobile while one is intoxicated is likely to injure others or their property. The distinction between ordinary and extreme negligence is important in determining a remedy.

Although compensatory damages are the normal remedy awarded in negligence cases, as we will see later in Chapter 9, punitive damages may be recoverable in cases involving gross negligence, or willful, wanton, and reckless conduct. Also, some states have special negligence statutes, such as automobile guest statutes, that make it difficult for guests in automobiles to sue their hosts without proving some form of extreme negligence. As we discussed earlier, some legal protections, such as Good Samaritan statutes, may protect certain persons from liability for negligent conduct, but they do not extend this protection where gross negligence or willful, wanton, and reckless conduct is present.

SIDEBAR

AUTOMOBILE GUEST STATUTES

Automobile guest statutes have been enacted in some states. These statutes generally provide that a driver, or perhaps owner, of an automobile is not liable for injuries sustained by a nonpaying passenger unless the driver is grossly negligent or reckless in causing the accident.

These statutes require a form of extreme negligence, beyond ordinary negligence, when a guest in an automobile wishes to sue the driver for injuries sustained in an accident. Some states require gross negligence on the part of the host, meaning the failure to use even a small amount of care to avoid foreseeable harm. Other states require a showing of willful, wanton, and reckless conduct, meaning the host had knowledge that the harm would probably result from his actions or inactions. Drag racing on a public street is an example of such extreme negligence for which a driver could be held liable under automobile guest statutes.

In essence, these statutes protect drivers from ordinary negligence liability by injured guests whom the driver voluntarily drives in an automobile, so long as no compensation is paid by the passenger for the ride. If the passenger pays compensation to the driver, the driver owes the passenger a duty of reasonable care.

CHAPTER **SUMMARY**

- Negligence is the largest of the three major categories of torts. This tort covers a wide variety of unreasonable conduct, both unreasonable acts and unreasonable failures to act, that cause harm or injury to others or their property. It is defined as harm caused by failure to use reasonable care.

- There are four essential elements of the tort of negligence. They are duty of care, breach of the duty of care, causation (including cause in fact and proximate cause), and damages.

- A duty of care is an obligation to conform to a standard of conduct prescribed by law. A duty of care arises when someone's conduct creates a foreseeable risk of harm to someone else's person or property. The duty is to take reasonable precautions to prevent the harm. What is reasonable depends on the facts and circumstances. The more foreseeable the harm, and the greater the harm, the more precautions must be taken to be "reasonable." The duty of care is triggered by the foreseeability of the harm.

- A duty of care is owed by a person if it is reasonably foreseeable that his conduct creates a foreseeable risk of harm to another's person or property. This test defines the normal case of who owes a duty of care, and to whom it is owed.

- In determining who is owed a duty of care, if the plaintiff is foreseeable, meaning a person can reasonably foresee that his actions create a foreseeable risk of harm to this plaintiff, then a duty of care is owed to her. A duty of care may be owed to an unforeseeable plaintiff as well.

- A person can be negligent through his actions or omissions. Under the Good Samaritan rule, in a gratuitous undertaking, once the person has voluntarily assumed a duty of care, she must act reasonably to avoid negligence liability. Good Samaritan statutes have been enacted in many jurisdictions to protect Good Samaritans who come to the emergency aid of others from ordinary negligence liability.

- Owners and occupiers of land owe a duty of care to those who enter their land. The extent of the duty depends on that status of the person coming onto their land: whether that person is a trespasser, a licensee, or an invitee. Landlords who retain control over the common areas of their properties assume the duty to reasonably maintain those areas to prevent others from foreseeable harm.

- Breach of the duty of care is the "reasonableness" element of the tort of negligence. The defendant's conduct must be reasonable. That standard used to make this determination is the reasonable person standard. A court will ask how a hypothetical reasonable person would have acted under the same or similar circumstances.

- *Res ipsa loquitur* means "the event speaks for itself." The *res ipsa loquitur* doctrine presumes negligence, and it was created to help plaintiffs prove the essential element of breach of the duty of care for certain types of accidents that would normally not occur in the absence of negligence.

- The negligence *per se* doctrine allows a court to infer a breach of the duty of care if the plaintiff can establish that the defendant's acts were in violation of a statute if certain requirements are met.

- Sometimes a defendant's conduct is so wholly unreasonable that is deemed to be willful, wanton, and reckless conduct, or gross negligence, which is more than ordinary negligence.

CONCEPT REVIEW AND REINFORCEMENT

QUESTIONS FOR **REVIEW**

1. What is the tort of negligence?
2. What are the essential elements of the tort of negligence?
3. What is the element of duty of care? Who owes it, and to whom and when?
4. When is a duty of care owed to an unforeseeable plaintiff?
5. How do you distinguish misfeasance and nonfeasance cases?
6. What is the Good Samaritan rule?
7. What duty of care is owed by owners or occupiers of land to trespassers or visitors?
8. What is the attractive nuisance doctrine?
9. What is breach of the duty of care?
10. What is the reasonable person standard and how it is applied?
11. What is *res ipsa loquitur* and how does it affect an essential element of negligence?
12. What is the doctrine of negligence *per se?*
13. What is gross negligence?

DEVELOPING YOUR PARALEGAL SKILLS

CRITICAL THINKING **EXERCISES**

1. In this chapter, we studied the essential elements of the tort of negligence. Research the law in your state on each of these elements to see in what way(s), if any, your state law differs from most states' laws. An excellent starting point for your research is a case law digest for your state. For example, in Maryland, the resource *Maryland Digest 2d* by West includes cases from Maryland defining the tort of negligence and establishing each of its essential elements. Compare your results to the Maryland common law, set forth in the *Bryant* case cited in the beginning of this chapter. Discuss your research results in class.

2. Veronica walks dogs for a living. Normally, she walks many dogs at one time, all on leashes. When she is walking a group of dogs down the street, she looks like a person leading a bouquet of puffballs. Unfortunately, during one recent walk, one of the dogs became agitated, seemingly by the crowd of dogs surrounding him, and attacked the poodle nearest him.

   a. *Regarding this incident, was a duty of care owed by Veronica? If so, to whom?*

   b. *When the poodle was attacked, who suffered damage (another essential element of the tort of negligence)? A dog is not a person; can it suffer damage and bring a negligence action?*

   c. On one of her walks, Veronica sees an unleashed, uncontrolled dog that is growling and snapping at a young child. Veronica does not want to be late for her next appointment, so she continues on her way (though she sincerely hopes the child will not be harmed).

   Did Veronica owe a duty of care to the child? If so, did she breach the duty of care by not coming to the child's aid?

   d. Now assume that Veronica, though she is in a hurry, immediately decides to come to the child's aid. Veronica ties all her dogs' leashes to a tree and carefully approaches the child and the threatening dog, placing herself between the two. The dog is owned by Jackson, who has not yet noticed that his dog has escaped from the yard.

   The dog attacks and bites Veronica, injuring her. Can she sue, in negligence, for the injuries she sustains from the dog bite? If so, who would she sue, and should she win (can she establish each of the essential elements of the tort)?

   e. Finally, assume that Veronica, in rushing to the child's aid in a frantic and panicked manner, further riles the dog, who then attacks and bites the poor child.

   Can Veronica be held liable, in negligence, for the injuries the child sustains from the dog bite under these circumstances?

ASSIGNMENTS AND PRACTICAL **APPLICATIONS**

1. Read and brief the *Palsgraf* majority opinion by Chief Judge Cardozo, in which he defines the zone of danger test. Read and brief the dissenting opinion by Judge Andrews, in which he defines the world at large test and comprehensively discusses the legal concept of proximate cause.

2. Perform legal research to determine whether your state recognizes the zone of danger test or the world at large test in determining whether a duty of care is owed to an unforeseeable plaintiff. Discuss your research results in class.

3. Research whether your state has a Good Samaritan statute. Compare yours to the Minnesota Good Samaritan statute (M.S.A. § 604A.01), which imposes an affirmative duty to assist under certain circumstances. Discuss the comparison in class.

4. The final episode of the vastly popular *Seinfeld* television series dealt with Good Samaritan law. Watch that episode and discuss it in class.

5. Review the federal Volunteer Protection Act found at 42 U.S.C. § 14503. This is a type of Good Samaritan statute that protects charitable volunteers from liability for negligent conduct or innocent errors (but not for gross negligence, recklessness, or intentional misconduct). Discuss in class the advantages and disadvantages of such legislation.

6. Research your state's dram shop act (if it has one). Does your state's statute extend liability to include not only tavern owners and servers, but also social hosts who are responsible for serving alcohol to people who then injure others? For class discussion, consider whether you think this law is reasonable, too broad, or too narrow.

7. For an interesting case on a landlord's duty of care (and breach of it) arising under a "no pets" clause in a lease and involving a fatal pitbull attack on a young child, read and brief *Matthews v. Amberwood Associates Ltd. P'ship, Inc.*, 719 A.2d 119 (Md. 1998). A pitbull named Rampage was being cared for by the owner's girlfriend while the owner was incarcerated. The unmuzzled and unrestrained dog, not being properly supervised by the adults, mauled the youngest child present.

8. Read and brief *Martin v. Wal-Mart Stores, Inc.*, 183 F.3d 770 (8th Cir. 1999) regarding the duty of care imposed on landowners toward store patrons.

9. The attractive nuisance doctrine protects trespassing children under certain circumstances. Read and brief *Mozier v. Parson*, 887 P.2d 692 (Kan. 1995), in which the court found that a swimming pool was not an attractive nuisance.

10. On the *res ipsa loquitur* doctrine, read and brief *Cox v. Northwest Airlines, Inc.*, 379 F.2d 893 (7th Cir. 1967), involving the principle that airplanes should not fall from the sky.

11. Negligence *per se* was found to exist in the case of *deJesus v. Seaboard Coast Line R.R. Co.*, 281 So.2d 198 (Fla. 1973). Read and brief this case.

12. Research whether your jurisdiction has an automobile guest statute. If it does, determine how much extreme negligence is required to trigger liability under that statute. Discuss your research results in class.

TECHNOLOGY RESOURCES AND INTERNET **EXERCISES**

For statistics on trends in tort cases filed, outcomes, and so on, review the U.S. Department of Justice's Bureau of Justice Statistics website (click on civil justice statistics to bypass the criminal justice statistics).

ETHICAL **APPLICATIONS**

Gerald, the supervising attorney, asks his paralegal, Nancy, to file a client's negligence complaint with the local county court no later than February 1. Nancy inadvertently forgets this deadline. On February 5, she realizes that the complaint has not been filed. Unfortunately, the statute of limitations on the client's negligence claim ran out on February 1, so the client's lawsuit can never be brought as a result of Nancy's failure to file the complaint by the requisite date.

Can Nancy be disciplined by the state's bar association for her actions (or omissions)? Can she suffer adverse employment consequences for her conduct? Can she be sued for malpractice by the client? Can Gerald be disciplined by the state's bar association for Nancy's actions? Can he, or his firm, be sued for malpractice because of Nancy's actions?

VIDEO **CASE STUDY**

Mechanic's Deposition: Duties of the Agent and Liability of the Principal

Synopsis: During the deposition of a truck mechanic for Ace Trucking Company, he admits that he violated company policy by purchasing "knockoff" brake parts in order to save his employer money. In addition, after the accident, the mechanic disposed of the brake parts despite the employer's written request that they be retained.

Questions

1. What must be established to hold a manufacturer liable for negligent manufacture of a product such as these brake parts?

2. What is the impact of the employee not preserving the evidence needed at trial in order for the collision victims to prove negligent manufacture of the brake parts?

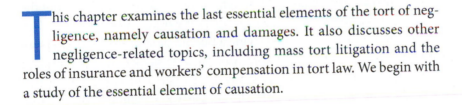

chapter **7**

NEGLIGENCE: THE ELEMENTS OF CAUSATION AND DAMAGES, PLUS OTHER NEGLIGENCE-RELATED TOPICS

This chapter examines the last essential elements of the tort of negligence, namely causation and damages. It also discusses other negligence-related topics, including mass tort litigation and the roles of insurance and workers' compensation in tort law. We begin with a study of the essential element of causation.

The Causation Element

A defendant is only responsible for harm caused by his unreasonable acts or omissions. That is the third essential element of the tort of negligence: *causation*.

The causation element is comprised of two parts: cause in fact and proximate cause. Note that some courts and practitioners combine these two causation concepts, including both of these parts within the term "proximate cause."

CAUSE IN FACT

The first part to causation is cause in fact, or causation in fact. *Cause in fact* means "actual cause." The defendant's act or omission must be the actual cause of the plaintiff's harm. In other words, actual cause is an act or omission without which an event/injury would not have occurred.

LEARNING OBJECTIVES

7.1 Define both cause in fact and proximate cause and explain the difference.

7.2 Define the essential element of damages.

7.3 Define and explain malpractice.

7.4 Define a mass tort and identify several examples.

7.5 Understand the role of insurance in tort law.

7.6 Explain the role of workers' compensation.

Causation
The essential element of negligence that limits negligence liability to harm caused by one's unreasonable acts or omissions.

Cause in fact
The part of causation brought about by an act or omission without which an event would not have occurred; also called causation in fact and actual cause.

CASE on Point

Bryant v. Better Bus. Bureau of Greater Md., Inc., 923 F.Supp. 720 (D. Md. 1996)

There must be a legally cognizable causal relationship between the breach of duty and the harm suffered, as the District Court of Maryland noted was required to state a claim for negligence.

Two tests are used to determine whether the defendant is the actual cause of the plaintiff's harm. One is the "but for" test: "But for" the defendant's action or omission, the harm to the plaintiff would not have occurred. In other words, without the defendant's act or omission, the plaintiff's injury would not have happened. This test is used when only one causal event is involved. For example, if John is driving his car and runs through a red light, colliding into Heather's car, John's act of running the red light was the cause in fact of the collision, as it was the only causal event involved. "But for" John's act of running the red light, Heather would not have suffered injury.

The other cause in fact test is the "substantial factor" test. This test is used when more than one causal event occurs, and the defendant's action or omission is a substantial factor in bringing about the harm. In other words, the defendant's act or omission had a substantial—that is, significant—role in bringing about the harm. Consider this example. Larry, a supermarket worker, recently washed an aisle floor, using too much water and leaving a puddle. Moe, a store stockperson, recently restocked the shelves in that aisle. Moe failed to stock one of the displays in compliance with store instructions, leaving the inventory in a precariously unstable stack. Mary, shopping in that aisle, slips in the water. Falling to the ground, she knocks into the display, which tumbles down on her. Mary is injured. The unreasonable actions of both Larry and Moe were significant factors in causing (in fact) Mary's injury, and each would pass the substantial factor test of cause in fact. Note that Mary would likely choose to sue the supermarket under the doctrine of *respondeat superior* (discussed in Chapter 2) rather than either or both of the individual store employees, as the store itself likely has much deeper pockets.

Only after cause in fact is established does proximate cause become an issue. If there is no cause in fact, meaning the defendant's action or omission did not actually cause the plaintiff's harm, then there is no negligence.

CASE on Point

Robb v. Wancowicz, 705 A.2d 125 (Md. Ct. Spec. App. 1998)

For wrongful conduct to be the proximate cause of a plaintiff's injury in negligence, you must first have cause in fact, as required by the Maryland Court of Special Appeals in this case.

PROXIMATE CAUSE

The second part of the causation element is ***proximate cause***, also called legal cause. Proximate cause is the part of causation that requires a sufficient connection or link between a person's act or omission and the plaintiff's injury in order to justify imposing negligence liability.

Proximate cause exists when the connection between the act and the injury is strong enough to justify the imposition of legal liability on the defendant. In other words, it is a cause that is legally sufficient to result in the wrongdoer being held responsible for the harm he, in fact, caused. Accordingly, a defendant is not necessarily liable for all harm resulting from his unreasonable acts or omissions, even if he set in motion the events that actually caused the harm. The proximate cause requirement establishes that the defendant may not be legally responsible for *all* the consequences of his actions, and foreseeability is key.

Proximate cause is a policy question. It deals with whether a wrongdoer should be held legally responsible for harms that he in fact causes, establishing a cutoff test for such liability. That cutoff test is applied using the concept of foreseeability, as follows.

In evaluating proximate cause, a court normally cuts off liability for unforeseeable harm, even if that harm was in fact caused by the defendant. In making this determination, the court evaluates whether it is fair for a defendant to avoid liability for his unreasonable action or omission. The test is whether the injury suffered by the plaintiff was the foreseeable consequence of the original risk of harm created by the defendant's unreasonable act or omission.

Consider this example. Rupert is on the slanted roof of a building, repairing loose shingles. Not paying careful attention to his task, Rupert mistakenly drops his hammer, which rolls down the roof and into a ladder being used to transport workers to and from the roof. Douglas happens to be on the ladder when the hammer hits, causing the ladder to shudder and Douglas to fall to the ground, injuring him. The homeowner, Nate, who is getting his mail from his mailbox at the time, sees Douglas fall and suffers heart palpitations and shortness of breath from seeing this horrible accident. Christine, Nate's wife, who is standing at the door of the home, observes what appears to be her husband having a heart attack. She faints, bumps her head, and falls unconscious.

Is Rupert liable for Christine's injuries? Is he liable for Nate's? What about Douglas's? Rupert did set in motion the series of events that led to all these injuries. His careless act of dropping the hammer on the roof was the cause in fact of all the injuries. Does that mean he is legally liable for all of them? For some of them? For none of them?

To answer these questions, apply the facts to the proximate cause test: Was the injury suffered by each of the plaintiffs the foreseeable consequence of the original risk of harm created by Rupert's unreasonable act of dropping the hammer on the roof? At least with respect to Christine and Nate, the answer is likely "no." A court would likely determine that the injuries they suffered were not the foreseeable consequence of the original risk of harm created by Rupert's act of dropping the hammer from the roof. Keep in mind that this is in spite of the fact that the injuries suffered by Christine and Nate would not have occurred, at least not at that time, in the absence of Rupert's unreasonable act.

Proximate cause
The part of causation that requires a sufficient connection between a person's act or omission and an injury to justify imposing liability; also called legal cause.

Key Point
Causation
The essential element of causation includes both actual cause and legal cause.

Key Point
Proximate Cause Test
Was the injury suffered by the plaintiff the foreseeable consequence of the original risk of harm created by the defendant's unreasonable act or omission?

CASE on Point

Rieck v. Med. Protective Co., 219 N.W.2d 242 (Wis. 1974)

In this case, parents brought a negligence action (wrongful birth) to recover the costs of rearing a child. Defendants in the action were a medical clinic and an obstetrician who failed to determine that the mother was pregnant in time to permit her to have an abortion to terminate the pregnancy.

The court discussed the negligence element of causation. It said that negligence plus an unbroken sequence of events establishing cause in fact does not necessarily lead to liability of the defendant for the plaintiff's injuries. The determination of whether to impose liability or not involves public policy considerations. Even when the chain of causation is complete and direct, recovery may be denied on public policy grounds (1) when the injury is too remote from the negligence; (2) when the injury is too wholly out of proportion to the culpability of the negligent tortfeasor; (3) when in retrospect it appears too highly extraordinary that the negligence should have brought about the harm; (4) because allowance of recovery would place too unreasonable a burden on the defendants; (5) because allowance of recovery would be too likely to open the way for fraudulent claims; or (6) because "allowance of recovery would enter a field that has no sensible or just stopping point." The court found multiple public policy grounds existed in the case to require a denial of recovery against the medical clinic and doctor. On the sixth ground noted, the court said that to permit the parents to keep their child and shift the entire cost of its upbringing to a physician who failed to determine or inform them of the pregnancy "would be to create a new category of surrogate parent." So the court in this case cut off the defendants' liability for their otherwise negligent conduct.

However, with respect to Douglas's injuries, a court is more likely to find that his injuries were the foreseeable consequence of the original risk of harm created by Rupert's careless dropping of the hammer on the slanted roof. A court would likely find proximate cause to exist.

Reconsider, for a moment, the *Palsgraf* case discussed in Chapter 6. In that case, the court found that injury to someone was foreseeable, but injury to the particular plaintiff, a bystander, was not. If, in that case, the world at large test was used and a duty of care was determined to exist, would proximate cause have been found? There is a close relationship between the duty of care and proximate cause; a plaintiff who successfully establishes a duty of care in an unforeseeable plaintiff case is far along in establishing proximate cause as well. The proximate cause test cuts off legal liability for negligence only if the injury was beyond the scope of the foreseeable risk of harm originally created by the defendant.

There are two main exceptions to the general rule of proximate cause, when liability will not be cut off despite the fact that either the extent of the injury was unforeseeable or the manner of its occurrence was unforeseeable. The first of these exceptions is the eggshell skull rule.

The Eggshell Skull Rule

An exception to proximate cause is the ***eggshell skull rule***. Under this rule, if it is foreseeable that the defendant's unreasonable act or omission will result in

Eggshell skull rule
An exception to proximate cause according to which, if it is foreseeable that the defendant's unreasonable act or omission will result in any harm to the plaintiff's person and harm does occur, then the defendant is liable for the full extent of the harm, including both the foreseeable and the unforeseeable injuries that result.

any harm to the plaintiff, and harm does occur, then the defendant is liable for the full extent of the harm, including both the foreseeable and the unforeseeable injuries that result. Therefore, the proximate cause test will not cut off liability for the unforeseeable *extent* of injuries that are unreasonably caused by a defendant's act or omission when it was foreseeable that the plaintiff would be harmed by the defendant's conduct.

Consider this example. Kevin, who is late for an appointment, is speeding in his car while eating a hamburger and fries, as well as drinking a soda. Looking away from the road to wipe a smear of mayonnaise off his shirt, he veers from his lane, side-swiping Megan's car. Megan's car careens out of control, hitting the median. Her car is totaled and Megan is injured. In fact, Megan is twelve weeks pregnant, and the injuries she sustains include a miscarriage. Is Kevin responsible for the full extent of the injuries suffered by Megan, including her miscarriage? The answer is "yes." Could Kevin have foreseen that she was pregnant? That fact is irrelevant to this determination.

Under the eggshell skull rule, a tortfeasor must "take the plaintiff as he finds him." This means that, if the plaintiff happens to be highly vulnerable to injury, such as by being pregnant or elderly or having heart disease, then the defendant is liable for the full extent of the injury, including both the foreseeable and unforeseeable harms suffered. This is true even if the extent of the injury was not within the foreseeable original risk of harm created by the defendant's act or omission. The only requirement is that at least some injury to the person, not just to property, of the plaintiff be foreseeable. The defendant is liable for the full extent of the injury, meaning for both the foreseeable and unforeseeable harms suffered.

The other exception to the general proximate cause rule is foreseeable harm that occurs in an unforeseeable manner.

CASE on Point

Castillo v. Young, 720 N.W.2d 40 (Neb. 2006)

This case involved a negligence lawsuit brought against the drivers of two other cars by a motorist who was injured as a result of a three car accident. Castillo was hit head on by a car driven by Young; then when she came to a stop after that collision, Castillo was hit from behind by a second driver (Sears). In the collision, Castillo suffered injury, including to her jaw.

From the testimony given at trial, it was determined that Castillo had a preexisting jaw condition. She had broken her jaw about seventeen years earlier and suffered from disk displacement in her jaw, a joint disorder. The court discussed the eggshell skull rule and its application to this case. It said that if a plaintiff has a preexisting condition and the defendant's conduct results in greater damages because of that preexisting condition, the defendant is liable for all damages proximately caused by the defendant's conduct. So a defendant "takes a plaintiff as the defendant finds him or her." Determining that the collision aggravated Castillo's jaw condition, the court ordered a new trial on the issue of damages so that proper instruction could be given to the jury on the eggshell skull rule—that the defendant could be held liable for the aggravation of Castillo's preexisting jaw condition.

Foreseeable Harm/Unforeseeable Manner

The other main exception to the general proximate cause rule involves the unforeseeable manner of occurrence of foreseeable harm. What if it is foreseeable that a defendant's act or omission will cause harm of some kind to the plaintiff, but the manner of its occurrence is unforeseeable? The fact that the manner of the injury is unforeseeable will not cut off the defendant's liability under the proximate cause test; the manner in which an injury occurs does not have to be foreseeable so long as the harm that results was within the risk originally created by the defendant's wrongful conduct.

Consider this example. Farley is helping to construct a bridge over a roadway. Pamela is driving her car well in excess of the speed limit, while talking on her cell phone. Not paying close attention to her driving, Pamela veers out of her lane and collides with the side of the bridge. Farley, who is welding steel beams near the point of collision, is severely burned when the car's impact with the bridge jostles him while he is welding. Is Pamela liable for Farley's burn injury? The answer is "yes." Although the precise manner of occurrence of Farley's injury (a burn from welding) was unforeseeable, that he would suffer harm in the nature of physical injury from Pamela's unreasonable act was foreseeable. Therefore, the proximate cause cutoff test would not apply to absolve Pamela from liability because she was the proximate cause of a foreseeable injury to Farley despite the fact that it occurred in an unforeseeable manner.

Sometimes intervening forces contribute to the plaintiff's injuries. These intervening forces, called intervening causes, if strong enough, may constitute superseding causes, cutting off the defendant's legal liability. These cases are discussed next.

INTERVENING AND SUPERSEDING CAUSES

Sometimes outside forces produce harm to the plaintiff after the defendant's act or omission. These are called intervening causes. An **intervening cause** is an event or occurrence that produces harm after the initial injury suffered by the plaintiff, which contributes to or aggravates the initial injury. An intervening cause may or may not be superseding.

A **superseding cause** is an event or occurrence that produces harm after the initial injury suffered by the plaintiff that cuts off the defendant's liability *for the later harm,* not for the original harm. A superseding cause is beyond the foreseeable risk of harm originally created by the defendant's unreasonable act or omission, which defeats proximate cause.

There are four types of intervening causes: (1) intervening forces of God or nature, (2) intervening innocent human forces, (3) intervening negligent human forces, and (4) intervening intentional and/or criminal human forces. An intervening cause is superseding, cutting off the defendant's liability for the harm caused by the intervening force, when the harm caused by the intervening force is outside the scope of the foreseeable risk of harm originally created by the defendant's unreasonable act or omission and/or when the harm caused by the intervening cause is extraordinary and highly unusual. The defendant's

Intervening cause
An event or occurrence that produces harm after the initial injury suffered by the plaintiff, which contributes to or aggravates the initial injury.

Superseding cause
An event or occurrence that produces harm after the initial injury suffered by the plaintiff, which cuts off defendant's liability for the later harm.

SIDEBAR

INTERVENING AND SUPERSEDING CAUSES

The four types of intervening causes are

1. Intervening forces of God or nature, which are natural occurrences, without human involvement, which cause subsequent additional harm, such as hurricanes, tornados, and earthquakes

2. Intervening innocent human forces, which are occurrences caused by people acting carefully who cause subsequent additional harm, such as a person, driving carefully behind another car, who cannot avoid hitting the pedestrian the car ahead of her just knocked down in the road, causing further injury to the pedestrian

3. Intervening negligent human forces, which are occurrences caused by people acting carelessly who cause subsequent additional harm, such as the situation above, but the driver of the second car could have avoided hitting the pedestrian the second time had he not been speeding and talking on his cell phone while driving

4. Intervening intentional or criminal human forces, which are occurrences caused by people engaging in intentional or criminal misconduct who cause subsequent additional harm, such as when the pedestrian hit by the car goes to the hospital for treatment, where she is killed during an escape by a prisoner who is also being treated in the hospital at that time

Key Point

When Intervening Causes Are Superceding

An intervening cause is superseding, cutting off the defendant's liability for the harm caused by the intervening force, when the harm caused by the intervening force is outside the scope of the foreseeable risk of harm originally created by the defendant's unreasonable act or omission and/or when the harm caused by the intervening cause is extraordinary and highly unusual.

CASE on Point

Puget Sound Elec. Workers Health Trust and Vacation Plan v. McKenzie Rothwell Barlow & Korpi, P.S., 2012 WL 280385 (Wash. Ct. App. 2012)[1]

This case, already discussed in Chapter 6 regarding duty of care owed by professionals, was a legal malpractice case brought against a law firm and some of its lawyers arising out of the firm's handling of certain trusts. The defendants tried to avoid liability by negating the causation element of the tort of negligence.

The court discussed the element of causation. It said that proximate cause can be divided into two elements, cause in fact and legal cause. Cause in fact is the actual, "but for" cause of the injury. Legal cause focuses on whether the connection between the result and the tortfeasor's act is too remote or insubstantial to impose liability. The court said that a superseding cause exists if a new, independent act breaks the chain of causation so that the original negligence is no longer a proximate cause of the injury sustained; in that case, the defendant's liability is cut off, or extinguished. It is for the trier of fact (the jury in a jury trial) to determine whether a third party's act is a superseding cause to cut off liability.

The defendants in the case argued that subsequent actions by a successor law firm severed the chain of causation so that they were no longer the proximate cause of the trusts' damages—that the other law firm's actions were a superseding cause. The court rejected this argument, finding that there was no evidence that the successor law firm was a proximate or superseding cause of any of the trusts' claims.

liability for the initial harm is not affected; only the defendant's responsibility for the additional harm caused by the intervening force is affected when the intervening force is superseding.

Remember, if the intervening cause is strong enough—in the jury's determination, during a jury trial—to relieve the wrongdoer of liability, it becomes a superseding cause. So if the intervening cause is superseding, it cuts off the defendant's liability for the subsequent, not the original, injury sustained by the plaintiff. The tortfeasor remains liable for the initial harm he caused, however. On the other hand, if the intervening cause is not superseding, then the tortfeasor is liable for *all* of the harm, including the subsequent harm, suffered by the plaintiff.

The final essential element of the tort of negligence is damages. Although damages are normally recoverable in tort actions, they must be established as an essential element of negligence claims. The essential element of damages is examined next.

The Damage Element

Damages
The essential element of negligence that requires a plaintiff to demonstrate that she suffered a legally recognizable injury.

In order for a plaintiff to recover in negligence, she must demonstrate that she suffered a legally recognizable injury, meaning she suffered ***damages***. To be able to receive compensation, she must show that she suffered some harm or damage, incurred some loss, or otherwise suffered some invasion of a legally protected interest. Such damages can be in the form of personal harm, damage to property, or monetary loss. Conversely, if no harm or injury results from a defendant's unreasonable conduct, there is no negligence.

Note that establishing damages is not an essential element of most intentional tort claims. Therefore, one can recover nominal damages on an intentional tort claim if the wrong was committed, even though no harm resulted. However, that is not the case with negligence. Damages are an essential element of the tort of negligence. There must be some demonstration of legally recognizable injury for a negligence action to succeed. Of course, the greater the harm suffered by the plaintiff, the greater will be the damage award that may be recovered if the negligence action succeeds.

What happens if, by the plaintiff's own conduct after suffering harm by the defendant's actions, the plaintiff suffers further harm by not taking reasonable steps to minimize his injury? Is the defendant liable for that subsequent harm? The next doctrine covers this situation.

AVOIDABLE CONSEQUENCES DOCTRINE AND MITIGATION OF DAMAGES

Avoidable consequences doctrine
Where a plaintiff is held legally responsible for any further injury or harm that, through his actions, he could have reasonably avoided after being injured by the defendant's negligence.

Under the ***avoidable consequences doctrine***, a plaintiff is held legally responsible for any *further* injury or harm that, through his actions, he could have reasonably avoided after being injured by the defendant's negligence. A plaintiff in a negligence action must take reasonable steps to mitigate the consequences

CASE on Point

Fuches v. S.E.S. Co., 459 N.W.2d 642 (Iowa Ct. App. 1990)

In this case, a contractor was injured at work when a scaffold on which he was standing collapsed. In receiving medical care, the plaintiff refused the doctor's advice to undergo surgery for an injury to his shoulder resulting from the fall. The contractor sued the lessor of the scaffold for his injuries. The court found that, by refusing the surgery recommended by his doctor, a question of fact was raised as to whether the plaintiff failed to reasonably mitigate his damages.

of his original injury. For example, he should seek prompt medical attention for any serious physical harm suffered because of the defendant's unreasonable conduct. Otherwise, the plaintiff's recovery may be reduced by the amount of harm he reasonably could have avoided.

Sometimes a plaintiff in a negligence action recovers funds or receives services because of the injury suffered that do not come from the defendant. How do these resources affect a plaintiff's recovery?

COLLATERAL SOURCE RULE

The **collateral source rule** is a rule of evidence recognized in some states. It deals with funds or services a person receives because of an injury that come from sources other than the defendant who caused the injury. **Collateral sources**, then, are funds or services received by a plaintiff from someone other than the defendant for injuries caused by the defendant's act or omission; they include items such as insurance benefits, Social Security payments, veterans' benefits, disability benefits, workers' compensation benefits, and sponsored medical care like Medicare and Medicaid. The defendant did not contribute to these sources of funds and services that the plaintiff received as a result of the harm the defendant caused. In jurisdictions that recognize it, the collateral source rule prohibits the jury from being told about these collateral sources of compensation and services, thereby preventing the defendant from avoiding liability because another source at least partially compensated the plaintiff. Obviously, letting the jury know that a plaintiff already received at least some compensation for the harm suffered, through insurance or other such benefits, might result in a jury reducing the plaintiff's recovery from the defendant for the amount of compensation or the value of the services provided by the independent source.

What happens after the plaintiff has established each of the essential elements of the tort of negligence? This is the next topic of discussion in our examination of the tort of negligence.

Collateral source rule
A legal doctrine that prohibits the defendant from avoiding liability for injuries caused to the plaintiff but compensated for by collateral sources.

Collateral sources
Funds or services that a person receives because of an injury caused by a defendant but that come from sources other than the defendant.

A *Prima Facie* Case

The plaintiff has the burden of establishing, through presentation of evidence, each of the four essential elements of the tort of negligence. Once the plaintiff has established all of the elements, then he has set forth a *prima facie* case of negligence.

At that point, the burden of proof shifts to the defendant to rebut one or more of the essential elements of the plaintiff's claim or to establish a legal defense in order to defend himself against the claim. Defenses to the tort of negligence are discussed in Chapter 9. If the defendant fails to defend himself successfully, then the plaintiff is entitled to remedies for negligence. Remedies are also discussed in Chapter 9.

The next topic we will consider relating to negligence is unreasonable conduct by professionals, such as lawyers and doctors, in the performance of professional services. This is the topic of malpractice.

Malpractice

Malpractice
The failure of a professional, such as a doctor or lawyer, to exercise reasonable care in the performance of professional services; also called professional negligence.

Malpractice is, in essence, professional negligence. It occurs when a professional, such as a doctor, lawyer, accountant, architect, engineer, or the like, breaches her duty of care in the performance of professional services, causing harm to another. Professionals are not liable for every mistake they make that causes injury to others; the injury must be caused by their wrongful conduct for a tort—namely, negligence—to be committed. Because malpractice cases are essentially negligence cases, by what standard of care are such professionals measured in determining whether there has been a breach of their duty of care?

Key Point

Standard of Care for Professionals
A professional must exercise the degree of skill and expertise commonly possessed by members of the profession in good standing.

As discussed in Chapter 6, professionals are held to a higher standard of care than ordinary persons because of their special knowledge, skill, training, education, and expertise in their profession. They are held to the standard of *a reasonable professional in similar circumstances*. In other words, the objective reasonable person standard is made partly subjective, taking into account the extensive knowledge, training, and so forth, that the professional possesses to be able to practice in her profession. The standard of care applied is this: A professional must exercise the degree of skill and expertise commonly possessed by members of the profession in good standing.

CASE on Point

Puget Sound Elec. Workers Health Trust and Vacation Plan v. McKenzie Rothwell Barlow & Korpi, P.S., 2012 WL 280385 (Wash. Ct. App. 2012)

Remember this case from Chapter 6 and earlier in this chapter. The Court of Appeals of Washington said that in order to breach the duty of care, an attorney must fail to exercise the degree of care, skill, diligence, and knowledge commonly possessed and exercised by a reasonable, careful, and prudent lawyer in the practice of law in Washington.

SIDEBAR

THE PRACTICE OF LAW AND MALPRACTICE INSURANCE

Legal practitioners and their firms routinely carry malpractice and errors and omissions insurance to insure themselves against claims of professional negligence and other errors that may be committed in the performance of legal services.

What differs from jurisdiction to jurisdiction is whether a national, or local, standard is used in making this determination. Some jurisdictions consider similar professionals across the nation in making this determination, thus using a broad, country-wide pool of similar professionals. Other jurisdictions limit this consideration geographically, to the pool of similar professionals in that geographic area. This distinction could matter if a doctor practices in a rural area in Alaska, for example. Would the standard of care against which he is measured include other doctors in his specialty area in his state or locality? Or would it be so broad as to include all doctors in his specialty area throughout the nation, including those practicing at such premier institutions as The Johns Hopkins Hospital and Health System and the Mayo Clinic, or other doctors practicing in major metropolitan areas such as New York City or Chicago? Whichever standard is applied, a breach of the duty of care by a professional, using a higher, more subjective, standard of care, is malpractice if the other elements of the tort of negligence are met.

Medical malpractice is professional negligence by medical practitioners. An example of medical malpractice is a surgeon operating on a patient's wrong ear. Legal malpractice is professional negligence by legal practitioners. An example of legal malpractice is a lawyer or paralegal missing a filing deadline set by a court. Other professionals, such as accountants, engineers, and architects, can be held liable for professional negligence by failure to use the reasonable care a similarly skilled and experienced professional in that field would use under the same or similar circumstances. An example of accountant malpractice is an auditor failing to review all material financial accounts of his client while performing a year-end audit.

Tort reform is concerned with malpractice actions, among other tort actions. Medical and legal malpractice actions, in particular, are plentiful and on the rise in our society, not so much because doctors and lawyers make more unreasonable mistakes than others, but because they often have "deeper pockets," making it more lucrative to sue them. Tort reformists would limit the types of cases and amount of damages one could recover in certain types of malpractice actions.

Next we will consider torts that involve one event or source that causes harm to numerous people. These are called mass torts.

Mass Torts

A *mass tort* is a tort involving the same event or source that causes harm to many people. It normally involves numerous plaintiffs and one or only a few defendants, usually corporate—that is, business—defendants. An example of a

Mass tort
A tort involving the same event or source that causes harm to many people.

mass tort is a commercial airline crash. Many people are harmed in the same event when a commercial airline crashes. These people, or their legal representatives in the event the passengers and crew did not survive, may all sue the airline responsible for the crash—the one defendant.

The main types of mass torts are mass accidents, mass marketing of defective products, mass toxic torts, and mass economic loss. A mass accident is a single event that injures a large number of people, such as a hotel fire, a commercial airline crash, a train derailment, or an oil or chemical spill. Mass marketing of defective products may cause mass injuries, and this is another kind of mass tort. Examples of defective products mass torts are litigation involving asbestos, tobacco, silicone breast implants, and the diet drug Fen-Phen (case briefing assignments at the end of the chapter consider Vioxx and PCBs). Mass toxic torts are torts involving injuries sustained from exposure to toxic substances, such as hazardous waste contamination at Love Canal in New York, Agent Orange herbicidal exposure in Vietnam, and nuclear power plant leaks. Mass economic loss torts are torts that involve injuries sustained by people who suffer monetary loss from fraud, including false representations made by companies to induce investors, such as those made by Enron executives preceding that company's collapse. Earlier, we noted that some mass torts arise out of a single event, whereas others are generated from a single source. Mass accident cases involve injuries arising out of a single event; the other mass torts deal with injuries coming from a single source.

Mass torts may give rise to mass tort litigation. Mass tort litigation is discussed next.

Key Points

The Four Main Types of Mass Torts

- Mass accidents
- Mass marketing of defective products
- Mass toxic torts
- Mass economic loss

Mass Tort Litigation

Mass tort actions are maintained to compensate for injuries to many people arising out of, for example, a single accident, a disaster, or an exposure to a toxin. The Federal Judicial Center's *Manual for Complex Litigation (Third)* notes that in mass disaster litigation, injuries occur at a single location, such as the site of a train derailment. Injuries often manifest immediately in these situations. However, in mass toxic tort or defective product litigation, injuries may occur in numerous widely dispersed locations or sites, and at different times, such as when consumers are injured by eating tainted beef sold throughout a wide geographic area. Further, the full extent of the harm they cause may take years to become known.[2] Mass tort litigation is often referred to as "complex litigation." Mass tort cases assert traditional tort causes of action, such as negligence, products liability, and misrepresentation. What differs is the scope of the cases. ***Mass tort litigation*** involves large numbers of plaintiffs in multiple jurisdictions, in both state and federal courts, and multiple venues, all injured by the same defendant and arising out of the same event or source. These complex cases create a significant burden on the courts. They consume significant resources, particularly in extensive discovery and document production, as well as generate large attorneys' fees (see the exercises at the end of the chapter for a case on this point). The legal issues involved are often complex and sophisticated, not uncommonly involving complicated scientific

Mass tort litigation
Litigation involving large numbers of plaintiffs in multiple jurisdictions, including both state and federal courts, and multiple venues, all injured by the same defendant and arising out of the same event or source.

CASE on Point

In re: Vioxx Products Liability Litigation, 574 F.Supp.2d 606 (E.D. La. 2008)

This case involved a federal district court's review of the reasonableness of attorneys' fees. The court held that contingent fee arrangements between attorneys and the claimants they represented would be capped at 32 percent plus reasonable costs. These fees were based on a settlement in the amount of $4.85 billion in mass tort litigation over the drug Vioxx.

Merck, a pharmaceutical company, researched, designed, manufactured, marketed, and distributed the pain and inflammation relief drug they called Vioxx (generically known as Rofecoxib). Though it was approved by the U.S. Food and Drug Administration on May 20, 1999, Merck withdrew it from the market on September 30, 2004, when data from a clinical trial evidenced that Vioxx increased a person's risk of heart attack and stroke. It was estimated that approximately 20 million patients took Vioxx in the United States during the period of time it was available. Thousands of people filed suit, both individually and in numerous class actions, alleging products liability, tort, fraud, and warranty claims.

or technical matters and requiring expert witnesses. They often generate inconsistent or conflicting rulings and judgments from different courts even though they involve the same facts, just different plaintiffs. It can be difficult for plaintiffs to establish "causation" in their tort claims for certain types of mass injuries, especially toxic torts, such as Love Canal, for example. Sometimes these cases involve novel legal theories. Imagine being the first person to bring a case against a tobacco company alleging that its cigarettes caused injury in the form of lung cancer. Mass tort cases take long periods of time to litigate or otherwise resolve, such as through settlement or arbitration. Mass tort litigation pressures the defendants involved to settle these cases in order to allow the companies to focus their energies and preserve their assets for conducting regular business activities, assuming they are not bankrupted by the litigation. Mass tort judgments can be financially devastating to the defendants.

Because mass torts involve similar cases, they are often certified as class actions or transferred to a multidistrict litigation court in order to expedite their adjudication. A **class action** is a lawsuit in which a large group of people bring

Class action
A form of lawsuit in which a large group of people bring a legal claim collectively.

SIDEBAR

BALANCING OF INTERESTS

In resolving mass tort cases, courts must balance the competing interests of compensating the injured parties for the harms they suffered against the societal interest in preserving the business or industry being sued.

Multidistrict litigation
A special federal litigation procedure designed to speed the process of handling complex cases.

a legal claim collectively. *Multidistrict litigation* is a special federal litigation procedure designed to speed the process of handling complex cases. Both of these methods of litigation help to make the bringing of mass tort claims more efficient and expedite their movement through the legal system.

In summary, a mass tort is a tort involving many plaintiffs and arising out of the same event or source. Mass torts require complex litigation to resolve the legal disputes involved.

Insurance is a contract law principle with tort law applications. The role of insurance in tort law is discussed next.

The Role of Insurance in Tort Law

Insurance law and negligence are distinguishable, as discussed in Chapter 6. Negligence is a tort action that can be brought when a tortfeasor engages in unreasonable conduct that causes harm to another. The distinguishing feature is that for the tort of negligence to occur, there must be conduct that is unreasonable. On the other hand, *insurance* is a type of contract. Insurance contracts have the same elements as other types of contracts but, unlike many other types of contracts, insurance policies are heavily regulated by state laws. Persons, including humans and entities, purchase insurance to manage their risk of loss in the event they suffer injuries to themselves or their property. Upon the occurrence of a covered event, as defined in the insurance contract, called an *insurance policy*, the insured receives compensation in accordance with the terms of the policy. Reasonableness of another's conduct is not a critical concern in the role of insurance.

Insurance
A type of contract utilized by persons to manage their risk of loss under certain circumstances.

Insurance policies, besides providing compensation for covered losses, also often contain "duty to defend" provisions. These contractual provisions, typical in automobile insurance policies, provide for an attorney to represent the insured if the insured is sued for any action covered by the policy. In other words, an insurance company has a duty to provide a defense for the insured when the insured is sued by someone and the legal action (i.e., a negligence action) is covered by the policy. The insurance company meets this duty by hiring

Insurance policy
A contract for insurance coverage.

an attorney to represent the insured in the lawsuit. This attorney represents the insured—so *the insured is the client,* not the insurance company—but the insurance company pays the legal fees. The attorney may be one employed by the insurance company, rather than one hired by it. Many insurance companies employ attorneys to defend actions on behalf of their insureds.

People and entities can purchase different types of insurance to protect themselves from certain risks of loss. For instance, professionals can purchase malpractice and/or errors and omissions insurance to protect themselves from risk of loss in the event they are sued for negligence in the performance of their professional services. Persons can purchase life insurance to protect their families in the event of their death. They can purchase premises insurance, such as homeowner's insurance, to protect their homes and personal property from risk of loss. Businesses can purchase various types of insurance to protect their worksites, their employees' safety, and their business deals. In addition, by law, drivers generally are required to maintain minimum levels of automobile insurance to protect themselves and others in the event of automobile accidents. The two types of insurance most relevant to personal injury tort cases are automobile insurance and homeowner's insurance.

Lawsuits involving automobile accidents are the most common form of personal injury actions. To better understand the role of insurance in tort law, we will examine automobile insurance in greater detail, as one example of insurance with which most people are familiar. Note that in the case of automobile accidents, police often fill out accident reports and these reports contain information about each driver's insurance. So police accident reports are a good way for a paralegal to determine what insurance coverage each party to a particular case has. The client should have a copy of the police accident report and can provide it to the paralegal. Because of the common occurrence of automobile accidents, all states require minimum levels of automobile insurance for drivers, or the posting of a bond or securities, or other demonstration that a driver has the ability to pay a tort judgment, at a minimum level, without insurance. Many drivers purchase additional insurance, in excess of the required minimum limits, to further protect themselves from risk of loss.

SIDEBAR

EXAMPLES OF DIFFERENT TYPES OF INSURANCE

- Liability insurance
- Life insurance
- Property insurance
- Automobile insurance
- Workers' compensation insurance
- Health insurance
- Casualty insurance
- Disability insurance

> **SIDEBAR**
>
> ## EXCLUSIONS FOR INTENTIONAL ACTS
>
> Most insurance policies contain exclusions for intentional acts of an insured. An exclusion is a person, damage, or type of loss not covered by an insurance policy. So if an insured purposefully runs another car off the road in an instance of road rage, the insurance company would not be responsible for the loss; the insured's intentional misconduct would be an exclusion under the policy.

Insurance premium
Consideration paid by the insured for the insurance protection set forth in the insurance policy.

Automobile insurance protects the insured, for up to the coverage amounts, for covered events, typically motor vehicle accidents, but may also cover events such as vandalism or theft of the covered automobile. The coverage amounts and what is a covered event are defined in the insurance contract, and the more comprehensive and higher the coverage, the more expensive the premium is likely to be. An **insurance premium** is the consideration (money) paid by the insured for the insurance protection he purchases, as evidenced by the policy. Note that the definition of what is a covered event for automobile insurance purposes will be different from what constitutes the tort of negligence. This is because automobile insurance policies typically cover harms caused by accidents that occur despite all drivers driving reasonably, and may exclude intentional or reckless misconduct by the driver, such as driving under the influence of drugs or alcohol or deliberately colliding with another vehicle.

Various types of automobile insurance coverage are available. Liability coverage covers bodily injury and property damage suffered by others, up to the stated policy limits. Collision coverage covers damage to the driver's vehicle in a collision. Comprehensive coverage covers other risks to a driver's automobile, such as vandalism or theft. Medical payments coverage covers medical expenses for persons injured in an accident. Uninsured/underinsured motorist coverage protects drivers and their passengers for personal injury and property damage caused by another motorist who is either uninsured or underinsured.

The cost of the automobile insurance, in the form of insurance premiums, will depend on many factors, including the size and nature of the insurer, the

STATUTE on Point

Mass. Gen. Laws Ann. ch. 90, § 34A (2012)

Massachusetts, in its Compulsory Motor Vehicle Liability Insurance Law, requires a policy of motor vehicle liability insurance that provides indemnity and protects the insured and anyone who operates the insured's motor vehicle with his express or implied consent. The policy must protect against liability for damages payable to others for bodily injuries, including death, and consequential damages for injuries or death sustained during the term of the policy by any person other than a guest occupant of the motor vehicle (which is treated under the Massachusetts automobile guest statute) or any employee of the owner or registrant of the motor vehicle. Coverage must be at least $20,000 for an accident resulting in injury to or death of one person and at least $40,000 for an accident resulting in injury to or death of more than one person.

FINANCIAL RESPONSIBILITY LAWS

Statutory minimum automobile insurance coverage consists of these parts:

- Liability coverage, to compensate any person the insured injures or whose property she harms
- Bodily injury
- Property damage
- Medical payments, for the insured and others covered by the policy
- Uninsured/underinsured motorist

Note that uninsured or underinsured drivers are violating state law. Although the law requires financial responsibility of registrants of cars, plenty of motorists fail to meet this requirement. So even though it is a legal requirement to have automobile insurance, some drivers operate automobiles without having it, or having enough of it—so uninsured and underinsured motorist coverage is required.

types and amount of coverage, the age, sex, and driving record of the driver, the geographic location of the driver and the car, the annual amount of driving, the use of the car (business or personal), the type and age of the car, and the amount of the deductible. All coverage other than liability insurance is subject to a deductible, meaning that the policy owner must pay up to a minimum amount of the claim, based on the deductible amount purchased in the contract.

Even in the presence of automobile insurance, tort lawsuits are common when automobile accidents are negligently, as opposed to accidentally, caused. In these cases, automobile insurance policies typically include a provision stating that the insurance company has a duty to provide a legal defense for the insured when he is sued by another for an incident covered by the policy (the "duty to defend" provision discussed earlier), and insurance companies have defense attorneys—many of them—who represent the insureds in these actions. If an insurance company makes a payout under a policy to compensate for harm

NO-FAULT INSURANCE

No-fault insurance is a type of insurance contract under which an insured is indemnified by his own insurance company, regardless of fault, for a covered loss he suffers. A minority of states requires or permits automobile insurance policy holders to operate under a no-fault system pursuant to which persons injured in automobile accidents obtain indemnification under their own policies and, in doing so, are limited in their ability to seek recovery from a driver or vehicle owner who operated or owned the vehicle that caused the collision.

Most states have traditional, rather than no-fault, tort liability schemes relating to automobile insurance, in which recovery is governed by principles of fault—the insurer for the vehicle or driver at fault traditionally is responsible.

SUBROGATION

Subrogation is the insurance company's right to sue the tortfeasor to recover money it has paid out to the insured. Consider this example. The insured is injured by a negligent driver and files a claim with his insurance company for compensation for those injuries. The insurance company pays the claim of the insured. Then, if the policy includes a subrogation provision, the insurance company can sue the negligent driver to recover for the damages he caused and the insurance company paid out to the insured. Subrogation permits the insurance company to substitute itself for the insured in order to be able to sue the negligent driver.

caused by a negligent tortfeasor it insured, the insurance company may have a right of subrogation (the right to recover from the person who caused the loss) to sue the insured tortfeasor for recovery of the money it expended. Further, an insurance company can file a subrogation claim against another insurance company if it has paid more than its fair share of a claim. So, although automobile insurance policies may pay out, under their contract terms, if there is an accident and no negligence, they may also pay out when negligence of a covered driver is involved.

Remember that collateral sources of funds may or may not be made known to and considered by courts, specifically juries, when determining the amount of a tortfeasor's liability. Insurance benefits are a type of collateral source. Depending on the jurisdiction, insurance benefits may or may not be made known to and considered by juries.

Insurance is very important to personal injury lawyers and their clients. In deciding whether to accept a case, a personal injury lawyer must consider the potential for the plaintiff to recover damages. This is so because most personal injury

SAMPLE COVERAGE AND LIMITS OF LIABILITY FROM A TYPICAL AUTOMOBILE INSURANCE POLICY

Liability: Bodily injury $300,000 per person and $500,000 per accident, property damage $50,000 per accident

Personal Injury Protection: $100,000 medical payments coverage per person

Uninsured Motorists: Bodily injury $300,000 per person and $500,000 per accident, property damage $50,000 per accident ($250 deductible)

Physical Damage: Comprehensive loss ($500 deductible) and collision loss ($500 deductible)

Note that many people carry automobile insurance protection far in excess of the minimums required by state law, such as those illustrated above, which are from the author's policy.

SPECIALTY PRACTICE AREAS

Attorneys who practice in the field of personal injury law often specialize in particular types of cases, such as automobile accident cases. Further, they often represent one particular side of the litigation, either representing those bringing the suits, as plaintiffs' attorneys, or defending the insurance companies, as insurance defense attorneys.

lawyers are paid a contingency fee, typically of about a third of the plaintiff's recovery. To be paid for their legal services, the clients need to recover. If the defendant has funds and/or assets that can be reached to pay a legal judgment rendered against him, it makes economic sense to sue him. But what if the defendant has no significant financial resources, at least not significant enough to pay an award a court may order? In such a case, whether the defendant has insurance matters. Plaintiff's attorneys often will not sue an individual defendant who does not have insurance coverage because that defendant may not have sufficient financial resources from which to pay a legal judgment or even a settlement. But if the defendant has insurance coverage, there is a much greater likelihood that a plaintiff may be able to recover from him, and from that recovery the lawyer collects his fee. So if the defendant has no insurance and no significant financial resources, it may make no economic sense to sue him even if you can win. But if the defendant has insurance, though he has no significant financial resources, it may make economic sense to sue him, depending on his insurance coverage and policy limits. Regarding policy limits, however, it may not make economic sense to sue a defendant for more than the insurance policy limits. The bottom line is that when a defendant has insurance, the possibility of obtaining a recovery against him increases, perhaps greatly. In personal injury cases, the types of insurance that are most relevant are automobile insurance and homeowner's insurance. These insurance coverages are specifically designed to pay out on these types of claims—it is an important reason why the insurance was purchased by the defendant in the first place.

Also, in negotiating possible settlements of lawsuits, policy limits are relevant and discoverable information in litigation. There may be no practical point in suing a tortfeasor for an amount in excess of the insurance policy limits if the tortfeasor would have no ability to pay an adverse judgment, thus encouraging settlement for an amount within policy limits.

Workers' compensation, as noted above, is a kind of insurance. It is examined next.

Workers' Compensation

Traditionally, workers who were injured on the job had to sue their employers in tort, for negligence in maintaining an unsafe workplace, to recover compensation for their injuries. Employees were often denied recovery in these actions when employers successfully asserted such common law tort defenses (discussed in Chapter 9)

Workers' compensation statutes
State laws that establish an administrative procedure to provide compensation to workers who suffer injury or illness as a result of their employment.

as contributory negligence on the workers' behalf, assumption of the risk by the worker who knew about the hazards of the job and voluntarily agreed to work it, and the fellow-employee rule, which stated that employers were not liable for injuries sustained by workers at the hands of most negligent fellow employees.

To counteract the common law result that often denied recovery to workers who were injured on the job, states have enacted workers' compensation statutes. *Workers' compensation statutes* establish an administrative procedure to provide compensation to workers who suffer injury or illness as a result of their employment. Note that workers' compensation laws are state statutes, not federal law.

State legislatures' purpose in enacting these statutes was to permit recovery, without the necessity of the employee proving employer negligence, for workplace injuries or illnesses, allowing an employee to receive a fixed monetary award in exchange for giving up the right to sue the employer in tort. Today, workers who are injured or killed as a result of workplace accidents or illnesses are covered by their state's workers' compensation statutes and follow the designated administrative procedure in seeking recovery. Under these statutes, employees can obtain compensation for their injuries (or their heirs, for their deaths) or illnesses without having to prove negligence of the employer, thus not having to combat the effective defenses noted earlier. Workers' compensation is a no-fault system, like strict liability, under which the worker's compensation is recovered regardless of fault—the worker's or the employer's. In other words, an employee is covered under a workers' compensation statute whether or not the injury or illness was a result of the fault of the employer, or whether or not the worker, through her conduct, contributed to her injury or illness.

Workers' compensation statutes cover private-sector employers, not government employers. Each state has an agency or commission, which may be part of the state's department of labor or may be an independent entity, which administers the workers' compensation statute for private-sector employees. Public employees are protected under separate workers' compensation systems covering their governmental employers. The workers' compensation statutes define who is an employer and who is an employee, what is employment, and other important terms that determine the right to compensation under that scheme. Workers typically excluded from workers' compensation statutes include independent contractors, employees of employers with less than a threshold number of employees, and domestic, farm, and casual workers. Employees who are not covered by workers' compensation statutes must sue their employers under negligence theory, and combat the defenses normally asserted by employers defending those lawsuits.

SIDEBAR

WORKERS' COMPENSATION AND FAULT

Workers' compensation eradicates the workers' need to prove fault of the employer in a tort suit to recover for on-the-job injuries or illnesses. Rather, the worker files a claim under the state's workers' compensation system to recover a set amount for the injury or illness, an amount based on a calculation set forth in the statutory scheme, which depends on the nature and extent of the injury or illness.

SIDEBAR

PRIVATE- VERSUS PUBLIC-SECTOR EMPLOYERS

State workers' compensation systems cover private-sector employers. Public employers, that is, government employers, are covered under separate systems.

To recover for workplace injuries or illnesses under workers' compensation statutes, the injury or illness must arise out of and occur in the course of employment. To "arise out of" the employment means that there must be a causal relationship between the injury or illness and the employment. In effect, the injury or illness must be caused by the employment, using one of various court tests to determine such causation, such as the increased-risk test, used by most jurisdictions, under which the risk of injury or illness to the employee is quantitatively greater than the risk of such to nonemployees. If particular workers are more vulnerable or susceptible to injury or illness, such as a worker who has a heart condition or asthma, then, if the employment aggravates the extent of the harm resulting from the injury or illness, that is enough to meet the "arising out of" requirement.

To occur "in the course of employment" under workers' compensation statutes means that the injury or illness must occur during a time, place, and under facts and circumstances that link it to the employment. Examples include injuries or illnesses that occur on the employer's premises (exclusions may apply if the employee engages in misconduct or horseplay on the premises), those that occur while on a business trip, and those that occur while taking a permitted break or using the restroom while on the employer's premises. Commuting to and from the workplace, and personal errands and other such deviations from work taking place during the workday, are examples of occurrences outside the course and scope of employment, to which workers' compensation does not apply.

To file a workers' compensation claim, employees must follow the administrative procedures set forth in their state statutes. These procedures normally include reporting the injury or illness to the employment supervisor or the insurance company, receiving medical treatment, providing paperwork (from the doctor, employee, and employer) to the workers' compensation agency or insurance carrier, and ultimately receiving workers' compensation benefits after a specified waiting period after the injury. Further, every state has a statute of limitations setting forth the time limit within which a worker must file a workers' compensation claim.

Most workers' compensation claims are uncontested. However, when there is a dispute as to whether workers' compensation benefits are owed, or their amount, such a dispute can be brought before a tribunal for resolution, such as before the state's workers' compensation commission or board. There, an administrative hearing is held to determine the validity of a claim, and a decision is rendered by an administrative law judge. That decision may be appealed to a court of law in the event a party to it is unsatisfied.

Workers' compensation systems are funded and financed through insurance, as discussed above. In effect, employers pay into the workers' compensation

Key Point

Arising Out of and Occurring In the Course of Employment
Under workers' compensation statutes, the injury or illness must arise out of and occur in the course of employment.

Key Point

Administrative Procedure for Compensation
Workers' compensation statutes establish an administrative procedure to provide compensation to workers who suffer injury or illness as a result of their employment.

STATUTE on Point

820 Ill. Comp. Stat. Ann. 305/4 (2012)

Illinois, in its Workers' Compensation Act, states that any employer required under the Act to provide and pay, or who elects to provide and pay, the workers' compensation provided for under the act must file annually with the worker's compensation commission an application (or renewal application) for approval as a self-insurer, including a current financial statement signed and sworn to by designated owners or officers of the employer.

If the sworn application and financial statement of an employer do not satisfy the commission as to the financial ability of the employer who has filed it to self-insure, then the commission requires the employer to furnish security, indemnity, or a bond guaranteeing the payment by the employer of the compensation provided for under the Act or to insure its entire liability to pay such compensation with an insurance carrier authorized, licensed, or permitted to do such insurance business in Illinois.

system. Either an employer must purchase insurance, through a state-operated insurance fund or through private insurers, or demonstrate that it is self-insured, meaning that it has the financial resources to be able to cover its workplace injury risks. You can see the Illinois funding requirement in the above Statute on Point.

Recovery under workers' compensation statutes is limited to the amount set forth in the statute, which is often less than might be recovered in a successful tort lawsuit. Statutes are very specific in detailing the weeks of compensation benefits to which a worker is entitled, depending on the nature of the injury or illness, in addition to the cost of medical treatment. This weekly benefit amount is based on a percentage of the worker's weekly pay, often 66⅔ percent. The percentages and payment periods differ depending on whether the employee has suffered a permanent or a temporary disability, whether the disability is total or partial, whether there was disfigurement, or even death. Both the nature and type of the injury or illness, and its permanence, affect the monetary award calculation. See the exercise at the end of the chapter on the amount of compensation to be paid for accidental injury not resulting in death under the Illinois workers' compensation statute; this provision addresses the compensation for specific injuries such as loss of a foot, arm, leg, eye, hand, hearing in one ear, and so on. Expert testimony may be required in order to determine the actual nature and relative permanence of an employee's workplace injury or illness. The following two Statutes on Point demonstrate compensation, in the state of Illinois, for death and for the loss of one big toe.

Now that we understand workers' compensation, what is its relationship to tort law? That relationship is discussed next.

Workers' Compensation's Relationship to Tort Law

Workers' compensation is typically the sole remedy for workplace injuries and illnesses. See the relevant provision in the Illinois workers' compensation Statute on Point. Accordingly, a covered worker may not sue his employer in tort

STATUTES on Point

820 III. Comp. Stat. Ann. 305/7 (2012) (for fatal cases); 820 III. Comp. Stat. Ann. 305/8(e)(6) (2012) (for nonfatal cases of injury to a big toe)

Fatal Cases

The Illinois Workers' Compensation Act provides the following compensation for fatal cases, meaning for accidental injuries to employees that result in death:

a. If the employee leaves a surviving widow, widower, child, or children, the applicable weekly compensation rate (as computed in another section) is payable during the life of the widow or widower, and if the surviving child(ren) is (are) not physically or mentally incapacitated, then until the later of the death of the widow or widower or until the youngest child reaches 18 years of age (25 years of age if a child is a full-time student at an accredited educational institution). If the surviving child(ren) is (are) physically or mentally incapacitated, the payments continue for the duration of the incapacity.

If the widow or widower remarries and the decedent did not leave any child or children who at the time of the remarriage are entitled to compensation benefits under the act, then the surviving spouse is paid a lump sum equal to two years' compensation benefits and all further rights of the widow or widower to compensation under this subsection are extinguished.

If the employee leaves any child(ren) under 18 years of age, who at the time of death is (are) entitled to compensation under this subsection (a), the weekly compensation payments provided for the child(ren) must continue for a period of not less than six years.

b. If no compensation is payable under subsection (a) and the employee leaves a surviving parent(s) who, at the time of the employee's accident, was (were) totally dependent on the employee's earnings, then weekly payments equal to the compensation rate payable in the case of a surviving widow or widower are paid to the parent(s). These weekly payments continue for the duration of the parent's (parents') lives, depending on the case, and in the event of the death of either parent, for the life of the surviving parent.

c. If no compensation is payable under subsection (a) or (b) and the employee leaves any surviving child(ren) who is (are) not entitled to compensation under subsection (a) but who, at the time of the accident, were dependent on the employee's earnings, or the employee leaves a surviving parent (parents) who, at the time of the accident, were partially (rather than fully) dependent on the employee's earnings, then weekly compensation payments are made to the dependent or dependents for eight years in the same proportion or share that would have applied if the employee had left a surviving widow or widower as the dependency bears to the total dependency. If any beneficiary dies during the compensation period, the share that beneficiary would have received is divided equally among the surviving beneficiaries. If the last beneficiary dies during the compensation period, all rights to compensation under this subsection are extinguished.

d. If no compensation is payable under subsection (a), (b), or (c) and the employee leaves surviving any grandparent(s), grandchild(ren), or collateral heirs (meaning relatives who are not direct descendants, such as brothers, sisters, aunts, uncles, nephews, nieces, and the like) dependent on the employee's earnings (for at least 50 percent of their support), then weekly compensation payments are paid to the dependent(s) for five years in the proportion or share that would have applied if the employee had left surviving a widow or widower as the dependency bears to the total dependency. If any beneficiary dies during the compensation period, the share that beneficiary would have received is divided equally among the surviving beneficiaries. If the last beneficiary dies during the compensation period, all rights to compensation under this subsection are extinguished.

Nonfatal Cases

The Illinois Workers' Compensation Act provides the following compensation for nonfatal cases of injury to a great toe: thirty-five weeks if the accidental injury occurred before February 1, 2006, and thirty-eight weeks if the accidental injury occurred on or after February 1, 2006.

STATUTE on Point

820 Ill. Comp. Stat. Ann. 305/5 (2012)

The Illinois Workers' Compensation Act provides that no common law or statutory right to recover damages from the employer or his insurer, other than the compensation provided for in the act, is available to an employee who is covered by the provisions of the act, to anyone who is dependent on him, the legal representatives of his estate, or anyone otherwise entitled to recover damages for the injury.

CASE on Point

Burton v. Phoenix Fabricators and Erectors, Inc., 670 S.E.2d 581 (N.C. Ct. App. 2009)

In this case, Michael Burton and Charles Davis were killed on October 30, 2002, while helping construct a water tower for their employer, Phoenix Fabricators and Erectors, Inc. (Phoenix). The work-related accident occurred in North Carolina but the men were employed by Phoenix's Indiana office. The plaintiffs were the wives of the decedents; they subsequently sued Phoenix for intentional tortious conduct resulting in their husbands' deaths.

The wives had accepted benefits for their husbands' deaths under the Indiana Workers' Compensation Act. The court held that the intentional tort action was barred by the exclusive remedy provision of Indiana's Workers' Compensation Act. Accordingly, the wives could not bring an intentional tort action against Phoenix in North Carolina.

for his workplace injury or illness if workers' compensation is available. Any related tort case is barred from being brought against the employer. See the exercises at the end of the chapter for a case on this point. Workers' compensation, then, replaces tort law as the means of recovery for workers who are injured or suffer illness in the workplace.

CHAPTER **SUMMARY**

- The causation element of negligence is comprised of two different parts, cause in fact and proximate cause. Cause in fact means "actual cause." The defendant must be the actual cause of the plaintiff's harm. The second part of the causation element is proximate cause, also called legal cause. Proximate cause is a policy question used to determine whether a defendant should be held legally responsible for injuries that he in fact caused.

- Damages are an essential element of the tort of negligence. In order for a plaintiff to recover for this tort, she must demonstrate that she suffered a legally recognizable injury. Under the doctrine of avoidable consequences, a plaintiff is held legally responsible for any further injury or harm that, through her actions, she could have reasonably avoided after being harmed by the defendant's negligence.

- Malpractice is professional negligence. It occurs when a professional, such as a doctor, lawyer, accountant, architect, engineer, or the like, breaches her duty of care in the performance of professional services, and the reasonable person standard is raised to account for the expertise, skill, knowledge, and training possessed by the professional.

- Once the plaintiff has established all of the elements of the tort of negligence, the burden of proof shifts to the defendant to rebut one or more of the essential elements of the plaintiff's claim or to establish a legal defense in order to defend himself.

- A mass tort is a tort involving the same event or source that has caused harm to many people. It normally involves numerous plaintiffs, and one, or only a few, defendants. Mass tort litigation is often called "complex litigation." Mass tort cases assert traditional tort causes of action, but the scope of the cases is much more broad.

- The main types of mass torts are mass accidents, mass marketing of defective products, mass toxic torts, and mass economic loss. Class actions or multidistrict litigation procedures may be used by the courts to expedite the handling of mass tort lawsuits.

- Insurance is a type of contract. People purchase insurance as a way to manage their risk of loss in the event they suffer an injury to their persons or property. Persons and businesses can purchase different types of insurance to protect themselves from certain risks of loss.

- Lawsuits involving automobile accidents are the most common form of personal injury actions. Because of the common occurrence of automobile accidents, all states require minimum levels of automobile insurance for drivers, or a demonstration that a driver has the ability to pay a tort judgment at a minimum level without insurance. Many drivers purchase additional insurance, in excess of the required minimum limits, to further protect them from risk of loss. Even where automobile insurance is present, tort lawsuits are common when automobile accidents are caused by negligence. Collateral sources of funds, including the presence and amounts of insurance coverage, may or may not be made known to and considered by courts when determining the amount of a tortfeasor's liability. In negotiating possible settlements of lawsuits, insurance policy limits are relevant and discoverable in litigation.

- States have enacted workers' compensation statutes to permit recovery for most workplace injuries and illnesses without the necessity of the employee proving employer negligence, thereby allowing an employee to receive a fixed monetary award in exchange for giving up the right to sue the employer in tort. Workers' compensation is a no-fault system that covers private-sector employers. To recover for workplace injuries or illnesses under workers' compensation statutes, the injury or illness must arise out of and occur in the course of employment. Workers' compensation systems are funded and financed through insurance.

CONCEPT REVIEW AND REINFORCEMENT

QUESTIONS FOR **REVIEW**

1. What is the essential element of causation?
2. What is cause in fact?
3. What is proximate cause and how is it different from cause in fact?
4. What is the eggshell skull rule? Explain how it is an exception to proximate cause.
5. What are intervening and superseding causes? Are all intervening causes superseding?
6. What is the essential element of damages?
7. What is the doctrine of avoidable consequences?
8. What are collateral sources, and what is the collateral source rule?

9. What is malpractice?

10. What happens in a negligence action once the plaintiff has established a *prima facie* case?

11. What is a mass tort?

12. What is mass tort litigation?

13. What is the role of insurance in tort law?

14. What is workers' compensation?

15. When and how does workers' compensation apply?

16. How does workers' compensation relate to tort law?

DEVELOPING YOUR PARALEGAL SKILLS

CRITICAL THINKING **EXERCISES**

1. Harvey is riding his bicycle, no-handed and at a very fast speed, down a park path. Trish, a jogger, accompanied by her dog, Rover, who is leashed, is approaching Harvey from the other direction. Because he knows that he is bigger and faster on his bike, Harvey expects Trish to move out of his way. Unfortunately, Trish does not, and as Harvey passes her, he side-swipes her, knocking her to the ground and injuring her. Rover is inadvertently released when Trish falls, and he runs off, into the road. Monty is driving carefully down the road. Seeing Rover running into his path and wanting to avoid hitting him, Monty drives off the road and onto the sidewalk, damaging his wheel alignment when he crosses the curb. Grandma Jenkins is babysitting young Elvis, her grandson. Elvis happens to be playing hopscotch on the sidewalk. Fortunately, Monty's veering car stops far short of Elvis, and all is well for the tot (except for anxiety he suffered when he looked up and saw Monty's car heading straight for him). Unfortunately, Grandma Jenkins, observing the car veering off the road and heading straight toward her grandson, suffers a heart attack.

   Is Harvey liable, in negligence, for Grandma Jenkins's heart attack? Is Harvey liable, in negligence, for the anxiety that Elvis suffered? Is Harvey liable for the damage to Monty's car? What about for Trish's injuries and the loss of Rover? Why or why not?

2. Research your state's workers' compensation statute. Who does it cover? How does it provide compensation? What does it exclude? Who administers your state's workers' compensation statute? Discuss your research results in class.

3. As a group assignment, students from different home states can research the workers' compensation statutes in their states, then compare and contrast the statutes.

4. Laurie Freeman is driving to work, where she is a law professor at a local university. That morning, it is pouring rain. Laurie, a good driver and acknowledging the poor driving conditions, slows down to a reasonable speed for the conditions. While she is driving down the road at 36 miles per hour in a 45-mile-per-hour zone, Laurie hits a large puddle and her car loses traction. The car hydroplanes. It spins out of control, into the lane of oncoming traffic, where it hits a passing car, damaging it, and injuring its driver and passenger. Laurie is also injured, and her car is damaged.

   a. *Is Laurie liable, in tort, for the injuries and car damage she caused? Why or why not? What theory(ies) would you consider?*

   b. *If Laurie's driving was reasonable under the conditions, what source of funds (outside of tort recovery) might be used to compensate both Laurie and the persons with whom she collided?*

5. Suppose that Laurie Freeman from Exercise 4 is not a law professor, but instead is a delivery person for a local soft drink bottler. At the time of the accident, she was not commuting to work; she was driving her employer's delivery truck to its next delivery.

   Given these facts, what other source of funds might be used to compensate Laurie for her injuries? Would the funds cover the damage to the vehicle? Why or why not?

ASSIGNMENTS AND PRACTICAL **APPLICATIONS**

1. Read and brief the *Palsgraf* dissenting opinion by Judge Andrews, in which he defines the world at large test and comprehensively discusses the legal concept of proximate cause.

2. Regarding the substantial factor test and multiple causes, read and brief *Landers v. East Tex. Salt Water Disposal Co.*, 248 S.W.2d 731 (Tex. 1952), in which

joint and several liability was found when two oil companies together polluted the plaintiff's lake, killing his fish.

3. Vioxx is an anti-inflammatory drug that was approved by the U.S. Food and Drug Administration in 1999 and marketed by Merck & Co. to treat chronic and acute pain. In 2004, Merck voluntarily withdrew

Vioxx from the marketplace when it was determined that the drug was increasing the risk of heart attack and stroke in its long-time users. Vioxx was one of the most widely used drugs ever withdrawn from the market; it had been prescribed to over 80 million people throughout the world. Read and brief the Case on Point from this chapter, *In re: Vioxx Products Liability Litigation*, 574 F.Supp.2d 606 (E.D. La. 2008), regarding mass torts and the use of contingency fees when a case ends in a $4.85 billion settlement.

4. Mass tort litigation is often referred to as complex litigation. Evidencing such complexity, read and brief *Abbatiello v. Monsanto Co.*, 569 F.Supp.2d 351 (S.D.N.Y. 2008). This case involved the denial of the plaintiffs' request to amend a briefing schedule and set focused discovery in a mass tort case against manufacturers of polychlorinated biphenyls (PCBs), which caused large-scale contamination and harm.

5. Locate and review the official Massachusetts Compulsory Motor Vehicle Liability Insurance Law summarized in the chapter. Notice how legislatures love a good run-on sentence! They frequently draft them.

6. Review your own automobile insurance policy, if you have one. If not, then review your parents' or guardian's. What are the coverage amounts? What types of events are covered? What exclusions are defined in your contract (meaning, what things are excluded from coverage, so that the insurer would not have to pay under the policy)? Contact your insurance carrier and ask what the increase in premium would be if you decreased your deductible amounts or increased your coverage amounts.

7. Research your state's workers' compensation statute. Prepare a summary of the administrative procedure used in your state to bring a workers' compensation claim.

8. Review the workers' compensation statutory provision from the Illinois Workers' Compensation Act scheduling the amount of compensation to be paid for accidental injury not resulting in death, for injuries such as loss of a leg, arm, great toe, index finger, foot, hand, loss of hearing in one ear, and so on. See 820 Ill. Comp. Stat. Ann. 305/8 (2012).

TECHNOLOGY RESOURCES AND INTERNET **EXERCISES**

Using Internet resources, research specific actions that a legal practitioner, such as a lawyer or paralegal, can take to minimize her exposure to malpractice claims when engaged in the practice of law or performing paralegal services. The first step is to insure against this risk, by purchasing malpractice and errors and omissions insurance. Who offers this type of insurance, and how much does it cost? What other things can a law practitioner do to minimize malpractice liability exposure? As a class, create a list of "good practices" a law practitioner can follow to minimize her malpractice liability exposure.

Damage determinations can be difficult to calculate. Personal injury lawyers and their firms may use computer software programs to help them determine the amount of damages they will request in a negligence action. What software programs are available? What specific functions do these programs perform?

The chapter references the *Manual for Complex Litigation (Third)*. Go to the website for the Federal Judicial Center at *www.fjc.gov/public/pdf.nsf/lookup/mcl.pdf/$File/mcl .pdf* and review this manual, the purpose of which is to assist lawyers and judges in the management of complex litigation.

For an interesting summary of the Love Canal tragedy, where toxic waste was buried beneath a neighborhood, over time resulting in tragic illnesses and deaths to many residents, go to the U.S. government's EPA website at *www .epa.gov/history/topics/lovecanal/01.htm*.

You may have seen notices in newspapers or magazines soliciting plaintiffs to join a class action lawsuit. See if you can find such a notice and bring it to share with the class.

Review the Illinois Workers' Compensation Act. See *www .state.il.us/Agency/IIC/act.pdf*.

For an interesting look at the Workers' Compensation Code for the Nez Perce Indian tribe, see *www.nezperce .org/&xim; code/workers%20comp.htm*.

ETHICAL **APPLICATIONS**

1. Rose Dawson, Esq., is a very successful and competent personal injury lawyer. Her reputation in her community (Denver, Colorado), which is well deserved, is as one of the best plaintiff's lawyers available. One day, just outside of Denver, there is a horrible commercial airline crash, caused by mechanical failure of the plane, and there are no survivors. Rose is able to obtain a list of the names of the victims of the crash. She contacts the families of the victims, by visiting them in person or calling

them on the telephone, and offers to represent them in a mass tort action against the airline that owned and operated the airplane. Rose is as competent as, if not more competent than, any lawyer to handle such claims, and the victims' families would be well represented by her and would do well to choose her as their lawyer.

Is there any problem with Rose contacting the families of the victims as she did and offering to represent them in a mass tort action? If so, what is the problem? Can it be overcome?

2. Jake Weber is a personal injury lawyer who specializes in complex litigation, handling many mass tort claims. Recently, he represented a class of victims harmed by the use of a formerly FDA-approved diet pill that was later found to cause heart problems and failure, and which was then banned by the FDA and recalled by the manufacturer. Under the terms of the fee arrangement, Jake will earn a contingency fee, as follows: 25 percent if the case settles prior to trial, 30 percent if the case settles during trial, and 40 percent if the case goes to verdict after trial. The case settles prior to trial after only one year in litigation, for $500 million. Typically, such a complex case takes many years in trial preparation alone. Jake's fee is 25 percent of the settlement, so he earns $125 million for a year's worth of work (and, presumably, he handled other cases for other clients during that year, as well).

Is Jake's fee ethical? Why or why not?

VIDEO **CASE STUDY**

Administrative Agency Hearing: The Role of the Paralegal

Synopsis: A paralegal is representing a school bus driver before an administrative law judge in a workers' compensation hearing.

Questions

1. Why did the bus driver make a workers' compensation claim?

2. How does workers' compensation relate to or affect tort liability?

3. Has the paralegal committed the unauthorized practice of law by representing the bus driver in the administrative hearing?

4. Regarding negligence and malpractice, what is the standard of care that must be exercised by the paralegal in representing the client at the hearing?

chapter 8

SURVIVAL, WRONGFUL DEATH, AND WRONGFUL BIRTH AND LIFE

This chapter examines certain effects of death and life on tort law. It covers the effect of a party's death on an existing tort claim. It also covers the tort theories available for the wrongful death, birth, and life of persons, which are all types of negligence actions. We begin our examination of death and life under tort law with a discussion of the topic of survival. What is survival?

Survival

Survival is the continuation of a cause of action, such as a tort action, after the death of either the victim or the alleged wrongdoer (the tortfeasor in a tort action). Whether a particular action survives the death of either the victim or the tortfeasor depends on the facts and circumstances of the case, and the law in this area has changed over the years. Now, survival statutes in many states govern whether certain tort actions survive the death of either of the parties, and many of them do. This is different from the old common law on survival (see Table 8-1).

Under the common law, a tort committed against a victim often did not survive the death of either the victim or the tortfeasor. If the

TABLE 8-1 Old Common Law Rules on Survival

For Torts Involving . . .	Result
Personal injury to persons	These causes of action did not survive the death of either the victim or the tortfeasor.
Harm to real property	These causes of action did not survive the death of either the victim or the tortfeasor.
Harm to personal property	These causes of action survived the death of the victim, but not the death of the tortfeasor.

victim died, the tort cause of action died with him, unless it was a tort involving only harm to personal property, which did survive the death of the victim, but not the death of the tortfeasor. So, unless it was a tort involving only harm to personal property, the victim's estate did not inherit the cause of action. Further, if the tortfeasor died, the tort cause of action died with him; the action could not be maintained against his estate.

Note that, in questions of survival of a cause of action, the death of the victim must be *unrelated to the tort*. For example, if Roger committed the tort of assault against Barry, and two years later, while the lawsuit filed by Barry remains pending, either Roger or Barry dies in a car accident, the tort suit for assault will not survive. This, under the old common law rules, was so because one, and it could be either or both, of the parties died while the action was pending, and the death was unrelated to the tort.

If the victim dies as a result of the tort, it is no longer a case of survival. Rather, it is a case of wrongful death. Consider the previous example. Suppose Roger had committed the tort of battery, rather than assault, against Barry, and Barry died a year later as a direct result of the injuries he sustained in Roger's attack. Because Barry died as a result of the tort Roger committed against him, the case involves wrongful death and does not involve the question of survival of a cause of action. Wrongful death is discussed in the next section.

Today, most states have enacted survival statutes to deal with the issue of when, and what types of, cases survive the death of either the victim or the tortfeasor. These statutes differ from jurisdiction to jurisdiction, but most provide that torts involving injury to persons' tangible interests—meaning injuries sustained through contact made with the body of the victim, such as via the tort of battery—survive the death of either party. However, some states do not permit, and others do permit, the survival of torts involving injury to persons' intangible interest—including invasions of privacy, such as false light, and injuries to reputation, such as defamation. Today, all states' survival statutes permit the survival of tort actions for injuries to real and personal property interests (see Table 8-2).

When a tort action survives the death of either of the parties, as is more common now because of survival statutes, the tort action is brought by the victim's estate, for the benefit of the estate, if the victim has died. It is brought against the defendant's estate if the tortfeasor has died. The action is brought or defended by the deceased party's legal representative, who is not necessarily

TABLE 8-2 Survival Statutes Today

For Torts Involving ...	Result
Injury to a person's tangible interests	In most jurisdictions, these causes of action survive the death of either the victim or the tortfeasor.
Injury to a person's intangible interests	These causes of action may, or may not, survive the death of either the victim or the tortfeasor, depending on the jurisdiction.
Injury to real or personal property interests	These causes of action survive the death of either the victim or the tortfeasor.

STATUTES on Point

Fla. Stat. Ann. § 46.021 (2012): Survival of actions

No cause of action dies with the person. All causes of action survive and may be commenced, prosecuted, and defended in the name of the person allowed by law to commence, prosecute, and defend the action.

Ind. Code Ann. § 34-11-7-1 (2012): Death of parties and survival of actions

If any person entitled to bring, or liable to, an action dies before the expiration of the time limit for bringing the action, the action survives to or against the person's personal representatives and may be brought at any time after the expiration

of the time limit within eighteen months after the death of the person.

Ind. Code Ann. § 34-9-3-1 (2012): Continuing a legal action after a party's death

If a person who is entitled or liable in a cause of action dies, the cause of action survives and may be brought by or against the representative of the deceased person except actions for libel, slander, malicious prosecution, false imprisonment, and personal injuries to the decedent (which survive only to the extent provided for in other provisions of the statute).

an heir. The action does not change. It is the same cause of action that existed before the death of either the victim or the tortfeasor, with the same applicable defenses available to the defendant's estate as would have been available to the defendant, in the case of the tortfeasor's death. Keep in mind that, in the case of the death of the victim from an unrelated cause, meaning a cause not related to the tort action, there is no recovery for the death of the victim because it is unconnected with the tort; wrongful death is the tort that deals with victims' deaths resulting from the tort itself. Wrongful death is examined next.

Wrongful Death

Wrongful death is death caused by a tort. It is also called tortious death, and it is a type of negligence action. Wrongful death can be distinguished from survival. Survival involves the death of a victim that is wholly unrelated to the tort committed. In wrongful death, the tort committed *causes* the death of the victim.

The old common law rule was that no cause of action existed for a tort resulting in the death of the victim. Although the wrongdoer could be criminally prosecuted if the conduct met the requirements of a criminal statute, there was no civil cause of action for tortiously caused death. Therefore, it was cheaper for a tortfeasor to kill his victim than merely injure him, because a civil suit could be brought against the tortfeasor for personal injury, but not for wrongful death.

The old common law result has been changed, by statute, in every state. Today, if a person is killed because of the wrongful conduct of another, the decedent's (dead person's) heirs may file a wrongful death action against the person(s) responsible for the decedent's death. This area of tort law is governed by statute now, not the common law. Each state has legislatively enacted some form of wrongful death cause of action. In every state today, a wrongful death

Wrongful death
Death caused by a tort; also called tortious death.

Key Point
Distinguish Survival from Wrongful Death
- Survival involves the death of a victim that is wholly unrelated to the tort committed.
- Wrongful death is death caused by a tort.

Key Point
Old Common Law Rule
No cause of action existed for a tort resulting in the death of the victim.

SIDEBAR

WRONGFUL DEATH STATUTES

Wrongful death statutes were originally designed to provide financial support to widows and orphans upon the loss of their spouse or parent, as well as to motivate persons to use reasonable care to prevent deaths of others.

Wrongful death statutes define who may sue for wrongful death and what, if any, limits may be applied to a damage award. These statutes vary, in their requirements and restrictions, from state to state.

action may be brought by the victim's estate, through its representative(s). What differs from state to state is the method for providing a wrongful death cause of action and the remedy that may be sought. States have enacted wrongful death causes of action in one of two major ways: either by enacting a separate wrongful death statute or by broadening the state's survival statute to include wrongful death.

STATUTES on Point

Ind. Code Ann. § 34-23-1-1 (2012): Death from wrongful act or omission

When the death of a person is caused by the wrongful act or omission of another person, the personal representative of the decedent may maintain a legal action against the wrongdoer. The action must be commenced within two years. The damages will be in the amount determined by a court or jury and can include, but are not limited to, reasonable medical, hospital, funeral, and burial expenses, and lost earnings of the decedent. The part of the damages that is recovered for reasonable medical, hospital, funeral, and burial expenses inures to the benefit of the decedent's estate to pay for those expenses. Any remainder of damages inures to the exclusive benefit of the widow/widower and dependent children, or to dependent next of kin.

Ind. Code Ann. § 34-23-2-1 (2012): Wrongful death of a child

A child means an unmarried person without dependents who is less than 20 years old or less than 23 years old and a student; it also means a viable fetus.

A legal action may be maintained against a person whose wrongful act or omission caused the injury or death of a child. The action may be brought by the parents jointly, by either of them, by the person who had legal custody of the child, or by the child's guardian.

In an action to recover for the death of a child, the plaintiff may recover damages for the loss of the child's services; for the loss of the child's love and companionship; and to pay the expenses of health care and hospitalization necessitated by the wrongful act or omission that caused the child's death, the child's funeral and burial expenses, the reasonable expenses of psychiatric and psychological counseling incurred by a surviving parent or minor sibling of the child that is required because of the child's death, uninsured debts of the child, and administration of the child's estate including reasonable attorney's fees.

Damages may be awarded only for the period of time from the death of the child until the date the child would have reached 20 years of age or 23 years of age if a student, or the date of the child's last surviving parent's death, whichever occurs first.

The statute expressly does not apply to an abortion.

The remedy that may be sought differs depending on the method used by the jurisdiction to recognize a cause of action for wrongful death. The damages that are normally recoverable when the wrongful death action is created by an expansion of the state's survival statute are often broader than those that are recoverable under a separate wrongful death statute. These damages typically include medical, hospital, and funeral expenses, pain and suffering of the victim from the time of the injury until his death, and lost earnings and savings the victim would have accumulated during his regular life expectancy. The underlying theory for this method of wrongful death treatment is that the tort action of the victim survives his death and covers damages that were incurred up to the time of death as well as damages resulting from the victim's death (all as part of the same survival action), including items such as funeral expenses and lost wages.

On the other hand, when a state legislature enacts a separate wrongful death statute, it defines who can bring the cause of action and what damages are recoverable. Many wrongful death statutes provide for recovery by a surviving spouse, children, or next of kin. Accordingly, a surviving spouse may bring suit for the wrongful death of the spouse. Ordinarily, children may bring suit for the wrongful death of their parents and parents may bring suit for the wrongful death of their children. In some states, only minor children are permitted to bring suit for the wrongful death of a parent. Some states do not permit a parent to bring suit for wrongful death of a child if the child was an adult who was financially independent or married.

The state statute delineates the amount of damages recoverable by the enumerated statutory beneficiaries (spouses, children, and next of kin). Compensatory damages, intended to make restitution to the injured party, are the most

CASE on Point

Branch Davidian Compound Seige

Beginning on February 28, 1993, and lasting for fifty days, the U.S. Bureau of Alcohol, Tobacco and Firearms (ATF) attempted to execute a search warrant at the Branch Davidian ranch near Waco, Texas. On the first day of the siege, shortly after the attempt was made to serve the search warrant, a gun battle erupted between the federal government agents and the Branch Davidian members. The battle lasted almost two hours, during which four ATF agents and six Branch Davidian members were killed. The siege ended on April 19, 1993, when a second assault was made on the compound and the compound was destroyed by fire. The compound was believed to house a hoard of weapons, which burst into flames during the assault, killing everyone inside. Seventy-six persons died in the fire, including the sect leader, David Koresh, two pregnant women, and around twenty children.

Following the siege, family members of the deceased Branch Davidians brought wrongful death lawsuits against the federal government. About one hundred plaintiffs sought $675 million in damages from the federal government, alleging the government agents used excessive force in the siege, resulting in the tragic fire. Ultimately, the judge found the federal government not responsible for the incident, and therefore not liable for the wrongful deaths of the compound inhabitants.

common damage award in wrongful death actions and include recovery for expenses such as medical and funeral expenses, as well as lost wages. Actuarial tables may be sued to determine life expectancy for people based on their age and gender in determining how much they would have earned had they lived, including an adjustment for inflation. Damages may also include compensation for grief and loss of services or companionship for the survivor beneficiaries. Punitive damages may be awarded in wrongful death cases where the defendant's actions were grossly negligent. Any damages recovered are distributed among the surviving beneficiaries in accordance with the state's statute.

Sometimes the damages recoverable under a wrongful death statute do not include all the damages that would be recoverable in a separate survival action. In that case, a separate survival action may be brought by the estate of the victim in addition to the permitted survivor's wrongful death action.

Remember that wrongful death actions are negligence actions. The essential elements of the tort of negligence must be proven. The tortfeasor must have breached a duty of care that he owed to the deceased person, causing the person's death. Any defense(s) that would have been available to the defendant had the victim lived remain available to the defendant in a wrongful death action. For instance, an assertion that the death was not wrongful, such as when the privilege of self-defense is involved, could be asserted by the defendant in defending a wrongful death claim.

Wrongful death actions are separate and distinct from criminal prosecutions against persons alleged of causing another's death. A defendant who is acquitted of murder in a criminal trial may still be sued, and found liable, in a civil action alleging wrongful death and brought by the victim's family. See the O. J. Simpson case, revisited, in the Sidebar.

Keep in mind that workplace deaths resulting from accident or disease are governed by states' workers' compensation statutes. Workers' compensation statutes were discussed in Chapter 7.

CASE on Point

Raum v. Restaurant Assocs., Inc., 252 A.D.2d 369 (N.Y. App. Div. 1998)

In this case, the same-sex partner of a decedent (person who died) sought to bring a wrongful death action under New York's wrongful death statute. The Supreme Court of New York held that "the wrongful-death statute . . . by its terms . . . does not give individuals not married to the decedent (other than certain blood relatives) a right to bring a wrongful-death action."

The court went on to address the same-sex partner's argument that the statute was discriminatory against same-sex partners. The court said that the statute "operates without regard to sexual orientation, in that unmarried couples living together, whether heterosexual or homosexual . . . lack the right to bring a wrongful-death action." The court determined that the statute did not discriminate against same-sex partners in spousal-type relationships because it treated opposite-sex cohabitating couples the same way.

Ultimately, in this case, the same-sex partner was not a "spouse," as specifically defined in the statute, so was not authorized to bring a wrongful death action.

THE O. J. SIMPSON CASE REVISITED

In Chapter 1, while distinguishing civil law from criminal law, we reviewed the causes of action against O. J. Simpson for the stabbing deaths of his ex-wife, Nicole, and her friend, Ronald Goldman. Remember that Simpson was found not guilty of their murders in the criminal action ending in 1995. However, in 1997, he was found liable for their wrongful deaths in a subsequent civil action brought by the families of the victims. A civil jury rendered a judgment of $33.5 million against Simpson for these wrongful deaths, which, to date, remains largely unpaid.

Wrongful death lawsuits are quite common, as, unfortunately, are deaths resulting from tortious acts. Less common, though still tortious under certain circumstances, are cases involving wrongful birth, wrongful life, wrongful pregnancy, and wrongful adoption. We examine these next.

Wrongful Birth, Life, Pregnancy, Adoption, and Other Family Tort Matters

WRONGFUL BIRTH

Wrongful birth is a tort cause of action, recognized in about half the states, which allows the parents of an impaired child to sue for their own damages. Like wrongful death actions, wrongful birth is a type of negligence action.

In particular, wrongful birth actions are a type of medical malpractice claim. In a wrongful birth action, the parents of an impaired child allege that the medical practitioner was negligent in giving advice or treatment to prevent the pregnancy from occurring or in giving the parents the opportunity to terminate it. Parents in these actions seek to recover damages for the cost of prenatal care and delivery, the cost of caring for the impaired child, and emotional distress.

Wrongful birth
A tort cause of action that allows the parents of an impaired child to sue for their own damages.

CASE on Point

Rieck v. Med. Productive Co., 219 N.W.2d 242 (Wis. 1974)

In this case (already discussed in Chapter 7 on the topic of causation), parents brought a wrongful birth action to recover the costs of rearing a child. They sued an obstetrician, and his employing medical clinic, who failed to determine that the mother was pregnant in time to permit an abortion of the fetus. In this case, the child was normal and healthy, but being the couple's fourth child, was an "unwanted addition to the family circle."

(continued)

The court acknowledged that the relief sought in the case was to shift the costs of rearing the child to the obstetrician, the clinic, and their insurer. It also acknowledged that the parents retained the benefits of keeping their child since they did not take steps to terminate their parental rights and place the child up for adoption. The court noted that many people would be willing to support the child if they were given the right of custody and adoption, but the parents did not want that. Rather, the parents wanted to keep the child but have the doctor support it.

The court ruled that it would "contravene sound public policy to hold recoverable the damages claimed for the negligence alleged in this case and under this circumstances." The court saw the action as an "endeavor on the part of the [parents] to determine the outer limits of physician liability for failure to diagnose the fact of pregnancy." The court said this case went well beyond those limits.

WRONGFUL LIFE

Wrongful life
A tort cause of action brought by or on behalf of a child, usually an impaired child, seeking his own damages.

Similar to wrongful birth, a few states recognize a tort cause of action for *wrongful life*, another type of negligence action. The tort of wrongful life is brought by or on behalf of a child, usually an impaired child, with the child seeking his own damages. However, most states do not recognize the legal right of a child not to be born. This is especially true if the child is born healthy but was unwanted by the parents. The *Berman* Case on Point illustrates a claim of wrongful birth and a claim of wrongful life.

CASE on Point

Berman v. Allan, 404 A.2d 8 (N.J. 1979)

This case, and another noted in the assignments at the end of the chapter, involves both wrongful birth and wrongful life theories. In *Berman v. Allan,* these two causes of action were alleged under the following facts.

Mrs. Berman, 38 years old and pregnant with her daughter, Sharon, was under the care and supervision of two OB/GYN specialists. When Sharon was born, it was immediately evident that she suffered from Down's syndrome, the genetic defect formerly known as mongolism. The Bermans alleged that the defendant physicians deviated from accepted medical standards by failing to inform Mrs. Berman during her pregnancy of the existence of an amniocentesis procedure in which a sample of amniotic fluid containing living fetal cells can be extracted from the uterus of the pregnant woman and subjected to karyotype analysis to determine the sex of the fetus and the presence of gross chromosomal defects, including Down's syndrome. The plaintiffs argued that because of Mrs. Berman's rather advanced age at the time of conception (38), the risk that her child would be afflicted with Down's syndrome was sufficiently great that sound medical practice required the defendants to inform her both of this risk and of the availability of amniocentesis as a method of determining the presence of this, or other, genetic defects. Mrs. Berman testified that had she been so informed of the risk, she would have submitted to

(continued)

the amniocentesis procedure, learned of the Down's syndrome defect, and aborted the fetus.

Wrongful Birth Theory

On their own behalf, the Bermans brought a wrongful birth action requesting damages for both the emotional anguish they experienced and would continue to experience because of Sharon's birth defect, and the medical and other costs they would incur in order to properly raise, educate, and supervise Sharon. The Supreme Court of New Jersey agreed that the Bermans had a cause of action against the physicians for wrongful birth. However, in evaluating the damages to which the parents were entitled, the court ruled that they could recover only for the emotional anguish that had been, and would later be, suffered by them because of Sharon's condition. The court denied recovery for the medical and other costs associated with raising, educating, and supervising Sharon. On this point, the court reasoned that the Berman's "desire to retain all the benefits inhering in the birth of the child, i.e., the love and joy they will experience as parents while saddling the defendants with the enormous expenses attendant upon her rearing . . . would be wholly disproportionate to the culpability involved . . . and would both constitute a windfall to the parents and place too unreasonable a financial burden upon physicians." (Note that in the *Marciniak* Case on Point (in the next section) on wrongful pregnancy, the Supreme Court of Wisconsin rejected the "benefits" argument that this court accepted.)

Wrongful Life Theory

On behalf of Sharon, the parents also brought a wrongful life cause of action against the physicians, seeking compensation for the physical and emotional pain and suffering that Sharon would endure throughout her life because of her condition. The complaint brought on Sharon's behalf was that had the defendants informed her mother of the availability of amniocentesis, Sharon would never have been born. The court distinguished this case from cases in which the medical malpractice increases the probability that an infant will be born with birth defects or in which the medical practitioner's negligence while a child is in gestation causes an otherwise healthy child to be born impaired. Rather, in this case, the defendants did not cause Sharon's condition, nor increase the risk of it occurring.

The court rejected Sharon's wrongful life claim. In doing so, it reasoned that it was impossible to measure damages because it was impossible to put a value on human nonlife. In addition, the court reasoned that Sharon did not suffer any damage cognizable at law by being "brought into existence." The court emphasized the sanctity of life, and a fundamental Constitutional right that "life whether experienced with or without a major physical handicap is more precious than non-life" (citing the notorious case of Karen Quinlan, which involved prolonged life support for a person who was in a vegetative state; that case is included in the assignments at the end of the chapter).

CASE on Point

Marciniak v. Lundborg, 450 N.W.2d 243 (Wis. 1990)

This was a case involving wrongful pregnancy. Paula Marciniak underwent a sterilization operation to avoid having further children (she already had two). Two years after the sterilization operation was performed, Paula Marciniak gave birth to a healthy child. When asked during litigation why she did not have an abortion, she replied, "I could not kill a baby. . . I am Catholic." She also did not consider giving her child up for adoption, saying, "It was my child."

Nonetheless, Paula Marciniak and her husband sued the physician to recover the costs involved in raising their healthy child, conceived subsequent to a negligent sterilization operation. The Supreme Court of Wisconsin held that the parents could recover the costs of raising a child until the age of majority, as damages caused by the negligently performed sterilization procedure.

The defendant argued that these costs should be offset by the benefits conferred on the parents by virtue of having the presence of a child in their lives (the argument made successfully in the *Berman* case discussed earlier). This court disagreed, reasoning that these parents made the decision not to have another child, and it was precisely to avoid that "benefit" that the parents went to the physician for a sterilization procedure in the first place; "any 'benefits' that were conferred upon them as a result of having a new child in their lives were not asked for and were sought to be avoided."

WRONGFUL PREGNANCY

Wrongful pregnancy
A tort cause of action brought when a woman conceives a child as a result of a tortious act by the defendant.

Most states allow a tort cause of action for **wrongful pregnancy**, involving a woman who conceives as a result of a tortious act of the defendant. Wrongful pregnancy, like wrongful death, wrongful birth, and wrongful life, is a type of negligence action.

In a wrongful pregnancy action, the parents of an unwanted but healthy child seek damages. This type of negligence case usually involves either (1) lack of informed consent, or (2) negligent performance of a sterilization procedure or a pharmaceutical company manufacturing and selling defective birth control devices. The *Marciniak* Case on Point involves negligent performance of a sterilization procedure. In the exercises at the end of the chapter, there is a case involving lack of informed consent.

WRONGFUL ADOPTION

Wrongful adoption
A tort cause of action by which an adoption agency can be held liable for wrongfully stating or failing to disclose material facts regarding the mental or physical health of the adoptive child, or for misrepresenting the medical history of the child's birth family, if such facts would have been relevant in the parents' decision about whether to adopt that child.

Some states permit a cause of action by adoptive parents for the tort of **wrongful adoption**. Like wrongful death, wrongful birth, wrongful life, and wrongful pregnancy, this is a type of negligence action.

With this tort, an adoption agency can be held liable for wrongfully stating or failing to disclose material facts regarding the mental or physical health of the adoptive child, or for misrepresenting the medical history of the child's birth family, if such facts would have been relevant in the parents' decision about whether to adopt that child.

CASE on Point

Halper v. Jewish Family & Children's Serv., 963 A.2d 1282 (Pa. 2009)

In this case, parents adopted their son, David, in 1964 through an adoption agency, Jewish Family and Children's Service of Greater Philadelphia. Throughout David's life, he suffered mental health problems, received mental health treatment, attempted suicide, continuously abused drugs, and was poor at maintaining social relationships. From 1980 through 1999, the parents and David sought his birth mother's medical records to facilitate David's treatment and provide insight into David's mental health issues.

The adoption agency had a file on David's birth mother that included a psychiatrist's letter stating that she suffered from schizophrenia. The letter was not in David's file but had been placed in the file of David's younger sibling who was also placed for adoption through this agency.

The parents brought legal action against the adoption agency alleging, among other things, wrongful adoption. The parents alleged that the agency improperly failed to notify them of David's birth mother's mental history. David's adoptive father died prior to trial; at trial the jury returned a verdict of liability, finding the agency negligent (awarding the parents $225,000 and David $75,000). On appeal, on the issue of wrongful adoption, the appellate courts (both the Superior Court and the Supreme Court) ruled against the plaintiffs. The court said that when this adoption occurred, schizophrenia was considered a product of the environment, not a mental health disorder. Because of this, the courts found that there was no foreseeable harm at the time of the adoption relating to David's birth mother's schizophrenia condition. Therefore, even if the information had been released to the parents, failing to provide it was "tempered by the lack of foreseeable harm." This negligence action required a foreseeability element, and the court found that was not present here.

Besides the negligence torts of wrongful death, wrongful birth, wrongful life, wrongful pregnancy, and wrongful adoption, there are other family torts that may be, or once were, allowed. These other family torts are discussed next.

OTHER FAMILY TORT MATTERS

Wrongful death, wrongful birth, wrongful life, wrongful pregnancy, and wrongful adoption torts can be brought by a family member because of what the defendant did to another family member. Certain other family torts may be, or once were, allowed to be brought by family members when other family members were harmed. Among these torts are heart balm actions and loss of consortium actions.

Heart Balm Actions

Although they have been largely abolished in most states today, under early common law, certain other tort actions, called *heart balm actions*, could be brought by a family member against a third party for something done to or with another family member. These heart balm actions were—and to the limited extent they have not been abolished today, are—breach of promise

Heart balm actions
Common law torts that historically could be brought by a family member against a third party for something done to or with another family member, including breach of promise to marry, alienation of affections, criminal conversation, and seduction.

TABLE 8-3 Heart Balm Actions

Breach of promise to marry	Brought by the innocent party to a broken engagement against the former fiancé.
Alienation of affections	Brought by an injured spouse against a person who intruded on his or her marital relationship and lured his or her spouse away.
Criminal conversation	Civil "adultery."
Seduction	Brought by a father against a man who had sexual relations with his daughter.

to marry, alienation of affections, criminal conversation, and seduction (see Table 8-3). Heart balm actions originated from the legal viewpoint that disfavored and discouraged intrusions into marital and family relationships. Recovery under one of these theories was thought to be the "balm" that healed the broken-hearted.

Breach of promise to marry actions could be brought to compensate a person who had been injured as a result of being the innocent party to a broken engagement. Early common law viewed a promise to marry as a legally enforceable promise.

Alienation of affections actions could be brought against a person who intruded on another's marriage relationship by luring away one of the spouses.

Criminal conversation is the tort of adultery, meaning sexual relations with another's spouse. Criminal conversation actions could be brought by a cheated-on spouse to recover from the third party with whom his or her spouse engaged in adultery. The purpose behind both alienation of affections and criminal conversation torts was to protect and preserve the sanctity of marriage.

Seduction actions could be brought by a father against a man who had sexual relations with his daughter. Interestingly, under the law, the harm caused by the seduction was regarded as an injury to the father rather than to the daughter.

Heart balm statutes
Legislative acts abolishing or limiting the heart balm actions.

Today, **heart balm statutes** have been enacted in most jurisdictions that abolish or severely limit the application of these torts. As morals and values in our society change, so do the laws—to reflect our current morals and values. See the California heart balm statute in the Statute on Point.

Another type of claim by family members is loss of consortium. Loss of consortium is discussed next.

STATUTE on Point

Cal. Civ. Code § 43.5 (2012)

No cause of action arises for
- Alienation of affections
- Criminal conversation

- Seduction of a person over the age of legal consent
- Breach of promise to marry

SIDEBAR

LOSS OF CONSORTIUM IN MARYLAND

Under Maryland law, a loss of consortium claim may arise when a seriously injured spouse cannot fully participate in the marriage because of the injury. Loss of consortium means the loss of society, affection, and assistance; it includes the loss or impairment of sexual relations. A claim for loss of consortium does not involve economic loss, but its monetary worth can be determined by the jury.

In Maryland, the loss of consortium claim must be brought together with the injured spouse's claim—in the same lawsuit. Termination of the injury claim will terminate the loss of consortium claim in Maryland (though not in some other jurisdictions). Because a loss of consortium claim is a derivative claim, meaning it is derived from the injured spouse's claim, a cap for noneconomic damages is applied to the whole action (so both the loss of consortium claim and the injured spouse's claim).

Loss of Consortium

Loss of consortium is a claim made by a spouse of an injured party for the loss of companionship from marriage that is caused by the injury. It includes recovery for things such as loss of love, affection, companionship, outside earnings, services performed around the house (cooking, cleaning, repairs, etc.), and sexual relations. Historically, loss of consortium claims could only be made by husbands, but today, in all states, this theory has become gender-neutral. However, most states will deny recovery for loss of consortium if the persons are not legally married, such as cohabitating couples and homosexual couples, though the law may develop in this area, as the right of homosexual couples to marry or enter into civil unions develops.

Loss of consortium is a derivative claim, meaning it is derived from other torts. For instance, if one spouse is seriously injured in a car accident caused by a negligent driver, the injured spouse can sue for negligence, and the other spouse can sue for loss of consortium.

Some states prevent double recoveries by requiring that the spouse claiming loss of consortium assert the claim in the same legal action maintained by the injured spouse. Other states allow the loss of consortium action to be brought as a separate and distinct cause of action from the injured spouse's action.

Some, but not all, jurisdictions permit claims of loss of consortium in other types of relationships, such as parent/child relationships. The right of a child to the companionship and affection of a parent is called **parental consortium**. Most states do not allow recovery for loss of parental consortium, though some states, in their wrongful death statutes, allow recovery for loss of parental consortium if the parent suffered a tortious death. The right of a parent to the companionship and affection of a child is called **filial consortium**. Many states deny recovery for loss of filial consortium, but some states permit a parent to recover for the loss of services the parent would have received from the child, such as loss of the child's performance of a share of the household chores. See the *Wachocki* Case on Point for a case denying a sibling's loss of consortium claim but allowing sibling loss of consortium claims generally.

Loss of consortium
A claim made by the spouse of an injured party for the loss of companionship from marriage that is caused by the injury.

Parental consortium
The right of a child to the companionship and affection of a parent.

Filial consortium
The right of a parent to the companionship and affection of a child.

CASE on Point

Wachocki v. Bernalillo County Sheriff's Dept., 265 P.3d 701 (N.M. 2011)

Bill Wachocki, the adult brother of Jason Wachocki (22 years old and 15 months older than Bill), brought a loss of consortium claim against a sheriff's office after Jason was killed when his vehicle was struck by a speeding van driven by a corrections officer for the jail. At the time of Jason's death, the brothers lived together as roommates in an apartment, where they split the bills and shared household chores. The brothers were close and spent their free time together.

The court said that in order to recover for loss of consortium, a claimant must show that (1) the claimant and the injured party shared a sufficiently close relationship, and (2) the tortfeasor owed a duty of care to the claimant. This court never ruled on the second element because it found the first element lacking, but said the second element was met where it is foreseeable that the harm inflicted upon the injured party would damage the relationship between the injured party and the claimant.

As to the first element, the court said that mutual dependence is the key element in a loss of consortium claim, regardless of the relationship between the claimant and the injured party. Applying that key element to these facts, the court held that the brothers were roommates and shared a small amount of financial responsibility; their relationship did not exhibit the mutual dependence required for Bill to recover for loss of consortium.

The court went on to note that many jurisdictions expressly reject sibling claims made for loss of consortium, recognizing that some jurisdictions draw the line at particular relationships. But the Supreme Court of New Mexico in this case said that its rejection of Bill's loss of consortium claim did not mean that a sibling cannot recover for loss of consortium; rather, the facts here merely did not demonstrate that these two siblings shared a mutually dependent relationship. Recovery for loss of consortium for a sibling may be available where two siblings share a mutually dependent relationship, said the court.

CHAPTER **SUMMARY**

- Survival is the continuation of a cause of action, such as a tort action, after the death of either the victim or the alleged wrongdoer. Today, most states have enacted survival statutes to deal with this issue. Although such statutes differ from jurisdiction to jurisdiction, most provide that torts involving injury to persons' tangible interests survive the death of either party, but some states do not permit, while others do permit, the survival of torts involving injury to person's intangible interests. All states' survival statutes permit the survival of tort actions for injuries to real and personal property interests.

- Wrongful death is death caused by a tort and is also called tortious death. The old common law rule was that no cause of action existed for a tort that resulted in the death of the victim. That result has been changed, by statute, in every state. Each state has enacted some form of wrongful death cause of action. What differs from state to state is the method for providing a wrongful death cause of action and the remedy that may be sought. States have enacted wrongful death causes of action in one of two major ways: either by enacting a wrongful death statute to deal with this issue or by broadening the state's survival statute to include wrongful death. Who can bring the action, and what damages are recoverable, depends on the method used by the jurisdiction in recognizing this cause of action.

- Wrongful birth is a tort cause of action that is recognized in about half the states and allows parents of an impaired child to sue for their own damages. A few states recognize a tort cause of action for wrongful life, which is brought by or on behalf of a child, usually an impaired child, seeking his own damages. However, most states do not recognize the legal right of a child not to be born. Most states allow a tort cause of action for wrongful pregnancy, in which the parents of an unwanted but healthy child may seek damages. Some states permit a cause of action by adoptive parents for the tort of wrongful adoption when an adoption agency wrongfully states or fails to disclose material facts regarding the mental or physical health of the child, or misrepresents the medical history of the child's birth family.

- Heart balm statutes have been enacted in most states to abolish or limit the old common law heart balm actions of breach of promise to marry, alienation of affections, criminal conversation, and seduction.

- Loss of consortium allows the spouse of a tortiously injured person to recover for the loss of companionship from marriage (or other significant relationship) suffered as a result of the injury.

CONCEPT REVIEW AND REINFORCEMENT

QUESTIONS FOR **REVIEW**

1. What is survival, and how does it affect existing tort claims?
2. What is wrongful death?
3. What is wrongful birth?
4. What is wrongful life?
5. What is wrongful pregnancy?
6. What is wrongful adoption?
7. What are heart balm statutes?
8. What is loss of consortium?
9. How do you distinguish consortium, parental consortium, and filial consortium?

DEVELOPING YOUR PARALEGAL SKILLS

CRITICAL THINKING **EXERCISES**

1. In this chapter, we studied tort causes of action for wrongful death, wrongful birth, wrongful life, wrongful pregnancy, and wrongful adoption. Research which of these causes of action are recognized in your jurisdiction, because although wrongful death and wrongful pregnancy causes of action are recognized in most states, wrongful birth, wrongful life, and wrongful adoption are recognized in fewer states. For causes of action recognized in your jurisdiction, what are their essential elements? An excellent starting point for your research is a case law digest for your state. For example, in Maryland, the resource *Maryland Digest 2d* by West includes cases from Maryland dealing with these applications. Discuss your research results in class.

2. Betty Goldsborough is walking home from class one day when she is mugged by John Fisher. While he is stealing her purse, John knocks Betty to the ground and then kicks her. John's kick cracks two of Betty's ribs and breaks the cell phone she is carrying in her pocket. Later, having rifled through the contents of Betty's purse, John discovers that Betty is carrying medication for a highly contagious venereal disease. John publishes a notice in the local paper stating (truthfully) that Betty has this venereal disease. Betty sues John for battery, invasion of privacy, and conversion of property. A month before trial is scheduled to begin, however, John is murdered during a drug deal gone bad.

   a. *Under today's survival statutes, will Betty's battery cause of action against John survive his death?*

   b. *Under today's survival statutes, will Betty's invasion of privacy cause of action against John survive his death?*

c. *Under today's survival statutes, will Betty's conversion cause of action against John survive his death?*

3. Felix and Oscar are street racing their cars (an illegal act) on a public road. A crowd of children has gathered to watch the race. Oscar, driving at high speed, loses control of his car and plows into the gathering of children. Susie is run over; five days later, she dies of her injuries while being treated in the hospital.

   Has Oscar committed the tort of wrongful death? If so, who can bring that action (because Susie is dead)? What damages are recoverable, if any?

4. Baby Johnny is born with a severe birth defect. The defect might have been known to the parents before his birth, but their doctor apparently did not notice irregularities in the sonograms and other screening devices used during the mother's pregnancy, so the parents were not aware of the condition before Johnny was born. Had the parents been made aware of the condition, they say they would have terminated the pregnancy.

   a. *What cause of action might the parents have against the medical practitioner? Would they likely succeed?*

   b. *What cause of action might Baby Johnny bring (through his representative, of course) against the doctor? Would he likely succeed?*

   c. *What if Baby Johnny was adopted, and was not the natural child of his parents? If the birth defect is an internal condition that is not realized until long after the adoption, what cause of action might be brought by the adoptive parents against the adoption agency? Would they likely succeed?*

5. Curlie is married to Laurie. Curlie develops a relationship with Annie, with whom he works. Over time, Curlie and Annie fall in love. One day, Curlie asks Laurie for a divorce, explaining to Laurie that he has fallen in love with Annie and wants to marry her.

   What legal action, if any, might Laurie bring against Curlie as a result of his conduct? What cause of action, if any, might she bring against Annie? Will Laurie likely succeed with either or both claims?

ASSIGNMENTS AND PRACTICAL **APPLICATIONS**

1. Research whether your state has a survival statute. Under the statute in your jurisdiction, which tort actions survive the death of either the victim or the tortfeasor? Prepare a list of these actions for discussion in class.

2. Research your state's wrongful death statute. Which type is it? Who can bring a wrongful death action? What are its remedies? Discuss your research results in class.

3. Should parents be able to recover for the wrongful death of an unborn child? Read and brief the following cases for contrasting court viewpoints: *Farley v. Sartin*, 466 S.E.2d 522 (W. Va. 1995); and *Wilson v. Kaiser Found. Hosps.*, 141 Cal. App. 3d Supp. 891 (1983).

4. Research whether your state recognizes tort causes of action for wrongful birth and/or wrongful life. If so, who can bring the action, and under what circumstances? Discuss your research results in class.

5. For another case involving both wrongful birth and wrongful life theories brought together, read and brief *Smith v. Cote*, 513 A.2d 341 (N.H. 1986), in which the court allowed recovery by the parents for wrongful birth, but denied recovery to the child for wrongful life.

6. For an interesting opinion on wrongful life as a cause of action in which unwanted life-saving treatment was administered by a medical provider, read and brief *Anderson v. St. Francis-St. George Hosp., Inc.*, 671 N.E.2d 225 (Ohio 1996), in which the court answers the question, "Is 'continued living' a compensable injury?"

7. For a wrongful pregnancy cause of action based on lack of informed consent, read and brief *Burke v. Rivo*, 551 N.E.2d 1 (Mass. 1990), in which a medical practitioner failed to advise a patient of certain risks associated with a sterilization procedure.

8. Read and brief *Dotson v. Bernstein*, 207 P.3d 911 (Colo. App. 2009), allowing a claim for negligent failure to terminate a pregnancy.

9. In stating a claim for loss of consortium, the claimant must provide facts showing the basis for the alleged damages, the periods of time in which they allegedly were suffered, and how the dollar amounts were determined; conclusory statements that loss of consortium was suffered are not enough. Read and brief *Chrismon v. Brown*, 246 S.W.3d 102 (Tex. Ct. App. 2008).

TECHNOLOGY RESOURCES AND INTERNET **EXERCISES**

Using online legal research, find two wrongful death statutes, one that is a separately enacted statute providing for a wrongful death cause of action and another that broadens its jurisdiction's survival statute to include wrongful death. Compare and contrast the requirements of these causes of action according to their source. Which is broader, and how is it broader? Consider doing this exercise in groups, dividing the class in half, and have the two groups compare and contract two such survival statutes.

Will a medical malpractice action lie for wrongful *abortion?* See *http://en.wikipedia.org/wiki /Wrongful_abortion.*

Genetic testing, as it relates to wrongful life suits, is discussed in a brief article at *www.eyeondna.com/ 2007/07/25/genetic-testing-to-prevent-wrongful-life.* Interestingly, the author of the article, a doctor, recommends the use of informed consent agreements signed by parents to minimize the medical professional's legal liability in these cases.

Using the Internet, determine if your state recognizes any of the heart balm causes of action examined in this chapter. If not, can you determine when these causes of action were abolished, how they were abolished, and why? See if your state has a heart balm statute, and if so, what it provides. These heart balm actions, and to what extent they have been abolished and why, make for interesting class discussion. Discuss these questions and answers in class.

The case of Karen Quinlan, mentioned in the chapter, is a famous U.S. right-to-die case. In 1975, when she was 21 years old, Quinlan became unconscious after returning home from a birthday party. Quinlan had been on a radical diet at the time, hardly eating in two days, and had consumed Valium, Darvon painkiller, and alcohol. In the hospital, she lapsed into a persistent vegetative state and was kept alive on a ventilator. Her parents requested that the hospital take Quinlan off life support, but the hospital refused. The parents brought legal action and, in 1976, the New Jersey Supreme Court ruled in their favor, permitting the removal of Quinlan's life support. After being removed from life support, Quinlan lived on in a coma (fed by artificial means) until 1985, when she died of complications from pneumonia. Research the Internet for information on the legal proceedings involving Quinlan and the right-to-die issue.

ETHICAL **APPLICATIONS**

Nelson Goldman, Esq., has an estates and trusts law practice. In that practice, he writes wills for some of his clients. From time to time, a client will ask Nelson to keep and safeguard the official copy of his or her last will and testament. Pamela was one of Nelson's clients. Nelson drafted Pamela's will and kept it safely for her, in a well-marked file on his desk. Upon her death, Nelson retrieved the will (it was just where he had put it, and easy to find) and delivered it to the administrator of Pamela's estate.

a. *Was Nelson's idea, to keep the will in a file on his desk, a good one? Why or why not? Did this meet his ethical duties as a lawyer? What if Nelson lost the file?*

b. *What if Pamela kept the official will, and Nelson maintained only a copy of it in his law office file? Is Nelson's method of storage of the copy of the will ethical? Why or why not?*

VIDEO **CASE STUDY**

Videotape Deposition: Deposing an Expert Witness for Use at Trial

Synopsis: An expert witness whose testimony is critical to the issue of negligence may not be available at the time of trial, so the parties have agreed to the videotaping of his deposition. The expert witness testifies regarding his opinion of the cause of the school bus and truck collision.

Questions

Note that this scenario, in its partial testimony, assumes that the school bus crash case is advancing under negligence theory.

1. Assume that one of the children on the school bus dies as a result of his injuries sustained in the crash. Does the tort cause of action survive the death of the child? Why or why not?

2. If the child dies before the legal action concludes, but of causes unrelated to this collision, would the cause of action survive? Why or why not?

3. When is a wrongful death lawsuit appropriate?

4. Would a wrongful death lawsuit be appropriate if a victim of the crash dies as a result of his injuries? Why or why not? What about if he dies from unrelated causes? Why or why not?

chapter **9**

DEFENSES TO NEGLIGENCE AND REMEDIES

T his chapter examines the major legal defenses rather specific to the tort of negligence. It also reviews the legal doctrine of immunity, which protects a person from legal responsibility for her actions, including her torts, under certain circumstances. In addition, it reviews the remedies available to plaintiffs who bring successful negligence actions.

Earlier, we studied certain defenses to intentional torts. Remember that defenses are asserted by defendants to show why a plaintiff's claim should be denied or his recovery reduced. In this chapter, we begin by studying certain defenses more specific to the tort of negligence.

LEARNING OBJECTIVES

9.1 Explain the defense of contributory negligence.

9.2 Understand the last clear chance doctrine.

9.3 Explain the defense of comparative negligence.

9.4 Define assumption of the risk.

9.5 Define immunity and identify the various types.

9.6 Understand the various remedies for negligence.

Three Major Defenses Rather Specific to the Tort of Negligence

Three major defenses relate rather specifically to the tort of negligence. These defenses do not apply to intentional tort cases, though they may apply in strict liability cases. Other defenses, such as certain privileges and immunities, may also apply in negligence cases, as well as in other kinds of torts actions. This chapter begins with a discussion of three more negligence-specific defenses: contributory negligence, comparative negligence, and assumption of risk. We will discuss each in turn, starting with contributory negligence.

Contributory Negligence

Contributory negligence is a common law doctrine that provides that when a plaintiff's own negligence contributes to the harm or injury caused by the defendant's negligence, he cannot recover. This is true no matter how slight the plaintiff's contribution is.

Contributory negligence
A common law doctrine that provides that when a plaintiff's own negligence contributes to the harm or injury caused by the defendant's negligence, the plaintiff is barred from recovery.

Contributory negligence is an affirmative defense. It is asserted by the defendant in a negligence action. In asserting contributory negligence, the defendant is arguing that the plaintiff's own unreasonable conduct contributed to the injury or harm he suffered. Where contributory negligence is established, it acts as a complete bar to the plaintiff's recovery. This is true even if the defendant was, in fact, negligent. Further, this is true no matter how slight the plaintiff's negligence is compared to that of the defendant.

Consider this example. Bruce, driving down the street on his way home from work, runs a red light. Bruce crashes into Samantha's car as Samantha drives through the intersection on a green light, meaning that she has the right of way. At the time of the collision, Samantha was talking on her cell phone and drinking a cup of coffee, and she did not check to make sure the intersection was clear before entering it. Samantha sues Bruce for negligence. Will she win? In a jurisdiction that recognizes contributory negligence, Samantha's unreasonable conduct, in driving without exercising due care, may be a complete defense to Bruce's negligence. Therefore, it may bar her recovery.

Consider this additional example, in which both the plaintiff and the defendant engage in unreasonable conduct. Marvin is driving faster than the speed limit and enters an intersection after the stoplight turns yellow. He hits Justin, a pedestrian who is jaywalking across the street at the time of the collision. Justin's unreasonable conduct may be a bar to his recovery against Marvin for negligence.

Not all negligence cases involve car collisions. Consider the following example. The public swimming pool posts a sign along the deepest end, which is 5 feet deep. The sign warns, "No Diving/Shallow Water." Lifeguards at the pool are trained to prohibit swimmers from diving into the pool. While the lifeguard on duty has her back turned from the pool so she can chat with friends, Lucy dives in. Lucy is injured when she hits her head on the bottom of the pool. After the fact, Lucy wishes the lifeguard had seen her and stopped her from diving into the pool. The lifeguard was negligent in performing her duties, but Lucy was also unreasonable in ignoring the warning and diving in such shallow water. Note that this scenario also illustrates assumption of the risk defense, which we discuss later in the chapter. However, suppose that Lucy is visiting from another country and does not speak English. Would the defense of contributory negligence still apply? Given these facts, the warning sign would not be effective against someone who cannot read English, so it is more likely that Lucy's conduct would not be negligent.

SIDEBAR

CONTRIBUTORY NEGLIGENCE DEFENSE TO STRICT LIABILITY TORT ACTIONS

Note that contributory negligence may be a defense in strict liability actions in jurisdictions that recognize it. Strict liability is discussed in Chapter 10.

CASE on Point

Wooldridge v. Price, 966 A.2d 955 (Md. Ct. Spec. App. 2009)

In this case, the widow of a 44-year-old skateboarder who was killed when the skateboard he was riding was struck by motorist Price's car brought a wrongful death and survival action against the motorist. The accident occurred on the street where all the parties lived. Mr. Price was driving Mrs. Price to go shopping and out to lunch. He was driving his car at 15 miles per hour in a 25-miles-per-hour speed zone. The decedent (the skateboarder) came out of his in-laws' driveway into the street to cross over to his own driveway when he struck the Prices' vehicle and ended up underneath it. He died from his injuries.

The court recognized that in Maryland, contributory negligence on the part of a plaintiff completely bars recovery against a negligent defendant. In wrongful death and survival actions, contributory negligence of the decedent bars recovery against a negligent defendant. Regarding the last clear chance doctrine (discussed below), the court said that it did not apply to the facts of this case because the Prices did not have a fresh opportunity to exercise due care and avoid the accident. The court ruled that because the decedent was contributorily negligent and the doctrine of last clear chance did not apply, the wife's claims of wrongful death and survival were barred.

Contributory negligence doctrine exists in only a few jurisdictions today. By barring a plaintiff's recovery no matter how unreasonable his conduct compared to the defendant, seemingly unfair rulings may result. Most jurisdictions, in order to prevent such unfair rulings, have adopted a form of comparative negligence and abandoned the doctrine of contributory negligence. Today, only a handful of states continue to apply the doctrine of contributory negligence: Alabama, Delaware, Maryland, North Carolina, South Carolina, and Virginia. All other states have adopted some form of comparative negligence.

One doctrine can change the effect of contributory negligence. It is called the last clear chance doctrine, and it is examined next.

The Last Clear Chance Doctrine

The **last clear chance doctrine** is a legal doctrine that applies only in contributory negligence jurisdictions, which are few and far between today, to offset the effects of contributory negligence when the defendant has the last clear chance to avoid the incident or accident. It applies when both the defendant and the plaintiff are negligent, and harm is suffered by the plaintiff, but the defendant had the last clear chance to avoid the incident or accident resulting in the harm. If the defendant had the last clear chance to avoid the incident or accident, then the plaintiff may recover in negligence for the defendant's wrongful conduct. The plaintiff's own contributory negligence is no longer a bar to his recovery.

Last clear chance doctrine
A legal doctrine that offsets the effects of contributory negligence when the defendant has the last clear chance to avoid the incident or accident and does not.

Key Point

Last Clear Chance Doctrine
The last clear chance doctrine offsets the effects of contributory negligence when the defendant has the last clear chance to avoid the incident/accident.

CASE on Point

Carter v. Senate Masonry, Inc., 846 A.2d 50 (Md. Ct. Spec. App. 2004)

In this case, a commercial plumber brought a negligence action against a forklift operator's employer after the plumber was injured at a construction site for a new Safeway supermarket. When the accident occurred, the plumber was kneeling on the ground searching for some pipe fitting parts when he perceived a forklift move in behind him. The forklift operator maneuvered the forklift to place a pan of mortar on a cube of cinder blocks that had just been delivered to a scaffold where the plumber was situated. This action caused several cinder blocks to fall and strike the plumber on the head, neck, shoulder, and back.

The court discussed the application of the last clear chance doctrine. It said that the last clear chance doctrine permits a contributorily negligent plaintiff to recover damages from a negligent defendant if (1) the defendant is negligent; (2) the plaintiff is contributorily negligent; and (3) the plaintiff makes a showing of something new or sequential that gives the defendant a fresh opportunity to avoid the consequences of his original negligence and he fails to avail himself of that opportunity. The theory behind this doctrine is that if the defendant had the last clear opportunity to avoid the harm, then the plaintiff's negligence is not a proximate cause of the result. The court noted that the last clear chance doctrine only applies if the acts of the parties are sequential (there is a "fresh opportunity") and not concurrent; the defendant must have had a chance to avoid the injury after the plaintiff's negligence was put in motion. This doctrine assumes that after the primary negligence of the plaintiff and defendant, the defendant could, and the plaintiff could not, avoid the accident.

The court held that whether the forklift operator had the last clear chance to avoid this accident was an issue for the jury to consider.

Consider the earlier example involving Samantha and Bruce. Suppose that Bruce had the last clear chance to avoid the accident because, while running through the red light, he could have swerved to the right and avoided the collision. How does this affect the result reached earlier? Well, the last clear chance doctrine offsets the effects of contributory negligence. This means that because Bruce had the last clear chance to avoid the accident and did not take it, he can be held liable for the damages that resulted from his negligence. Samantha's contributory negligence no longer bars her recovery.

So, when evaluating the defense of contributory negligence in a jurisdiction that recognizes it, be sure to remember that the last clear chance doctrine allows the plaintiff to recover for his injuries in a negligence action against the defendant, even if the plaintiff contributed to them, if the defendant had the last clear chance to avoid the accident and did not do so.

The last clear chance doctrine does not apply to comparative negligence. Most states recognize comparative negligence rather than contributory negligence. What, then, is comparative negligence? That question is answered next.

STATUTE on Point

Hawaii's Comparative Negligence Statute: Haw. Rev. Stat. § 663-31 (2012)

Hawaii's comparative negligence statute states that contributory negligence shall not bar recovery in any action to recover damages for negligence resulting in death or in injury to person or property if the negligence was *not greater than* the negligence of the person against whom recovery is sought; any damages allowed shall be diminished in proportion to the amount of negligence attributable to the person alleging injury. If the proportion of the person alleging injury's fault is greater than the negligence of the person against whom recovery is sought, the court will enter judgment for the defendant.

Comparative Negligence

Comparative negligence is an apportionment of damages between negligent plaintiffs and defendants according to their relative degrees of fault, which may limit or bar a plaintiff's recovery. Comparative negligence is a defense similar to contributory negligence. It is asserted by a defendant in a negligence action (or sometimes, in a strict liability action). In asserting comparative negligence, the defendant is arguing that the plaintiff's own unreasonable conduct contributed to the injury or harm he suffered. Where the doctrines of contributory negligence and comparative negligence differ is in the allocation of fault and its effect on recovery.

With contributory negligence, when the plaintiff's own unreasonable conduct contributes to the injury or harm he suffers, that acts as a complete bar to the plaintiff's recovery. With comparative negligence, the plaintiff's unreasonable conduct may either bar his recovery or reduce his recovery proportionate to his relative degree of fault.

Comparative negligence schemes fall within two major categories. Comparative negligence states have adopted, by statute or case law, either a pure comparative negligence or a modified comparative negligence scheme.

Comparative negligence
An affirmative defense used to limit or bar recovery when a plaintiff's own negligence contributes to the injury or harm caused by the defendant's negligence, in which recovery is based on relative degrees of fault of the plaintiff and the defendant.

CASE on Point

Steigman v. Outrigger Enter., Inc., 267 P.3d 1238 (Haw. 2011)

In this case, a hotel guest brought a legal action against Outrigger Enterprises' Ohana Surf Hotel, alleging negligence. The hotel guest slipped and fell on a lanai (the name used in Hawaii for an outside porch furnished like a living room) while she was a guest at the hotel; at the time of the slip and fall accident, it was raining.

The court discussed Hawaii's comparative negligence statute (see the above Statute on Point). It said that the legislative purpose of the comparative negligence statute was to allow a person who is partly at fault in an accident that results in injury to be compensated for the damages attributable to the fault of another person so long as the person seeking recovery was not the primary cause of the accident.

MORE AT FAULT VERSUS EQUALLY OR MORE AT FAULT

For modified comparative negligence, some states require that the defendant be *more* at fault than the plaintiff. This means the defendant's fault must be more than 50 percent for the plaintiff to recover, *pro rata*, from the defendant. Other states require that the defendant's fault must be *equal to or greater than* the plaintiff's for the plaintiff to recover. That means the defendant's fault must be 50 percent or more for the plaintiff to recover, *pro rata*, from the defendant.

With pure comparative negligence, the plaintiff's own negligent conduct is never a bar to his recovery. Rather, the plaintiff's recovery is reduced so that his damage award reflects only the defendant's respective share of the fault. For instance, what if the plaintiff is injured by the defendant's negligence? The plaintiff's own negligent conduct contributed to the injuries he suffered. The jury determines that the defendant is 40 percent responsible for the harm, and the plaintiff is 60 percent responsible for it. If the damages suffered total $100,000, the plaintiff would be able to recover $40,000 (40 percent of $100,000) from the defendant in a pure comparative negligence jurisdiction.

In a modified comparative negligence jurisdiction, relative degrees of fault are determined just as with pure comparative negligence. Depending on the jurisdiction, the plaintiff may recover for his *pro rata* share of the harm caused by the defendant so long as the defendant was either *more* at fault than the plaintiff *or equally or more* at fault than the plaintiff. Otherwise, the plaintiff's unreasonable conduct acts as a complete bar to his recovery, just as with contributory negligence. Using the previous example, because the plaintiff was more at fault than the defendant—60 percent at fault, according to the jury— that would be a complete bar to recovery in a modified comparative negligence jurisdiction. What if the plaintiff was only 20 percent at fault, and the damages incurred were $100,000? In that case, the plaintiff could recover $80,000 (80 percent of $100,000) in a modified comparative negligence jurisdiction.

Comparative negligence is a popular defense used to limit or bar recovery when a plaintiff's own negligence contributes to the injury or harm caused by the defendant's negligence. Another defense to completely bar a plaintiff's recovery for a defendant's negligence is assumption of the risk. Assumption of the risk is discussed next.

Assumption of the Risk

Assumption of the risk
The knowing and voluntary acceptance of the risk of being harmed or injured by another's negligent conduct, which acts as a defense and bars the plaintiff's recovery.

Assumption of the risk is the knowing and voluntary acceptance of the risk of being harmed or injured by another's negligent conduct. It is another defense that can be asserted by the defendant in a negligence action (or sometimes, in a strict liability action). For assumption of the risk to apply, a plaintiff must knowingly and voluntarily assume the risk of being harmed by the negligence of the defendant. If that is the case, the defendant is not liable for the injury or harm suffered by the plaintiff. It is a complete bar to the plaintiff's recovery.

SIDEBAR

VICARIOUS LIABILITY

Notice that Joseph would choose to sue the team, in addition to or instead of the individual player. This is because the team has "deeper pockets"—it is better able to pay a large judgment. Why would the team be responsible for the individual player's misconduct? The answer is vicarious liability. One can be held liable for the misconduct of another through the doctrine of vicarious liability, which we studied in Chapter 2. The doctrine of *respondeat superior* is one form of vicarious liability pursuant to which an employer can be held liable for the misconduct of an employee acting within the course and scope of his employment. That is the case here, subjecting the team to potential liability for the player's actions.

As a simple example, a jockey assumes the risk of being injured or killed by riding young thoroughbred race horses.

Consider this hypothetical situation. Joseph loves ice hockey. Several times a year, he attends games of the local professional hockey team. One fateful night, Joseph is sitting in his seat enjoying the game. A player on the home team slaps a puck, which is mis-hit and is hurled into the fan seats. Joseph is hit in the head by the puck and is injured. Joseph sues the team (see the Sidebar on vicarious liability), and the player who hit the puck, for negligence. Will he win? The player and team could defend themselves by asserting that, by coming to the game where being possibly hit by a puck flying into the stands is a reality, Joseph assumed the risk of his injury. The questions for the jury are whether Joseph had knowledge of that risk, and whether he voluntarily assumed it. Likely, the answer is "yes" to both questions.

But what if Joseph is injured not by being hit by a puck, but by an excited stampede of people when the arena catches fire because of faulty electrical circuits, which were improperly maintained by the arena owners? Joseph then sues the arena for his injuries caused by the arena's negligent maintenance of the facility. Could the arena successfully defend itself that Joseph assumed the risk of injury by attending the hockey game? The answer is "no." Although Joseph had knowledge of the obvious risk of being hit by a puck while attending a hockey game, he had no knowledge of the faulty electrical circuits in the arena, and so he did not assume *those* risks. This risk is a different one than the one Joseph assumed. A different or greater risk takes the conduct outside the defense of assumption of risk.

SIDEBAR

APPLICATION TO STRICT LIABILITY TORTS

While assumption of risk is often alleged as a defense to the tort of negligence, it can be a defense to strict liability. Remember from Chapter 1 that strict liability is one of the three main classifications of torts, along with intentional torts and negligence. Strict liability defenses are covered in Chapter 12.

CASE on Point

Thomas v. Panco Mgmt. of Md., LLC, 31 A.3d 583 (Md. 2010)

This case involved a tenant who slipped and fell on black ice on a sidewalk that led to her apartment building when she was leaving it at 8:00 P.M. one evening to pick up her granddaughter from a church youth group meeting. She filed legal action against her landlord and the management company that ran the apartment complex, alleging negligence. The defendants asserted the defense of assumption of the risk.

The court recognized three requirements that a defendant must prove to establish the defense of assumption of the risk: (1) the plaintiff had knowledge of the risk of the danger; (2) the plaintiff appreciated the risk; and (3) the plaintiff voluntarily confronted the risk of danger. The court ruled that whether the tenant knew of the risk of slipping on black ice and whether she voluntarily chose the more dangerous route when she exited her apartment building were questions of fact to be answered by the jury.

Remember also that the assumption of risk must be knowingly made: The plaintiff must have full knowledge of the danger and risk involved. In addition, the plaintiff must voluntarily assume the risk; the defendant cannot force the plaintiff to assume the risk through coercion, or trick the plaintiff into assuming the risk.

Immunity can be a defense to negligence liability. However, immunity is a broad defense that can apply to all kinds of tort actions, as well as other types of legal actions. So immunity is a defense that can be asserted in a negligence action but that is not a defense specific only to negligence actions. Immunity is reviewed next.

Definition of Immunity

Immunity
A defense to legal liability or criminal prosecution that, when applied to tort law, under certain circumstances, protects a tortfeasor from liability for his tortious conduct.

Absolute immunity
Legal immunity without limits or conditions, such as a good faith requirement, which acts as a complete defense to liability.

Qualified immunity
Legal immunity that has limits or conditions, such as a requirement of good faith, which can be lost as a defense.

Immunity is a legal doctrine that provides a defense to liability, including tort liability, or criminal prosecution. It is an exemption from legal responsibility. A person can be immune from civil liability for wrongful conduct such as tort liability. A person can also be immune from criminal prosecution for the commission of criminal acts. In effect, immunity bars one person from suing another, or the government from prosecuting a person.

Immunity can be absolute or qualified. *Absolute immunity* is immunity that, basically, cannot be lost. Absolute immunity is a complete defense to liability and is typically given to public officials who perform legislative or judicial functions. It is immunity without limits or conditions, such as a good faith requirement, meaning there is no requirement that a person's tortious act be performed in good faith for absolute immunity to act as a complete defense. *Qualified immunity* is immunity that can be lost. It is immunity that has limits or conditions, such as a requirement of good faith. For instance, if the acts are performed with malice, meaning with an improper motive, qualified immunity may be lost as a defense. If absolute immunity is not present, qualified immunity may protect the defendant in a tort action. See the following Case on Point on this distinction, and its effect.

CASE on Point

Forrester v. White, 484 U.S. 219 (1988)

In this case, a female probation officer was demoted, then fired, by an Illinois state court judge who had originally hired her. Under Illinois law at the time, a state judge had the authority to hire probation officers, and their removal was within the judges' discretion. The former court employee brought a sex discrimination action under Section 1983 of the federal Civil Rights Act against the judge who hired and then fired her. The judge defended himself, in part, by alleging immunity.

The U.S. Supreme Court held that a state court judge does not have absolute immunity from a damages action for his decisions to demote and dismiss a subordinate court employee. In so holding, the Court reasoned that the judge's employment decisions were not "judicial acts for which he should be held absolutely immune." Rather, these acts were administrative in nature.

Although the threat of liability can "create perverse incentives that operate to inhibit officials in the proper performance of their duties," thus supporting the need for immunity from suit for certain government officials, the Court adopted a "functional" approach to immunity questions. Using this functional approach, the Court said that immunity is justified and defined by the functions it protects and serves, and not by the person to whom it attaches. Judicial immunity, therefore, attaches to judicial functions, but not to administrative, legislative, or executives ones that judges may be assigned by law to perform.

Ultimately, the Court said that personnel decisions made by judges, though crucial to the efficient operation of public institutions such as courts, do not give rise to absolute immunity of judges from liability for wrongs such as discrimination. The Court expressly did not rule on whether the judge might be able to claim qualified immunity but instead remanded the case for further proceedings, thus leaving open the question of whether qualified immunity, like that available to executive branch officials making similar discretionary decisions, might be available for judges making employment decisions.

In the *Forrester* case, the Supreme Court did not decide whether qualified immunity applied to protect the state court judge's employment decisions. Qualified immunity protects government employees from personal legal liability for their wrongful conduct, including tortious conduct, that is committed within the scope of their employment so long as they have not acted with malice, or in some federal civil rights cases, so long as they should not have reasonably known that their actions were in violation of established law.

In its application to tort law, under certain circumstances, immunity protects a tortfeasor from liability for his tortious conduct. Immunity normally operates as an absolute defense in intentional tort, negligence, and strict liability actions, making the wrongdoer immune from suit. Examples of immunity applicable to tort law include the following:

- Family immunity protects certain family members from liability for harm caused to other family members, in order to preserve family harmony.
- Governmental, or sovereign, immunity prevents a lawsuit against a government or sovereign, such as a monarch or other ruler, without the government or sovereign's consent.

Key Point

Sources of Immunity

Immunity is derived from

- Who a person is
- What a person does
- A person's relationship with another person

- Charitable immunity is immunity from legal liability granted to charitable organizations to help them fulfill their charitable missions.
- Official and diplomatic immunity protects public officials, like judges and legislators, as well as diplomats, from liability in the performance of their duties.

Immunity is derived from three main sources: (1) who a person is (such as a government or charitable organization), (2) what a person does (such as acts as a government official, judge, legislator, etc.), or (3) a person's relationship with another person (such as a spouse).

Next, we will consider the reasons behind the doctrine of immunity and its application as a defense to tort, such as negligence, liability.

Public Policy Behind Tort Immunity

Why should a person be immune from tort liability just because of who he is, what he does, or his relationship with another person? The reason is based on public policy.

Public policy behind immunity in tort law is that certain persons, including humans and entities, warrant special legal protection in order to fulfill their missions and functions. For example, if a judge could be subjected to a tort lawsuit for injuries caused by a defendant released from incarceration after being acquitted in a criminal case, the judge would not feel free to act as the judicial office demands, for fear of such liability.

Further, certain relationships deserve special legal protections in order to preserve them. For example, if personal injury lawsuits could be maintained by one spouse against another, harmony in marriage would be disrupted (seriously).

Keep in mind, however, that immunity that applies to persons acting in an official or special capacity does not extend to their off-duty conduct. For instance, the immunity of certain governmental officials, such as mayors or legislators, does not extend to their off-duty conduct. Public official immunity protects only their conduct committed within the course and scope of their official duties, such as while performing mayoral or legislative functions.

Next, we will examine each of the different types of immunity that are applicable to tort law. Family immunity is one of these several types of immunity. What is family immunity, and when does it apply?

Family Immunity

Family immunity
Protects certain family members from liability for harm caused to other family members.

Family immunity is immunity from legal liability between certain family members. It protects certain family members from liability for harm caused to other family members under certain circumstances.

The purpose for family immunity is grounded in public policy. The notion is that certain family members should have some protections against other family members in order to foster better family relationships by limiting the ability of certain family members to sue each other. In other words, family immunity,

SIDEBAR

OTHER FAMILY TORTS

Recall our discussion of heart balm actions from Chapter 8. Heart balm statutes have abolished or limited many of the old common law torts involving family members, including alienation of affections suits and the like.

where it is allowed, promotes family harmony. There are two main types of family immunity: interspousal immunity and parent–child immunity.

Interspousal immunity is the immunity that exists between legal spouses. It is meant to protect marriage. Interspousal immunity is just one example of a bias in the law in favor of, and toward preserving, the institution of marriage. Under common law, spouses were considered one person. Therefore, one spouse could not sue the other in tort because one cannot sue oneself. Over time, state law evolved in this area, abolishing the old common law notion of "one person" to permit certain types of tort suits between spouses. Other types of tort suits continue to be disallowed. What types of torts suits are allowed, and what types are disallowed, vary from jurisdiction to jurisdiction, but here are the general rules.

Most states today permit spouses to sue each other for torts against property. Regarding torts involving personal injury, some states permit one spouse to sue another for intentional torts, but other states do not. All states disallow negligence suits between spouses for personal injury. The theory behind distinguishing among different types of personal injury torts in terms of

Interspousal immunity
The immunity that exists between legal spouses.

CASE on Point

Lusby v. Lusby, 390 A.2d 77 (Md. 1978)

When the tort is an intentional one, more states allow such a claim and deny interspousal immunity. In this case, a husband and two accomplices forced the husband's wife off the road by threatening her and pointing a high-powered rifle at her as she drove her car. Then they kidnapped her, her husband raped her, the accomplices attempted to rape her, and the husband threatened to kill her if she informed anyone of what he had done. The Court of Appeals of Maryland found the application of interspousal immunity inappropriate when the intentional torts of battery, assault, and false imprisonment are committed.

In rendering its decision, the court said: "There is no reason to think that in the case of intentional, willful, and wanton injury an action would disrupt domestic harmony, since the conduct leading to the action has already caused the disruptions." The court noted that the conduct at issue in this case was beyond mere intentional conduct, being outrageous in nature. Accordingly, the court stated that it found "nothing in our prior cases or elsewhere to indicate that under the common law of Maryland a wife was not permitted to recover from her husband in tort when she alleged and proved the type of outrageous, intentional conduct" alleged in the case, despite its recognition of the doctrine of interspousal immunity.

CASE on Point

Squeglia, Jr. v. Squeglia, Sr., 644 A.2d 378 (Conn. App. Ct. 1994)

In this case, a 4-year-old boy, through his mother, brought a tort suit against his father for injuries he sustained when his father's dog attacked him. The Appellate Court of Connecticut recognized that the doctrine of parental immunity barred an action by an unemancipated minor against his parents, pursuant to the Connecticut General Statutes § 22-357 (discussed in the next section on the "tender years doctrine"). The court recognized four exceptions to the parental immunity doctrine, but it held that these facts did not fall under any recognized exception. As a result, the child's suit was barred because of the father's parental immunity.

Parent–child immunity
The immunity that exists between parents and their children; also called parental immunity.

interspousal immunity, for those jurisdictions that make a distinction, is the belief that one spouse should be able to recover for harms caused intentionally by the other spouse, but not for those caused innocently or mistakenly, even if unreasonably.

Another family relationship that receives some family immunity protection is the parent–child relationship. *Parent–child immunity*, also called *parental immunity*, is immunity between parents and their children. Historically in the United States, immunity developed between parents and their children to prevent tort suits between them. The purpose of parent–child immunity is to foster harmonious relationships between parents and their children. However, many states have significantly abolished or limited parent–child immunity by creating exceptions to the immunity rule. Like interspousal immunity, all states today permit a child to sue a parent for torts against property. However, only some states permit an *unemancipated child*—meaning a child who is not yet "of age" or married, self-supporting, or in military service—to sue a parent for personal injury torts, and normally for intentional torts only, not negligence. Further, parents have the privilege to discipline their children.

Unemancipated child
A child who is not yet "of age" or married, self-supporting, or in military service.

What about other family relationships? Does immunity apply? The answer is "no." Family immunity does not apply to grandparents, grandchildren, siblings, aunts, uncles, nieces, nephews, and cousins; thus, these persons can sue each other in tort.

What about children? Are they immune from suit for their tortious acts? Can they even perform tortious acts? Those questions are answered next.

Immunity for Children of Tender Years

Children of tender years
Young children, normally under the age of 7.

What are children of tender years? Very young children, under the law, are considered *children of tender years*. The rule of thumb is that a child under the age of 7 is of tender years. A minor is a child under the age of 18 or 21, depending on the jurisdiction. Being a child of tender years, then, is distinguishable from being a minor. To what extent are very young children liable for their tortious conduct? Alternatively, to what extent are they immune from liability for their torts?

Only these very young children enjoy immunity under the ***tender years doctrine***, a legal doctrine that, under certain circumstances, offers special treatment and protections to them. Older children, who are still minors, may be held liable for their tortious misconduct, as well as prosecuted for their criminal misconduct. Although 7 years of age is an age that is commonly recognized by courts in defining tender years, some courts include older children under the doctrine, though today most courts do not include teens. This means that children ranging in age from 8 to 12 years may be immune from tort liability, depending on the jurisdiction. Teenagers, however, are not normally immune from tort liability merely because they are minors.

Whether children of tender years are held liable for their torts varies based not only on their age but also on the nature of the torts committed, that is, whether they are negligent or intentional. Strict liability theory usually does not apply to minors, simply because most minors normally do not keep dangerous animals, engage in abnormally dangerous activities, make or sell defective products, or the like. Most courts grant children in their tender years absolute immunity from liability for the commission of intentional torts. The reasoning of the courts is that such young children are incapable of having the "intent" necessary to commit the intentional torts, because of their level of mental and emotional maturity and development. These young children are deemed to be incapable of fully appreciating the significance of what they do.

Regarding the tort of negligence, most courts consider the age of the child as a factor in determining the standard of care a similarly situated child should meet—recall the discussion of "standard of care" in Chapter 6. For instance, the conduct of a 10-year-old would be judged against the conduct of other, reasonably behaving 10-year-olds to determine whether there was a breach of a duty of care. However, courts do not necessarily grant absolute negligence immunity to young children. Note that a few states grant immunity for children below a certain very young age by finding such children incapable of committing even negligence.

Tender years doctrine
A legal doctrine that, under certain circumstances, offers special treatment and protections to very young children.

STATUTES on Point

Connecticut General Statutes: § 22-357 (2012) and § 52-217 (2012)

Consider the Connecticut statute (Conn. Gen. Stat. § 22-357) applied in the *Squeglia* case, discussed earlier. The statute says that if a dog damages the person or property of another, the owner or keeper of the dog, or if the owner or keeper is a minor, the parent or guardian of the minor, can be held liable for the damages unless the person damaged was committing a trespass or other tort or was teasing, tormenting, or abusing the dog. In the case of a minor bringing suit (through his parents or guardians) under this provision, if the minor was under 7 years of age at the time the damages occurred,

it is presumed that the minor was not committing a trespass or other tort or teasing, tormenting, or abusing the dog.

Another Connecticut statute (Conn. Gen. Stat. § 52-217) says that in lawsuits to recover damages for injury to person or property when the plaintiff or defendant was a minor under 16 years of age at the time the cause of action arose, it is a question of fact to be submitted to the judge or jury to determine whether the minor plaintiff or minor defendant was exercising due care if there was a violation of a statutory duty by the minor plaintiff or minor defendant.

Read and brief the case on applying immunity theory to minors that appears at the end of the chapter, which notes that the law does not grant minors complete immunity from liability for their torts. This case also illustrates the application of negligence analysis to minors, including the effects of age, judgment, and experience on this determination.

Not only may certain family members be immune from particular suits, either by other family members or because of their young age, governments may be immune from suit as well. Next we consider governmental, or sovereign, immunity.

Governmental, or Sovereign, Immunity

Governmental immunity
Prevents a lawsuit against a government or sovereign, without the government or sovereign's consent; also known as sovereign immunity.

Governmental immunity is immunity of the government from certain lawsuits. Government, in this context, refers to all levels of government, including federal, state, and local. Government immunity extends to all such levels.

A governmental unit, because it is not itself human, "acts" through its employees and agents. Accordingly, vicarious liability, as studied in Chapter 2, applies for the government to be held legally responsible for the wrongful acts of its employees committed within the course and scope of their employment. Normally, governments cannot be held liable for the tortious acts of their employees, even under the doctrine of *respondeat superior*, unless either the government sanctioned the misconduct or the government waived its immunity and consented to be sued. Governmental immunity usually must be waived, then, in order for the government to be sued, including being sued in tort.

Sovereign immunity
A type of governmental immunity that prevents a lawsuit against a sovereign, such as a monarch, without the sovereign's consent.

Governmental immunity stems from the traditional English rule of *sovereign immunity*. Historically, the king (a sovereign) could not be sued by a subject unless he consented, because, as king, he could do no wrong. The reason was that, in early times, sovereigns were considered divine. More recently, since the twentieth century, the doctrine of sovereign immunity has been remodeled to protect governments run by those other than kings. In the United States, the term "government" has replaced the term "sovereign" where immunity still exists.

Modern courts, including those in the United States, found the result of sovereign immunity to be unfair to many plaintiffs, who might be wronged by their sovereigns or governments, yet had no opportunity for redress. In whittling away sovereign immunity as a defense, courts in the United States began to distinguish two types of functions performed by governments and their agencies, namely, governmental functions and proprietary functions, and to treat them differently, especially when considering immunity of local government units.

Governmental functions
Activities performed by government in the best interest of and to protect the public, which often can be performed only by the government.

Governmental functions are activities that are performed by the government in the best interest of and to protect the public, such as providing courts, city councils, jails, schools, sanitation, and fire and police departments. Governmental functions are ones that are typically only performed by the government. Generally speaking, governmental immunity applies when governmental functions are involved.

Proprietary functions are activities that are performed in the government's discretion, for the benefit of its citizens; often, they are functions that cannot be performed adequately only by the government, and many of them are revenue-producing. These functions tend to be business-like, or quasi-private-sector, activities. Further, proprietary functions tend to be those activities that a government is not required to perform, but may perform, in its discretion. Examples of proprietary functions are the operation of airports, garages, utilities, public hospitals, and the like.

Normally, governmental immunity extends only to governmental functions. It does not extend to proprietary functions, according to most modern courts. However, it is not always clear whether a function is governmental or proprietary.

When the government provides a service for profit, then that function is likely to be considered proprietary. When the government provides the service for the public good, then the function is likely to be considered governmental. In addition, courts consider whether fees are charged by the government for the service or activity, such as utility fees, park fees, parking fees, and the like, tending the function toward a proprietary nature.

In dealing with governmental immunity issues, many legislatures, at the federal, state, and local levels, have enacted statutes stating explicitly when and to what extent the government waives its immunity.

In the United States, federal government immunity today is governed by the Federal Tort Claims Act (FTCA) of 1946. Under the Federal Tort Claims Act, the federal government can be sued, subject to many exceptions as noted below, as if it was a private person under the local laws of the place where the tort occurs, constituting a waiver of governmental immunity. Jurisdiction is in the federal district courts. However, no jury trials are permitted, and a two-year statute of limitations applies.[1]

The Federal Tort Claims Act does not abolish governmental immunity for the federal government. Rather, the statute delineates many exemptions, which are exceptions to its waiver of governmental immunity. The Federal Tort Claims Act excludes—meaning it does not waive its governmental immunity for—claims arising out of the commission of many of the intentional torts, including assault, battery, false imprisonment, false arrest, malicious prosecution, abuse of process, libel, slander, misrepresentation, deceit, and interference with contract rights; claims arising out of the exercise of a discretionary function by an employee at the planning or leadership level, involving policy decisions and the exercise of judgment; strict liability claims; claims arising out of war, mail delivery, admiralty, customs, quarantine, and tax collection; and claims arising in the course of their duties by armed forces personnel. These exclusions are set forth as exceptions under the FTCA in 28 U.S.C. § 2680.

The types of misconduct that are not excluded by the Federal Tort Claims Act, and for which governmental immunity is waived, include those torts not specifically excluded and that arise out of the exercise of nondiscretionary functions by federal government employees. The Federal Tort Claims Act also includes many of the property torts, such as trespass to land, conversion, and trespass to chattels; invasion of privacy torts; and assault, battery, false

Proprietary functions
Activities performed in the government's discretion, for the benefit of its citizens, and that often cannot be performed adequately only by the government.

Key Point

Governmental Versus Proprietary Functions
Courts distinguish governmental from proprietary functions in determining the application of immunity to a governmental unit. Governmental immunity normally extends only to the performance of governmental functions.

Key Point

Waiver of Immunity by Statute
Today, federal, state, and local statutes often define the scope of governmental immunity that applies, via waiver of immunity under certain circumstances, perhaps up to certain dollar limits.

SIDEBAR

FEDERAL TORT CLAIMS ACT EXCLUSIONS

Claims excluded under the Federal Tort Claims Act (for which the federal government does *not* waive its governmental immunity) include

- Assault, battery, false imprisonment, false arrest, malicious prosecution, abuse of process, libel, slander, misrepresentation, deceit, and interference with contract rights
- Claims arising out of the exercise of a discretionary function by a federal government employee
- Strict liability claims
- Claims arising out of war, mail delivery, admiralty, customs, quarantine, and tax collection
- Claims arising in the course of their duties by armed forces personnel[2]

imprisonment, false arrest, abuse of process, or malicious prosecution committed by law enforcement personnel. Accordingly, the U.S. government has limited, but not abolished, its governmental immunity under the FTCA.

State government immunity today varies by jurisdiction. Some states have virtually abolished governmental immunity for the torts of their employees. Other states have enacted statutory schemes similar to the Federal Tort Claims Act, which set forth when the state waives governmental immunity and when it does not. Many such statutes limit the state's liability for certain governmental functions, for judicial and legislative acts, and for the exercise of discretionary decision making.

Local government immunity today also varies by jurisdiction. Some local governments, such as cities, municipalities, counties, towns, and villages, have completely or substantially waived governmental immunity, or follow whatever scheme their states use. For example, the mayor and city council of Baltimore are covered under the state of Maryland's Local Government Tort Claims Act, which waives governmental immunity for certain torts, up to a certain dollar limit, and essentially mirrors the Maryland Tort Claims Act.

Recall our discussion of the distinction between governmental and proprietary functions. Local governments typically distinguish propriety functions from governmental functions, waiving immunity for proprietary functions but maintaining immunity for governmental ones. This is so

STATUTE on Point

Md. Code Ann., State Gov't § 12-104 (2012)

Maryland, in its Maryland Tort Claims Act, provides (subject to certain exclusions and limitations) that the immunity of the state and its units is waived in tort actions in courts of the state for up to $200,000 in damages per claimant for injuries arising from a single incident or occurrence.

STATUTE on Point

Md. Code Ann., Cts. & Jud. Proc. § 5-301 to 5-304 (2012)

What about Baltimore City, a local government in the state of Maryland? Maryland's Local Government Tort Claims Act requires Maryland counties and other entities defined in the statute as local governments to pay, up to certain limits, judgments for compensatory damages rendered against their employees as a result of tortious acts committed within the course and scope of employment. The statute contains some procedural requirements; for example, it requires plaintiffs to give local government defendants notice of claims within 180 days of sustaining their injuries, and that such notice be given to designated government officials. The purpose of this statute is to provide a remedy for people who are injured by local government officers and employees acting without malice and within the scope of their employment and at the same time ensuring that the financial burden of compensating the victims is carried by the local government that is ultimately responsible for the public employee's conduct.

because local governments, rather than the federal or state governments, are often the ones that perform proprietary functions, such as operating airports or parking garages.

Another type of immunity is charitable immunity. Charitable immunity is examined next.

Charitable Immunity

Charitable immunity is immunity granted to charitable organizations—schools, churches, animal shelters, foundations, some hospitals, and the like—to help them fulfill their missions and objectives. Charitable organizations are defined by federal law under Section 501(c)(3) of the Internal Revenue Code as being organized for purposes such as prevention of or relief from poverty or the advancement of religion, education, human rights, environmental protection, animal welfare, the arts, and culture; such organizations receive favorable tax treatment.

Charitable immunity
Immunity from legal liability granted to charitable organizations to help them fulfill their charitable missions.

CASE on Point

Mayfield-Brown v. Sayegh, 667 S.E.2d 785 (Va. 2008)

In this case, a university's medical practice group (a foundation) sought to avoid liability for medical malpractice based on the doctrine of charitable immunity. The Supreme Court of Virginia recognized the doctrine of charitable immunity. However, in applying the facts of the case, the court held that the doctrine of charitable immunity did not apply. The court reasoned that the foundation was not immune from tort liability under the doctrine of charitable immunity because it conducted its affairs like a profitable commercial business, despite the fact that it treated some indigent patients. The court said the foundation's charity work was small compared to the rest of its work.

CHARITABLE IMMUNITY AND THE *RESTATEMENT (SECOND) OF TORTS*

The *Restatement (Second) of Torts* rejects the doctrine of charitable immunity, stating that a person who is engaged in charitable, religious, educational, or similar benevolent activities is not, for that reason of charity or benevolence, immune from tort liability.[3]

The original purpose of charitable immunity was to prevent depletion of the charity's resources and to encourage continued donations by protecting the charitable organization from tort lawsuits in which the organization could be held vicariously liable for wrongful acts of its employees committed within the course and scope of their employment.

Today, however, most states have either abolished or significantly restricted this form of immunity via statute. Accordingly, most jurisdictions allow charitable organizations to be sued, including in tort. Among states that statutorily reject the notion of charitable immunity, some limit the liability of the charity to a specific amount, or provide more narrow legal protections in the form of specific immunities for particular persons engaged in certain charitable activities (such as volunteers), or permit charitable immunity for particular charitable activities themselves. Consider the illustrations from several different state codes in the Statutes on Point.

STATUTES on Point

Ark. Code Ann. § 16-120-103 (2012); Me. Rev. Stat. Ann. tit. 14, § 158 (2012); Conn. Gen. Stat. § 52-557d (2012); Ga. Code Ann. § 51-1-29.1 (2012)

Arkansas limits charitable immunity from tort liability. The Arkansas statute says that charitable immunity does not extend to acts or omissions of directors of nonprofit corporations or members of boards, authorities, commissions, or other governing bodies of governmental entities when the acts or omissions constitute negligence, gross negligence, or an intentional tort. Further, the statute states explicitly that it does not limit the liability of a nonprofit corporate entity itself for damages resulting from any negligent act or omission of its employees.

Maine also limits charitable immunity. By statute in Maine, charitable immunity for tortious conduct is waived to the extent that the organization is insured for its liability. Maine's statute says that a charitable organization waives its immunity from tort liability (both negligence and any other torts) during the period when an insurance policy

is in effect that covers the liability of the charitable organization for such tort. The amount of damages cannot exceed the limits of coverage specified in the policy. The statute requires that each insurance policy state that the insurer cannot assert the defense that the organization is immune from liability on the ground that it is a charitable organization.

Connecticut statutorily provides that the common law doctrine of charitable immunity is abolished and is not a valid defense to any cause of action, including a tort action.

Georgia permits charitable immunity for particular activities. The Georgia statute provides immunity from liability for certain health care providers who provide professional services without expecting or receiving compensation. It states that unless the injury or death was caused

(continued)

by gross negligence or willful or wanton misconduct, no health care provider licensed under certain chapters of the statute who voluntarily and without the expectation or receipt of compensation provides professional services at the request of a hospital, public school, nonprofit organization, or an agency of the state or one of its political subdivisions (or who provides the services for pay but at the request of such an organization and the organization does not expect to or receive compensation for the services from the recipient) will be liable for damages for injury sustained by the person or for the death of the person when the injury or death is alleged to have occurred by reason of an act or omission in the rendering of the professional services.

Other types of immunity include official immunity and diplomatic immunity. These are examined next.

Official and Diplomatic Immunity

Official immunity protects public officials for certain conduct committed within the course of their official functions. Earlier, we discussed immunity from vicarious liability for units of government for the torts committed by their employees and other agents. Official immunity deals with liability of individuals, namely, certain government employees considered public officials, as opposed to liability of the governmental unit that employs the public officials.

A *public official* is a person who holds a governmental position, called an office, in which he serves in the public interest. Public officials, such as executive officers of the government, judges, and legislators, normally are not held liable for torts they commit without malice during the discharge of their official duties. This is public official immunity, or official immunity.

By granting such immunity, the law allows certain freedom to public officials to perform their official duties without fear of tort liability resulting from their public service. As the U.S. Supreme Court reasoned in the *Forrester* case, discussed earlier in distinguishing absolute and qualified immunity:

> [T]he threat of liability can create perverse incentives that operate to *inhibit* officials in the proper performance of their duties. In many contexts, government officials are expected to make decisions that are impartial or imaginative, and that above all are informed by considerations other than the personal interest of the decision-maker. Because government officials are engaged by definition in governing, their decisions will often have adverse effects on other persons. When officials are threatened with personal liability for acts taken pursuant to their official duties, they may well be induced to act with an excess of caution or otherwise to skew their decisions in ways that result in less than full fidelity to the objective and independent criteria that ought to guide their conduct. Such considerations have led to the creation of various forms of immunity from suit for certain government officials.[4]

As an illustration, judges normally are immune from tort liability for their official conduct in the performance of their function as judges. Without such immunity, their ability to make and interpret laws might be hampered by considerations regarding their own exposure to potential legal liability. For instance,

Official immunity
Legal immunity that protects public officials in the performance of their duties; also called public official immunity.

Public official
A person who holds a governmental position, called an office, in which he serves in the public interest.

if a judge feared being sued by the victim of a crime for letting the criminal defendant "off" on a procedural technicality, the judge's decision regarding upholding the Constitution, as, ultimately, many criminal procedure technicalities involve guarantees provided to criminally accused persons under the Constitution, would be affected by the possibility of such a lawsuit.

Recalling our earlier discussion of absolute versus qualified immunity, judges, legislators, and high administrative officials are more likely to have absolute official immunity for acts committed within the scope of their official duties. As we discussed earlier, absolute immunity is immunity that cannot be lost. That said, the U.S. Supreme Court has stated that it "has generally been quite sparing in its recognition of claims to absolute official immunity" (from the *Forrester* case).[5]

Lower-level administrative officials who exercise considerable discretion in performing their jobs, such as assistant city solicitors, who are lawyers in a city's legal department, are likely to have qualified immunity. Qualified immunity is immunity that is limited or conditioned and may be lost, for instance, if the act is committed with malice.

Lower-level administrative officials whose functions are ministerial and who exercise no or little discretion in the performance of their duties, such as public trash collectors or road repairmen, likely have no immunity unless a specific statute protects them.

Specifically regarding the immunity of executive officers of the government, as opposed to other public officials such as legislators or judges, very high administrative officials, such as the U.S. President, enjoy *absolute* immunity. See the case at the end of the chapter involving the official immunity of former President Richard Nixon [*Nixon v. Fitzgerald,* 457 U.S. 731 (1982)]. However, the Supreme Court has confined such absolute immunity to the President himself, because of his "unique position in the constitutional scheme," quoting the Court in the *Forrester* case.[6] It has not extended absolute immunity to the President's personal aides or cabinet members, nor to the highest executive officials in the state governments under federal law, all of which are examined in cases at the end of the chapter.

Even when absolute immunity is not granted, qualified immunity may be granted to public officials, including higher- and lower-level ones.

CASE on Point

Forrester v. White, 484 U.S. 219 (1988)

Recall the Supreme Court ruling in *Forrester v. White,* discussed earlier, which involved a state court judge who dismissed a probation officer from employment, which was one of his official duties. The Court in this case said that the judge did not enjoy absolute public official immunity for that act, even though it was part of his job function. It reasoned that, because the act was not "judicial" in nature—in other words, it was not related to his work as a jurist, but rather was part of his role as a supervisor of subordinate employees—he did not have absolute immunity for this action. The Court left open the question of whether qualified immunity might apply to the judge's conduct when it remanded the case for further proceedings.

CASE on Point

Beato v. Pakistan Embassy, 301 A.D.2d 459 (N.Y. App. Div. 2003)

In this case, the Supreme Court, Appellate Division, of New York rejected the defendant's assertion of diplomatic immunity. Instead, the court held that this personal injury action, which arose out of a traffic accident, fell within the "tortious act" exception of the Foreign Sovereign Immunities Act. Accordingly, the defendant could not avoid suit on the grounds of diplomatic immunity.

Official immunity, both absolute and qualified, does not extend to conduct engaged in outside the scope of public officers' official duties, for which they can be held liable, including in tort. For a simple illustration, if the deputy mayor of a town unreasonably causes a car accident while returning from a social engagement, injuring a third party by her conduct, that third party could sue the deputy mayor for negligence, and public official immunity would not apply. Remember that the conduct covered by official immunity is that which is committed while performing official public duties.

Though it is not a traditional common law tort, a cause of action for deprivation of federal civil rights is sometimes called a constitutional tort. Under 42 U.S.C. § 1983 of the Civil Rights Act, a person who deprives another of a civil right is liable to that person in a legal action, called a Section 1983 action. Public officials who, in the course of their duties, deprive someone of federal civil rights appear to have qualified immunity with respect to a Section 1983 action. The *Forrester* case, examined earlier, involved a Section 1983 gender discrimination claim.

Diplomatic immunity protects diplomats in the performance of their official duties. A diplomat is a person who is appointed by the national government to maintain and manage relations with another foreign nation. To allow diplomats freedom in the performance of their duties, they are granted immunity from tort suits for their official actions. This immunity can be waived by the government of the diplomat, for instance, if the diplomat engages in criminal conduct outside the scope of his duties. Diplomatic immunity may be limited by statute. See the above Case on Point for a case denying diplomatic immunity.

Diplomatic immunity
Legal immunity that protects diplomats in the performance of their official duties.

Public official and diplomatic immunity are similar, in both definition and application. They cover either public officials or diplomats acting within their official functions. Their immunity may be absolute or qualified.

If no defense succeeds in barring the plaintiff's recovery completely, what remedies may be awarded to the successful plaintiff in a negligence action? Remedies are examined next.

Remedies for Negligence

As with intentional torts, remedies in negligence actions may be awarded at law and in equity. The normal remedy awarded in negligence actions is the remedy at law, namely, damages.

SIDEBAR

PUNITIVE DAMAGES

Remember that punitive damages are recoverable in intentional tort cases, in which "intent" is an essential element of the tort involved. Punitive damages are more common in the areas of intentional torts and strict liability (we will discuss strict liability in Chapter 10) than they are in negligence.

Also similar to the study of intentional torts, the same types of damages may be awarded: compensatory, nominal, punitive, and pain and suffering. Remember that compensatory damages are awarded to compensate the victim for the harm or injury he suffered and to attempt to make him whole again. Compensatory damages are the typical negligence remedy.

Nominal damages are awarded when very little harm is suffered by the plaintiff. Keep in mind that actual damages are an essential element of the tort of negligence. This means that some harm must be suffered by the plaintiff for him to win a cause of action in negligence. Without actual harm, there is no tort. Because of this requirement, nominal damages are not a typical award in negligence cases. Remember that there must be some amount of damage for negligence to be found; that amount is recoverable, even if it is small.

Regarding punitive damages, recall that they are a way to punish a defendant for her wrongful conduct and to deter future similar misconduct. Punitive damages may be awarded in addition to compensatory or nominal damages. However, punitive damages are rarely awarded in regular negligence cases. The unreasonable conduct required to meet the essential elements of this tort may not be heinous enough that an award of damages meant to punish or deter would be appropriate. Normally, to recover punitive damages in the realm of

SIDEBAR

INTERNATIONAL LAW COMPARISON

Punitive damages are common in U.S. tort law, where they are often left to the discretion of a jury (hence tort reform); other countries, however, are much more restrictive in their approaches to damage awards. For instance, throughout Europe, damages are generally limited to compensatory awards. These awards are designed to compensate the plaintiff for the loss suffered and to make him "whole" again, rather than to punish the defendant or deter future misconduct. Many of these countries believe that punishment should be left to the criminal justice system rather than to private lawsuits. Unlike the United States, these countries view punishment as a governmental function, not a private one.

Also, other countries may allow damage awards to be reduced if the awards would cause undue economic hardship to the party who has to pay them. On the other hand, in the United States, companies can be bankrupted by adverse legal judgments, so they normally insure themselves to protect against such risk. In the United States, ability to pay a judgment is not a consideration in determining punitive damage awards.

the tort of negligence, the unreasonable conduct involved must be more than mere negligence; extreme negligence such as gross negligence or willful, wanton, and reckless conduct (defined in Chapter 6) might be necessary.

Pain and suffering damages also may be recovered in negligence cases. Remember that pain and suffering damages include recovery for harms such as actual pain, fear, anxiety, humiliation, depression, loss of companionship, and the like. These forms of emotional harm may be suffered by a plaintiff in a negligence case, depending on its facts and circumstances. They are considered noneconomic damages. Refer to Table 9-1 for a summary of the types and classifications of damages that may be recoverable in negligence cases.

A plaintiff has a duty to mitigate, or lessen, his damages whenever it is reasonable to do so. This mitigation doctrine applies in tort law as well as in other areas of law, such as contract law. Failure to mitigate damages may reduce or limit the plaintiff's recovery. For instance, if a plaintiff is injured by the defendant's negligent conduct, yet refuses reasonable medical care and is harmed further by lack of proper medical treatment, the defendant is responsible only for the original harm. The defendant is not responsible for the further harm caused by the plaintiff's failure to mitigate his damages by obtaining reasonable medical care and treatment. The plaintiff has a duty to mitigate his damages by obtaining reasonable medical care, and is responsible for the consequences for not doing so.

The facts and circumstances surrounding negligence actions lend themselves more to an award of damages. Yet if the case warrants, when remedies at law are inadequate to make the plaintiff whole, a court, in its discretion, may award equitable remedies, such as injunctions.

TABLE 9-1 Types and Classifications of Damages

Type	Description
Compensatory	Money awarded to indemnify, or compensate, an injured person for the harm suffered; typically awarded in negligence cases
Nominal	Small monetary awards when a legal injury is suffered but there is no material injury to be compensated; not typically awarded in negligence cases because an essential element of the tort is that the plaintiff must suffer actual harm or loss
Punitive	Money awarded in addition to actual damages to punish the defendant and deter others; not typically awarded in negligence cases unless gross negligence or willful, wanton, and reckless conduct is involved
Pain and suffering	Money awarded when the plaintiff has suffered emotional harm such as pain, fear, anxiety, humiliation, depression, loss of companionship, and the like
General	Monetary awards that the law presumes will flow from the type of wrong committed, such as medical bills resulting from injuries sustained in an automobile collision caused by the defendant's negligence
Special	Monetary awards particular to the plaintiff's circumstances, such as lost wages, and which must be specially plead and proved by the plaintiff in order to recover
Economic	Monetary awards for economic losses sustained by the plaintiff, such as for medical bills, lost wages, and damage to property
Noneconomic	Monetary awards for pain, suffering, loss of companionship, loss of consortium, and the like; sometimes the law limits recovery for these in torts actions

CHAPTER **SUMMARY**

- There are three defenses that relate specifically to the tort of negligence: contributory negligence, comparative negligence, and assumption of the risk.

- Contributory negligence is a defense asserted by a defendant in a negligence action. The defendant is arguing that the plaintiff's own unreasonable conduct contributed to the injury or harm he suffered. When contributory negligence is established, it acts as a complete bar to the plaintiff's recovery. Contributory negligence doctrine exists in only a few jurisdictions today. Most jurisdictions have adopted some form of comparative negligence.

- The last clear chance doctrine is a legal doctrine that applies only in contributory negligence jurisdictions. This doctrine offsets the effect of contributory negligence. It applies when both the defendant and the plaintiff are negligent, and harm is suffered by the plaintiff, but the defendant had the last clear chance to avoid the incident resulting in the harm. If the defendant had the last clear chance to avoid the incident or accident and did not do so, then the plaintiff may recover in negligence for the defendant's wrongful conduct. The plaintiff's own contributory negligence is no longer a bar to his recovery.

- Comparative negligence is a defense similar to contributory negligence. It is asserted by a defendant in a negligence action. In asserting comparative negligence, the defendant is arguing that the plaintiff's own unreasonable conduct contributed to the injury or harm he suffered. The plaintiff's unreasonable conduct may either bar his recovery or reduce his recovery proportionate to his relative degree of fault.

- Comparative negligence schemes fall within two major categories. Comparative negligence states have adopted, by statute or case law, either a pure comparative negligence or a modified comparative negligence scheme.

- With pure comparative negligence, the plaintiff's own negligent conduct is never a bar to his recovery. Rather, the plaintiff's recovery is reduced so that his damage award reflects only the defendant's respective share of the fault.

- In a modified comparative negligence jurisdiction, relative degrees of fault are determined. The plaintiff may recover for the *pro rata* share of the harm caused by the defendant so long as the defendant was either equally or more at fault than the plaintiff. Whether "equal" or "more" is the threshold depends on the jurisdiction. However, if the plaintiff's fault is equal to or greater than the defendant's, again depending on the jurisdiction, then the plaintiff's conduct acts as a complete bar to recovery.

- Assumption of the risk is a defense that can be asserted by the defendant in a negligence action when the plaintiff knowingly and voluntarily accepts the risk of being harmed by the negligence of the defendant. If that is the case, the defendant is not liable for the injury or harm suffered by the plaintiff.

- Immunity is a defense to legal liability, including tort liability. A person can be immune from civil liability for wrongful conduct, including tort liability. Immunity may be absolute or qualified, depending on whether it can be lost or not. Immunity is derived from three main sources: (1) who a person is, (2) what a person does, or (3) a person's relationship with another person.

- The public policy behind immunity in tort law is that certain persons, including humans and entities, warrant special legal protection in order to fulfill their functions. Further, certain relationships deserve special legal protections in order to preserve them.

- Family immunity is immunity between certain family members. Family immunity is meant to foster better family relationships.

- There are two main types of family immunity: interspousal immunity and parent–child immunity. Interspousal immunity exists between legal spouses and is meant to protect marriage. Parent–child immunity exists between parents and their children.

- Interfamily immunity does not extend to other family members, such as grandparents, aunts, uncles, nieces, nephews, and cousins.

- Very young children, under the law, are considered children of tender years. Only very young children enjoy immunity under the tender years doctrine.

- Governmental immunity is immunity of the government, including federal, state, and local government, from certain lawsuits. In dealing with governmental immunity issues, many legislatures, at the federal, state, and local levels, have enacted statutes stating explicitly when and to what extent the government waives its immunity. Federal government immunity today is governed by the Federal Tort Claims Act; state and local government immunity varies by jurisdiction. Local governments typically distinguish propriety functions from governmental functions, waiving immunity for proprietary functions but maintaining immunity for governmental ones.

- Charitable immunity is immunity granted to charitable organizations, such as schools, churches, animal shelters, and the like, to help them fulfill their missions and objectives. It is restricted, by statute, in many states today.

- Official immunity protects public officials for certain conduct in the course of their official functions. A public official is a person who holds a governmental position, called an office, in which he serves in the public interest.

- Diplomatic immunity protects diplomats in the performance of their official duties. A diplomat is a person who is appointed by the national government to maintain and manage relations with another foreign nation.

- The normal remedy awarded in negligence actions is damages. The types of damages that may be awarded are compensatory, nominal, punitive, and pain and suffering. Normally, to recover punitive damages for the tort of negligence, the unreasonable conduct involved must be more than mere negligence; gross negligence or willful, wanton, and reckless conduct may be necessary.

- A plaintiff has a duty to mitigate, or lessen, his damages whenever it is reasonable to do so. Failure to mitigate damages may reduce or limit the plaintiff's recovery.

- Although equitable remedies may be awarded, in the court's discretion, the facts and circumstances surrounding negligence actions lend themselves mostly to awards of compensatory damages.

CONCEPT REVIEW AND REINFORCEMENT

QUESTIONS FOR **REVIEW**

1. What are the three major defenses specific to the tort of negligence?
2. What is contributory negligence? When and how does it apply?
3. What is the last clear chance doctrine? When and how does it apply?
4. What is comparative negligence? When and how does it apply?
5. What are the two types of comparative negligence schemes?
6. What is assumption of the risk?
7. What is immunity?
8. What is the difference between absolute and qualified immunity?
9. What is the public policy behind immunity from tort law?
10. What is family immunity?
11. What are the two types of family immunity, and to what extent do they apply today?
12. Are children of tender years immune from tort liability?

13. What is governmental, or sovereign, immunity?

14. When is governmental immunity typically waived today?

15. What is charitable immunity, and to what extent does it apply today?

16. What is official immunity and what is diplomatic immunity, and when does each apply?

17. What remedies are available in negligence actions?

DEVELOPING YOUR PARALEGAL SKILLS

CRITICAL THINKING **EXERCISES**

1. In this chapter, we studied the defenses specific to the tort of negligence. Research the laws in your state on each of these defenses and determine in what way(s), if any, they differ from most states' negligence defenses. Does your state recognize contributory negligence or comparative negligence? By statute or case law? If your jurisdiction is a comparative negligence state, what scheme does it follow, pure or modified? Review your research results with the class.

2. Tamara purchases a certain over-the-counter hair-removal product from her local pharmacy. The package, the product, and an insert in the packaging all contain labeling warnings stating that the product may cause irritation on some people. The labels warn that users should first test their skin reaction by using the product on a small area. Tamara reads the warning but does not expect to experience any problems. She uses the product to remove the hair on her legs and underarms. Unfortunately, Tamara experiences an allergic reaction to certain chemicals in the product. She obtains medical treatment to mitigate her damages.

   Will Tamara succeed in a lawsuit alleging that the company making the product was negligent? Why or why not?

3. a. Jose is riding his bicycle down a country road, training for an upcoming race. He has been riding for about seven hours, with about two more to go before stopping for the day. Jose's back feels achy and stiff. Taking his hands off the handle bars, Jose sits up, puts his hands behind the small of his back, and stretches. While Jose is riding no-handed, Steve is driving down the same road on his way home from work. Steve is tired after a long and draining day at the office, and he is exceeding the speed limit and listening to loud music. Steve decides to change the CD he is listening to, so he reaches behind his seat to grab his CD case. He cannot feel the CD case, however, so he looks behind the seat and finds it. Unfortunately, while Steve is looking backwards, his car veers toward the road's shoulder.

   Jose, no-handed, cannot move quickly enough to get out of the way. The two collide, Jose is injured, and his bike is ruined. Jose sues Steve for negligence, asking for recovery of $75,000 in compensatory damages for his injuries and damage to his racing bike.

   In a contributory negligence jurisdiction, will Jose recover from Steve for negligence?

   b. What if Steve, at the last minute, by honking his horn to warn Jose, and slowing down his vehicle by taking his foot off the accelerator, could have avoided the collision?

   In a contributory negligence jurisdiction, will Jose recover from Steve for negligence?

   c. Now assume that you are in a pure comparative negligence jurisdiction. The jury determines that Jose is 30 percent at fault in the incident, and Steve is 70 percent at fault.

   Can Jose recover from Steve for the tort of negligence? If so, how much?

   d. Now assume that you are in a modified comparative negligence jurisdiction and the jury determines that Jose is 60 percent at fault, and Steve is 40 percent at fault.

   Can Jose recover from Steve for the tort of negligence? If so, how much?

4. In this chapter, we examined various types of immunity and how such immunity applies as a defense to tort actions. Research the laws in your state (and city/county in the case of governmental immunity) to see to what extent your jurisdiction recognizes family, governmental, charitable, and official immunity. Does your jurisdiction grant immunity to children of tender years? If so, what is the age cutoff for this application of immunity? Because of the degree of variation in the law on immunities, this can be performed as a group project. Neighboring jurisdictions' laws on the various immunities can also be compared, as a group project, with different groups researching different states' laws. Discuss your research results in class.

5. Rick and Bernadette are married. Kayla is their 6-year-old daughter. One evening, while she is making dinner, Bernadette accidentally knocks a pot of boiling water off the stove because she is watching television as she cooks and is not really paying attention to what she is doing. Boiling water splashes on her husband and daughter, burning them both.

   a. *Can Rick successfully sue Bernadette, in tort, for the injuries he sustained? Why or why not?*

   b. *Can Kayla successfully sue her mother, in tort, for the injuries she sustained? Why or why not?*

6. Heather is driving to work when her car is struck by a police cruiser that is speeding to an accident scene. The police cruiser is owned by the city of Orlando, and its driver is an officer of the Orlando police department.

   a. *Can Heather successfully sue the city of Orlando for her injuries? Why or why not?*

   b. *Can Heather successfully sue the police officer who caused the collision? Why or why not?*

7. a. Mayor Dixon, the mayor of a major metropolitan city in the United States, is accused of misdeeds in inappropriately awarding city contracts for personal gain. As a result of the investigation into the mayor's misdeeds, the city is sued, in tort, for the misuse and wrongful conversion of city funds arising out of the mayor's wrongful actions.

      Can the city successfully defend this suit based on the doctrine of governmental immunity? Why or why not? On what might this success depend?

   b. Now assume that Mayor Dixon is sued, personally, for her wrongful conduct in misusing her position for personal financial gain.

      Can Mayor Dixon successfully defend this suit based on the doctrine of public official immunity? Why or why not?

ASSIGNMENTS AND PRACTICAL **APPLICATIONS**

1. As a group exercise, divide into groups and role-play contributory negligence, the last clear chance doctrine, comparative negligence and assumption of risk as defenses, and doctrines to defenses, to negligence. Students should make up their own hypothetical negligence situations for this exercise.

2. Read and brief *Butterfield v. Forrester,* 103 Eng. Rep 926 (1809) for a fun, old case involving contributory negligence and a transportation (horseback) injury.

3. Maryland is one of only a handful of jurisdictions that still recognize contributory negligence. See *Stanley Martin Co., Inc. v. Universal Forest Products Schoffner, LLC,* 396 F.Supp. 606 (D. Md. 2005) on this point.

4. Most jurisdictions are comparative negligence jurisdictions. Should the plaintiff's failure to use a seat belt be considered in determining the amount of fault to be allocated to her in a comparative negligence jurisdiction, when failure to wear a seat belt does not contribute to the cause of the accident but only to the extent of the injuries sustained? Read and brief *Foley v. City of W. Allis,* 335 N.W.2d 824 (Wis. 1983) for the Supreme Court of Wisconsin's answer to that question.

5. A high school teacher was injured during a fund-raising donkey basketball game when the donkey she was riding put its head down and she fell off and permanently injured her left arm. She sued the board of education and the Buckeye Donkey Ball Company, the company that supplied the donkeys, for negligence. Did the teacher assume the risk of this harm? Read and brief *Arbegast v. Board of Educ. of S. New Berlin Cent. Sch.,* 480 N.E.2d 365 (N.Y. 1985).

6. Research interspousal immunity in your jurisdiction. Prepare a short PowerPoint presentation identifying the types of torts that may be brought against a spouse, and what types are disallowed because immunity applies.

7. Regarding the abrogation of interspousal immunity in Utah, read and brief *Ellis v. Estate of Ellis,* 169 P.3d 441 (Utah 2007).

8. For a case that recognized parent–child immunity and barred an unemancipated minor from suing her mother for injuries caused by the mother's negligence, read and brief *Dubay v. Irish,* 542 A.2d 711 (Conn. 1988).

9. Does parent–child immunity extend to stepparents? Read and brief *Zellmer v. Zellmer,* 188 P.3d 497 (Wash. 2008) on this issue.

10. For a case that applies Connecticut General Statutes Annotated § 22-357 on the issue of immunity in tort for minors, read and brief *Gangemi v. Beardsworth,* 1995 WL 781424 (Conn. Super. Ct. 1995) (this is an unpublished opinion available on Westlaw). In determining the negligence of a minor, the law applies to the child a standard of conduct that varies according to his age, judgment, and experience but does not grant him complete immunity from liability for his torts, including negligence [see *Overlock v. Ruedemann,* 165 A.2d 335 (Conn. 1960)].

11. Research the Federal Tort Claims Act. In a short PowerPoint presentation, summarize when, and to what extent, the U.S. government waives its governmental immunity.

12. Charitable immunity has been abolished or curtailed in many states. Research whether, and to what extent, charitable immunity exists in your state. Summarize your research results in a PowerPoint presentation to present to your class.

13. The Supreme Court of Arkansas has ruled that it is for the legislature, not the courts, to abolish charitable immunity in that state. Read and brief *Scamardo v. Sparks Reg'l Med. Ctr.,* 289 S.W.3d 903 (Ark. 2008).

14. The President of the United States enjoys absolute immunity from legal liability predicated on his official acts as President, including those within the "outer perimeter" of his duties as President. Read and brief *Nixon v. Fitzgerald,* 457 U.S. 731 (1982). However, absolute immunity does not extend indiscriminately to the President's personal aides [see *Harlow v. Fitzgerald,* 457 U.S. 800 (1982)] or cabinet members [see *Mitchell v. Forsyth,* 472 U.S. 511 (1985)]. Nor, under federal law, does it extend to the highest executive officials in the state governments [see *Scheuer v. Rhodes,* 416 U.S. 232 (1974)].

15. For an interesting case involving diplomatic immunity and vicarious liability, read and brief *Tikhonova v. Ford Motor Co.,* 830 N.E.2d 1127 (N.Y. 2005), in which a passenger was injured in an automobile collision while riding in a vehicle driven by a Russian diplomat.

16. Punitive damage awards and the *Exxon Valdez:* In 1989, the oil tanker *Exxon Valdez* ran aground on a reef in Prince William Sound, off the coast of Alaska. As a result, it spilled 11 million gallons of crude oil into the Sound and devastated the local environment, becoming the worst oil disaster to date in U.S. history. In 1994, in the District Court in Alaska, a jury awarded fishermen and local business owners $287 million in actual damages and $5 billion in punitive damages. Exxon vowed to appeal all the way to the U.S. Supreme Court, and did. Its first appeal was to the 9th Circuit Court of Appeals in 2001, where the court found the $5 billion punitive damage award excessive. After that appeal, Exxon continued to appeal the punitive damage award, with it being reduced time and time again by the U.S. Supreme Court. It took nearly two decades for the case to be finally resolved in 2008, and many of the claimants died prior to final resolution. To read and brief that final Supreme Court case, see *Exxon Shipping Co. v. Baker,* 128 S. Ct. 2605 (2008). For class discussion, consider the impact of this long-appealed punitive damage award on both the plaintiffs and the defendant in this case.

17. As a group exercise, determine all the damages the students would suffer and to which they would be entitled to recover if they were seriously injured in a car collision caused by another's negligence. List the relevant types of damages.

NEGOTIATION AND SETTLEMENT EXERCISE

THIS EXERCISE SHOULD BE DONE IN **PAIRS**.

Facts: The defendant is a company that owns and operates a chain of grocery stores. The defendant has established policies to clean up spills that occur on the premises of the stores in order to safeguard its customers and employees. Among these policies is a requirement that, upon notification that there has been a spill in a store, employees will promptly set up an orange cone to warn passersby of the spill, and thoroughly clean up the spill as soon as possible.

A customer, while removing a jar of maraschino cherries from the shelf, inadvertently dislodges the display, causing several jars to fall to the floor and break. The customer scoots quickly away, embarrassed. Another customer who comes down the aisle a few minutes later, upon seeing the spill, reports it to customer service. An employee responds to customer service's request to clean the spill, and proceeds to the maraschino cherry aisle to check it out and see what cleaning supplies he will need, bringing an orange cone with him and placing it at the scene of the spill.

While the employee is off collecting the cleaning supplies, another store customer walks down the aisle toward the spill. This customer is throwing his child's birthday party that weekend and is in the store to pick up party supplies, including ice cream sundae fixings. He needs hot fudge, butterscotch sauce, caramel sauce, and maraschino cherries from this aisle, all located in the same section of shelves. The customer, in selecting these items, must walk on the spill, and does. Unfortunately, the customer slips on the wet floor and broken glass and falls to the floor, where he is cut by some of the broken glass, requiring many stitches. He also suffers a broken hip as a result of the fall.

The customer subsequently files a personal injury tort action against the defendant, alleging negligence. Recovery is sought in the amount of $75,000 in damages. This is a comparative negligence jurisdiction.

Tasks: Neither party wants to go to trial. The parties hire you to represent them. Your job is to settle this case. Each student represents one of the parties. First, you must negotiate a settlement of all issues in this dispute. Once you have reached a settlement, draft a settlement agreement to reflect your resolution. (Remember that if one party pays money to the other, the party paying the money is going to want a release.)

TECHNOLOGY RESOURCES AND INTERNET **EXERCISES**

To review the various defenses to the tort of negligence, visit *www.findlaw.com* and search for negligence defenses.

Using the Internet, track the U.S. Supreme Court appeals of the *Exxon Valdez* case on the issue of excessiveness of punitive damage awards. Decisions were rendered from 2002 through final resolution in the summer of 2008.

For a review of interspousal tort immunity under Connecticut law, see *http://www.jud.ct.gov/lawlib/Notebooks /Pathfinders/SpousalImmunity/spousal.pdf*.

For a comprehensive look at torts committed by minors in the state of Connecticut, including parental liability for torts committed by minor children, see *www.jud.ct.gov /LawLib/Notebooks/Pathfinders/TortsofMinors.htm*.

For the U.S. Justice Department's explanation of the types of cases it litigates under the Federal Tort Claims Act, see *www.usdoj.gov/civil/FTCA.htm*.

Using the Internet, locate your state's tort claims act. Determine when, and to what extent, your state government waives governmental immunity for torts. Next, determine whether the local government (city, county, municipality, etc.) where you live is governed by a local tort claims act. If so, under that act, determine when, and to what extent, your local government waives governmental immunity for torts. Discuss your research results in class.

Search the Internet for material on former Vice President Richard Cheney's controversial assertion of public official immunity from liability arising out of his role in the disclosure to reporters about the identity of undercover CIA Officer Valerie Plame and her husband, former Ambassador Joseph C. Wilson.

The Volunteer Protection Act of 1997 provides immunity for volunteers of nonprofit, charitable organizations from tort claims that might be filed against them arising out of their performance of volunteer work. For a discussion of this federal act and charitable immunity, see *www.texmed .org/Template.aspx?id=2107*.

ETHICAL **APPLICATIONS**

1. Miranda is a paralegal working for the law firm of Kirk, Melon and Rogers, P.A. The firm is representing Clint Blackstone in a personal injury action he brought against a taxi company for injuries sustained in a car collision. Clint has been out of work, on disability, since the accident, as a result of his severe back injuries. One pretty summer day a week before trial of Clint's case is set to begin, while Miranda is enjoying a picnic at the local lake with her husband, she sees Clint waterskiing on the lake. The firm has worked for almost two years on this case, and it expects to earn a large contingency fee as a result of it.

    a. *What are Miranda's ethical responsibilities upon learning that Clint is faking his injuries? Does the legal ethics duty of confidentiality prevent Miranda from disclosing this information? If so, to whom does it prevent disclosure? Can Miranda tell her supervising lawyer? Do the confidentiality rules, or other legal ethics*

    rules, compel Miranda to disclose this information? If so, to whom? What should Miranda do?

    b. *Given that negligence is, by far, the largest category of tort litigation, can someone other than a lawyer represent clients in court in negligence actions? For instance, can a paralegal represent a client in court during negligence litigation? If not, what can a paralegal or other nonlawyer do to assist the lawyer with negligence litigation?*

2. Mayor Dixon, the mayor of a major metropolitan city in the United States, is accused of misdeeds in inappropriately awarding city contracts for personal gain. As a result of the investigation into the mayor's misdeeds, the city is sued, in tort, for the misuse and wrongful conversion of city funds arising out of the mayor's wrongful actions.

    You are the city solicitor, the head lawyer for the city. You are responsible for defending against the legal action on behalf of the city. Mayor Dixon, who has worked with you for years and knows your great competence as a litigator, asks if you will represent her in the legal action that has also been filed against her. Should you accept the representation of Mayor Dixon, in addition to your representation of the city, as the matters are related and it may be efficient for you to handle them both? Does this potential dual representation present any legal ethics issue(s)? Identify any issue you see, and if you think it can be overcome. If so, is this dual representation a good idea?

VIDEO **CASE STUDY**

Court Hearing to Decide Who Represents a Minor: The Court's Duty to Protect the Child

Synopsis: The parents of a child injured in a school bus accident are in the process of divorcing and are battling over child custody and their opposing views of medical treatment for the injured child. The father wishes the child to receive traditional, prompt medical treatment, but the mother opposes traditional medical treatment because of her religious views. The court is now asked to decide what is in the child's best interest.

Questions

1. Do parents have the right to determine what type of medical treatment their child will receive?

2. What is the court's role in overseeing this, and should the child have her own attorney representing her interests, which may be different from those of either parent?

3. Must the court permit the practice of nontraditional religious beliefs such as the mother in this case holds?

4. How would a parent's decision to forego traditional medical treatment for a child affect a damage award in a tort suit if such traditional medical treatment could have healed the child?

5. What is mitigation of damages, and how would mitigation apply in this situation?

chapter 10

INTRODUCTION TO STRICT LIABILITY: HARM CAUSED BY ANIMALS AND OTHER ABNORMALLY DANGEROUS CONDITIONS OR ACTIVITIES

This chapter introduces strict liability tort theory and two of its three major applications, to harm caused by animals and to harm caused by other abnormally dangerous conditions or activities. Before studying the application of strict liability theory, we must understand what strict liability means in tort law.

Definition of Strict Liability

Strict liability is one of the three major classifications of torts, besides intentional torts and negligence, as discussed in Chapter 1. It is also called "absolute liability" or "liability without fault." Strict liability is distinguished from the other classifications of torts in its approach to the concept of fault.

Strict liability is tort liability imposed regardless of the fault or blameworthiness of the defendant. Remember, with regard to intentional torts, the defendant must *intend* the act that causes the injury. That is why they are "intentional" torts. Similarly, for the tort of negligence, the defendant must fail to exercise reasonable care either by

LEARNING OBJECTIVES

10.1 Define strict liability.

10.2 List and discuss the situations in which strict liability applies.

10.3 Explain strict liability as applied to harm caused by animals.

10.4 Explain strict liability as applied to harm caused by abnormally dangerous conditions or activities.

Strict liability
Tort liability imposed regardless of fault or blameworthiness of the defendant; also called absolute liability or liability without fault.

SIDEBAR

CAVEAT

Persons who permit abnormally dangerous conditions to exist, or who engage in abnormally dangerous activities, do so at their own peril; under strict liability theory, they are responsible for any harm these conditions or activities may cause to others.

act or by omission. Thus, fault in the form of unreasonable conduct is required for the tort of negligence. Under strict liability theory, fault, or lack of fault, of the defendant is irrelevant in determining whether legal liability is imposed for harm he causes. It is truly liability without regard to fault or blameworthiness.

The social policy behind strict liability is that persons who allow certain dangerous conditions to exist, or who engage in certain dangerous kinds of activities, should be responsible for any harm that is caused by those conditions or activities. Simply because of the risky nature of these conditions or activities, the persons responsible for them should bear the burden of the costs of those injuries. In effect, persons who permit the conditions to exist or who undertake the activities become insurers against harm. In being so responsible, such persons are liable for the injuries or damage caused by these dangerous conditions or activities, whether they acted intentionally, negligently, or even carefully in allowing the conditions to exist or in conducting the activities. In other words, they allow these conditions to exist or engage in these activities at their peril, knowing that they are assuming responsibility for any harm they may cause others. That they acted with utmost care in allowing the conditions to exist or in conducting the activities is irrelevant.

Three main categories of harm can lead to strict liability in tort. In other words, strict liability applies in the three situations discussed below.

Applying Strict Liability Theory

Strict liability applies in three types of situations: harm caused by animals, harm caused by abnormally dangerous conditions or activities, and harm caused by defective products (see Table 10-1). The first two types of strict liability application are discussed in this chapter; the last type, products liability, is discussed in the next chapter.

TABLE 10-1 Three Applications of Strict Liability

Applies to	Covers
Animals	Harm caused by wild animals, or domesticated animals with known dangerous propensities
Abnormally dangerous conditions or activities	Harm caused by allowing abnormally dangerous conditions to exist or by conducting abnormally dangerous activities
Products liability	Harm caused by defective products

Strict liability cases are often asserted against corporate defendants, such as against manufacturers in products liability cases involving defective products, or manufacturers of poisons, the manufacturing of which is an abnormally dangerous activity, in industrial situations. Strict liability exists in these cases to encourage defendants engaged in strict liability activities, such as transporting hazardous materials, to exercise the utmost care in what they do, as they become virtual guarantors of the cost of any harms caused by their activities. In implementing strict liability theory, courts must balance the need to protect people from harm against the need to allow the existence of dangerous conditions or the carrying out of dangerous activities that are necessary and unavoidable in society, such as dumping toxic waste. In essence, strict liability theory allows certain dangerous conditions to exist and certain dangerous activities to be conducted when their social utility and value to the community outweigh the risk of preventing harm, so long as those responsible for the dangerous conditions or activities pay for any harm that results.

The first application of strict liability theory we will examine is harm caused by animals. One of the courts' early applications of strict liability theory involved the care and maintenance of animals.

Application to Harm Caused by Animals

When a person's animal injures another person, that animal's owner or caretaker may be held liable, in tort, for those injuries. Liability, whether under the strict liability theory or another tort theory, such as negligence, is imposed not only on the owner of the animal but on anyone who keeps, cares for, possesses, or harbors it (see the *Noble* Case on Point).

Several tort theories may apply to harm caused by animals, depending on the facts and circumstances. Often, however, tort claims involving injuries caused by animals are brought under the strict liability theory. In these cases, the owner or caretaker of the animal can be held strictly liable for any harm caused by the animal. These cases are easier for plaintiffs to prove, because no fault on behalf of the tortfeasor, in the form of "intent" or "unreasonableness," must be established under strict liability theory.

SIDEBAR

THE MATTER OF TRAVIS THE CHIMPANZEE

In February 2009, a pet and television commercial star chimp named Travis surprisingly mauled the friend of its owner, tearing off her face, among other serious injuries, and leaving her in critical condition and blind in both eyes. The local prosecutor considered, but declined, to file criminal charges against Travis's owner. Under strict liability theory, could the owner be held liable for the harm Travis caused her friend? Certainly!

CASE on Point

Noble v. Yorke, 490 So.2d 29 (Fla. 1986)

In this case, the Supreme Court of Florida held that a victim of a dog bite could sue a property owner who cares for but does not own the offending dog under common law tort theory.

SIDEBAR

"ANIMAL HARM" THEORIES

Several tort theories may apply to situations in which persons are hurt by other persons' animals. However, strict liability theory is often the one chosen for these suits, because it is easier for plaintiffs to establish a *prima facie* case.

Other legal theories, besides strict liability, may be used to bring a tort action against an animal owner or caretaker for harm caused by the animal. We have already studied two of them, namely, negligence and the intentional tort of battery. For example, a dog owner who fails to use reasonable care in controlling his dog in a public park might be held liable, in negligence, for his unreasonable actions that cause injury to another. In such a case, the burden is on the plaintiff to establish the four essential elements of the tort of negligence, and the dog owner, in defending the action, may assert any applicable defense to negligence, including the plaintiff's contributory negligence, such as that the plaintiff incited the dog's aggression by taunting him.

What if the dog is a guard dog, and, feeling threatened, the dog's owner "sics" the dog on an apparent attacker, causing him injury? The injured person might bring suit under an intentional tort theory, such as battery, considering that the dog's owner intended to cause the dog to attack the plaintiff. In such a case, the plaintiff would have to establish the essential elements of that intentional tort, including the "intent" requirement. The dog owner, in defending the battery claim, might assert the privilege of self-defense if he could show that he was being threatened at the time.

Because the essential elements of these other tort theories require that the plaintiff prove some sort of "fault" on the defendant's part, it is oftentimes easier for plaintiffs to establish strict liability claims, for which they need only demonstrate that the animal caused them harm. Fault on the defendant's part is entirely irrelevant under strict liability theory. In these cases, from early common law to the present, the owner or caretaker of the animal can be held strictly liable for any harm caused by the animal. However, an important distinction is made under the law in this area as to whether the animal is "wild" or "domestic."

WILD ANIMALS

Wild animal
An animal that is not domesticated and is a kind of animal that is wild in its natural state.

An animal is considered a **wild animal** if it has not been domesticated and if it is a kind of animal that is wild in its natural state. "Wild," for these purposes, means a type of animal that is normally wild in nature, but the specific animal is kept by a person, usually as an exotic pet. For examples, lions, tigers, bears, monkeys, and snakes, although they may be kept by people as pets, are wild in nature, and are considered wild for strict tort liability purposes.

What is the effect of thoroughly training a wild animal? Does that mean it is no longer "wild" for strict liability purposes? The answer is "no." Even if the owner or caretaker trains the animal as thoroughly as possible, the animal still falls under the "wild" animal rule. What is the rule for wild animals, then?

The rule for wild animals is that their owners and/or caretakers are strictly liable for any harm the animals cause to others. Period. It does not matter how well the animal is trained, whether the animal had ever exhibited a dangerous propensity, or how much care the owner or caretaker took in trying to prevent harm to others. Therefore, anyone who owns or keeps a wild animal is strictly liable for any harm the animal causes to others. The owner or caretaker bears the risk.

Consider the following examples. Kimberly keeps a pet tiger. It is very well trained and is often used in public exhibitions and in movies and television shows. One day, Kimberly's friend brings her daughter over to see the tiger. While Kimberly is making lunch and the child's mother is not supervising her, the child reaches her hand into the tiger's cage and is bitten by the tiger. Is Kimberly strictly liable for that injury? Yes. What if the child is bitten while Kimberly is holding the tiger, allowing the child to pet it? Kimberly is still strictly liable. What if Kimberly is holding the tiger, instructing the child on how to pet the tiger, and the child purposefully pulls the tiger's whiskers, triggering an attack? Is Kimberly strictly liable for that harm? Yes, unless a defense to strict liability applies, such as the comparative negligence of the plaintiff (defenses to strict liability are discussed in Chapter 12). It is questionable whether a child would be deemed negligent via these actions, but perhaps if the child were an older one, such as an older teen, that defense might apply. As these examples illustrate, an owner or caretaker of a wild animal keeps it at his peril and is responsible for harm that animal causes to others.

The courts' reasoning behind this rule is that these wild animals are inherently dangerous, and keeping them is an inherently dangerous activity. These

> **Key Point**
>
> **Wild Animal Rule**
> Owners and caretakers of wild animals are strictly liable for any harm these animals cause to others.

CASE on Point

Johnson v. Swain, 787 S.W.2d 36 (Tex. 1989)

In this case, Swain was seriously injured when he was gored by a bull elephant owned by Johnson. Swain sued Johnson under both negligence and strict liability theory.

The Supreme Court of Texas acknowledged the legal principle "that strict liability for damages attaches to injuries caused by vicious animals" and that the animal's owner could be held strictly liable for possession of a wild animal if such possession caused the injury. Interestingly, the court found the element of causation lacking in the plaintiff's case because of a stipulation entered into between the parties and the jury finding that the plaintiff's negligence was the sole cause of this injury.

animals need particular care and experienced handlers; no matter how well trained and used to humans the animals may be, they pose a more significant threat of injury to people than do domesticated animals, such as dogs and ponies.

Is a deer a wild animal? What about a ferret? Are bees in a beehive wild animals? What about a camel, which is domestic in virtually all places where it is found, but is not native to the United States? It is not always clear whether a particular animal is wild or domesticated. The "wild" versus "domestic" animal distinction has led to some interesting classification problems for the courts, which can affect how the strict liability rule is applied. See the exercises at the end of the chapter for cases that illustrate this classification issue.

DOMESTIC ANIMALS

Domestic or **domesticated animals** are those animals that are domesticated and habituated to live with and among humans, and their normal populations are pets. For example, dogs, cats, and horses are domesticated animals, whose populations in the United States are mostly pets. Although there are some wild horses, dogs, and cats in the United States, these kinds of animals typically are bred and kept by humans.

The common law strict liability rule for domesticated animals is slightly different than that for wild animals. An owner or caretaker of a domestic animal may be held strictly liable for any harm the animal causes to others if (1) the owner or caretaker had *reason to know* the animal had a specific propensity to cause harm and (2) the harm caused by the animal was due to that specific propensity.

For example, if Devlin knows his dog loves to chase bicyclists and snap at their heels, and one day the dog succeeds in catching up to and biting a cyclist, Devlin can be held strictly liable for that harm. Devlin knew of the dog's dangerous propensity to chase and threaten cyclists, and the harm was caused by that propensity. However, what if the dog jumps on a visiting neighbor's child, knocking her over and causing her harm? Is Devlin strictly liable for that harm? No, not under strict liability theory, because the harm that resulted was not due to the dog's dangerous propensity to chase cyclists.

Remember that if the owner or caretaker of the domesticated animal does not know of the animal's dangerous propensity, he cannot be held strictly liable for harm caused to others by the animal. However, the plaintiff may be able to recover under another tort theory for his injuries, such as negligence, if he can establish a *prima facie* case.

In summary, an owner or caretaker of a domesticated animal must know or have reason to know of the dangerous propensity of the animal in order to be held strictly liable for harm caused by it. In other words, the owner or caretaker must, or should, know that the animal is dangerous. There is quite an interesting body of case law, including creative arguments by plaintiffs' counsel, on the issue of whether an animal owner knew or should have known of an animal's propensity to be dangerous or vicious. See the materials at the end of this chapter for a selection of some of these cases.

Domestic animal
An animal that is habituated to live with and among humans, and its normal population is pets; also called a domesticated animal.

Key Point

Domesticated Animal Rule
Owners and caretakers of domestic animals may be held strictly liable for any harm to others caused by the animals if they had reason to know of the animals' specific propensity to cause harm, and the harm suffered was due to that propensity.

What about the old axiom that "every dog is entitled to one free bite"? Does this common law rule, then, mean every dog is "entitled to one free bite"? No. The "one free bite" rule is more myth than law. Under the common law today, every dog is *not* entitled to one free bite, or every dog owner, for one free bite by his dog. If a dog has bitten a person before, then the owner or caretaker obviously knows of its propensity to bite. But what if the dog has never bitten a person before? Yet the dog does snap and snarl, threateningly, at visitors to the home. Although the dog has never before bitten anyone, that it gets aggressive and threatens humans is enough to put the dog owner or caretaker on notice of the dog's dangerous propensities. So if, one day, the dog decides to bite a visitor, the owner was aware of that dangerous propensity in his dog, and the harm was caused by that propensity, triggering strict liability. An owner or caretaker of a domesticated animal is on notice of its dangerous propensity if the animal has acted aggressively toward others in the past.

Note, however, that many jurisdictions have changed the common law regarding liability for dog bites by enacting statutes in this area. These statutes change the common law in different ways. They may do away with the requirement that the plaintiff prove *scienter*, which means "knowing"; in other words, the plaintiff is not required to show that the owner knew or had reason to know of the animal's dangerous propensity. Such statutes treat domesticated animals the same as wild ones. They may set forth defenses, such as that the plaintiff was a trespasser, or the defendant had posted a warning sign to "beware of the dog."

CASE on Point

Matthews v. Amberwood Assoc. Ltd. P'ship, Inc., 719 A.2d 119 (Md. 1998)

Recall the pitbull case in the materials at the end of Chapter 6. In that case, a pitbull named Rampage fatally mauled a young boy when the boy's mother and her friend, the dog's caretaker, were not supervising the children (testimony at trial was conflicting as to whether the adults were even present in the apartment at the time of the mauling). Testimony was clear that, although the dog was usually muzzled and restrained, at the time of the incident, he was neither.

The victim's mother and father sued the landlord, under a "no pets clause" in the friend's lease, for the mauling death of the young child. The landlord was found liable for the child's wrongful death upon a finding by the court that the landlord owed a duty of care to the parents and child, and that the duty was breached. Why did the parents choose to sue the landlord rather than Rampage's caretaker (recall that Rampage's owner was incarcerated at the time of the incident, and the dog was being kept by the owner's girlfriend)? Clearly, this case demonstrates an appropriate situation for the application of strict liability theory against a caretaker for harm caused by a domesticated animal with a known propensity to attack people. However, the landlord, being the "deep pocket," was the party sued for this tragic occurrence.

Who was in the best position to protect the child from this harm? Was it the person held liable for it, namely, the landlord? Or was it the child's mother and/or the dog's caretaker?

SIDEBAR

"BAD DOG"

The state of Florida enacted a dog bite statute that supersedes the common law and provides an exclusive remedy in dog bite actions. The statute imposes absolute liability on the owner of a dog for any injury caused by the dog regardless of scienter, meaning intent.[1] Further, it provides absolute defenses to dog owners when either the victim provokes the dog or the dog owner displays an easily readable sign warning that a "Bad Dog" is on the premises.[2] The purpose of this last defense is to protect dog owners who give genuine and bona-fide notice to others in warning about the dog's presence. Florida, in applying this statute, requires that the statutory requirements for this defense be strictly met. In the following *Noble* Case on Point, already studied on the issue of whether a nonowner can be sued for dog bites under the common law, the defense was not met because genuine, bona-fide notice was not given.

CASE on Point

Noble v. Yorke, 490 So.2d 29 (Fla. 1986)

In this case, already discussed earlier in this chapter, the Supreme Court of Florida found that although the Nobles prominently posted a "Bad Dog" sign, they directed the Yorkes, business invitees to the premises, to ignore it and enter the property, saying that the dog would be secured. Unfortunately, when the Yorkes arrived at the Nobles' property, the dog was not secured, and Mrs. Yorke's finger was bitten by the dog. The court ruled that tort immunity under the "Bad Dog" statute did "not extend to a dog owner who affirmatively directs a business invitee to ignore the 'Bad Dog' sign displayed on the premises." In other words, the Nobles' actions, in directing the Yorkes to ignore the "Bad Dog" sign, did not give the required genuine, bona-fide notice of warning required by the statute for tort immunity to apply.

They may require leash or muzzle use, as well. Some states have adopted rules that establish a presumption of dangerousness for certain dog breeds, such as pitbulls. What pet owners should know in keeping their animals, whether tigers or tabby cats, is that they may be strictly liable for harm caused by the animals, and so they should always take care to prevent these occurrences.

TRESPASSING PEOPLE RULE

Is a distinction made when the person who is injured by the animal is a trespasser on the property of the animal owner or caretaker, or if he is invited or otherwise permitted to be there? In other words, what is an animal owner or caretaker's liability to third parties who come onto the owner or caretaker's premises and are then injured by an animal on the premises? That depends on

SIDEBAR

STATUS OF PERSONS ENTERING THE LAND OF ANOTHER

Recall from the discussion of negligence in Chapter 6 with regard to the duty of care:

A *trespasser* is a person who intrudes on the land of another without permission or privilege. Remember the discussion of the intentional tort of trespass to land (in Chapter 4) and the discussion of the duty of care owed to trespassers.

A *licensee* is a person who enters the land of another, with permission, for his own purposes or benefits. A social guest, such as a dinner party guest, is an example.

An *invitee* is a person who enters the land of another, with permission, for the benefit of the landholder or for their mutual benefit, or for the purposes for which the owner or occupier holds the property open to the public. A customer in a retail store and a client in a business office are two examples.

whether the person coming onto the owner or caretaker's property is a licensee, an invitee, or a trespasser. Here is the distinction.

Strict liability applies to injuries to both licensees and invitees, both of whom come onto the premises of another with permission. However, strict liability does not apply to trespassers. Rather, trespassers must sue under negligence theory. Accordingly, they must establish a *prima facie* case of negligence and must be able to overcome any asserted defenses to negligence.

Further, under negligence theory, a possessor of land does not owe a duty of care to trespassers to protect them from harm from either a wild animal or a dangerous domestic animal unless they are known trespassers or another trespass exception applies (as discussed in Chapter 6), and even then, the duty is merely to warn of known dangers—such as by posting a sign warning of the presence of guard dogs.

TRESPASSING ANIMALS RULE

What about trespassing animals that cause harm to the property of others? For centuries, courts have recognized the strict liability of owners or caretakers for harm caused by animals who trespass on the land of others. The types of animals for which such liability is typically extended under the common law are livestock and other types of barnyard animals, including cattle, horses, hogs, goats, sheep, turkeys, chickens, and the like. Strict liability is not normally extended by courts to trespassing animals that are not categorized as livestock or other barnyard animals, such as dogs and cats.

Today, some states continue to apply the common law rule of strict liability for trespassing animals, particularly livestock. This is particularly true in the eastern part of the United States. See the case entitled *King v. Blue Mountain*

CASE on Point

Adams Bros. v. Clark, 224 S.W. 1046 (Ky. Ct. App. 1920)

In this case, Mrs. Clark's 250 to 400 chickens trespassed on the unfenced land of the Adams Bros., eating and destroying the Adams Bros.' grain and garden vegetables. The Court of Appeals of Kentucky found this chicken owner liable for the harm caused by her trespassing chickens.

Forest Ass'n in the exercises at the end of the chapter for an illustration. However, many jurisdictions have enacted statutes or local ordinances to alter the common law rule. Some states, particularly states out West, where livestock more often roam freely, permit livestock to roam at large. Other jurisdictions have adopted either "fencing in" or "fencing out" statutes or ordinances, under which liability is affected by whether a landowner "fenced out" others' animals or "fenced in" his own. Still other jurisdictions have enacted laws that provide for liability only if fault is established. The Missouri Statute on Point is an example of a statute that modifies the common law regarding certain types of trespassing livestock.

On April 26, 2005, in Baltimore, Maryland, a herd of beef bison escaped from their pasture and roamed neighboring properties just outside the Baltimore beltway (and very near the university campus of this author!). Fortunately, no person was injured or property was damaged, and much good humor came of this unusual "beef-alo" escape, in which the animals were later corralled on a tennis court. However, the bison owner could have been held strictly liable for any harm caused by the escaped livestock, had such occurred, under the common law.[3]

Keeping wild animals, or keeping domesticated animals with known propensities to cause harm, is considered a kind of abnormally dangerous condition or activity, to which strict liability theory applies. How does strict liability theory apply to other types of abnormally dangerous conditions or activities?

STATUTE on Point

Mo. Rev. Stat. § 272.030 (2009)

A Missouri statute governs liability of owners for damages caused by their livestock. The statute covers horses, cattle, and other stock that go through or over a fence, resulting in access to or trespass on the property of another and causing damage as a result. Such liability can result in making reparation for damages to the injured party (for the first offense) and paying damages as well as compensation for taking up and caring for the trespassing animals (for subsequent offenses).

SIDEBAR

RESTATEMENT (SECOND) OF TORTS SECTION 504 LIVESTOCK RULE

With some exceptions, noted below, a person who possesses livestock that intrude on the land of another may be liable for the intrusion even if the person exercised the utmost care to prevent the intrusion. The possessor of the livestock is liable for any harm caused to the land, or to the land's possessor or a member of his household, or to their chattels, but only so long as the harm is a reasonably expected result of the intrusion by the livestock.

Exceptions to liability occur when the harm that results is not a reasonably expected result of the livestock intrusion, when the harm is caused by animals straying onto abutting land while being driven on a highway, or when the harm is caused by unexpected operation of a force of nature, action of another animal, or intentional, reckless, or negligent conduct of a third party.

A further exception to liability occurs when the possessor of the land fails to erect and maintain a fence required by common law or statute to prevent the intrusion of livestock.[4]

Application to Harm Caused by Abnormally Dangerous Conditions or Activities

Persons who permit abnormally dangerous conditions to exist or who engage in abnormally dangerous activities may be held strictly liable in tort for harm that results. The interest protected by this application of strict liability theory is the right to be free from harm caused by abnormally dangerous conditions or activities. The essential elements of this tort are (1) the existence of an abnormally dangerous condition or activity, (2) the defendant knows of the abnormally dangerous condition or activity, (3) damages, and (4) causation. We will discuss each of these essential elements in turn.

The first element of this tort is the existence of an abnormally dangerous condition or activity. Courts have grappled with this concept for some time. "Abnormal" has come to mean unusual or not natural for the location or area. For instance, keeping a lion as a pet in an apartment is an abnormal activity—a lion is an unusual pet to keep, and an apartment is an unusual location to keep it. To be "dangerous" means to create a substantial likelihood of great harm to persons or their property that cannot be eliminated by the use of reasonable care by the defendant.

Putting these concepts together, ***abnormally dangerous conditions or activities*** are ones that are not usual for the area and create a substantial likelihood of significant harm, which cannot be eliminated by the exercise of reasonable care. In other words, these conditions cannot exist, or the activities be carried out, safely, even if the defendant exercises due care. They are sometimes referred to as "ultrahazardous" conditions or activities, the terminology preferred in the

Key Point

Essential Elements of Strict Liability for Harm Caused by Abnormally Dangerous Conditions or Activities

1. There is existence of an abnormally dangerous condition or activity
2. The defendant has knowledge of the abnormally dangerous condition or activity
3. Damages
4. Causation

Abnormally dangerous conditions or activities Conditions or activities that are not usual for the area and that create a substantial likelihood of significant harm that cannot be eliminated by the exercise of reasonable care.

first *Restatement of Torts*, but replaced in the second *Restatement* in favor of the phrase "abnormally dangerous." Keeping a pet lion in an apartment meets the definitions of both "abnormal" and "dangerous." In applying strict liability, courts reason that some conditions and activities are so dangerous to persons and their property that the defendant will be held liable for any harm they cause, even if the defendant did not intend the harm, and even if the defendant exercised reasonable care. Common examples of abnormally dangerous conditions or activities include making, storing, and using explosive devices; conducting blasting activities; manufacturing poisons; operating nuclear power plants; and transporting, storing, and dumping toxic and other dangerous substances.

The landmark case in this area of law is *Rylands v. Fletcher*. In that early English case, considered radical and highly debatable at the time, an English court first established the "abnormally dangerous condition or activity" application of the strict liability theory.

Modeled after the principles established in the *Rylands* case, Section 520 of the *Restatement (Second) of Torts* sets forth six factors to be used in determining the appropriate application of strict liability for abnormally dangerous conditions and activities.

Normally, the circumstances involving strict liability for abnormally dangerous conditions or activities on land involve the way the defendant uses his

CASE on Point

Rylands v. Fletcher, L.R. 3 H.L. 330 (1868)

This often-quoted landmark case from the House of Lords in England first established strict liability for abnormally dangerous conditions or activities. In this case, the defendants owned and occupied a mill near, but not adjoining, the plaintiff's coal mine. In order to supply the mill with water, the defendants constructed a reservoir. Abandoned coal shafts from the plaintiff's coal mine extended underneath the defendant's land. Water from the reservoir leaked through the old coal shafts and flooded the plaintiff's mine.

The court found that "the plaintiff was damaged by his property being flooded by water which, without any fault on his part, broke out of a reservoir constructed on the defendants' land by the defendants' orders, and maintained by the defendants." The court went on to consider the following question of law: "[W]hat is the obligation which the law casts on a person who, like the defendants, lawfully brings on his land something which though harmless whilst it remains there, will naturally do mischief if it escape out of his land[?]" The court pondered "whether the duty which the law casts upon him . . . is an absolute duty to keep it in at his peril, or is . . . merely a duty to take all reasonable and prudent precautions, in order to keep it in, but no more."

The court ultimately ruled, "We think that the true rule of law is that the person who for his own purposes brings on his lands and collects and keeps there any thing likely to do mischief if it escapes, must keep it in at his peril, and if he does not do so, is prima facie answerable for all the damage which is the natural consequence of its escape[,]" holding the defendants strictly liable for the harm the plaintiff suffered.

SIDEBAR

RESTATEMENT (SECOND) OF TORTS FACTORS

The *Restatement (Second) of Torts* sets forth several factors that can be used in determining whether a condition or activity is an abnormally dangerous one. These factors include

- The existence of a high degree of risk to people or to property
- The likelihood that the harm resulting from the condition or activity will be great
- The inability to eliminate the risk by the exercise of reasonable care
- The extent to which the activity is not a matter of common usage
- The extent to which the activity is appropriate to the place where it is conducted
- The extent to which the value of the activity to society is outweighed by its dangerous attributes[5]

own land, such as by manufacturing poisons in a factory; however, this tort also can be committed on the land of another, such as by transporting a dangerous substance over a public highway or another's private land.

The second essential element of this tort is that the defendant must have knowledge of the dangerous condition or activity. This means that the defendant must actually be *aware* of the dangerous condition or activity, and the plaintiff must be able to prove this. If the condition exists or the activity is occurring and the defendant is not aware of it, such as when there is a latent, or hidden, defect in the defendant's building, making it abnormally dangerous, but the owner has no knowledge of it, as it was not discovered in a prepurchase inspection or disclosed by the seller of the property, he cannot be held strictly liable for harms resulting from it—though he may be liable under some other tort theory.

Damages are another essential element of this type of strict liability claim. The damages element means that actual harm must be suffered by the plaintiff, either to his person or to his property. This requirement is similar to the tort of negligence, for which damages must also be proven as an essential element of that tort claim. Slight harm is sufficient, so long as some harm is incurred. Of course, the extent of the harm affects the amount of damages that may be recovered, but there may be no nominal damage recovery under this application of strict liability theory if no actual damages are suffered by the plaintiff. For example, if the defendant's blasting activities cause a rock to be propelled into the plaintiff's eye, injuring it, then the plaintiff has suffered actual harm. However, if the blasting activities scare the plaintiff, but there is no contact with his person and he suffers no actual harm, an action in strict liability is not available.

The fourth essential element of this tort requires that the harm be *caused* by the abnormally dangerous condition or activity. This causation element encompasses both actual cause and proximate cause. Actual cause, or cause in fact, is determined using either the "but for" or "substantial factor" test, depending on the number of causal factors: either (1) but for the defendant's conduct, the

CASE on Point

Madsen v. East Jordan Irr. Co., 125 P.2d 794 (Utah 1942)

In this case, the Madsen Mink Farm, whose owners bred and raised minks for sale, was located 100 yards from the defendant's irrigation canal. One day, the defendant, in order to repair his canal, "blasted with explosives, causing vibrations and noises which frightened the mother mink and caused 108 of them to kill 230 of their" kittens. The mink farm sued the defendant for damages, valuing each mink kitten at $25.

The Supreme Court of Utah acknowledged that "the rule of absolute liability prevails when someone uses explosives and the blasting of the explosives results in hurling of rock, earth, or debris which causes injury to another." However, the court found that the actions of the mother mink, a result of "peculiarity of disposition," was not "within the realm of matters to be anticipated" and broke the chain of causation. The owners of the mink farm were found not to be within the class of persons that could foreseeably be harmed by blasting activities conducted on another's property.

plaintiff would not have been injured, or (2) the defendant's conduct was a substantial factor in producing the plaintiff's harm. Proximate cause is the second part of the causation element that must be present. The harm suffered by the plaintiff must be a foreseeable consequence of the condition or activity. As with the tort of negligence, proximate cause, as applied in strict liability cases, is a policy question establishing a cutoff point beyond which a defendant will not be held liable in tort for harm he in fact caused. Strict liability will be imposed when the harm that results is included within the type of harm that was initially foreseeable *and* it covers only those classes of people who were within the foreseeable risk of harm posed by the abnormally dangerous condition or activity. See the *Madsen* Case on Point as an illustration.

In application, courts more narrowly construe proximate cause in strict liability cases involving abnormally dangerous conditions and activities than they do in negligence cases. In strict liability cases, intervening causes, such as acts of God or acts of third persons, are more likely to be considered superseding, thereby cutting off the defendant's liability, as demonstrated in the *Madsen* case. Courts' reasoning in being more restrictive in the application of proximate cause to strict liability cases is that there may be an absence of fault on the part of the defendant in strict liability cases; with the tort of negligence, when fault on behalf of the defendant exists, courts are more willing to extend liability.

What if the condition or activity that causes harm is not deemed to be sufficiently abnormally dangerous? In such cases, other legal theories may be used by plaintiffs when the condition or activity is not abnormally dangerous enough to warrant strict liability protection. These tort theories include trespass to land, nuisance, wrongful death, and negligence in permitting the condition to exist or in engaging in the activity.

The final major application of strict liability theory is products liability. Products liability is discussed in the next chapter.

CHAPTER **SUMMARY**

- Strict liability is one of the three major classifications of torts; the others are intentional torts and negligence. Strict liability is tort liability imposed regardless of fault or blameworthiness of the defendant and is also called "absolute liability" or "liability without fault."

- Strict liability theory applies in three types of situations: harm caused by animals, harm caused by abnormally dangerous conditions or activities, and harm caused by defective products.

- Tort claims made for injuries caused by animals may be brought under the strict liability theory, among other theories. In these cases, the owner or caretaker of the animal can be held strictly liable for any harm caused by the animal, but a distinction is made under the law as to whether the animal is a "wild" or "domestic" one.

- The animal is considered a wild animal if it has not been domesticated and if it is the kind of animal that is wild in its natural state. The common law strict liability rule for wild animals is that their owners and/or caretakers are strictly liable for any harm to others the animals cause. It does not matter how well the animal is trained, whether the animal had ever exhibited a dangerous propensity, or how much care the owner or caretaker took in trying to prevent such harm. The issue for courts is often classifying an animal as either wild or domesticated.

- Domesticated animals are those animals that are domesticated and habituated to live with and among humans, and their normal populations are pets, such as dogs, cats, and horses. The common law strict liability rule for domesticated animals is that an owner or caretaker of a domesticated animal may be held strictly liable for any harm the animal causes to others if (1) the owner or caretaker had reason to know the animal had a specific propensity to cause harm, and (2) the harm caused by the animal was due to that specific propensity.

- Persons who permit the existence of abnormally dangerous conditions or who engage in abnormally dangerous activities may be held strictly liable in tort for harm caused by them. The essential elements of this tort are the existence of an abnormally dangerous condition or activity, knowledge of it by the defendant, damages, and causation.

- Other legal theories may be used by plaintiffs if the condition or activity is not abnormally dangerous enough to warrant strict liability protection, such as the torts of trespass to land, nuisance, wrongful death, and negligence in permitting the condition to exist or in engaging in the activity.

CONCEPT REVIEW AND REINFORCEMENT

QUESTIONS FOR **REVIEW**

1. What is strict liability, and how does it relate to the other major tort classifications?

2. When does strict liability apply?

3. How does strict liability theory apply to harm caused by wild animals?

4. How does strict liability theory apply to harm caused by domesticated animals?

5. What is the fallacy in the statement, "Every dog is entitled to one free bite"?

6. How does strict liability theory apply to harm caused by abnormally dangerous conditions or activities?

7. What constitutes an abnormally dangerous condition or activity, triggering strict liability application?

DEVELOPING YOUR PARALEGAL SKILLS

CRITICAL THINKING **EXERCISES**

1. In this chapter, we studied strict liability theory and two of its three applications: harm caused by animals and harm caused by abnormally dangerous conditions or activities. Research the laws in your state on each of these applications of strict liability theory to see in what way(s), if any, they differ from most states' laws. An excellent starting point for your research is a case law digest for your state. For example, in Maryland, the resource *Maryland Digest 2d* by West includes cases from Maryland dealing with these applications. Discuss your research results with the class.

2. Barney has a very friendly and well-trained pet monkey, Clyde. One day, while Fran is visiting Barney, she is bitten by Clyde when she tries to feed him a banana. At the time, Barney was controlling his monkey, and that Clyde bit Fran surprised everyone. Clyde has never bitten anyone before, and has never acted aggressively or meanly.

   a. *Can Barney be held strictly liable for the injuries sustained by Fran from Clyde's bite? Why or why not?*

   b. *What if Clyde is a cheetah, not a monkey, and Fran is trying to feed him a hamburger? Does that change your answer?*

   c. *What if Clyde is a pony, and Fran is trying to feed him a carrot at the time she is bitten? Does that change your answer?*

3. XYZ Company is the industry leader in blasting holes through mountains so roadways can be constructed. Known for using the utmost care in conducting its operations, the company has the safest record in the business, with by far the fewest incidents of injuries from blasting reported. One day, while conducting blasting activities to widen an existing thoroughfare, the plaintiff is injured when a dislodged rock hits his car as he drives past the construction site.

   a. *Is XYZ Company strictly liable for the harm suffered by the plaintiff? Why or why not?*

   Suppose XYZ Company, although it is an industry leader in terms of operating safety, was careless in its operations at this site, using an inexperienced site manager and cutting corners to save time and money on the project.

   b. *Does this change your answer to the previous question? Why or why not?*

4. Metropolitan Chemical Company manufactures chemical pesticides at its facility in Rockville, Maryland. A semitruck, transporting medical devices to Johns Hopkins Hospital in Baltimore, crashes into the plant when the truck driver suffers a heart attack, veering off the road and onto the company's property. In the collision, a chemical storage tank is ruptured, and noxious fumes are released into the surrounding atmosphere. Workers at neighboring industrial sites suffer illness as a result of inhaling the noxious fumes released from Metropolitan Chemical's ruptured tank.

   Is Metropolitan Chemical Company, in manufacturing chemical pesticides, strictly liable for the harm caused by the spread of the noxious fumes? Why or why not?

ASSIGNMENTS AND PRACTICAL **APPLICATIONS**

1. Read and brief *Olson v. Pederson*, 288 N.W. 856 (Minn. 1939) regarding household pets not being included in the trespassing animal rule; also see *King v. Blue Mountain Forest Ass'n*, 123 A.2d 151 (N.H. 1956) applying the common law rule.

2. For another case on Florida's "Bad Dog" statute, this one finding no liability when proper notice was given pursuant to the statute, see *Carroll v. Moxley*, 241 So.2d 681 (Fla. 1970).

3. Are these animals considered wild or domestic? Deer [*Congress & Empire Spring Co. v. Edgar*, 99 U.S. 645 (1878)]; raccoon [*Andrew v. Kilgour*, 19 Man.L.Rep.

544 (1910)]; ferret [*Gallick v. Barto*, 828 F.Supp. 1168 (M.D. Pa. 1993)]; hive of bees [*Ammons v. Kellogg*, 102 So. 562 (Miss. 1925)]; and camel [*McQuaker v. Goddard*, 1 K.B. 687 (1940)].

4. Did this animal owner have knowledge of the animal's dangerous propensity? A rider-throwing mule [*Walters v. Grand Teton Crest Outfitters, Inc.*, 804 F. Supp. 1442 (D. Wyo. 1992)]; an often-snarling dog [*Zarek v. Fredericks*, 138 F.2d 689 (3d Cir. 1943)]; when children are warned to keep away from the dog [*Perkins v. Drury*, 258 P.2d 379 (N.M. 1953)]; whether an entire breed may be classified as

dangerous or vicious [(*Briscoe v. Graybeal*, 622 A.2d 805 (Md. Ct. Spec. App. 1993) (Thoroughbred horse) and *Slack v. Villari*, 476 A.2d 227 (Md. Ct. Spec. App. 1984) (Doberman Pinscher dog)].

5. Compare the *Madsen* case from the chapter with *Foster v. Preston Mill Co.*, 268 P.2d 645 (Wash. 1954), another case involving blasting activities that frightened mother mink on a neighboring mink farm, causing them to kill their kittens. In the *Foster* case, another limitation on application of strict liability was imposed when the court found the nervous disposition of the mink, rather than the normal risks inherent in blasting operations, to be the true cause of the harm. The court held that the "risk of causing harm of the kind here experienced … is not the kind of risk which makes the activity of blasting ultrahazardous."

6. Does your state or locality have a dog bite statute? Research whether it does, and if so, what it provides. Discuss your research results in class.

7. Read and brief the following cases involving strict liability applied to a variety of abnormally dangerous conditions or activities: *Vern J. Oja & Assoc. v. Washington Park Towers, Inc.*, 569 P.2d 1141 (Wash. 1977) (pile driving); *Langan v. Valicopters, Inc.*, 567 P.2d 218 (Wash. 1977) (crop dusting); *Smith v. Lockheed Propulsion Co.*, 247 Cal. App. 2d Supp. 774 (1967) (testing rocket fuel); *State Dept. of Envtl. Prot. v. Ventron*, 468 A.2d 150 (N.J. 1983) (disposing of hazardous waste); and *Hudson v. Peavey Oil Co.*, 566 P.2d 175 (Or. 1977) (storing gasoline in a residential area).

8. Despite automobile accidents being a leading cause of death, injury, and property damage in the United States, driving an automobile is not considered an abnormally dangerous activity to which strict liability theory applies. Read and brief *Goodwin v. Reilley*, 176 Cal. App. 3d 86 (1985) on this point of law.

TECHNOLOGY RESOURCES AND INTERNET **EXERCISES**

Tatiana, a tiger kept at the San Francisco zoo, bit a zookeeper on December 22, 2006, and then on December 25, 2007, escaped from her cage, attacking three people, killing one. The tiger was shot and killed by police officers during the 2007 attack. Legal proceedings regarding the 2007 incident are under way at the time of this text's writing, but the evidence so far suggests that the victims, who admitted to smoking marijuana and drinking vodka before the attack, were provoking the tiger, perhaps climbing into her enclosure, throwing objects at her, causing her agitation, and inciting her escape. Go to *http://en.wikipedia.org/wiki/Tatiana _(tiger)* for more information. Should the zoo, as keeper of the tiger, be held strictly liable for the harm she caused if she was provoked by her victims? For a case involving an attack by a neighbor's boar on a plaintiff who provoked and taunted him, see *Marshall v. Ranne*, 511 S.W.2d 255 (Tex. 1974).

Perform an Internet search for the facts and legal issues in the "Travis the Chimpanzee" mauling case. The victim received a face transplant at the Ohio hospital that had recently performed the first total face transplant in the United States.

Research, online, whether your state or county has a statute or ordinance dealing with the liability of owners for trespassing livestock. Does your jurisdiction have a "fencing in" or "fencing out" statute, or some other statutory rule that modifies the common law rule of strict liability? What does it provide? Share your results with the class.

Perform Internet research to determine if your locality has leash and/or muzzle laws for dogs. If so, what requirements are imposed? When, and to what types of dogs, do these rules apply? What are the penalties for violation of the leash or muzzle law? For class discussion, consider the advantages and disadvantages of these types of laws and regulations.

For a review of some West Virginia cases defining abnormally dangerous activities, see *www.state.wv.us/wvsca /jury/inherently.htm*.

ETHICAL **APPLICATIONS**

Colleen comes to your office and asks you to represent her in a personal injury action she wishes to bring. Colleen was disfigured and permanently disabled when the car she was riding in experienced axle failure, causing a terrible highway accident. After hearing the facts of the case and being a practitioner in products liability law, you agree to represent Colleen in this matter.

Poor Colleen has been down on her luck in many ways lately, and she has no money to pay for the representation. You agree to take the case on a contingency fee basis. Compassionate as you are, you would like to provide Colleen with some financial assistance, loaning her some money to help pay for rent, medical bills, and groceries until she is recovered and receives compensation from the lawsuit.

In addition, you agree to advance her the costs of the litigation, such as court fees and discovery expenses. You feel that you can trust Colleen to repay you once she recovers from the car manufacturer.

Is it permissible for you, as Colleen's attorney, to provide Colleen with financial assistance? If so, what kind of financial assistance may you provide? Can you provide her with funds to pay her living or medical expenses? Can you advance her the costs of litigation?

VIDEO **CASE STUDY**

Closing Argument: A Lawyer's Last Chance to Convince the Jury

Synopsis: The parents of a child injured when file boxes fell on her during a sudden school bus stop are in the process of divorcing and are battling over child custody and their opposing views of medical treatment for the injured child. Because of the mother's religious views and contrary to the father's wishes, the child did not receive traditional medical treatment for her injuries, causing her further harm.

Questions

1. The injuries sustained by this child were caused by a stack of file boxes being transported by the bus, which toppled onto the child when the bus driver stopped the bus abruptly. Is the transport of file boxes in a bus full of children an abnormally dangerous activity to which strict liability would apply?

2. What if the cargo was not file boxes, but rather lab supplies, including acid, which fell and spilled when the bus stopped abruptly? Is the transport of that cargo on a school bus full of children an abnormally dangerous activity?

chapter **11**

PRODUCTS LIABILITY

This chapter thoroughly examines products liability and the tort theories under which products liability actions may be brought. We begin our study of products liability with its definition and its relationship to strict liability tort theory.

Definition of Products Liability

Products liability is legal liability of manufacturers, sellers, and others for harm caused by products. Under certain products liability theories, the products must be defective. Under others, the term "defective" may not be used, but the products may not be "merchantable" or "fit for their ordinary purposes."

Those who can be held liable for harm caused by defective products include product manufacturers, component part manufacturers, parts suppliers, wholesalers, distributors, retailers, and lessors of the products (sometimes called goods rather than products, depending on the legal theory involved). Who can be held liable for harm caused by products depends on the theory under which the suit is brought. Certain theories define this category of potential defendants much more broadly than others, so this is one factor that plaintiffs consider in selecting a legal theory under which to bring products liability actions.

The legal liability for injuries caused by defective products extends to harm caused both to persons and to their property. What harm is redressed, and how, also affects the plaintiffs' decision-making process when selecting a legal theory under which to bring a products liability action. If you have any doubt whether consumer products, such as automobiles, drugs, food, tools, furniture, toys, household appliances, and the like, cause injury or death to persons and property, do the exercise at the end of the chapter involving research of the U.S. Consumer Product Safety Commission's website.

Those who can bring products liability actions include consumers (the products' "buyers"), lessees ("renters" of the products), users (who

LEARNING OBJECTIVES

11.1 Define products liability.

11.2 Identify and explain the five legal theories that can be used to bring products liability actions.

11.3 List and discuss the essential elements of a strict products liability claim.

Products liability
Legal liability of manufacturers, sellers, and others for harm caused by defective products.

THE U.S. CONSUMER PRODUCT SAFETY COMMISSION

Congress enacted the Consumer Product Safety Act in 1972. Under this federal statute, the U.S. Consumer Product Safety Commission (CPSC) was established as an independent agency of the federal government. The overall purpose of the CPSC is to protect the public from potentially dangerous consumer products and to adopt rules and regulations to interpret and enforce the Consumer Product Safety Act.

The CPSC has the authority to regulate the sale and manufacture of consumer products other than those regulated by other agencies, such as automobiles, which are regulated by the National Highway Traffic Safety Administration, foods and drugs, which are regulated by the Food and Drug Administration, and guns, which are regulated by the Bureau of Alcohol, Tobacco, Firearms and Explosives. In fulfilling its mission to protect consumers against unreasonable risks of harm from consumer products, the CPSC develops both voluntary and mandatory standards, bans dangerous consumer products, issues recalls of products already in the marketplace, and researches potential hazards relating to consumer products.

did not buy the products), and sometimes even bystanders. Who can bring an action is another factor considered by plaintiffs in selecting a legal theory under which to bring a products liability action. Some theories define this concept much more broadly than others do.

Product defect
Something is wrong with a product that makes it dangerous, increasing the risk of harm to persons and their property.

Most products liability cases arise because of a ***product defect***. A product is defective if something is wrong with it that makes it dangerous. A product is dangerous if it increases the risk of harm to persons and their property. For example, a ladder manufactured using weak screws is a defective product if the weakness of the screws makes the ladder dangerous by increasing the risk of harm to persons who use the ladder, or to their property. In other words, if the weak screws affect the ability of the ladder to hold weight, such as to hold an adult, or a can of paint, then the ladder is a defective product.

However, not every product that causes harm is necessarily defective. Consider the following example. While moving furniture, Jeff drops a sofa on his foot, breaking his big toe. Was the sofa defective? It is true that Jeff was injured by the sofa he dropped on his foot. However, the injury was not the result of a defect in the product. Jeff just dropped the sofa on his foot. The result might be different if the sofa fell on Jeff's foot because the sofa's arm broke off as a result of poor adhesive used in its construction. If the adhesive was defective, that could render the entire sofa defective and lead to a products liability action.

Manufacturing defects
Product defects resulting because the manufactured product does not conform to its design, and a problem occurred during the making of the product that caused it to be dangerous to use.

There are three categories of product defects: manufacturing, design, and warning defects (see Table 11-1). ***Manufacturing defects*** exist if the manufactured product does not conform to its design and a problem occurs during its manufacture that makes it dangerous to use. The defective product is different from the rest of the products made on the manufacturing line. If a product is not properly assembled, or properly tested, or its quality checked adequately, a manufacturing defect may exist.

TABLE 11-1 Three Categories of Product Defects

Manufacturing defect	The product does not conform to its design, making the product dangerous to use.
Design defect	All products on the line conform to the product design, but something is wrong with the design that makes the entire line of products dangerous to use.
Warning defect	All the products on the line contain no, or insufficient, warnings or instructions, making the products dangerous to use.

For example, a foreign substance left in a can of peaches before it is sealed for shipment and sale renders that can of peaches a defective product, and the defect is a manufacturing one—it occurred during the manufacturing process. As another example, the ladder made using weak screws, discussed above, has a manufacturing defect.

Design defects exist when all products on the line conform to the design, but something is wrong with the design itself that makes the product dangerous to use. Different from manufacturing defects, design defects occur when all the products manufactured on this line have the same feature, making them all unreasonably dangerous. This condition of dangerous design increases the risk of harm to persons and their property. For example, a car design in which windows are unusually small, reducing driver visibility to a dangerous level, would constitute a design defect in the product. All automobiles made in accordance with that design would be defective, not because of what went into them during the manufacturing process, but because they were designed with too small windows.

Warning defects exist when all the products contain no, or insufficient, warnings or instructions, which makes the products dangerous by increasing the risk of harm to persons and their property. In other words, the product labels are insufficient to provide users with the information they need to use the product safely and properly. "Reasonableness" is the test applied to determine whether warnings and instructions are sufficient to alert consumers to the risks of using a certain product. With warning defects, both the manufacture and the design of the product are fine; the problem is that foreseeable users of the product are not given enough information to use it safely. For example, a toxic household cleaner should contain a label warning that the liquid should not be ingested; failure to provide such a warning, especially if the bottle is one that could be opened by a child, may constitute a warning defect. As is discussed further later in the chapter, the seller's duty is to warn purchasers of the harm that can result both from the product's use and from its foreseeable misuses.

Did you ever wonder why your hair blow dryer has a thick tag attached to its electric cord (which you have to cut off, because it is too strong to tear) bearing large, bold, colored lettering and images, warning to keep it AWAY FROM WATER, UNPLUG IT, and warning of a RISK OF SHOCK? Now you know—this tag is a warning, given by the manufacturer, to instruct consumers on how to use the product properly, and what precautions a user must take to avoid being injured while using the product. Such warnings serve to minimize harm caused by products and to reduce legal exposure for the products' manufacturers and sellers.

Design defects
Product defects where all the products on the line conform to the product design, but something is wrong with the design that makes the entire line of products dangerous to use.

Warning defects
Product defects where all the products on the line contain no, or insufficient, warnings or instructions, making the products dangerous to use.

PACKAGING DEFECTS AND TAMPERING

A manufacturer owes a duty to design and provide safe product packaging and containers. The products should be packaged in containers that either are tamper-resistant or indicate when the product has been tampered with and should not be used.

A manufacturer also has a duty to put products in child-safe containers if the products can foreseeably harm children.

Remember the McDonald's coffee case discussed in Chapter 1? Today, McDonald's and many other coffee sellers place warnings on their coffee cups to warn consumers that the coffee is hot. That coffee is served hot may seem obvious, but in light of that case, failure to provide a warning might constitute a warning defect.

There is no need to warn about risks that are obvious or commonly known, however. That a risk is obvious or commonly known constitutes a valid defense to strict products liability and is discussed in Chapter 12. Of course, as the McDonald's coffee case illustrates, what constitutes obvious or commonly known dangers is not always clear. Note that an important question in that case was *how* hot the coffee was served, and McDonald's now serves its coffee *less* hot as a result of that adverse ruling (in addition to providing a warning that the coffee is hot).

The *Restatement (Second) of Torts* did not clearly define the term "defect." Courts were left to grapple with that issue, over time coming to recognize the three types of product defects discussed above. The *Restatement (Third) of*

RESTATEMENT (THIRD) OF TORTS ON PRODUCTS LIABILITY

The *Restatement (Third) of Torts: Products Liability* was issued by the American Law Institute in 1998 specifically to deal with the liability of commercial product sellers and distributors for harm caused by their products. It is the first part of the American Law Institute's revisions and updates to its *Restatement (Second) of Torts*. Superseding Section 402A of the *Restatement (Second)*, this new *Restatement* part covers the complex and evolving field of products liability. It addresses products liability issues that have become points of serious contention and debate in the courts, but that were not part of the products liability tort arena when the *Restatement (Second)* was published decades ago.

The *Restatement (Third)* specifically addresses the important issue of when a product is defective. It defines the traditionally recognized three types of product defects, namely, manufacturing, design, and warning defects, and sets forth the legal standards appropriate to each category of defect. In addition, it develops rules for special products, such as component parts, prescription drugs, medical devices, foods, and used products.

Torts, in updating its guidance on the law of products liability, defines the three traditionally recognized types of product defects, and expands on certain legal standards appropriate to each category. It says that a *manufacturing defect* exists when a product departs from its intended design even though all possible care was exercised in the preparation and marketing of the product.[1] Further, it says that a *design defect* exists when the foreseeable risks of harm posed by the product could have been reduced or avoided by the seller, distributor, or a predecessor in the commercial chain of distribution adopting a reasonable alternative design.[2] It is the failure to use the alternative design that renders the product not reasonably safe. This *Restatement* prescribes a new test for design defects: The plaintiff must be able to establish that there was a reasonable alternative design available, so that the harm was reasonably preventable by the manufacturer or other defendant.[3] Later in this chapter, we will examine other tests that have been traditionally used by the courts in determining whether a defective product is unreasonably dangerous and warrants strict products liability application. Finally, this *Restatement* says that a *warning defect* exists when inadequate instructions or warnings are given on a product and the foreseeable risks of harm posed by the product could have been reduced or avoided by providing reasonable instructions or warnings.[4] This failure may be the fault of the seller, distributor, or a predecessor in the commercial chain of distribution.[5] It is the omission of the instructions or warnings that renders the product not reasonably safe.[6] In a comment on this section of the *Restatement,* certain factors for a court to consider in evaluating the risks of a product are stated. These include the content and comprehensibility and intensity of expression of warnings and instructions, and the characteristics of expected user groups, such as children.[7]

A seller must warn those who purchase or use its product of the harm that can result not only from the product's intended use but also from certain types of product misuse. What is product misuse?

Courts must identify the intended use of a product and distinguish that from the product's unintended uses, called product misuses. For instance, a consumer who uses a pair of scissors to unclog a bathtub drain, cutting herself in the process, has misused the product; scissors are intended to be used for cutting, not fixing clogged drains.

As discussed in Chapter 12, although sellers of products must protect consumers from risks of harm resulting from both the intended use(s) and the foreseeable misuses of their products, the *unforeseeable* misuse of a product is a complete defense to strict products liability claims. Of course, courts must grapple with the issue of whether a particular product misuse is foreseeable or not, and the next chapter includes several interesting cases on this point.

With regard to warnings and labeling, remember that the *Restatement (Third) of Torts* provides a list of factors that courts should consider in evaluating the reasonableness of warnings and instructions, including the risks of a product (consider the different risks involved depending on whether the product is a pencil or a pencil sharpener), the "content and comprehensibility" and "intensity of expression" of the instructions and warnings (look for bold and colored lettering on blow dryer warning labels), and the "characteristics of expected user groups" who are anticipated to use the product (an important

THE FDA'S DEFECT ACTION LEVELS

The U.S. Food and Drug Administration (FDA) sets guidelines, called food defect action levels, that detail how much of certain natural or unavoidable defects in specific foods present no health hazards to humans. For example, the guidelines state that contaminants in amounts less than the following are acceptably safe for human consumption:

- *Frozen broccoli:* 60 or more aphids and/or thrips and/or mites per 100 grams
- *Maraschino cherries:* 5 percent or more pieces are rejects due to maggots
- *Cherry jam:* mold count is 30 percent or more
- *Chocolate:* 60 or more insect fragments per 100 grams and 1 or more rodent hairs per 100 grams
- *Coffee beans:* 10 percent or more by count are insect-infested or damaged
- *Macaroni:* 225 insect fragments or more per 225 grams and 4.5 rodent hairs or more per 225 grams
- *Mushrooms:* 20 or more maggots per 100 grams and 75 mites per 100 grams
- *Ground pepper:* 475 or more insect fragments per 50 grams and 2 or more rodent hairs per 50 grams

Yum!

consideration for manufacturers is whether the expected users might include children).

Remember, too, that there is no duty to warn about risks that are obvious or commonly known, such as that scissors can cut—scissors, in fact, should cut. This is because such warnings would not add to the product's safety, and they could detract from warnings that will enhance the product's safety. For example, pencils have sharp points (once they are sharpened!), and so do knives; saws can cut; hammers can pound. As you will see in the next chapter, it is a defense to a products liability claim that a person was harmed as a result of a commonly known danger, such as being cut by a steak knife while using it to cut meat.

Some jurisdictions have codified products liability by enacting statutes covering these actions. Indiana, for example, has enacted the Indiana Product Liability Act, which governs products liability actions in its jurisdiction, and its

STATUTE on Point

Ind. Code § 34-20-1-1 (2009)

The Indiana Code says that products liability actions may be brought by a user or consumer of a product against a manufacturer or seller of that product for physical harm caused by the product.

courts enforce, and interpret, that statute. The first part of that statute is summarized in the Statute on Point, demonstrating the scope of its coverage.

Now that we have defined and discussed the concept of products liability, we will consider how products liability relates to strict liability tort theory.

The Relationship Between Products Liability and Strict Liability Tort Theory

Products liability actions may be brought under five different tort theories. One of these theories, and the one most often used for a variety of reasons to be discussed later in this chapter, is strict liability. Therefore, products liability relates to strict liability in that products liability actions may be brought under strict liability theory, among other tort theories.

Five Products Liability Causes of Action

Five legal theories may be used by plaintiffs, defending on the facts and circumstances, to bring products liability actions. They are negligence, misrepresentation, breach of express warranty, breach of implied warranty, and strict liability. Several theories may be alleged in the same lawsuit. The requirements and applications of each are discussed below, starting with the tort theory of negligence.

NEGLIGENCE

Negligence theory may be used to bring an action for harm caused by a product. This theory applies if the plaintiff is injured because of the defendant's unreasonable act or failure to act. In order to succeed in a products liability suit under this theory, the plaintiff must first establish each of the four essential elements of the tort of negligence: a duty of care was owed to the plaintiff by the defendant; the duty of care was breached; causation; and damages. Further, in such an action, the defendant may assert any relevant defense to negligence, including contributory or comparative negligence, and assumption of the risk, to bar or reduce the plaintiff's recovery.

Negligence
A person suffers harm because of another's unreasonable act or omission.

SIDEBAR

PRODUCTS LIABILITY AND CLASS ACTION SUITS

Sometimes products that are dangerous cause injury to numerous people, in numerous separate incidents. These common incidents may be joined in one legal action, called a class action. Class actions are lawsuits brought by multiple—meaning a group of—persons in the same situation, with interests so similar that common legal representation is adequate to meet their needs. For example, a drug that causes very harmful side effects, such as stroke or heart attack, may become the subject of one class action lawsuit by many plaintiffs who used the drug and were injured. Class action lawsuits were discussed more fully in Chapter 7.

Privity of contract
The requirement that because a contract is a private agreement between or among the parties to it, those who are not parties to the contract normally have no rights under it.

Accordingly, a product's manufacturer can be held liable under negligence theory for failure to exercise reasonable care toward any person who suffers injury caused by a defective product. For example, if a person is injured by a coffee maker that sprays scalding hot water when he tries to use it and sues under negligence theory, that plaintiff must establish that the manufacturer owed him a duty of care, that the manufacturer breached its duty of care by acting unreasonably or unreasonably failing to act, that the manufacturer's breach of the duty of care both "in fact" and "proximately" caused the harm, and that actual damages were suffered by the plaintiff.

If the plaintiff was not injured because the scalding water did not touch him, nor was his property damaged because the scalding spray did not harm his kitchen counter or floor (and assuming the coffee maker was not damaged), then the plaintiff suffered no actual damages. In such a case, the plaintiff could not recover under negligence theory, despite the fact that the product malfunctioned, because damages are an essential element of that tort.

If the plaintiff did suffer harm, in the form of either personal injury or property damage, he could establish a *prima facie* case of negligence. At that point, the defendant could assert any relevant defenses to the tort of negligence. What if the plaintiff had placed the coffee maker on an unstable surface, such as on a pile of books, and the hot water sprayed out of it when the coffee maker toppled off the pile? Under negligence theory, the defendant might defend itself by asserting that the plaintiff was either contributorily or comparatively negligent, depending on which defense is recognized in the jurisdiction, or perhaps assumption of the risk, for the plaintiff is at least partially at fault for using the coffee maker on an unstable surface.

Under negligence theory, the plaintiff need not be in **privity of contract** with the negligent manufacturer of the product, which means that he need not

CASE on Point

MacPherson v. Buick Motor Co., 111 N.E. 1050 (N.Y. 1916)

In the early days of automobiles, the plaintiff was injured when a vehicle in which he was riding suddenly collapsed and he was thrown from it. The vehicle collapsed as a result of crumbling spokes in one of the vehicle's wooden wheels.

The defendant, Buick Motor Company, had sold the car to a retail dealer, who in turn had sold the vehicle to the plaintiff. The wheel that crumbled was purchased by Buick Motor Company from another manufacturer, and incorporated into the automobile by Buick.

The Court of Appeals of New York, in an opinion written by Judge Benjamin Cardozo (the author of the majority opinion in the *Palsgraf* case discussed in Chapter 6), held that Buick Motor Company, the automobile's manufacturer, was liable to the plaintiff, in negligence, for failure to exercise reasonable care in manufacturing the automobile. That the plaintiff was not an immediate purchaser from Buick did not bar his recovery. The court found that Buick Motor Company, as a manufacturer and more than a mere dealer in automobiles, "was responsible for the finished product," including its component parts.

PRIVITY OF CONTRACT

Privity of contract is the requirement that, because a contract is a private agreement between or among the parties to it, those not a party to a contract normally have no rights under it. Privity of contract must exist between a plaintiff and a defendant before an action based on the contract may be brought.

Privity of contract recognizes the legal relationship that exists between the promisor(s) and the promisee(s) under a contract. Normally, outside persons, called third parties, have no rights under contracts to which they are not parties.

The *Restatement (Second) of Torts* does not require privity of contract in products liability actions based on negligence theory. Rather, the *Restatement* says that a manufacturer may be held liable for physical harm caused to people who use its product in ways the product is expected to be used and who are those expected to be endangered by its use. Negligence liability may be imposed if the manufacturer fails to exercise reasonable care in the manufacture of a product that involves an unreasonable risk of harm if the product is not carefully made.[8]

be the immediate purchaser of the product, as illustrated in the *MacPherson* Case on Point. Today, a duty of care is owed to foreseeable users of products, not just those in privity of contract with the manufacturer, if it is reasonably foreseeable that harm will result if the product is defective.

Note that, under negligence theory, manufacturers and sellers of products are not made virtually insurers of the safety of their products, as you will see is the case with strict liability theory. Rather, the defendant's duty under negligence theory in products liability cases is to provide a reasonably safe product. If manufacturers or sellers have not breached their duty of care to provide a reasonably safe product to foreseeable users, then there is no negligence, even if an injury is suffered by the plaintiff. Only when a person is foreseeably injured by a product because the manufacturer or seller acted unreasonably may there be negligence liability.

Because of these restrictions, most importantly the fault requirement, plaintiffs may choose a different legal theory when bringing a tort action for harm caused by a defective product. Another possible theory is misrepresentation.

MISREPRESENTATION

Misrepresentation theory may also be used to bring a products liability action. **Misrepresentation**, also called fraud, fraudulent misrepresentation, or the tort of fraud or deceit, is the intentional making of a false statement, or the failure to disclose when a duty to disclose exists, which causes the plaintiff a pecuniary (financial) loss. This tort was already examined in Chapter 4, as it applies to other factual situations beyond, but including, products liability.

In bringing a misrepresentation claim against a product manufacturer, seller, or lessor, the plaintiff must establish a *prima facie* case. To do this, the plaintiff must show that the defendant made a material, meaning important,

Misrepresentation
The intentional making of a false statement, or the failure to disclose when a duty to disclose exists, which causes the plaintiff harm; also called fraud, fraudulent misrepresentation, or the tort of fraud or deceit.

Key Point

Essential Elements of the Tort of Misrepresentation

1. A false statement of material fact, or nondisclosure when a duty to disclose exists
2. Made with the intent to induce the plaintiff's reliance
3. Justifiable reliance by the plaintiff
4. Causation
5. Damages

With regard to the second element, some jurisdictions also recognize a tort of negligent misrepresentation. See the assignments at the end of the chapter for a products liability case brought under a negligent misrepresentation theory.

statement of fact that was false. The statement must have been made by the defendant with the intent to mislead the plaintiff—meaning the intent to induce the plaintiff's reliance on the statement. Note that some states recognize "negligent" misrepresentation, in addition to the intentional tort of misrepresentation, a topic that we discussed already, in Chapter 4. The plaintiff must justifiably rely on the defendant's false statement. Finally, the plaintiff must suffer actual damages as a result of relying on the defendant's false statement. Notice, however, that a product need not be defective under this theory; it need only be misrepresented.

Note that the essential elements of this tort are very numerous and particular, and a fairly narrow set of facts and circumstances involving harm caused by products falls within the scope of this tort theory. Also note that the plaintiff must justifiably rely on the false statement or omission; if the statement is not made to the plaintiff in order to induce his reliance, there can be no misrepresentation. This type of privity requirement limits who can bring a products liability claim under this theory, and it prohibits bystanders from bringing such actions under this theory.

Once the plaintiff has established a *prima facie* case of misrepresentation, the defendant may assert any relevant defense to this intentional tort, such as that the statement was one of opinion rather than fact, that the statement was not material to the plaintiff's decision making, that it was a true statement, that the defendant is immune from suit, or that the plaintiff failed to mitigate her damages.

An example of misrepresentation theory being used to bring a products liability action is a manufacturer intentionally mislabeling a pharmaceutical product, not disclosing the full extent of the side effects known to result from using the drug. If a manufacturer knowingly makes a false statement of fact to a consumer about a product with the intent to deceive that consumer, a misrepresentation action may be possible. The following Case on Point is another

CASE on Point

Ford Motor Co. v. Lonon, 398 S.W.2d 240 (Tenn. 1966)

In this case, the Supreme Court of Tennessee relied on a theory of misrepresentation to hold a manufacturer liable for injuries caused to a consumer by a defective, though not dangerous, product.

Lonon was a farmer who needed a large tractor with certain features to use in his farming work. He had purchased Ford Motor Company tractors before, so he went to Haywood Tractor Company, a local Ford dealership, to purchase the needed tractor. After reviewing a Ford Motor Company sales brochure describing its tractors, including detailed information about the power and special features of each tractor, and discussing quality and other characteristics of the tractor he was considering with both a manager and a mechanic at Haywood Tractor Company, Lonon purchased a Fordson Major Diesel. When it was put into service, however, the tractor quickly proved to be mechanically defective,

(continued)

and it never functioned properly. Lonon sued Ford Motor Company, the manufacturer of the tractor, along with the distributor and retailer of the tractor.

The court held that a manufacturer of a product that has been found to be seriously defective and unsuitable for use can be held liable for a resulting commercial loss to the purchaser even though there was no direct contractual relationship between the purchaser and the manufacturer (meaning no privity of contract), when the buyer relied on the manufacturer's booklets and trade name in making the purchase. Using the misrepresentation theory, though breach of warranty had been pled by the plaintiff, the court expanded misrepresentation theory in this commercial loss case (rather than a personal injury or property damage case) to permit recovery in the absence of privity of contract between the manufacturer and the purchaser when the manufacturer made material misstatements regarding the character or quality of its product in its sales brochure.

Note that the court distinguished this case from another Case on Point, *General Motors Corp. v. Dodson* (in the breach of warranty theory section following this section), in which both products (a tractor and a car) were defective, but only one (the car) was dangerous. Although the *Dodson* case was decided under a breach of warranty theory, this court said that the case could have been decided using strict liability theory because the product was both defective and dangerous, and the case need not have been brought under a breach of warranty or misrepresentation theory.

illustration of the use of the misrepresentation theory in bringing a products liability claim.

The essential elements of the tort of misrepresentation are numerous and factually specific. They apply to a fairly limited scope of situations or circumstances involving harm caused by products. Accordingly, products liability suits are often brought under tort theories other than misrepresentation. Another available theory is breach of express warranty.

BREACH OF EXPRESS WARRANTY

Breach of express warranty is another theory under which a products liability action may be brought. To understand breach of warranty, the term "warranty" must first be understood, and express and implied warranties must be distinguished.

Warranties are express or implied assurances, or promises, made by sellers of goods that the goods meet certain descriptions or standards of

Warranties
Express or implied assurances made by sellers of goods that the goods meet certain descriptions or standards of quality or performance on which buyers may reasonably rely.

SIDEBAR

THE UNIFORM COMMERCIAL CODE

The Uniform Commercial Code (UCC) is a uniform code governing commercial transactions that was written by legal experts and scholars to address commercial law issues and to provide uniform guidance to jurisdictions. The UCC has been adopted, in whole or in part, by most states. Article 2 of the UCC governs contracts for the sales of goods, including express and implied warranty rules.

Express warranties
Assurances made by a seller, either orally or in writing, that address the quality, description, or performance of the goods being sold.

Implied warranties
Warranties that arise by operation of law under a state's commercial code.

quality or performance on which buyers may reasonably rely. Notice that warranty law, governed by Article 2 of the states' commercial codes, uses the term "goods," not "products," as modeled in the Uniform Commercial Code (UCC). Warranties relate to contract law, rather than tort law, because they involve legal promises.

Warranties can be either express or implied. *Express warranties* are warranties that are made, either orally or in writing, by the seller of the goods. They usually address the quality, description, or performance of the goods being sold. *Implied warranties* are warranties that arise by operation of law because of the nature of the transaction or the relative situations of the parties. There are two main types of implied warranties, both of which are discussed in the next section: implied warranties of merchantability and implied warranties of fitness for a particular purpose. In this chapter, we discuss implied warranties as they relate to products liability.

An express warranty is created when the seller of goods makes an affirmation of fact or promise to the buyer that relates to the goods, in the form of any description, sample, or model of the goods that is made a part of the bargain, meaning the sale or lease of goods transaction under Article 2 of a state's commercial code. The representations made may concern the goods' description, quality, condition, or performance ability. The warranty created is that the product will conform to the promised description, sample, or model. For example, the statement, "The tires will conform to this sample," creates an express warranty. Express warranties may be made in writing or orally, though of course it is easier to prove the existence of written ones. The seller of the goods need not use the word "warranty" or "guarantee" or the like, nor must the seller have the specific intention to make a warranty in order for an express warranty to be created. However, a statement that merely suggests the value of the goods or is simply the seller's opinion or recommendation of the goods is not enough to create an express warranty.

CASE on Point

Baxter v. Ford Motor Co., 12 P.2d 409 (Wash. 1932)

Baxter purchased a Model A Ford town sedan after representations were made to him by the local Ford dealer and the automobile's manufacturer, Ford Motor Company, that the windshield of the vehicle was made of nonshatterable glass that would not "break, fly, or shatter" under the hardest impact. While he was driving the car, a pebble from a passing car struck the automobile's windshield, causing small pieces of glass to break off and fly into Baxter's eyes, resulting in loss of vision in his left eye and injuries to his right eye.

The Supreme Court of Washington held that the catalogs and printed material furnished by Ford Motor Company for distribution and assistance in sales contained representations concerning the product's qualities, on which purchasers might reasonably rely, even without privity of contract between the parties. (The court found that the sales contract between the Ford dealership and Baxter effectively disclaimed warranties as to the retailer, absolving the retailer from liability.)

Breach of warranty means a legal failure to fulfill the assurances made in a warranty, whether express or implied. To breach a warranty, the maker of the warranty must fail to live up to the promises made in the warranty. For example, if a manufacturer warrants that an automobile's windshield is made of shatter-proof glass, and the windshield shatters and injures the driver, a breach of express warranty action is an appropriate claim. See the *Baxter* Case on Point for an illustration.

Breach of warranty, both express and implied, is part of contract law, not tort law. Contract law deals with the enforceability of promises. It does not deal with wrongful conduct *per se*, as tort law does, though, arguably, it may be wrong to breach one's promises in a contract, depending on the circumstances. Because breach of warranty theories involve contract law principles rather than tort law principles, the plaintiff need not establish negligence, or intent, or any other type of fault of the seller of the goods in setting forth a *prima facie* case, as is normally required of tort theories other than strict liability. Rather, to establish a claim for breach of express warranty, the plaintiff must establish that the seller made an express warranty to the buyer when she sold the buyer the goods, that the goods failed to meet the affirmations made in the warranty, which caused the plaintiff to suffer actual harm, and the plaintiff gave notice to the seller of the breach of warranty within a reasonable time.

Note that notice is an essential element of a claim of breach of express warranty. Within a reasonable time after the buyer discovers or should have discovered the breach of warranty, he must notify the seller of the breach or he will be barred from suing under it. In other words, notice is a necessary preceding condition for a cause of action for breach of express warranty, and it is the plaintiff's responsibility to demonstrate that he met this condition.

Breach of warranty
A legal failure to fulfill the assurances made in a warranty.

Key Point

Essential Elements of a Breach of Express Warranty Claim

1. A sale of goods
2. Privity of contract between the buyer (plaintiff) and the seller (defendant) (required in some states)
3. An express warranty was made by the seller to the buyer and relied on by the buyer
4. The product failed to conform to the express warranty
5. Causation
6. The buyer gave reasonable notice of the breach of warranty to the seller
7. The buyer suffered damages

CASE on Point

General Motors Corp. v. Dodson, 338 S.W.2d 655 (Tenn. Ct. App. 1960)

Mr. and Mrs. Dodson purchased a new Oldsmobile automobile from Kemp Motor Company, an authorized dealer of General Motors Corporation (GM), which manufactured Oldsmobiles. The brakes of their new automobile were defective. Mrs. Dodson was severely and permanently injured and the automobile was damaged when her brakes locked and the car plunged into a ditch. The couple sued GM under breach of warranty theory.

At the time of the automobile purchase, GM required its dealers to deliver a booklet to each purchaser entitled "Oldsmobile Owner Protection Policy and Operating Manual." This booklet contained warranties identical to those appearing in another booklet entitled "Direct Dealer Selling Agreement," which was given by GM to its dealers. Among the warranties stated were that "each new motor vehicle, including all equipment or accessories . . . [shall be] free from defects in material and workmanship under normal use and service. . . ."

(continued)

The Court of Appeals of Tennessee found that express warranties were created by GM in the booklets. It also found that implied warranties of quality or fitness were created, under the jurisdiction's Uniform Sales of Goods Act, covering the automobile made by GM and extending to the consumer. The court rejected GM's argument that lack of privity of contract prevented the Dodsons recovery from GM, stating that GM "was the actual person or entity with whom plaintiffs were dealing, and Kemp was a conduit or subterfuge by which [GM] tried to exempt itself from liability to consumers who are the plaintiffs."

Although this court did not address strict liability theory, the court in the *Lonon* case (discussed earlier, in the section on misrepresentation theory), six years later, distinguished this case by noting that the vehicle was not only defective but also dangerous, whereas the tractor in the *Lonon* case was merely defective, not dangerous. The *Lonon* court went on to say that, while it agreed that the decision in the *Dodson* case was sound, "whenever a manufacturer . . . places on the market a chattel which is defective and unreasonably dangerous to potential users, and harm does result from the defect, while the product is in normal use, the manufacturer should incur a *strict liability* [emphasis added] in tort, apart from any warranties or representations which he may have made."

An important consideration in selecting a theory under which to bring a products liability action is the privity of contract requirement. For breach of warranty actions, either express or implied, some states require that there be privity of contract between the plaintiff and the defendant, meaning that the action must be between the buyer and the seller of the goods. This requirement limits who can bring suit under breach of warranty theories. Other states permit a breach of warranty action between the seller and the buyer's family or household, and still others extend those with standing to sue to include any persons

SIDEBAR

STANDING TO SUE

Only those with standing to sue may bring valid lawsuits. Having standing to sue means that one has a legal "right" to bring a court action against another.

To have standing to sue means that a person has a sufficient stake in a legal matter or dispute to justify allowing him or her, or "it" in the case of an entity, to seek a remedy in court. Normally, to demonstrate standing to sue, a plaintiff must be able to demonstrate that she has a legally protected interest in the subject matter of the suit or is otherwise directly affected by the issues raised in the case.

Consider this example. Jill is seriously injured in a car accident caused by Morty's negligent driving. Becky, who hears of the accident while watching the news that night, and who knows neither Jill nor Morty, is very upset by the news story. She sleeps poorly that night, disturbed by Jill's suffering, which Becky feels deeply because she is such a compassionate person. Who has standing to sue Morty? Does Becky? Does Jill? Jill, who was injured by Morty's actions, has standing to sue him—in tort, for negligence. Becky, who was not involved in the accident and suffered no injury because of it, has no standing to sue—even though the news of it triggered her feelings of compassion and caused her to sleep poorly that night.

LEMON LAWS

"Lemon laws" are state and federal statutes that protect consumers who purchase automobiles that repeatedly fail to meet certain standards of quality and performance. Such cars are called "lemons." Although these types of laws are referred to generically as lemon laws, each state has its own specific name for its relevant statute.

The federal lemon law, called the Magnuson-Moss Warranty Act, covers citizens of all states. State lemon laws vary from jurisdiction to jurisdiction. For instance, some states' laws cover leased or used cars, whereas others' do not. What these statutes provide is an administrative procedure that is less formal, costly, and time-consuming than litigation to resolve a legal dispute involving a car that is a "lemon."

Generally, the statutes require that an arbitrator decide the dispute between the consumer and the car dealer. These laws may provide that if the dealer or manufacturer does not correct the recurring automobile defect within a specified number of tries within a specified period of time, the purchaser can rescind the purchase contract and obtain a full refund of the purchase price paid. As such, rights afforded to consumers under lemon laws may exceed the warranty protections provided by the manufacturers.

who may reasonably be expected to be affected by the product, such as a bystander. If the jurisdiction requires privity of contract between the plaintiff and the defendant and the plaintiff cannot establish it, he is limited to nonwarranty theories in bringing a products liability action.

A defendant may defend a breach of express warranty action by showing that no express warranty was made, that it was not made to this plaintiff, that it was not relied on by this plaintiff, that there was no privity of contract between the plaintiff and defendant if the jurisdiction requires privity, that the plaintiff failed to give the defendant timely notice, or that the plaintiff failed to prove some other essential element(s) of the claim. Further, a defendant may defend on the grounds (1) that the warranty was disclaimed, in a statement limiting the scope of the warranty or stating that no warranty exists—as the Ford dealership did in the *Baxter* case—or (2) that the plaintiff assumed the risk of harm.

Breach of express warranty is a legal theory that can be used to bring a products liability action, depending on the facts and circumstances of the case, but another type of breach of warranty action may also be used. Next we will examine this other type of breach of warranty action, namely, breach of implied warranty.

BREACH OF IMPLIED WARRANTY

Breach of implied warranty is another theory on which a products liability action may be brought. As indicated earlier, an implied warranty is a warranty that is imposed by law, derived from the nature of the transaction or from the relative situations of the parties. There are two types of implied warranties: implied warranties of merchantability and implied warranties of fitness for a particular

Implied warranty of merchantability
A warranty imposed by law that promises that goods are of proper quality and fit for the ordinary purposes for which such goods are used.

Key Point

Essential Elements of a Breach of Implied Warranty of Merchantability Claim

1. A sale of goods by a merchant doing business in goods of that kind
2. Privity of contract between the plaintiff and the defendant (required in some states)
3. The goods were defective, meaning not of proper quality or reasonably fit for their ordinary purposes, when they left the control of the defendant
4. Causation
5. Notice to the defendant of the breach
6. Damages suffered by the plaintiff

purpose. These implied warranties are established in statutes enacted by state legislatures, found in the states' commercial codes, many of which are modeled after the Uniform Commercial Code. The breach of either of these warranties may be an appropriate theory for a products liability action, depending on the facts and circumstances. As with breach of express warranty, the intent, negligence, or innocence of the seller of the goods is irrelevant under these causes of action.

An ***implied warranty of merchantability*** is a warranty imposed by law that promises that the goods are of proper quality and fit for the ordinary purposes for which such goods are normally used. For example, in selling a can of interior house paint, the seller, limited to a "merchant" under this implied warranty, makes an implied warranty that the can of paint is fit for the ordinary purposes of being applied to interior house walls. This warranty is made only by merchants, and the term "merchant" is defined in the statute. "Merchant" is normally defined as a regular seller in the business of selling goods of that kind, and not an occasional seller. Also, this warranty applies only to sales of goods, not to sales of services. For an example, see Florida's statute on the implied warranty of merchantability in the Statute on Point below.

"Breach of the implied warranty of merchantability" means that the goods did not live up to their promise of proper quality or being fit for their ordinary purposes. The elements of a claim of breach of implied warranty of merchantability are that there was a sale of goods made by a merchant in the business of selling goods of that kind, that the goods were not merchantable, meaning not of proper quality or fit for their ordinary purposes, and the unmerchantable condition caused the plaintiff damages. Finally, the plaintiff must give timely notice of the breach to the defendant. Further, some jurisdictions require that the plaintiff and defendant be in privity of contract. An example of a good that is not fit for its ordinary purpose is a foreign substance in a food product, such as in the famous Wendy's case involving a human finger found in a bowl of chili, which was ultimately determined to have been a hoax, as the finger was planted in the chili by the plaintiff in the case. See the *Webster* Case on Point regarding foreign substances found in food products and the breach of implied warranty of merchantability theory.

What if the goods are fit for their ordinary purposes but are not fit for the special purpose for which the buyer purchased them? In that case, breach of implied warranty of fitness for a particular purpose may apply.

STATUTE on Point

Fla. Stat. § 672.314 (2009)

Under a Florida statute, when a seller sells a product that is of the kind of product it regularly sells, in the sales contract there is an implied warranty that the product (goods) will be merchantable. To be merchantable, goods must pass without objection in the trade under the contract description, and in the case of fungible goods (goods whose units are capable of substitution, such as wheat or crude oil) be of fair average quality within the description, be fit for the ordinary purposes for which these goods are used, be of even kind, quality, and quantity within each unit and among all units involved, be adequately contained, packaged, and labeled, and conform to any promises or affirmations of fact made on the container or label.

CASE on Point

Webster v. Blue Ship Tea Room, Inc., 198 N.E.2d 309 (Mass. 1964)

This is a classic case of a foreign substance found in food. Ms. Webster was dining at the Blue Ship Tea Room, a quaint wharf-side Boston seafood restaurant. After ordering a cup of fish chowder because the restaurant was out of her first choice (clam chowder), Ms. Webster ate three or four spoons full of the milky broth containing chunks of haddock and potatoes, as well as milk, water, and seasoning. Ms. Webster became aware of something lodged in her throat when she found she could not swallow or clear her throat, and felt something in it. Later, at Massachusetts General Hospital, a fish bone was discovered in her throat, and removed. Ms. Webster sued the Blue Ship Tea Room for breach of implied warranty of merchantability. She lost.

The Supreme Court of Massachusetts, in answering the question of whether a fish bone "lurking" in fish chowder constituted a breach of implied warranty of merchantability under the UCC, ruled that it did not. The court distinguished this case from other foreign-substance food cases when the food is rendered unwholesome because of some foreign substance in it, such as stones in beans. In this case, a restaurant patron found a fish bone in fish chowder. The court said, "We should be prepared to cope with hazards of fish bones, the occasional presence of which in chowders is . . . to be anticipated, and which . . . do[es] not impair [its] fitness or merchantability."

An ***implied warranty of fitness for a particular purpose*** is an implied warranty imposed by law that promises that the goods are fit for the particular purposes for which this buyer purchased them. For example, in selling a can of interior house paint to a customer based on a color swatch the customer asked the seller to match, the seller makes an implied warranty that the can of paint is fit for the particular purpose for which this customer, the buyer, requested it. This implied warranty is made by a seller, who does not have to be a merchant under this theory, who knows the particular purpose to which the buyer intends to put the goods, and the buyer is relying on the seller's skill and judgment in selecting the goods.

Breach of the implied warranty of fitness for a particular purpose means that the goods have not lived up to their promise of being fit for the special purpose for which the buyer sought the seller's expertise. The elements of a claim

Implied warranty of fitness for a particular purpose
A warranty imposed by law that promises that goods are fit for the particular purposes for which the buyer purchased them.

STATUTE on Point

Fla. Stat. § 672.315 (2009)

Under this Florida statute, an implied warranty of fitness for a particular purpose arises when, at the time of contracting, the seller had reason to know of a particular purpose for which the goods are required, and the buyer relied on the seller's skill or judgment to select or furnish suitable goods for that purpose.

This implied warranty arises in situations where the seller has certain expertise that the buyer does not, and the seller recommends a particular product to meet one or more of the buyer's needs. The buyer must rely on the seller's expertise, skill, or judgment to select the proper product for the buyer's purpose.

Key Point

Essential Elements of a Breach of Implied Warranty of Fitness for a Particular Purpose Claim

1. A sale of goods
2. Privity of contract between the plaintiff and the defendant (required in some states)
3. The defendant knowingly sold the product, or had reason to know the product was sold, for a particular purpose
4. The plaintiff bought the product for a particular purpose in reliance on the defendant's judgment
5. The product was defective, meaning not fit for the particular purpose for which the defendant knowingly sold it to the plaintiff, when the product left the defendant's control
6. Causation
7. Reasonable notice to the defendant of the breach of warranty
8. Damages suffered by the plaintiff

of breach of implied warranty of fitness for a particular purpose are that there was a sale of goods (and some jurisdictions require privity of contract between the plaintiff and the defendant, meaning the buyer must be the original purchaser of the goods from the seller), the defendant knew or had reason to know (the defendant does not have to *actually* know, but can) the plaintiff's particular purpose in buying the goods, the plaintiff relied on the defendant's skill or judgment in selecting the goods, and the goods were not fit for the particular purpose, which caused the plaintiff damages. Also, the plaintiff must give the defendant reasonable notice of the breach of warranty.

Consider this example. The seller is a dealer in custom skates. This seller is told by his customer that she is selecting skates to be used in international figure skating competitions. The seller recommends certain skates to the customer, who relies on the seller's recommendation and purchases the skates. The raw materials used in these skates are of insufficient strength and quality to withstand landing the triple jumps that are common in international figure skating competitions. If the skates break during use because of this weakness and cause the skater injury, the seller may be liable under breach of implied warranty of fitness for a particular purpose theory.

Note that the notion of product "defects" in strict liability actions is applicable to breach of warranty actions, but in a different way. Although the Uniform Commercial Code uses the terms "not merchantable" and "not fit for

CASE on Point

Deichl v. Savage, 216 P.2d 749 (Mont. 2009)

In this case the buyer of a horse, Deichl, brought an action against the sellers for, among other claims, breach of implied warranty of fitness for a particular purpose. The sellers sold a horse to Deichl in Yellowstone County, Montana. To sell the horse, the sellers placed a classified newspaper advertisement offering a gelding for sale. Deichl contacted the sellers and told them he was interested in purchasing a gentle and broken horse for use by a friend's teenage daughter, who was a novice rider. The sellers told Deichl that their gelding was gentle and would be suitable for riding by a teenager with little or no riding experience. Deichl went to look at the horse, rode it in a pen, and then purchased it. Several months later, Deichl was thrown from the horse while riding it, knocked unconscious, sustaining a head injury.

The court said that Deichl's claim for breach of implied warranty of fitness for a particular purpose was governed by Montana's Uniform Commercial Code. That UCC states that "where the seller at the time of contracting has reason to know any particular purpose for which the goods are required and that the buyer is relying on the seller's skill or judgment to select or furnish suitable goods, there is . . . an implied warranty that the goods shall be fit for such purpose." The court went on to say that Deichl's claim for breach of implied warranty of fitness for a particular purpose "sounds in contract," meaning arises out of contract law. The issue in the case was what was the proper venue to bring this action; the court determined that venue is proper for a contract claim in the county where the contract is performed—Yellowstone County here because the contract for the sale of the horse was performed there (though Deichl lived in another county, where the horseback riding accident occurred).

its ordinary purpose," many courts consider those terms to be interchangeable with the term "defect" in the context of products liability.

Defendants can defend breach of implied warranty actions by establishing that the plaintiff has failed to prove one or more of the essential elements of his claim, that the implied warranty was disclaimed, or that the plaintiff assumed the risk of harm.

Remember that actions for breach of implied warranties require privity of contract between the plaintiff and the seller in some states. If privity of contract is not present, another theory must be used to bring a products liability action. Next, we will discuss the most common theory under which products liability actions are brought: the strict liability theory.

STRICT LIABILITY

Strict products liability is another theory on which products liability actions may be brought, and it is often the preferred theory, for a variety of reasons discussed in the following section. **Strict liability**, as examined in the previous chapter, means legal liability imposed regardless of fault of the tortfeasor; it is also called "absolute liability" or "liability without fault." The interest protected by this tort is the right to be free from harm caused by defective products that are unreasonably dangerous.

Generally speaking, strict liability is liability imposed by law, as a matter of public policy, to prohibit actions that tend to injure the public, whether or not the defendant was at fault. The purpose in allowing strict products liability recovery in the absence of fault on the part of the defendant is threefold. First, consumers should be protected against harm from unsafe products. Second, manufacturers, distributors, sellers, and the like should not be able to avoid legal liability for their defective products merely because they were not in privity of contract with the injured person. Third, manufacturers, distributors, sellers, and the like are in a better position to bear the burden of the costs of the injuries sustained than the injured consumers.

The first case to impose strict products liability in tort on manufacturers of defective products was *Greenman v. Yuba Power Products, Inc.* Leading the way in strict products liability, the California Supreme Court reasoned that "the costs of injuries resulting from defective products are borne by the manufacturers that put such products on the market rather than by the injured persons who are powerless to protect themselves."

Strict liability
Liability imposed regardless of fault; also called absolute liability or liability without fault.

CASE on Point

Greenman v. Yuba Power Products, Inc., 377 P.2d 897 (Cal. 1962)

The plaintiff was injured when a Shopsmith combination power tool (saw, drill, and wood lathe) he was using malfunctioned, causing him to be struck in the forehead with a piece of wood. The plaintiff brought suit against the manufacturer and retailer, alleging breach of warranty and negligence. The California Supreme Court decided the case on another theory—strict liability.

(continued)

> The court said that liability in this case was not "governed by the law of contract warranties but by the law of strict liability in tort." Rather, "[a] manufacturer is strictly liable in tort when an article he places on the market, knowing that it is to be used without inspection for defects, proves to have a defect that causes injury to a human being. Recognized first in the case of unwholesome food products, such liability has now been extended to a variety of other products that create as great or greater hazards if defective," quoting cases, including *General Motors Corp. v. Dodson*, on this point. "The purpose of such liability is to ensure that the costs of injuries resulting from defective products are borne by the manufacturers that put such products on the market rather than by the injured persons who are powerless to protect themselves."
>
> The plaintiff could establish the manufacturer's liability by proving "that he was injured while using the Shopsmith in a way it was intended to be used as a result of a defect in design and manufacture of which plaintiff was not aware that made the Shopsmith unsafe for its intended use."

Before examining the essential elements of the strict products liability tort, we will consider the advantages of electing to bring a products liability action under the strict liability theory, because this theory is the most common one for bringing products liability actions.

Strict Liability Theory Election

In choosing a legal theory under which to bring a products liability action, plaintiffs consider whether they have standing to sue under a particular theory, whom they can sue, what essential elements they need to prove, and what they can recover.

A plaintiff has many theories under which to bring a products liability action. We have already discussed the theories of negligence, misrepresentation, breach of express warranty, and breach of implied warranty. Having examined the essential elements of each of those torts, it should be clear by now that the theory chosen depends on the facts and circumstances surrounding each case. As you have seen, some theories have more narrow application than others in terms of the situations in which they fit. As you will see when we examine the essential elements of the tort of strict products liability in the following section, many plaintiffs choose this theory for the simple reasons that it applies to a broader spectrum of fact patterns and it is easier for many plaintiffs to establish a *prima facie* case.

Many plaintiffs choose the strict liability theory when bringing products liability actions. Under strict products liability theory, defendants may be held liable regardless of fault or blameworthiness. In other words, the plaintiff need not establish fault on the part of the defendant. Further, strict products liability theory covers a broad range of possible defendants, defining "sellers" of defective products very broadly, to include almost everyone in the chain of manufacture, distribution, and sale of a product other than an occasional seller. Similarly, a broad range of plaintiffs may recover under this theory, oftentimes including bystanders, and privity of contract is not required. Also, the essential elements of this tort action are often easier for plaintiffs to establish than for the other tort and breach of warranty theories discussed earlier. These many reasons make strict liability theory an attractive one for plaintiffs injured by others' defective products.

In bringing a products liability suit under the strict liability theory, what are the essential elements that a plaintiff must establish to set forth a *prima facie* case? Those requirements are discussed next.

Essential Elements of a Strict Products Liability Claim

As for all tort claims, the plaintiff must establish each of the essential elements of a strict products liability claim in order to establish a *prima facie* case. The essential elements of strict products liability are that there be a seller of a defective product, a product which is unreasonably dangerous to persons or property, and which causes a user or consumer (or even a bystander) to suffer physical harm. These elements are now discussed in turn.

A SELLER

A seller is any person who is engaged in the business of selling the product for use or consumption. This is a very broad definition. It includes manufacturers, suppliers of component parts, wholesalers, distributors, retailers, and lessors of products. *Any* of these persons may be sued under strict liability theory

Key Point

Essential Elements of a Strict Products Liability Claim

1. A seller
2. A defective product that is unreasonably dangerous to persons or property
3. A user or consumer (most courts have expanded this to include bystanders)
4. Damages (usually physical harm is required, not just economic harm)
5. Causation

CASE on Point

MacPherson v. Buick Motor Co., 111 N.E. 1050 (N.Y. 1916)

Recall this landmark case from earlier in this chapter, in which the New York Court of Appeals held that Buick Motor Company (Buick) owed a duty of care to persons beyond the immediate purchaser of the car (the immediate purchaser was the Buick dealer, who purchased the automobile from Buick). The defective product in this case was an automobile, which collapsed as a result of spokes crumbling in one of the car's wooden wheels. Although Buick had not manufactured the wheel itself, the court held that Buick had a duty to inspect the wheels and that Buick "was responsible for the finished product."

Under current law, both Buick and the manufacturer of the wheels, a component part of the finished product, can be held strictly liable for harm caused by their defective products (the wheels, in the case of the component part supplier, and the automobile itself, in the case of Buick), as can be the distributors and retailers of defective automobiles. Consider how this liability relates to remedies available under lemon law statutes (discussed earlier in this chapter), which deal with automobiles that never work properly but that have not caused personal injury or property damage.

for harm caused by their defective products. However, the term "seller" does not include the occasional seller of a product, who is not in the business of selling the product—such as an individual who sells her personal automobile before buying a new one.

For a particular defendant to be held liable under strict products liability theory, the plaintiff must be able to show that the defective product was essentially in the same condition as when it left the hands of that defendant manufacturer, distributor, retailer, lessor, or other seller. For instance, if an automobile is defective because its wheels were not properly assembled by the car manufacturer when on the assembly line, the component part supplier who made the wheels, which are not themselves defective, would not be liable.

A DEFECTIVE PRODUCT THAT IS UNREASONABLY DANGEROUS TO PERSONS OR PROPERTY

Product

Under this cause of action, there must be a product. There is no strict products liability application for sales of services or, as illustrated in the school shootings Case on Point that follows, when there is a *reaction* to a product.

Defect

The product must be defective at the time it leaves the seller's hands, because of a manufacturing, design, or warning defect, as discussed earlier, and defined in the *Restatement (Third) of Torts*.

CASE on Point

James v. Meow Media, Inc., 300 F.3d 683 (6th Cir. 2002)

On December 1, 1997, Michael Carneal entered the lobby of Heath High School in Paducah, Kentucky, and shot several of his fellow students, killing three of them and wounding several others. This case was brought by the parents of some of the students who were killed in the attack.

Carneal regularly played video games, watched movies, and viewed Internet sites produced by the defendants in this case. Many of these games, movies, and sites were violent in nature, and the plaintiffs argued that they "desensitized" Carneal to violence and "caused" him to shoot the students at his school.

Among the many issues in the case, the 6th Circuit Court of Appeals was asked to determine whether video games, movies, and websites were "products" for purposes of strict products liability. The court answered that they were not. Accordingly, the producers and distributors of the games, movies, and websites could not be held liable for the harm inflicted by Carneal under strict products liability theory. The court said that "video game cartridges, movie cassette, and internet transmissions are not sufficiently 'tangible' to constitute products" and that those killed by Carneal were "not directly injured by the products themselves, but by Carneal's reaction to the products."

Unreasonably Dangerous

The defective product must be unreasonably dangerous to persons or property. Traditionally, many courts have held that the product must be dangerous to an extent beyond what is contemplated by the ordinary consumer who purchases it, with the ordinary knowledge common to the community as to its characteristics. Said simply, the product must be dangerous beyond the expectation of the ordinary consumer. With this test, the court defines the defect in relation to consumer expectations and reasonably foreseeable uses of the product. This "ordinary consumer" test, sometimes called the "consumer contemplation test," has been used by most courts and is defined in Section 402A of the *Restatement (Second) of Torts.*

However, not all courts have adopted the "ordinary consumer" test for determining whether a defective product is unreasonably dangerous. Some courts apply a risk-utility test, instead considering the foreseeability, probability, and seriousness of the harm, the importance of the product and its social utility, and the ability or burden and inconvenience on the manufacturer to redesign the product to make it safer. Even the *Restatement (Third) of Torts* now recommends a broader test for design defects than the ordinary consumer test, defining a design defective as where the foreseeable risks of harm posed by the product could have been reduced or avoided by the adoption of a reasonable alternative design, and the omission of the alternative design renders the product not reasonably safe. The *Restatement's* new test for design defects based on the availability of a reasonable alternative design has been controversial, and its adoption by courts is not universal, at least not yet. Table 11-2 provides a summary of the tests used by courts to determine whether a defective product is unreasonably dangerous. The law in this area continues to emerge as courts struggle with the definition of "unreasonable danger."

A product must not be unreasonably dangerous for its *intended use.* A product's intended use is that use which the manufacturer of the product

SIDEBAR

RESTATEMENT (SECOND) OF TORTS, SECTION 402A (1965)

The *Restatement (Second) of Torts* sets forth the most widely recognized articulation of the doctrine of strict products liability, which has been adopted, in whole or in part, by most states. It provides that anyone who sells a product in a defective condition, when the product is unreasonably dangerous to the user or consumer or to his property, is subject to liability for physical harm caused to the ultimate user or consumer or to his property if certain conditions are met. First, the seller must be engaged in the business of selling such a product. Second, the product must be expected to and must reach the user or consumer without substantial change in the condition in which it is sold by this seller. Liability is imposed even if the seller has exercised all possible care in the preparation and sale of its product, and even if the user or consumer has not bought the product from or contracted with the seller.

TABLE 11-2 Tests to Determine Whether a Defective Product Is Unreasonably Dangerous

Ordinary consumer test	The product is dangerous to an extent beyond what would be contemplated by an ordinary consumer who purchased it with ordinary knowledge common to the community.
Risk-utility test	The product is dangerous because the seriousness of the risk of danger outweighs the product's usefulness.
Restatement (Third)'s alternative design test	The harm caused by the defective product was preventable by adoption of a reasonable alternative product design.

planned for and is the purpose for which it made the product. For example, the intended use of a stepladder is to climb on to reach items otherwise out of reach.

A product also must not be unreasonably dangerous for its *foreseeable misuse.* Manufacturers can reasonably anticipate that their products may be used in certain ways, other than their intended ways, by consumers. Accordingly, under the law, manufacturers must consider how persons might misuse their products. If a type of misuse is one that the manufacturer can reasonably anticipate—for instance, that a consumer might stand on a chair, even though a chair is made for sitting on—the misuse is considered "foreseeable." So even though the manufacturer intends the chair to be used as something to sit on, it must anticipate that users may also stand on it, and take reasonable precautions to protect the public from harm caused by both sitting and standing on the chair in order to avoid legal liability.

A consumer can legally expect a product to be reasonably safe for all its foreseeable uses, including both its intended and its unintended ones. Of course, if a manufacturer can reasonably anticipate a certain type of product misuse, she should either redesign the product and/or warn consumers about risks of harm that may result from such product misuse. Consider bleach as an example. Bleach is used as a cleaning solution, normally for clothes, but also for sterilizing surfaces, such as bathroom and kitchen fixtures. Using bleach to clean is the manufacturer's intended use of its product. However, a bleach manufacturer also realizes that bleach is a liquid and is commonly found in the home. Accordingly, manufacturers must include warning labels on bottles, and perhaps design safety caps for lids, to protect persons from risks of harm from foreseeable misuses such as ingesting the bleach, mixing it with other cleaners, or pouring it on skin. As noted in the *Restatement (Third) of Torts,* factors such as the content and comprehensibility, and the intensity of expression of the warnings and instructions, as well as the characteristics of expected user groups, affect the determination of whether a product's warnings or instructions are reasonable.

Although strict products liability extends beyond products' intended uses to their foreseeable misuses, it does not extend to *unforeseeable* misuses of products; as discussed in the following chapter, unforeseeable misuse is a valid defense to strict products liability.

A USER, CONSUMER, OR BYSTANDER

The plaintiff in a strict products liability action need not be the product's original purchaser. A user or consumer of the product may bring suit. Today, by judicial decision or statute, most jurisdictions also permit bystanders to bring suit.

DAMAGES

Physical harm, in the form of personal injury or property damage, must be suffered by the plaintiff. Most courts say that economic damage, by itself, is not enough for strict products liability recovery.

CAUSATION

The product defect must cause the harm. The plaintiff must establish that the product was defective at the time it left the control of the specific defendant, and that this defect caused the harm the plaintiff suffered.

Similar to the tort of negligence, in a strict products liability case the seller's conduct must be the cause in fact and the proximate cause of the plaintiff's

CASE on Point

Giberson v. Ford Motor Co., 504 S.W.2d 8 (Mo. 1974)

Ford Motor Company sold the city of Springfield, Missouri, an automobile. On May 6, 1969, a police officer was driving the automobile in a line of traffic when its motor exploded. The explosion caused "a dense cloud of steam, smoke and gas which restricted visibility of other drivers to such an extent that a multiple automobile collision occurred," and the Gibersons were injured.

The parties agreed that existing law in the state of Missouri called for the application of strict liability in tort in the area of products liability. The question faced by the Supreme Court of Missouri was whether the rule should be extended to cover bystanders who were not purchasers or users of the defective product.

The court ruled that strict products liability applied to bystanders who were not purchasers or users of the defective products. The court acknowledged the "logic of placing the burden on the one with the best opportunity of avoiding the distribution of a defective product" and the "one controlling the making and inspection of a product should be held responsible for damage caused by defects in that product."

SIDEBAR

BAD FOOD IN RESTAURANTS AND CAUSATION

Plaintiffs can experience problems when suing food suppliers over bad food in restaurants. The causation element requires that the plaintiff establish that the product was defective at the time it left the control of the food supplier. Improper food handling by the restaurant, however, might be the cause of the bad food. For example, improper hot holding temperatures at a restaurant may cause food spoilage, and improper pest control at the facility may cause rodent or insect infestation.

injury. See the materials at the end of the chapter for a strict products liability case that fully discusses the distinction between cause in fact and proximate cause. In establishing causation, the plaintiff must demonstrate actual cause using either the "but for" (but for the defective product, the plaintiff would not have suffered harm) or "substantial factor" (the defective product was a

CASE on Point

Sindell v. Abbott Laboratories, 607 P.2d 924 (Cal. 1980)

This case involved a class action suit brought by women who had been injured when their mothers were administered the drug diethylstilbestrol (DES), a synthetic compound related to the female hormone estrogen, for the purpose of preventing miscarriage during their pregnancies. DES was manufactured and used in this capacity from 1941 until 1971. DES was later determined to be both carcinogenic and ineffective in preventing miscarriage. The prebirth exposure to DES in the daughters of the women who took it caused cancerous vaginal and cervical growths, called adenocarcinomas, a form of cancer that may lie dormant for at least ten to twelve years, and then emerge as a fast-spreading and deadly disease requiring radical surgery to contain it. Manufacturers of the drug DES were sued together, because the injured daughters could not determine which particular manufacturer produced the DES taken by their respective mothers.

The Supreme Court of California found that all the defendants, manufacturers of DES, produced a drug from an identical formula, which caused the plaintiffs' injuries. That a particular manufacturer could not be traced to each specific plaintiff's mother was not the fault of the plaintiffs. The court determined that it was reasonable to "measure the likelihood that any of the defendants supplied the product which allegedly injured plaintiff by the percentage which the DES sold by each of them for the purpose of preventing miscarriage bears to the entire production of the drug sold by all for that purpose." Although about 200 manufacturers produced DES, only about 6 companies produced 90 percent of the DES marketed. The court held, "Each defendant will be held liable for the proportion of the judgment represented by its share of that market unless it demonstrates that it could not have made the product which caused the plaintiff's injuries." One DES manufacturer/defendant was able to do this by proving that it did not manufacture DES until after a plaintiff was born.

substantial factor contributing to the harm suffered by the plaintiff) test. This part of causation is normally fairly straightforward. Sometimes it is unclear, however, and the plaintiff may have difficulty, through no fault of her own, proving that the defective product that caused her injury was the product of a specific defendant. For instance, if a product goes through many stages in its manufacture and ultimate sale, causation may be hard to determine and prove because the product must be defective when it leaves the defendant's control. Another difficult "causation" situation is one involving market-share liability, in which a plaintiff cannot establish which manufacturer made the product that caused her injury, as the Case on Point on the previous page illustrates.

In a market-share liability case, a plaintiff may suffer harm from a product but be unable to determine who made the particular product that caused her harm. For example, if a woman is injured by her mother taking DES pills to prevent miscarriage, she may not be able to determine which particular company manufactured the drug her mother took. This presents a causation issue because the plaintiff cannot determine who caused her injury and, in many jurisdictions, defeats her claim. However, a minority of jurisdictions will permit a plaintiff to sue the manufacturers together, and if she wins, to hold each manufacturer liable for its proportionate share of her damages based on each manufacturer's relative share of the market. In effect, if the plaintiff is injured by a product and it is difficult to determine which manufacturer made the product that injured this plaintiff, then some courts require all manufacturers to pay their proportionate share of the damage based on their market share. Only if a particular manufacturer can prove that it could not have manufactured the product in question can it avoid its proportionate share of liability. When these cases are successful, they deal with identical or very similar products, and a large number of manufacturers must be sued in order to have representation of a substantial share of the industry defending the suit. Tobacco, breast implant, pesticide, and drug cases are areas to which this theory is typically applied.

Proximate cause is the second part of the causation element. For the plaintiff to recover, the court must determine that the harm suffered by the plaintiff was the foreseeable consequence of the defective product. Similar to the tort of negligence, proximate cause, as applied in strict products liability cases, is a policy question, establishing a cutoff point beyond which a defendant will not be held liable in tort for harm she in fact caused.

Once the plaintiff has established a *prima facie* case of products liability under any of these theories, the defendant can assert defenses to the claim. Defenses related specifically to strict products liability theory are discussed in the next chapter, as part of strict liability defenses.

CHAPTER **SUMMARY**

- Products liability is legal liability for harm caused by defective products. Those who can be held liable for such harm include manufacturers, component part manufacturers, parts suppliers, wholesalers, distributors, retailers, and lessors of goods. Legal liability extends to injuries to persons or their property that are caused by defective products. Those who can bring products liability actions include consumers, lessees, users, and sometimes even bystanders.

- Most products liability cases arise because of a product defect. A product is defective if something is wrong with it that makes it dangerous, increasing the risk of harm to persons and their property. However, not every product that causes harm is necessarily defective.

- There are three categories of product defects: manufacturing, design, and warning defects.

- Manufacturing defects exist when the manufactured product does not conform to its design, and a problem occurs in the making of the product that causes it to be dangerous to use. The defective product is different from the rest of the products made on the line.

- Design defects exist when all products on the line conform to the design, but something is wrong with the design itself, which makes the product dangerous and increases the risk of harm to persons and their property.

- Warning defects exist when all the products contain no, or insufficient, warnings or instructions, which make the products dangerous, increasing the risk of harm to persons and their property. In the case of warning defects, the product labels are insufficient to provide users with the information they need to use the product safely and properly.

- Five legal theories may be used by plaintiffs, defending on the facts and circumstances, to bring products liability actions: negligence, misrepresentation, breach of express warranty, breach of implied warranty, and strict liability.

- Negligence theory may be used to bring an action for harm caused by a product if a plaintiff can establish the four essential elements of that tort claim, namely, a duty of care was owed, the duty of care was breached, causation, and damages. In such actions, the defendant may assert any relevant defenses, including contributory or comparative negligence, and assumption of the risk, to bar or reduce the plaintiff's recovery.

- In bringing a misrepresentation claim against a product manufacturer, seller, or lessor, the plaintiff must establish a *prima facie* case by showing that the defendant made a statement of fact that was false, the statement was made with the intent to mislead, the plaintiff justifiably relied on the false statement, and the plaintiff suffered actual damages as a result. The defendant can assert any relevant defenses to this intentional tort, such as that the statement was one of opinion rather than fact, that the statement was not material to the plaintiff's decision making, that it was a true statement, that the defendant is immune from suit, or that the plaintiff failed to mitigate her damages.

- Breach of warranty means a legal failure to fulfill the assurances made in a warranty, whether express or implied. To establish a claim for breach of express warranty, the plaintiff must establish that the seller made an express warranty to the buyer when she sold the buyer goods, that the goods failed to meet the affirmations made in the warranty, which failure caused the plaintiff to suffer actual harm, and the plaintiff gave notice to the seller of the breach of warranty within a reasonable time.

- A defendant may defend a breach of express warranty action by showing that no express warranty was made, that it was not made to this plaintiff, that it was not relied on by this plaintiff, there was no privity of contract between the plaintiff and the defendant, the plaintiff failed to give the defendant timely notice, or the plaintiff failed to prove some other essential element(s) of the claim. Also, a defendant may defend on the grounds that the warranty was disclaimed or that the plaintiff assumed the risk of harm.

- Breach of the implied warranty of merchantability means that the goods did not live up to their promise of being fit for their ordinary purposes. The elements of a claim of breach of implied warranty of merchantability are that there was a sale of goods made by a merchant of goods of that kind, that the goods were not merchantable, which unmerchantability caused the plaintiff harm, and the plaintiff gave the defendant reasonable notice of the breach of warranty.

- Breach of the implied warranty of fitness for a particular purpose means that the goods did not live up to their promise of being fit for the special purpose for which the purchaser sought the seller's expertise in selecting the goods. The elements of a claim of breach of implied warranty of fitness for a particular purpose are that there was a sale of goods, the seller knew or had reason to know the buyer's particular purpose in buying the goods, the buyer relied on the seller's skill or judgment in selecting the goods, the goods were not fit for the particular purpose, which unfitness caused the plaintiff damages, and the plaintiff gave the defendant reasonable notice of the breach of warranty.

- Under strict products liability theory, defendants may be held liable regardless of fault or blameworthiness. Strict products liability theory covers a broad range of possible defendants. Similarly, a broad range of plaintiffs may recover under this theory, including bystanders, and privity of contract is not required. Also, the essential elements of this tort action are often easier for plaintiffs to establish than for the other tort and breach of warranty theories.

- The essential elements of a claim of strict products liability are that there was a seller of a defective product that was unreasonably dangerous to persons or property, which caused a user or consumer, or even bystander, to suffer physical harm.

- A seller is any person who is in the business of selling the product for use or consumption. This is a very broad definition, which includes manufacturers, suppliers of component parts, wholesalers, distributors, retailers, and lessors of products. However, it does not include the occasional seller of the product. There must be a product, not a service or reaction to a product. The product must be defective at the time it leaves the seller's hands, via a manufacturing, design, or warning defect. The product must be unreasonably dangerous to persons or property, both in its intended uses and in its foreseeable misuse. A user or consumer of the product must bring suit; the plaintiff need not be its purchaser. Additionally, most courts extend standing to sue to include bystanders. Physical harm, in the form of personal injury or property damage, must be suffered by the plaintiff and must be caused by the defective product.

- Once the plaintiff has established a *prima facie* case of products liability under any of these theories, the defendant can assert defenses to the claim.

CONCEPT REVIEW AND REINFORCEMENT

QUESTIONS FOR **REVIEW**

1. What is products liability?
2. How does products liability relate to strict liability tort law?
3. What are the five tort theories under which plaintiffs may bring products liability actions?
4. Why would someone choose to bring a products liability claim under the strict liability theory? Why might someone choose a different theory?
5. What are the essential elements of a strict products liability claim?

DEVELOPING YOUR PARALEGAL SKILLS

CRITICAL THINKING **EXERCISES**

1. In this chapter, we examined products liability and the theories on which products liability actions may be brought. Among the most commonly used of these theories, for reasons discussed in the chapter, is strict liability theory. Research the essential elements of a strict products liability claim in your jurisdiction. Compare those state-specific requirements to the requirements of most states, as set forth in the chapter. Are they similar? Are there any differences? Who may bring a strict products liability action in your state? Against whom may such an action be brought? What must be proven by the plaintiff to establish a *prima facie* case? Discuss your research results in class.

2. For her birthday, Cindy, an avid cook, receives a top-quality stainless steel carving station from her husband. The knife that is included in the set was patterned after an old style of Japanese cutlery, in which the sharp edge of the knife extends for 8 inches, and the last 5 inches of the knife constitute the handle. In this artistic style, there is no transition from cutting blade to handle, unlike most knife blades, which have a transition between blade and handle where the blade is not sharp. The knife carries no warning label on it.

   a. *Cindy, while carving a roast beef for a dinner party, is injured when her hand slips off the knife handle and is cut on the blade. If she wishes to sue the manufacturer of the carving station, what type of product defect might she successfully allege?*

   b. *Cindy, when getting ready to carve the roast beef, grabs the knife by the blade to pick it up, cutting herself. Is the knife defective because no warning label was on it?*

   c. *Cindy, while carving the roast beef, is injured when the knife blade comes apart from the handle and falls on her foot. If she wishes to sue the manufacturer of the carving station, what type of product defect might she successfully allege?*

3. Balmer Corp. manufactures electric space heaters. Sara, who purchased one of Balmer's electric heaters, and Joel, Sara's boyfriend, are injured when the mechanism's fan malfunctions, causing an explosion.

   a. *Can Sara sue Balmer Corp., under negligence theory, for her injuries sustained in the explosion? If so, what must she prove?*

   b. *Can Joel sue Balmer Corp., under negligence theory, for the injuries he sustained in the explosion even though he was not the purchaser of the space heater? Why or why not?*

   c. *What if Sara mistakenly spilled a cup of water into the electric space heater, triggering the explosion? Does this affect either Sara or Joel's recovery under negligence theory?*

4. Larry, in the market for a car, goes to the local Auto-Max, Inc., dealership. There, he is told by Sam, a salesman, that a particular car of interest to Larry has "new tires, with less than 5,000 miles on them." In fact, the tires are not new; they are about due to be replaced. Larry purchases the car. A month later, Larry is injured when one of the tires blows out while Larry is driving down the highway. It is determined that the cause of the blowout was that the tire, well worn, was pierced when it went over a sharp rock lying on the roadway.

   Can Auto-Max, Inc., be held liable, under misrepresentation theory, for the harm Larry sustained?

5. Brian purchased an electric weed cutter from Lawn Products, Inc. At the time he purchased the weed cutter, the seller told Brian that the machine was safe to use with plastic line no. 462. One day, while Brian was cutting down weeds, the line detached from the machine and put out the eye of Billy, a nearby neighbor.

   Can Billy successfully bring a products liability action under the theory of breach of express warranty for the injury he sustained? Why or why not?

6. Charles and some friends go out to eat at Great Plains Steak House. Charles takes a bite of a "blooming onion" giant fried onion ring, and cuts his mouth on a piece of glass embedded in the onion.

   a. *If Charles wishes to bring a products liability action against Great Plains Steak House under a breach of implied warranty theory, what warranty would apply? Do you think he would succeed?*

   b. *If Charles had not bitten into glass in the "blooming onion," but rather had bitten into a live insect in a fresh salad, do you think these factual changes would affect your answer to question a?*

7. Fred has an electric train set that he inherited from his grandfather many years ago. Fred needs some extra money and is not really interested in electric trains, so he offers the train set for sale, at auction, over the Internet. Stella purchases the set as a birthday present for her son. When Stella and her son set up the train to operate it, the train malfunctions due to a product defect; it shocks them, causing them injury.

   Can Stella successfully sue Fred for the injuries sustained using the strict products liability theory? Why or why not?

8. Georgia purchased a top-of-the-line alarm clock from KeepTime Co. On the day Georgia was to interview for an important employment position, she overslept because her alarm clock malfunctioned, and the alarm did not sound at the time for which it was set. Because she missed her interview, Georgia lost any chance she might otherwise have had to secure that great job.

   a. *If Georgia sues KeepTime Co. under strict products liability theory, will she win? Why or why not?*

   b. *What if, when the alarm clock malfunctioned, it exploded. A piece of the clock hit Georgia in the eye, injuring her. Does this change your answer to question a? If so, how?*

   c. *What if Georgia is not injured when the alarm clock explodes. However, Georgia's grandmother, who is visiting her from out of town, is injured when the clock explodes while she is standing near it. Can Georgia's grandmother recover from KeepTime Co. under strict products liability theory? Why or why not?*

ASSIGNMENTS AND PRACTICAL **APPLICATIONS**

1. You are a law school student performing a summer clerkship with a law firm in which you are hoping to work, full-time, after graduating and achieving membership in the state's Bar Association. Your supervising attorney asks you to research "what constitutes a product defect" under products liability law in your state. Perform the legal research required to answer this question and outline your research results for class discussion.

2. Read and brief the following cases on product defects: *Rix v. General Motors Corp.*, 723 P.2d 195 (Mont. 1986), in which the plaintiff alleged both manufacturing and design defects in a 2-ton chassis-cab; *Prentis v. Yale Mfg. Co.*, 365 N.W.2d 176 (Mich. 1984), about a design defect involving a forklift; and *Anderson v. Owens-Corning Fiberglas Corp.*, 810 P.2d 549 (Cal. 1991), a warning defect case involving asbestos exposure.

3. Pick three products you have at home or in your dorm room and examine the warning labels and instructions that came with the products. What warnings and instructions are there? How are they expressed? Where are they expressed? How do they differ from product to product? Share your favorite with the class.

4. For another products liability case involving express warranty theory, see *Collins v. Uniroyal, Inc.*, 315 A.2d 16 (N.J. 1974), in which the plaintiff's decedent (the plaintiff is administratrix of her dead relative's estate) was killed in an automobile accident involving a tire blowout, and the tire manufacturer had advertised, "If it saves your life once, it's a bargain."

5. For a case involving products liability under a negligent (as opposed to intentional) misrepresentation theory, see *Hanberry v. Hearst Corp.*, 276 Cal. App. 2d Supp. 680 (1969), involving a woman who was injured when she slipped and fell on a vinyl kitchen floor while wearing shoes that had been advertised as certified with the "Good Housekeeping's Consumers' Guaranty Seal."

6. Read and brief *Mazetti v. Armour & Co.*, 135 P. 633 (Wash. 1913), which was the first case to extend the implied warranty of a seller in the absence of privity of contract in a products liability case involving bad food. For another interesting breach of implied warranty case, see *Henningsen v. Bloomfield Motors, Inc.*, 161 A.2d 69 (N.J. 1960), involving injuries sustained in an automobile accident caused by defects in a newly purchased automobile.

7. For a criminal case allowing a certain amount of insect fragments in butter, illustrating the application of the FDA guidelines on natural and unavoidable defects in food for human consumption, see *U.S. v. Capital City Foods, Inc.*, 345 F.Supp. 277 (D.C.N.D. 1972).

8. Strict products liability theory requires the sale of a product, not a service. Is the receipt of tainted blood in a blood transfusion the sale of a product or of a service? Some states, by statute, define blood transfusions as a service, taking them outside the realm of strict products liability. Research how your state treats blood transfusions. Discuss your research results in class.

9. For a classic case of a foreign substance (a decomposed mouse) found in a bottle of Squirt, in which strict products liability was found even though the seller exercised all reasonable care and was not in a contractual relationship with the buyer, see *Shoshone Coca-Cola Bottling Co. v. Dolinski*, 420 P.2d 855 (Nev. 1967).

10. What about if the product is altered by someone after manufacture, such as by someone in the marketing chain, the consumer-purchaser, or a third person? Any substantial alteration of a product that was not contemplated by the manufacturer is likely to break the causal connection. The *Restatement (Second) of Torts*, section 402.A(1)(b), provides for liability only if the product is expected to and does reach the user or consumer without substantial change in the condition in which it was sold. Read and brief the case of *Glass v. Allis-Chalmers Corp.*, 789 F.2d 612 (8th Cir. 1986), about a combine that was substantially changed after leaving the control of the manufacturer but before being purchased by the owner.

11. For a full discussion of the distinction between cause in fact and proximate cause in a strict products liability case, see *E.J. Stewart, Inc. v. Aitken Prod., Inc.*, 607 F.Supp. 883 (D.C. Pa. 1985).

TECHNOLOGY RESOURCES AND INTERNET **EXERCISES**

Research the Internet website for the U.S. Consumer Product Safety Commission at *www.cpsc.gov*. Search "consumer injuries" and see what you find. From what you find, how big an issue is product safety in this country? Do consumers really need government protection in this area? Discuss the pros and cons in class.

The U.S. Food and Drug Administration sets food defect action levels that state the levels of natural and unavoidable defects in foods that present no health hazards for humans. See *http://vm.cfsan.fda.gov/~dms/dalbook.html* for the published booklet on food defect action levels. For example, an average of 30 or more insect fragments per 100 grams, or an average of 1 or more rodent hairs per 100 grams, of peanut butter is considered a natural and unavoidable defect, not rendering the product unsafe for human consumption. Have a class discussion on these defect action levels and permitted contamination.

Lemon laws are statutes that protect consumers against automobiles (and other products, in some jurisdictions) that fail to meet certain standards of quality and performance. Using the Internet, research whether your state has a lemon law, and if so, what it protects, and how. How does a consumer invoke the protections of your state's lemon law? Assuming the role of the attorney, write a legal letter to your client explaining the steps involved in invoking protections provided under the lemon law.

ETHICAL **APPLICATIONS**

Peter Marshall was injured in a motorcycle accident caused by the steering mechanism becoming dislodged while the cycle was in motion. It appears that the steering mechanism was defectively manufactured and, once assembled into the finished product, caused the motorcycle to be unreasonably dangerous.

Peter asks you, a lawyer known for specializing in personal injury plaintiff's work, to represent him in bringing an action against the manufacturer, distributor, and retailer of the motorcycle. After interviewing Peter, you would like to represent Peter in this matter. He asks what your fee is and you explain that you charge a contingency fee of 40 percent. This means that any recovery he receives in the suit, either at trial or via settlement, will be distributed 60 percent to him and 40 percent to you as your fee. You ask Peter to sign a fee agreement agreeing to this fee arrangement, as well as a retainer agreement.

Is this fee arrangement, and the amount of the fee, ethical under your state's legal ethics rules?

Are contingency fees appropriate in class action tort claims? Sometimes, in class action personal injury cases, the attorney (or attorneys) receives millions of dollars in fees while members of the class, who are the ones harmed, get little recovery. Is this fair? Read the novel *The King of Torts*, by John Grisham, for a fictional account of such cases.

VIDEO **CASE STUDY**

The Judge Instructs the Jury Before Deliberations

Synopsis: The trial judge gives the jurors instructions on the law at the conclusion of the presentation of evidence and closing statements.

Questions

1. When is a manufacturer of a defective product that causes injury strictly liable for that injury under the law in this jurisdiction?

2. What is the purpose of the judge telling the jurors what the relevant law is?

3. What is the jury's purpose, then, if not to decide the law?

chapter 12

STRICT LIABILITY DEFENSES AND REMEDIES

This chapter discusses the defenses applicable to strict liability torts as well as remedies available for successful strict liability actions. First, we examine strict liability defenses. What are they?

Defenses to Strict Liability

Remember from earlier in the text that a ***defense*** is a response by a party to the claim of another party, setting forth the reason(s) why the claim should be denied or recovery reduced. A defendant can defend a strict liability action in two ways. First, to defend a strict liability action, a defendant can defeat one or more of the essential elements of the plaintiff's claim. Remember that the ***essential elements*** of a claim are each of the component parts that must be established by the plaintiff in order for her to make a *prima facie* case. If a defendant can defeat one or more of the essential elements of the plaintiff's claim, then he defeats the claim entirely.

For instance, with a claim involving an abnormally dangerous condition or activity, a defendant could show that the condition or activity was not abnormally dangerous, the defendant was not aware of the condition or activity, or the condition or activity did not cause the harm that the plaintiff suffered. For a case involving harm caused by a domesticated animal, the defendant could assert that he had no reason to know of the animal's dangerous propensity, or that the harm suffered by the plaintiff was not due to that dangerous propensity. For a strict products liability claim, a defendant could assert that the product was not defective, the defendant was not a seller of the product, the product was not unreasonably dangerous, the product did not cause the injury, or the like. To defeat one of the plaintiff's essential elements of a strict liability claim is to defeat the claim itself.

The defendant can also assert the following affirmative defenses in a strict liability action: assumption of the risk, commonly known dangers, knowledgeable users, unforeseeable misuse of the product,

LEARNING OBJECTIVES

12.1 Discuss the various defenses to strict liability torts.

12.2 Identify and discuss the remedies available in strict liability actions.

12.3 Explain how the mitigation of damages doctrine applies in strict liability actions.

Defense
A response by a party to the claim of another party, setting forth the reason(s) why the claim should be denied or recovery reduced.

Essential elements
Each of the component parts that must be established by the plaintiff in order to make a *prima facie* case.

Affirmative defense

The defendant's response to a plaintiff's claim setting forth new factual allegations that were not included in the plaintiff's original claim.

immunity, and statutes of limitations and repose. In some states, the defendant may also be able to assert comparative negligence as a defense to a strict products liability claim. Remember that an *affirmative defense* is the defendant's response to a plaintiff's claim setting forth new factual allegations that were not included in the plaintiff's original claim. Each of these defenses to strict liability will be discussed in turn. When the defense applies to other tort theories, such as negligence or intentional tort theories, in addition to strict liability theory, that is pointed out as well. The first of the affirmative defenses to strict liability we will discuss is assumption of the risk.

ASSUMPTION OF THE RISK

Assumption of the risk

An affirmative defense in which the plaintiff knowingly and voluntarily agrees to accept the risk of being injured by certain conduct of the defendant.

A plaintiff assumes the risk of harm when he knowingly and voluntarily agrees to accept the risk of being injured by another's conduct; this is the affirmative defense known as *assumption of the risk*. It is a defense to all classifications of torts, including strict liability torts, and bars a plaintiff's recovery, even in strict liability cases (note that this defense was discussed earlier, in Chapter 9, as a defense to negligence).

Assumption of the risk may be expressed in words, either written or oral, or may be implied by the plaintiff's conduct and the surrounding facts and circumstances. Normally, to assert this defense successfully in a strict liability action, the defendant must show not only that the plaintiff knowingly and voluntarily assumed the risk, but that the plaintiff's assumption of the risk was unreasonable. This is because, under the law, a person has the right to the reasonable use and enjoyment of his own property. It is only when the plaintiff's use of his own property is unreasonable that the courts will deny him recovery in strict liability for harms he suffers by the conduct of others when using his own property.

Consider the following application of the assumption of the risk defense to a strict liability case involving a vicious captive bear.

CASE on Point

Ervin v. Woodruff, 119 A.D. 603 (N.Y. App. Div. 1907)

This action was brought to recover damages caused by injuries inflicted by a bear kept by the defendant at his camp in the Adirondacks. The bear "was a ferocious animal, dangerous to mankind." Both the plaintiff and the defendant knew this because, on "various occasions" prior to this one, the bear had "attacked, bitten, and injured" others while the defendant kept it. The bear was "safely chained up, and the length of the chain was known to the plaintiff" and the defendant. The court said, "[t]he plaintiff knew and understood, if he went within reach of the bear as so chained, he was likely to be attacked and injured." On the day of the plaintiff's injury, the plaintiff was asked by the defendant's guests to make the bear stand up so they could take its picture. The plaintiff went "within reach of the bear, and put himself in a position to be attacked, and did this knowingly, voluntarily, and unnecessarily, and as a result, was attacked and injured." The

(continued)

court said that the plaintiff could have accomplished this safely, without getting within reach of the bear. The plaintiff "knew the chain sometimes got wound up, so that the bear would be temporarily more closely confined than when the chain was free and at full length, and he knew it was not safe to get within the limits which the full length of the chain permitted the bear to go."

In citing cases decided as much as thirty years before, and concluding that those cases continued to state the law correctly and to apply to this case, the Supreme Court of New York found the defendant was not liable. The court reasoned that the plaintiff "knew the vicious disposition of the bear. He knew it had frequently attacked persons before who came within its reach. He knew the length of the chain by which it was confined, and though it was sometimes wound up by the bear itself, so as to confine him within a more limited circle, yet it was liable to be, and generally was, unwound so as to permit it the full length of the chain. Knowing all these things, the plaintiff voluntarily and unnecessarily put himself within reach of the bear and was injured. He brought the calamity upon himself, and could not recover damages therefor."

Accordingly, the plaintiff's knowing and voluntary assumption of the risk of harm is a complete bar to recovery. Closely related to the defense of assumption of the risk is the "commonly known dangers" defense.

COMMONLY KNOWN DANGERS

In strict products liability actions, if a defendant can demonstrate that the plaintiff's injury was a result of a *commonly known danger*, such as being shot by a gun or cut by a knife, the defendant will not be liable. This is because some dangers associated with certain products are so obvious that manufacturers need not warn users of them.

The law imposes no duty to warn about risks that are obvious or commonly known. Warnings about obvious or commonly known dangers do not make a product safer. In fact, they may do the opposite, by reducing the significance of the other warnings and instructions, to the detriment of the consumer.

Commonly known dangers
Dangers associated with certain products which are so obvious that manufacturers need not warn users of them.

CASE on Point

Jamieson v. Woodward & Lothrop, 247 F.2d 23 (C.A.D.C. 1957)

In this case, Mrs. Jamieson purchased an elastic rubber exercise rope similar to a jump rope. While she was exercising with it one day, the rope slipped from Mrs. Jamieson's foot and struck her in the eye, detaching the retina.

Mrs. Jamieson sued the manufacturer of the exercise rope, alleging that the rope was inherently dangerous and that the manufacturer failed to properly warn users that it might slip off a foot and cause injury. The elastic exercise rope was not defective and did not break or fail in any way.

The District of Columbia Circuit Court of Appeals held that the manufacturer was not liable even though it failed to warn any user that the exercise rope might slip off a foot in such a way. The court reasoned that "[a]lmost every

(continued)

physical object can be inherently dangerous or potentially dangerous in a sense. A lead pencil can stab a man to the heart or puncture his jugular vein, and due to that potentiality it is an 'inherently dangerous' object; but if a person accidentally slips and falls on a pencil-point in his pocket, the manufacturer of the pencil is not liable for the injury. . . . A tack, a hammer, a pane of glass, a chair, a rug, a rubber band, and myriads of other objects are truly 'inherently dangerous,' because they might slip. They cause accidents and injury even more often, we expect, than do rubber exercisers. . . . A hammer is not of defective design because it may hurt the user if it slips. A manufacturer cannot manufacture a knife that will not cut or a hammer that will not mash a thumb or a stove that will not burn a finger. The law does not require him to warn of such common dangers."

The court recognized that it was common knowledge that an elastic band of any kind, once stretched, would snap back. Accordingly, no duty was imposed on the manufacturer to warn of that simple fact.

Key Point

Commonly Known Dangers Defense

The commonly known dangers defense is a defense to strict products liability actions under which the defendant can show that the plaintiff's injury was a result of a commonly known danger.

Keep in mind, then, that in cases involving products liability, if the defendant can demonstrate to the court that the plaintiff's injury resulted from a commonly known danger, then the defendant will not be liable for the plaintiff's injuries.

Similar to the commonly known dangers defense, it is a defense to strict liability if a specific danger is commonly known by a particular user of a product. This is the "knowledgeable user" defense.

KNOWLEDGEABLE USER

Similar to commonly known dangers, if a specific danger is or should be commonly known by *particular users* of a product, the manufacturer need not warn these users of the danger. This defense is the knowledgeable user defense, sometimes called the sophisticated user defense. Note, however, that this defense is not recognized in all jurisdictions. See the Internet exercises at the end of the chapter for an online article about this defense and its application.

Knowledgeable users

Particular users of a product who should, because of experience and training, know of the particular dangers of that product; also called sophisticated users.

For example, electricians are aware of the danger of electric shock in the course of their work with electrical products. They are **knowledgeable users**, and manufacturers need not warn them of such dangers.

CASE on Point

Miller Metal Fabrication, Inc. v. Wall, 999 A.2d 1006 (Md. 2009)

This case involved, among other claims, a products liability claim and the knowledgeable user defense. Dawn Wall worked at Hanover Foods Corporation (Hanover) as a quality control coordinator. Miller Metal Fabrication, Inc. (MMF) made custom manufactured machinery; one of the products it made was a brine-filling machine used at Hanover's facility in Ridgely, Maryland, to fill buckets of mushrooms with brine. This machine was constructed by MMF according to the design provided by Hanover.

Wall's job was to test samples of the mushroom brine. While performing her duties one day, Wall rested her hand on a table behind the machine while she waited

(continued)

for some buckets to fill so she could take more samples. Unexpectedly the machine's carriage system descended and before Wall could remove her hand, lowered onto her hand, and pulled it inside the carriage system up to her forearm. Wall's arm was trapped for ten minutes before the carriage system ascended and released her arm. She suffered bone fractures in her hand and wrist, lacerations, and scarring.

In defending against the products liability claim, MMF asserted it supplied the brine-filling machine to Hanover, a "sophisticated user"—because Hanover provided the design for the machine and was an experienced and knowledgeable buyer. This shifted the duty to warn from MMF to Hanover, asserted MMF. The court said that under the sophisticated user defense, a manufacturer is insulated from liability for injuries allegedly arising out of the manufacturer's failure to warn if the purchaser was a knowledgeable industrial user who had reason to know of any dangerous condition that might be inherent in the product.

Key Point
Knowledgeable User Defense
The knowledgeable user defense is a defense to strict products liability actions under which manufacturers need not warn knowledgeable users of specific dangers of a product that are or should be known to these users.

What if a person misuses a product and is injured as a result? Is misuse of a product a defense to a strict products liability claim?

UNFORESEEABLE PRODUCT MISUSE

Manufacturers design and produce products for certain intended uses. Sometimes consumers use products for purposes not intended by the manufacturers, such as using a solution of vinegar and water as a window cleaner rather than using the vinegar in a recipe. *Unforeseeable product misuse* is a defense to strict tort liability if the consumer used the product for purposes not intended nor reasonably foreseeable by the manufacturer.

Under strict products liability theory, a manufacturer must consider and take precautions not only for expected uses of its product but also for its foreseeable misuses. For example, a manufacturer of a chair, in planning its product design and manufacture, must consider that consumers not only will sit in the chair but may also stand on it. Standing on a chair is a foreseeable misuse of the product, and strict products liability theory extends to cover injuries caused both by a product's intended use and by its foreseeable misuse.

If the misuse is unforeseeable, however, that is a valid defense to liability. For instance, if a leg from the chair is removed and fashioned into a lance, and the lance is then used in a playful "jousting" match during which the plaintiff suffers an injury, the manufacturer of the chair would not be liable for that injury because that misuse of the product was unforeseeable.

Unforeseeable product misuse
A defense to strict tort liability if the consumer used the product for purposes not intended nor reasonably foreseeable by the manufacturer.

Key Point
Unforeseeable Product Misuse Defense
Unforeseeable misuse of a product is a defense to strict tort liability if the consumer used the product for purposes not intended nor reasonably foreseeable by the manufacturer.

SIDEBAR

MISUSE OF PRODUCTS AND STRICT PRODUCTS LIABILITY THEORY

Sellers of products must consider how consumers may misuse their products. They must take precautions to protect consumers from foreseeable misuses, and they can be held strictly liable for harm caused both by the products' intended uses and from foreseeable misuses.

However, it is a defense to strict products liability if the consumer misuses the product in a way that is not foreseeable by the seller. Unforeseeable misuse is an affirmative defense to strict products liability.

It is not always clear whether a misuse of a product was foreseeable. Courts must decide this issue, and many interesting cases have been heard on it, such as the following Cases on Point.

CASES on Point

Larue v. National Union Elec. Corp., 571 F.2d 51 (1st Cir. 1978); *Erkson v. Sears, Roebuck & Co.*, 841 S.W.2d 207 (Mo. Ct. App. 1992)

Compare and contrast the following cases.

Larue v. National Union Elec. Corp. was a case brought against a vacuum cleaner manufacturer to recover damages for injuries sustained by an 11-year-old boy who suffered a partial amputation of his penis while riding a vacuum cleaner "as if it were a toy car." The manufacturer argued that the accident resulted from an unforeseeable misuse of the product for which it should not be held liable.

The First Circuit Court of Appeals disagreed. It found there was a sufficient basis for holding that the vacuum cleaner "presented an unreasonable risk of harm to children who might reasonably be foreseen to explore and fiddle with" it. The court reasoned that the manufacturer realized the vacuum cleaner "would be used in households where children would be present and appreciated the risks of children playing with the insides of the machine."

Accordingly, it was determined that the injury fell within the class of dangers foreseeable to the manufacturer, "even though the precise circumstances of the accident might have been improbable."

On the other hand, in *Erkson v. Sears, Roebuck & Co.*, a products liability action was brought against the retailer and manufacturer of a riding lawn mower (as well as a great grandmother) to recover for injuries sustained by a 2-year-old child in a mower accident. The child's great grandfather built and installed a small, open wooden box on the right fender of the mower, directly over the deck housing the mower blades. The box was built to be a "dog box" in which the great grandmother's dog could ride while she was mowing.

One day, the great grandmother decided to give the child a ride on the mower and placed her in the dog box, with no seat belt or other restraint, and with her feet dangling over the edge. While the great grandmother was cutting the lawn, the mower hit a stump and the child was thrown off the mower, which ran over her foot.

Proceeding on the strict liability theory, the plaintiffs argued that the great grandmother's use of the mower was proper or should have been reasonably anticipated by the manufacturer or retailer. The Missouri Court of Appeals disagreed.

The court said that in order to recover under strict liability theory, the plaintiffs must prove, among other elements, that the product was being used in a manner that could be reasonably anticipated. The court considered several factors in making this determination: the young age of the child and her lack of physical maturity to react to bumps, dips, and stops; the lack of any sort of restraint on the child; the child being placed in the most precarious position, directly over the housing covering the mower blades; and the great grandmother had activated the blades to cut a clump of grass.

The court ruled that the great grandmother's misuse of the mower as a "motorized baby buggy" to transport a child was not objectively foreseeable. Rather, neither the manufacturer nor the retailer could have reasonably anticipated this use: "[t]hat was not its intended use nor a use reasonably anticipated."

Another defense to strict liability torts is immunity (already discussed at length in Chapter 9 on defenses to negligence).

CASE on Point

Pope v. Edward M. Rude Carrier Corp., 75 S.E.2d 584 (W. Va. 1953)

The plaintiff was injured when an explosion occurred during the lawful transportation of a shipment of dynamite on a public highway.

The Supreme Court of Appeals of West Virginia found that the contract carrier, manufacturer, and shipper of the explosives were immune from absolute liability because they were lawfully engaged in the transport of the explosives. The court said that licensed contract carriers, manufacturers, and shippers of high explosives are not insurers against or absolutely liable for injuries caused by an explosion occurring during their transport (although liability could be found under negligence theory).

IMMUNITY

Immunity from strict liability may arise by legal sanction, where statutes authorize a defendant to perform a particular activity. For instance, where common carriers are required by law to ship explosives, they may be immune from strict liability (though not negligence) for their actions, which may result in injury to others. See the above Case on Point, which was discussed previously in relation to nuisance liability and the doctrine of *res ipsa loquitur,* involving the lawful transport of explosives.

Immunity, more generally, is a defense to tort liability that protects certain tortfeasors from liability for their tortious conduct. Immunity is derived from who the person is (such as a government agency or a charitable organization), what the person does (such as a public official, judge, or legislator), or his relationship with another (such as a spouse). Immunity bars one person from successfully suing another, and is a complete defense. Examples of such immunity include family immunity, governmental immunity, and public official immunity, already discussed in Chapter 9 because this type of general immunity applies to all torts.

Sometimes, too much time passes for it to be fair to require a defendant to defend herself in a lawsuit. Statutes of limitations and statutes of repose define time limits within which lawsuits must be brought. Many jurisdictions have enacted such statutes to require that strict liability tort actions be brought within a prescribed time period, or else they are barred. Statutes of limitations and repose are examined next.

Immunity
A defense to tort liability that protects certain tortfeasors from liability for their tortious conduct because of who they are, what they do, or their relationship with another.

STATUTES OF LIMITATIONS AND REPOSE

Statutes of limitations are enacted by legislatures to limit the time period within which plaintiffs may file certain legal actions, including strict liability actions. Statutes of limitations ensure that actions are brought within a certain time after the cause of action accrues. A products liability action normally accrues when the product causes harm, so the relevant statute of limitation begins to run once the injury occurs.

Statutes of limitations
Laws enacted by legislatures to limit the time period within which a plaintiff may file certain types of legal actions, and that begin to run upon the accrual of a cause of action.

What if a consumer is harmed by a product he had purchased ten years earlier? Is it fair for the seller of the product to have to defend the suit a decade after its purchase? Pursuant to a statute of limitations, which is normally a fairly short period of time, such as two or three years, the cause of action does not begin to accrue until the injury occurs. The fact that ten years passed before the injury occurred is irrelevant to a statute of limitations, and a statute of limitations would not bar the suit, a decade after the purchase of the product, so long as the suit is brought within the prescribed number of years after the injury occurs. Nonetheless, the suit may be barred by a relevant statute of repose.

Statutes of repose
Laws enacted by legislatures that place outer time limits on certain claims but are not dependent on the accrual of a cause of action.

In the absence of statutes of limitations in jurisdictions, or in conjunction with them, *statutes of repose* have been enacted in many states. These statutes are like statutes of limitations in that they place outer time limits on certain claims. They are enacted so that a defendant will not be expected to defend itself indefinitely, especially as access to evidence and to witnesses diminishes over time. However, unlike statutes of limitations, statutes of repose are not dependent on the accrual of a cause of action; rather, they begin to run sooner than statutes of limitations, such as when the product is purchased, or when it is delivered or installed.

Consider the previous example, in which the product caused injury ten years after it was purchased. Although the statute of limitations may not have run (meaning expired), a statute of repose may impose an earlier lawsuit deadline, such as six years after the purchase, delivery, or installation of the product. In that case, the products liability suit for an injury that occurred ten years after the purchase would be barred. In other words, a six-year statute of repose, which begins to run on the date the product is purchased, might bar a claim even if the statute of limitations, which begins to run on the date of injury, does not.

Statutes of repose, which impose an absolute bar on actions against manufacturers, usually after the goods are purchased, delivered, or installed rather than when they cause harm, are favored by industry trade groups representing manufacturers and opposed by consumer rights organizations (and perhaps tort lawyers). Statutes of repose are a part of legislative proposals for tort reform in this country, and more and more states are enacting them. Do the Internet exercise at the end of the chapter to see which states, so far, have enacted products liability statutes of repose.

STATUTE on Point

Ind. Code § 34-20-3-1 (2009)

According to the Indiana Code, products liability actions, whether based on negligence or on strict liability theory, must be brought within two years after the cause of action accrues (the statute of limitations part) or ten years after delivery of the product to the initial user or consumer (the statute of repose part).

Indiana has a statute of limitations *and* repose on products liability actions. Examine the language of that statute, summarized in the Statute on Point, and consider its implications on products liability suits.

One final defense that may apply to strict products liability claims, depending on the jurisdiction, is the defense of comparative negligence.

COMPARATIVE NEGLIGENCE

Earlier in the text, in examining the defenses to negligence in Chapter 9, we discussed the defenses of contributory and comparative negligence. Contributory negligence is no defense to strict tort liability. The plaintiff's conduct, even if unreasonable, will not bar his strict liability recovery in jurisdictions that recognize contributory negligence. However, some jurisdictions do permit the plaintiff's comparative negligence as a defense to a strict products liability claim. *Comparative negligence* is the tort theory under which injuries resulting from negligent conduct are shared by all persons responsible, including the plaintiff, in proportion to each person's relative degree of fault.

The Case on Point below illustrates the application of comparative negligence as a defense to a strict liability claim. In that case, the Alaska Supreme Court held that a defendant in a strict products liability suit could assert the plaintiff's ordinary negligence in its defense.

In comparative negligence cases, including strict liability actions, the damages suffered by the plaintiff are proportionately reduced by that portion which was caused by the plaintiff's own unreasonable conduct. In other words, the plaintiff who shares in the fault also "pitches in" with the remedy in a jurisdiction that permits the strict liability application of the comparative negligence defense.

Comparative negligence
A tort defense under which injuries resulting from negligent conduct are shared by all persons responsible, including the plaintiff, in proportion to each person's relative degree of fault.

CASE on Point

Smith v. Ingersoll-Rand Co., 14 P.3d 990 (Alaska 2000)

Smith was injured when the door of an air compressor fell on his head. He sued the defendant, the manufacturer of the air compressor, in a strict products liability action. At trial, it was determined that Smith contributed to the harm he suffered by failing to wear a hard hat and by propping the door to the compressor open in a manner that was unsafe.

In 1986, the state of Alaska enacted a Tort Reform Act. Case law in Alaska up until that time limited the application of comparative negligence in strict products liability actions to cases involving either product misuse or unreasonable assumption of the risk by the plaintiff. It was not extended to include the plaintiff's ordinary negligence.

The Supreme Court of Alaska held that the 1986 Tort Reform Act expanded the definition of comparative negligence in products liability cases to include a plaintiff's ordinary negligence. The court noted that its decision corresponded with a national trend toward such expansion, and that its decision was supported by the new *Restatement (Third) of Torts: Products Liability.*

What damage award, or other remedy, is a successful strict liability plaintiff normally able to recover? Remedies in strict liability are examined next.

Remedies in Strict Liability Actions

Remedies
The judicial awards by which legal rights are enforced and the violations of rights are compensated.

Remember that *remedies* are the judicial awards by which legal rights are enforced and the violations of rights are compensated.

Damages are the usual remedy in actions involving strict liability. Compensatory damages may be recovered to compensate for the harm to persons and property caused by abnormally dangerous conditions or activities and by defective products. Punitive damages may be awarded if the plaintiff can establish that the defendant acted recklessly or maliciously in allowing the harm to occur.

CASE on Point

Anderson v. General Motors Corp., BC 116926 (Cal. Superior Ct. 1999)

On Christmas Eve, 1993, Patricia Anderson was driving her 1979 Chevrolet Malibu, manufactured by General Motors (GM), home from church. In the car with her were her four young children and her neighbor. While she was stopped at a stoplight, Ms. Anderson's vehicle was hit by a drunk driver, who rear-ended her car at high speed (over 70 miles per hour). The impact caused the Malibu's gas tank to explode, and the car went up in flames. Although no one died in the accident, some occupants were seriously burned (others suffered only minor injuries) because the children were trapped in the back of the car while the adults in the front of the car were able to escape.

The driver and passengers sued GM for products liability, alleging that the fuel tank of the Malibu was defectively designed and placed too near the rear bumper of the car (10 inches from it). Evidence at trial showed that GM knew the car's fuel tank design was not safe, but the company had not changed the design because of cost considerations. Key evidence was a 1973 memo written by GM engineer Edward Ivey, reporting an estimate that "fatalities related to accidents with fuel-fed fires are costing General Motors $2.40 per automobile in current operation." GM argued that the driver of the other car caused the accident, not its fuel tank design, and that the Malibu met all safety standards. The jury was not told that the driver who caused the accident was drunk or that he was speeding. Although more than 98 percent of all cars built during the 1970s had their gas tanks in the same location, the jury did not hear that evidence either.

After a ten-week trial, the jury returned a verdict in favor of the plaintiffs. The jury awarded $107 million in compensatory damages to compensate them for their injuries, disfigurement, and pain and suffering. The jury also awarded $4.9 billion in punitive damages to punish GM. This was the largest amount awarded in a personal injury lawsuit in the United States up to that time. Upon posttrial motion, the trial court agreed that the punitive damage award was excessive, and reduced it to $1.09 billion, which GM appealed.

Tort reform advocates such as the American Tort Reform Association point to verdicts like this one in making their case for tort reform.

DEATH VERSUS DISMEMBERMENT/DISFIGUREMENT/INJURY

As the GM Case on Point suggests, sometimes injury, disfigurement, or dismemberment of a person may bring a larger damage award than his or her death would. Typically, juries render these large awards, and they can be deeply swayed in serious injury and dismemberment/disfigurement cases, sometimes even more than in cases resulting in death. Unfortunately, as a result, defendants sometimes delay and drag out their cases in hopes that the plaintiff will die before trial, thereby possibly reducing their liability.

The plaintiff must take reasonable steps to avoid the consequences of the harm caused by the defendant. In other words, the plaintiff must mitigate his damages to fully recover under strict liability theory. Any damages that could have been avoided by the plaintiff undertaking reasonable measures, such as seeking prompt medical treatment for her injuries, may not be recovered from the defendant.

CHAPTER **SUMMARY**

- To defend a strict liability action, a defendant can defeat one or more of the essential elements of the plaintiff's claim. The defendant can also assert the following affirmative defenses: assumption of the risk, commonly known dangers, knowledgeable user, unforeseeable product misuse, immunity, and statutes of limitations and repose. In some states, the defendant may also assert comparative negligence as a defense.

- A plaintiff assumes the risk of harm when he knowingly and voluntarily agrees to accept the risk of being injured by the defendant's conduct. It is a defense to strict liability and other torts, and it bars a plaintiff's recovery.

- In strict products liability actions, if a defendant can demonstrate that the plaintiff's injury was a result of a commonly known danger, the defendant will not be liable. This is because some dangers associated with certain products are so obvious that manufacturers need not warn users of those commonly known dangers.

- If a specific danger is or should be commonly known by particular users of a product, the manufacturer need not warn these users of the danger. This defense is the knowledgeable user defense.

- Under strict products liability theory, a manufacturer must consider and take precautions not only for expected uses of its product, but also for its foreseeable misuses. However, if the misuse is unforeseeable, that acts as a valid defense to liability.

- Immunity from strict liability may arise as a result of a legal sanction, where laws are enacted that authorize a defendant to perform a particular activity. Immunity, more generally, is a defense to legal liability that protects a tortfeasor from liability for his tortious conduct. It bars one person from suing another. Examples of such immunity include family immunity, governmental immunity, and public official immunity.

- Statutes of limitations are enacted by states to limit the time period in which plaintiffs may file certain lawsuits, including strict liability actions. Even in the absence of statutes of limitations in some jurisdictions, statutes of repose may be enacted to place outer time limits on products liability claims so that the defendants will not be expected to defend themselves indefinitely, especially as access to evidence and witnesses diminishes over time. Unlike statutes of limitations, statutes of repose are not dependent on the accrual of a cause of action; rather, they begin to run sooner than do statutes of limitations, often upon the initial purchase, delivery, or installation of the product.

- Contributory negligence is no defense to strict tort liability. However, some jurisdictions permit the plaintiff's comparative negligence as a defense to a products liability claim. In such cases, the damages suffered by the plaintiff are proportionately reduced by that portion which was caused by the plaintiff's own unreasonable conduct.

- Damages are the usual remedy in actions involving strict liability. Compensatory damages may be recovered to compensate for the harm, both to persons and their property, caused by the abnormally dangerous condition or activity or by the defective product. Punitive damages may be awarded if the plaintiff can establish that the defendant acted recklessly or maliciously in allowing the harm to occur.

- The plaintiff must take reasonable steps to avoid the consequences of the harm caused by the defendant under the mitigation of damages doctrine.

CONCEPT REVIEW AND REINFORCEMENT

QUESTIONS FOR **REVIEW**

1. What are the defenses to strict liability torts?
2. How does the defense of assumption of the risk apply in strict liability actions?
3. What are "commonly known dangers" and "knowledgeable users"? What is their effect?
4. How does unforseeable misuse of a product affect strict products liability actions?
5. What immunity defenses are available in strict liability actions?

6. Do statutes of limitations apply to strict liability actions?
7. What are statutes of repose, and how do they affect strict liability actions?
8. Which defenses are available in other tort actions, and which are specific to strict liability actions?
9. What remedies are available for strict liability torts?
10. How does the mitigation of damages doctrine apply in strict liability actions?

DEVELOPING YOUR PARALEGAL SKILLS

CRITICAL THINKING **EXERCISES**

1. Find a products liability case in your state or federal district that deals with (1) a hair dryer, (2) a chain saw, (3) a prescription drug, (4) a ladder, (5) a firearm, (6) a motorcycle, (7) a shop tool, (8) a child's toy, (9) a feature of a car (such as a tire or gas tank), or (10) a medical apparatus. What legal theory or theories were asserted by the plaintiff? What defenses were asserted by the defendant? What remedies were sought by the plaintiff? Review your research results with the class.

2. Harold keeps a bear in a cage at a circus. One day, Joy crawls under the rope fencing in front of the bear's cage and gets within inches of the bars to the cage; she is hoping to pet the bear. The bear reaches through the bars and claws Joy's body, injuring her.

   Is Harold (or the circus, under the doctrine of respondeat superior) strictly liable for the harm caused by the bear (under the "wild animal" rule)? Has Joy, by her conduct, made a valid defense available to Harold? If so, which one?

3. Cody is injured when the Smith & Wesson shotgun with which he is hunting discharges, shooting him in the foot. Cody did not mean to pull the trigger; he accidentally knocked the trigger while repositioning the gun to take aim at a deer.

   Is Smith & Wesson, the gun's manufacturer, strictly liable for Cody's injury? Why, or why not?

4. Gerald, who has lived in Indiana his entire life, purchased a hair dryer from his local department store in September 1990. Over the years, he has used the dryer from time to time, but very irregularly. On December 17, 2008, Gerald turns on the dryer to dry his hair for a special occasion; the dryer explodes and injures him.

   Is the seller of the hair dryer strictly liable for Gerald's injuries? Why or why not? What defense(s) might the seller assert, eighteen years after the sale of the product?

5. Lisa is getting ready for an evening date. She is using an electric curling iron to style her hair. Though the curling iron has a warning tag on its electric cord instructing users to keep the appliance away from water, Lisa brushes her teeth, using running water from her sink, while curling her hair. Unfortunately, the curling iron slips from Lisa's hand and lands in the water, causing an electric shock that injures Lisa.

   a. *Is the seller of the curling iron strictly liable for Lisa's injuries? Why or why not? In answering the question, assume that Lisa is in a jurisdiction that recognizes comparative negligence. Explore all the defenses that might apply.*

   b. *Now assume that the jurisdiction recognizes contributory negligence, not comparative negligence. Does this affect your answer? If so, how?*

6. Carmen, an avid bike rider, has a newborn baby. The baby is too young and small to be able to ride in a baby bike seat, so Carmen decides to tuck the baby in a top-quality bicycle basket strapped on Carmen's front handlebars. While Carmen is riding to the grocery store for formula, the bicycle basket's straps break because of the baby's weight. The baby falls to the ground and is injured.

   Is the seller of the bicycle basket strictly liable for the harm suffered by Carmen's baby? What defenses might apply? Would they likely succeed?

ASSIGNMENTS AND PRACTICAL **APPLICATIONS**

1. As a follow-up to Critical Thinking Exercise 2, read and brief *Heidemann v. Wheaton*, 34 N.W.2d 492 (S.D. 1948), involving a person's failure to exercise ordinary care by approaching captive bears in an unsafe manner, acting as a valid defense to strict liability.

2. Read and brief *Campo v. Scofield*, 95 N.E.2d 802 (N.Y. 1950), which found, like the *Jamieson* court, that a manufacturer of an onion topping machine has no duty to protect the user against a danger that is perfectly obvious.

3. Consider the case of *Baker v. Int'l Harvester Co.*, 660 S.W.2d 21 (Mo. Ct. App. 1983), which was similar to the *Erkson* case. In this case, a hunter carrying a gun "hitched" a ride on an operating combine, without the knowledge of the combine operator. The hunter fell from the combine, was run over by it, and was killed. The court found the hunter's actions to be "a species of abnormal use which bars recovery under the doctrine of strict liability."

4. For another case involving immunity from strict liability when the defendant is performing an activity he is required by law to perform, namely, transporting explosives, read and brief *Actieselskabet Ingrid v. Central R. Co. of N.J.*, 216 F. 72 (2d Cir. 1914).

5. On the issue of whether certain product misuses are foreseeable or not, read and brief the following cases involving cigarette lighters causing injury to children who play with them: *Griggs v. BIC Corp.*, 981 F.2d 1429 (3rd Cir. 1992); and *Bean v. BIC Corp.*, 597 So.2d 1350 (Ala. 1992).

6. Research whether your state has a statute of repose governing products liability actions. Research to find your state's statute of limitations on strict liability actions. If your state recognizes both, are they combined? Discuss your research results in class.

7. For another case involving contributory negligence and strict products liability, see *General Motors Corp. v. Farnsworth*, 965 P.2d 1209 (Alaska 1998), involving product misuse when a plaintiff wore a car seat belt under her arm rather than across her body.

8. Products liability actions are often in the news. Bring to class and share a news item from the newspaper, a magazine, or the Internet that deals with a current products liability action. On what theory or theories is the lawsuit based? What defenses are asserted by the defendant? What remedies are sought by the plaintiff?

TECHNOLOGY RESOURCES AND INTERNET **EXERCISES**

The Massachusetts Supreme Judicial Court ruled that cigarette manufacturers cannot use commonly known dangers as a defense to products liability suits. See *www.physorg .com/news67264256.html*. Everyone knows that cigarette smoking is the leading cause of lung cancer, one of the most deadly forms of cancer. Is this fair?

For a discussion of the knowledgeable user defense and its application to strict products liability, see *www.riskvue .com/articles/rb/rb0503c.htm*.

Using the Internet, research how many states have statutes of repose governing products liability actions, and compare and contrast when their time periods begin and how long they last.

North Carolina has enacted a six-year statute of repose governing products liability actions in order to limit the liability of manufacturers and sellers. Accordingly, in North Carolina, consumers have protection for six years from the date of purchase of a product (any type of product). After six years from the date of purchase, suit is barred. Using the Internet, locate and review this statute.

Read the appellate brief in the GM Malibu case at *www .appellate.net/briefs/Anderson%20final%20DMG.pdf*.

For arguments in favor of tort reform as it applies to strict products liability, see the American Tort Reform Association's website at *www.atra.org*.

ETHICAL **APPLICATIONS**

Statutes of limitations and statutes of repose limit the time period during which a plaintiff may bring a legal action, including the various types of tort actions. Consider the implication of a lawyer or paralegal missing a case filing deadline, and failing to file a client's lawsuit in time to fall within the relevant statute of limitations or statute of repose. Certainly, that could be grounds for adverse employment action (such as termination or demotion) for the attorney or paralegal, and disciplinary action for an ethical violation by the state bar association for the attorney. In addition, the client could sue the attorney, paralegal, and/or firm for malpractice, another term for professional negligence.

What are some steps a lawyer or paralegal can take to minimize his or her exposure to malpractice liability?

Note that, although it is prudent for law firms and attorneys to carry malpractice insurance, not all states require attorneys to carry malpractice insurance (though some states do). Do you think a client has a right to know if the attorney carries malpractice insurance before retaining her? What is the risk to the client if he is represented by an attorney who does not maintain malpractice insurance?

VIDEO **CASE STUDY**

Zealous Representation Issue: When You Are Asked to Lie

Synopsis: A paralegal has been instructed by his supervising attorney to do whatever is necessary to obtain information needed in a particular case in order to prove that the plaintiff in the case was not badly injured.

Questions

1. Why is the supervising attorney interested in finding witnesses who can show that the plaintiff in the case was not badly injured?

2. How is evidence regarding extent of injuries and amount of damages obtained?

3. According to legal ethics rules regarding zealous representation, is the requested conduct ethical? Does it make a difference whether the conduct is performed by a paralegal rather than an attorney?

chapter 13

DEFAMATION AND DISPARAGEMENT

This chapter examines torts involving harm caused by making false statements that injure the reputation or business of others. We begin our examination with a definition of defamation. What is defamation?

Definition of Defamation

Tort law imposes a duty on persons to refrain from making false, defamatory statements of fact about others that cause injury to their reputations. **Defamation** is the publication of false statements of fact that cause injury to a person's good name, character, and reputation.

The interest protected by this tort is a person's right to her good name and reputation. The harm caused by defamation is the loss of reputation a person suffers in the community or that causes others to stop associating with her. The *Swenson-Davis* Case on Point illustrates the definition of the tort of defamation and its application.

There are two types of defamation: slander and libel. We will now examine and distinguish these two types of defamation.

Distinguishing Slander and Libel

Slander and libel are the two types of defamation. Generally speaking, slander is "oral" defamation; libel is "written" defamation. To help remember this difference, remember that "s"lander is "s"poken, and "l"ibel is in "l"etters.

What is slander? **Slander** is defamation in oral form. Normally, it is spoken defamation. However, it can also be committed via gesture. Some jurisdictions refer to slander as nonwritten, rather than oral, defamation, to acknowledge the gesture component of this form of defamation. Consider these ways of orally publishing defamatory statements: speaking them in a conversation, making them by waving a hand, pointing two thumbs down, sign language, or nodding one's head.

Because slander is, by definition, oral, to prove it, plaintiffs must produce witnesses to testify to the statement being made, heard, and

LEARNING OBJECTIVES

13.1 Define defamation and discuss its essential elements.

13.2 Distinguish between slander and libel.

13.3 Describe the element of actual malice and when it applies.

13.4 Identify the defenses to and the remedies for defamation.

13.5 Define disparagement and identify the two types.

13.6 Explain the relationship between disparagement and injurious falsehood.

13.7 List the essential elements of disparagement of property.

13.8 Identify and discuss the defenses and remedies applicable to disparagement.

Defamation
Published false statements of fact that cause injury to a person's good name, character, and reputation.

Slander
Defamation in oral, or nonwritten, form.

CASE on Point

Swenson-Davis v. Martel, 354 N.W.2d 288 (Mich. Ct. App. 1984)

The plaintiff was an Ann Arbor, Michigan, high school teacher who had the defendant's son, Jonathan, in her "honors" English class. The plaintiff announced to the class that each student's final grade would be determined by a mathematical formula. Under that formula, Jonathan should have received a final grade of A–, but he was given a B+. Jonathan complained to the plaintiff, but she claimed that, notwithstanding the formula, determination of a student's final grade was within her discretion.

Jonathan told his father about the plaintiff's refusal to change his grade. The defendant, Dr. Martel, contacted the school principal. Pursuant to the first step of the school system's "fair treatment policy," a conference was held with the plaintiff, Dr. and Mrs. Martel, Jonathan, and the principal. The plaintiff claimed that the conference consisted of the defendant berating her. After the conference, the defendant, pursuant to the fair treatment policy grievance procedure, wrote a letter to the principal expressing his dissatisfaction with the plaintiff's performance as a teacher and with her treatment of his son. In his letter, the defendant accused the plaintiff of treating Jonathan "most unfairly" and of displaying "remarkable insensitivity and behavior that was most unprofessional" and "inconsistent with good teaching practice."

The plaintiff then filed a lawsuit, alleging that the statements in the defendant's letter were libelous. The Court of Appeals of Michigan said, "[A] communication is defamatory if it tends so to harm the reputation of another as to lower him in the estimation of the community or to deter third persons from associating or dealing with him."

See the discussion of qualified privilege later in this chapter to learn the outcome of this case.

understood. Unlike libel, there is no written or physical evidence of the statement that can be produced for the court to inspect.

Libel, on the other hand, is defamation in written or other tangible form. Normally, libel is written, such as in a letter, book, newspaper, or magazine, on a chalkboard, or even on the Internet. However, defamation is also libel if it is embodied in some other physical form, other than a writing, such as on a photograph, videotape, DVD, or film.

The importance of the statement appearing in a physical form of expression is this: By embodying the statement in a physical form, it becomes a more permanent mode of expression than an oral statement. Some writings can last a very long time. Also, people tend to put more thought into their written communications than their oral ones (with the exception, perhaps, of e-mail expression); oral statements are more likely to be expressed spontaneously. Written statements, such as those in books, magazines, newspapers, photographs, and videotapes, can reach more people over a longer time period than mere oral statements. They can also be produced in court and inspected. Because of these facts, courts consider libel to be more serious than slander. Courts will broaden their protection against it by extending liability for libel more than for slander.

Libel
Defamation in written or other tangible form.

CASE on Point

Shor v. Billingsley, 158 N.Y.S.2d 476 (1956)

Is the defamation libel or slander? It is not always clear. In *Shor v. Billingsley,* the plaintiff brought a defamation action as a result of a nationwide telecast of *The Stork Club Show.* The defendants in the case included the operator of *The Stork Club Show,* its producer, and Mr. Billingsley, its master of ceremonies and a performer on the show. The plaintiff was the operator and manager of The Toots Shor Restaurant, with which The Stork Club competed. The following conversation, between Mr. Billingsley and Mr. Brisson, a guest on the program, occurred during the show, and the plaintiff's picture was telecast in conjunction with the conversation:

MR. BILLINGSLEY: I see, I would like to show you a few pictures taken here lately. The first-now, how did this picture get in here?

MR. BRISSON: That is Toots Shor and a man I don't know.

MR. BILLINGSLEY: You want to know something?

MR. BRISSON: Want to know something? I saw Toots Shor, he's a good-looking fellow, isn't he?

MR. BILLINGSLEY: Yes, he is. Want to know something? I wish I had as much money as he owes.

MR. BRISSON: Owes you or somebody else?

MR. BILLINGSLEY: Everybody—oh, a lot of people.

MR. BRISSON: He doesn't owe me anything, but he is a good-looking fellow just the same. A little (indicating)—you know.

MR. BILLINGSLEY: I wish I could agree with you.

The court addressed the issue of whether the telecast conversation, which was ad-libbed and not part of a prepared script, constituted libel or slander. Defamatory remarks read from a script and broadcast constituted libel under the law at that time, but this question was one of first impression in that jurisdiction, meaning that it was being heard for the first time.

In finding that this type of defamation was libel and not slander, the Supreme Court of New York ruled that a defamatory broadcast or telecast could be treated as libel even though no prepared script was used.

These differences are behind the variations that exist in the essential elements of slander and libel. Overall, however, the essential elements of the two types of defamation are very similar. These essential elements are discussed next.

Essential Elements of Defamation

Like all torts, defamation can be broken down into its essential elements. Each of these elements must be established, by a demonstration of evidence, by the plaintiff to present a *prima facie* case of defamation.

The essential elements of slander and libel are virtually the same except for the element of damages. These are the essential elements: a defamatory

Key Point

The Essential Elements of Defamation

1. A defamatory statement made by the defendant
2. Of and concerning the plaintiff
3. Publication of the statement
4. Damages
5. Causation

Actual malice also must be established if the plaintiff is suing a media defendant (see the discussion of the actual malice requirement in the next section).

CASE on Point

Haegert v. McMullan, 953 N.E.2d 1223 (Ind. Ct. App. 2011)

In this case, a university professor, Haegert, was terminated from his employment at the University of Evansville for alleged sexual harassment of his female supervisor, the English department chair named McMullan. Haegert filed legal action against his supervisor alleging defamation, as well as intentional infliction of emotional distress and tortious breach of employment contract.

The court defined defamation as "that which tends to injure reputation or to diminish esteem, respect, goodwill, or confidence in the plaintiff, or to excite derogatory feelings or opinions about the plaintiff." To recover for defamation, a plaintiff must demonstrate (1) a communication with a defamatory imputation; (2) malice; (3) publication; and (4) damages. The determination of whether a communication is defamatory is a question of law for the court, said this court.

The court found that Haegert's complaint failed to state a claim for defamation. The court said that a person who sues for defamation must set out the alleged defamatory statement in the complaint. In his complaint, Haegert merely stated that "McMullan impugned the character of [Haegert] when she made false statements to no fewer than 30 people regarding [Haegert]." The court determined that no specific statements alleged to be defamatory were identified in the complaint. Accordingly, his cause of action for defamation failed.

In fact, all of Haegert's claims failed when this court affirmed the lower court's granting of summary judgment in favor of McMullan in this case. As to his claim for intentional infliction of emotional distress, the court said that there was no evidence that McMullan intended to cause emotional distress to Haegert; rather, she acted according to her responsibilities at the university when she filed a sexual harassment complaint because she believed Haegert violated the employer's zero-tolerance policy prohibiting sexual harassment.

statement made by the defendant, of and concerning the plaintiff, publication of the statement, damages, and causation. Sometimes claims of defamation are made in conjunction with claims for intentional infliction of emotional distress. See the above Case on Point for one example (as well as the *Hustler Magazine* Case on Point found later in the chapter as another example).

A defamatory statement is a statement of fact, rather than merely an opinion, which subjects the plaintiff to public ridicule, hatred, or contempt. To be defamatory, the statement must be false. However, the burden is not on the plaintiff to establish the falsity of the defamatory statement as an essential element of the claim. Rather, a defamation defendant may defend himself by establishing the truth of the statement as a defense. A true statement that causes injury, although it is not defamation, may constitute another tort, such as one of the invasion of privacy torts that are discussed in Chapter 14. An example of a defamatory statement about attorney Jack Jones is "Jack Jones never passed the Michigan Bar Examination," if Jack, in fact, did pass it.

The defamatory statement must be of and concerning the plaintiff. In other words, the harmful statement must be understood to be about the person bringing the defamation action. Consider the previous example concerning Jack Jones and the Michigan Bar Examination. Can Julie Smith sue the maker of that false statement for defamation? No, because the statement is not "of and concerning" her; that defamatory statement is of and concerning Jack Jones.

If a defamatory statement is made by a defendant who is referencing someone within a group of people, such as by pointing to a group of people and stating, "She is a thief," the plaintiff must establish that she was the person referred to by the statement. The defendant need not name the plaintiff specifically, but it must be clear, through his actions and words, that the defendant meant the statement to refer to the plaintiff. The issue for the court is whether the defamatory statement could reasonably be interpreted to refer to the plaintiff, thus being of and concerning her.

The defamatory statement must be published. This means that it must be shared with another. Courts also use the term "communication" in setting forth this element. Publication and communication, for purposes of this tort, describe the same action.

Although a defamatory statement can be shared with the general public, or a large group of people, it may also be shared with another person, meaning someone other than the plaintiff. Just one other person is enough to meet the publication requirement of defamation, unlike certain invasion of privacy torts with publicity requirements, which require broader communication as you will learn in Chapter 14. When the defamation is slander, the statement must be heard (in the case of a conversation) or seen (in the case of a gesture) and understood by at least one other person. When it is libel, the statement must be read (in the case of a writing) or seen (in the case of a photograph, videotape, or the like) and understood by at least one other person. Note that the statement, to be published, must be *understood* by at least one other person. This means that, to meet this publication element, a statement expressed in words, whether oral or written, must be in a language that the other knows.

Can a communication that is made accidentally meet the publication requirement? If the communication to a third person is accidental and occurs through no fault of the publisher, most courts will find that there was no publication. Without publication, there is no defamation.

The defamatory statement must damage the reputation or good character of the plaintiff. A distinction between libel and slander, and their different types, namely, *per se* or *per quod*, must be made to understand this essential element. There is libel *per se* and libel *per quod;* there is slander *per se* and slander *per quod*. This distinction affects the damage element.

Libel *per quod* is a libelous statement that is not defamatory on its face. Such a statement must be interpreted before it is considered defamatory, meaning it requires its reader to know extrinsic facts to understand that it is defamatory. For example, a society pages piece about John Parker and his date at a charity event, while not defamatory on its face, becomes libelous to a reader who knows that Father John, a Catholic priest, is the subject of that piece. Libel that is not libel *per quod* is libel *per se*.

Key Point

The "Publication" Requirement for Defamation

Regarding the essential element of "publication" for the tort of defamation, sharing the defamatory statement with *one* other person is enough.

Just as there are two types of libel, there are two types of slander: slander *per se* and slander *per quod*. Slander *per se* is oral defamation that injures the plaintiff in one of four ways:

1. By accusing the plaintiff of a serious crime (such as stealing a car)
2. By accusing the plaintiff of having a loathsome communicable disease (such as a venereal disease)
3. By accusing the plaintiff of sexual misconduct (such as adultery) or an unmarried woman of being unchaste (meaning sexually active)
4. By stating that the plaintiff has committed improprieties while engaged in his trade, business, or profession (such as by falsifying financial statements)

Any slander that is not slander *per se,* meaning it is not one of these four types, is slander *per quod.* Note that in a few states, slander that requires extrinsic facts to understand that its meaning is defamatory is included in the category of slander *per quod.*

In cases of libel *per se* and slander *per se,* the defamatory statement is considered serious enough that damage to the plaintiff's reputation is presumed. In other words, damages are assumed if such a defamatory statement is made and published. The plaintiff need not produce specific evidence of the harm he suffered.

However, in cases of slander *per quod* and, in some states, libel *per quod,* the plaintiff is required to prove special damages. Special damages are damages beyond mere embarrassment or humiliation. They are economic or pecuniary losses that can be demonstrated and quantified, such as lost income or medical expenses incurred. In proving special damages, a plaintiff must establish, by producing evidence, that the defamatory statement actually caused damage to her reputation.

An additional essential element must be proven by plaintiffs in certain kinds of defamation actions. That element, and when it is applicable, is examined next.

SIDEBAR

GENERAL VERSUS SPECIAL DAMAGES

An injury that results from an invasion of a legally protected right may cause either general or special damages. General damages are damages that flow as a natural and necessary result of an act. No special pleading is required for general damages.

On the other hand, special damages are damages that result from an act by reason of the special circumstances of the case and are not a necessary result of the act. Special damages must be pled "with particularity" and proven by plaintiffs in cases of slander *per quod,* and in some jurisdictions, in cases of libel *per quod.* Actual economic or pecuniary losses, when they can be shown and quantified, constitute special damages. For example, lost income resulting from the defendant's defamatory statement constitutes special damages. To specially plead and prove special damages, a plaintiff must set forth the factual matters that give reasonable notice of the nature and extent of the claim. See the Case on Point of *Porter v. Crawford & Co.* in Chapter 4 for an illustration of the difference between general and special damages in a case involving the *prima facie* tort doctrine.

The Actual Malice Requirement

To preserve the freedom of the press protected by the First Amendment of the U.S. Constitution, the U.S. Supreme Court made it harder for public figures to win defamation lawsuits against media defendants. It did this by requiring such "public figure" plaintiffs to prove an additional essential element—actual malice—to succeed in defamation actions against media defendants, thus constitutionalizing the law of defamation for these parties.

In *New York Times Co. v. Sullivan*, described in the following Case on Point, the U.S. Supreme Court set forth the requirement that defamatory statements made about public figures on matters of public concern, when published by the media, are privileged unless they are made with actual malice. A statement is made with ***actual malice*** when the maker of the statement makes it knowing that the statement was false or with reckless disregard for its truth or falsity. Accordingly, public figures have a greater burden of proof in establishing defamation cases than do private persons because they must prove an additional essential element, that of actual malice.

Actual malice
The requirement that a defamatory statement be made knowing that it is false or with reckless disregard for its truth or falsity.

CASE on Point

New York Times Co. v. Sullivan, 376 U.S. 254 (1964)

In the case, the U.S. Supreme Court addressed, for the first time, the extent to which the constitutional protections of free speech and of the press limit a state court's power to award damages in a libel action brought by a public official against critics of his official conduct. In doing so, it created an additional essential element for certain defamation actions involving public figures and media defendants.

L. B. Sullivan was one of the three elected commissioners of the City of Montgomery, Alabama. Among his duties as a commissioner, Sullivan supervised the Police Department. Sullivan brought a defamation action against four African American clergymen and the publisher of *The New York Times*, alleging that he had been libeled by statements made in a full-page, ten-paragraph advertisement that was carried in *The New York Times* on March 29, 1960.

The advertisement carried the title, "Heed Their Rising Voices," and stated, "As the whole world knows by now, thousands of Southern Negro students are engaged in widespread non-violent demonstrations in positive affirmation of the right to live in human dignity as guaranteed by the U.S. Constitution and the Bill of Rights. . . . [I]n their efforts to uphold these guarantees, they are being met by an unprecedented wave of terror by those who would deny and negate that document which the whole world looks upon as setting the pattern for modern freedom." Later paragraphs in the advertisement purported to illustrate the "wave of terror" by describing certain alleged events. The advertisement ended with an appeal for funds to support the student movement, the struggle for the right to vote, and the legal defense of Dr. Martin Luther King, Jr., leader of the movement, against a perjury indictment pending at the time in Montgomery, Alabama.

The text appeared over the names of sixty-four people, many widely known for their activities in public affairs, religion, trade unions, and the

(continued)

performing arts. Below these names and the statement, "We in the south who are struggling daily for dignity and freedom warmly endorse this appeal," were the names of the four defendant clergymen, among others.

The basis for the plaintiff's libel action was the third and a portion of the sixth paragraph of the advertisement. The third paragraph read as follows:

> In Montgomery, Alabama, after students sang "My Country, 'Tis of Thee" on the State Capitol steps, their leaders were expelled from school, and truckloads of police armed with shotguns and tear-gas ringed the Alabama State College Campus. When the entire student body protested to state authorities by refusing to re-register, their dining hall was padlocked in an attempt to starve them into submission.

A portion of the sixth paragraph read:

> Again and again the Southern violators have answered Dr. King's peaceful protests with intimidation and violence. They have bombed his home almost killing his wife and child. They have assaulted his person. They have arrested him seven times—for "speeding," "loitering" and similar "offenses." And now they have charged him with "perjury"— a felony under which they could imprison him for ten years.

Neither of these paragraphs mentioned Sullivan by name. However, he argued that the use of the word "police" in the third paragraph referred to him as the Montgomery commissioner who supervised the Police Department, and that the paragraph read as imputing to the police, and therefore to him, the acts of ringing the campus with police and padlocking the dining hall to starve the students into submission. Sullivan contended that the sixth paragraph referred to him because arrests are ordinarily made by the police, and that the "They" who did the arresting were equated with the "They" who committed the other described acts and with the Southern violators. Sullivan and six other Montgomery residents testified that they read some or all of these statements as referring to Sullivan in his capacity as commissioner. The court found that it was uncontroverted that some of the statements included in the two paragraphs relied on by Sullivan in his claim were not accurate descriptions of events that had occurred in Montgomery. Further, the court found that Sullivan made no effort to prove that he suffered actual pecuniary loss as a result of the alleged libel.

In its decision, the Supreme Court held that the rule of law applied by the Alabama courts was constitutionally deficient because it failed to provide the safeguards for freedom of speech and of the press required by the First and Fourteenth Amendments to the U.S. Constitution in a libel action brought by a public official against critics of his official conduct. The Court reasoned that the expression of grievance and protest on a major public issue of the time, as found in the advertisement, qualified for constitutional protection. The Court posed the question of whether that constitutional protection was forfeited because of the falsity of some of the advertisement's factual statements and by its alleged defamation of Sullivan. The Court said, "The constitutional guarantees require, we think, a federal rule that prohibits a public official from recovering damages for a defamatory falsehood relating to his official conduct unless he proves that the statement was made with 'actual malice'—that is, with knowledge that it was false or with reckless disregard of whether it was false or not." Upon establishing this rule, the Court found actual malice not present under the facts of the case.

This landmark case demonstrates the balancing of interests between the freedom guarantees in the U.S. Constitution and tort law protections provided by states to their citizens. The notion of courts balancing competing interests was discussed in Chapter 5. In balancing these interests, courts consider that public persons, such as celebrities, politicians, and other well-known people, have placed themselves in the public eye. As a result, they are afforded less protection from defamation than are private citizens. Note that the purpose behind the "actual malice" requirement regarding media defendants and public matters is to protect the constitutional rights of free speech and of the press; the requirement recognizes that statements made by the media about public figures usually deal with matters of public interest, and that public figures have the means and opportunity to respond publicly that private persons do not share.

Once a plaintiff establishes a *prima facie* case of defamation by proving the essential elements of libel or slander, a defendant may defend the claim. If the defense is unsuccessful, the court may award the plaintiff a remedy. Defenses to defamation actions and remedies are examined next.

Defamation Defenses and Remedies

The defendant may defend a defamation action in several ways. For example, the defendant may prove that the statement was not defamatory, thus rebutting an essential element of the plaintiff's claim of defamation. If the statement was merely embarrassing, insulting, annoying, or the like, it is not actionable defamation because it is not serious enough. Or the defendant may prove that the statement was one of opinion, not fact, so not actionable. The defamatory statement must actually cause injury to a person's reputation, and if it does not, the defendant can rebut the plaintiff's claim. Sometimes a person's reputation is bad to begin with. Another way to defend a defamation claim is to show that the plaintiff's reputation was already bad; that the plaintiff had a bad reputation before the alleged defamatory statement was made.

Truth is an absolute defense to defamation claims. If the defendant can prove that his statement was true, he has not committed the tort of slander or libel.

The First Amendment is another important defense to defamation. Speech that might otherwise be considered defamatory may be protected by the Constitution's free-speech guarantee. See the *Hustler Magazine* Case on Point for an example.

CASE on Point

Hustler Magazine v. Falwell, 485 U.S. 46 (1988)

In this well-known Supreme Court case, *Hustler* magazine published an advertisement "parody" that depicted the nationally known minister and political commentator, Jerry Falwell, engaged in a drunken incestuous rendezvous with his mother in an outhouse. Like the *Haegert v. McMullan* Case on Point, this case alleged both defamation (libel) and intentional infliction of emotional distress.

(continued)

At trial, the jury ruled against Falwell on the libel claim, finding that the parody could not reasonably be understood as depicting actual facts or events. However, the jury ruled in Falwell's favor on the intentional infliction of emotional distress claim (for $150,000). The Court of Appeals affirmed the trial court's determinations. The Supreme Court felt otherwise.

The Supreme Court said that "[i]n order to protect the free flow of ideas and opinions on matters of public interest and concern, the First and Fourteenth Amendments prohibit public figures and public officials from recovering damages for the tort of intentional infliction of emotional distress by reason of the publication of a caricature such as the ad parody at issue without showing in addition that the publication contains a false statement of fact which was made with 'actual malice,' i.e., with knowledge that the statement was false or with reckless disregard as to whether or not it was true." The court reasoned that the interest in protecting public figures from emotional distress was not sufficient to deny First Amendment protection to speech that was patently offensive and intended to inflict emotional injury when that speech could not reasonably have been interpreted as stating actual facts about the public figure involved. Here the court said that Falwell was clearly a public figure for First Amendment purposes; accordingly, the lower courts' findings that the ad parody was not reasonably believable "must be accepted." Regarding the claim of intentional infliction of emotional distress (also known as the tort of outrage; see Chapter 3), "[o]utrageousness in the area of political and social discourse has an inherent subjectiveness about it which would allow a jury to impose liability on the basis of the jurors' tastes or views . . . and cannot, consistently with the First Amendment, form a basis for the award of damages for" the conduct involved here. Accordingly, the Supreme Court reversed the earlier judgment in favor of Falwell on the intentional infliction of emotional distress claim.

Also, statements made about deceased people are not normally actionable defamation. The rationale for this rule is that, once someone is dead, his reputation cannot truly be damaged.

Privilege is another important defense to defamation. Some communications, both oral and written, are privileged, thus rendering their maker immune from defamation liability. Certain persons at certain times are protected under the law from defamation actions. The purpose behind the privilege defense is to allow persons to express themselves freely, without fear of being sued, in the performance of certain duties that necessitate free expression.

There are two types of privileged communications: those that are absolutely privileged and those that are qualifiedly privileged. An ***absolute privilege*** cannot be lost; it includes such communications as those between attorneys and their clients, judges, witnesses, parties, jurors, and attorneys while performing their courtroom functions, legislature members (federal, state, and local) in the course of legislative proceedings, and executives and officers of the government in carrying out their official duties.

A ***qualified privilege*** can be lost if it is abused, such as if it is not exercised in a reasonable manner and for a proper purpose. This privilege may apply in

Privilege
A defense to defamation and other tort actions under which certain communications can be made and their maker remains immune from liability.

Absolute privilege
A privilege that cannot be lost.

Qualified privilege
A privilege that can be lost if it is abused.

CASE on Point

Swenson-Davis v. Martel, 354 N.W.2d 288 (Mich. Ct. App. 1984)

We discussed this case at the beginning of the chapter in relation to the definition of defamation. In this case, the Court of Appeals of Michigan noted: "The Michigan Supreme Court has held that a citizen who complains to the appropriate official about the fitness of a public school teacher enjoys a qualified privilege." The defendant in this case "had both an interest and a right to see that his child was being competently taught. His letter and the complained-of statements reflect defendant's legitimate concern with his child's education and fall within the scope of Michigan's qualified privilege." Thus, the court held that a qualified privilege protected the defendant's statements about his child's teacher.

several situations. Normally, it applies to statements made by persons to protect their own private interests. The above Case on Point is an example. It also applies to statements made that are related to a matter of public interest, called fair comment. Also, many jurisdictions recognize a privilege permitting members of the media to publish stories on government proceedings and reports so long as their reporting is fair and accurate; this is called the fair report privilege.

The usual remedy in a successful defamation case is a remedy at law, namely, damages. Compensatory damages are typically recoverable in these cases. Note that defamation is not an intentional tort. Accordingly, punitive damages are not normally recoverable in defamation actions. Because a lot of money is not usually involved or recoverable in these cases, they are not commonly accepted by attorneys. Remember that damages are an essential element of the plaintiff's defamation claim, and in some cases, the plaintiff must prove special damages, as discussed earlier.

As we have examined, defamation deals with tortious injury to a person's name, reputation, and character. Disparagement is similar to defamation, but it deals with injury to a person's property rather than his reputation. Disparagement is examined next.

Definition of Disparagement

Disparagement, or disparagement of property, is an injurious false statement made by a person to damage another person's business or title to property. The disparagement of property torts are intentional torts, knowingly committed. The false statement must either attribute an undesirable quality to a product, thereby dissuading third parties from dealing with the plaintiff in his business or in transactions involving the product, or cast doubt on the plaintiff's title to property.

Disparagement of property is similar to defamation. What distinguishes these torts is that defamation involves harm to a person's reputation. Disparagement involves harm to a business or property.

Disparagement
An injurious false statement made to damage a person's business or title to property; also called disparagement of property.

FOOD OR "VEGGIE" LIBEL

Food libel laws, also known as food disparagement laws, veggie libel laws, or veggie hate laws, have been passed in several states. These laws make it easier for the various food industries to sue others for libel.

In 1996, on her popular television talk show, Oprah Winfrey and Howard Lyman, a guest on her show and a vegetarian activist, were discussing the U.S. cattle industry and how U.S. beef was largely infected with bovine spongiform encephalopathy, otherwise known as "mad cow disease":

WINFREY: You said this disease could make AIDS look like the common cold?

GUEST: Absolutely.

WINFREY: Now doesn't that concern ya'll a little bit right here, hearing that? It has just stopped me cold from eating another burger.

These statements created a media frenzy, giving rise to a famous, though not the first, lawsuit involving food libel. The case was the first one brought under Texas's food libel statute, called the Texas Food Disparagement Act.

Food libel laws vary greatly from state to state, but they typically allow a food manufacturer or processor to sue a person or group who makes disparaging comments about its food products. In some states, these laws lessen the burden of proof required of plaintiffs from that normally required under traditional common law libel or disparagement suits. For instance, in Oprah's Texas case, under that state's law, the plaintiffs, beef feedlot operator Paul Engler and the beef company Cactus Feeders, merely had to show that the statements made on the Oprah Winfrey show deviated from reasonable and reliable scientific inquiry, facts, or data. Even under that lesser burden, however, the plaintiffs lost their case (see the assignments at the end of the chapter to research the reason(s) why Winfrey won this case), though pursuing it took six years and cost millions of dollars in attorneys' fees alone.

These food libel cases are hard for plaintiffs to win. One important reason is that it is difficult to prove that the statements are false. Also, some courts look with disfavor on allegations of disparagement when the statements are not directed at a particular food grower or producer, but rather are directed toward a group. Further, it would not be a giant leap for the U.S. Supreme Court to impose constitutional limitations on these suits when they are brought against media defendants, as the Court has done with defamation and the "actual malice" requirement.

There are two main types of disparagement: slander of title and slander of quality, also called trade libel. These two types of disparagement are discussed next.

Two Types of Disparagement

Slander of title
A disparagement of property tort that involves the publication of a false statement which casts doubt on or denies the plaintiff's title to property.

The two types of disparagement are slander of title and slander of quality. *Slander of title* is a disparagement of property tort that involves the publication of a false statement casting doubt on or denying the plaintiff's title to—meaning legal ownership of—property, which causes pecuniary harm—meaning financial loss—to the plaintiff. The tortfeasor, by making the statement, desires to dissuade others from dealing or doing business with the plaintiff. Note that the publication requirement for this tort is similar to that for defamation in that the statement must be made to at least one other person, but need not be made to the general public or a large group of people as is required of certain invasion of privacy torts.

Consider this example. A tortfeasor publishes an untrue statement that a plaintiff's inventory of Rolex watches consists of stolen property. That statement constitutes slander of title because it casts doubt on the plaintiff's legal title to the watches he is offering for sale.

Slander of quality, also called trade libel, is the disparagement of property tort that involves publication of a false statement about the plaintiff's product, attributing a quality to it that makes it undesirable for sale or other commercial use. In other words, the disparaging statement claims that the product is not

> **Slander of quality**
> A disparagement of property tort that involves the publication of a false statement about the plaintiff's product, attributing a quality to it that makes it undesirable for sale or other commercial use; also called trade libel.

CASE on Point

Horning v. Hardy, 373 A.2d 1273 (Md. Ct. Spec. App. 1977)

In this case, the Hardys filed suit against the Hornings, claiming that the Hardys owned certain real property that the Hornings were developing (the Hornings were building five houses on the tract of land). The Hornings filed a counterclaim, claiming, among other things, that the Hardys' interference with their development, by claiming ownership of part of the tract of land that they were developing, constituted slander of title regarding the disputed land.

The Court of Special Appeals of Maryland said that disparagement (which it called, more broadly, injurious falsehood, as discussed in the Sidebar) may "consist of the publication of matter derogatory to the plaintiff's title to his property, or its quality, or to his business in general, or even to some element of his personal affairs, of a kind calculated to prevent others from dealing with him, or otherwise to interfere with his relations with others to his disadvantage." The court went on to say that although the tort resembles defamation, it differs in that a greater burden of proof rests on the plaintiff. For this tort, the plaintiff must prove special damages, must establish the falsity of the statement as part of his cause of action, and must show that the publication "played a material and substantial part in inducing others not to deal with" the plaintiff, and that "as a result he had suffered special damages."

In reaching its decision, the court adopted Prosser's (the original author of *Law of Torts*, the renowned law school torts text) term, "injurious falsehood," as a broader designation than slander of title. It reasoned that the tort has grown beyond interference with commercial relations, to encompass interference with noncommercial relations as well, such as the right to remain in the United States rather than be deported or the right of expectancy in marriage. Having previously decided only two cases on slander of title, the Court of Special Appeals of Maryland expressly adopted the broader terminology suggested by Prosser, considering the tort to be one of "injurious falsehood."

This case also addressed the defense of privilege. We will examine this part of its holding in the section on defenses, later in this chapter.

INJURIOUS FALSEHOOD

As the *Horning* case illustrates, "injurious falsehood" is a legal term that is sometimes used interchangeably with "disparagement," but that is actually a broader concept than disparagement. Disparagement is a kind of injurious falsehood involving commercial matters. Other injurious falsehoods dealing with noncommercial matters, and not involving harms to reputation—for that would be defamation—also fall within this broader category.

Examples of injurious falsehoods occurring outside the realm of commercial matters, as described in the *Horning* case, include disparaging statements that interfere with the expectancy of marriage, the right to remain in the United States rather than be deported, and false reporting of payments to an employee by an employer which subjects the employee to prosecution for income tax evasion.

Therefore, an ***injurious falsehood*** is a statement of fact that injures another economically, by disparaging either her business or her property, or in a noncommercial way.

Injurious falsehood
A statement of fact that harms the interests of another, which includes disparagement when commercial matters are at issue but is broader and also includes noncommercial matters.

what the seller says it is, causing others to not want to transact with the plaintiff regarding the product.

Consider this example. A tortfeasor publishes a statement that the plaintiff's microwave oven emits a dangerous level of electromagnetic waves. Although the oven is perfectly safe, this false statement of fact dissuades retailers from carrying the oven and offering it for sale.

What, then, are the essential elements of disparagement of property? That topic is discussed next.

Essential Elements of Disparagement of Property

Key Point

Essential Elements of Disparagement of Property

1. A false statement of fact
2. That is disparaging to the plaintiff's business or property
3. Publication of the disparaging statement to at least one other person
4. Intent
5. Special damages
6. Causation

The essential elements of the tort of disparagement of property are a false statement of fact that is disparaging to the plaintiff's business or property, publication of the disparaging statement to at least one other person, intent, special damages, and causation.

For there to be disparagement of property, the defendant must make a false statement of fact. The statement cannot be true. The statement cannot be merely an opinion. That statement must be disparaging to the plaintiff's business or property, rather than damaging to his personal character or reputation, as is the case with defamation. Like defamation, that statement must be published to at least one other person, and can be published to lots of people—it just need not be published to more than one person.

Disparagement is an intentional tort. The intent required is that the disparaging statement be intentionally made. In other words, the statement must be made by the defendant with knowledge that it is false or in reckless disregard for its truth or falsity. Note that the statement must be made intentionally.

CASE on Point

Brown v. Hanson, 798 N.W.2d 422 (S.D. 2011)

In this case, landowners brought a slander of title claim (as well as a tortious interference with a business relationship claim) after a neighboring landowner tried to rescind a common well and road easement agreement the parties had on file with the county register of deeds in Meade County, South Dakota.

The court said that in order to prove slander of title, a plaintiff must show that a publication was false and that the publication (1) was derogatory to the title to the plaintiff's property, its quality, or the plaintiff's business in general, calculated to prevent others from dealing with the plaintiff or to interfere with the plaintiff's relations with others to the plaintiff's disadvantage; (2) was communicated to a third party; (3) materially or substantially induced others not to deal with the plaintiff; and (4) resulted in special damage.

This court found that Hanson's letter to the Meade County register of deeds, seeking to unilaterally rescind the common well and road easement agreement between the parties, constituted slander of title. The court reasoned that Hanson's letter disparaged the Brown's property because Hanson had no authority to unilaterally rescind the agreement and his reasons given in the letter were false.

However, it can be published intentionally, negligently, or accidentally; the *publication* need not be intentional.

To recover for disparagement, the plaintiff must prove special damages. To do this, he must establish that he suffered actual, pecuniary harm. It is not enough to show a general loss of business caused by the disparaging statement. Finally, the plaintiff must establish that the disparaging statement is what caused the plaintiff's harm.

Once the plaintiff has established a *prima facie* case of disparagement, the defendant can defend against that claim. If the defendant fails to successfully defend against the claim, the plaintiff will be awarded a remedy. Possible defenses to and remedies for disparagement are examined next.

Disparagement Defenses and Remedies

As for the tort of defamation, a defendant can defend himself from a claim of disparagement by rebutting one of the plaintiff's essential elements, such as by showing that the statement was not disparaging, that it was not published, or that it did not cause the plaintiff to suffer special damages.

Further, as for defamation, truth of the statement is a defense. There is no disparagement if the statement of fact is a true one, though some other tort may be involved, such as an invasion of privacy tort discussed in Chapter 14, depending on the facts and circumstances.

Finally, the defense of privilege applies to disparagement as it does to defamation. Any absolute or qualified privilege that applies to defamation applies to disparagement, and to injurious falsehood, more broadly. See the following Case on Point.

CASE on Point

Horning v. Hardy, 373 A.2d 1273 (Md. Ct. Spec. App. 1977)

In addition to the issues discussed earlier in this chapter in relation to this case, the Court of Special Appeals of Maryland discussed the essential elements of a slander of title case. Pursuant to the facts of the case, once the claim of slander of title was presented by the Hornings, a relevant defense was raised by the Hardys. That defense was privilege.

The court found that the Hardys were not liable for slander of title because they possessed a conditional privilege to protect their "present economic interest" in the property by asserting an honest legal claim to it. The privilege was conditional because it could be lost if it was abused or forfeited. However, the Hardys did not act with malice, ill will, or spite, or with knowledge of the falsity of their claim or reckless disregard for its truth or falsity. Accordingly, the court determined that the privilege had not been abused or forfeited by the Hardys. Thus, their statements claiming title to the disputed property were qualifiedly privileged.

The usual remedy for disparagement is a remedy at law, namely, damages. Compensatory damages are typically recoverable in these cases. Remember that special damages are an essential element of the tort of disparagement of property and must be specially pled by the plaintiff. Because disparagement is an intentional tort, punitive damages may be recoverable as well.

CHAPTER **SUMMARY**

- Defamation is the publication of false statements of fact that cause injury to a person's good name, character, and reputation. Tort law imposes a duty on persons to refrain from making false, defamatory statements of fact about others that cause injury to their reputations.

- Slander and libel are the two types of defamation. Slander is defamation in oral form. Normally, it is spoken defamation, but it can be committed via gesture. Libel is defamation in written or other tangible form. Normally, it is written down. However, defamation is also libel if it is embodied in some physical form other than writing.

- The essential elements of slander and libel are virtually the same except for the element of damages. They are a defamatory statement made by the defendant, of and concerning the plaintiff, publication of the statement, damages, and causation.

- A defamatory statement is a statement of fact, rather than merely an opinion, which subjects the plaintiff to public ridicule, hatred, or contempt, and it must be false. The defamatory statement must be of and concerning the plaintiff. The defamatory statement must be published to, and understood by, at least one other person. The defamatory statement must cause damage to the reputation or good character of the plaintiff.

- In cases of slander *per quod* and, in some states, libel *per quod,* the plaintiff is required to prove special damages. Otherwise, the plaintiff need not produce specific evidence of the harms suffered, as they are presumed from the making of the defamatory statement.

- Stemming from a U.S. Supreme Court requirement, a public figure suing a media defendant for defamation must prove the additional essential element of actual malice by showing that the statement was made by the defendant knowing it was false or with reckless disregard for its truth or falsity.

- A defendant may defend a defamation action by rebutting an essential element of the plaintiff's claim. Truth is an absolute defense to a defamation claim. The First Amendment's free-speech guarantee is another defense to defamation. Privilege is a defense to defamation that renders the maker of certain communications immune from defamation liability. Damages are the typical remedy in defamation cases.

- Disparagement of property includes those intentional torts that protect against harm caused by injurious false statements made by someone against another's business or property. The statement either must cast doubt on the plaintiff's title to property, which is slander of title, or must attribute an undesirable quality to a product that dissuades third parties from dealing with the plaintiff in his business or in transactions involving the product, which is slander of quality, also called trade libel. Disparagement is a form of injurious falsehood.

- The essential elements of the tort of disparagement of property are a false statement of fact that is disparaging to the plaintiff's business or property, publication of the disparaging statement to at least one other person, intent, special damages, and causation. The same defenses apply to disparagement cases as to defamation ones. Damages are the typical remedy in disparagement cases.

CONCEPT REVIEW AND REINFORCEMENT

QUESTIONS FOR **REVIEW**

1. What is the tort of defamation?
2. What is the difference between slander and libel?
3. What are the essential elements of a defamation action?
4. How does actual malice apply to defamation actions?
5. What are the defenses to and remedies for defamation?
6. What is disparagement of property?
7. How does disparagement relate to the tort of injurious falsehood?
8. What are the two types of disparagement of property?
9. What are the essential elements of the tort of disparagement of property?
10. What defenses and remedies apply to the tort of disparagement?

DEVELOPING YOUR PARALEGAL SKILLS

CRITICAL THINKING **EXERCISES**

1. In this chapter, we examined the related torts of defamation and disparagement. Research the essential elements of these torts in your jurisdiction. Compare those state-specific requirements to the requirements of most states, as set forth in the chapter. Are they similar? Are there any differences? Discuss your research results in class.

2. Fred Bergen wishes to purchase a boat, and he is looking for a personal loan to help him finance the acquisition. Unfortunately, Fred has a blemished credit history, and he has filed for personal bankruptcy twice.

   a. *During consideration of Fred's loan application, Louis Jeffries, who knows Fred, tells the loan officer that "Fred is a deadbeat." Fred's loan application is denied. Has Louis defamed Fred? If so, is the defamation libel or slander?*

   b. *Suppose instead that Louis tells the loan officer, "Fred has filed for bankruptcy three times before." The loan officer denies Fred's loan application as a result of this statement and Fred's credit reports. Has Louis defamed Fred? If so, is this libel or slander?*

c. *Now suppose that Louis writes the loan officer a note stating, "Fred has filed for bankruptcy twice before." Fred's loan application is rejected as a result. Has Louis defamed Fred? If so, is this libel or slander?*

3. Joe Reynolds, a commentator for a major sports television network, makes an on-air comment one day that Aligatoraid, a sports beverage made by Extreme Beverages of America, Inc., "is so full of sugar it will rot your teeth." The beverage actually contains no sugar, only a sugar substitute. Shortly after that statement is made, sales of Aligatoraid decline.

a. *If Extreme Beverages sues Joe for disparagement of property, might it win? Why or why not?*

b. *Which of the two types of disparagement is at issue?*

c. *What if the beverage is made using sugar, not sugar substitute? Does that affect your answer?*

Now assume that Joe's statement is that the beverage, which is made using real sugar, "is so full of sugar it will rot your teeth faster than it will quench your thirst."

d. *How does this change in the statement affect your answer to part a?*

ASSIGNMENTS AND PRACTICAL **APPLICATIONS**

1. Read and brief the following libel case involving an unsuccessful gubernatorial candidate whose campaign was thwarted, at least in part, by misleading headlines and subtitles running in the defendant's newspaper on the eve of the election: *Sprouse v. Clay Commc'n, Inc.*, 211 S.E.2d 674 (W. Va. 1975).

2. In a defamation action, such as the following slander action, the plaintiff must be able to establish that the persons to whom the statement was published understood that it referred to the plaintiff (in this case, a statement that a woman had a child with a man other than her husband): *Gnapinsky v. Goldyn*, 128 A.2d 697 (N.J. 1957). What about the case in which a plaintiff, a Spanish stewardess on a steamer ship routed between the United States, Cuba, and Spain, was called a "cocotte" by her jealous suitor. The word "cocotte" is French for either a prostitute or a poached egg; the issue before the court was which of the two meanings of the term was understood by those who heard it: *Rovira v. Boget*, 148 N.E. 534 (N.Y. 1925).

3. Locate and examine the Texas Food Disparagement Act, the food libel statute under which Oprah Winfrey was sued by certain representatives of the beef industry. Research that law and determine how it compares to and contrasts with the common law of disparagement of property. Discuss your results in class.

4. Read and brief the first case involving a form of injurious falsehood, under facts very similar to the much more recent *Horning* case, but in which the plaintiff knew that her claim to a castle was based on forgery: *Gerard v. Dickenson*, 76 Eng.Rep. 903 (1590).

5. In the chapter, it was said that it might not be a giant leap for the U.S. Supreme Court to impose constitutional limitations on disparagement cases, as it did in defamation cases. Read and brief *Bose Corp. v. Consumers Union of U.S., Inc.*, 466 U.S. 485 (1984), an action brought by the speaker manufacturer against the publisher of *Consumer Reports* magazine for an adverse rating of its model 901 speakers. In that case, the Court discussed imposing an "actual malice" requirement when a media defendant is sued by a public figure, as Bose Corp. was determined to be.

TECHNOLOGY RESOURCES AND INTERNET **EXERCISES**

You can listen to the oral arguments before the U.S. Supreme Court in the famous *New York Times v. Sullivan* case at *www.oyez.org/cases/1960-1969/1963/1963_39/argument*.

Using the Internet, research whether your state is one of the several that have a food libel statute. If it does, does the statute ease the burden of proof, making it easier for plaintiffs to establish their cases than under traditional, common law disparagement theory? In what way(s)? Discuss your research results in class.

Using computerized legal research methods and the Internet, research the reasons why Oprah Winfrey won her Texas food libel suit.

ETHICAL **APPLICATIONS**

Susan Slater is a paralegal with the law firm of Day, Riley, & Warner, P.C. Susan wonders what title she may use in informing clients and others of her role on the legal services delivery team.

What titles, if any, may Susan use besides "paralegal" or "legal assistant"? May she use the title "lawyer's assistant," "nonlawyer assistant," or "nonlawyer paralegal"? What about the term "legal associate"? What guidance do the legal ethics rules in your state provide?

VIDEO **CASE STUDY**

Solicitation in the E.R.: Ethical Duties of the Professions

Synopsis: A hospital clerk works with a mother of a student who was injured when file boxes fell on her while the school bus carrying her, other students, and the boxes made a sudden stop. The clerk shares the student's treatment report with a paralegal. In addition, he whispers to the student's mother that the bus driver may have been intoxicated. The paralegal tries to solicit the mother's injured child as a new client for her firm.

Questions

1. What are the elements of the tort of defamation?
2. Do you think the hospital clerk defamed the bus driver in this scenario?

chapter **14**

INVASION OF PRIVACY

LEARNING OBJECTIVES

14.1 Define invasion of privacy.

14.2 List and discuss the four invasion of privacy torts.

14.3 Identify the defenses applicable to the invasion of privacy torts.

14.4 Explain the remedies available for invasion of privacy.

Right to privacy
The right a person has to be left alone.

Invasion of privacy
Interference with a person's right to be left alone; also called invasion of the right to privacy.

T his chapter examines the four invasion of privacy torts: intrusion, appropriation, public disclosure of private facts, and false light.

Americans have a reasonable expectation of privacy in their lives, and it may be an invasion of their privacy to intrude on their solitude. To understand the four invasion of privacy torts, one must first understand what invasion of privacy is.

Definition of Invasion of Privacy

Before invasion of privacy can be examined, the right to privacy must be understood. The **right to privacy** is the right a person has to be left alone. The right to privacy is acknowledged by the U.S. Supreme Court, which has held that a fundamental right to privacy is implied by various amendments to the U.S. Constitution, as illustrated in the *Griswold* Case on Point.

Some states, in their constitutions, specifically grant certain privacy rights. For a review of these, see the Internet exercise at the end of the chapter involving a state-by-state comparison of the states' constitutional right to privacy. Both federal and state legislatures have codified the right to privacy in statutes that protect persons in specific situations; some examples are given in Table 14-1, and others are included in the exercises at the end of the chapter.

Tort law's contribution to the protection of an individual's right to privacy is the tort of invasion of privacy. **Invasion of privacy**, or the invasion of the right to privacy, is the interference by another with one's privacy rights. In other words, it protects a person's right to be left alone.

There are four different invasion of privacy torts: intrusion, appropriation, public disclosure of private facts, and false light. Each of these torts will be examined, in turn, starting with intrusion.

CASE on Point

Griswold v. Connecticut, 381 U.S. 479 (1965)

In this case, the Griswolds were convicted of violating the Connecticut birth control law by using contraceptives. In its review of the case, the U.S. Supreme Court held that the Connecticut law forbidding use of contraceptives unconstitutionally intruded on the right to marital privacy.

The Court recognized a constitutional right to privacy implied by various amendments to the U.S. Constitution, saying that:

> [S]pecific guarantees in the Bill of Rights have penumbras, formed by emanations from those guarantees that help give them life and substance [citation omitted]. Various guarantees create zones of privacy. The right of association contained in the penumbra of the First Amendment is one, as we have seen. The Third Amendment in its prohibition against the quartering of soldiers "in any house" in time of peace without the consent of the owner is another facet of that privacy. The Fourth Amendment explicitly affirms the "right of the people to be secure in their persons, houses, papers, and effects, against unreasonable searches and seizures." The Fifth Amendment in its Self-Incrimination Clause enables the citizen to create a zone of privacy which government may not force him to surrender to his detriment. The Ninth Amendment provides: "The enumeration in the Constitution, of certain rights, shall not be construed to deny or disparage others retained by the people." There have been "many controversies over these penumbral rights of 'privacy and repose' [citations omitted]. These cases bear witness that the right of privacy which presses for recognition here is a legitimate one."

In its opinion, the Court said that the case involved a relationship "lying within the zone of privacy" created by numerous fundamental constitutional guarantees. It said that a law forbidding the use of contraceptives, rather than regulating their manufacture and sale, sought "to achieve its goals by means having a maximum destructive impact" on the marital relationship. The law could not "stand" because a "governmental purpose to control or prevent activities constitutionally subject to state regulation may not be achieved by means which sweep unnecessarily broadly and thereby invade the area of protected freedoms." The idea that the police could search the "sacred precincts of marital bedrooms for telltale signs of the use of contraceptives" was, said the Court, "repulsive to the notions of privacy surrounding the marriage relationship."

TABLE 14-1 Examples of Federal and State Legislation Protecting Privacy Rights*

COPPA (Children's Online Privacy Protection Act)	Requires websites directed at children under 13 years of age to obtain "verifiable parental consent" before collecting personal information online from children.
DPPA (Driver's Privacy Protection Act)	Prevents states from disclosing or selling drivers' personal information without their consent.

(continued)

TABLE 14-1 (Continued)

Drug and alcoholism abuse confidentiality statutes	Prohibit disclosure of information collected for federally funded research and treatment of drug abuse and alcoholism.
Equal Employment Opportunity Act	Restricts the collection and use of information that would result in employment discrimination.
Fair Credit Reporting Act	Regulates the collection and use of personal data by credit reporting agencies.
FERPA (Family and Educational Rights and Privacy Act)	Protects the privacy of education-related student records retained by colleges and universities.
HIPAA (Health Insurance Portability and Accountability Act)	Protects the privacy of patients' medical records retained by medical and health care providers.
Telephone Consumer Protection Act	Requires those who use the telephone to solicit to provide the persons solicited with the ability to prevent future telephone solicitations.
Wiretap statutes	Prohibit the use of eavesdropping technology and the interception of electronic mail, radio communications, data transmission, and telephone calls without consent.
Various state laws	Protect items such as bank records, criminal justice information, employment records, insurance records, medical records, school records, and genetic information, and restrict conduct such as wiretapping, telephone and facsimile solicitation, polygraph usage, and the collection of information about individuals by state governments.

*See the exercises at the end of the chapter for more examples.

SIDEBAR

WEBSITE PRIVACY POLICIES

Companies that conduct online business with consumers must gather information about and from those consumers to carry out their transactions. To avoid liability under privacy and other laws, and to relieve consumers of fear regarding the security and privacy of their personal information, most online businesses create and implement online privacy policies. Such website privacy policies normally provide guidelines regarding what types of information are collected, how the information will be used, and to whom the information will be disclosed. Some organizations, including the Federal Trade Commission and the Better Business Bureau, provide guidance to companies in developing and implementing online privacy policies.

Intrusion

Intrusion
Invasion into a person's private affairs or concerns; also called intrusion on seclusion.

Intrusion, or intrusion on seclusion, is an invasion into a person's private affairs or concerns. Another way of describing intrusion is an interference with another person's solitude. This interference with another's solitude must be one that is highly offensive to the ordinary person, as the essential elements of the

CASE on Point

Galella v. Onassis, 533 F. Supp. 1076 (S.D.N.Y. 1982)

In this case, a freelance photographer, Ronald Galella, sued Jackie Kennedy Onassis for false arrest, malicious prosecution, and interference with his business of photography. Onassis counterclaimed, alleging intrusion, and along with her daughter, Caroline Kennedy, sought an order holding Galella in contempt of court for violating an earlier restraining order dated January 8, 1975, that permanently enjoined Galella from approaching, touching, harassing, alarming, frightening, and the like, Onassis and both her children, Caroline and John, Jr. Galella had hounded Onassis relentlessly by photographing her at point-blank range on sidewalks, tennis courts, and riding trails, and by hiding in cloakrooms and bribing employees of businesses patronized by Onassis.

The court said that "under certain circumstances, surveillance may be so overzealous as to render it actionable." The "systematic public surveillance" of another could be construed as a plan to intrude on that person's privacy. The court recognized Onassis's constitutional right to privacy, calling it the right to be left alone. This right to be left alone was "exactly what Galella relentlessly and shockingly invaded—goaded on because, as he put it, . . . my favorite, and to me the biggest celebrity in the world is Jacqueline Onassis."

The court found that Galella purposefully violated the provisions of the 1975 court order on twelve different occasions by grossly disrupting and intruding on the lives of Onassis and Caroline Kennedy. Accordingly, the court found Galella in contempt of court twelve times.

tort require. Therefore, it is not the tort of intrusion for someone to peek into the window of an unoccupied car parked in a public lot because that, while perhaps interfering with another's private matters, is not highly offensive to a reasonable person. The interest this tort protects is the right of a person to be free from unreasonable intrusions into his or her private affairs or concerns. The "Jackie O" case is a famous case on the tort of intrusion (see the *Galella* Case on Point).

The essential elements of the tort of intrusion are (1) an act of intrusion (2) into a person's private affairs or concerns (3) that is highly offensive to a reasonable person.

What is an act of intrusion? An act of intrusion is an act that encroaches on another person's private affairs or concerns. It includes such acts as prying, peering, or probing into the private affairs or concerns of another.

As suggested, the intrusion must be into a person's *private* affairs or concerns, not a public matter. What distinguishes a private affair or concern from a public one? Courts consider several factors in determining whether a concern or affair is public or private. For example, courts may consider whether the plaintiff was in a public or private place at the time of the intrusion. If the plaintiff was in a public place, such as a shopping mall or a park, the matter is more likely to be considered a public one. On the other hand, if the plaintiff was in a stall of a restaurant bathroom, with the door closed, the matter is more likely to be considered a private one even if the restaurant is a public facility—the occupied bathroom stall is not.

Key Point

The Essential Elements of the Tort of Intrusion

1. An act of intrusion
2. Into another's private affairs or concerns
3. The intrusion is highly offensive to a reasonable person

Courts may also take into account whether the plaintiff was observable by normal methods of observation at the time of the intrusion. In other words, could the plaintiff be seen simply by looking, or was an instrument such as a telephoto lens needed? The facts will affect a court's determination of whether the matter was public or private. What about paparazzi using telephoto lenses to photograph celebrities who are on private property, perhaps sunbathing on a balcony at home? What if the balcony is at a resort hotel rather than the celebrity's home? The first scenario seems more private than the second one, given that the first involves private property (a balcony at a private home) while the other involves more public property (a hotel balcony), though both scenarios involve the use of technology to capture the image.

Whether the plaintiff was trying to draw attention to herself at the time of the intrusion is another factor that courts may consider. For instance, if a plaintiff was "walking the red carpet" for an event, the matter is more likely to be considered a public one than a private one. Suppose a celebrity dons a hat and dark sunglasses to go shopping on Worth Avenue in Palm Beach. In that case, the celebrity is not trying to draw attention to herself, thus taking the matter farther from the "public" side of the public/private spectrum. However, what if it is nighttime and the celebrity is walking down the street wearing dark sunglasses? In that case, because sunglasses are not needed at night, the celebrity might be trying to draw attention to herself by wearing sunglasses when no one else would be. Thus, the matter may swing back toward the "public" side of the public/private spectrum.

Courts may also consider whether the plaintiff was caught off guard, through no fault of her own, at the time of the intrusion. For example, if someone peers under a bathroom stall partition in a public bathroom, that act would constitute intrusion involving a private matter. What about a celebrity touching up her makeup in a public restroom during a publicity event? There may be a reasonable expectation of privacy in a bathroom, even a public one, but a distinction might perhaps be made by a court between a bathroom stall and the sink and mirror areas in the bathroom, because one is more private than the other—in fact, the bathroom stall doors lock from the inside, but the bathroom door itself does not lock at all.

Whether the plaintiff's activity was something that society would consider private, and not a matter of public concern, is another factor that courts may take into account. Consider the previous example of a celebrity reapplying her makeup in the mirror of a public bathroom, which also illustrates this factor.

Also, courts may consider whether the defendant took advantage of the plaintiff's vulnerable position in determining whether a matter is public or private. For example, photographing a person immediately after he is involved in a car collision would constitute taking advantage of that person while he was in a vulnerable position, making the matter more likely a private one.

Finally, courts may consider whether the plaintiff's activity was already a matter of public record before the defendant became involved. For example, if a plaintiff is testifying in a court proceeding, she has no reasonable expectation of privacy because the activity is a matter of public record.

Courts take into account each of these factors to the extent that they are relevant to the facts of the case in determining whether the affair or concern

Key Point

Public Versus Private Concern Factors

- Whether the plaintiff was in a public or private place at the time of the intrusion
- Whether the plaintiff was observable by normal methods of observation at the time of the intrusion
- Whether the plaintiff was trying to draw attention to himself at the time of the intrusion
- Whether the plaintiff was caught off guard through no fault of his own at the time of the intrusion
- Whether the plaintiff's activity was something that society would consider private, and not a matter of public concern
- Whether the defendant took advantage of the plaintiff's vulnerable position
- Whether the plaintiff's activity was already a matter of public record before the defendant became involved

CASE on Point

Pearson v. Dodd, 410 F.2d 701 (C.A.D.C. 1969)

This was a case of first impression (that is, being heard for the first time) on the tort of intrusion in the District of Columbia.

Thomas Dodd was a U.S. Senator from Connecticut. Two members of Dodd's staff, along with two of his former employees, entered his office after hours, without authority to do so, and removed numerous documents from the senator's files. They copied the documents, returned the originals, and then turned the copies over to investigative journalist Jack Anderson. Anderson was aware of the unauthorized manner in which these copies had been obtained. Anderson and Drew Pearson, another journalist, then wrote nationally released newspaper columns using information obtained from those copied documents. The newspaper articles portrayed the columnists' view of Dodd's relationship with certain lobbyists and gave an interpretive biographical sketch of Dodd's career in public service, in effect portraying Dodd as a politician who engaged in misdeeds. The columns implied that Dodd was not qualified to serve as a U.S. Senator.

Among the legal theories alleged in a lawsuit brought by Senator Dodd against the columnists was intrusion. The U.S. Court of Appeals of the D.C. Circuit said:

> [It] has been held that unauthorized bugging of a dwelling, tapping a telephone, snooping through windows, and over-zealous shadowing amount to invasions of privacy, whether or not accompanied by trespasses to property . . . . Unlike other types of invasion of privacy, intrusion does not involve as one of its essential elements the publication of the information obtained. The tort is completed with the obtaining of the information by improperly intrusive means.

The court had to decide, for the first time in D.C., whether it would recognize the tort of intrusion. The court held:

> We approve the extension of the tort of invasion of privacy to instances of intrusion, whether by physical trespass or not, into spheres from which an ordinary man in a plaintiff's position could reasonably expect that the particular defendant should be excluded. Just as the Fourth Amendment has expanded to protect citizens from government intrusions where intrusion is not reasonably expected, so should tort law protect citizens from other citizens. The protection should not turn exclusively on the question of whether the intrusion involves a technical trespass under the law of property. The common law, like the Fourth Amendment, should "protect people, not places."

After recognizing the tort of intrusion, the court found that Pearson and Anderson did not improperly intrude on Dodd's "protected sphere of privacy." The court reasoned that the columnists did not intrude on Dodd's privacy because they were merely ones who received information from intruders, despite knowing that it had been obtained by improper intrusion. In this case, the court

(continued)

was unwilling to extend liability for intrusion to include mere recipients of information and documents (although the court stated that Dodd's employees and former employees committed the tort of intrusion when they removed the confidential files with the intent to show them to unauthorized outsiders, but Dodd had not sued *them* for intrusion).

is public or private. If it is a private affair or concern, the person involved may have a reasonable expectation of privacy, depending on how offensive the intrusion is.

The intrusion into another's private affairs or concerns must be highly offensive to a reasonable person. This is an objective test, as it is with the tort of negligence. It means the intrusion must be more than embarrassing. It must be so displeasing and insulting that no ordinary, prudent person would find it tolerable. Even if the particular plaintiff was humiliated or offended by the conduct, the test is whether an ordinary, reasonable, prudent person would be. Remember the earlier example of someone peering in the window of an unoccupied car parked in a public parking lot. This may be an intrusion, but it is not one that would be considered highly offensive to an ordinary person—given that the car is in a public parking lot and its windows are not covered, it is likely a public matter anyway.

A classic example of an intrusion that is highly offensive to a reasonable person is a "peeping Tom." One who "peeps" and peers into the windows of another's residence to observe private occurrences within the residence has intruded on the seclusion of others, and likely has committed a crime as well. The following types of conduct may also constitute intrusions on seclusion, depending on the facts and circumstances: invading a person's real property (home or office) or personal property (rifling through her purse, briefcase, or bed stand), eavesdropping using wiretapping devices, compulsory drug testing, or opening another person's mail or answering his telephone (without permission, obviously).

Intrusion is one of the four invasion of privacy torts. Another is appropriation. We examine appropriation next.

Appropriation

Appropriation Use of another person's name, likeness, image, or other identifying characteristic, without permission, for the benefit of the user.

Key Point

The Essential Elements of Appropriation

1. Use of the plaintiff's identity
2. For the benefit of the defendant

Appropriation is the use of another person's name, likeness, image, or other identifying characteristic, without permission, for the benefit of the user. This invasion of privacy tort protects a person's right to the exclusive use of her identity. The essential elements of this tort are fairly simple: There must be a use of the plaintiff's identity for the benefit of the defendant.

How does a tortfeasor use another person's identity? He does so by using another's name, likeness, image, or other identifying characteristic. In using another's identity, the use must specifically identify the plaintiff. This means that others must know the defendant's use refers to and identifies the particular plaintiff.

CASE on Point

White v. Samsung Elecs. America, Inc., 971 F.2d 1395 (9th Cir. 1992)

In this case Vanna White, the "letter turner" on the TV game show *Wheel of Fortune*, sued Samsung Electronics America, Inc., and David Deutsch Associates, Inc., under the theory of appropriation, among other theories. The facts of the case were that the defendants made and aired an advertisement that featured a robot, dressed in a wig, gown, and jewelry, which had been consciously selected by Deutsch, the advertising company, to resemble White's hair and dress. The robot appeared next to a game board that was easily recognizable as the *Wheel of Fortune* game show board and set. Further, the defendants referred to the ad as the "Vanna White" ad. White did not authorize or consent to the ad, and she was not paid for it.

Under California law at the time, White brought a common law right of publicity claim, which had the following essential elements: "(1) the defendant's use of the plaintiff's identity; (2) the appropriation of plaintiff's name or likeness to defendant's advantage, commercially or otherwise; (3) lack of consent; and (4) resulting injury."

In applying the facts of the case to the law, the Ninth Circuit found that the ad did not make use of White's name or likeness. However, the court expanded the appropriation theory to include, more broadly, the plaintiff's identity, rather than merely use of her name or likeness. The court stated that "the common law right of publicity reaches means of appropriation other than name or likeness, but that the specific means of appropriation are relevant only for determining whether the defendant has in fact appropriated the plaintiff's identity. The right of publicity does not require that appropriations of identity be accomplished through particular means to be actionable." The court said, "It is not important *how* the defendant has appropriated the plaintiff's identity, but *whether* the defendant has done so." Based on the facts presented in the case, the court determined that White had established that the defendants had appropriated her identity, though they did not necessarily appropriate her name or likeness, when using the robot to depict her.

In addition, for there to be appropriation, the defendant must derive some benefit or gain some advantage from the use of the plaintiff's identity. Some jurisdictions require a commercial benefit, with a financial or other pecuniary advantage being derived by the defendant, such as increased sales by using a celebrity's name in conjunction with marketing a product. Other jurisdictions require only that the defendant derive some sort of benefit from the use of the plaintiff's identity, such as by impersonating a celebrity to gain admittance to a popular nightspot.

Examples of appropriation are using a celebrity's name or picture to endorse a product or service without permission, or using the identifying information of another to take his identity, perhaps to obtain credit or to make a fraudulent purchase.

Of course, the use of another's identity must be without authorization for the tort of appropriation to be committed. If a person has been given authority or consent to use another's identity, such as a celebrity agreeing to endorse a product in exchange for a rather substantial endorsement fee, the tort of appropriation is not committed. Thus, consent to use is a defense to the tort of appropriation. Defenses to invasion of privacy torts are discussed more fully at the end of this chapter.

Appropriation is another of the invasion of privacy torts. A third invasion of privacy tort is public disclosure of private facts. It is examined next.

Public Disclosure of Private Facts

Public disclosure of private facts is the unreasonable public disclosure of private facts about a person that are not matters of legitimate public concern. The interest protected by this tort is the right to be free from such unreasonable disclosures of private facts about a person that are not legitimate matters of concern for the general public. The essential elements of this tort are (1) publicity (2) concerning the private life of the plaintiff (3) that is highly offensive to a reasonable person.

In analyzing each of these essential elements, first we must consider the meaning of publicity. "Publicity" means more than the "publication" requirement of the tort of defamation. For the defamation torts of slander and libel, the defamatory statement must be published to at least one other person. The publicity requirement for this invasion of privacy tort is broader. Publicity, for this tort, means communication to either the public at large (such as through a newspaper announcement) or a large group of people (such as making a statement to an audience during a performance).

The disclosed fact must be a private, not public, one. In other words, it must concern the private life of the plaintiff and not be a matter of public concern. Courts consider many of the same factors as discussed in relation to the tort of intrusion in determining whether a disclosure is one of private or public fact. This element merits greater analysis, as it is not always clear. Consider the following examples.

There is no disclosure of a private fact if the fact is already a matter of public record, such as the conviction record of an adult or the names of contributors to a particular political campaign. Legally protected confidential documents and information, such as Social Security numbers, tax returns, and privileged attorney–client communications, are private facts. Publishing the name of a rape victim who is a minor is disclosure of a private fact; publishing the name of a sex offender who is listed in a state's sex offender registry is a public fact—that information is publicly available. Some facts are considered private by custom rather than law, such as a person's sexual conduct or preference. However, a person who self-discloses information normally considered and kept private may be found to have consented to public disclosure of that information by others.

The First Amendment right to free speech limits a public figure's recovery under this tort. For public figures, such as celebrities, politicians, and other well-known people, in whom the public has a legitimate interest because of their occupations, achievements, and the like, it is more difficult to establish that a fact is a private one, for which public disclosure would be highly

---

Public disclosure of private facts
Unreasonable public disclosure of private facts about a person that are not a matter of legitimate public concern.

Key Point

The Essential Elements of Public Disclosure of Private Facts

1. Publicity
2. Concerning the private life of the plaintiff
3. That is highly offensive to a reasonable person

Key Point

Publicity (Invasion of Privacy) Versus Publication (Defamation)

For the invasion of privacy torts for which publicity is an element, this concept is broader than the "publication" requirement for defamation (discussed in Chapter 13). For defamation, while publication can be to the public at large or a group of people, sharing the statement with one other person is enough. However, the "publicity" requirement for the invasion of privacy torts that have it requires communication to the public at large or a large group of people—communication to one other person is not enough.

CASE on Point

Pearson v. Dodd, 410 F.2d 701 (C.A.D.C. 1969)

Let us reconsider this case, discussed earlier with reference to the tort of intrusion. In this case, the court stated that "we have separately considered the nature of [the columnists'] publications concerning [Dodd], and have found that the matter published was of obvious public interest. The publication was not itself an invasion of privacy."

Had the information gleaned from the files been private facts about Senator Dodd's life, the tort involved might have been public disclosure of private facts rather than intrusion. However, the facts disclosed in the case involved matters of public concern, namely, Dodd's relationship with certain lobbyists and a biographical sketch of his public career. Because Dodd was a U.S. Senator at the time, more facts concerning him, his life, and his actions fall within the "public" realm than they would for a private citizen (meaning someone not well known and not in the public eye).

offensive. Celebrities and politicians, when they become public figures, give up some expectations of privacy that private citizens maintain, and the application of this tort is one example.

Concerning the last essential element, the published statement of a private fact must be highly offensive to a reasonable person. As for the tort of intrusion, an objective standard is used in making this determination. The question asked is whether an ordinary, prudent person would find the disclosure highly offensive. It must be more than merely embarrassing or insulting. It must be so highly offensive that a reasonable person would be mortified by its public disclosure, such as publicly playing a close-up videotape of a woman privately nursing her infant, or a news story concerning a private person's financial affairs or sex life.

Note that the truth or falsity of the fact disclosed is irrelevant. Truth or falsity is not an essential element of this tort. If the statement is false, it may also constitute the tort of defamation if all the other essential elements of that tort are met. For instance, a false news report that John Smith is a child molester could constitute both defamation, if it is a false statement and the other defamation elements are present, and the invasion of privacy tort of public disclosure of private facts, if all its elements are met. Remember that a true statement can serve as the basis for an invasion of privacy action.

The final invasion of privacy tort is false light. We examine that tort next.

False Light

False light is publicly making or giving a highly offensive and inaccurate portrayal or impression of another person. With false light, a defendant is imparting to the public an inaccurate impression about a person, which inaccurate impression is highly offensive.

Like the tort of defamation, false light involves false statements made by a defendant about a plaintiff. Unlike the tort of defamation, however, the tort

False light
Publicly making or giving a highly offensive and inaccurate portrayal or impression of another person.

of false light does not require that the published statement cause harm to the plaintiff's reputation. A defendant's conduct can constitute both the tort of defamation and the tort of false light if all the essential elements of both torts are met.

The interest protected by this tort is the right to be free from the wrongful making of false statements that unreasonably and publicly place a person in a false light. The essential elements of the tort of false light are (1) publicity, (2) which places the plaintiff in a false light, and (3) which is highly offensive to a reasonable person. For media defendants, an additional essential element of actual malice must be established by the plaintiff. For example, publishing a story attributing to a person ideas he does not hold or actions he has not undertaken, such as that the plaintiff, as a young woman, spent five years in a polygamist compound, may constitute the tort of false light if the public statement places the woman in a false light that she perhaps supports or even engaged in the practice of polygamy.

The first essential element, publicity, means the same thing for this tort as it does for the tort of public disclosure of private facts. The communication must be made to the public in general, or to a large group of persons. Unlike defamation, one person is not enough.

To place the plaintiff in a false light, the defendant's publicity must leave an impression or offer a conclusion about a plaintiff that is not accurate. In other words, the portrayal must be false and misleading. If the portrayal is accurate and true, even if it is offensive, it is not the tort of false light, though it might be another of the invasion of privacy torts, depending on the facts and circumstances. Beyond being a mere false impression, the false impression must be highly offensive to a reasonable person.

The element that the false impression be highly offensive to a reasonable person is the same as for the other invasion of privacy torts, other than appropriation, which does not require this element. This is an objective test and requires that a reasonable person, not just the plaintiff, find the publicity to be highly offensive. Consider this example.

The defendant makes public statements giving the impression that the plaintiff is very compassionate and is a selfless philanthropist. In reality, the plaintiff is a heartless, selfish pig. Has the defendant committed the tort of false light? No, there is no tort of false light, as the public impression given by the defendant of the plaintiff is not offensive. Rather, it is complimentary. What if the plaintiff is a rich, well-known community member who never contributes to charity? If a story is published by the defendant that, according to his tax records, the plaintiff has never taken a charitable deduction for making a charitable contribution, would that constitute false light? Not if it is a true statement. Although it may be another invasion of privacy tort, making an accurate public portrayal of someone, even if it is embarrassing to that someone, is not false light. However, suppose the statement was false because the plaintiff had, in fact, made many charitable contributions in the past, but he did so through a trust and thus left no public record. Would the tort of false light be committed under such circumstances? Because the impression left by the defendant's public statement is a false one, it is the tort of false light if the court determines the portrayal was

CASE on Point

Kolegas v. Heftel Broad. Corp., 607 N.E.2d 201 (Ill. 1992)

In this case, two radio disc jockeys and their broadcasters were sued under false light theory, among other theories, for statements they made during a broadcast. By way of background, Anthony Kolegas called into the radio show one day and had an on-air conversation with the disc jockeys. The subject of the conversation involved Kolegas promoting a cartoon festival to benefit the National Neurofibromatosis Foundation and to promote public awareness of neurofibromatosis, commonly known as "Elephant Man disease." During the conversation, Kolegas stated that his wife and son suffered from the disease, and one of the disc jockeys responded, "You're gone," and hung up the phone. After disconnecting the call, the disc jockeys engaged in the following banter: "Why would someone marry a woman if she had Elephant Man disease? It's not like he couldn't tell—unless it was a shotgun wedding." The other disk jockey responded that it must have been a shotgun wedding. Then the first retorted, "If he is producing it, he's only producing it part-time. The rest of the time he's too busy picking out their wardrobe. You know, he has to make sure they have large hats to cover their big heads and make sure that all of their collars are big enough to fit." The other disk jockey acknowledged her agreement.

In suing under the false light invasion of privacy theory, the Kolegas family alleged that those statements placed them in a false light before the public because they implied that the couple were married in a shotgun wedding (they were not) and that the wife and son had abnormally large heads (they did not). The Supreme Court of Illinois agreed with the Kolegas family.

The court set forth three elements needed for a false light cause of action. First, the plaintiffs must establish that they "were placed in a false light before the public as a result of the defendants' actions." Second, the plaintiffs must show that the false light in which they were placed "would be highly offensive to a reasonable person." That element is met "when the defendant knows that the plaintiff, as a reasonable man, would be justified in the eyes of the community in feeling seriously offended and aggrieved by the publicity." Third, the plaintiffs must show "that the defendants acted with actual malice, that is, with knowledge that the statements were false or with reckless disregard for whether the statements were true or false." The court found all elements established in this case.

highly offensive to a reasonable person—creating a public impression that such a rich man is not at all charitable.

If the defendant is a media defendant, an additional element of actual malice must be established by the plaintiff. This is required to overcome the defendant's First Amendment right of free speech—just as for the tort of defamation. As discussed with regard to the tort of defamation, actual malice means that the publicity that placed the plaintiff in a false light was made by the defendant either knowing it was false or with reckless disregard for its truth or falsity.

Once a plaintiff has established the essential elements of one or more of the invasion of privacy torts, the defendant may assert any defenses available in an effort to defeat the plaintiff's claim. If the defendant is unable to successfully assert a defense to such tort(s), then the plaintiff is entitled to recovery, in the form of one or more remedies. Defenses and remedies are examined next.

Defenses and Remedies Applicable to the Invasion of Privacy Torts

In defending an invasion of privacy action, a defendant can defeat one or more of the essential elements of the plaintiff's claim. For instance, for the tort of intrusion, the defendant can show that there was no act of intrusion or that the intrusion was not highly offensive to a reasonable person; or for the tort of false light, that there was no publicity, that the impression left was accurate (rather than false), or that the portrayal was not highly offensive to a reasonable person.

Consent is a defense to all four of the invasion of privacy torts. If the plaintiff consents to the intrusion, disclosure, use, or publicity, no invasion of privacy tort has been committed.

Certain immunities also apply to the invasion of privacy torts. For example, intrafamily immunity may bar suit by one family member against another family member for invasion of privacy, and official immunity may bar a suit against a public official for invasion of privacy. Immunity was discussed in Chapter 9.

Further, depending on the facts and circumstances of the case, certain privileges may apply. For example, if the defendant's conduct occurred while he was defending himself or his property or arresting the plaintiff, the self-help privileges or the privilege to arrest might apply to bar recovery for invasion of privacy.

Unlike defamation, truth is *not* a defense to invasion of privacy torts. A true statement can be the basis for an invasion of privacy claim, such as a true statement that constitutes the public disclosure of private facts.

The normal remedy in an invasion of privacy action is damages. The plaintiff can recover compensatory damages for harm suffered, such as for physical or mental illness suffered by the plaintiff as a result of the defendant's commission of the tort. Compensatory damages can include damages for humiliation and embarrassment caused by the intrusion, disclosure, or the like, so long as all the essential elements of the tort are met. Punitive damages may be recoverable if the defendant acted maliciously, with harmful intent.

As with other tort actions, the plaintiff must take reasonable steps to mitigate his damages. This means he must take reasonable action to minimize the harm caused by the defendant's invasion of his privacy. The plaintiff cannot recover for damages he sustains as a result of his own failure to take reasonable steps to reduce the amount of harm he suffers.

CHAPTER **SUMMARY**

- Invasion of privacy, or invasion of the right to privacy, is interference with another's right to be left alone. There are four different invasion of privacy torts: intrusion, appropriation, public disclosure of private facts, and false light.

- Intrusion, or intrusion on seclusion, means invasion into a person's private affairs or concerns. The essential elements of this tort are that there be an act of intrusion into a person's private affairs or concerns that is highly offensive to a reasonable person.

- Appropriation is the use of another person's name, likeness, image, or other identifying characteristic, without permission, for the benefit of the user. The essential elements of this tort are that there is a use of the plaintiff's name, likeness, or image for the benefit of the defendant.

- Public disclosure of private facts is the unreasonable public disclosure of private facts about a person that are not matters of legitimate public concern. The essential elements of this tort are publicity concerning the private life of the plaintiff that is highly offensive to a reasonable person.

- False light is the invasion of privacy tort involving an untrue and misleading public portrayal of another person. The essential elements of the tort of false light are publicity that places the plaintiff in a false light and that is highly offensive to a reasonable person. For cases involving a media defendant, an additional essential element of actual malice must be established by the plaintiff, just as for the tort of defamation.

- A defendant can assert defenses in invasion of privacy actions, such as immunity, privilege, or consent, as well as defeat one or more of the essential elements of the plaintiff's case. If the defendant cannot successfully defend the action, the plaintiff is entitled to recovery of one or more remedies, the most common of which is damages.

CONCEPT REVIEW AND REINFORCEMENT

QUESTIONS FOR **REVIEW**

1. What is invasion of privacy?
2. What are the invasion of privacy torts?
3. What is intrusion?
4. What is appropriation?
5. What is the tort of public disclosure of private facts?
6. What is false light?
7. What defenses and remedies apply to the invasion of privacy torts?

DEVELOPING YOUR PARALEGAL SKILLS

CRITICAL THINKING **EXERCISES**

1. In this chapter, we examined the four invasion of privacy torts. Research the law in your state on each of these torts to see in what way(s), if any, your state's law differs from most states' laws. An excellent starting point for your research is a case law digest for your state. For example, in Maryland, the resource *Maryland Digest 2d* by West includes cases from Maryland dealing with these torts. Review your research results in class.

2. a. Julie Robins, a famous movie actress, is attending a charity event at which she will speak on behalf

of an environmental organization to solicit funds for its efforts in educating people about the effects of global warming. As she is walking into the event venue, using a "private" back entrance, a member of the paparazzi takes her picture, to sell to the tabloid press.

Has the tort of intrusion been committed by the photographer against Julie? Why or why not?

b. What if the picture was taken not while Julie was walking into the building, but while she was riding to the event in a dark-windowed limousine?

Was there intrusion into Julie's seclusion under these facts? Why or why not?

c. What if the picture was taken not while Julie was riding in the limousine, but while she was in her hotel room, working with a fashion stylist, makeup artist, and hair stylist, to prepare for the event. At the time, she was wearing only her undergarments. The photographer was able to get the shot by using a telephoto lens and shooting into the hotel room through an open window.

Was there an intrusion into Julie's seclusion under these modified facts? Why or why not?

d. What if the picture was taken by a guest at Julie's wedding, and sold to a tabloid newspaper that expected its readers to be interested in seeing a picture from Julie's wedding. The wedding was held in a remote location, with only those needing to know about it having advance knowledge of it, and with comprehensive security measures taken to ensure that only those invited to the wedding were in attendance, to help maintain the privacy of the couple at this special and sacred event.

Was there an intrusion into Julie's seclusion under these circumstances? Why or why not?

3. a. Juan, in an effort to generate interest in a website he recently launched, posts pictures of celebrities throughout the site, hoping to give site users the impression that these celebrities endorse his website.

Has Juan committed the tort of appropriation? Why or why not?

b. Now know that Juan took the celebrity photos himself, while living in the Los Angeles area, where certain celebrities (mostly actors) can be seen, publicly, in large numbers, compared to other locations besides New York.

Did Juan commit the tort of appropriation when he took the photos of the celebrities while they were in public places? Why or why not?

c. Now assume that Juan seeks, and gets, permission from each celebrity (or his representative) before posting the picture on his website. Juan does not pay the celebrities for the use.

Has the tort of appropriation been committed? Why or why not?

4. Mrs. Baines, a high school science teacher, announces to her class of twenty-five seniors that Mr. Holmes, the school's principal, "did some jail time for illegal drug use" before he became an educational administrator.

a. *If that statement is true, has Mrs. Baines committed the tort of public disclosure of private facts? Why or why not?*

b. *If that statement is false, has Mrs. Baines committed the tort of public disclosure of private facts? Why or why not?*

c. *If the statement is true, has Mrs. Baines committed the tort of false light? Why or why not?*

d. *If the statement is false, has Mrs. Baines committed the tort of false light? Why or why not?*

e. *If the statement is false, what tort, other than any of the invasion of privacy torts, may Mrs. Baines have committed?*

ASSIGNMENTS AND PRACTICAL **APPLICATIONS**

1. Your supervising attorney has asked you to draft a privacy policy to be posted on client ABC Inc.'s website. Research privacy policies on several of the websites you often use; then draft a privacy policy for your client, which you will submit to your supervising attorney for review and approval. Matters to consider in drafting your privacy policy: where the privacy policy will be accessed, how you will give users notice of it, what safeguards you will use to secure the users' private information, how you will let users know how the information you collect will be used (and not used or shared), how you will obtain parental consent if a child is using the website, and how you will allow users to opt out of sharing of their information with others. Discuss your privacy policies in class.

2. Read and brief these additional cases on intrusion: *Morrissey v. Nextel Retail Stores, L.L.C.,* 2009 WL 387750 (Mich. Ct. App. 2009) (unpublished opinion) on the essential elements of the tort of intrusion and how they were not met when an employee's personal cell phone calls were tracked by the employer who paid for the phones; contrast that with *In re Marriage of Tigges,* 758 N.W.2d 824 (Iowa 2008), in which the

tort of intrusion was committed when a husband covertly videotaped his wife's bedroom activities.

3. Read and brief these additional cases on appropriation: *Kirby v. Sega of Am., Inc.,* 144 Cal. App. 4th Supp. 47 (2006), in which a celebrity (Lady Miss Kier, lead singer for the 1990s musical group Deee-Lite) sued distributors of a video game for use of her likeness and identity to create a character in a game; *Minnifield v. Ashcraft,* 903 So.2d 818 (Ala. Civ. App. 2006), about whether the right to privacy protects the commercial value of a public figure's identity when a tattoo artist and studio photographed the client's upper-breast tattoo and submitted the photo for publication in a national tattoo magazine.

4. Read and brief these additional cases on public disclosure of private facts: *Hoff v. Spoelstra,* 2008 WL 2668298 (Mich. Ct. App. 2008) (unpublished opinion), in which it was found that there was no public disclosure of private facts when a city attorney's e-mails were disclosed because the attorney had no reasonable expectation of privacy in e-mails in the city's computer system; *Cawood v. Booth,* 2008 WL 4998408 (Tenn. Ct. App. 2008) (unpublished opinion) in which it was found that there was no public disclosure when a videotape, showing sexual

misconduct by an attorney with his client, was shown to only a small group of people as part of a criminal investigation (though it was viewed by sheriff's department employees not working on the case and a bail bondsman in the office at the time; see the Ethical Applications, below, on this case).

5. Read and brief these additional cases on false light: *O'Connor v. Meyer,* 2008 WL 5481704 (Conn. Super. Ct. 2008) (unpublished opinion), in which false light was committed by a mother of a high school student who recklessly made untrue statements to the school and police department that the plaintiff, another student at the school, was showing pornographic photographs to other students and had threatened to kill her daughter; *Frohriep v. Flanagan,* 754 N.W.2d 912 (Mich. Ct. App. 2008), in which a list comparing registered educational personnel (teachers) and criminal convictions was distributed to affected school districts to correct any erroneous matches, and the court found that this distribution did not constitute the publicity required for the tort of false light.

6. Using newspapers, magazines, and the Internet, find a recent case involving one of the invasion of privacy torts. Share your current event with the class.

TECHNOLOGY RESOURCES AND INTERNET **EXERCISES**

For a review of privacy rights provided by state constitutions, see *www.ncsl.org/programs/lis/privacy/state constpriv03.htm.*

California has a government office called the Office of Privacy Protection, which is devoted specifically to privacy protection. Read about what this office does at *www.oispp .ca.gov/consumer_privacy/default.asp.*

For a comprehensive review of federal and state privacy laws, see *www.bbbonline.org/UnderstandingPrivacy /library/fed_statePrivLaws.pdf.*

What information is included in a website privacy policy? Go to some of the websites you often use and examine their privacy policies. Review the privacy policy on Westlaw's website (*www.westlaw.com*). Where do you find Westlaw's online privacy policy, what does it protect, and how?

ETHICAL **APPLICATIONS**

Polly Pringle, Esq., is a solo practitioner specializing in personal injury cases, and she is a very competent and likeable attorney. She would like to increase the number of clients and cases she handles. In an effort to do this, Polly engages a telemarketing firm to make telephone calls on her behalf to prospective new clients. In particular, she wishes to target people from her area who have recently been treated in a hospital emergency room because they may have been injured by the tortious conduct of another, such as in a car accident caused by another driver's negligence.

Is Polly's marketing plan a good one from a legal ethics perspective? Why or why not?

Consider the case of *Cawood v. Booth,* noted in the assignments above. In that case, Cawood was an attorney representing a client in a divorce case. During the postjudgment phase of that representation, the attorney and the client engaged in a sexual relationship. The attorney would masturbate in the presence of the client in return for reducing her legal bill by $100 per episode. After this happened twice, the client complained to a local judge, who referred the client to the sheriff's department. The sheriff's department began an investigation of the complaint and provided electronic equipment to the client so that she could audio- and videotape her next sexual encounter with the attorney, which she did (and which depicted the attorney masturbating in his office while the client slapped his buttocks with a belt and pinched his nipples). Unfortunately, the video equipment malfunctioned during that episode, but the audiotape was successful. The sheriff's department asked the client to return to the attorney's office one more time, to obtain both an audio- and a videotape, which she did successfully. The attorney sued several of the tape viewers under theories of public disclosure of private facts, outrageous conduct, and violation of the federal Wiretapping and Electronic Surveillance Act of 1994.

Do you see a legal ethics problem with the attorney's conduct? Is there a problem with the attorney having a sexual relationship with the client while the representation is ongoing, though the matter is in the postjudgment phase? Is there a problem with his "fee arrangement"? Note that the attorney was arrested and initially found guilty on two counts of attempting to patronize prostitution, but the convictions were reversed on appeal due to insufficient evidence to support the guilty verdict.

VIDEO **CASE STUDY**

A School Principal Reacts: Student Rights Versus School's Duty

Synopsis: The student responsible for attacking another student on the school bus is brought to the school principal's office by the bus driver and a school security officer. Before the student's parent arrives at school, the student is taken to be searched for a weapon by the school nurse.

Questions

1. Was the search of the student's person and his property a tortious invasion of his right to privacy?

2. Should the principal have waited for the parent of the student to arrive before authorizing the school nurse to conduct the search?

3. If the child did not object to the search and participated willingly, knowing he had nothing to hide and that no weapon would be found, what defense might apply to insulate the school from liability?

chapter **15**

TORT PRACTICE AND APPLICATIONS

This chapter examines the practice and applications of torts as a distinct field of law. It discusses how tort cases, as civil cases, proceed in the process of litigation. It also introduces practical employment skills, including drafting tort-related documents and conducting client interviews, factual investigations, and negotiations.

Given today's marketplace, the study of tort law is not complete until the student understands the practical application of the substantive law of torts in the employment arena. Accordingly, in this chapter, we will develop practical employment skills useful to a paralegal beginning employment in this field.

Many of the practical employment skills discussed here are the subject of thorough study in civil litigation courses and in legal research and writing courses. They are introduced here to an extent sufficient for students who have not yet taken those other courses to be able to perform assignments and exercises using these skills. Such assignments and exercises are included in this chapter.

We begin our introduction to practical tort applications by examining how a civil case such as a tort case proceeds through the legal system.

LEARNING OBJECTIVES

15.1 Explain how a tort case proceeds through the legal system.

15.2 Describe the documents customarily used in tort law practice and how they are drafted.

15.3 Explain how to conduct interviews, investigations, and negotiations in tort law cases.

Overview of a Tort Case

A civil case, such as a tort case, proceeds through the legal system in the process of litigation. **Litigation** is the process of carrying on a civil lawsuit. The vast majority of civil cases are settled between the parties before trial begins, or even during trial but before a verdict is reached. So at any point during the litigation process, a plaintiff may settle the legal dispute with the defendant and have the case dismissed by the court. Terms of settlement are evidenced in a written settlement agreement, signed by the parties. A **settlement agreement** is a contract entered into by the parties to a legal dispute that sets forth the terms and conditions of the resolution and settlement of the dispute. Paralegals may draft settlement agreements for their supervising attorneys. How

Litigation
The process of carrying on a civil lawsuit.

Settlement agreement
An agreement, or contract, entered into by the parties to a legal dispute that sets forth the terms and conditions of the resolution and settlement of the dispute.

Key Point

Litigation Process

A civil case proceeds as follows:

- Pleadings
- Discovery
- Pretrial procedures
- Trial
- Post-trial procedures

> **SIDEBAR**
>
> ## OTHER LAW COURSES
>
> Some of these skills, such as conducting legal research and drafting litigation-related legal documents, are covered, in depth and in a broader context than just tort law, in legal research and writing as well as in civil litigation courses. Their inclusion in this text is to demonstrate how these skills apply specifically to the practice of tort law. Students should refer to texts and materials in those other courses for detailed study of these skills.

Retainer agreement
A contract authorizing an attorney to represent a client in a matter and setting the fee to be charged for that representation.

Pleading
A legal document used by a party to set forth or respond to allegations, claims, denials, or defenses.

Key Point

Rules for Pleadings and Discovery
The rules regarding the content and form of both pleadings and discovery documents vary from jurisdiction to jurisdiction. As a litigation paralegal, you must research to know these rules for your jurisdiction.

Discovery
The process of searching for and obtaining information and evidence relevant to a case.

to draft settlement agreements is covered later in this chapter. Unless or until settled, the case proceeds in the following order: pleadings, discovery, pretrial procedures, trial, and post-trial procedures.

Now we will examine each step in the litigation process. A client often seeks legal representation for help adjudicating her claim. The attorney will have the client sign a retainer agreement. A **retainer agreement** is a contract authorizing an attorney to represent a client in a matter and setting the fee to be charged for that representation. The attorney or her paralegal will conduct an interview of the client to gather information about the case. How to conduct interviews is examined later in this chapter. Then the attorney initiates the lawsuit on behalf of the client by filing a complaint with the court and having it, along with the court's summons, served on the defendant. The defendant usually files an answer to the plaintiff's complaint, admitting or denying the allegations made in the complaint or stating that he has insufficient knowledge to admit or deny an allegation, and perhaps makes counterclaims and/or cross-claims against the plaintiff (counterclaims) or other defendants (cross-claims). The complaint and answer are the pleadings in the case. A **pleading** is a legal document used by a party to set forth or respond to allegations, claims, denials, or defenses. Drafting pleadings is a task commonly performed by paralegals, to assist their supervising attorneys. How to draft pleadings is covered later in this chapter. Time limits for filing pleadings and the rules for service of process vary from jurisdiction to jurisdiction, so local court rules must always be consulted when paralegals file and serve pleadings. The defendant may make a motion to dismiss the complaint; both parties may make a motion for judgment on the pleadings or a motion for summary judgment. One or more parties may try to settle the case.

If the case is not resolved through motions or settlement, discovery is conducted. **Discovery** is the process of searching for and obtaining information and evidence relevant to a case. The most commonly used discovery devices include interrogatories, depositions, requests for production, requests for examination, and requests for admission (all discussed further later in this chapter). One of the most time-consuming and expensive processes in civil litigation can be the discovery process, depending on the nature of the particular case. Paralegals are often involved in preparing and responding to discovery requests. How to prepare discovery requests and responses is covered later in this chapter.

Filing motions to dismiss for failure to state a claim on which relief can be granted or motions for summary judgment are types of pretrial procedures. A *motion to dismiss* for failure to state a claim on which relief can be granted, also called a *demurrer*, is a motion filed by the defendant that asserts that the plaintiff has failed to state a legally valid claim in bringing the legal action. A *motion for summary judgment* is a motion brought by a party asking the court to enter judgment in its favor—as a matter of law—because there is no material fact at issue for the jury to decide and the court has all the information that it needs to render a decision. To rebut a motion for summary judgment, the opposing party must show the court that at least one genuine factual issue exists, making trial of the matter necessary. Discovery responses and affidavits can be used in bringing and defending against motions for summary judgment.

Another important pretrial procedure is a pretrial conference. Before trial, a *pretrial conference* is conducted by the judge assigned to the case and attended by each party's attorney. At this conference, pretrial issues are resolved. Parties are encouraged to reach a settlement of their dispute at the pretrial conference. If the case does not settle, it proceeds to trial.

At trial, the parties have their day in court where, through presentation of their evidence and witnesses, they can explain their version of what occurred. A jury is selected through a process called *voir dire* if a right to jury trial exists and has not been waived by the parties. *Voir dire* is the process of attorneys or the judge asking questions of potential jurors to help them select jurors for the case. If there is no right to jury trial in that type of case (jury trials are typical in tort cases) or the right to jury trial has been waived by all parties, a bench trial, meaning a trial where the judge decides both factual and legal issues, is conducted. Attorneys for the parties make opening statements, with the plaintiff's side going first and the defendant's side going last. In an opening statement, the attorney typically provides an overview of his case and the evidence he plans to present, introduces the parties

Motion to dismiss
A motion filed by the defendant that asserts that the plaintiff has failed to state a legally valid claim in bringing the legal action; also called a demurrer.

Motion for summary judgment
A motion brought by a party asking the court to enter judgment in its favor—as a matter of law—because there is no material fact at issue for the jury to decide and the court has all the information that it needs to render a decision.

Pretrial conference
A meeting between the attorneys and the judge, held prior to trial, to discuss possible settlement as well as trial matters.

Voir dire
The process of attorneys or the judge asking questions of potential jurors to help them select jurors for the case.

SIDEBAR

TRIAL NOTEBOOKS

Trial notebooks are commonly prepared by litigation paralegals. Preparing them is a way paralegals assist attorneys with trial. Trial notebooks are used to assemble in one place all the important and necessary information relevant to a case. By creating a trial notebook, all important information is easily accessible and handy for the attorney during trial of the case. Trial notebooks typically are made using three-ring binders holding 8½ × 11-inch paper with tabs separating the different sections (and perhaps a table of contents). Sections of a trial notebook can include a section on the law relevant to the case (often case law in a tort case), pleadings and pretrial motions filed with the court, jury selection charts and information, the attorney's notes for her opening statement, a witness list containing names and contact information, exhibits (if there are many, they may need to be put in a separate book), questions to ask witnesses on direct examination and cross-examination, notes the attorney makes during trial to be included in her closing argument, and jury instructions relevant to the claims and defenses asserted in the case.

and witnesses who will be involved in the trial, and offers his theory of the case and how it should be resolved by the jurors or judge. Then the parties present their evidence. The evidence presented at trial includes witness testimony and exhibits. Witness testimony obtained by counsel who calls the witness is gotten through direct examination; witness testimony obtained by opposing counsel (the side not calling the witness) is gotten through cross-examination, the function of which is to try to impeach, meaning discredit, the witness's testimony. Redirect (a second direct examination) and recross-examination (a second cross-examination) of witnesses may be conducted by counsel where needed and as permitted. Again, the plaintiff goes first in presenting the evidence, and the defendant goes last—because the plaintiff bears the burden of proving her case by a preponderance of the evidence (and if she fails to, she loses—as well as if the defendant proves an affirmative defense that bars the plaintiff's recovery). The defendant's counsel may make a motion for directed verdict after the close of the plaintiff's case—meaning after all of the plaintiff's evidence has been presented. In a ***motion for directed verdict***, the defendant argues to the court that the plaintiff has failed to meet her burden of proof and that a verdict should be made in the defendant's favor. While motions for directed verdict are often made, they are rarely successful. If a motion for directed verdict is not made or is made but not granted, the defendant presents his evidence. After the presentation of all evidence, attorneys for the parties make closing arguments. The plaintiff's side typically goes first again—because she bears the burden of proof. In closing arguments, attorneys typically summarize their cases, emphasize how the evidence supports their side, and argue to try to convince the jury or judge to rule in their side's favor. The judge then instructs the jury on the relevant rules of law to be applied to the case if it is a jury trial. This is called ***charging the jury***. Standard jury instructions are used in some states. In other states, attorneys for the parties draft proposed jury instructions for the judge to consider; attorneys can object to any instructions that the judge gives or fails to give to the jury—providing a common basis for an appeal. Then the jury retires to deliberate and to reach a verdict. Once the verdict is rendered, the jury is dismissed.

Post-trial procedures can then occur. For example, the losing party may file a motion for judgment notwithstanding the verdict, arguing that the verdict is contrary to the evidence and the law, and/or a motion for a new trial, arguing that errors made during the trial necessitate a new one be conducted. Either party may appeal the verdict if they are unhappy with the outcome—such as they lost, or they won but not enough. If a party wins a judgment, it must enforce that judgment to collect it.

To bring a lawsuit, from beginning to end, takes months, if not years. It is not a quick process. In addition, litigation is a very expensive process. Not only is it customary and advisable to engage legal counsel, for which legal fees normally must be paid, but costs associated with the litigation process, especially discovery, can be enormous. Further, the process of litigation is public, not private. It is an adversarial process that pits two opposing sides against one another. The goal is winning rather than the pursuit of justice. Whether a jury or bench trial is conducted, the outcome of litigation is never predictable or controllable. Though the outcome is not predictable or controllable, however, litigation will resolve the dispute—one way or the other.

Motion for directed verdict
A motion made by the defendant at the close of the plaintiff's case where the defendant argues to the court that the plaintiff has failed to meet her burden of proof and that a verdict should be made in the defendant's favor.

Charging the jury
Where the judge instructs the jury on the relevant rules of law to be applied to the case.

Given the disadvantages of litigation as a means of resolving legal disputes, alternative dispute resolution methods are often used. ***Alternative dispute resolution (ADR)*** is the resolution of legal disputes in ways other than the traditional judicial process of litigation. As noted above, the vast majority of civil cases settle before or during trial. Settlement of cases is achieved through a method of alternative dispute resolution. There are many forms of alternative dispute resolution. The three most common are negotiation, mediation, and arbitration. ***Negotiation*** is a process where the parties to a legal dispute informally communicate, themselves or via their attorneys, to discuss possible settlement of their legal dispute. It can be conducted in person, over the telephone, or through correspondence (using letters or electronic technology—e-mail). The skill of negotiation is discussed later in this chapter. ***Mediation*** is a nonadversarial process where a neutral third party, called a ***mediator***, facilitates communications between parties to a legal dispute to help them resolve it. Mediation is sometimes called "assisted negotiation" because it is the process of negotiation, assisted by a neutral third party. ***Arbitration*** is an out-of-court process where parties submit their legal dispute to a neutral third party or parties for resolution. Either one arbitrator or an arbitration panel presides over the arbitration proceedings. The parties, who may or may not be represented by counsel, submit evidence in a more informal process than a trial in court. The process is an adversarial one, similar in that way to a trial. The evidence is considered by the arbitrator or arbitration panel in rendering a decision, called an ***award***. Arbitration awards usually are enforced by courts if the parties agreed, in advance, that they would be binding.

Besides preparing case briefs, discussed in Chapter 2, attorneys and paralegals who practice in tort law may prepare other types of legal documents. These documents include pleadings, discovery requests and responses, and settlement agreements, already discussed, as well as legal memorandums and legal correspondence. These documents are discussed next.

Alternative dispute resolution (ADR)
The resolution of legal disputes in ways other than the traditional judicial process of litigation.

Negotiation
A process where the parties to a legal dispute informally communicate, themselves or via their attorneys, to discuss possible settlement of their legal dispute.

Mediation
A nonadversarial process where a neutral third party facilitates communications between parties to a legal dispute to help them resolve it.

Mediator
A neutral third party who conducts a mediation session.

Arbitration
An out-of-court process where parties submit their legal dispute to a neutral third party or parties, called an arbitrator or arbitration panel, who hears evidence and renders an award.

Award
The decision made by an arbitrator or arbitration panel.

Drafting Tort-Related Documents

Several different types of legal documents are commonly used in tort practice. These include documents such as correspondence, legal memoranda, pleadings, discovery requests and responses, and settlement agreements as examples. Successful tort attorneys and paralegals possess strong writing skills and are able to draft effective legal documents. How to draft each of these documents should be the subject of detailed study and practice in legal research and writing, as well as civil procedure, courses for law and paralegal students.

LEGAL CORRESPONDENCE

Paralegals and attorneys engaged in tort practice regularly draft and send letters to clients, opposing counsel, witnesses, and others. ***Legal correspondence*** means legal letters. Such correspondence may be informative, such as to inform the client of a deadline or a settlement offer. It may be an opinion letter, providing a legal opinion about the matter. However, legal opinions may only be given

Legal correspondence
Legal letters.

LEGAL ETHICS NOTE

When the sender of legal correspondence is a paralegal, it is recommended that the paralegal state his title, conveying to the recipient his role as a paralegal, and making it clear that he is not an attorney. This helps to prevent issues relating to the unauthorized practice of law.

by attorneys per legal ethics rules and criminal statutes, so paralegals should not draft opinion letters. Frequently, legal correspondence is used to confirm information that was already conveyed orally, either in person or over the telephone.

FIGURE 15-1 Sample Legal Correspondence

Murphy, Smith & Payne, P.C.
9385 South Charles Street, Suite 100
Baltimore, Maryland 21210
Telephone: 410-372-6600
Facsimile: 410-372-6601
E-mail: MSPlaw@laol.com

July 17, 20 __

<u>Via Facsimile and First Class Mail</u>
Sylvia Russell
265 Schwann Valley Road
Hunt Valley, Maryland 21110

Re: Deposition Scheduled for July 20, 20__ (Case No. CV-649684)

Dear Ms. Russell:

This letter is to confirm your attendance at your deposition, scheduled for 9:30 a.m. on Wednesday, July 20, at our offices. Please arrive at least one half hour early so that I may answer any final questions you may have before the deposition begins. The deposition is expected to take most of the day, as we discussed during our preparation meeting last week.

I have enclosed our firm's deposition preparation tip sheet for you to review prior to the taking of your deposition. It summarizes what we discussed last week.

If you have any questions or concerns prior to your arrival for the deposition, please let me know so that I may address them. I look forward to seeing you on July 20th.

Very truly yours,

Lucas R. Payne

Lucas R. Payne, Esq.

LRP/nrt

Enclosure

cc: Linda M. Duncan, Esq.

These letters are called confirmation letters. Attorneys may draft demand letters, in which the sender of the letter demands a third party to cease and desist from some action based on a legal claim the sender is threatening to assert. Demand letters, also known as cease and desist letters, are often used to try to resolve legal disputes prior to litigation. As an example of such legal correspondence used in tort matters, an attorney may send a cease and desist letter to a third party who continues to trespass across his client's land. This letter, with the goal of resolving the dispute without the need for litigation, would inform the third party of the client's legal position and both firmly and professionally request the third party to stop performing the activity the client believes is infringing on his rights, such as repeatedly entering upon the client's land.

Written correspondence is better evidence of what was said between the parties than is oral communication, so legal professionals, perhaps even more than other professionals, often write their communications to preserve them. Also, if the oral communication was vague or ambiguous, writing can clarify the understanding of those involved. It can also be used to fill in any gaps in fact or understanding.

Legal correspondence is written on the letterhead of the firm or corporate legal department from which it is sent. The basic components of a legal letter include the following: the date, the method of delivery (first-class mail, hand delivery, FedEx, facsimile, etc.), the name, title, and address of the recipient, a reference line (identifying the subject matter of the letter), a salutation or greeting, the body (the "meat" of the letter), a closing ("Sincerely," "Very truly yours," etc.), the signature and title of the sender, the initials of the author and the typist (set forth as "ABC/abc" where the author's initials are capitalized and the typist's are lowercase), a notation if there are any enclosures, and a notation for any recipients of copies. A sample legal letter is given in Figure 15-1.

LEGAL MEMORANDA

Lawyers and paralegals engaged in tort practice also draft legal memoranda. *Legal memoranda* are documents that thoroughly analyze and summarize the law in a particular area, on the basis of legal research, and inform the requestor of the strengths and weaknesses of the client's legal position. They are prepared for internal use by a law firm or corporate legal department. Attorneys, and paralegals at the request of their supervising attorneys, often prepare these documents to better understand a client's matter and to formulate a realistic legal opinion on the merits of the client's legal position. A well-written legal memorandum is an objective analysis of the law on a matter. It includes both the strengths and the weaknesses of the client's position, whether that position is a legal claim or a defense. Thus, it is an evaluation tool, used by the preparer or requester to formulate a realistic opinion on the strength of the client's position. An example of a legal memorandum used in tort practice is to evaluate whether the client/plaintiff was contributorily or comparatively negligent by speeding through an intersection when the defendant, who ran a red traffic light, collided with her.

How a legal memorandum is organized and formatted depends on office protocol or the directions of the supervisor requesting the memorandum. There

Legal memoranda
Documents that thoroughly analyze and summarize the law in a particular area, on the basis of legal research, and inform the requestor of the strengths and weaknesses of the client's legal position.

Key Point

Parts of a Legal Memorandum

1. Heading
2. Statement of the facts
3. Questions presented
4. Analysis/discussion
5. Conclusion

is no universally accepted way to structure a legal memorandum, but legal memoranda are typically divided into the following distinct parts: heading, statement of the facts involved, questions presented, analysis or discussion, and conclusion.

The heading sets forth the date of the memorandum, identifies the person for whom it is prepared, includes the name of the person who prepared it, and includes a reference line briefly describing its nature. The statement of the facts sets forth the material facts of the dispute at issue, both those favorable to the client's position and those detrimental to it. The section on questions presented should set forth clearly the legal issues being addressed by the memorandum. Note that one, or multiple, questions may be presented in a legal memorandum, depending on its nature. Some legal memorandum preparers include brief answers to the questions presented in this part of the legal memorandum, whereas others provide answers later, in the conclusion. The fourth part of the memorandum is the analysis, or discussion, section. In this part, the writer provides a legal analysis and discussion of each issue presented for resolution. When multiple questions are presented, it is a good idea to organize the analysis section into parts, each examining a particular legal issue. Legal research is performed by the writer, who then applies the research results to the facts of the client's matter. This application of the law to the facts is what is embodied in the analysis and discussion section of a legal memorandum. This section contains appropriate citations to legal authority setting forth the relevant law being applied, using appropriate citation style. The analysis section is the longest, most detailed, and comprehensive part of a legal memorandum. The final part of a legal memorandum is the conclusion. After the legal issues have been fully evaluated, the writer gives her opinion on the relative strength of the client's legal position, and may make recommendations regarding a course of action to take—such as to make a settlement offer if the client's position does not appear to be strong as a result of the research and analysis performed. A sample legal memorandum is given in Figure 15-2.

FIGURE 15-2 Sample Legal Memorandum

MEMORANDUM

To: Martin I. Boone, Partner

From: Jennifer Clayton, Paralegal

Date: September 6, 20___

Re: Application of Contributory Negligence Defense and Last Clear Chance
          Doctrine in Maryland

STATEMENT OF FACTS

Jane Smith, the firm's client, was involved in a car collision caused by the alleged negligence of the defendant, Jackson Doe, another driver. At the time of the collision, Mrs. Smith was driving north on the Jones Falls Expressway, near the Druid Hills Parkway entrance ramp. In her complaint, Mrs. Smith alleged that Mr. Doe

---

(continued)

failed to yield the right-of-way to her as he attempted to merge onto the Jones Falls Expressway from the Druid Hills Parkway entrance ramp. In his answer to the client's complaint, Mr. Doe asserted that the client was speeding at the time of the collision, contributing to its cause, and asserted the client's contributory negligence as a defense.

In an interview, Mrs. Smith stated that the defendant had the opportunity to avoid the accident by yielding the right-of-way or by driving on the shoulder of the road when the collision seemed imminent. Mr. Doe failed to do so, and the collision occurred.

You asked me to research the law in the state of Maryland on the defense of contributory negligence and the last clear chance doctrine as they relate to this case.

QUESTIONS PRESENTED

1. Does Maryland recognize the defense of contributory negligence and if so, how would it apply to these facts?

2. Does Maryland recognize the last clear chance doctrine, and if so, how would it apply to these facts?

BRIEF CONCLUSION

1. Yes, Maryland is one of few remaining jurisdictions recognizing contributory, rather than comparative, negligence, and the client's alleged speeding may constitute contributory negligence, barring her recovery. However, another law in Maryland, the boulevard rule, may change this result.

2. Yes, Maryland recognizes the last clear chance doctrine, and if the defendant had the last clear chance to avoid the collision by driving onto the shoulder of the road, the client may recover for the harm she suffered despite her contributory negligence.

DISCUSSION

I. Contributory Negligence Defense

Maryland recognizes the defense of contributory, rather than comparative, negligence. Under Maryland law, the plaintiff's contributory negligence completely bars recovery against a negligent defendant. *Wooldridge v. Price*, 184 Md. App. 451 (Md. Ct. Spec. App. 2009). Accordingly, if the defendant can "adduce some evidence of negligence on the part of the [plaintiff], her claims against [him] would be barred." *Id.* at 462.

In applying that law to our client's case, if the defendant can produce evidence that our client was speeding at the time of the collision, and that speeding contributed to its cause, then the defense of contributory negligence could bar her recovery. However, this bar is subject to both the last clear chance doctrine (see II., below) and the boulevard rule.

The boulevard rule is a law in Maryland which imposes a duty on drivers entering or crossing a highway from another highway or private roadway to stop and yield the right-of-way to through traffic on the highway. If the driver of a vehicle approaches a through highway, the driver shall: (1) stop at the entrance to the through highway; and (2) yield the right-of-way to any other vehicle approaching on the

(continued)

through highway. Md. Code Ann., Transp. § 21-403 (b) (2009). Accordingly, the boulevard rule imposed a duty on the defendant to yield to our client's automobile when merging onto the Jones Falls Expressway. The boulevard rule has been held inapplicable where the favored driver (the one traveling on the highway) fails to exercise due care. However, speeding alone is not ordinarily considered sufficient to strip a driver on a through highway of his favored status. *Palenchar v. Jarrett*, 507 F.Supp.2d 502 (D. Md. 2007). Accordingly, even if the client was speeding at the time of the collision, that alone should not strip her of her favored status under the boulevard rule.

II. Last Clear Chance Doctrine

In some contributory negligence situations, the last clear chance doctrine can apply to allow the plaintiff's recovery. *Wooldridge* at 462. Under Maryland law, for the last clear chance doctrine to apply, these requirements must be met: (1) the defendant must be negligent; (2) the plaintiff must be contributorily negligent; and (3) the plaintiff must make "a showing of something new or sequential, which affords the defendant a fresh opportunity (of which he fails to avail himself) to avert the consequences of his original negligence." *Id.*

The third requirement has been interpreted to mean that the doctrine will apply only if the acts of the parties were sequential rather than concurrent; in other words, the defendant must have had the opportunity to avoid the injury after the plaintiff's negligent action was put in motion. *Id.* The last clear chance doctrine assumes that, after the primary negligence of the plaintiff and the defendant, "the defendant could, and the plaintiff could not, by the use of the means available avert the accident." *Id.* The defendant should recognize and respond to the plaintiff's position of "helpless peril." *Id.*

To apply the last clear chance doctrine, courts require a showing that the plaintiff be in a position of helpless peril and the defendant have a fresh opportunity to exercise due care to avoid the injury. If driving off the shoulder of the road to avoid the collision was considered a fresh opportunity for Mr. Doe to avoid the collision, then his failure to so act could trigger the application of the last clear chance doctrine in this case, permitting our client's recovery.

CONCLUSION

Under current Maryland law, if Mr. Doe can prove that the client was speeding at the time the collision occurred, and that her speeding contributed to the personal injury and property damage she suffered, that contributory negligence could bar her recovery from the defendant for his negligence. However, the application of the boulevard rule in Maryland, where the plaintiff's speeding is all that is alleged to constitute her contributory negligence, would likely change this result, permitting her recovery.

Even if the client's contributory negligence can be established by the defendant, if the client can prove that the defendant had the last clear chance to avoid the collision, such as by driving onto the shoulder of the road, then the effect of her contributory negligence is negated and she can recover, fully, from the defendant for her injuries and other harm suffered. To establish the application of the last clear chance doctrine, the client must demonstrate that the defendant had a fresh opportunity to avoid the collision.

PLEADINGS AND DISCOVERY REQUESTS/RESPONSES

Attorneys and paralegals engaged in tort practice also draft pleadings and discovery requests and responses. Pleadings and discovery requests and responses are part of the process of civil litigation, including tort litigation. These documents, written for the court in advocating a particular legal position on behalf of the client, are written persuasively, from the position of an advocate for a client's position, unlike legal correspondence and legal memoranda, which are written objectively, from a neutral position. Both attorneys and paralegals typically prepare pleadings in tort, and other civil litigation, cases.

Pleadings are the initial documents prepared by the parties either in bringing a lawsuit, when the pleading is called the "complaint" and is filed by the plaintiff, or in responding to the complaint when sued, called the "answer," which is filed by the defendant. Whether a complaint, answer, counterclaim (a claim initiated by the defendant against the plaintiff), or cross-claim (a claim initiated by one plaintiff against another, or by one defendant against another), the pleadings inform the other side of the claims or defenses asserted against them and the facts alleged in support of those claims or defenses.

To initiate a tort lawsuit, the plaintiff files a complaint with the appropriate court, probably a state court, because most tort law is state law (although via diversity of citizenship jurisdiction, a tort case may be brought in federal court). In addition, the complaint is served on the defendant, called "service of process," within the time limit set by the jurisdiction's rules, to notify the defendant of the action filed against him so that he can defend himself to the court. The complaint typically contains the following information: a caption (like the heading of a legal memorandum, which names the parties, the court, and the case number, and identifies the document as a complaint); allegations supporting jurisdiction of the court and over the persons and subject matter of the dispute (alleging that the court has authority to hear this case); the body, meaning the "meat" of the complaint (which sets forth the general allegations, or claims, being made by the plaintiff and the facts supporting her position, where the degree of factual detail required is set by the procedural rules of the jurisdiction); a request for the court to grant a remedy (called a "prayer for relief"), the plaintiff's signature (and that of her attorney, if she is represented by counsel), and a demand for jury trial if there is a right to one and it is not waived. Note that some states require a verification to be filed along with the complaint; a *verification* is an affidavit made by the plaintiff acknowledging that he has read the complaint and that, to the best of his knowledge, it is true and accurate. A sample negligence complaint is given in Figure 15-3.

To avoid a default judgment being entered against her, the defendant must respond to the complaint in a pleading called an answer. A *default judgment* is a judgment of the court made in favor of the plaintiff when the defendant fails to oppose the plaintiff's legal action against him. The answer should parallel the plaintiff's complaint and be organized in paragraphs and by counts, like the complaint. In the defendant's answer, the defendant responds to the allegations made by the plaintiff in the complaint by admitting or denying each of them, or stating that she has insufficient knowledge at the time to admit or deny any of

Key Point

State Civil Procedure Rules
Remember that each state's civil procedure rules, such as rules on how to file and serve a complaint, are unique; these rules vary from state to state. It is a litigation paralegal's job to research and know these rules, and to follow them, for the appropriate jurisdiction and court.

Verification
An affidavit made by the plaintiff acknowledging that he has read the complaint and that, to the best of his knowledge, it is true and accurate.

Default judgment
A judgment of the court made in favor of the plaintiff when the defendant fails to oppose the plaintiff's legal action against him.

FIGURE 15-3 Sample Negligence Complaint

JANE SMITH,	)	IN THE CIRCUIT COURT
Plaintiff	)	FOR
	)	BALTIMORE CITY,
v.	)	MARYLAND
	)	
JACKSON DOE,	)	Civil Action No. 01-C-01-12345
Defendant	)	

COMPLAINT FOR NEGLIGENCE AND DEMAND FOR JURY TRIAL

Plaintiff, Jane Smith, by her undersigned counsel, sues Defendant, Jackson Doe, and in support, alleges as follows:

1. Plaintiff Jane Smith is a resident of Baltimore City, Maryland.

2. Defendant Jackson Doe is a resident of Baltimore City, Maryland.

3. This action arises out of an automobile collision which occurred on July 6, 20__, on the Jones Falls Expressway, near the ramp for Druid Hills Parkway, both public roads in Maryland.

4. At approximately 9:50 a.m., while driving north on the Jones Falls Expressway, Plaintiff's vehicle was violently struck on the passenger's side by Defendant's vehicle while Defendant was merging onto the Jones Falls Expressway from the Druid Hills Parkway ramp.

5. Plaintiff was driving in a careful and prudent manner in the moments before and at the time of the collision.

6. It was the duty of Defendant to use reasonable care to watch where he was driving, to maintain a proper lookout for other automobiles, to drive at an appropriate speed, to yield the right of way to oncoming traffic while performing a merge onto the expressway, and to operate and control his automobile in a reasonable manner when performing a merge onto the expressway in order to avoid a collision.

7. Defendant breached his duty of care to Plaintiff by failing to use reasonable care when performing a merge onto the expressway, by failing to watch where he was driving, by failing to maintain a proper lookout for other automobiles, by failing to drive at an appropriate speed on the merge lane, by not yielding the right of way to oncoming traffic while performing a merge onto the expressway, and by failing to operate and control his automobile in a reasonable manner when performing a merge onto the expressway in order to avoid a collision.

8. Plaintiff suffered severe physical injuries and mental anguish, and her automobile extensive damage, as a direct and proximate result of Defendant's negligence in causing the collision. Plaintiff has incurred expenses for medical care and treatment, medicines, nursing services, physical therapy, and other medical services. Plaintiff has lost wages and will continue to lose wages in the future due to the injuries she sustained. Plaintiff continues to suffer physical pain and discomfort due to injuries sustained. Plaintiff's automobile was towed to an auto body shop, where it underwent extensive repairs. All the above damages were directly and proximately caused by the aforementioned negligence of Defendant and were incurred without contributory negligence or assumption of the risk on the part of Plaintiff, and Plaintiff also did not have the opportunity to avoid this accident.

(continued)

WHEREFORE, Plaintiff demands judgment against Defendant for ONE HUN-
DRED THOUSAND DOLLARS ($100,000) in damages, plus interests and costs of
the action, and any further relief the court considers proper.

DEMAND FOR JURY TRIAL

Plaintiff demands a trial by jury.

This 27th day of October, 20___.

Respectfully submitted,

LOWELL, ROWE & TURNBILL, P.A.

By:_____

Sylvia G. Rowe, Esq.
Maryland State Bar No. 5397045
3000 N. Charles Street, Suite 100
Baltimore, Maryland 21210
(410) 372–6500
Attorney for Plaintiff

them. She also asserts affirmative defenses in her defense, such as contributory
or comparative negligence, which tell the court the reasons why she believes she
is not liable to the plaintiff. An ***affirmative defense*** is a response to a plaintiff's
complaint that asserts why the defendant should not be held liable to the plaintiff. Affirmative defenses raise new issues to the court, based on additional facts,
that negate the defendant's liability even if the plaintiff's allegations in the complaint are true. The defendant may also assert counterclaims against the plaintiff relating to the same incident, such as that the plaintiff's negligence caused
the collision, or cross-claims against other defendants named in the complaint
(cross-claims are claims raised against a co-party, so they can be raised by a
plaintiff against another plaintiff, or by a defendant against another defendant),
for example, that the defendant was the passenger, not the driver, of the car that
caused the collision that injured not only the plaintiff but also this defendant.
Like other pleadings, answers are signed by the defendant (and her attorney, if
she is represented by counsel), include a prayer for judgment, and can include a
demand for jury trial. A sample answer is given in Figure 15-4.

Both attorneys and paralegals routinely draft pleadings in tort cases, and
styles, formatting, and the like can often be obtained from the law firm's or corporate legal department's form files. In preparing litigation documents, requirements of the particular court must be followed, both in content and in formatting.

Attorneys and paralegals also draft discovery requests and responses, as
well as calendar and track discovery due dates. Paralegals play a particularly
important role in drafting discovery requests and responses. The purpose of
discovery documents is to facilitate factual investigations and gather evidence
relating to the case. The attorney wants to learn as much about the claims and
defenses in a case as possible through the discovery process, and discovery
allows each party to gather nonprivileged information (so not information to
which the attorney–client privilege applies) about the other party's case.

Affirmative defense
A response to a plaintiff's complaint
that asserts why the defendant
should not be held liable to the
plaintiff.

FIGURE 15-4 Sample Answer to the Complaint from Figure 15-3

JANE SMITH,	)	IN THE CIRCUIT COURT
Plaintiff	)	FOR
	)	BALTIMORE CITY,
v.	)	MARYLAND
	)	
JACKSON DOE,	)	Civil Action No. 01-C-01-12345
Defendant	)	

ANSWER

Defendant, Jackson Doe, by his undersigned counsel, and in answer to the Complaint filed herein, states as follows:

1. Defendant is without knowledge or information sufficient to form a belief as to the truth of the allegations contained in Paragraph 1 of the Plaintiff's Complaint.

2. Defendant admits the allegations of Paragraphs 2 and 3.

3. Defendant denies the allegations of Paragraphs 4, 5, 6, and 7.

4. Defendant is without knowledge or information sufficient to form a belief as to the truth of the allegations contained in Paragraph 8.

AFFIRMATIVE DEFENSE

If Plaintiff was injured as alleged, then those injuries were caused by the sole and/or contributory negligence of Plaintiff.

WHEREFORE, Defendant respectfully prays that the Complaint be dismissed, with costs to be adjudged against Plaintiff, or such other relief as the court considers proper.

Respectfully submitted,

HARDY & JAMES, P.A.

By:_____

Glenn S. Hardy, Esq.
Maryland State Bar No. 9548347
485 Pratt Street
Baltimore, Maryland 21202
(410) 546-7345
Attorney for Defendant

Interrogatories
Written questions prepared by a party, submitted to the other party, to be answered under oath.

In terms of written discovery, ***interrogatories***, which are written questions asked of parties, to be answered in writing, under oath, need to be drafted by the party seeking the answers, and responded to in writing by the party asked. Sample interrogatories are given in Figure 15-5. Note that interrogatories can only be sent to parties to the litigation; they are not used with witnesses. Some courts limit the number of interrogatories that can be asked, so the drafter must be aware of the relevant court rules. In responding to interrogatories, it is important that the answers be drafted both truthfully, as they are given under oath, and skillfully, to support the client's position (to the extent possible) and not

FIGURE 15-5 Sample Interrogatories

Based on pattern motor vehicle tort interrogatories under the Maryland Rules of Civil Procedure

JANE SMITH, Plaintiff	)))	IN THE CIRCUIT COURT FOR BALTIMORE CITY,
v.	))	MARYLAND
JACKSON DOE, Defendant	)))	Civil Action No. 01-C-01-12345

PLAINTIFF'S FIRST INTERROGATORIES TO DEFENDANT

TO: JACKSON DOE, Defendant
FROM: JANE SMITH, Plaintiff

The Plaintiff, Jane Smith, by her attorneys Sylvia G. Rowe and Lowell, Rowe & Turnbill, P.A., requests that the Defendant, Jackson Doe, answer the following Interrogatories separately and fully, in writing and under oath, within 30 days and in accordance with Rule 2-421 of the Maryland Rules of Civil Procedure, subject to the instructions and definitions set forth below. If an objection is made, please state the reason for the objection.

INSTRUCTIONS AND DEFINITIONS

a. These Interrogatories are continuing in nature so as to require you to file supplementary answers if you obtain further information or different information before trial.

b. Unless otherwise stated, these Interrogatories refer to the time, place, and circumstances of the occurrence complained of in the Complaint, namely the automobile collision that occurred on July 6, 20__.

c. Where name and identity of a person is required, please state the person's legal name, residence address, and business address, if known.

d. Where knowledge or information in possession of a party is requested, such request includes knowledge of the party's agents, representatives, and unless privileged, the party's attorneys.

e. "You" refers to the party to whom these Interrogatories are addressed and the persons mentioned in instruction (d).

f. "Identify" means to set forth the legal name, present or last known residence address, occupation or business, and name and address of employer if an individual, and its principal place of business address if a corporation or other entity.

INTERROGATORIES

1. Identify yourself and state all names by which you have been known, your date of birth, your marital status, and the identity of your spouse.

(continued)

2. State all addresses at which you have resided for the past five years and the dates that you resided at each.

3. Describe in detail how the occurrence took place.

4. Identify all persons who were witnesses to the occurrence and state their locations at the time of the occurrence.

5. Identify all persons who were at or near the scene at the time of the occurrence.

6. If you were in a vehicle at the time of the occurrence, identify all other persons who were in that vehicle.

7. Identify all persons who arrived at the scene within two hours after the occurrence.

8. If you were in a vehicle at the time of the occurrence, state the itinerary of the vehicle, including the time and place of the beginning of the trip, the time and duration of each stop, the destination, and the expected time of arrival.

9. If you were engaged in any activity for an employer or other person at the time of the occurrence, state the nature of the activity and identify the employer or other person.

10. If a report with respect to the occurrence was made in the ordinary course of business, state the date on which the report was made, the identity of the person who made the report, and whether the report was written, oral, or in some other form. Identify each document containing information concerning the report and the custodian of the document.

11. Identify all photographs, videotapes, plats, diagrams, or other depictions of the scene or of things connected with the occurrence that are in your possession.

12. Identify all persons who have given you statements concerning the action or its subject matter. For each statement, state the date on which it was given and identify the custodian.

13. If you were charged with any offenses arising out of the occurrence, state the nature of the charges, the court and case number, and the disposition of the charges.

14. If you contend that any party to this action caused or contributed to the occurrence, state concisely the facts on which you rely.

15. If you contend that a person not a party to this action caused or contributed to the occurrence, identify each such person and state concisely the facts on which you rely.

16. If you owned or were in a vehicle damaged as a result of the occurrence, describe any damage to the vehicle. If the vehicle was repaired, identify the person who performed the repairs, the dates of the repairs, and the cost. If the vehicle is unrepaired, state the address where and the hours when it may be seen.

17. If you owned or were in a vehicle involved in the occurrence, state: when the vehicle was last repaired before the occurrence; the nature, dates, and costs of the repairs; the identity of the persons making the repairs; and

(continued)

the extent of any unrepaired damage to the vehicle immediately prior to the occurrence.

18. If you contend that mechanical failure caused or contributed to the occurrence, state concisely the facts on which you rely.

19. If you were in a vehicle at the time of the occurrence, identify the owner and driver of the vehicle. If you were not the owner, state whether you had the permission of the owner to be in the vehicle and the purpose for which permission was given.

20. If you were the driver of a vehicle involved in the occurrence, state whether you have or have ever had any disability, illness, disease, or injury that could affect your ability to operate a motor vehicle, and describe its nature and extent. If treated or evaluated, identify all treating or examining health care providers and the approximate date of each examination or treatment.

21. State whether you used any alcoholic beverages or drugs, whether controlled or otherwise, within 24 hours before the occurrence, the places where they were obtained, the places where they were used, and the nature and amount used.

22. State the substance of all discussion concerning the occurrence that you or others in your presence had with any party to this case. State when and where each discussion took place and identify all persons who were present.

23. State whether you have possession or knowledge of any recordings or transcripts of testimony in any proceeding arising out of the occurrence. If so, state the date and subject matter, and identify each person who recorded the testimony and the custodian of each recording or transcript.

24. If you were in a vehicle involved in the occurrence, state whether the driver of the vehicle has a current driver's license. If so, state when and where the license was issued, its number, the nature of any restrictions on the license, and whether the license was ever suspended or revoked.

25. State whether, at the time during the fifteen year period preceding the date of your answers to these Interrogatories, you have been convicted of any crime other than a minor traffic offense. If so, for each conviction identify the court in which you were convicted and state the amount of any time and the date and length of any incarceration imposed.

> Respectfully submitted,
> Lowell, Rowe & Turnbill, P.A.
> Sylvia G. Rowe, Esq.
> 3000 N. Charles Street, Suite 100
> Baltimore, Maryland 21210
> (410)372-6500
> Attorney for the Plaintiff

volunteer information not specifically requested in the interrogatories. Usually the paralegal prepares draft responses with the help of information provided by the client. Then the attorney or paralegal meets with the client to review the responses before final answers are drafted, along with objections to questions (such as relevance, privilege, or overbroad), if any are made by the attorney.

Depositions are used to obtain the sworn testimony of parties and witnesses before trial. A *deposition* is the sworn testimony of a party or witness, given during an oral examination in the form of a question and answer proceeding that is conducted before trial—and typically held in a conference room in the attorney's law office. A court reporter is present during the deposition and prepares a transcript of the testimony given. The transcript can be used at trial for two purposes; it can take the place of live testimony of a witness who does not appear for trial (maybe the witness died, or moved away and cannot be located) and it can be used to impeach (meaning discredit) the party's or witness's testimony at trial. While the legal ethics rules prohibit nonlawyers from taking and defending depositions, paralegals may attend depositions and they often prepare deposition summaries by summarizing deposition transcripts. Paralegals often schedule depositions, draft and send deposition notices, and arrange to have court reporters for the depositions.

Requests for production, also called *requests for the production of documents* or *requests for the production of documents and other tangible things*, are written requests by a party to another party for documents or other tangible things, such as written contracts or defective products, or for permission to enter on the land or the property of a party for the purpose of conducting an inspection if the "thing" is not capable of being delivered to the requesting party, such as if it is a storage unit. They are often used to gather

Deposition
The sworn testimony of a party or witness given during a question and answer proceeding conducted before trial.

Requests for production
Written requests by a party to another party for documents or other tangible things or for permission to enter on the land or other property of a party for the purpose of conducting an inspection; also called requests for the production of documents or requests for the production of documents and other tangible things.

SIDEBAR

PREPARING CLIENTS AND WITNESSES FOR DEPOSITION AND TRIAL

A task commonly performed by paralegals, as well as attorneys, is to prepare clients and witnesses to testify at depositions and at trial. To do this, the paralegal or attorney should:

- Explain what a deposition is and go over deposition procedures.
- Review with the client or witness questions that will probably be asked at the deposition or trial.
- Review pleadings, discovery responses, medical records, and potential exhibits with the client or witness.
- Review any prior statements made by the client or witness.
- Instruct the client or witness to tell the truth, listen to the question and be sure it is understood before beginning to answer, pause to think about the answer and allow the attorney a chance to object to the question, state you "don't know" when you do not know the answer to a question rather than guess at an answer, not to volunteer additional information and instead answer only the question asked, not to make jokes or laugh while giving testimony, and dress in appropriate business attire and be well-groomed.

documents and other tangible things relevant to the case that are in the possession of the opposing party. Requests for production are useful for finding out what evidence the opposing parties has, such as accident reports, witness statements, medical records, employment records, photographs, income tax records/returns, correspondence, computer records, and so on. ***Requests for examination*** are written requests by a party to the court asking the court to order the other party to submit to a physical or mental examination. ***Requests for admission*** are written requests by a party to the other party asking her to admit the truth of certain matters or facts relating to the lawsuit. Once a party admits a matter or fact, it is deemed to be conclusively established and cannot be disputed at trial. Requests for the production of documents or other tangible things (such as records), requests for access to property or records, as well as requests for physical and mental examinations need to be drafted when they are relevant to a particular case. These requests are often drafted by paralegals, subject to review and approval by their supervising attorneys. A sample request for physical examination is given in Figure 15-6. When requests for admissions are submitted, the person responding must carefully draft any admissions, for what is admitted is considered conclusively established as true and cannot be disputed at trial.

Requests for examination
Written requests by a party to the court asking the court to order the other party to submit to a physical or mental examination.

Requests for admission
Written requests by a party to the other party asking her to admit the truth of certain matters or facts relating to the lawsuit.

FIGURE 15-6 Sample Request for Physical Examination

```
IN THE SUPERIOR COURT OF THE STATE
            OF DELAWARE

COUNTY:      NEW CASTLE  ____   KENT ____   SUSSEX ____
                                    :
                                    :
_____                :
  Plaintiff(s)                      :
                                    : C. A. No.: _____
                                    :
                                    :
  v.                                :
                                    :
                                    :
                                    :
_____                :
  Defendant(s)                      :


            REQUEST FOR PHYSICAL EXAM

Defendant, _____, hereby requests a medical
examination of plaintiff, _____, regarding the injuries
alleged. The examination is to be conducted by _____, at
his/her office at _____,
on ____, _____, 20___ at _____ o'clock.

_____


_____
Attorney for Defendant
DATED: _____
```

FORM BOOKS

Form books are secondary sources of law that can be useful for tort practitioners who regularly represent clients in litigation. Form books contain sample forms that drafters can use in preparing legal documents, including litigation-related documents such as pleadings and motions. Some of the better form books also include annotations on the law relating to particular forms. *American Jurisprudence Pleading and Practice Forms Annotated* is an example of a form book set found in most law libraries that can be useful to tort litigators. Forms also may be found online, though their reliability depends on their source. See the materials at the end of the chapter for exercises in finding both print and online legal forms.

SETTLEMENT AGREEMENTS

Settlement agreements are frequently drafted by tort practitioners. As defined earlier, a settlement agreement is an agreement, or contract, entered into by the parties to a lawsuit that sets forth the terms and conditions of the resolution and settlement of the dispute. So in tort practice, when litigation is settled out of court, settlement agreements are drafted to evidence the terms and conditions of the parties' legal settlement. The settlement agreement typically is submitted to the court in which the litigation is pending and serves as the basis for dismissal of the legal action. A sample settlement agreement is given in Figure 15-7.

FIGURE 15-7 Sample Settlement Agreement
Based on form compromise agreements from American Jurisprudence Legal Forms 2d. (Note that release language has been added.)

SETTLEMENT AGREEMENT

THIS SETTLEMENT AGREEMENT (the "Agreement") is made and entered into this 15th day of July, 20__, by and between John M. Douglas, an individual residing at 84 Westbury Court, Syracuse, New York 13201 (the "Claimant"), and Robert F. Jones, an individual residing at 16 Simsbury Circle, Brookfield, Wisconsin 53005 (the "Opponent").

WHEREAS, the parties have been involved in a legal dispute resulting in the litigation noted below, where the Claimant filed a legal action and the Opponent denied any liability and asserted certain counterclaims related thereto;

WHEREAS, this Agreement is made as a compromise between the parties for the complete and final settlement of their claims, differences, and causes of action with respect to the dispute now pending in Circuit Court in Onondaga County, New York entitled *Douglas v. Jones,* and identified as case number CV-9384756 (the "Action"); and

WHEREAS, the parties desire to reach a full and final compromise and settlement of all matters and all causes of action arising out of the facts and claims as set forth, pursuant to the terms and conditions hereof.

(continued)

NOW, THEREFORE, in consideration of the foregoing and other good and valuable consideration, the receipt and sufficiency of which is hereby acknowledged, the parties hereto agree as follows:

1. The Opponent agrees to pay the Claimant eighty-five thousand dollars ($85,000), to be paid in a lump sum cash payment (the "Payment") on or before July 30, 20_____.

2. Both parties hereto agree that all claims, demands, rights, and causes of action that either has or may have against the other with respect to the above-described dispute are satisfied, discharged, and settled.

3. The Claimant shall seek, obtain, and be bound by a dismissal with prejudice of the Action, which dismissal shall be obtained on or before August 1, 20_____.

4. Each party hereto releases and discharges the other, and their heirs and legal representatives, from any and all claims, damages, and causes of action of any kind, for personal injuries or property damage suffered by either in connection with the above-described dispute and the Action, whether now known or to become known, and whether existing or subsequently arising.

5. This Agreement shall be binding on and enure to the benefit of the parties and their respective legal representatives, successors, and assigns.

IN WITNESS WHEREOF, the parties hereby execute this Settlement Agreement on the day and year first written above.

_____

John M. Douglas

_____

Robert F. Jones

I, Lucy Stewart, Esq., attorney for the Claimant, have explained to my client all the terms and conditions of this Agreement, and my client has represented to me that all the terms and their significance are understood, and my client has signed this Agreement on my advice.

Dated: _____   _____

Lucy Stewart, Esq.

I, Marcy Abrams, attorney for the Opponent, have explained to my client all the terms and conditions of this Agreement, and my client has represented to me that all the terms and their significance are understood, and my client has signed this Agreement on my advice.

Dated: _____   _____

Marcy Abrams, Esq.

Sworn and subscribed before me this _____ day of July, 20__.

_____

Jordan Michaels
Notary Public
State of New York

WRITTEN COMMUNICATION SKILLS

Communication, both oral and written, is paramount in the legal profession and to legal professionals. Now we will examine written communication skills and how to exhibit good ones. In the following section, we will examine oral communication skills for legal professionals more closely.

Good writing skills are critical to success for both attorneys and paralegals. No matter what type of document you are drafting, the following suggestions will help to improve your written work.

First and foremost, write for your audience. It is important to remember that the document you are drafting is being created to communicate some information to a specific reader, and you should keep your target audience in mind. Accordingly, remember to tailor your document for your intended audience. In addition, what you draft should follow (exactly!) the directions of the person requesting it—normally, the supervising attorney for a paralegal or associate attorney. If the reader is not a lawyer or paralegal, use plain English that a layperson can understand rather than legalese. *Legalese* is the body of terms used by the legal profession, also called *legal jargon*. Avoid the use of legalese if your target audience is not a legal professional. Draft well-written sentences with appropriate use of grammar and sound sentence structure, well-organized paragraphs, including topic sentences with supporting detail sentences, and appropriate introductions, transitions, and conclusions. Organize and structure your written work so that it makes sense and is clear and concise. Use the active voice (subject/verb/object order), rather than the passive voice (object/verb/subject order), unless your use of the passive voice is purposeful. Write efficiently by being concise and to the point in your writing. Concise statements are more powerful and persuasive than rambling ones, so avoid unnecessary verbiage. Avoid redundancy unless it is needed for emphasis. Format your document so that it is easy to read and attractive, and where appropriate, give it headings, subheadings, and the like, to improve its organization and readability. Law firms typically have styles and formats they require for documents prepared by their employees, such as the use of Times New Roman font in 12-point size. If you are drafting a document for filing with a court, remember that the court will have established rules for filed documents, to which your document must conform. Keep your writing and formatting consistent within a document. Be gender-neutral in your writing where reference to specific gender is not required. Most important, proofread your work very, very carefully. Nothing speaks more about your professionalism than your ability to produce written documents that are free from errors—especially grammatical and typographical ones.

Oral communication skills are as important to the tort law practitioner as are written communication skills. In particular, attorneys and paralegals working in the field of tort law often conduct interviews, factual investigations, and negotiations, in which oral communication skills are critical. These skills are examined next.

Legalese
The body of terms used by the legal profession; also called legal jargon.

Key Point

Tips for Legal Writing

- Write for your audience.
- Follow directions.
- Use plain language; avoid legalese.
- Pay attention to sentence, paragraph, and overall structure.
- Be organized, clear, and concise.
- Use active voice.
- Avoid redundancy.
- Use appropriate formatting and style.
- Be gender-neutral.
- PROOFREAD.

Conducting Interviews, Factual Investigations, and Negotiations

CONDUCTING INTERVIEWS OF CLIENTS AND WITNESSES

Attorneys and paralegals may conduct client and witness interviews in the course of their legal work. An *interview* is a meeting held for the purpose of asking questions and eliciting responses. An attorney typically conducts the initial client interview, sometimes called the *intake interview*, when the decision is made whether to accept representation of the client in a particular matter and when the fee agreement is established. Legal ethics rules require that an attorney handle these issues directly, though paralegals may be, and sometimes are, present at these meetings. Afterward, the attorney or paralegal may conduct further client interviews to obtain more detailed information from the client. In addition, attorneys and paralegals may interview witnesses as part of the investigation of the client's claim(s) or defense(s). Both client and witness interviews are important parts of the evidence-gathering process.

To be an effective interviewer takes practice, advance planning, organization, and good communication skills. Certain preparation should be undertaken before the interview is conducted. For example, a paralegal typically schedules the interview with the client or witness. He locates the witness (hopefully the location of the client is known), determines where the interview will be held, reserves the interview location, and arranges transportation for any witness who is not local. As an important part of the preparation for the interview, the attorney or paralegal conducting the interview should carefully review the file.

Planning the interview is as important as the interview itself to ensure that the right questions are asked and all of the necessary information is elicited from the client or witness. In advance of the interview, the attorney or paralegal should determine the information to obtain from the client or witness (if the interview is being conducted by a paralegal, this advance planning should be done with the assistance of the attorney), decide what questions to ask, and prepare an outline or checklist of these questions for use during the interview. If the purpose of

Interview
A meeting held for the purpose of asking questions and eliciting responses.

Intake interview
The initial client interview.

SIDEBAR

PREPARING FOR AN INTERVIEW

A paralegal should prepare for a client or witness interview by:

- setting the appointment (date, time, location) for the interview with the client or witness;

- confirming the appointment with the client or witness (by letter is a good idea) and marking the appointment on his calendar;

- reviewing the file and organizing its contents;

- preparing the interview location so it is quiet, clean, and interruption and distraction-free;

- determining if the interview will be recorded and getting the interviewee's permission to record the interview;

- gathering a standardized interview form or a legal form that needs to be filled out, or preparing an interview checklist or outline; and

- discussing the interview plan with the supervising attorney.

Key Point

Before Concluding an Interview

Before concluding an interview, the interviewer should refer back to and review her checklist or outline, or standardized or legal form if one was used, to be sure she has asked all the pertinent questions and obtained all the necessary information.

the interview is to elicit information to enable the attorney or paralegal to fill out a legal form, such as a bankruptcy filing, then that legal form should be used as the basis, or outline, for the questioning. Some law offices have standardized interview forms for particular types of interviews, such as client intake interviews. These forms may be used in lieu of an outline or checklist.

During the interview itself, the interviewer should refer to the interview checklist or outline as a *guide.* Using this guide, the interviewer can "stay on track" and succeed in eliciting all the information she planned to obtain. Of course, while the interviewer is questioning the interviewee, the interviewer should use the checklist or outline flexibly. The interviewer, using effective listening skills and modifying her questions accordingly, should adjust and adapt her questions based on the responses provided by the interviewee. The guide should not be used as a script. A good interviewer will know when to ask follow-up questions or modify her questions based on the responses she receives from the interviewee. That is, the interviewee's responses should direct the flow of the interview. Accordingly, during the interview it is important for the interviewer to be both flexible in departing from her pre-interview outline where appropriate, and interactive, responding to the interviewee's answers even when they lead to a departure from the interview outline. Before concluding the interview, however, the interviewer should refer back to and review her checklist or outline to be sure she has asked all the pertinent questions and obtained all the necessary information. Although it is important to pursue leads that arise during the course of the interview, it is also important for the interviewer to circle back and be sure she has obtained all the information she originally planned on eliciting, for the interviewer needs all of the "who, what, where, when, and how" of the matter.

Interviewers may wish to make recordings of their interviews so they can review them again later, or so another member of the legal team can review them. Before recording an interview, the interviewer should obtain the written consent of the interviewee. In addition, at the start of the interview, the

STANDARDIZED INTERVIEW FORMS

Some attorneys and firms have standardized interview forms they use. These forms may be generalized initial client intake forms or they may be more specific, relating to a particular type of legal claim, such as a personal injury action. Using standardized forms can help ensure that all essential information is gathered from the client or witness during the interview. An example of an initial client interview checklist is found in Figure 15-8.

FIGURE 15-8 Initial Client Interview Checklist

Date:

Interviewee information

Full name:

Address:

Home telephone number:

Work telephone number:

Cell phone number:

Facsimile number:

E-mail address:

Employer's name:

Employer's address:

Occupation:

Salary:

Birthdate:

Social security number:

Driver's license state/number:

Marital status:

Spouse's name (if any):

(continued)

Children or other dependants (name, sex, age):

Education (last level completed and degrees held):

Certificates and/or licenses:

Military experience:

How did you learn about this firm/attorney?

Why are you seeking legal representation?

Nature of the legal problem (criminal, divorce/family law, business, bankruptcy, personal injury, employment/workers' compensation, immigration, other):

Are there other parties involved? If so, who are they? Do you have a relationship with them, such as family member, friend, or neighbor?

Are there any documents involved?

Have you seen any other attorney? If so, who? What was the result?

Have you seen a doctor? If so, what is the doctor's name, address, and telephone number?

Briefly describe the facts of your case.

Provide the names of any witnesses and their contact information, if available.

What is the outcome you seek?

What other outcomes would satisfy you?

How urgent is your matter?

How will you pay your fee?

interviewer should state that the interview is being recorded on the interviewee's grant of consent and include on the recording the names of the interviewer, the interviewee, and anyone else present at the interview, as well as the date, time, and location of the interview. If an interviewer believes that recording an interview will stifle the responses of the interviewee, she may prefer to take notes during the interview rather than record it. If the interviewer is an attorney, she may request her paralegal be present to take detailed notes of the interview while she is conducting it.

After the conclusion of the interview, it is a good idea for the interviewer to review and complete any notes she has taken before much time passes. It is easier

SIDEBAR

"INTERVIEWER" / "INTERVIEWEE"

The *interviewer* is the person conducting the interview; the *interviewee* is the person being interviewed.

to remember the details of the interviewee's responses immediately after the interview than at some later time. A written summary of the interview, prepared either by the interviewer or by a paralegal present to observe the interview, is a great way to preserve the information obtained during the interview. If a standardized interview form was used, the completed form itself serves as the interview summary.

Conducting interviews is a skill that a person develops through practice. In other words, it is a learned skill. Interviewing skills combine the use of communication, listening, and interpersonal skills. Just as a person becomes better at interviewing for a job through interview practice, a paralegal or attorney becomes better at interviewing clients and witnesses through interview practice. What are some things interviewers can do to improve their interview skills?

SIDEBAR

TIPS FOR CONDUCTING AN INTERVIEW

Here are some tips for how to conduct an interview:

- Greet the interviewee and introduce yourself.
- If you are a paralegal, inform the interviewee that you are a paralegal and not an attorney (in compliance with legal ethics rules on the unauthorized practice of law).
- Practice the art of conversation and be friendly, courteous, and polite to establish rapport and build trust with the interviewee.
- Act professionally in greeting and questioning the interviewee.
- Explain the purpose of the interview—that it is to gather and record information.
- Demonstrate confidence, for you control how the interview is conducted.
- Allow the interviewee to speak in his own words.
- Extract from the interviewee the pertinent information by asking the right questions.
- Follow up with additional questions based on the information the interviewee provides during the interview.
- Remember the importance of effective listening.
- Take good notes, even if the interview is being recorded.
- Obtain copies of all documents and records relating to the matter that the interviewee has in her possession or mentions in the interview.
- Arrange for the possibility of follow-up with the interviewee if you think that might become necessary.
- Thank the interviewee for participating and conclude the interview.

Key Point

Effective Interviewers . . .

- plan and prepare for interviews in advance;
- are active listeners;
- use direct eye contact;
- conduct interviews in a flexible manner, listening to interviewees and adapting their questions based on the interviewees' answers;
- ask clear and thoughtful questions;
- are efficient and use the interview time wisely;
- put their interviewees at ease;
- develop a rapport with their interviewees; and
- treat each interviewee with courtesy and respect.

Effective interviewers do not go into interviews unprepared. Rather, they plan and prepare for their interviews in advance. Effective interviewers are active listeners. Active listeners focus not only on what the interviewee is saying, but they respond to the interviewee as well by providing feedback such as nodding their head, repeating what the interviewee said, asking the interviewee to "go on," and so forth. Importantly, active listeners provide feedback to the interviewee by summarizing what was said by the interviewee and repeating it back. This process demonstrates that the listener understood what the interviewee said. In other words, an active listener openly participates in the listening process. Effective interviewers also maintain direct eye contact with their interviewees. Effective interviewers are flexible in how they conduct their interviews, using a checklist or outline, but being willing to depart from that plan to adapt lines of questioning based upon the interviewee's answers. Effective interviewers ask clear and thoughtful questions to their interviewees, avoiding legalese and speaking to interviewees using language they understand. Effective interviewers are efficient, using the interview time wisely. Effective interviewers have the ability to ease the nervousness and discomfort of their interviewees by making them comfortable with the situation. Finally, effective interviewers develop a rapport with their interviewees and treat them with courtesy and respect.

As mentioned above, effective interviewers ask clear and thoughtful questions. Learning how to ask questions is another skill that interviewers develop through practice. There are different types of questions that interviewers can ask depending on the situation. These question types include open-ended questions, close-ended questions, and leading questions.

Open-ended questions are phrased to elicit a broad response. They give the interviewee much latitude in answering by allowing the client or witness to "tell his story." For example, "Why are you seeking legal representation?" from Figure 15-8 is an open-ended question. "What happened next?" is another

Key Point

Three Types of Interview Questions

The three main types of interview questions are

- Open-ended questions, phrased to elicit a broad response
- Close-ended questions, phrased to elicit a narrow response
- Leading questions, suggesting to the interviewee the response

SIDEBAR

EFFECTIVE LISTENING

To be a successful interviewer, a paralegal must listen to what her clients and witnesses say. Here are some tips for becoming a more effective listener:

- Maintain eye contact with the interviewee to show that you have focused your attention on what he is saying.
- Pay attention to the interviewee and demonstrate your interest by showing signs of active listening such as nodding your head.
- Minimize interruptions and distractions by turning off electronic devices, forwarding telephone calls, closing doors and windows, not allowing visitors, and the like.
- "Read" the body language of the interviewee, because nonverbal communications (tone, expression, posture, and so on) can say as much as words.
- Repeat back to the interviewee what was said to ensure understanding of the communication.

example of an open-ended question used not only in interviews but in eliciting testimony at deposition or trial. This type of question works best when interviewing a client or a "friendly" witness, meaning a witness favorable to your client, for these interviewees are more likely to be forthcoming in their responses than a hostile witness, meaning a witness favorable to the opposing side, also called an adverse witness.

Close-ended questions, on the other hand, are phrased in a way to elicit a "yes" or "no" or other very narrow response. They are often used to clarify an interviewee's statement, to keep an interviewee on track, or to draw out information when interviewing an adverse or otherwise reluctant witness. They are a good way to gather more details. For example, "Were you driving the truck?" is a close-ended question. So is "What color was the traffic light at the time you entered the intersection?"

Leading questions are questions that suggest to the interviewee the answer. Leading questions typically are used in interviews to get information from adverse or other reluctant witnesses. "Isn't it true that you were driving 65 miles per hour in a 45-mile-per-hour zone at the time the accident occurred?" is an example of a leading question. Another example is, "As you approached the intersection, the signal light was red, wasn't it?" Knowing what types of questions to ask what types of interviewees, and when, is a component part of the skill of conducting interviews of clients and witnesses.

We have reviewed conducting interviews of both clients and witnesses. Interviewing skills that we have discussed apply to interviews of both types of interviewees, clients and witnesses. **Clients**, obviously, are the parties that you represent. Witnesses, on the other hand, establish facts relating to the client's case. A **witness** is a person who is not a party and who testifies under oath in a trial or in a deposition in a lawsuit. When interviewing witnesses, the types of questions you use depends on whether they are friendly or hostile witnesses—meaning whether they are favorable to your client or not.

There are other different kinds of witnesses. One type is an eyewitness. An **eyewitness** is a person who observed an event and can testify about it. For example, someone who observes a car crash is an eyewitness to it. Another type of witness is a lay witness. A **lay witness** is a person who can testify about factual knowledge he possesses. The eyewitness noted in the previous example is also a lay witness. Another type of witness is an expert witness. A lay witness is any witness who is not an expert witness. What is an expert witness? An

Client
A party who engages an attorney as counsel in a legal matter.

Witness
A person who is not a party and who testifies under oath in a trial or in a deposition in a lawsuit to establish facts relating to a client's case.

Eyewitness
A person who observed an event and can testify about it.

Lay witness
A person who can testify about factual knowledge he possesses.

SIDEBAR

FRIENDLY OR HOSTILE WITNESS?

A friendly witness is a witness who is sympathetic toward a client, or biased against a client's adversary, in a legal matter.

A hostile witness, also called an adverse witness, is a witness who is sympathetic toward a client's adversary, or biased against a client, in a legal matter.

THE TIME FACTOR

The sooner you interview a witness, the better. A witness will be easier to locate and will have better recollection of the event or occurrence if you interview her sooner rather than later.

Expert witness
A person possessing professional training or skill, advanced knowledge or education, and/or substantial experience in a specialized area who is hired to testify in court or to render an opinion on a matter related to a client's case.

expert witness is a person possessing professional training or skill, advanced knowledge or education, and/or substantial experience in a specialized area, such as forensics, medicine, or computer technology, who is hired to testify in court or to render an opinion on a matter related to a client's case. An example of an expert witness is a doctor hired by the plaintiff's lawyer to testify about the extent of harm suffered by the plaintiff.

When you interview a witness, you should consider how this person would appear to a court in the event she eventually will be called to testify at trial or to give testimony at a deposition. At the interview stage, you do not yet know whether the witness's testimony will be needed at trial or even if there will be a trial. However, because the witness could potentially be called to give testimony at trial or deposition, you should consider her qualifications as a witness. In doing so you evaluate her credibility. Credibility means a witness's believability—whether the witness appears truthful and reliable. You also evaluate a witness's competence. A lay witness is competent so long as she possesses personal knowledge of the matter on which she will testify. An expert witness, on the other hand, is considered competent only if she possesses special training, skill, knowledge, education, and/or experience relating to the subject matter for which she is called to testify. Finally, you evaluate a witness's potential bias. If a witness has an interest in the matter—for example, is a family member or friend of one of the parties or is prejudiced against one of the parties—she is considered biased and her testimony may be discredited because she lacks impartiality.

In addition to conducting interviews, tort practitioners also conduct factual investigations in representing their clients. Factual investigations are discussed next.

WITNESS STATEMENTS

A witness statement is a written record of what the witness said during an interview. It is a formal summary of a witness interview. After being drafted, a witness statement is given to the witness to review for accuracy. Then the witness signs the statement to verify the accuracy of the statement's contents.

Court rules and statutes differ on how witness statements may be used. Depending on the relevant law or rule in the court or jurisdiction, the witness statement may be used as evidence (rarely), may be used to impeach (cast doubt on) the credibility of the witness, or may be used to refresh the witness's memory (if she forgot something about the matter on which she is testifying).

CONDUCTING FACTUAL INVESTIGATIONS

Paralegals and attorneys regularly conduct factual investigations in representing clients in legal matters, including tort matters. A *factual investigation* is an examination or inquiry into the facts of a legal matter. The goal of a factual investigation in a tort case is to gather information on liability and on damages. The outcome of a legal dispute, including a tort action, depends largely on the facts of the case and the quality of the evidence obtained. This makes factual investigation a crucial part of a tort practitioner's job.

Interviewing the client and witnesses, just discussed, is one form of factual investigation. Remember from our earlier discussion that before a witnesses can be interviewed, he must first be located. Locating a witness is another type of preliminary factual investigation. Other factual information a tort practitioner may need, besides testimony from the client and witnesses, may include police reports, weather condition information, traffic condition information, medical records, employment records, business records, property ownership records, and insurance records, as some examples.

Just as for conducting interviews, a preliminary investigation plan should be established before conducting a factual investigation. An *investigation plan* is a list of tasks an investigator plans to perform to obtain or verify factual information about a legal matter. In creating an investigation plan, the investigator should consider the factual information needed. An investigator may want to verify information, such as weather conditions testified to by a witness. He may also want

Factual investigation
An examination or inquiry into the facts of a legal matter.

Key Point
The Importance of Factual Investigations
The outcome of a legal dispute depends largely on the facts of the case and the quality of the evidence obtained.

Key Point
Planning a Factual Investigation
An investigator should plan her factual investigation before she begins it. When a paralegal drafts an investigation plan, it should be reviewed and approved by the supervising attorney.

Investigation plan
A list of tasks an investigator plans to perform to obtain or verify factual information about a legal matter.

SIDEBAR

MEDICAL RECORDS

Discovery and review of medical records is an important part of personal injury litigation. Common tasks for personal injury paralegals include obtaining, reviewing, and summarizing medical records.

Regarding discovery of medical records, access to medical records today is regulated by law to protect patients' privacy rights. Largely due to the Health Insurance Portability and Accountability Act (HIPAA), a paralegal must follow proper procedures to obtain medical records from health care providers such as doctors and hospitals. There are two main ways of accessing these records: (1) to obtain an authorization from the patient and give it to the medical provider, and (2) to serve a subpoena on the custodian of the medical records. Paralegals can prepare these authorizations for the client's signature. Medical records obtained through discovery may be used at trial (medical records fall within the business records exception to the hearsay rule).

In reviewing medical records, a paralegal is determining whether the plaintiff's allegations of physical injury are substantiated, whether the injury is as severe as is alleged, and if the amount of damages claimed is reasonable.

In summarizing medical records, a paralegal is condensing the plaintiff's medical information by providing the provider's name and a brief summary of the medical record. The most common way to summarize medical records is chronologically, by date, but other methods, such as by subject matter (neck injury, broken right arm, and so on), may be used.

to obtain new information or evidence, such as title documents to property involved in a dispute or photographs of an accident scene. It is important for an investigator to thoroughly review the information she already possesses about the matter in preparing an investigation plan, which information is gained from the file, from documents and records already obtained, and from any client or witness interviews already conducted. Before the investigation begins, attorneys should review the investigation plans of their paralegals, just as they would do for interview checklists, to ensure that the investigation plans are complete and meet all of the attorney's objectives. Supervising attorneys may also be able to suggest some investigative shortcuts that will save the paralegal time and the client money.

After the planning stage, the factual investigation is conducted. Computer searches and databases are often good starting points. Computerized databases contain useful information, such as driver's license numbers and history of residences, driving records (tickets, arrests, alcohol use, and so on), vehicle title and registration, credit reports and financial records, criminal histories, past civil lawsuits, property deeds and liens, and business records. Using computerized databases is a good way for a defense paralegal to identify any previous claims or lawsuits brought by the plaintiff, to discredit the plaintiff's testimony by showing a tendency to bring legal claims against others. Interviewing clients and witnesses is another good way to begin a factual investigation. Reviewing records is another important task in conducting a factual investigation. For example, employment and lost wage information can be verified through tax returns, W-2s, affidavits from employers, pay advices, and employment contracts. Many different medical records can be reviewed and summarized to understand the extent of a party's injuries, such as hospital bills, doctor bills, ambulance bills, physical and occupational therapy bills, x-ray and MRI bills, prescription and over-the-counter medicine receipts, and medical equipment and supply receipts for items such as walkers, crutches, casts, and bandages. Receipts for in-home nursing care, housekeeping, and cook expenses for disabled parties also shed light on the extent of a party's injuries. Follow-up investigations, such as finding and reviewing records, visiting accident scenes, confirming weather conditions, and obtaining incident reports, are an example of factual investigation.

SIDEBAR

FACTUAL INVESTIGATION OF A TYPICAL AUTOMOBILE ACCIDENT CASE

The factual investigation of a typical automobile accident case often includes:

- Interviewing the client and witnesses.
- Obtaining and reviewing the police accident report. This can be used to identify witnesses and get their contact information, determine the location of the accident, see if any tickets were issued and to whom/for what, verify weather conditions at the scene at the time of the accident, determine if any persons needed immediate hospitalization, determine if any cars were so damaged that they needed to be towed from the scene, identify insurance coverages, and see

(continued)

if the reporting officer made comments in the report about fault factors such as texting, drinking, medicine use, or fatigue.

- Photographs of parties' injuries and the vehicles involved, as well as of the scene of the accident.
- Medical records of any parties who sought medical treatment.
- If mechanical malfunction is at issue, expert witnesses to inspect the automobile and testify about its condition.

If the paralegal represents the defendant, she will also:

- Identify other possible defendants, such as any person responsible for the street maintenance or road conditions at the scene of the accident.
- Evaluate the professional reputation of the doctor who treated the plaintiff's injuries.
- Investigate whether any act(s) of the plaintiff contributed to the accident that the defendant can use to defend against the plaintiff's claims.
- Investigate whether the plaintiff made prior accident claims or brought similar personal injury/property damage lawsuits in the past.
- Determine whether the plaintiff had any preexisting injuries that she should not claim again now.

As part of their factual investigation role, paralegals often document the scene of an accident. They do this by photographing or videotaping the place where the accident occurred. They may describe the physical condition of the location, such as that visibility at the intersection was impeded on the right hand side by dense vegetation in a forest at that time of year, or by a 5-foot high privacy fence surrounding a property to the right of the intersection. They may take measurements of the features of the scene of the accident, such as measure how far the crosswalk is from where the pedestrian was hit by the car and injured. The sooner the paralegal documents the scene, the better, if conditions on the scene could be changed; for example, if a terrible accident occurred because vegetation blocked visibility to the right of an intersection, that vegetation may be removed or cut back to prevent future such occurrences. If the paralegal waits to document the scene until after that condition is changed (improved in this situation), the value of her scene documentation is greatly diminished.

SIDEBAR

CRIMINAL ACT

If the event that gave rise to the tort lawsuit also involves a criminal act (e.g., one person stabbed another person—which constitutes the tort of battery and the crime of assault and battery), the criminal investigation offers much information to a paralegal conducting a factual investigation for the tort case. The paralegal can gain information from the police report, the criminal prosecution transcript and exhibits used in the criminal trial (such as maps of the area or incident location), 911/emergency telephone audiotapes or transcripts, and criminal records of the defendant.

SIDEBAR

TYPICAL PARTS OF A FACTUAL INVESTIGATION

Depending on the nature of the legal matter being investigated, here are some common searches paralegals perform in conducting factual investigations:

- Search records, such as employment records, medical records, and business records.

- Locate and interview witnesses who observed or have personal knowledge about the event.

- Contact police departments to get copies of incident reports, names of witnesses, names of investigating officers, and pictures of the scene and evidence found there.

- Contact the national weather service to obtain information about weather and daylight conditions at the date and time of the event.

- Search property records, such as land records or motor vehicle title and registration records.

- Contact insurance companies for information about policies and coverages.

Key Point

Value of Investigations in Resolving Legal Disputes

Knowledge gained through the investigative process is useful in trying to negotiate the resolution of legal disputes. The more that is known about the facts of a particular legal matter, in conjunction with the applicable law in the jurisdiction, the more able a party to litigation is to be able to evaluate the likely success of his claim or defense. This evaluation of possible success impacts settlement offers and acceptances.

Although paralegals and attorneys regularly conduct factual investigations, some lawyers enlist the services of professional investigators, at least for certain investigative tasks. Engaging a professional investigator, though it incurs additional fees for which the client is ultimately responsible, relieves the attorney or paralegal of that responsibility and gives it to a professional who is trained, licensed, and experienced in the conduct of investigations, and who may have access to people and records that a nonprofessional investigator might not. At the request of the supervising attorney, paralegals may work with the professional investigator.

During and after the conduct of the investigation, the attorney or paralegal should document and record his results, preserving his findings for later review and use. On the conclusion of the investigation, the attorney or paralegal should document and summarize the findings and present recommendations based on the results of the investigation.

Factual investigations should be well planned and thoroughly executed. After they are completed, they should be thoroughly and carefully documented. That way, the best quality and quantity of evidence is obtained to

SIDEBAR

PROFESSIONAL INVESTIGATORS

Sometimes attorneys hire professional investigators to perform certain investigative tasks. For example, an attorney for an insurance company might hire a professional investigator to observe a person who is claiming disability to determine if the person is as disabled as he claims.

help resolve the legal dispute, whether through negotiation and settlement or through trial.

In addition to conducting interviews and factual investigations, tort practitioners, typically attorneys but sometimes paralegals, conduct negotiations. The skill of conducting negotiations is examined next.

CONDUCTING NEGOTIATIONS

Because most tort cases are settled prior to trial, negotiation is a valuable skill. Attorneys can often resolve a tort dispute through negotiation rather than litigation. Remember from earlier in the chapter that negotiation is a process where the parties to a legal dispute informally communicate, themselves or via their attorneys, to discuss possible settlement of their legal dispute. It is an informal process. Negotiation can be conducted in person, over the telephone, or through correspondence such as letters or e-mail. Negotiation is considered a form of alternative dispute resolution (ADR). In fact, it is the most commonly used form of ADR. The vast majority of cases, including tort cases, are resolved this way before, or even during, trial.

Sometimes the parties themselves may negotiate to try to resolve their dispute, but often the negotiation is conducted via the parties' attorneys. Note that attorneys do not delegate this task of negotiating the resolution of legal disputes to their paralegals. During the negotiating process, both sides make offers and counteroffers in an effort to resolve the dispute. In presenting offers and counteroffers, each side may provide additional information about their claim(s) or defense(s), sharing what they believe are the strengths of their legal position to resolve the matter more efficiently than through a costly and time-consuming trial. Many courts require parties to a lawsuit to engage in settlement discussions before the start of trial, possibly at a settlement conference together with the judge assigned to the case.

If a settlement of the legal dispute is reached between the parties as a result of negotiation, a settlement agreement containing the terms of the resolution is executed by the parties. Settlement agreements were discussed earlier in the chapter, and a sample settlement agreement was provided.

In conducting both interviews and negotiations, attorneys and paralegals need to be skillful communicators. By using appropriate interpersonal skills, such as putting a nervous witness at ease by spending the early moments of an interview establishing a friendly rapport with him, an interviewer can be more effective. By asking appropriate open-ended questions to clients and friendly witnesses, close-ended questions to elicit specific responses, and leading questions to draw out responses from witnesses who are reluctant to cooperate, an interviewer can be more successful in gaining useful information. In both interviews and negotiations, listening to the other side helps the interviewer or negotiator understand the statements or position of the other, advancing her cause of either eliciting useful information or reaching a settlement of a dispute. Whether paralegals are conducting interviews, factual investigations, or negotiations, their skills and abilities improve with practice and experience.

Key Point

Legal Dispute Settlement

Remember that attorneys are the only legal representatives who should negotiate the settlement of legal disputes. In doing so, they must abide by their clients' directions regarding making settlement offers and accepting them. It is ultimately a decision for the client whether or not to make or accept any settlement offer.

Key Point

Negotiation and the Paralegal

Negotiation is a skill used more often by attorneys than paralegals. Attorneys are the legal representatives who negotiate the settlement of legal disputes unless the clients prefer to negotiate the settlement themselves. Paralegals can assist the attorneys in preparation for negotiation by conducting factual investigations and by performing legal research to determine the likely success of the client's claim or defense.

CHAPTER **SUMMARY**

- A civil case, such as a tort case, proceeds through the legal system in the process of litigation. Litigation is the process of carrying on a civil lawsuit. The litigation process, very generally, involves pleadings, discovery, pretrial procedures, trial, and posttrial procedures.

- Most civil cases settle either before or during trial. A settlement agreement is a contract entered into by the parties to a legal dispute that sets forth the terms and conditions of the resolution and settlement of the dispute.

- Besides case briefs, attorneys and paralegals typically prepare other legal documents when engaged in tort practice, including legal correspondence, legal memoranda, pleadings, discovery requests and responses, and settlement agreements. Good writing skills are critical to success for both attorneys and paralegals.

- Attorneys and paralegals may conduct client and witness interviews in the course of their legal work. An attorney typically performs the initial client interview, when the decision is made whether to accept representation of the client in a particular matter and when the fee agreement is established. Afterward, the attorney or paralegal may conduct further interviews to obtain additional information from the client and witnesses.

- Paralegals and attorneys regularly conduct factual investigations while representing clients in tort matters. The outcome of a legal dispute, including a tort action, depends largely on the facts of the case and the quality of the evidence obtained. This makes factual investigation a crucial part of a tort practitioner's job.

- Because most tort cases settle prior to trial, negotiation is a valuable skill for attorneys who practice tort law. During the negotiation process, both sides make offers and counteroffers in an effort to amicably resolve their dispute. If a settlement is reached between the parties as a result of negotiation, a settlement agreement containing the terms of the resolution is executed by the parties and submitted to the court in which the litigation is pending to serve as the basis for dismissal of the legal action.

CONCEPT REVIEW AND REINFORCEMENT

QUESTIONS FOR **REVIEW**

1. How does a tort case proceed through the process of litigation?

2. What legal documents typically apply in tort practice?

3. How do you draft these tort-related documents?

4. How do you conduct interviews, factual investigations, and negotiations in practicing tort law?

DEVELOPING YOUR PARALEGAL SKILLS

CRITICAL THINKING **EXERCISES**

1. You are conducting a factual investigation of your client's negligence matter. Your client was injured when he was struck by a car while walking across Jade Street in Pasadena, Texas. Your client said it was 6:45 p.m. on September 15, and light outside, when he walked into a pedestrian crossing while the pedestrian crossing light was green, telling him to cross, and was struck by the defendant's car. The defendant has asserted that the plaintiff was not in the crosswalk but was jaywalking at the time of the incident, and that it was dusk and the plaintiff was attired in dark clothes, making him difficult to see. In conducting a factual investigation of the incident, where would you search for the following:

a. *To find any videotapes or cameras near that crossing that would show the incident?*

b. *To find out if there were any other witnesses to the incident?*

c. *To get a copy of the police report relating to the incident?*

d. *To get an understanding of the intersection involved, such as whether the intersection is in a busy area, and to see how the road and pedestrian crossing are configured? Remember, you want to preserve this scene for trial.*

e. *To find the daylight conditions at that time on that day?*

f. *To find out the weather conditions at the time of the incident?*

g. *To get information about the extent and permanence of the plaintiff's injuries?*

h. *To find out whether the defendant has a clean driving record or perhaps a history of DUIs (driving under the influence) or other driving infractions?*

2. You are a paralegal specializing in tort law and products liability. Your firm is representing a client who is suing a hairdryer manufacturer, alleging strict product liability. Remember that a strict products liability claim can be brought when a defective product causes harm to a person and/or her property, and fault of the defendant need not be established. The claim arose out of an incident when the client was blow-drying her hair and the dryer exploded, causing her injury. Lauri, the client's best friend, was in the room when the incident occurred and witnessed the explosion. Your supervising attorney asks you to interview Lauri and obtain from her the information the firm will need to bolster the client's claim.

   Prepare an outline of the questions you plan to ask the witness during the interview, for submission to your supervising attorney for review prior to conducting the interview. Share your outline with the class.

3. Exactly three months ago today, Judy Miller went grocery shopping at Waul's Food Market in Lutherville, Maryland, located in Baltimore City. While strolling past the soda aisle, a display of soda bottles became unstable, toppling to the ground in a noisy crash. Unfortunately, several of the falling bottles struck Judy, causing her to be knocked to the floor, where she hit her head and suffered a mild concussion. Judy also broke her left arm and sprained her right ankle in the incident. Several other customers witnessed the occurrence, causing Judy embarrassment in addition to her physical injuries. One of these customers came to Judy's aid, calling 911 on her behalf, when no store employee came to render assistance.

   Pretend you are a lawyer and have agreed to represent Judy in her tort action, specifically, her negligence claim, against the store. Draft the complaint you will file in Baltimore City Circuit Court to initiate the lawsuit. You may follow the format in this chapter for a negligence complaint or, even better, the format specific to your jurisdiction if you know or can find it.

4. The Crestview Country Club pool has both a diving board and a slide at its deep end. Whenever swimmers are in the water, at least two lifeguards must be on duty, per pool policy. A warning sign posted on the slide says, "Rider must ride feet first, on his/her back, with hands crossed over the chest, to avoid serious injury." Lifeguards are trained to monitor that swimmers use the pool slide properly. Timothy, a bit of a daredevil, rides down the slide head first, on his stomach. Unfortunately, he enters the water in a dive posture and slices to the bottom of the pool, where he hits his head and traumatizes his neck and spine, suffering serious injury, including permanent paralysis. At the time of the incident, the lifeguards were in the staff lounge, playing cards and having an afternoon snack. Timothy sues the Crestview Country Club for the tort of negligence (in Circuit Court of Norfolk County, case number CV-962547), seeking $1,250,000 in compensatory damages, alleging that the country club failed to use reasonable care by not having lifeguards on duty who could have saved him or instructed him to ride the slide properly. The country club will defend the action by asserting that Timothy's own negligence, in riding the slide in the dangerous head-first position, contrary to pool policy and the warning sign posted on the slide itself, caused or contributed to his injuries. The country club carries liability insurance in the amount of $750,000 and is in a state of financial difficulty. If the country club is ordered to pay an adverse judgment of more than $250,000, it will be bankrupted.

   Partner with another student in class and each take a role as one of the parties (or the attorney representing one of the parties). Negotiate a settlement of this legal dispute. Next, draft a settlement agreement reflecting your terms of settlement of this case. Share your settlement terms with the class.

ASSIGNMENTS AND PRACTICAL **APPLICATIONS**

1. You are an associate attorney with a plaintiff's firm that specializes in tort cases, especially products liability matters. Draft a letter to your client, Sara Whitman, confirming your appointment with her, at your firm's offices (Franklin, Whiting & Sullivan, P.A., 145 Charles Avenue, Sparks, Maryland 21110) next Thursday. You plan to meet at 10:00 a.m. to prepare her to testify at her upcoming products liability trial. The meeting should last about two hours. Remind her to bring with her records of the physical therapy she is receiving, including the treatment plan prepared by her physician.

2. Your client, who is purchasing a fleet of trucks for use in his business, asks you what he needs to do to comply with automobile owners' liability insurance or other financial responsibility requirements. Research your state's requirements for automobile liability insurance, bonding, or other financial responsibility requirements. Using the results of your research, write a letter to your client advising him of these obligations, and his options, under your state's motor vehicle liability insurance law.

3. You are a paralegal working in a personal injury law firm. A prospective client comes to the law office seeking representation. During an interview, the person tells you that he was seriously injured when a speeding car struck him while he was crossing the street in a pedestrian crossing zone. He learned from the police that the driver of the car that hit him died of a heart attack about six months after the incident. Research whether your state has a survival statute. Under the statute in your jurisdiction, would this prospective client's tort action survive the death of the tortfeasor? Write a legal memorandum to your supervising attorney evaluating the prospective client's claim.

4. Form books are excellent secondary sources of law for tort practitioners who need litigation forms. *American Jurisprudence Pleading and Practice Forms Annotated* is an example of a comprehensive and accurate multivolume form book set, published by West and found in most law libraries. Go to your school's or a local law library and locate this form book resource. Browse through its index and review some of its forms that would be useful to practitioners engaged in tort litigation.

TECHNOLOGY RESOURCES AND INTERNET **EXERCISES**

Model jury instructions, also called pattern jury instructions, are forms of jury instructions approved by a state bar association or similar group regarding matters arising in a typical case. A good way for students to learn the essential elements of the different torts and how those elements are defined is to review the jury instructions used in their state. These can often and easily be found on the Internet. Locate jury instructions used in your state for the various torts discussed in this text.

FindLaw.com is a useful resource to find legal forms for use in drafting tort-related legal documents. Using the website's "Legal Forms" database, you can find forms for different types of legal letters, as well as for litigation-related documents including complaints, answers, motions, and the like. Review the different types of legal forms available on this popular website.

Using the Cornell Law School website, perform a search for the legal ethics code in Maryland (*www.law.cornell.edu /ethics/md/code*). Use this resource or your state's legal ethics rules to answer the questions in the following Ethical Applications section.

ETHICAL **APPLICATIONS**

Jonathan Sweeney is a paralegal in the boutique firm of Jones, Masters, and Serio, P.C., a plaintiff's firm. Jonathan is an experienced paralegal who is excellent at what he does. One day, one of the firm's clients, Tax-Made-EZ Software, Inc., calls the firm to speak to Jonathan's supervising attorney, Gloria Milford. Gloria is in a meeting and will be unavailable all day, as the receptionist tells the client. The client's vice president for development, who has placed the call on behalf of his company, asks to speak to Jonathan, who is available, in lieu of Gloria. In speaking with Jonathan, the client's representative asks Jonathan whether the earned income credit will be repealed by federal legislators for the upcoming tax year so that the company may finalize the updating of its federal tax return software for copying, distribution, and sale. Jonathan, who is up to date and very knowledgeable about federal tax law, responds, "I'm sure that it's safe to finalize your software; the earned income credit will not be repealed by Congress this year." In fact, although there were some discussions during recent legislative sessions about repealing the earned income credit, the credit was not repealed, and Jonathan is correct (and confident that he is).

Was Jonathan's conduct appropriate? If so, why? If not, what was wrong with it? What can happen to Jonathan because of this conduct? What, if anything, can happen to Gloria because of Jonathan's conduct?

At the law firm of Sweeney & Barry, LLC, the tort law specialist, Brian Ludwig, is busy preparing for a hearing he will be attending later in the day. A prospective client comes to the office, wishing to discuss a legal issue involving tort law and wanting to know if Brian will represent him and handle the matter. Although Brian appreciates the opportunity for new business, he is just too busy to meet with the prospective client at that time. Not wanting to lose the new

business, he sends his very capable paralegal, Brenda Todd, to meet with the visitor and gather information about the legal issue.

Is it okay for Brenda to meet with the prospective client to gather information about the matter? Why or why not?

What if, in addition to gathering information about the matter, Brenda, under Brian's direction and with his authority, agrees that Brian and the firm will represent the client in that matter, and also sets the fee arrangement pursuant to which the client will pay the standard hourly fees charged by both herself and Brian for work performed on the case.

Is it okay for Brenda's interview with the prospective client to cover these issues (accepting the representation and setting the legal fee)? Why or why not?

VIDEO **CASE STUDY**

Preparation for Trial: Preparing Witness for Deposition and Trial

Synopsis: A paralegal is preparing a fact witness for deposition and trial in a tort case. The paralegal is explaining the procedure to the witness and attempting to put the witness at ease and answer her questions.

Questions

1. Is it proper to prepare a witness for the giving of a deposition or to testify at trial? Is it necessary?

2. Do legal ethics rules regarding unauthorized practice of law permit a paralegal to prepare a witness for deposition or trial, or should an attorney perform this function?

3. What do you think are the most important pieces of advice that the paralegal gives in preparing this witness?

4. Is there anything else you would do or say in preparing this witness for the giving of testimony at deposition or trial?

ENDNOTES

Chapter 1

1. 1995 WL 360309 (this is an unpublished opinion).
2. There are those, including one reviewer of this manuscript, who feel strongly that the media reaction was not in line with the law and the parties' conduct in this case, and support the large jury verdict in favor of Liebeck.
3. The author of this text operates a tax law clinic where she and her paralegal students prepare tax returns for low-income taxpayers as part of the Internal Revenue Service's Volunteer Income Tax Assistance (VITA) program. Because of the Volunteer Protection Act, the clinic participants are protected from liability for damages they may cause clients if they negligently prepare a tax return.

Chapter 2

1. Colo. Rev. Stat. Ann. § 13-21-107 (2009).
2. Fla. Stat. Ann. § 741.24 (2009).

Chapter 3

1. *Restatement (Second) of Torts*, section 8A.
2. 2011 WL 290509 (this is an unpublished opinion).
3. 2011 WL 6782438 (this is an unpublished opinion).
4. 2011 WL 6057930 (this is an unpublished opinion).
5. 2011 WL 6270529 (this is an unpublished opinion).

Chapter 5

1. *Restatement (Second) of Torts*, section 63(1).
2. *Restatement (Second) of Torts*, section 65(1).
3. *Id.*
4. Model Penal Code, section 3.06(1)(b).
5. *Restatement (Second) of Torts*, section 147.
6. *Id.*
7. *Liebeck v. McDonald's Restaurants, P.T.S., Inc.* No. D-202 CD-93-02419, 1995 WL 360309 (this is an unpublished opinion).

Chapter 6

1. From the Minnesota Statutes Annotated, M.S.A. § 604A.01 (2009).
2. *Id.*

3. 2011 WL 3903241 (this is an unpublished opinion).
4. *Restatement (Second) of Torts*, section 289.
5. *Id.*
6. 2012 WL 280385 (this is an unpublished opinion).

Chapter 7

1. 2012 WL 280385 (this is an unpublished opinion).
2. Federal Judicial Center's *Manual for Complex Litigation*, p. 309, http://www.fjc.gov/public/pdf.nsf/lookup/mcl.pdf/$File/mcl.pdf.

Chapter 9

1. 28 U.S.C. §§ 1346(b), 2671-2680 (2012).
2. *Id.* at § 2680.
3. *Restatement (Second) of Torts*, section 895E.
4. *Forrester v. White*, 484 U.S. 219 (1988).
5. *Id.*
6. *Id.*

Chapter 10

1. Fla. Stat. § 767.04 (2009).
2. *Id.*
3. See www.wbaltv.com/beachandbayforecast/4415797/detail.html for the local news story, including a fun picture of a buffalo roaming a tennis court while being rounded up by officers.
4. *Restatement (Second) of Torts*, section 504.
5. *Restatement (Second) of Torts*, section 520.

Chapter 11

1. *Restatement (Third) of Torts: Prods. Liab.*, section 2.
2. *Id.*
3. *Id.*
4. *Id.*
5. *Id.*
6. *Id.*
7. *Id.* at Comment i.
8. *Restatement (Second) of Torts*, section 395.

GLOSSARY

Abnormally dangerous conditions or activities
Conditions or activities that are not usual for the area and that create a substantial likelihood of significant harm that cannot be eliminated by the exercise of reasonable care.

Absolute immunity Legal immunity without limits or conditions, such as a good faith requirement, which acts as a complete defense to liability.

Absolute liability Strict liability.

Absolute privilege A privilege that cannot be lost.

Abuse of process The use of civil or criminal proceedings for an improper purpose or for an ulterior motive.

Actual cause Cause in fact.

Actual malice The requirement that a defamatory statement be made knowing that it is false or with reckless disregard for its truth or falsity.

Affirmative defense The defendant's response to a plaintiff's claim that sets forth new factual allegations that were not included in the plaintiff's original claim to assert why the defendant should not be held liable to the plaintiff or why the defendant's liability should be reduced.

Alternative dispute resolution (ADR) The resolution of legal disputes in ways other than the traditional judicial process of litigation.

Appropriation Use of another person's name, likeness, image, or other identifying characteristic, without permission, for the benefit of the user.

Arbitration An out-of-court process where parties submit their legal dispute to a neutral third party or parties, called an arbitrator or arbitration panel, who hears evidence and renders an award.

Assault A purposeful act that causes an apprehension of a harmful or offensive contact.

Assumption of the risk The knowing and voluntary acceptance of the risk of being harmed or injured by another's negligent conduct, which acts as a defense and bars the plaintiff's recovery.

Attractive nuisance doctrine A legal doctrine that states that a duty of care is owed to trespassing children of young age who cannot fully appreciate certain dangers and who may be attracted to artificial conditions or dangerous activities on the premises.

Automobile consent statutes Legislative acts that make the owners of automobiles vicariously liable for the negligence of any person to whom they entrust their automobiles.

Avoidable consequences doctrine Where a plaintiff is held legally responsible for any further injury or harm that, through his actions, he could have reasonably avoided after being injured by the defendant's negligence.

Award The decision made by an arbitrator or arbitration panel.

Battery Purposeful and unwanted harmful or offensive contact with another person.

Beyond a reasonable doubt The standard of proof applied in a criminal case by which the prosecution must prove the case sufficiently so that there is no reasonable doubt in the mind of any juror that the defendant committed the crime.

Binding authority Legal authority that a court must follow in deciding the issue at hand.

Breach of the duty of care Failure to use reasonable care under the circumstances, judged by the reasonable person standard.

Breach of warranty A legal failure to fulfill the assurances made in a warranty.

Briefing a case Case briefing.

Burden of proof A party's duty to prove a disputed assertion in a lawsuit or prosecution.

Case brief A mechanism for summarizing, in written form, a court case.

Case briefing The process of reading, analyzing, and summarizing court cases.

Case citation A case's locator reference, which includes the volume number of the reporter where the case is published, the name of the reporter, the page number on which the case begins, identification of the court rendering the decision, and the year of the decision.

Case law Common law.

Case name Identifies the parties to a court case.

Case on point A previous court decision involving similar facts and legal issues.

Case title Case name.

Causation The essential element of negligence that limits negligence liability to harm caused by one's unreasonable acts or omissions.

Causation in fact Cause in fact.

Cause in fact The part of causation brought about by an act or omission without which an event would not have occurred.

Cause of action A legal theory in a lawsuit.

Charging the jury Where the judge instructs the jury on the relevant rules of law to be applied to the case.

Charitable immunity Immunity from legal liability granted to charitable organizations to help them fulfill their charitable missions.

Chattels Personal property.

Children of tender years Young children, normally under the age of 7 years.

Civil law The system of law dealing with the definition and enforcement of all private or public rights.

Class action A form of lawsuit in which a large group of people bring a legal claim collectively.

Client A party who engages an attorney as counsel in a legal matter.

Collateral source rule A legal doctrine that prohibits the defendant from avoiding liability for injuries caused to the plaintiff but compensated for by collateral sources.

Collateral sources Funds or services that a person receives because of an injury caused by a defendant but that come from sources other than the defendant.

Common law Judge-made law created by the courts and found in court opinions.

Commonly known dangers Dangers associated with certain products which are so obvious that manufacturers need not warn users of them.

Comparative negligence An affirmative defense used to limit or bar recovery when a plaintiff's own negligence contributes to the injury or harm caused by the defendant's negligence, in which recovery is allocated based on relative degrees of fault between the plaintiff and the defendant.

Compensatory damages Damages awarded to compensate, or reimburse, the plaintiff for the actual harm suffered and awarded to make the plaintiff whole again.

Concurring opinion An opinion written by a judge or judges who agree with the court's majority opinion, but for different reasons.

Consent A plaintiff's voluntary willingness to let the defendant's conduct occur and to accept its consequences.

Consequential damages Special damages.

Contingency fee A legal fee based on a percentage of the plaintiff's recovery.

Contract A legally enforceable agreement between parties.

Contribution The right of a joint tortfeasor who has paid a judgment to be proportionately reimbursed by the other joint tortfeasors for their share of the harm.

Contributory negligence A common law doctrine that provides that when a plaintiff's own negligence contributes to the harm or injury caused by the defendant's negligence, the plaintiff is barred from recovery.

Conversion Intentional exercise of dominion and control over another's personal property which seriously interferes with the owner or possessor's right to possession.

Course and scope of employment Conduct of an employee performed in the interests, or on behalf, of the employer.

Covenant not to sue A legally enforceable promise by the plaintiff not to sue the person in whose favor the covenant is made.

Criminal law The system of law dealing with wrongful actions perpetrated against society, for which society demands redress.

Damages A remedy awarded at law, in the form of money; also one of the essential elements of the tort of negligence that requires a plaintiff to demonstrate that she suffered a legally recognizable injury.

Danger invites rescue doctrine A legal doctrine under which rescuers who are injured while coming to another's aid may recover from the person who caused the danger.

Defamation Published false statements of fact that cause injury to a person's good name, character, and reputation.

Default judgment A judgment of the court made in favor of the plaintiff when the defendant fails to oppose the plaintiff's legal action against him.

Defendant The party being sued in a civil case or the party being prosecuted in a criminal prosecution.

Defense A response by a party to the claim of another party, setting forth the reason(s) why the claim should be denied or recovery reduced.

Defense of others The right of a person to use reasonable force to prevent an immediate harmful or offensive contact by another against someone other than himself.

Defense of property The right of a person to use reasonable, but never deadly, force to prevent immediate interference with his property or to end interference already occurring.

Demurrer Motion to dismiss.

Deposition The sworn testimony of a party or witness given during a question and answer proceeding conducted before trial.

Design defects Product defects when all products on the line conform to the product design, but something is wrong with the design that makes the entire line of products dangerous to use.

Dicta Nonlaw statements made by judges in an opinion.

Diplomatic immunity Legal immunity that protects diplomats in the performance of their official duties.

Direct damages General damages.

Discipline The privilege to use reasonable force or confinement to control, train, or educate a child.

Discovery The process of searching for and obtaining information and evidence relevant to a case.

Disparagement An injurious false statement made to damage a person's business or title to property.

Disparagement of property Disparagement.

Dissenting opinion An opinion written by a judge or judges who disagree with the court's majority opinion.

Doctrine of avoidable consequences Mitigation of damages.

Doctrine of *respondeat superior* A legal doctrine under which an employer can be held vicariously liable for the wrongful conduct, including the tortious conduct, of its employees committed within the course and scope of their employment.

Doctrine of transferred intent The intent to commit a tort against one person may be transferred to another person (the "unintended plaintiff"), or the intent to commit one tort may be transferred when the tortfeasor commits a different tort against that person (the "unintended tort").

Domestic animal An animal that is habituated to live with and among humans, and its normal population is pets.

Domesticated animal Domestic animal.

Duty of care An obligation to conform to a standard of conduct prescribed by law.

Eggshell skull rule An exception to proximate cause according to which, if it is foreseeable that the defendant's unreasonable act or omission will result in any harm to the plaintiff's person and harm does occur, then the defendant is liable for the full extent of the harm, including both the foreseeable and the unforeseeable injuries that result.

Employee A worker who is subject to an employer's control over the details of the work.

Employer One who hires another to perform work on his behalf, and who has the right to control the details of how the work is performed.

Equitable remedies Remedies in equity.

Essential elements The building blocks, or component parts, of a cause of action, which must be established by the person bringing the action.

Exemplary damages Punitive damages.

Expert witness A person possessing professional training or skill, advanced knowledge or education, and/or substantial experience in a specialized area who is hired to testify in court or to render an opinion on a matter related to a client's case.

Express warranties Assurances made by a seller, either orally or in writing, that address the quality, description, or performance of the goods being sold.

Eyewitness A person who observed an event and can testify about it.

Factual investigation An examination or inquiry into the facts of a legal matter.

False arrest The unprivileged arrest of an individual.

False imprisonment Intentional confinement of another within fixed boundaries set by the defendant.

False light Publicly making or giving a highly offensive and inaccurate portrayal or impression of another person.

Family car doctrine The family purpose doctrine.

Family immunity Protects certain family members from liability for harm caused to other family members.

Family purpose doctrine A doctrine that allows a plaintiff to sue the owner of an automobile for the negligent acts of members of the owner's family when an immediate family member is driving the automobile for family purposes.

Filial consortium The right of a parent to the companionship and affection of a child.

Foreseeability In tort law, the predictability of an event or occurrence.

Fraud Misrepresentation.

Fraudulent misrepresentation Misrepresentation.

Frolic and detour When an employee deviates from or abandons the employer's business interests and acts in furtherance of her own personal interests.

General damages Those compensatory damages that are normally and reasonably expected from the defendant's actions.

Good Samaritan rule Absent a special relationship, in nonfeasance cases, no duty of care is imposed on a person to come to the aid of another in an emergency.

Good Samaritan statutes Statutes enacted in many states to limit the ordinary negligence liability of Good Samaritans who come to the emergency aid of others.

Governmental functions Activities performed by government in the best interest of and to protect the public, which often can be performed only by the government.

Governmental immunity Prevents a lawsuit against a government or sovereign, without the government or sovereign's consent.

Gratuitous undertaking Voluntarily assuming a duty of care when none is imposed by law.

Gross negligence A form of extreme negligence in which a tortfeasor fails to use even a small amount of care to avoid causing foreseeable harm to others or their property.

Heart balm actions Common law torts that historically could be brought by a family member against a third party for something done to or with another family member, including breach of promise to marry, alienation of affections, criminal conversation, and seduction.

Heart balm statutes Legislative acts abolishing or limiting the heart balm actions.

Immunity A defense to legal liability or criminal prosecution that, when applied to tort law, under certain circumstances, protects tortfeasors from liability for tortious conduct because of who they are, what they do, or their relationship with another.

Implied warranties Warranties that arise by operation of law under a state's commercial code.

Implied warranty of fitness for a particular purpose A warranty imposed by law that promises that goods are fit for the particular purposes for which the buyer purchased them.

Implied warranty of merchantability A warranty imposed by law that promises that goods are of proper quality and fit for the ordinary purposes for which such goods are used.

Indemnity A method of forcing a person who has not paid the judgment to reimburse the person who paid it for the full amount of the judgment paid.

Independent contractor One who works for another but whose working conditions and methods are not controlled by the hiring party.

Injunction A court order requiring a person to do or refrain from doing a certain act.

Injurious falsehood A statement of fact that harms the interests of another, which includes disparagement when commercial matters are at issue but is broader and also includes noncommercial matters.

Insurance A type of contract utilized by persons to manage their risk of loss under certain circumstances.

Insurance policy A contract for insurance coverage.

Insurance premium Consideration paid by the insured for the insurance protection set forth in the insurance policy.

Intake interview The initial client interview.

Intent The desire to bring about the consequences of the act or knowledge with substantial certainty that the consequences will flow from the act.

Intentional infliction of emotional distress The purposeful causing of severe mental anguish by an act of extreme or outrageous conduct.

Intentional torts Those torts in which the tortfeasor either desired to bring about the result or knew with substantial certainty that the result would follow from the person's actions or failure to act.

Intentional torts against property Those torts in which the defendant acts purposefully to interfere with another person's rights in property.

Interrogatories Written questions prepared by a party, submitted to the other party, to be answered under oath.

Interspousal immunity The immunity that exists between legal spouses.

Intervening cause An event or occurrence that produces harm after the initial injury suffered by the plaintiff, which contributes to or aggravates the initial injury.

Interview A meeting held for the purpose of asking questions and eliciting responses.

Intrusion Invasion into a person's private affairs or concerns.

Intrusion on seclusion Intrusion.

Invasion of privacy Interference with a person's right to be left alone.

Invasion of the right to privacy Invasion of privacy.

Investigation plan A list of tasks an investigator plans to perform to obtain or verify factual information about a legal matter.

Invitee A person who enters the land of another, with permission, for the benefit of the land owner or occupier or the mutual benefit of both parties, or for the purposes for which the owner or occupier holds his property open to the public.

Joint and several liability A legal doctrine under which a plaintiff, in a tort or other action, may sue all of the responsible parties, jointly, or any one or more of them, severally, at his option.

Joint enterprise liability A legal doctrine under which persons who are working together for some common business purpose may be held vicariously liable for the acts of the others in the joint enterprise.

Joint tortfeasors Persons who act with other persons in causing a tortious wrong, who can be sued together by the injured party.

Justification A reasonable belief by the court that the defendant's actions were justified and it would be unfair to hold the person liable for his actions.

Knowledgeable users Particular users of a product who should, because of experience and training, know of the particular dangers of that product.

Last clear chance doctrine A legal doctrine that offsets the effects of contributory negligence when the defendant has the last clear chance to avoid the incident or accident and does not.

Lawsuit A civil legal action brought by a party against another.

Lay witness A person who can testify about factual knowledge he possesses.

Legal cause Proximate cause.

Legal correspondence Legal letters.

Legal jargon Legalese.

Legal memoranda Documents that thoroughly analyze and summarize the law in a particular area, on the basis of legal research, and inform the requestor of the strengths and weaknesses of the client's legal position.

Legalese The body of terms used by the legal profession.

Liability Legal responsibility.

Liability without fault Strict liability.

Libel Defamation in written or other tangible form.

Licensee A person who enters the land of another, with permission, for his own purposes or benefit.

Litigation The process of carrying on a civil lawsuit.

Loss of consortium A claim made by the spouse of an injured party for the loss of companionship from marriage that was caused by the injury.

Majority opinion A court opinion in which a majority of the judges agree.

Malicious prosecution Initiation of a criminal prosecution or a civil lawsuit against another party with malice and without probable cause.

Malpractice The failure of a professional, such as a doctor or lawyer, to exercise reasonable care in the performance of professional services.

Mandatory authority Binding authority.

Manufacturing defects Product defects resulting because the manufactured product does not conform to its design, and a problem occurred during the making of the product that caused it to be dangerous to use.

Mass tort A tort involving the same event or source that causes harm to many people.

Mass tort litigation Litigation involving large numbers of plaintiffs in multiple jurisdictions, including both state and federal courts, and multiple venues, all injured by the same defendant and arising out of the same event or source.

Mediation A nonadversarial process where a neutral third party facilitates communications between parties to a legal dispute to help them resolve it.

Mediator A neutral third party who conducts a mediation session.

Misfeasance Misconduct by affirmative act.

Misrepresentation The intentional making of a material false statement, or the failure to disclose when a duty to disclose exists, which causes the plaintiff harm in the form of a pecuniary loss.

Mitigation of damages doctrine The legal requirement that a person who has suffered injury because of another's misconduct must take reasonable steps to mitigate, or lessen, the damages she suffers or her recovery may be denied or reduced by the amount of harm she could have avoided.

Motion for directed verdict A motion made by the defendant at the close of the plaintiff's case where the defendant argues to the court that the plaintiff has failed to meet her burden of proof and that a verdict should be made in the defendant's favor.

Motion for summary judgment A motion brought by a party asking the court to enter judgment in its favor—as a matter of law—because there is no material fact at issue for the jury to decide and the court has all the information that it needs to render a decision.

Motion to dismiss A motion filed by the defendant that asserts that the plaintiff has failed to state a legally valid claim in bringing the legal action.

Multidistrict litigation A special federal litigation procedure designed to speed the process of handling complex cases.

Necessity The privilege to make reasonable use of another's property in order to prevent immediate harm or damage to persons or real or personal property.

Negligence The failure to use reasonable care, resulting in harm to a person or to his or her property.

Negligence _per se_ An act or omission in violation of a statute; it literally means "negligence by itself."

Negligent infliction of emotional distress Causing emotional distress by an act of unreasonable conduct.

Negotiation A process where the parties to a legal dispute informally communicate, themselves or via their attorneys, to discuss possible settlement of their legal dispute.

Nominal damages Damages awarded when wrongdoing has occurred, but little or no injury or harm is suffered by the plaintiff.

Nonfeasance Misconduct by failure to act.

Nuisance A common law doctrine under which persons can be held liable for using their property in a manner that unreasonably interferes with other persons' use and enjoyment of their property.

Official immunity Legal immunity that protects public officials in the performance of their duties.

Omnibus clause A clause in many standard automobile insurance policies that provides that liability insurance for the designated automobile applies to the named insured in the policy, any member of the named insured's household, and any person using the automobile with the named insured's permission.

Opinion The formal, usually lengthy, analysis, decision, and reasoning of the court in ruling on a case.

Pain and suffering damages Damages awarded to recover for actual pain, fear, anxiety, humiliation, depression, loss of companionship, and similar emotional harms suffered.

Parent–child immunity The immunity that exists between parents and their children.

Parental consortium The right of a child to the companionship and affection of a parent.

Parental immunity Parent-child immunity.

Penalty What is imposed on a defendant found guilty in a criminal prosecution.

Personal injury cases A name for negligence cases resulting in personal injury to a plaintiff, often known by the abbreviation PI.

Personal property All property that is not real property.

Persuasive authority Legal authority that is not binding on a court but that may be used as guidance in making its decision.

Plaintiff The party bringing suit in a civil case.

Plaintiff's attorney A lawyer who represents an injured person in a tort lawsuit.

Pleading A legal document used by a party to set forth or respond to allegations, claims, denials, or defenses.

Preponderance of the evidence The standard of proof typically applied in a civil case, by which the party must demonstrate that it is more likely than not that the allegations are true.

Pretrial conference A meeting between the attorneys and the judge, held prior to trial, to discuss possible settlement as well as trial matters.

Prima facie tort doctrine A catch-all tort doctrine recognized in a few states to cover certain wrongful conduct that is intentional but does not fit the essential elements of the other recognized intentional torts.

Primary sources of law Resources that establish the law on an issue, such as a court decision, constitution, statute, or administrative regulation.

Private nuisance Unreasonable interference with another's interest in the private use and enjoyment of his or her land.

Privilege A defense that justifies otherwise tortious conduct and is derived from the right of a person to act contrary to the right of another person without being subject to liability for his actions.

Privity of contract The requirement that because a contract is a private agreement between or among the parties to it, those who are not parties to the contract normally have no rights under it.

Product defect Something is wrong with a product that makes it dangerous, increasing the risk of harm to persons and their property.

Products liability Legal liability of manufacturers, sellers, and others for harm caused by defective products.

Professional negligence Malpractice.

Proprietary functions Activities performed in the government's discretion, for the benefit of its citizens, and that often cannot be performed adequately only by the government.

Prosecution The legal action brought against a defendant alleging the commission of a crime.

Protected interest A right that a person has, under the law, to be protected from certain kinds of conduct.

Proximate cause The part of causation that requires a sufficient connection between a person's act or omission and an injury to justify imposing liability.

Public disclosure of private facts Unreasonable public disclosure of private facts about a person that are not a matter of legitimate public concern.

Public nuisance Unreasonable interference with a right that is common to the general public.

Public official A person who holds a governmental position, called an office, in which he serves in the public interest.

Public official immunity Official immunity.

Punitive damages Damages awarded to the plaintiff to punish the defendant and to deter future wrongdoing.

Qualified immunity Legal immunity that has limits or conditions, such as a requirement of good faith, which can be lost as a defense.

Qualified privilege A privilege that can be lost if it is abused.

Real property Land and anything permanently affixed thereto.

Reasonable person standard The standard of behavior expected of a hypothetical reasonable person under the same or similar circumstances.

Recapture of chattels The limited right to use reasonable force to regain possession and control over one's personal property.

Reentry onto land The limited right to use reasonable, nondeadly force to reenter and reclaim real property when the plaintiff has wrongfully dispossessed the defendant.

Release A document that formally relinquishes a plaintiff's legal claim.

Remedies The judicial awards by which legal rights are enforced and the violations of rights are prevented, redressed, or compensated.

Remedies at law Recovery in a civil lawsuit in the form of money damages.

Remedies in equity Forms of recovery in a civil lawsuit other than money damages, which are awarded by a court, in its discretion.

Remedy The relief given to a party to enforce a right or to compensate for the violation of a right.

Requests for admission Written requests by a party to the other party asking her to admit the truth of certain matters or facts relating to the lawsuit.

Requests for examination Written requests by a party to the court asking the court to order the other party to submit to a physical or mental examination.

Requests for production Written requests by a party to another party for documents or other tangible things or for permission to enter on the land or other property of a party for the purpose of conducting an inspection.

Requests for the production of documents Requests for production.

Res ipsa loquitur doctrine A legal doctrine that infers negligence simply because an event occurred, if it is the type of event that would not normally occur in the absence of negligence; res ipsa loquitur means "the event speaks for itself."

Retainer agreement A contract authorizing an attorney to represent a client in a matter and setting the fee to be charged for that representation.

Right to privacy The right a person has to be left alone.

Sales puffery The sales talk engaged in by salespersons in order to induce a sale.

Satisfaction Full payment of a judgment by a liable party.

Secondary sources of law Resources that summarize or interpret the law but are not law themselves.

Self-defense The right of a person to use reasonable force to prevent an immediate harmful or offensive contact by another against himself.

Settlement agreement An agreement, or contract, entered into by the parties to a legal dispute that sets forth the terms and conditions of the resolution and settlement of the dispute.

Slander Defamation in oral or nonwritten form.

Slander of quality A disparagement of property tort that involves the publication of a false statement about the plaintiff's product, attributing a quality to it that makes it undesirable for sale or other commercial use.

Slander of title A disparagement of property tort that involves the publication of a false statement which casts doubt on or denies the plaintiff's title to property.

Sophisticated users Knowledgeable users.

Sovereign immunity A type of governmental immunity that prevents a lawsuit against a sovereign, such as a monarch, without the sovereign's consent.

Special damages Those compensatory damages that are incurred beyond and in addition to the general damages suffered and expected from the defendant's conduct, which are specific, or peculiar, to the plaintiff and which must be specifically pled.

Statement of fact A statement that can be objectively verified (proven), as distinguished from a statement of opinion.

Statement of opinion A vague statement or value judgment that is not objectively verifiable, as distinguished from a statement of fact.

Statute A law enacted by a legislature.

Statutes of limitations Statutes enacted by legislatures that set time limits during which plaintiffs may bring certain types of legal actions, including tort actions.

Statutes of repose Laws enacted by legislatures that place outer time limits on certain claims but are not dependent on the accrual of a cause of action.

Strict liability Tort liability imposed regardless of fault or blameworthiness of the defendant.

Subrogation Indemnity.

Superseding cause An event or occurrence that produces harm after the initial injury suffered by the plaintiff, which cuts off the defendant's liability for the later harm.

Survival The continuation of a cause of action, such as a tort action, after the death of either the victim or the tortfeasor.

Tender years doctrine A legal doctrine that, under certain circumstances, offers special treatment and protections to very young children.

Tort A civil wrong, other than a breach of contract.

Tort liability Arises when a person commits a wrongful act.

Tort of fraud or deceit Misrepresentation.

Tort of outrage Intentional infliction of emotional distress.

Tort reform Changing the rules and applications of tort law to reverse the upward trend in compensation being awarded by juries today, particularly in personal injury cases.

Tortfeasor A person who commits a tort.

Tortious death Wrongful death.

Tortious interference Harm caused intentionally to a plaintiff's contractual or other business relationships.

Tortious interference with a business relationship Where a tortfeasor interferes with a business or activity of another, causing harm.

Tortious interference with a contractual relationship Where a tortfeasor induces a party to breach its contract with the plaintiff, or otherwise disrupts the party's performance under the contract, causing the plaintiff harm.

Tortious interference with employment The taking of adverse employment action by an employer, in violation of the law.

Trade libel Slander of quality.

Trespass to chattels Intentional dispossession or intermeddling by the defendant with the plaintiff's right to use or possession of personal property.

Trespass to land Intentional and unlawful entry onto or interference with the land of another, without permission.

Trespasser A person who intrudes on the land of another without permission or privilege.

Unanimous opinion A court opinion in which all the judges agree.

Unemancipated child A child who is not yet "of age" or married, self-supporting, or in military service.

Unforeseeable product misuse A defense to strict tort liability if the consumer used the product for purposes not intended nor reasonably foreseeable by the manufacturer.

Verification An affidavit made by the plaintiff acknowledging that he has read the complaint and that, to the best of his knowledge, it is true and accurate.

Vicarious liability Legal responsibility of one person for the wrongful conduct of another.

Voir dire The process of attorneys or the judge asking questions of potential jurors to help them select jurors for the case.

Warning defects Product defects where all the products on the line contain no, or insufficient, warnings or instructions, making the products dangerous to use.

Warranties Express or implied assurances made by sellers of goods that the goods meet certain descriptions or standards of quality or performance on which buyers may reasonably rely.

Wild animal An animal that is not domesticated and is a kind of animal that is wild in its natural state.

Willful, wanton, and reckless conduct A form of extreme negligence in which a person's act or omission is likely to cause harm to others or their property.

Witness A person who is not a party and who testifies under oath in a trial or in a deposition in a lawsuit to establish facts relating to a client's case.

Workers' compensation statutes State laws that establish an administrative procedure to provide compensation to workers who suffer injury or illness as a result of their employment.

World at large test A duty of care is owed to an unforeseeable plaintiff if, as a result of the defendant's unreasonable conduct, someone (not necessarily the plaintiff) was within the foreseeable zone of danger.

Wrongful adoption A tort cause of action by which an adoption agency can be held liable for wrongfully stating or failing to disclose material facts regarding the mental or physical health of the adoptive child, or for misrepresenting the medical history of the child's birth family, if such facts would have been relevant in the parents' decision about whether to adopt that child.

Wrongful birth A tort cause of action that allows the parents of an impaired child to sue for their own damages.

Wrongful death Death caused by a tort.

Wrongful life A tort cause of action brought by or on behalf of a child, usually an impaired child, seeking his own damages.

Wrongful pregnancy A tort cause of action brought when a woman conceives a child as a result of a tortious act by the defendant.

Zone of danger test A duty of care is owed to an unforeseeable plaintiff, such as a bystander, when the plaintiff was within the foreseeable zone, or orbit, of danger.

INDEX